CON

ACKNOWLEDGEMENTS

This being the final edition of our series of books looking at the development of the local coal industry and therefore social conditions in the three villages of Thornley, Ludworth and Wheatley Hill from the 1830's, to their demise in the 1960's and 70's, I am sure that our volunteer word processor operators are breathing a sigh of relief!

It is not an easy job to word process newspaper articles which are sometimes lengthy and not very well written, however, undeterred, our team have continued to support these publications over the last ten years and without their support, there wouldn't be any books.

Wheatley Hill is a small village and the History Club only has a small number of members, and yet the continued dedication by a small number of people in producing a series of five substantial books charting local history over 140 years is magnificent and completely under-rated and often unacknowledged by outsiders.

We have had tremendous support this year from outside funders, especially the Coal-field Regeneration Trust, Wheatley Hill Parish Council, The Durham Miners Association and Thornley Parish Council and without their support the book or the book launch would not have been possible.

Owen Rowland, our researcher, must also be pleased that his task is at an end, for sitting in the local records office for hours on end must have its drawbacks, but Owen is passionate about preserving local history, and it is this passion that has kept him going throughout this ten year research task.

Our word processor operators have been: Sheila Brown, Catherine Goodrum, Margaret Hedley, Janet McGraw, Joan Scott and Mary Walker to whom we are eternally grateful. In terms of the word processing, we must also mention Alf Carr, our proof reader, whose exacting standards and critical eye have made possible such a professional publication.

Bill Burrell from the Heritage Centre is always willing to help with the images and once again has offered support and advice on the photographs contained within this edition.

To those who have provided photographs, information etc that I am unaware of, thank you for your interest and thank you to all who have purchased previous editions of the book, without your interest, we wouldn't be in a position to produce the final one.

INTRODUCTION

This edition of the book takes a look at the final years of the three collieries and their associated communities from the late 1950's through the 1960's and eventually to the death of a young boy who fell down the shaft of the closed Thornley pit in 1976.

This book reports on events from the communities which shows a good, strong community spirit with many organisations thriving. There is less emphasis on the mining industry in the newspapers and we can assume, that under National Coal Board ownership, that safety and conditions improved and thankfully, there were fewer fatalities to report.

The closure of Wheatley Hill pit in 1968 and then Thornley in 1972 were sad occasions for both villages with many men being transferred to other pits in the area. Some took the opportunity to leave the mining industry altogether and retrained in the many new factories that were springing up in the surrounding area. The pit closures may have been seen as a time for new opportunities by some but a time of great sadness and loss to others.

Alongside the closure of our major industries in Thornley and Wheatley Hill, came the inevitable decline of our villages. No longer were there local opportunities for young men leaving school and this led to the slow demise of people leaving to relocate to more prosperous areas. There are articles in the newspapers at this time, of some families and their emigration plans.

We know from our involvement in local history and heritage that the days of the pits and their associated communities are still remembered with pride by the people of Thornley, Ludworth and Wheatley Hill and this book will remind us all of what it was like living through those halcyon times.

1956

THORNLEY FUNERAL OF MR T SCULLY

The funeral of Mr Timothy Scully (72), Ashford Grove, Thornley, who was well-known in the cinema business in South-East Durham, took place on Saturday. Interment at Thornley cemetery followed Requiem Mass said in the Church of the English Martyrs by Dr H McNeil and Father F Robinson. The body had been received in the church on Friday evening by Father Robinson.

Mr Scully had been ill for some time, and this caused him to retire recently from the post of manager at the Thornley Hippodrome. He had been manager of the Wheatley Hill cinema for a period. After a fall in his bedroom he was taken to Durham County Hospital, where he died.

As a young man he was a builder in company with his brother, the late Mr Dan Scully. They built the Hippodrome theatre and the houses in the Garden Terrace area. He served in the Royal Engineers in the first world war.

Chief mourners were: Mrs Scully (widow), Miss M Scully (daughter), Mr and Mrs J Davison (cousins), Mr G Bland (brother-in-law), Mr and Mrs Bartlett, Mr and Mrs G Brown (nephews and nieces).

Representatives of the DRC Cinemas were Mr T G Armstrong (manager of the DRC Cinemas, Wingate), Mr Phil Jones (manager of the Hippodrome Cinema, Thornley). Miss Davis represented the Thornley staff.

Friends of the family included Mr H Tunney, Mr M Fleming, Mr and Mrs F Blanch and Miss Mary Elliott.

Floral tributes included wreaths from the DR Cinemas Ltd, Newcastle, and the staff of the Hippodrome.

6 January 1956

WHEATLEY HILL

CLUB ELECTIONS – Though opposed by three other members, Mr Thomas Cowie was re-elected chairman of Wheatley Hill Workmen's Club, following a ballot. Mr W Walker was re-elected door-keeper, and officials re-elected unopposed were: secretary, Mr S Hughes; treasurer, Mr J Dunn; librarian, Mr J Walton. With 227 votes, Mr W Gibson topped the poll for election to the committee. Others elected to the committee from 19 nominations were Messrs N Carr, W Banks, R Bradley, J Maddison and T Wilson.

BALLOT FOR CHAIRMAN – Balloting takes place this week-end at Wheatley Hill Discharged and Demobilised Soldiers' and Sailors' Club for a new chairman to succeed Mr Alfred Carr, who is not seeking re-election after filling the position for a number of years. Nominated for the position are Messrs Charles Curry and George Reay. The secretary, Mr W Hackworth, treasurer, Mr R Burnip, and door-man, Mr T

Cain, have all been returned unopposed. Nine nominations have been received for six vacancies on the committee.

PLAYING CAROLS in the streets on Christmas Day, Thornley Colliery Band collected £4.18s.4d for their maintenance fund.

CHILD KILLED - Four-year-old Eddy McMenam, son of Mr and Mrs James McMenam, 1 Percy Street, Thornley, was fatally injured when knocked down by a bus inHartlepool Street, Thornley, not far from his home, on Tuesday. The bus belonged to Shotton 'Bus Company, Shotton Colliery. The young boy ran off the pavement into its path.

20 January 1956

GOLDEN WEDDING AT THORNLEY
Mr and Mrs A Abbs

When our reporter called at the home of Mr and Mrs Alfred Abbs, 6 High Street, Thornley, on Wednesday, to congratulate the couple on celebrating their golden wedding, he arrived at the same time as the Vicar, the Rev H W Jackson. The Vicar had also called to offer his good wishes and administer Holy Communion to the couple.

Mr Abbs (72) has been confined indoors since a stroke two years ago and receives a regular visit from the Vicar of the church, where he has worshipped for so many years. Mrs Abbs, like her husband, has been a member of Thornley Parish Church since moving to the village. She has been associated with the Mothers' Union since 1917.

Born at Langley Park

Born at Langley Park, Mr Abbs began work at the colliery there as a joiner at 13, earning a shilling a day. He continued there until he was nearly 20, when he moved to Chopwell colliery. It was while living at Chopwell that he was married at Hookergate St Patrick's Church, near High Spen. His wife's maiden name was Hannah Ellwood.

After a short spell at Lintz Green, Mr Abbs and his wife moved to Thornley 47 years ago. Mr Abbs continued his mining career as a banksman at Thornley colliery but, unfortunately lost his left eye in an accident 36 years ago. Later he was appointed explosives magazine attendant and filled this position for some 20 years before retiring at the age of 65. Throughout the First World War he served in the Royal Engineers.

Mrs Abbs, who enjoys quite good health, was born in Thornley 74 years ago but later lived at Brandon. From the age of 15 until her marriage she was in domestic service.

"When I started work in domestic service," she said, "I received a wage of 5s 6d a week, and even as a cook general just before I was married I was only getting 7s 6d. And young people nowadays have no idea what a 'domestic' had to do in those days! I was up at six o'clock every morning and often never finished until ten or eleven at night!"

Mr and Mrs Abbs have a family of three sons and five grandchildren. All their sons are employed at Thornley colliery – James, the eldest, as a blacksmith, Alfred, who lives at Wheatley Hill, in the lamp-cabin, and Robert as a lorry-driver.

WHEATLEY HILL ROVERS

During a recent visit to the children's ward of Durham County Hospital, which they "adopted" some three years ago, the Rover Crew of the 2nd Wheatley Hill Group of Boy Scouts took with them a gift of six nursery chairs – a gesture which was warmly appreciated both by the young patients and the hospital staff. The chairs will be used at mealtimes and at the children's desks during their school hours.

The Rovers took the opportunity of entertaining the children with comic items and songs and later visited the men's ward and gave the pantomime, "Jack and the Bean-stalk". The women's ward, too, was visited and there the Rovers sang "special request" songs. The Scout-master, Mr Barker, also took part in the entertainment.

The Rover Crew, who were in charge of Mr Pattison, were thanked for their visit on behalf of the patients by the Matron, Miss Harding. A further visit to the hospital is to be made in the near future by the Boy Scouts.

THORNLEY & WHEATLEY HILL – New Combined Washery – Mr Watson reported that the following information had been received from the Coal Board in connection with the Washery:

NATIONAL COAL BOARD
(Durham Division)

25th January 1956

Sam Watson Esq.,
NUM
Red Hill
Durham

Dear Mr Watson

NEW COMBINED WASHERY AT THORNLEY AND
WHEATLEY HILL COLLIERIES

I am to inform you that the new Washery, which is being erected to deal with the coals drawn from the Thornley and Wheatley Hill Collieries, will be complete and ready to commence operations on 1st March, 1956. The working of the Washery and the change-over of men will take place slowly, in order to allow it to be worked up to capacity by about the end of April.

As a result of this re-organisation there will be a reduction in the number of workmen required at both pits and at the moment the Area cannot determine from which pit the staff to operate the new Washery will be drawn, as this will depend, to some extent, on the reaction of the Lodges at both pits.

With regard to the workmen, the proposals are as follows:

1	**Total number now working on the surface screen and dry cleaners**	97
	Number of workmen required to operate the new Washery	<u>40</u>
		<u>57</u>
2	**Of the surplus workmen (subject to training in the cases of some Juveniles) it is proposed to employ underground**	45
3	**Number of workmen over 65 years of age to be declared redundant**	6
4	**Number of workmen who are not suitable or not willing to undertake underground employment to be declared redundant**	<u>6</u>
		<u>57</u>

There may be some inter-Lodge difficulty in regard to the selection of men to operate the Washery and some conflict as to Lodge Membership and I shall be glad of any assistance you can render to clear up this problem.

The Board has decided that the Scheme shall be regarded as a Scheduled Project within the provisions of the Redundancy Agreement and any men declared redundant will receive the compensation benefits.

I have advised the Area General Manager that he is now free to consult both Colliery Consultative Committees.

Yours sincerely
N F Nattrass

(DMA Publications, July – Dec 1956)

NEW CLUB CHAIRMAN - By the narrow majority of three votes, Mr Charles Curry was elected chairman of Wheatley Hill Discharged and Demobilised Soldiers' and Sailors' Club in a ballot at the week-end, in succession to Mr Alfred Carr, who retired from the position. Mr Curry polled 73 votes against the 70 votes of his opponent, Mr George Reay. The other officials were returned unopposed, and from nine nominations Messrs G Frost, G Hargreaves, T Christopher, J Chapman, K Pratt and J Fishwick were elected to the committee for the ensuring year. Messrs R Dodds and P Gair were scrutineers.

27 January 1956

NEWS FROM THE COURTS
INCIDENT AT A DANCE –
THORNLEY EX-BOXER FINED FOR ASSAULT

When a 24-year-old insurance agent, Colin Thackeray, 8 Shakespeare Street, Wheatley Hill, summoned William Williamson, 4 Percy Street, Thornley, for assault it was alleged that Williamson, an ex-boxer, struck the complainant a "vicious blow" on the chin at a dance in Thornley Welfare Hall.

Williamson, stated to be engaged by the committee of the Welfare Hall to keep peace and order at their Saturday night dances, pleaded "Not guilty". The magistrates, however, found the case proved and he was fined 20s, with three guineas costs. "We feel you exceeded your duties on this occasion", Williamson was told by the chairman, Mr J V Carter.

Appearing for Thackeray, Mr Kenneth D Hodgson said his client had gone to the dance with a friend and was sitting in the hall when a youth tripped over his feet. When Thackeray told the youth "to be careful", the youth started swearing and then some of his friends "set about" Thackeray.

This disturbance brought Williamson on the scene, continued Mr Hodgson. He grabbed Thackeray by the arm and ordered him outside. "Thackeray attempted to explain what had happened", said Mr Hodgson, "but Williamson struck him a vicious blow, cutting his chin, and blood poured down his shirt and jacket."

Thackeray told the bench that he and his friend, Mr Tony Carr, 4 Durham Street, Wheatley Hill, had only been in the dance hall about ten minutes when the trouble started with the youth who tripped over his feet. When Williamson reached the scene, he was not aware, said Thackeray, that he was the door-man. "I was in the act of explaining the trouble when he struck me", witness added.

Some days later, continued Thackeray, Williamson said he was sorry for what he had done. "He said he was a boxer and had been knocked about once or twice himself and was not going to let it happen again", Thackeray added.

Cross examined by Mr John N Goldsbrough (defending), Thackeray declared he had never raised his arm to Williamson. He admitted that only one blow was struck.

Williamson, in court, said he was told about the trouble by a committee-man. He saw Thackeray and a youth "brawling" but did not know who had started it. Thackeray refused to leave the hall when ordered. "I got hold of his arm", continued the defendant, and he flung me around. I thought he was going to hit me because he had his arm up and so I hit him first. It was only my intention to take him outside when I got hold of him."

Called in by the defence, George Smart, 17 High Street, Thornley, a member of the committee of the Welfare Hall, said it was Williamson's duty, along with the committee, to maintain order at the dances.

There was no doubt that a blow was struck, said Mr Goldsbrough, addressing the magistrates, but there were justifying circumstances. Williamson had acted in self-defence because he thought Thackeray was going to strike him.

FIFTY YEARS MARRIED – MR AND MRS COWELL, WHEATLEY HILL

The days when there was a toll-gate at the entrance to Wheatley Hill near the railway crossing were recalled by Mrs Margaret Cowell, 27 Handel Terrace, Wheatley Hill, when she celebrated her golden wedding on Friday. She and her 73-year-old husband, John, were married in Thornley Parish Church on 27 January 1906, and have lived in Wheatley Hill all their married life. Both enjoy quite good health.

Toll-gate recalled

Mrs Cowell, whose maiden name was Meechin, was born at Hesleden 69 years ago and was only a girl of eight when she went to live at Wheatley Hill. "It was a very small village then," she told our reporter. "Only the colliery streets had been built and there was scarcely a road in or out. There was a toll gate near the colliery farm and carts entering the village either had to pay a sixpenny toll or make a four-mile detour round what we now call "the four-mile walk", via the Fir Tree, Wingate. The street where Mrs Cowell first lived – Emily Street – was demolished years ago.

11d a shift

Mr Cowell was born at Haswell Moor and started work at Haswell colliery, shortly before he was 13, as a trapper-boy. His first wages were at the rate of 11d per ten-hour shift. He was at Haswell only a year and later worked for a short spell at Wearmouth colliery before going to Wheatley Hill when he as 16. For 20 years he was a deputy at Wheatley Hill colliery, where he retired on light duties at the age of 65 after a mining career of 52 years.

Mr Cowell was formerly a member of the RAOB lodge at Wheatley Hill – he reached the rank of Primo – and in his younger days he served on the committee of Wheatley Hill Constitutional Club.

For the past 25 years Mrs Cowell has been a keen member of Wheatley Hill women's section of the British Legion and she also regularly attends the local Over-60 Club. During the last war she devoted most of her spare time to helping various local war organisations. She was a member of the Women's Voluntary Service and an ardent National Savings collector. "I counted it a joy to give whatever help I could", said Mrs Cowell.

The couple, who have an only son Robert who is unmarried, held a quiet family party at their home on Sunday.

3 February 1956

FIRE NEAR CHURCH – Breathing apparatus had to be used by members of Peterlee and Wheatley Hill Units of the Durham County Fire Brigade when they were summoned last Thursday afternoon to a fire in the boiler-house beneath St Godric's Roman Catholic Church, Thornley. The fire had started among logs and spread to the wooden flooring. Though hampered by dense clouds of smoke, the firemen quickly had the blaze under control. An electric wiring fault is believed to have been the cause of the outbreak.

VARIETY SHOW – Thornley Mothers' Club concert party, led by Mrs Margaret Hobbs, gave their new variety show to a large audience in the Welfare Hall for the benefit of Thornley War Memorial Fund. Mr Jack Toye, Thornley's blind accordionist and pianist, was accompanist. Taking part in the programme, which included two humorous sketches, were Mesdames Hobbs, Mason, Chapman, Parker, Ramage, Robson, Luke, Peacock, Featonby, Hughes, Lowther, Humes, Wilson, Turner and Robinson and Miss Irene Horner. Mr T H Holder and Mr J Pattison thanked the party on behalf of the Memorial Committee.

10 February 1956

THORNLEY IMPRESS IN CUP TIE

Probably the proudest man in Thornley on Saturday night was Coun J R Bosomworth, secretary of Thornley CW FC. His team gave a great performance in beating Cockfield 4-1 at Cockfield in a Durham Central League Cup replay.

Thornley, on the snow-clad ground, were in complete command in the first 15 minutes, and it was smart work by the home team goalkeeper that prevented them from establishing a substantial lead. He made several miraculous saves. "Shots from Smith, Allan, Barrass and Stoker, with goal written on them, were frustrated by this wonder custodian," said Mr Bosomworth.

Then Smith beat him with a cannonball effort from five yards. Thornley continued to exert tremendous pressure, but Cockfield defence refused to yield one inch. Most miserable player on the field was goalkeeper McGee (Thornley). He had nothing to do, with the result the Arctic conditions almost froze him stiff. He certainly appreciated the hot drink given by the thoughtful secretary, Mr Bosomworth.

Cockfield improved in the ten minutes before half time, but were unable to make headway against a well-organised defence. Five minutes before the interval Goyns offended in the penalty area, and the "ref" had no hesitation in awarding a spot kick, with which Mulrooney equalised.

Thornley on Top

Cockfield monopolised the play in the first 15 minutes of the second half to the delight of goalkeeper McGee, who was called upon to deal with several hot shots that kept him warm. But the "freeze" took hold of him soon afterwards, for Thornley re-asserted their superiority for the remainder of the game. Thompson punched clear a great shot from Allan. Then Allan made the goalkeeper go full-length to save a penalty kick.

10

Thornley, showing some fine constructive play, took the lead through Allan, but before this O'Brien missed an easy chance. Then Thompson saved another "spot" kick, this time from O'Brien. This was certainly Thornley at their best, and midway through the half Smith rattled in No 3. Just before the end, Border completing the scoring with a great shot from 15 yards.

Thornley now meet Cornsay Park Albion in the semi-final of this competition. They are also in two other semi-finals. "The football now being served up by the team will probably be appreciated by a big increase in 'gates'," said Coun Bosomworth.
17 February 1956

FIREMEN'S QUIZ – WHEATLEY HILL TEAM GOES FORWARD

Wheatley Hill Firemen
L-R: Frank Horner, Stan Poulson, Thomas Ayre, Percy Whynn, Jack Starkey, Fred Winnard, Joe Craig, Mark O'Brien, Jim Cairns, Eric Snowdon

Five happy men returned to Wheatley Hill on Saturday, safe in the knowledge that they have a good chance to reach the final of the national firemen's technical quiz sponsored by the Fire Services Research and Training Trust, organised, with Home Office approval, by the Chief Fire Officers' Association.

The five men who represent the county will travel in the same capacity to Wakefield on Saturday 17 March for the Northern semi-final, and, if successful, will compete in the national final at the Fire Service College, Dorking, Saturday 14 April.

It was the third time Wheatley Hill had got to the district final. On the two previous occasions they finished second. Their success was gained in convincing fashion, for they answered every question correctly right up to the last one, and then only one-and-a-half points were dropped.

Their final score was 43½ points. Northallerton, representing the North Riding were second with 22, and Gosforth, representing Northumberland, finished third with 18½.

Questions of high standard

Captain of the Wheatley Hill team was Sub-Officer S Poulson. He said afterwards that the questions were of a "high standard".

No question seemed too difficult for the Wheatley Hill men. They answered promptly and to the point, so gaining maximum marks each time. And it was only because he was "a bit hasty" that Fireman T W Ayre answered only part of the last question asking a cause for a sudden "big increase" on the pressure gauge while delivering water.

Other members of the Wheatley Hill team were: Leading Fireman F Horner, Firemen P E Whinn and J Cairns.

Sub-Officer Poulson said his team had studied hard for their success and he paid tribute to the help given during their studies by Station Officer R Gatenby.

Cash awards

Cash awards of £15 to the winners. £8 and £5 to second and third teams respectively were presented by County Coun H Lavery, chairman of the County Fire Brigade Committee.

The teams and guests were welcomed by the district chairman, Fire Officer A J Leyland, who thanked Durham County Council for the use of the hall and amenities provided, and also the County Fire Brigade and Assistant Chief Officer C Tozer for their hospitality.

Mr Leyland referred to the presence of County Coun E Leggett, a past chairman of the County Fire Brigade Committee, and he thanked him for displaying such a keen interest in the competition.

The vice-chairman of the committee, County Coun W Hirst, responded on behalf of the guests and paid tribute to the efficient manner in which the quiz had been conducted.

Mr J McIntyre, Cumberland County Fire Brigade, presided, and the Question Master was Mr R H Patterson, Darlington. Mr N Kettlewell, West Hartlepool, was adjudicator, Mr L Allison, Sunderland, timekeeper, and recorder Mr W T Taylor, South Shields.

CONCERT – Given by Thornley Mothers' Club, raised £23.10s for the Thornley War Memorial Fund.

2 March 1956

HARDISTY TEAM FOR THORNLEY

Youthful sportsmen in the Thornley and Wheatley Hill area are to have the opportunity next Wednesday of seeing an exhibition football match, played by present and past amateur and professional football stars, Thornley and District Boys' Club are to play a team brought by Bob Hardisty, the Bishop Auckland and England right half-back.

Until recently, the Boys' Club had no place to meet except the home of the leader, Mr George Greymore, a Thornley businessman. Just before Christmas a hall was secured in Hartlepool Street, Thornley. The members themselves did a lot to clean and decorate the building. Their weekly subscriptions, however, were inadequate to meet the expenditure of all that needed to be done in the way of repairs.

As a result of an interview between Mr W Morley, Youth Organiser of Durham County, and Mr Greymore, the former agreed to interest Bob Hardisty in the Club's need. Hardisty promised to bring a team to play the Thornley and District Boys' Club, who have got together a team that is doing very well. Besides Hardisty himself,

Warney Cresswell, the old Sunderland favourite and Frank Brennan, the idol of Tyneside, is turning out.

The match takes place at Wheatley Hill School Field (5 pm). Mr J Forrester is to be the referee.

Hardisty's Team - T Dormand (ex-County PT Organiser); J Shurben (ex-Sunderland); Warney Cresswell (ex-Sunderland and England); R E Hardisty (Bishop Auckland and England); Frank Brennan (ex-Newcastle and Scotland); G Wardle (Middlesbrough and Darlington); J Thompson (Evenwood); W Morley (County Youth Organiser); Corbett Cresswell (Bishop Auckland and England); D Lewin (Bishop Auckland and England); J Sowerby (ex-Glasgow Rangers and Scotland). Mothers of the members are to provide tea for this notable occasion.

Mr Greymore appeals for the support of the district to help the Boys' Club to modernise their new quarters and to show appreciation for the kindness of these past and present stars of football.

16 March 1956

BOXING AT THORNLEY

Event was huge success – The boxing show in Thornley Welfare Hall by the Thornley CW Amateur Boxing Club, with the help of the local Welfare Committee and the NCB Welfare organisation, was a huge success. Mr Jimmy Nicholson, the local secretary, expressed himself as highly delighted with the big attendance and the exhibition given by the competitors, who came from places as distant as Darlington, Gateshead and Ushaw Moor.

1   The official in charge was Mr A S Wilson, of West Hartlepool, with Messrs E F Jenkinson, Gatenby, C A Litherland, J H Walton, A H Ronald, R T Williamson, J A Wilkinson and J Robinson taking part in carrying the enterprise through to success. Dr McLean, Wheatley Hill, was also in attendance.

1   The ring was on the hall floor alongside the platform, and all available space, including the platform, was filled with spectators, many other would-be spectators being crowded out.

1   As each winner of the 14 bouts all under ABA rules, left the ring he was presented with a prize by Mr C R Knaggs, group agent of the NCB Castle Eden area.

1   The principal contest was between middleweights K Jones of Blackhall, who knocked-out A Eccles, of Darlington. In welterweights, John Harvey, of Thornley, knocked-out J Fellow, of Trimdon, and a bout between J Bambrough, of West Hartlepool and G Rowland, of Thornley, was stopped by the referee and declared Bambrough the winner.

1   Three Thornley brothers, John Harvey (22), Ron (20) and Ken (17) won their bouts, but their schoolboy brother, Joe (13) failed against E Jackson of Wheatley Hill.

1   The other results (decided on points were: A Brown (Ushaw Moor) beat T Harrison (Thornley); G Ponton (Gateshead) beat W Williams (Easington); A

13

Roddy (Fishburn); K Harvey (Thornley) beat D Keenan (Hesleden); Ron Harvey (Thornley) beat G Ray (Murton); P Germon (Shildon) beat J Tidyman (Wingate); J Pollock (Darlington) beat J Allison (Murton); P Jones (Blackhall) beat A Kirby (Thornley); J Freeman (Thornley) beat C Raine (Shildon); A Beer (Murton) beat D O'Brien (Darlington).

WHEATLEY HILL FARMER'S FUNERAL

The farming community and agricultural interests throughout the North-East and in particular from the county, were well represented among the large cortege attending the funeral on Wednesday of Mr James Alfred Robinson (59), Thornley Hall Farm, Wheatley Hill, who died with tragic suddenness at his home on Saturday.

Mr Robinson appeared to be in his usual good health when he went to bed on Friday night – he had been to Durham railway station to meet his son-in-law who had come up from Lancashire for the week-end – but complained of feeling unwell on Saturday morning and died soon afterwards.

Mr Robinson was particularly well-known at the Castle Eden and Haswell cattle markets – for many years, including the whole of the last war, he had been chief farmer cattle grader there – and was a noted breeder of fat-stock.

Well-known Freeman

Born at East Farm, Tunstall, he was only 17 when he took complete charge of Murton Moor Farm, Murton, which his grandmother had bought for him. Earlier he had worked for a short spell at Ryhope Co-operative Society. The farm at Murton covered 200 acres and Mr Robinson quickly became known among the neighbouring farming community.

He remained at this farm until his marriage in 1922 and then left to take over Tunstall Lodge Farm, Burdon, Sunderland. He spent six years there and then for nine years farmed at Low Newport Farm, Silksworth, before going to Thornley Hall as a tenant farmer 19 years ago. Mr Robinson was one of the best known farmers in South-East Durham, his farm with the surrounding woodland covering about 500 acres.

Mr Robinson was also a well-known figure in Masonic circles, having been a member of the Thornhill (Sunderland) Lodge of Freemasons for the past 25 years. He is survived by his wife, an only son, Alfred, who is also at Thornley Hall, and two daughters, and six grandchildren.

St Bartholomew's Church, Thornley, was filled to capacity for the funeral service, conducted by the Rev H W Jackson, Vicar of Thornley, which preceded cremation at Sunderland.

23 March 1956

WHEATLEY HILL BARITONE'S SUCCESS

Though in his 65th year – he celebrates his birthday in September – Mr Billy Williams, 31 Henderson Avenue, Wheatley Hill, a well-known local baritone, continues to meet with success in singing competitions in East Durham.

From eight competitors, he won first prize in an open contest in Easington Colliery Workmen's Club on Monday night, and the night before he won his heat in an open singing contest at Thornley Workmen's Club, and so qualified to compete in the final on Sunday night.

Mr Williams, who has given loyal service to Wheatley Hill Over-60 Club as its entertainments secretary since the club was formed two years ago, has also reached the final of an open singing contest at Wheatley Hill Workmen's Club. He was placed third in the semi-final of this contest on Saturday night. Mr T Foster, of Sunderland, being first, and Miss Bell, of Horden, second. These three winners compete against the three winners of the other semi-final, which has yet to be held.

Mr Williams, who has been responsible for bringing many concert parties to the Over-60 Club, has been singing now for close on 50 years. "And I still love it!" he told me the other day.

WHEATLEY HILL HOSTEL'S "NEW LOOK"
For the past three weeks painters have been busy with their brushes in the Aged Miners' Hostel at Wheatley Hill, giving a refreshing "New Look" to the eight bedrooms, television lounge, reading-room and dining-room.

"A wonderful change has been made," the aged miners' secretary, Coun E Cain, told me, "and the delightful colour scheme has been more than welcomed by the old miners who live there." It was the first major redecoration scheme carried out at the hostel for many years, added Coun Cain, and cost approximately £168.

30 March 1956

PASSION PLAY AT WHEATLEY HILL
In the Church Hall on Good Friday night, newly decorated for the event, with new curtains made by the wives of the churchwardens, Mrs J White sen and Mrs E Marshall, members of Wheatley Hill All Saints' Church presented a moving Passion play entitled "Golgotha". It was produced by Mrs A Woodward.

Taking part were Mrs M Orton, Mrs M Alderton, Mr C Perkins, Mr G Alderton, Mrs I Scott, Mrs J Smith, Mr B Blenkinsop, Mr S Woodward, Mr N Blakemore, Mrs E Poulson, Mrs E Hutchinson, Mrs E Marshall, Mrs N Kelly, Mr W Marshall, Miss L Sweeting, Miss J Adams, Mrs S Woodward, Mr A Alderton, Miss D Stark and Mrs B Robson.

The scenery was painted by Mr and Mrs J White, jun, art teachers at Wheatley Hill Boys' and Girls' Modern Schools. They had the assistance of the Misses Jean Musgrave, I Venables, J Stark and Ann Walker. Mr C Raffell was in charge of lighting effects. Mrs J White and Mrs E Marshall did excellent service in making costumes.

Proceeds were in aid of the repairs and renovations fund.

6 April 1956

DEATH OF MR JOHN THOMAS LUKE
ENDS MARRIAGE PARTNERSHIP OF 57 YEARS

The death has occurred of Mr John Thomas Luke (76), 23 Ruskin Crescent, Thornley. He leaves a widow – they had been married 57 years – four sons, one daughter and 23 grandchildren. He was born in Thornley and with the exception of the 1914-18 war, in which he served with the Royal Artillery in France, had never lived away from the village. He spent most of his mining life at Thornley and was for four years in an Aycliffe factory before retiring at 66.

Mr Luke had two great interests – football, and although he was not a musician, the colliery band.

Played for Thornley Rising Star

He played football for Thornley Rising Star 50 years ago. When playing for Sunderland "Co-op", he won a medal at Roker Park. For many years after his playing days were over, he was trainer to the Rising Star Club.

Mr Luke travelled all over the country with the Thornley Colliery Band for concerts and competitive events. Two of his sons, John and Lloyd, played in the band. He, himself, was chairman of the committee for more than 12 years. Up to three years ago, Mr Luke was caretaker for the premises in Nelson Street where the band holds its practices.

13 April 1956

WED FOR 50 YEARS

On 5 May 1906, Mr and Mrs Christopher George Dobbin, 2 Fred Peart Square, Wheatley Hill, were married in St Bartholomew's Church, Thornley. The Rev John Grey was the officiating clergyman. On Saturday the couple celebrated their golden wedding. Both are 74 in a few months' time and on the whole enjoy good health.

Mr Dobbin was born at the Wood Houses, Wingate. Like many people in the early days of the century, his parents moved from pit to pit.

Started as Trapper Boy

"As a boy," he said, "I remember the people in one village helping men who were on strike at another colliery. I recall the first soup kitchens that were opened at West Cornforth to aid miners' children whose fathers were on strike."

Mr Dobbin started work as a trapper boy at Thornley Colliery when he was 14 where he earned 11d a shift. He worked from six in the morning till half-past five at night. In winter he only saw the sun at the week-end.

He moved to Wheatley Hill 56 years ago but continued to work at Thornley for the whole of his working career. He retired after working for 53 years in the mine at the age of 67. For some years he was a member of the local Union committee.

Mrs Dobbin was born at Spennymoor. Her parents died early in her life and she was brought up by her uncle and aunt, the late Mr and Mrs John Walker.

She said, "Ties were much harder in the old days but people preserved their independence by working for themselves. Before I was married I used to do a day's washing for people. In those days, it was washing! Families were large and pit clothes were dirty. It meant boiling your water on the fire as it was wanted and using the old "dolly" or "poss" stick. For a ten-hour day I received 2s. I reckon I earned it!"

Mrs Dobbin has been associated with Wheatley Hill Church Street Methodist church and has worked in the Sisterhood.

Commenting on mining as a career Mr Dobbin said, "In the old days wages were small and hours long. Accidents through explosion, fire and flooding often high-lighted the dangers surrounding the miner's calling. If a man had 30s a week, he was reckoned to be doing well. The frequency of strikes and the trade slumps, which meant slack times, bred a sense of insecurity. But taking the good with the bad, if I had my time to begin again, I would still be a miner. Wages and conditions are much better today. The pitman is worth every penny he is paid."

18 grandchildren

Mr and Mrs Dobbin recall the days when Wheatley Hill was an isolated village with no social amenities. "In those days," said Mr Dobbin, "we were even cut off from our neighbours at Thornley. There was only a field path. Public men like the late Peter Lee pressed for a road to be built, houses to be improved, water and better sanitary conditions to be laid on."

Mr and Mrs Dobbin reared a family of four sons and two daughters; Alfred, John and Robert have followed in "father's footsteps" and are in the mines and Arthur, living in Leeds, a male nurse. Their two daughters are Mrs Barbara Lowther and Mrs Margaret Wigham. There are 18 grandchildren.

The couple are both members of the Wheatley Hill Over 60 Club.

Mr Dobbin had an association with Wheatley Hill Colliery Band for 22 years. He played the cornet and travelled with the band all over the county. He also qualified as a member of St John Ambulance Brigade. His services have been in great demand for minor accidents and ailments in the home.

The golden wedding was celebrated on Sunday with a family party.

WHEATLEY HILL SCOUTS' PROGRESS

Successful reports were presented at the annual meeting of Wheatley Hill Scouts Group Committee presided over by Scoutmaster L Barker. The secretary, Coun R Watson, gave a review of the activities of the committee since it was formed 21 years ago. Three original members Mrs Hinds, Mrs W L Watson and Dr A P Gray, were still rendering yeoman service, said Mr Watson.

Scoutmaster Barker reported on the work of the Boy Scouts and Cubmaster A C Watson reviewed the activities of the Cubs. During the recent "Bob-a-job Week" the Scouts raised £23 and the Cubs £29 8s 9d. A satisfactory financial statement was presented by the treasurer, Mr J Ford. This summer the Boy Scouts are to hold their annual camp at Knaresborough.

Officers elected

Chairman, Dr A P Gray; secretary, Mr Ralph Watson; treasurer, Mr J Ford; commit-tee, Mesdames Hinds, W L Watson, Cowan, Dunn, R Watson, Walker, Richardson,

Cook, J Andrew and Burnside, Miss E Shutt and Mr R Booth, together with the Group Scoutmaster, Mr T Meechin, the Scoutmaster and Cubmaster.

THORNLEY PARISH COUNCIL

Mr W N Fleming, area land agent of the NCB, attended Thornley Parish Council meeting on Tuesday and asked for diversions of the colliery yard footpath and the Gassy Gutter footpath. He instanced a case in which children were severely injured on colliery premises and said the Area General Manager was afraid something similar might happen in each of the above cases. He suggested that the path which entered by the colliery gates might be diverted by way of the Ritz Cinema, rejoining the old path near the pit baths. The Council agreed that they would not object if the Coal Board made an application for this diversion.

In the other case members pointed out that this was much more difficult. To make a diversion fro the Gassy Gutter across the waste land to the highway was undesirable because of the narrowness of the bridge at that point. It was decided to make an inspection before coming to a decision and to invite the Wingate Parish Council to arrange for their Wheatley Hill members to attend, owing to the footpath being used by residents of Wheatley Hill.

Bus stop request

A request was received from residents in Dunelm Road for alterations of the bus stop near the Half Way House Inn. They asked for it to be placed nearer the houses on the ground that elderly and infirm people found that the distance "inclines them to exhaustion". The Council decided to ask the highway authority and the police to support the request.

Other matters

An application to pay the expenses of representatives to the Public Lighting Engineers' Conference at Blackpool in September was turned down in a letter from the Ministry of Housing and Local Government. "The Minister does not feel that he would be justified in issuing a sanction," said the letter. In previous years when the Minister had made similar refusals an appeal had been made to Mr E Shinwell, MP, but it was decided not to proceed further this time. "We'll have to wait until we get a Labour Government," remarked one member.

In reply to the Council's request for information, the North-Eastern Electricity Board wrote that it was anticipated that the electricity change over from the Coal Board to the Electricity Board would be started in about 12 months' time and that all work would be completed in two to three months.

Mr Martin Fleming, of Thornley, was appointed Clerk of the Council in succession to Mr T H Holder, who retires on 30 June.

11 May 1956

LIGHTING IN A THORNLEY STREET – Sir, I am rather amused to read about Thornley Parish Council being very perturbed that their application to pay expenses to the Public Lighting Engineers' conference had been turned down by the Ministry of Local Government and that one member said that we will have to wait until we have a Labour Government.

Surely if these people have the interests of the people of Thornley at heart they need not go to Blackpool to find where public lights are required. Have they ever gone along Hartlepool Street, Thornley, after dusk, to see where lights are required? I think that this is among the worst streets in County Durham.

Traveller
Wheatley Hill

WHEATLEY HILL WIN

After skittling out Littletown for 76, Wheatley Hill won by four wickets in their away Coast League (Division 1) game on Saturday. Bowling unchanged, George Allison, their pro, took five wickets for 40 and Dennis Chisholm four for 25

The "Hill" had five wickets down for 30 but skipper Jack Martin was unbeaten for 22 and only another wicket was lost before they passed the home score. Chisholm took batting honours with 29, including four fours. Details:

Littletown : 76

Wheatley Hill : R Taylor b Mechin 9, H Simpson run out 2, E Simpson c Adamson b Squires 7, G Allison lbw b Mechin 2, D Chisholm b Cowley 29, E Smart c Mechin b Squires 0, J K Marti not out 22, W E Simpson not out 2, extras 5; total (for 6) 78.

Wheatley Hill seconds tried eight bowlers in a vain effort to dismiss Littletown II whom they entertained in a Division 2 game on Saturday. Littletown declared at 172 for seven and then sent the home team back for 106. Young Bob Battye was Wheatley Hill's best bowler. He took four wickets for 20, three of his victims being clean bowled.

Bobby Patterson had a brisk knock of 47 for the "Hill". He hit nine fours and had only two singles. Jack Wright was second-best scorer with 29 and Billy Gibson contributed 14. The last seven wickets produced only 26 runs.

Wheatley Hill Teams – Tomorrow Wheatley Hill visit Ryhope in Div 1 of the Coast League and on Monday entertain Silksworth. The second eleven entertain Ryhope II tomorrow and on Monday visit Silksworth CW II.

The selected teams are the same for both days, namely: 1st XI, J K Martin, H Simpson, E C Simpson, R Taylor, B Winter, D Chisholm, A Fishwick, W E Simpson, J Jordan, E Smart, G Allison. 2nd XI, R Patterson, W Gibson, G Carr, T Hall, K Farn, J Wright, J Nicholson, R Battye, P Barlow, F Aunger, A Carter; res T Simpson, R Wlson, D McBriar, G Battye.

18 May 1956

LEGION TO SUPPORT MEMORIAL - Mrs H Slater presided over the weekly meeting of Thornley Women's Section of the British Legion. There was a good attendance. Mrs C Cooper (secretary) read the business details. Mrs Cooper presented a report on the Thornley Road Safety and War Memorial committee meetings. It

19

was agreed that the Legion should support the idea of a Garden of Remembrance with a Cenotaph.   Although the Legion Women have already raised £40, the meeting expressed a willingness to work and make their target £100.
25 May 1956

THORNLEY WELFARE

Speaking at a social gathering at Thornley, Mr J C Robinson, of Easington, chairman of the No 3 Area Sports Committee of the National Coal Board, said the Welfare Committee were proud of a number of things it had done.

"We are proud of having provided your Thornley Welfare Institute, the football field at Horden and quite a number of other things we are getting done." Mr Robinson was accompanied by Mr J L Bell, of Wingate, of the No 3 Welfare Committee.

Mr T Scollen, Division Welfare Officer, presented the Thornley Welfare billiards and snooker teams with personal gifts and trophies for winning the championships of the NCB Divisional billiards and snooker competitions and the championship of the Northern Amateur Billiards League. Mr J Watson, the Thornley captain acknowledged Mr Scollen's congratulations.

The teams were also congratulated by Mr W Henderson (secretary of Thornley Committee), Coun J Williams, Mr E Carter (chairman of the Miners' Lodge), and Mr J Adamson.

Teams were: Billiards, Messrs J Watson (capt), J Lennox, L Williamson, J McCoy, G Wake; snooker, Messrs W Norrie, J Mills, H Taylor, E Dawson, L Williamson.
1 June 1956

SCHEME OF REORGANISATION
THORNLEY MEN TO RECEIVE REDUNDANCY PAY

Thornley Colliery workmen have approved a Coal Board reorganisation scheme which will shortly cause about 35 men over and nearly 65 years old to be redundant, partly because of the stoppage of an underground district known as Clark's and partly because of the recent completion and coming into use of a large modern cleaning plant for the cleaning of Wheatley Hill as well as Thornley coal. This has entailed the transfer of 18 men from Wheatley Hill to Thornley.

The men who will be retired will receive "redundancy pay" for 26 weeks. Mr Edward Carter, secretary of the Thornley Colliery Workmen's Federation, said the underground workers would receive £3 7s per week plus their State pension, and the surface men would be paid £4 per week plus State pension.

"Home" Colliery For Thornley Boys

An advantage of the reorganisation will be that 30 surface workers, including 20 boys, will go to work underground.

Mr Carter said that for about three years Thornley Colliery has not been able to take all the school-leaving boys who wished to work there. These have had to go to collieries as far away as Easington. While boys who have gone to other collieries will have to remain there, Thornley in future will be in a position to employ all the leaving boys from the local school.

Thornley Colliery, now 122 years old, employs over 1,400 workers and has a weekly target of 8,000 tons, which has frequently been reached.

The acceptance of the reorganisation scheme was decided upon at a Federation meeting of the men, presided over by Mr James Hedley (chairman), supported by Mr E Carter (secretary) and M J Cherry (treasurer).

15 June 1956

BOW STREET ANNIVERSARY – Thornley Bow Street Methodist Church Sunday School anniversary services were a notable success this year. The musical director was Mr Alan Lincoln and accompanist on piano and organ was Mr Malcolm Galloway.

THORNLEY MEMORY – VALOROUS MAN WHO DIED IN ACTION

The celebrations next week of the centenary of the Victoria Cross will recall to elderly people of Thornley the sadness which fell upon the village while the country was rejoicing over signing the amistice in November 1918. It was during that period the sad news came through that the 21-year-old VC, 2nd Lieut "Jack" Youll, Northumberland Fusiliers, had been killed in action in Italy on 27 October, only a few days after he had been at home receiving. from Thornley folk, a gold watch and silver cigarette case to make the honour he had brought to the village.

His widowed sisters, Mrs Tully, Thornley, and Mrs Robinson, Haswell, are to attend the celebrations. "I know there will be a good deal of sadness," remarked Mrs Tully, whose husband was lost in the same war.

Was electrician at Thornley

Born in Thornley, 2nd Lieut Youll, then the first officer of the Northumberland Fusiliers to win the VC since the Siege of Lucknow, served his apprenticeship as an electrician at Thornley Colliery. Meritorious service in France brought him a commission.

He won the VC in Italy on 15 June 1918 for most conspicuous bravery and devotion to duty during enemy attacks when in command of a patrol which came under the hostile barrage. Sending his men back to safety, he remained to observe the situation. Unable subsequently to rejoin his company, 2nd Lieut Youll reported to as neighbouring unit, and when the enemy attacked he maintained his position with several men of different units until the troops on his left had given way and an enemy machine gun had opened fire from behind him. He rushed the gun and, having himself killed most of the team, opened fire on the enemy with captured gun, inflicting heaving casualties. Then, finding that the enemy had gained a footing in a portion of the front line, he organised and carried out with a few men three separate counter-attacks. On each occasion he drove back the enemy, but was unable to maintain his position by reason of reverse fire. Throughout the fighting his complete disregard of personal safety and very gallant leading set a magnificent example to all. King George V presented him with the VC and the King of Italy handed him the Italian Silver Medal for Valour.

We also mention Pte Thomas Kenny, VC, born at South Wingate on 4 April 1882 to Darby and Mary Kenny.

He joined the army in 1914, serving as 17424 Private Thomas Kenny in the 13th (Service) Battalion, the Durham Light Infantry, 67th Infantry Brigade, 47th (London) Division. It was at Lahoussie, France, that he earned the Victoria Cross for most conspicuous bravery and devotion to duty on the night of 4 November 1915. Lieutenant Brown had been shot through both thighs, Private Kenny, although heavily and repeatedly fired upon , crawled about for ore than an hour with his wounded officer on his back, trying to find his way through the fog to our trenches. He came to a ditch which he recognised, placed Lieutenant Brown in it, and went to look for help, he found an officer and a few men at a listening post, and after guiding them back, with their assistance, Lieutenant Brown was brought in.

Thomas Kenny spent the last 21 years of his life at Wheatley Hill, where he worked at the local colliery, living at 13 Darlington Street. At the age of 66 years he died on 30 November 1948, the burial took place at Wheatley Hill cemetery.
22 June 1956

THORNLEY CW FOOTBALL "ANNUAL"

Mr J R Bosomworth (secretary) said at the annual meeting of Thornley Colliery Welfare Football Club that last season was successful both from a playing and a financial point of view. The team won the National Orphanage Cup, and finished in a respectable position in the Durham Central League.

"We will be competing in the Wearside League next term," he said, "but greater support will be needed if we are to operate successfully in this higher status." Mr Bosomworth appealed to football supporters in the village to rally round to help to restore the local team to its former position in minor soccer in East Durham. The team will play on the new Colliery Welfare ground which has cost £5,000.

Election of officers resulted: Patron, Mr A Welsh; president, Mr E Luke; vice-presidents, Messrs C Lamb, W Henderson and T Wetherall; chairman, Mr R Lewis; vice-chairman, Mr R Richardson; secretary, Mr J R Bosomworth; treasurer Mr G Armstrong; trainer, Mr J Potts; committee, Messrs M Walton, S Harrison, J Hall, F Telford N. Howe, R Patterson, G Pattison, N. Mains, R Bosomworth, J Kellett, P Potts and Coun James Nicholson.

Mr Richardson, who presided, thanked the Thornley Workmen's Club Committee, the Welfare Committee and the Ladies' Supporters' Club, for the valuable help they had given during the past year.

THORNLEY PARISH COUNCIL

Martin Fleming, a former chairman of Thornley Parish Council, attended his first meeting as Clerk on Tuesday and was welcomed by the chairman, Coun James Nicholson.

He reported on a meeting held earlier in the day to consider a request by Dunelm Road residents that the bus stop on the south side of the highway near the Half Way House dog track be moved eastwards. Mr Fleming said the highway and police authorities, the Easington RDC and Thornley parish representatives, and a representative of the bus operators all agreed the stop be moved about 65 yds eastward. The Council approved.

Regarding the complaint of danger from road vehicles turning from the openings in Hartlepool Street into the back of that street; Mr Fleming said this was a county road and could on no account be stopped. The meeting of representatives recommended that danger notices be put up and paid for as road safety expenses. It was agreed that this should be referred to the local road safety sub-committee.

A resident of Ruskin Crescent wrote asking if the Council could provide a playing ground for the children of Ruskin and Shinwell Crescents. The Council decided that members should inspect and consider the matter at the next meeting.

Other matters

The chairman said he had received a request for some seats to be placed outside the Miners' Welfare Institute but on Welfare ground. Mrs Bosomworth said a number of people had asked for this to be done. She thought it would be of great benefit to old people and many others who wanted to sit outside. On the chairman's suggestion it was agreed to make the request to the welfare committee.

A report from the Deputy Surveyor of Easington Rural Council about a meeting with members of the Council regarding bus shelters was approved. Brickwork shelters were suggested for the stop near the Workmen's Club on vacant land next the hairdresser's shop in Hartlepool Street South, and in the Market Place next to the Colliery Inn. The stop at the colliery office corner would need to be of the tunnel type.

Speaking about the recent re-naming of the council houses in Thornlaw South, the chairman said there appeared to be some confusion regarding re-numbering. It was agreed to ask Easington RDC if and when the re-numbering was likely to be carried out.

6 July 1956

THORNLEY COLLIERY WELFARE FC

More than 150 guests, representing various organisations of the village, attended Thornley CW Football Club's supper in the Club Hall, to celebrate the winning of the National Orphanage Cub. Mr R Lewis, presiding, introduced Mr Wetherall to present souvenirs to the following players: M O'Brien, W Goyns, W Laverick, A Abbs, M Carter, W Stobbs, W Border, D Allen, J Croft, S Slack, G Stoker, A Barrass, J McGee and D Brown.

Coun James Nicholson, one of the speakers, said last season's success was mainly the result of fine team spirit. He congratulated the officials on their success in seeking admission to the Wearside League, and hoped local "soccer" fans would turn up in large numbers to give the club a flying start. They will play on the new welfare ground which has cost £5,400.

Coun Bosomworth (secretary) said officials and committee were determined to build up a strong side for next term, and he was sure that they would finish with distinction in the Wearside League.

The supper was arranged by the ladies' supporters' club, Mesdames G Armstrong, C Bosomworth, R Lewis and R Richardson.

CLUB COMMITTEE – From a record number of 42 nominations the following have been elected by ballot to serve on the committee of Wheatley Hill Workmen's Club for the ensuing year: Messrs Kit Hackworth, Kit Carr, G Henderson sen, G Tempest, W Jones and W Wood.

SCOUT CAMP – Thirty-eight members of the 1st Wheatley Hill Troop of Boy Scouts are leaving tomorrow for their annual week's camp at Sandsend. In charge of the party will be Scoutmaster L Barker and Assistant Scoutmaster W Mowbray. Last week the Rovers spent an enjoyable time at Ayr, in charge of Rover Leader Colin Thackeray, for their annual camp.

MINERS' HOLIDAY – Miners at Wheatley Hill colliery begin their fortnight's holiday this weekend, and to enable them to get off to a good start the management have agreed to a request from the miners' lodge for all three shifts to be advanced today. Both the fore-shift and back-shift are to start three hours earlier today, while the night-shift will commence four hours earlier.

OUTING – Retired miners of Wheatley Hill Colliery and their wives had a happy outing to Redcar. Widows over 55 whose husbands last worked at Wheatley Hill Colliery also accompanied the party of over 300. Ten motor coaches conveyed the party from the colliery village to the sea. Each tripper was given 7s 6d pocket money. Officials and members of the Aged Miners' Committee accompanied the old people. Arrangements were made by Coun Edward Cain.

MINISTER 'GROOM FOR THORNLEY MUSIC TEACHER

A former insurance clerk at Newcastle, who entered the Methodist ministry in 1951 and is to be ordained at next year's Methodist Conference at Nottingham in July, was married on Saturday in Thornley Bow Street Methodist Church.

He was the Rev Edward Harrison, only son of Mr and Mrs J J Harrison, 12 Burns Street, Wheatley Hill, and his bride a well-known local music teacher, Miss Madge Harris, youngest daughter of Mr and Mrs J W Harris, 26 Shinwell Crescent, Thornley.

The couple have both had a long association with Wheatley Hill Youth Fellowship, which the bridegroom's father formed more than 20 years ago.

Mr Harrison, whose father is a magistrate at Castle Eden and chairman of the Hartlepools Hospital House Committee, spent a year on circuit work in Norwich before entering Wesley College, Headingley, Leeds, in 1952, to study for the ministry. He spent three years at college and since last September has ministered in the Glasgow Toll Cross Circuit. He was actively associated with Wheatley Hill Church Street Methodist Church before entering the ministry.

Given away by her father, the bride, who is a fellow and gold medallist of the Victoria College of Music, was dressed in white lace over taffeta, with a full-length veil and diamante coronet. She carried a sheaf of lilies. Attending her was her cousin, Miss Glenis Boniface, who wore gold brocade with headdress to match, and carried a bouquet of multi-coloured sweet peas. A college friend of the bridegroom, the Rev Peter Sutcliffe of Portobello, was best man.

The Rev George H Ireland, supt minister of the Thornley Methodist Circuit, officiated, assisted by the Rev Noel Catherall, Wheatley Hill.

Reception was held in Thornley Welfare Hall and later the happy couple left for their honeymoon at Dunoon.

Actively associated with Thornley Bow Street Methodist Church, the bride has been a Sunday School teacher and junior class leader there for some years and was formerly assistant organist and a member of the choir.

20 July 1956

YOUTH CLUB AT THORNLEY
Fine Achievement by Leader and Members

Some months ago, Mr George W Greymore, a Thornley tradesman, threw open his house to entertain Thornley Boys Club. This was necessary if the club was to be kept in being. No other premises were available.

Then came a turn in the affairs of the club. They were able to rent the Thornley Catholic Club Hall. To make the premises attractive they had to be cleaned and decorated. Mr Greymore and his boys did not grumble. They rolled up their sleeves and cleaned and decorated the building. Soap, mops, scrubbing brushes, elbow grease and paint has transformed the premises. The last touch of artistic design was the installation of coloured electric lights.

The Turning-Point

Mr Greymore said in an interview, "The gaining of new premises has meant the turning-point in our club history. With increased accommodation we have been able to widen the scope of our activities. We can now cater for the girls of the village. Thirty girls are now enrolled and are in regular attendance. They also helped in cleaning and decorating the hall."

Mr Greymore said that the club had no grants and by their own efforts had bought a billiards table, table tennis sets, football and cricket gear. Boys pay a subscription of 1s and girls 6d.

Speaking of the club's future plans Mr Greymore said, "This winter we shall have two football teams operating in junior leagues. We shall go all out for providing netball facilities on a competitive basis for the girls."

Mr Greymore wishes it to be known that there are vacancies for both boys and girls aged 14 to 17 in his club, which is now known as Thornley and District Mixed Youth Club.

Mr G Thompson assists Mr Greymore with the boys and Mrs Greymore acts as club leader to the girls She is assisted by Mrs B Thompson and Miss J Sewell.

OFF TO RUSSIA

Mr Anthony D Wharrier, 52 Liddell Terrace, Wheatley Hill, one of the eight Durham miners who left Durham on Wednesday on the first stage of their journey to Russia, where they are to spend about three weeks, is a married man with a ten-year-old son, Gregory.

Mr Wharrier, who is 46, is included in the delegation as a representative of the Durham Miners' Executive Committee on which he has served since the beginning of the year. He has been employed at Wheatley Hill colliery for the past 20 years and has always shown a keen interest in trade union affairs. A month ago he was elected president of Wheatley Hill miners' lodge in succession to Mr H Bradshaw, who resigned from that position.

Since 1939, shortly after moving to Wheatley Hill from Thornley, Mr Wharrier has frequently served on the committee of Sherburn Hill Co-operative Society.

He has been chairman of Wheatley Hill Colliery Checkweigh Fund for two years and he formerly served on Wingate Parish Council as a representative of the Wheatley Hill Ward for three years.

Mr Wharrier commenced his mining career at East Hetton colliery when he was 14. He has never before been abroad and is quite thrilled at the prospect of visiting "behind the Iron Curtain".

27 July 1956

SLUM CLEARANCE IN THORNLEY
"People don't want to go to Peterlee"

The question of people being forced to leave the colliery villages to go to live at Peterlee was raised at Thornley Parish Council meeting on Tuesday by Coun James Hoban.

"It has been said that the County Council is going to take the letting of council houses over from Easington Rural Council and that this means that many will have to go to Peterlee," said Coun Hoban. "Can we get any information about this?"

Coun James Nicholson, presiding, and a member of Easington Rural Council, said that the "slums" in Thornley were all supposed to be cleared up in ten years. About 1,700 people would be affected and there would only be accommodation provided in Thornley for 900. "The rest will have to go to Peterlee," he said.

"Is it possible for us to write a letter to Easington Council deploring this attitude? Our people don't want to go to Peterlee," said Coun Hoban.

The Clerk, Mr M Fleming, said they could ask Easington Rural Council for their support. He added that Easington Council had upheld the building of Peterlee, and now, after ten years, they were wanting the slum clearance property built in their own area. It was agreed to seek information from the Easington Council.

During the discussion there were references to the lack of information in the Press about the proceedings of the Easington Rural Council.

Other Matters

A request for a seat to be placed on the welfare institute property, near the main entrance to the hall, was agreed to by the Thornley Miners' Welfare Committee.

The District Council agreed to receive an estimate of the cost of renovating the Coronation clock in the Market Place. The Parish Council will obtain the estimate and forward it to the District Council for approval. It will include the lighting of the clock as well as renewing the clock face.

REDUNDANCY AT THORNLEY COLLIERY

About 35 underground and surface men of Thornley Colliery completed 14 days' notice to terminate their employment on Saturday. They left under a redundancy scheme agreed upon by the NCB and their trade union. The period of their notice coincided with the pit holiday fortnight. Along with the other men they drew their holiday pay of £22.

For the next 26 weeks they will receive a weekly redundancy allowance, the underground men £4 and the surface men £3 7s per week. A few who are not quite 65 years old, attracted by the redundancy allowance, elected to be included in the scheme, the others are all 65 and over. The erection of new coal cleaning plant is a partial cause of the redundancy.

ON LAST DAY OF HOLIDAY WHEATLEY HLL MINER IN HOSPITAL

On the last day of his fortnight's pit holiday, a 22 year old Wheatley Hill miners, Joseph Pratt, youngest son of Mr and Mrs Ralph Pratt, 11 Sunderland Street, and his girl pillion passenger, Miss Mary Luke (16), 31 Laurel Crescent, Thornley, were taken to Durham County Hospital about midnight on Saturday when their motor-cycle crashed into a tree after mounting the kerb.

The accident occurred at a bend near Thornley Hall Farm, on the main road between Halfway House, Thornley, and Wheatley Hill. Pratt and Miss Luke, who had not long left a dance at Thornley, were thrown from the motor-cycle and received extensive facial injuries. Miss Luke sustained a suspected facture of the skull and Pratt a fractured nose, and both suffered from shock.

The motor-cycle, which Pratt bought only two months ago – it was a new model – was extensively damaged at the front.

10 August 1956

BACK TO WHEATLEY HILL
Mrs Ethel Shepherd's 30 years in Canada

After 30 years in Ontario, Canada, a former teacher at Wheatley Hill infants' school, Mrs Ethel Shepherd, has returned to Wheatley Hill to spend the rest of her days. But it has been a sad home coming for Mrs Shepherd, who was 67 on Tuesday.

Her husband, Joseph William, died last December at the age of 65, only a few months before he was due to retire from his work as a winding-engineman in a Canadian gold mine, and only a week after Mrs Shepherd had returned to Wheatley Hill for the first time since emigrating in 1926, one of her two brothers, Mr Jonathan P Howarth, 69 Wordsworth Avenue, died. He was cremated at Sunderland on Saturday.

"It was after my husband's death that I decided to come back to England for good," Mrs Shepherd told our reporter. "We made many good friends in the small town where we lived in Ontario, and we never regretted going abroad. But when he died I felt I had to come back to Wheatley Hill; it was loneliness which brought me back. When you are as old as I am it is nice to be able to look into somebody's face and say, 'You belong to me'."

Mrs Shepherd is to live at Wheatley Hill with her brother's widow. She has another brother living in the same village, Mr John J Howarth.

Born at Ludworth

Mrs Shepherd was born at Ludworth but most of her young days before emigrating with her husband, who was a winding-engineman at Wheatley Hill colliery, were spent at Wheatley Hill. The couple, who had no family, had been married 11 years when they decided to embark upon a new life in Canada. Mr Shepherd worked in a number of gold mines but for the last 18 years before his death was employed at the Young Davidson mine at Matachewan.

Canada offered wonderful opportunities, especially for young people. "But they don't want to go there thinking they can pick money off the streets," said Mrs Shepherd. "They must be prepared to work, and to work hard. Times are sometimes hard through strikes, closing of mines etc, and you have to be prepared for these."

Cost of living is higher

The cost of living is higher than in this country but wages are higher, too. "I think you can save a little more money out there than you can here," Mrs Shepherd added.

Before emigrating Mrs Shepherd was actively associated with the Church Street Methodist Church, Wheatley Hill – she was a Sunday School teacher and chorister there – and she soon began to play an active parting the United Church of Canada after emigrating.

For 18 years she was organist and choir leader at the at the Matachewan Church and when she left last month to come back to England the members organised a farewell party at which they presented Mrs Shepherd with a flashlight camera. "They were wonderful folk," said Mrs Shepherd. "I told them I was coming back to England for good, but they smiled and said they would give me only six months: but I am afraid they'll be wrong! In the circumstances, I am glad to be back home at Wheatley Hill again!"

Before emigrating Mrs Shepherd spent 13 years on the teaching staff of Wheatley Hill Infants' School.

GIFTS FOR REV AND MRS N CATHERALL

Bearing the inscription, "In appreciation of their unstinted love and devotion during their term of six years amongst us," a china cabinet was presented to the Rev and Mrs Noel Catherall, who are leaving Wheatley Hill at the end of this month for a new circuit, from the members and friends of Wheatley Hill Church Street Methodist Church, at a farewell social gathering in the church on Saturday night.

The presentation was made by one of the church officials, Mr Jack Harrison, JP, who spoke in glowing terms of the fine service both Mr Catherall and his wife had rendered since the minister came to take charge of Wheatley Hill section of the Thornley Methodist Circuit six years ago. Nothing had been a trouble to either the minister or his wife and they had devoted themselves unselfishly and wholeheartedly to their work, declared Mr Harrison. Mr Catherall had also given valuable help with the Wheatley Hill Young People's Fellowship, of which Mr Harrison himself was the founder.

As well as the gift of a china cabinet – their own choice – Mr and Mrs Catherall received a money gift, and three Sunday School scholars, Ann and Barbara Galley and Derek Langley, presented Mrs Catherall with a bouquet of red roses on behalf of the Sunday School.

Others paying tribute to the excellent service of Mr and Mrs Catherall were Mrs P H Galley, sen, (on behalf of the Sisterhood), Mr George Poulson, senior Society steward (on behalf of the Society), Miss Irene Lewis (on behalf of the Young Guild).

Expressing thanks, Mr and Mrs Catherall both spoke of the six happy years they had spent in the area. They had made many friends and would long cherish happy memories of their ministry at Wheatley Hill. Mr and Mrs Catherall, who have a four-year-old daughter Jean, are going to the St Helens and Prescot Circuit in the Liverpool District, where Mr Catherall has been appointed one of the ministerial staff of five.

Refreshments were served after the presentation and contributing to a short concert were Mr Ernest Goyns (organist), the Misses Joan and Irene Lewis (pianoforte duets) and Mr George Todd (bass), Trimdon Grange.

CIVIL DEFENCE TEST
Consett and Thornley in Competition

It might have been any area in any city or town in Britain, Birmingham or Brighton, Wigan or Wolverhampton. A bomb had dropped. It could have been hydrogen, atom, or a thousand times less powerful, just high explosive, but the effect was the same to the eye.

Buildings leaned crazily, walls were crumpled and cracked, and broken spars of timber jutted out of the shattered roof-tops. It could have been fact – but it was only make-believe. A scene of what could happen and the action that would be taken, played out in Durham on Tuesday night by volunteers of the Country Civil Defence.

Narrow win for Thornley

Conditions as near as possible to the "real thing" were created on a council plot when the two teams, Consett UDC "A" and NCB No 3 Area, Thornley competed. And though the crowd of interested spectators who watched them shivered in the August weather, the two teams of eight strained and perspired at the onerous tasks that were set them. The result was a narrow one indeed when the Thornley team won by only a three points lead – 108 to 105.

The tests were varied and brought out all the skill and teamwork of the contestants – to say nothing of the dangers. Four situations were created where the men had to plan and carry out rescue operations within a time limit. In two of these "casualties" were used but the two adjudicators made constant inspection to make sure that the rescuer handled the "bodies" as though they were injured.

The Thornley team began first by "bridging a gap," a tricky operation that meant scaling a high wall, bridging a 20 foot gap with an extension ladder and rescuing a victim, returning with him on a stretcher from a building about to collapse. This had to be achieved in 25 minutes including getting the equipment out of a five ton column rescue vehicle – which held tools ranging from a clasp knife to a 15 ton jack – and replacing it.

Consett's test

While spectators watched this real situation, the Consett team was involved in the second of the tests – erecting a ladder near a perpendicular derrick held by guy ropes and large spikes. The purpose again was to rescue a "casualty" but it was not so simple. Imagine the difficulties if there is an 18 foot wall of an unsafe building between the rescuers and the victim. But these men in their uniforms of dark blue and tin hats were equal to the occasion and with brisk orders from their section leader the task was completed successfully and in time for them to earn valuable points.

The whole floor of a building was assumed to have collapsed in the third test – and underneath was a dummy "casualty" this time. The floor, covered in a pile of bricks and rubble, had to be raised and one of the men crawled underneath with a rope round his waist to facilitate the removal of the dummy. But again the examiner was close at hand – though from a safe distance – to see that everything was performed correctly. How smartly and gently did they carry out this operation! Only 15 minutes allowed for this.

Entering a high building

The final test in this hour and a quarter of high-pressure rescue work was placing an extended ladder in a vertical position so that rescuers could climb up in order to enter a high building carrying rescue equipment such as shovels, blankets or picks. The test was completed by two men having to mount the ladder, go over the top and down the other side – and then there was an eight-man rush to return the equipment to finish on time.

30

There was loud applause as the two teams lined up looking dishevelled but with smiles of satisfaction that meant they were both confident of their success.

For members of both teams the competition had meant cancelling their holidays. In the case of Alf Peters, in the Consett team, he was already on holiday at Newbiggin but was brought through by car so that the team would not be changed. Mr Simpkin, surveyor of Consett UDC took him back by car after the competition to continue his holiday.

The two men who had the biggest smiles in the Thornley team were Section Leader F Bradley and his son Frank, who had both worked like Trojans to see their team through.

The winners were presented with the W H B Cotton Trophy by County Coun E Colgan who congratulated both teams for fine performances, and the organisers for the programme going without a hitch.

The Teams

Consett UDC "A" team – section leader R Peel; deputy leader J Henderson; L Collins, G Herbert, A W Wagner, J W Hickin, H Peters, G W Johnston.

NCB No 3 Area, Thornley – section leader F Bradley, sen, F Carter, L Mitchell, W Hutchinson, N Fort, T Bullock, F Bradley, jun, M Converry.

THORNLEY BOY'S DISTINCTION
Chosen to play in National Orchestra

Fifteen-year-old Malcolm Galloway, a pupil at Wellfield A J Dawson Grammar School, eldest of the four sons of Mr and Mrs David Galloway, 55 Dunelm Road, Thornley, is pleased at being chosen to play the viola in the National Youth Orchestra's concert at the Edinburgh Festival on May 31.

The concert will be repeated at Carlisle on the following day. Malcolm has been playing the viola about three years under Miss Florence Wilson in the Durham County Youth Orchestra. He also played under Sir Adrian Boult in the Schools Musical Festival at the Albert Hall, London.

But in his home village he is better known as a gifted young pianist. Taught by his father, a miner, who had about two years' tuition on the pianoforte, he has gained high marks in his examinations. It is unlikely, however, that he will seek to make music his career.

He is keen on scientific subjects and is hoping to obtain sufficient qualifications in these to enable him to earn his livelihood.

17 August 1956

VICAR TO SIT IN COLLIERY YARD

Today is St Bartholomew's Day. As usual it is also pay day at Thornley Colliery. As St Bartholomew is the patron saint of the parish church, the Vicar, the Rev Hilary Jackson, is to take the opportunity of sitting in the colliery yard to receive gifts towards the £2,000 the parochial church council hopes to raise during the next five years for the church restoration fund.

He will sit in the yard during the morning while the colliery workers are being paid, and in the afternoon, he will move into the Market Place among the large number of pay-day shoppers. He will have with him a large model of the church, made for the occasion.

In the evening there will be a service to mark the start of the appeal, and taking part will be the Rev G R Renwick, who was in charge of Thornley Church during the war. He is now at Tyne Dock.

In the next few weeks voluntary workers will be going round to supply boxes to those who wish to help and also calling upon those who wish to make small regular donations. Although the Vicar will not be able to see the work completed, he hopes to see the scheme fully launched before he goes to his new parish at Beamish next month.

THORNLEY PEOPLE WATCHED IN COMFORT

The soaked players in the Wearside League match on Saturday – the first to be played on the Thornley Welfare Committee's new football and cricket ground – may have thought that the half-dozen standing around the railings were their only spectators. In an upstairs room in the Welfare Institute, 150 yards away, there were 40 others, some on the floor and others standing on chairs.

When the occasion arose they go quite excited, particularly when Thornley scored the only goal of the match against Wingate.

At half-time Thornley officials appeared and took a collection, which suggests that at all the home matches in dirty weather this wise move will have to be repeated if the Welfare Committee are willing to allow this comfortable centrally heated grandstand to be used in the financial interests of the football club.

24 August 1956

DEATH OF A BOER WAR VETERAN – The funeral took place at Wheatley Hill of Mr Hugh Murray. In his 85th year, Mr Murray spent most of his working career at Thornley Colliery and during that time had lived at Wheatley Hill and Thornley. A Boer War veteran he was a survivor of Ladysmith. He served as a sergeant in the King's Liverpools during the first world war and was mentioned in despatches.

WHEATLEY HILL ARE CHAMPIONS

Playing at home on Saturday in a Durham Coast league cricket match, Wheatley Hill CC defeated Washington in a low scoring match and so made sure of the league championship.

On a soft wicket, Wheatley Hill knocked up a total of 60, Tommy Simpson 19 and Jack Martin 11, were the only players to reach double figures. C Williams was the visitors' most successful bowler with six for 20. Washington made 25 for the loss of seven wickets. G Allison took three for ten and D Chisholm three for 15. Scores:

WHEATLEY HILL: R Taylor c and b Johnson 9, G Allison c Plender b Williams 4, J Martin c Trotter b Williams 11, E Simpson c Trotter b Williams 9, T Simpson c Trotter b Williams 19, D Chisholm c Johnson b Trotter 4, H Simpson c Johnson b Trotter 1, G Carr b Williams 0, E Smart b Trotter 3, J Wright not out 0, Battye b Williams 0; total 60.

WASHINGTON: 25

Wheatley Hill owe much to the bowling of G Allison their "pro." In each of the six seasons he has been with them he has taken 100 wickets.

31 August 1956

PLANS FOR THORNLEY
Explained to the Parish Council

Chairman of Thornley Parish Council, who is a member of Easington Rural Council, gave the Council important information respecting the future development of the villages in the rural district.

Quoting from the county planning proposals, he said that of the 4,610 people resident in Thornley 1,260 were in need of new homes. About 14 acres of clearance land in the older part of the village would be developed to accommodate 560 people as well as some shops, leaving 700 to be housed at Peterlee.

Of the shopping and social centre of the village, the report stated that the existing shopping and social centre consisted mainly of sub-standard property, but some public buildings would remain as there was no other site which could suitably be developed as a new centre. It was therefore proposed that the existing centre be redeveloped with shops and houses but the housing development should not take place too near the colliery or the colliery railway line.

ELECTRICITY NETWORK – In reply to the Council's enquiry, the North Eastern Electricity Board said they would consider setting up a cash-receiving agency in The Villas, Thornley, when they took over the electricity network from the National Coal Board. Some time ago the Board said they expected to start the work of taking over the network next year.

LIGHTNING STRIKE – Normal working was resumed at Wheatley Hill Colliery last Friday morning following a lightning strike, involving 300 miners in the previous day's night shift. One shift's work was lost, coal production being affected by several hundred tons. It was because of an alleged wages grievance that the men came out on strike in the shift due to start work at 4.20 pm. On Sunday, Mr Sam Watson, Durham Area secretary NUM, paid a special visit to Wheatley Hill to address the local miners' lodge.

NEW MINISTER WELCOMED – A large congregation gathered in Wheatley Hill Patton Street Methodist Church on Saturday evening to welcome the Rev George L Nelson and his wife to the Wheatley Hill section of Thornley circuit. Mr Nelson, who

succeeds the Rev Noel Catherall previously served in Scotland and Carlisle. Mr T A Walker, circuit steward, presided and the Rev J W Dickinson led the devotions. Addresses of welcome were given by the superintendent minister, the Rev G H Ireland, Mr A Johnson, circuit steward and Mrs J Craig. The Rev C L Nelson, who entered the ministry from the Houghton circuit, responded. Mrs D Venables was at the organ.
7 September 1956

VETERAN BOWLERS – Competition was keen when two veteran Wheatley Hill bowlers, Messrs J T Hodgson and W Crisp, defeated Messrs R Taylor and G Harrison in the final of the veterans' pairs tournament for the MacLean Cup at Wheatley Hill Welfare ground on Monday evening. The scores were level when the 21 ends were up but in the extra end played Mr Hodgson and his partner won by one shot, the final scores being 21-20 in their favour. Mrs MacLean, wife of Dr W G MacLean, donor of the cup, presented the trophy to the winners and also handed over the prizes. A bouquet of flowers was presented to Mrs MacLean.

FIRE OUTBREAK – Peterlee and Wheatley Hill Units of the Durham County Fire Brigade, together with the Houghton fire and Rescue Brigade, quickly dealt with a fire which broke out on Friday night at the dry cleaner plant at Wheatley Hill colliery. Floor-boards at the plant caught fire when a spark from an acetylene cutter ignited coal dust ling on the floor. Only slight damage was done.
14 September 1956

"TEDDY BOYS"

When "Teddy boys" were said to have been connected with a disturbance in a Wheatley Hill dance hall during the hearing of a court case at Castle Eden on Tuesday, the chairman, Coun E Cain, who lives at Wheatley Hill, declared that not all those who dressed in "Edwardian fashion" were ruffians.

"Whilst they may be classed as 'Teddy boys' I have no doubt there are some very decent young men among them," said Coun Cain.

The magistrates, however, were very concerned about the way certain youths went about trying to break up local dances and they intended to do their utmost to stamp out such conduct, whether the culprits were "Teddy boys" or not, added Coun Cain.
21 September 1956

"NEWS OF THE WORLD" LEEK, FLOWER AND VEGETABLE SHOW AT THE TOWN HALL, DURHAM
Winning Exhibits from Thornley

A 33-year-old miner, Mr Alan Hutchinson, Thornley, followed up his last year's successes in the vegetable section by winning four prizes. In the class for four varieties for vegetables he was the first-prize winner and he had first, second and third places in the class for three varieties.

This is a remarkable achievement, because he scored exactly the same success as last year in each class.

28 September 1956

WAR MEMORIAL AT THORNLEY

After lengthy negotiations Thornley War Memorial Committee have been promised a free gift of the old colliery institute site on which to erect a new war memorial. It will replace the first war memorial which was destroyed when the Welfare Institute was burned down in 1944.

The old memorial bore the names of 132 men lost in the first war, including a good many who did not live in Thornley but worked at Thornley colliery. So far as is known there are 23 names of Thornley men lost in the second world war which will need to be added to the new memorial.

The committee hope to be in a position soon to start the demolition of the old Institute and the clearance of the site in readiness for the erection of the memorial, the design of which will be finally settled in the near future.

The fund now stands at £744, including the balance of £286 from the comforts fund run by the War Committee during the last war. The Committee intend to run a publicity campaign to raise the amount still required, estimated at from £300 to £400.

THORNLEY PARISH COUNCIL

The road to Thornley's beauty spot, "The Hilly" now being filled up with pit refuse, was the subject of a strong complaint by Coun James Hoban at Thornley Parish Council meeting on Tuesday. The Council agree to take up the matter with the National Coal Board.

Vandalism was complained of in and about the churchyard and in the Council allotments. The Council is to refer the case of damage to the churchyard wall to the Church Council. Consultation with the Thornley Allotments Society is to take place respecting the considerable damage done in the council allotments, and if the Allotments Society undertake to prosecute the Council will give support.

The Clerk (Mr M Fleming) said that in a recent case an allotment holder suffered from £30 to £40 damage. His grape vine was destroyed, with the loss of a large quantity of grapes. His tools were damaged, and some were taken away. This was a very serious case.

The chairman, Coun J Nicholson, said that in another case someone had torn the head off a pigeon.

This raised the question of people keeping pigeons without cultivating their allotments. The Council were informed that all applicants for allotments signed an agreement that they would cultivate them, though they did not always do so. Other members agreed that there were allotment holders who kept pigeons without causing any trouble.

Other matters

Estimates for renewing the face and the lighting of the parish clock in the Market Place are to be obtained and submitted for approval by Easington Rural Council.
5 October 1956

WHEATLEY HILL RETIREMENT

After 16½ years' service as an attendant at Wheatley Hill pithead baths – he took up his duties there six months after the baths were opened in 1939 – Mr Benjamin Venables, 7 Henderson Avenue, Wheatley Hill, retired from work on Tuesday. The following day he celebrated his 65th birthday and to mark this and his first day of retirement, Mr Venables took his wife for a day's outing at Stockton.

About 1,200 workmen used the baths when Mr Venables began work as an attendant but this number gradually dwindled through redundancy among the workmen and other causes until Mr Venables told me, only 700 now use them.

Mr Venables, who has two sons – the elder, Thomas, is assistant winding-engine-man at the colliery – was born at Quebec. He began his mining career at Wheatley Hill colliery at the age of 12, earning 10½d for a ten-hour shift on the "screens". Two years later he went down the pit and was employed there on various duties until 1935 when he was among about 400 who were given their notices. He was out of work for a period but spent three years at Kelloe colliery before returning to Wheatley Hill as baths attendant.

In his younger days Mr Venables was a member of the Wheatley Hill Male Voice Choir for many years and recalls singing both in Durham Cathedral and in Shire Hall.

Mr Venables has two brothers living and five sisters. His younger brother, Charles, is secretary of Wheatley Hill miners' lodge, and elder brother Jack (70), who lives in the local Aged Miners' Homes, was formerly chairman of Wheatley Hill Workmen's Club for 27 years.
12 October 1956

WHEATLEY HILL PLAYER IS SPENNYMOOR "FIND"

Wolves, Newcastle, Bury, Grimsby Town, Bristol City, Workington and Middlesbrough – they are all after 19-year-old Dave Carr, Spennymoor United's "find" of the season. Our reporter called at Dave's training quarters this week and the young bricklayer from Wheatley Hill knew nothing of the fight for his services.

One thing is certain though; Dave won't join any club until both he and Spennymoor United are certain he will get a fair deal. "If the right offer came along I would go. I would like to turn professional with a league club," he remarked.

This is what Spennymoor secretary Mr S W Greaves had to say about centre-forward Dave: "He has a lot to learn. He is a sensible boy though and if he gets the right club I am certain he will make the grade." Mr Greaves was with Wolves, Port Vale, Shrewsbury and Charlton in his playing days.

So far only Grimsby Town have made an official approach to the club although representatives have been making non-stop enquiries.

Asks for Guidance

Dave has turned to the Spennymoor club for guidance and advice. He will make no decision without the consent of the Brewery Field officials. It is also very unlikely that Dave will move while the club is interested in the FA Cup.

Spennymoor do not want to lose the services of this colliery apprentice who has suddenly shot into the limelight. "He is worth more to us in that No 9 shirt than cash in the bank," one official remarked. It was only this season that he came to the "Moor" from Easington Lane. He had played for Ludworth Juniors and Wheatley Hill Modern School before that.

Keen Trainer

He trains three evenings each week, twice at the gymnasium in Spennymoor and on the roads near his home. Once each week he has a five mile run with team mates Alan Fishwick and Walter Miller. Two years ago Dave was on trial with Huddersfield Town.

What does he think of Spennymoor's chances at Horden on Saturday? "I think we are going to win, we have the right boys to break the 'jinx' this time," he replied.

Footnote: It isn't often that Bobby Gurney lets centre-forwards slip through his fingers. But it happened with Dave. He had three outings with Darlington Reserves last year!

19 October 1956

ERNEST ADDING TO HIS LAURELS

Fourteen-year-old Ernest Peachey, son of Mr and Mrs Peachey, Emmerson Square, Thornley, and already well known in East Durham as a singer, is steadily adding to his laurels.

Recently, while on holiday at Blackpool, he was first (for the second time) in a talent-spotting competition in Peter Webster's show on the Central Pier. At this year's Royal Show at Newcastle he sang in the presence of the Queen Mother, and at Scarborough this summer he won a competition in the Galaland theatre.

He is a favourite at Crimdon, the East Durham lido, having appeared there on three August Bank Holidays when Mr E Shinwell MP has attended the beauty queen competition. On another Crimdon occasion he was chosen to sing at a reception given by Easington Rural District Council to German visitors. Ernie has had a big part in the Thornley team's success in winning the Council's "Top Town" competition three years in succession.

He began singing when he was six, and those who have followed his career have been pleased to note the gradual refinement of his voice due, no doubt, to professional tuition during the past three years. Ernest's father and his younger sister, Elizabeth, are also well known to East Durham audiences, Elizabeth as a singer and dancer, and father as a singer.

WHEATLEY HILL BAND IN TOMORROW'S CHAMPIONSHIP

Wheatley Hill Silver Prize Band left for London yesterday. In the motor coach there were 27 bandsmen. By gaining second place at the area contest in Newcastle they earned the right to take part in the national championship (Section 2) in the Royal Albert Hall tomorrow.

Mr J Gair, secretary of the band for five years, Mr J L Smith chairman, and Mr R Harker, treasurer, have worked hard to raise the money necessary for the trip – estimated cost about £130.

Mr Gair thanks the people of the area for all they have done, and says that if there is a deficit the bandsmen themselves will meet it. "Their enthusiasm is so great," he said, "that there has not been a grumble from any one of them at having to 'fork out'."

Through the years their headquarters have changed several times – first in Quarry Street, then in the old workmen's club; afterwards the Discharged Soldiers and Sailors Club and in 1944 they got their own headquarters – a wooden hut tucked away behind Front Street. Mr Harold Strong, Blackhall, conductor, was formerly a cornet player in the Horden band.

A Great Year

This has been a great year for the band with Mr Strong as leader: third at an NCB contest on first attempt; first in the second section of the County Brass Band contest; and then second in the Northern Area final.

Mr Strong said, "We have a fine blend of experience and youth. Alf Cartwright has given 50 years' service to Blackhall and Wheatley Hill bands. Jackie Halsall (63) has played in this band for 40 years. Jim Beresford is another experienced hand. He has served at Wheatley Hill for 26 years and many years previously at Thornley.

Family Associations

"The band also has family associations. We have two long serving brothers, Arthur and Peter Donaldson. Both joined the band in 1914, having put in 42 years. Arthur joined the band when he was 10. Ned and Alan Mordica are father and son." Alan is 15½. He said he started to train for taking a place in the band when he was 10.

While the band is mainly composed of men working in the mines, there are exceptions. Mr R Harker, treasurer, is an ex-miner, now a school teacher at West Cornforth. There is one lady performer (cornet). She is 24-year-old Olive Strong, sister of the conductor. Miss Strong is employed on a milk round at Blackhall. "Olive is a grand trouper," said one of the men. "She pulls – or should it be – blows her weight. We are glad to have her in the band."

The test piece on Saturday is "Sirius" by Frank Wright.

"We'll do our best"

Asked what he thought of the band's prospects in London, Mr Strong replied, "We shall do our best to play in a manner which will bring credit to the North in general and Wheatley Hill in particular. There are 22 bands in our section; bands from all over the country. If we are in the first three I shall be very satisfied. The lads are as keen as mustard. The band is in grant shape, I should say peak form."

On the eve of their departure, the band gave a free concert in the Workmen's Club's new concert hall.

While their fellow bandsmen are enjoying the excitement of a contest in London, two old players will be left at home owing to illness. They are John Lewis, treasurer for more than 20 years, and George Chadbourne, who fractured a leg in the mine. Both will be sad at heart at missing this great weekend but will be with the band in spirit in the Royal Albert Hall.

26 October 1956

TRAINING TO PROTECT MINES INSTALLATIONS
Competition at Tursdale

An atom bomb has exploded in the county! There is a huge area of devastation, death, ruin and destruction. The poisonous vapour spreads around the fringe, contaminating the air, spreading disease as it did at Hiroshima. What should we do? Indeed what could we do?

This came into my mind on Saturday as I stood watching the first competition of the Civil Defence to incorporate Durham coal-miners. A ladder was being held in a vertical position by four guy ropes. One of the team climbed to the top. Then he climbed down the other side. It was like an Indian rope trick in a way: it was as if the climber expected to find something at the top of the ladder. He was followed by others members in turn.

Held in a field within the grounds of Tursdale Colliery, the competition had attracted as many officials from collieries as it had competitors.

From Chilton, Brancepeth, Louisa, Thornley and Harton: from Boldon, South Hetton, Langley Park, Wheatley Hill, Thrislington and Morrison Busty, officials watched patiently their team's efforts to put out a fire of straw and lift a girder off a "body" – a wide-hipped, lumpy thing in Civil Defence uniform, and stuffed with wooden chips.

Teams of Eight

The star attraction, as a switchback is to a coconut shy, was a construction of steel pipes, as large, nearly, as a two-storey building. In the middle, one floor up, was a platform. The space between the platform and the end of the construction was 18 feet wide and represented a gap. The end of the construction represented a wall 16 feet high.

The teams of eight had to remove the casualty with the aid of an extending ladder, a stretcher, blankets and a considerable amount of rope. Given the word to go the team leader took over. "Number!" They numbered. "Bridging-the-gap – Right turn! Get to work!"

They ran the ladder against the "wall," and shook out ropes, fastening the stretcher at its four corners. One after another the first five men went up the ladder, their yellow leather gloves sticking out of their back pockets. "Extend the ladder," they were ordered. "Stretcher on the ladder."

Then the ladder was swung off the ground and through a quarter circle so that the extended part came to rest on the platform, 18 feet away across the gap.

Hauled Back and Swung Back

The first two men crawled across, pulled the stretcher over with ropes and set the casualty on it, fastening him in a blanket, and trussing him, with ropes tied round his chest, stomach, thighs and ankles. Then they blind-folded him, and he was hauled back across the extended ladder, which was still bridging the gap.

Mr R Carling, Spennymoor, was the "casualty" in the Chilton team which came second to Thornley in this event.

He said he had no worries at being shifted across a gap, tied hand and foot, with a 16-foot drop below. "It was a bit worrying in the early stages of training but I grew confident in their skill after a while." He said the Coal Board had allowed them a fortnight's "holiday" to train in Civil Defence at Westerton. Now and again they were given time off to train, and more recently they had been training in their own time for the competition.

Imaginary Post on Fire

In the Wardens' Section an imaginary post caught fire. The fire was symbolised by a brazier filled with burning straw and the efforts of a man fighting this conflagration with a stirrup pump almost single-handed suggested a 20th century Don Quixote tilting at a dragon. Langley Park mastered the situation most satisfactorily, with South Hetton second, and Thrislington third.

Organising this competition was Brig P Kirkup, Civil Defence Officer, Durham Division of the NCB. Asked if it was true that miners were apathetic and uninterested in Civil Defence, he answered, "Who told you that? It's utter nonsense! The men are as keen as mustard."

The Langley Park team answered to this description. Civil Defence would always be valuable, they said, because there were always the outside areas of devastation where rescue work had to be done.

"We used to play football or watch it on Saturday afternoons," said one, "but this is more important." They thought everyone should take an interest in civil defence work; "There is a lot of apathy among miners – because there is no war on. If anything happened they would come forward quickly enough. That was proved in the last war."

Prizes of eight large and attractive clocks, and a cup were presented to the winners of the Rescue Section competition by Mr E H D Skinner, Chairman, Durham Division, NCB.

High Level of Efficiency

The runners-up each received bedside lamps. Winners of the Warden Section competition received carving sets.

Mr Skinner said that 2,870 men had been enrolled in Durham mines; the object in mind being to protect installations of mines and coke ovens belonging to the Board.

"The very noble response demonstrates the splendid spirit exhibited," he said. "You have shown the utmost keenness and reached high levels of efficiency. It pleases me that in essence you are all volunteers. I hope that the Press will give it wide publicity to serve as a stimulus."

1   Results: Rescue Section Competition: 1st Thornley, Messrs Bradley, sen, Bradley, jun, Carter, Mitchell, Hutchinson, Bullock, Convery, Fort (188 points). Warden Section Competition: 1st Langley Park, Messrs Atkinson, Rose, Clegg, Thompson (87 points).

1   Judging was carried out by members of the staff of Durham County Council Civil Defence Department.

1   NEWS FROM THE COURTS – WHEATLEY HILL MINER FINED £10

Crash near Thornley

When a 22-year-old miner, Joseph Pratt, 11 Sunderland Street, Wheatley Hill, was accused of driving his motor-cycle dangerously, Supt J G Rowell declared he had ridden the machine in a "suicidal manner".

After crashing into a tree on his wrong side at a bend in the road between Halfway House, Thornley and Wheatley Hill, Pratt and his 16-year-old pillion passenger, Miss Mary Luke, Laurel Crescent, Thornley, were hurled into the air and both were seriously injured. The girl, in fact, was still in hospital, though the accident occurred on 4 August.

Pratt pleaded "Not guilty," but the magistrates found the case proved and he was fined £10, with £10 5s 2d costs. He was disqualified from driving for 12 months. "We think it was the excessive speed which caused this accident," said the chairman, Mr C H Wreford.

The accident, said Supt Rowell, occurred about midnight at the entrance to Thornley Hall Farm on the Durham road. Earlier, Pratt and the girl had been to a dance at Thornley. Pratt was riding towards Wheatley Hill from the direction of Halfway House and after colliding with the kerb on his wrong side of the road appeared to have completely lost control of the machine. "The prosecution claims that he struck the kerb because of the high speed at which he was travelling – this made him incapable of taking the left-hand bend in the road," said Supt Rowell.

Loud, Screeching Noise – There was no other traffic on the road at the time and motoring conditions were good. Douglas Alderton, 30 East View, Wheatley was walking along the footpath and had just passed the entrance to the farm when he heard the motor-cycle coming from behind. He then heard a loud screeching noise and then the crash and on looking round saw the motor-cycle lying in the middle of the road. Pratt was lying on the grass verge and the girl was lying 80 ft from him down the hill in the centre of the road.

When police later examined the road they found a tyre scrub mark on the kerb. From their examination it appeared that the motor-cycle had "jumped into the air" and come down some distance away and then collided with the kerb again and then struck a tree. A piece of bark was found torn from the tree ten feet above the ground. From the first scrub-mark on the kerb to where the girl was found lying on the road was a distance of 147 feet.

When Pratt later told the police the accident must have been due to a "blow-out" on one of the tyres both wheels were removed and examined at the Forensic Science Laboratory where it was stated that this was not so. The front wheel valve was torn out of the tube when the wheel became buckled and the back wheel was punctured when the mudguard was driven into it.

Later, when Sgt York interviewed Pratt in hospital, accused said, "I am sorry I cannot help you. I only wish I could. It must have been a flat type." The girl, said Sgt York, received a compound fracture both of the jaw and the pelvis and severe lacerations to her body. "She is still in hospital, but is improving," the officer added.

Cross-examined by Mr Crute (defending) Sgt York agreed that the speedometer could have "jumped up or down" when the accident occurred.

The Defence

Pratt did not give evidence in court. "He was unconscious seven days after the accident," Mr Crute told the Bench, "and has no recollection of the events leading up to the accident or the accident itself." The solicitor declared there had been no evidence whatever to show the cause of the accident. The police case was "all presumptions and assumptions". The motor-cycle had certainly gone on to its wrong side but there was no evidence to show why. "No-one saw the accident and no-one can explain how it happened," the solicitor added.

THORNLEY COLLIERY BAND

Mr Arthur Welsh, manager of Thornley Colliery, and Mr Edward Carter, secretary of the Mining Federation Board, gave a hearty send-off to the members of the Thornley Colliery Silver Prize Band, when they left on Friday morning to compete in the national contest on Saturday in London.

Mr Teddy Kitto, the bandmaster, who has led the Thornley band for 35 years, must have recalled days of signal success in London and elsewhere. One success which received considerable public notice was when the band wore their pit clothes to play to a large audience in a London entertainment. People who stayed at home will recall the thrill they got when on another occasion a radio announcer told listeners that Thornley band were the winners of a BBC contest.

Another veteran who has been with Thornley band in its ups and downs over the years is Joe Oswald, drummer of the past and now secretary. Failure to bring honours back on Saturday does not reduce his confidence. He believes their young players will keep up Thornley's prestige. This is borne out by their winning ten prizes in eight contests during the past two years, including the NCB (C) Sectional Divisional championship.

2 November 1956

WHEATLEY HILL'S NEW VICAR - Many clergymen from the surrounding area were among the congregation filling All Saints' Church, Wheatley Hill, on Wednesday, when the Rev George Gordon Graham was admitted to the perpetual curacy of All Saints by the Bishop of Jarrow.

The new Vicar, a bachelor, took up residence at the Wheatley Hill Vicarage a week ago. Before entering St Chad's College, Durham, Mr Graham was employed for nine years as a metallurgical and analytical chemist near Sheffield.

9 November 1956

SACRISTON MAN'S MISHAP AT THORNLEY – A man narrowly escaped death when he touched electrical equipment powered at 20,000 volts. He was 19-year-old Arthur Pallister, 14 Sowerby Street, Sacriston. He suffered severe burns. Latest report indicated he was comfortable.

He was admitted to Dryburn Hospital following an accident at Thornley Electric Sub-station when it is thought he touched the bared wire on an electrical apparatus.

Pallister's accident led to a black-out in parts of Thornley and Wheatley Hill for about half-an-hour.

WHEATLEY HILL PRESENTATIONS
Cricketers' League and Cup Double

To mark their league and cup "double" last season – they won Div I of the Durham Coast League as well as the Andrew Dixon Cup – members of Wheatley Hill Welfare Cricket Club held a successful supper and social evening on Saturday.

More than 120 club members and friends assembled in the Constitutional Club under the chairmanship of Mr J Soulsby, when miniature inscribed plaques were presented to the following players associated with the club's dual success: J K Martin, H Simpson, R Taylor, D Chisholm, W E Simpson, E C Simpson, A Fishwick, G Allison, J Wright, D McBriar, B Winter, R Battye, G Battye, J Jordan, R Patterson, W Gibson, T Hall, E Smart, G Carr, K Nicholson, T Forster, A Carter, P Barlow and T Simpson.

The presentations were made by the club president, Mr J L Snaith, a former manager of Wheatley Hill colliery. Mr Snaith also presented miniature plaques to the following members of Castle Eden Divisional Police cricket team, winners of a novices' tournament, which attracted 15 entries: PC W Northcote (capt), PCs R Stott, S Wilde, J Weetman, J Blair, C Pickering, G Waters, J Wilkinson, L Battersby, J Reed and G Galley and Insp W A Herbert. Members of the Thornley St Godric's team, who were runners-up in the tournament, received miniature cups.

23 November 1956

BOY INJURED – Just after alighting from a bus in North Road, Wingate, on Saturday, Raymond Churlish (13), 20 Shakespeare Street, Wheatley Hill, was knocked down by a motor-cycle. He received injuries to his legs and arms and was taken to Hartlepools Hospital.

SOCIAL EVENING – The weekly meeting of Wheatley Hill Mothers' Club was held in the Welfare Hall, Mrs E Powell presided and welcomed about 150 members to the annual social evening. Whist winners were Mrs E Colvine, Mrs D Walker and A Armstrong, Mesdames Walton, Harker and Thubron, and dominoes awards went to Mrs Heal and Mrs Storey. Tea was served by committee members. A programme of games and dancing was organised by the entertainment committee, with Mrs Powell as MC. Competition winners were Mrs H Newton and Mrs A Armstrong.

WOMEN BOWLERS'AWARDS – Officials of the North-Eastern Ladies' Bowling League and most of the clubs in the league were among the 140 guests at the supper and prize giving of Wheatley Hill Welfare Ladies' Bowls Club. Mrs E Hall, secretary of Wheatley Hill club, and president of the league, welcomed the visitors, and the trophies and prizes were presented by Mrs McLean, wife of Dr McLean, who was introduced by Mrs J Hodson. All three trophies – The Club Cup, William Jones Cup and Festival Bowl – were won by Mrs Hall. Mrs Atkinson was runner-up for the William Jones Cup and the Festival Bowl, and Mrs J Hodson for the Club Cup. Mrs G Harker (vice-president) presented Mrs McLean with a spray of flowers. After supper Mrs Hall was MC for whist and dancing, and whist prizes were presented by Mrs McLean to Mesdames Brown, C Robson, E Hedley, Healer, Colvine and Mills. **30 November 1956**

CLUB TREAT – About 120 guests were present when retired members of Wheatley Hill Discharged and Demobilised Soldiers, and Sailors' Club, and their wives and widows of retired members were entertained to tea and their annual concert at the club headquarters on Wednesday. They were welcomed by the cub officials, Messrs C Curry (chairman), W Hackworth (secretary) and R Burnip (treasurer). Each retired club member received a Christmas gift of £1 and his wife 10s. At night a concert, presided over by Mr Curry, was given by Mr William Pratt's party.

AMATEUR DRAMATICS –
With old-age pensioners from the village forming a guest audience, Wheatley Hill Amateur Dramatic Society scored another success when they presented the two-act play, "The Winslow Boy," in the Welfare Hall on Wednesday night. In the title role, Norman Winter, a 14-year-old Wellfield Grammar School boy, gave an excellent performance. Others taking part were

Cast of the Winslow Boy

Tom King, Minnie Galloway, Ivy Scott, Jean Willan, William Walton, Charles Lister,

John Robson, Eva Wharrior, Les Barker and Donald Willan. The play was produced by Mrs Vera Fairclough. Stage managers were Nora Abbs and Ivy Scott, and Minnie Galloway and Maureen Abbs were wardrobe mistresses. Mr R Horner was responsible for the special effects and Mr C Raffell for the lighting. The play is to be repeated tonight and tomorrow night.

7 December 1956

LEGION WORKER'S DEATH – Mrs Mary Forster (72), 23 Cain Terrace, Wheatley Hill, who was actively associated with Wheatley Hill Women's Section of the British Legion since its inception, died on Monday. Mrs Forster, who had lived in the village for 46 years was formerly chairman of the section for 12 years and had latterly served as vice-chairman. She was also Poppy Day organiser for a number of years. She served for 12 months on the North-Eastern Area committee and for five years on the county committee. While on the North-Eastern Area committee, Mrs Forster was chosen as a member of the Legion guard of honour for the Queen Mother – then the Duchess of York – when she visited the North-East in 1936. Mrs Forster did much voluntary work for local committees during the last war, including the WVS and Comforts Fund.

14 December 1956

WHEATLEY HILL

POPPY SALES – Last month's Poppy Day effort organised by Wheatley Hill Women's Section of the British Legion realised £118 10s – an increase of £12 6s 6d on last year. Mrs N Briggs was organising secretary and the collectors were Mesdames Kime, Bradley, Brain, Duggan, Jackson, Parkin, Taylor, Tatters, Telford, Worthington, Jones, Harnby, Robinson, Hildrew, Carter, Bishop, E Richardson and Bowes, Miss Snowden and Mrs Galley.

CAROL SERVICE – A carol service by Wheatley Hill Peter Lee Girls' Modern School was held in the school hall attended by 220 girls and the 11 teachers on the staff. The service was conducted by the headmistress, Miss G Alderslade. The singing of new and traditional carols reached a high standard. Mrs J Grey (Darlington), was musical director and Mrs J Standish accompanied on the piano. The nine Lessons were read by girls.

SCOUTS' REUNION – Old Scouts who still take an active part in the 2nd Wheatley Hill Group were among those present when former Scouts held their first reunion at the Marine Hotel, Seaton Carew. Among the 30 old Scouts present were Mr R Cowpethwaite of Stockton, founder of the Group, Mr Leslie Barker, the present Scout-master, Mr A Watson, Cub-master and Coun R Watson, secretary of the Parents' Committee. After diner Mr J Cain entertained at the piano. It is hoped to make the reunion an annual function.

BIG CELEBRATIONS AT WHEATLEY HILL

This is an enjoyable week for schoolchildren but rather harassing for the teachers. One thousand three hundred Wheatley Hill schoolchildren enjoyed their parties.

At Thornley RC Infants' School 60 scholars (5-7) were given tea and enjoyed games and carol singing. Miss M B Kevany and her assistant, Mrs T Wilson, carried out the arrangements. The Rev Dr McNeill and Father Smith were present and also Miss B O'Hara, who was headmistress for over 40 years. Prior to the Christmas festivities, in which the children enjoyed the usual good things, a concert was given by the children. Arrangements were planned by the headmaster, Mr J Finnerty and his staff. There were 120 children entertained to tea.

Modern School

The party at modern school was a "four-decker" affair, the parties being held in the evenings. Team and party games and competitions created much fun and laughter. Arrangements were made by Messrs A Harris (head teacher), T Ward, G Potts, A Jones, N Norton, T Holder, A Stabler, T Edwards and J Etherington.

Peter Lee School

In the hall of Wheatley Hill Peter Lee Girls' Modern School two school parties for 220 were held amid gay decorations. A Christmas tree dominated the scene and the walls were adorned with murals depicting scenes from "Snow White and the Seven Dwarfs". These were painted by fourth form girls under the supervision of Mrs D White, art mistress. Tea was served. All the members of the staff assisted.

Junior Mixed School

Two parties for 310 scholars were organised by the staff of Wheatley Hill Junior Mixed School in the Miners' Welfare Hall. The guest of honour was Miss A Hutchinson, who retired as a teacher from the school 18 months ago. The programme, which included a display of country dancing, was in the hands of Mr J W Willan (headmaster), Messrs A Wright, J Thompson, F Alderson and R Lister and the Misses J Hart, J Grieves, E Punshon and J Blenkiron.

County Infants' School

Miss E P Snowden and her staff worked hard to entertain 300 children attending the Wheatley Hill County Infants' School. Tea was provided, favourite games played and carols were sung.

DEATH OF MRS BURRELL, THORNLEY

The death has taken place of Mrs Emily Burrell (65), 7 Dunelm Road, Thornley, after a long period of ill-health. She is survived by her husband, Mr J T Burrell, a retired deputy, one son and two daughters. The couple were married 44 years and lost a son, killed in the recent war.

Mrs Burrell, who had lived in Thornley for 34 years, was born in Durham, where her father was well known in Conservative circles. She was a regular communicant member of St Bartholomew's Church, an active member of the Mothers' Union and a member of the Over-20 Club.

Interment took place on Wednesday at Thornley Cemetery, after a funeral service in St Batholomew's Church, conducted by the Vicar of Shotton. Mothers' Union was represented by Mesdames H Hird, E Anderson, J Vincent, A Thomas and other members.

21 December 1956

DEATH OF WHEATLEY HILL BANDSMAN

The death took place last Thursday of Mr John Henry Lewis (60), 73 Wordsworth Avenue, Wheatley Hill, after a long illness. He is survived by his wife, Mrs Ruby Lewis, three daughters and a son. The couple had been married 36 years and came to Wheatley Hill from Craghead 23 years ago.

Music, particularly the brass band, has always been Mr Lewis's great interest outside his work and from the age of 12 he has been a bandsman, playing the cornet. He played for many years with Craghead and Burnhope bands. It was this interest in bands that brought him to Wheatley Hill 23 years ago. He played in the West Hartlepool Old Operatic band.

He has been a member of the Wheatley Hill band since going to the colliery. He was treasurer for 21 years.

One of his proudest moments occurred a week or two ago. Bandmaster Harold Strong, secretary John Gair and Robert Harker, who succeeded him as treasurer, visited Mr Lewis in his sick room. On behalf of the band, in recognition of his loyal and devoted service, he was presented with a wallet of notes. At the time of his death he was training officer at Wheatley Hill colliery.

The Funeral

On Monday, Wheatley Hill Church Street Methodist Church was well filled when the Rev L Nelson conducted the funeral service, followed by interment in Wheatley Hill cemetery.

Members of Wheatley Hill band attended with their bandmaster Mr H Strong, secretary, Mr J Gair and treasurer, Mr R Harker.

28 December 1956

1957

SCOUTS' ENTERTAIN – As a result of carol singing in the village during the festive season the 2nd Wheatley Hill Group of Boy Scouts raised £22. Some of this money as spent on gifts and sweets which they distributed personally among the patients of the children's ward of Durham County Hospital, which they "adopted" some four years ago. At the same time as they distributed the gifts, the Scouts entertained with songs, choruses and comedy items. Leading the Scouts in their hospital visit were Scoutmaster Leslie Barker, assistant Scoutmaster W Mowbray, Rovermaster Colin Thackeray and Cubmaster Alfred Watson.4 January 1957

SCOUTS' PARTY – Rovers, Scouts and Cubs joined in the fund when the 22nd birthday party of 2nd Wheatley Hill Boy Scouts was held in the Welfare Hall. Guest of honour was Mr R Cowperthwaite, Stockton, the group's founder. He was accompanied by his wife and two sons, and also among the guests were Mr F Richardson, Miss Harding, matron, Durham County Hospital, Sister Sutton, of the children's wad, and Mrs L Barker and Mrs R Watson, captain and lieutenant, respectively, of 1st Wheatley Hill Girl Guides. A birthday cake, made by Mrs S Watson and iced by Mrs J Lindsay, was cut by Dr A P Gray, chairman of the committee. The entertainment included a sketch, "School-days," by the senior Scouts, with Mr T Howe as the headmaster, a sketch, "The Wallpaperers," by Scoutmaster L Barker and assistant Scoutmaster D Mowbray, and a "potted" pantomime, "Robin Hood," by the Rovers, principals being Messrs C Thackeray, R Turnbull, J Watson, W Saxby and K Brown. The party ended with a camp sing-song under the direction of Mr Barker. In charge of the supper arrangements were Coun R Watson (secretary), Mr J Ford (treasurer), and Mesdames S Watson, J Hind, M Watson, S Cook, H Dunn, T Andrew, G Burnside and E Cowan.
11 January 1957

FATAL ACCIDENT IN THE MINE
Wheatley Hill Boy The Victim

The funeral took place at Wheatley Hill on Monday of 16 year old Brian Bell, only child of Mr and Mrs Richard Bell, 10 Eighth Street, Wheatley Hill, who was killed in an underground accident in the main coal Hutton seam of Thornley colliery.

Employed as a datal hand for the past twelve months, Brian, who would have celebrated his 17th birthday on January 28, was caught by a set of moving tubs. First on the scene was his father, a wagonwayman, who was working close by.

"Though we never liked the idea, Brian was always keen to get a job down the pit," Mrs Bell told our reporter, "and the day he was told he could start work there, it was as good as giving him a £10 note!"

Brian was born at Thornley, but had lived in Wheatley Hill since he was four.

The Funeral

The National Coal Board, colliery management and miners' lodge were well represented among the large cortege which made its way to Thornley R C Church, where Requiem Mass was conducted by the Rev Dr H McNeil. At the last rites at the graveside. Dr McNeil was assisted by Father Smith.

Three of the dead boy's uncles, Messrs D Bell, John Bell and Joseph Bell, and a cousin, Mr William Barber (Station Town) were under-bearers. The parents were among the family mourners, together with the boy's grandmother, mr I Bell, and there were many floral tributes.

11 January 1957

FUNERAL AT THORNLEY OF MR R CLOUGH

Memories of the early days of struggling trades unionism are recalled by the death of Mr Richard Clough (64) 12 Laurel Crescent, Thornley. Mr Clough's great–grandfather brought his family to Thornley in 1837 and played an active part in forming the first miners' union at the local colliery.

Mr Richard Clough was born in Thornley and had lived most of his live in the village. He is survived by his wife, Jane and a son George.

Mr Clough had experience of Yorkshire mining. He was at Doncaster for some time. He also had a spell of six years in the Raisby Hill quarries at Garmondsway, Coxhoe. During the war he served in a munitions factory at Aycliffe.

His death in Winterton Hospital after a short illness ended a marriage partnership of 42 years. Interment took place on Saturday in Thornley cemetery after a service in Bow Street Methodist church, conducted by the Rev H Ireland.

18 January 1957

FATHER'S TRAGIC DISCOVERY
Wheatley Hill Pit Lad Struck By Tubs

"It is very, very seldom in our history that a father has been called to the death of his own son in the pit." commented Mr Sam Watson, general secretary, Durham Area NUM, at the inquest at Thornley on Monday night, on a 16 year old datal hand, Brian Bell, 10 Eighth Street, Wheatley Hill, who was killed instantly when he was struck by a set of tubs at Thornley colliery on January 3.

Mr Watson was expressing sympathy with the dead boy's father, Richard Bell, who had told the Coroner, Mr T V Devey, that while working in the same district as his son he had been summoned by telephone to the bank top, where a set of tubs was "of the way." "I went there," said Mr Bell, "and saw a set of 16 tubs off the way. The two front tubs were upside down. I went to them and saw my son lying on his back with a tub on top of him. He was dead."

Bell added that he tried to lift the tub off his son but was unable to move it and had to telephone for assistance.

Dr G H Wallace said that the boy had died of cerebral haemorrhage caused by a blow on the head. The jury returned a verdict of "Accidental death."

"Rapper" And Refuge Hole

A 21 year old datal hand, Richard A Champley, 118 Bernard Avenue, Ludworth, who was working in the same district, said when Bell or any other boys rapped, he could hear the raps in his own bell, but on this occasion he was too far away to hear whether Bell had rapped for the set to stop. "The signalling has always worked quite satisfactorily in the five or six months I have been at my job," witness added.

Under cross-examination by Mr Watson, Robert Wigham, overman, 69 Dunelm Road, Thornley, admitted that since the accident the "rapper' had been moved to a refuge hole. Previously the refuge hole was about two yards away.

Summing up, the Coroner said they had no exact information as to how the accident occurred except perhaps that the girder falling on the wires had stopped the raps which the dead boy might have given.

Main Rope Broke

The engineman in charge of the movement of the tubs, William Henderson, 66 Dunelm Road, Thornley, said he received a signal of three raps from the in-bye landing to bring out a set of tubs in the Main Coal seam. He complied with the signal and brought out a set to the bank head. He did not, however, receive a signal to stop his main ropes.

"Not receiving a rap," went on witness, "I continued to haul the set out-bye until it ran into the box. When the set went into the box the main rope broke. I clamped the tail rope brake down immediately and shouted, 'what's happened? Receiving no reply, I 'phoned to the wagonwayman (Richard Bell) to come out and attend to the set.'

Henderson then went on to the scene of the accident and found a girder resting on the tail-rope and one of the bell signalling wires. The dead lad, said witness, had been at his job about five weeks and was "perfectly efficient." Replying to the Coroner, Henderson said the lad was found about ten yards from the rapper point.

"Mr Watson has quite rightly brought up this question of a refuge-hole," the Coroner added. "No doubt there should have been a refuge-hole where the rapper was – on the other hand of course, he was not caught very near the refuge-hole."

Expressing his sympathy with the boy's parents the Coroner said that apparently the boy was a lad of great promise who did his work "efficiently and well." Sympathy was also expressed by Mr W Kinghorn (legal department, NCB), Mr S B Wilson (HM Inspector of Mines), Mr J H Pattison (representing Thornley branch Colliery Officials Association), Mr A Emmerson (foreman of the jury) and Sgt J W Hastings (on behalf of the police).

HAPPY MARRIED LIFE
"Concentrate On The Family" – says Wheatley Hill Couple

Mr and Mrs Thomas W Trisnan, 4 Aged Miners' Homes, Wheatley Hill, celebrated their golden wedding. They were married in Hutton House R C Church of St Peter and St Paul. The ceremony was performed by Father O'Dowd, who was in charge at Hutton Henry in 1907.

"I was living at Hart at the time, said Mrs Trisnan "and my husband was living at Wellfield. We were married according to the fashion of the early part of the century. We went to the church in a carriage and pair."

Mr Trisnan who is a hale and hearty 77, was born at Castle Eden. He started his working career at Nimmo's brewery. The mines attracted him and in 1914 he moved to Wheatley Hill colliery. He worked there for over 40 years and retired at the age of 68 as master's weighman.

Lived At Hart

Mrs Trisnan, (72) was born at Hartlepool. She spent her early years in Hart Village. "I missed the beauty of Hart when I moved into the mining area," she said, "but I have never regretted it."

Mr and Mrs Trisnan have a daughter, they lost a son, Mr Thomas Trisnan, in the Easington Pit disaster.

Giving her views on happy married life, Mrs Trisnan said, "Concentrate on training a family in the way it should go. When a family turns out well, nothing can give a couple more happiness nor satisfaction in a job well done."

MEMORIES REVIVED AT THORNLEY
Old Literary Institute To Go

Thornley Literary Institute, Later Thornley School

Thornley's old "Literary Institute" (to give it its proper name) is to be demolished soon to make way for the new war memorial, which will take the place of the first war memorial that was destroyed when the Miners' Welfare Institute was burned down.

The new memorial is to carry the names of the men lost in both wars. For something like 100 years the old limestone institute has served Thornley people in many ways. Built by one of the old colliery companies as a school (so people say), it was later used for a variety of purposes, including a reading room, mechanics' library, child welfare centre (bedevilled by smoke), and (unofficially) a place where a good deal of money changed hands.

In the memory of Thornley's elderly people the larger of the two rooms was the scene of much healthy heckling in the days when elections were really exciting. Two habitual hecklers were Joe Quinn, who teased everybody who didn't speak for the miners, and Andrew Dent, who teased Peter Lee.

In Election Times

Meetings in this room were addressed by Jack Lawson (now Lord Lawson) and Evan Hayward (Gladstonian Liberal) and the Hon F W Lambton when they were wooing the electors as Parliamentary candidates. There were also the late Col Rowland Burdon (who described himself as a "political chrysalis") and Sir Charles Trevelyan (who arrived in a fur coat).

When Ramsey MacDonald, Sidney Webb and Emanuel Shinwell came on to the political scene they addressed their audiences in the comparatively palatial Welfare Institute – the one that was lost in the fire but has since been replaced.

WHEATLEY HILL METHODISTS MEET

Members of the Christian Endeavour Society of Wheatley Hill Patton Street Methodist church held their annual meeting with the resident minister the Rev George L Nelson presiding. In days when the Christian Endeavour is said to have lost its appeal to young people, the society at Patton Street is in a healthy condition.

The secretary, Mr C Lister, reported that membership was being well maintained and real progress was being made in the junior society. He reported that the average attendance for senior CE meetings was 20 with an average junior attendance of 50.

Mr Wilf Warnes, treasurer, gave a satisfactory financial statement which revealed a substantial balance in hand. It was agreed to make the Trust Board a donation of £30.

Officers elected were: Present, Mr Tom King; vice-president, Miss M Alderton; secretary, Mr Charles Lister; treasurer, Mr Wilf Warnes, roll call secretary, Miss Rita Maughan; pianist, Mrs T Venables; assistant pianist, Miss Margaret Winnard; auditor, Mr Arthur Burrows; Junior C E Society leaders, Mrs M Lee and Miss F Hood.

25 January 1957

THORNLEY AMBULANCE CLASS

A 100 per cent pass list was achieved in the examination of Thornley Ambulance Class. Results:

Certificates: A J Brown, A H J Kimber, D Barker, A Fleetham, R Humphries, M Convery.

Re-examination: J R Symons, R Major, J Rutherford, W Docherty, R Raine, M Hopkins, F Carter, F Bradley, L Mitchell, B Smith, T Robson, J W Convery, J Nuttall, R Thompson, N Osbaldstin, J Burnip, W Routledge, R Conway, J Troupe, H Lonsdale, C Woodward, J Orange.

Messrs Woodward and Orange have been students together in this class for 40 years. The former is the holder of 35 labels and is a Serving Member of the Order of St John. Mr Orange holds 31 labels and is also Serving Brother.

Dr J Barry Scott was examiner; Dr A Todd surgeon instructor, Mr Woodward class instructor and Mr Orange class secretary, a position he has held since 1918.

HER 80TH BIRTHDAY

Congratulations were showered upon Mrs Jennie Tyson, 15 Patton Crescent, Wheatley Hill, when she was guest of honour at a party to celebrate her 80th birthday, organised by the Women's Own of Patton Street Church. Greetings to Mrs Tyson, oldest member, were extended by the president, Mrs G Wilson, and other members, and a birthday cake which Mrs Tyson had made herself and which had been beautifully decorated by Mrs Winnard, was cut.

Mrs Tyson, who has been actively associated with organisations in the village since she moved to Wheatley Hill from Cumberland 42 years ago, was presented with a bouquet of red carnations from the Women's Own. She also received a bouquet of pink carnations from the president and committee of Wheatley Hill WI, a bouquet of tulips from Miss A E Hutchinson, and a spray of mixed tulips from her only granddaughter, Miss B Baxter. Like her husband, Mr Peter Tyson, who was 80 last October, Mrs Tyson enjoys good health and leads an active life. Mr and Mrs Tyson have been married 52 years.

TWINS MISS EXAM – The 11-year-old twin children – a boy and a girl – of a Wheatley Hill miner cheerily shouted "Good-bye" to their father when they left their home in Johnson Estate on Tuesday to sit their 11-plus examination at the local school. But they never sat the exam. Shortly after they had left home their father, Mr J T Saiger (43), collapsed and died. The twins were told the sad news at school. They will now sit the examination at a later date. Their only sister, aged 15, is a pupil at Wellfield A J Dawson Grammar School – her form-mistress and head-master, Mr G A Carr, sent letters of sympathy to the family.
8 February 1957

RC CLUB – Mr James Regan, appointed secretary of Thornley Roman Catholic Club when it opened on 19 October, has resigned. At this week's meeting Mr Hugh McCoy, 2 Shinwell Crescent, Thornley, was appointed as his successor. A whist and dominoes drive was held. The following were prize-winners: Whist, Mrs M McCoy and Miss M Lewis; dominoes, Mr B Heslop and Mrs J Trisnan. MC was Mr J Oban.

FAREWELL GIFTS – A presentation, without being present to receive it, was the lot of Mr Thomas W Simpson, a former resident of Thornley, now living at Harrogate, where his son, Mr Robert Simpson is games master at a school. Mr Simpson, senior, was chief electrician at Thornley Colliery until last December, when he retired owing to ill-health. Mr Arthur Woodward, Mr Simpson's successor, on behalf of the colliery staff and workmen, forwarded to him a space heater and an electric drilling machine. Mr Simpson was chief electrician at Thornley for 20 years.

WHEATLEY HILL LONG SERVICE

To mark completion of 30 years' membership of Wheatley Hill branch of the Union of Shop Distributive and Allied Workers, three employees of Wheatley Hill branch Sherburn Hill Co-operative Society, were presented with long-service certificates and badges from the national union headquarters on Tuesday.

They were Mr Nichol Wharrier (grocery warehouse foreman), Mr William Gibson (travelling shop manager) and Mr Albert Atkinson (hardware department manager). The presentations were made during a dance by the Northern Area organiser, Mr T Hamilton. Mr Hamilton, introduced by the branch chairman, Mr N Cook, congratulated the recipients on the interest they had always shown in union affairs. Coun A Bishop and Mr H Howarth were MC's for the dance, which was attended by more than 200. Arrangements were made by the branch secretary, Coun John Fenwick.

15 February 1957

RC CLUB – Entertainment was provided for members of Thornley Roman Catholic Club by Mr John Quinn's concert party. Taking part were John Quinn, Bob Armstrong, Billy Williams, Kenny Bell, Bob Maycock and Miss Irene Bell. Billy Bell accompanied on the piano. Mr J Trisnan was MC for a dominoes drive. Prizewinners were: Whist, Mrs M Atkin, and Mr B Heslop; dominoes, Messrs M Hopkins, R Youll and J Darby.

MOTHERS CLUB – Mrs M Hobbs presided over meeting of Thornley Mothers' Club. The secretary, Mrs N Mason, read the correspondence. The main attraction was a 'bring-and-buy' stall, organised to raise funds for the club's target for the War memorial. A sum of £3.4s.6d was raised. Competition winners were Mesdames J Clark, J Hargreaves, M Barrass and F Lowther. A special prize presented by Miss Hannah Robson (Wheatley Hill) was awarded to Mrs E McMennam.

22 February 1957

ROAD SAFETY QUIZ AT WHEATLEY HILL
Children's Teams

When children's teams from Wheatley Hill and South Hetton were in opposition at the Welfare Hall, Wheatley Hill, on Monday, in the preliminary round of the Road Safety quiz organised by Easington Rural Area Road Safety Committee, Wheatley Hill won the junior section but were beaten by South Hetton in the senior section. PC J L Jackson, Accidents Prevention Officer, was question-master.

In the senior section South Hetton team, comprising J Howlett, T Kitchen V Dowell and B Howie, won by 54 points to 40. Members of the Wheatley Hill team were Margaret Simpson, Joyce Burgin, Raymond Errington and James Johnson.

In the junior section the Wheatley Hill team, comprising William Morgan, Robert Inchcliffe, Betty Woodward and Margaret Poole, won by 46 points to 44. The defeated South Hetton team comprised M Emery, G Evans, G Young and D Quin.

Top Boys And Girls

The two top boys and two top girls in the cycling proficiency test at Wheatley Hill were presented with vouchers by P C Jackson. They were Barry Hodgson (who also received a cup), Brian Thomas, Margaret Simpson and Linda Craggs. Proficiency certificates and badges were also presented to James Stanford, David Richards, Edward Dobson, Martin Foster, Ian Graves, Godfrey Goynes, Billy Middleton, William Haswell, Frank Bennett and Billy Banks.

Enjoyable entertainment was by South Hetton "Top Town" concert party. Arrangements were made by Mrs O Slater (secretary) and her committee.

The winning quiz teams visit Haswell in the first round of the competition.

RC MEN'S CLUB – twenty-two nominations have been received for ten seats on the management committee of Thornley Roman Catholic working Men's Club. Secretary, Mr J English and treasurer, Mr T McCoy are unopposed. The chairman, Mr P Ellward will be opposed by Mr T Lennox and Mr E Morrow. The ballot will take place in the near future.

MAY DAY SPORTS REVIVAL AT WHEATLEY HILL

The children's May Day sports programme of years ago it to be revived at Wheatley Hill this year following a decision taken at a well-attended representative meeting in Wheatley Hill Welfare Hall, convened by the local Mining Federation Board. Mr A Wharrier presided, and representatives of most local organisations in the village were present, together with a good representation from the teaching profession.

The various branches of the miners' union associated with the Federation said Mr Wharrier, had promised a total of £400 to cover the day's expenses. It was agreed to run sports on the lines of those organised on Coronation Day and to investigate the possibility of providing tea for all the children. All Wheatley Hill children will be eligible to join in the day's programme, together with those from outside the village whose fathers are employed at Wheatley Hill colliery.

Huge Sports Day

Mr Wharrier was elected chairman of the organising committee, Mr E Ward vice chairman, Coun J Cowie secretary, Mr C W Venables assistant secretary, and Mr J Hedley treasurer.

Sports and catering committees were also formed and these are to draw up rough plans for the sports day to put before a full meeting of the organising committee in the near future.

"It will be a huge sports day, catering for about 2,000 children," Coun Cowie told our reporter, "and in order to get the exact number of children we hope to visit every house in the village and draw up a comprehensive list of names. We are sparing no effort to make the venture a huge success and bring back the old May Day community spirit,"

1 March 1957

THORNLEY PARISH COUNCIL

Criticism of the County Ambulance Service was voiced by Coun J Hoban at a meeting of Thornley Parish council. He said that one patient had complained that on three occasions the ambulance had never called to collect him.

Coun M Murray said there were so many factors involved that the blame could not be put down to any particular one; on many occasions the patient was to blame.

Coun A Bushby said the muddle was typical of all centralised organisations. The further administration if away from the people the greater the chaos.

The Clerk (Mr M Fleming) was instructed to ask the Easington RDC Health Committee to take up the matter with the County Health Committee.

A circular from the County Surveyor stated that preliminary estimates for the making up of the roads of Garden Terrace, Thornley, were now being considered and would be submitted to Easington RDC and Thornley Parish Council for approval.

Coun J Nicholson (chairman) said he was very pleased that some attempt was being made to ease the mode of travel at the bottom end of Thornley.

The turning of buses in the Market Place and the breaking up of land in front of the clock were discussed. It was decided that the NCB be asked to ballast the open space and that some attempt was being made the bus companies be informed of the damage done.

8 March 1957

RC MEN'S CLUB – The ballot for officers and committee of Thornley Catholic Club returned Mr Pat Ellward as chairman, Mr James English and Mr Tom McCoy were unopposed as secretary and treasurer. From 22 nominations for the committee Mr John French, past chairman of Thornley Working Men's Club was returned at the top of the poll. The committee is: Messrs J French, T Smyth, J Hoban, T Ellward, E Hutchinson, J regan, O Filon, M Hoban, W Graney and J Darby. The scrutineer was Mr George Dryden.

MOTHERS' CLUB – Mrs M Hobbs presided at a meeting of Thornley Mothers' Club. The evening was given over to organising future events. Arrangements were made for the club's sixth birthday party on April 11. It was agreed to hold the annual meeting on April 25 and nomination for officers and committee will be taken on April

18. It was agreed that the annual outing should be on June 8 with the venue being Bridlington.

AID FOR BLIND – Mrs J Ord, secretary of Wheatley Hill branch of the Guide Dogs for the Blind Association, announces that their latest effort in the village realised £7.15s. Mrs Ord told our correspondent that the work of the Association can best be helped by steady effort through the year. It was announced that the film "Eyes for the Blind" will be shown on March 20, at the Royalty Picture House and a collection for the Association will be made. A social evening is to be organised on April 6 in the Welfare Hall.

WHEATLEY HILL CHILDREN IN PANTOMIME

The staff of Wheatley Hill Patton Street Methodist Sunday School organised a successful pantomime, "Babes in the Wood," which was presented in the Welfare Hall on Friday and Saturday evenings. The show was played to capacity audiences each night and over £50 was raised by the effort.

The producers were Mr and Mrs T Venables, Mr W Walton and Mr G Robson. The dancing troupe was trained by Mrs G L Nelson, and Mrs T Venables was accompanist. Stage manager was Mr P Harper; lighting effects were in the hands of Mr J Raffell and sound effects were in the hands of Mr R Horner. The costumes, which were charming and colourful, were designed and made by Mesdames Barker, Horner, Maughan and Ruth.

The Sunday School children played their parts excellently. "Babes" were David and Janice Harker. Other characters were played by Linda Craggs, Brian Cairns, Keith Green, Charles Hargreaves, Colin Butterfield, William Haswell, Pat Berry, Alan Scrafton, Jean Stark, Judith Sangster, Margaret Winnard and Marjorie Ruth.

At the end of the performances on Saturday evening, the 'babes' presented Mrs Nelson and Mrs Venables with a bouquet. The dress makers were not forgotten. Mesdames Barker, Horner, Maughan and Ruth received chocolates, presented by Linda Craggs and Judith Sangster.

TV SET FOR HOSPITAL
Gift From Thornley Women's Institute

Ever since she received severe injuries as a result of a motor-cycle accident in August, pretty 17 year old Mary Luke, 31 Laurel Crescent, Thornley Colliery, has been visited nearly every day by her mother. But on Wednesday, in No 6 women's ward at Durham County Hospital, she not only saw her mother but 23 other women from her village,

The occasion – a happy one for Mary and her five fellow patients – was the presentation of a 17-inch television set to the ward by Thornley Colliery Women's Institute.

Besides providing the set, the Institute also gave the aerial and a table for the set to stand on. The gifts have cost over £90, most of which has been raised as the result of special efforts organised by the Institute Working Party.

The handing-over ceremony was performed by Mrs J H C Scott, the Institute President, who was introduced by the Matron, Miss M C Harding.

A Wonderful Gift

The Matron described the set as a "wonderful gift" and said the Institute had always been considerate and helpful to the hospital in the past.

Mrs Scott said: "There must be times when patients must get fed-up just looking through the windows. We hope this will help you to forget your aches and pains. I wish you all good viewing."

Mary Luke, expressing thanks on behalf of the hospital said it was a "marvellous and generous gift."

Included in the party of Institute members who attended the presentation were Mrs D Miller (secretary), Mrs A Todd (treasurer), Mrs A Tully (past chairman of the Working Party committee) and Mrs M Walton (secretary of the committee).

THORNLEY'S FIGHTING HARVEYS
Ken's Manchester Test

The enthusiasm displayed by officials and supporters of Thornley Miners' Welfare Boxing Club at Ken Harvey's approaching fight at Manchester in the North of England ABA contests was fully repaid y the brilliant performance put up by Ken on Friday.

There is little doubt that Ken, the Thornley Club's 18 year old 11st middleweight Northern champion, is going ahead. He will meet Chic Calderwell, Scottish middleweight champion, at Liverpool in the near future in the elimination contests that will send one of them to Wembley.

The fighting Harveys, the term that denotes the five fighting brothers, are meeting to discuss the approaching fight, and there are no wild decisions here. Jack, the father, says, "Foresight and vision comes from experience; we will eliminate the small errors and cultivate only the best of tactics. We are in no way pessimistic. The lads have a good trainer in Pat Gorman and he has got a wealth of experience behind him, and what is more he can talk to the lads like a father."

15 March 1957

COLLIERY OFFICIALS' GIFT
Wheatley Hill Presentation to Mr J J Harrison

Many tributes to his long service at the colliery and his work among the young people of the village were paid to Mr John J Harrison at a social gathering of the officials of Wheatley Hill colliery, when he was presented with a farewell gift of a clock, suitably inscribed.

Mr Harrison, who lived in Burns Street, Wheatley Hill, has ended 35 years' service at the colliery to take up a new post as warden of the Eden Hill Community Centre at Peterlee. With the exception of six years at Bearpark colliery, all his working career has been spent at Wheatley Hill, mostly as pit heap weighman.

Mr R S Chisholm, chairman of Wheatley Hill branch of the officials' Union, presided at the presentation, which was made on behalf of the officials by Mr F Simpson, colliery under manager.

Mr Simpson said that he had many others in Wheatley Hill had lost a fine friend with the departure to Peterlee of Mr Harrison. Mr Harrison's activities in the village had been many and varied and not least important was his splendid work among the young people.

"He has now taken up duties which have been dear to his heart for many years," added Mr Simpson, "and will be most happy doing what he can to brighten and enrich the lives of others. Wheatley Hill has lost a man respected by all, but our loss is undoubtedly the new town's gain!"

22 March 1957

WHEATLEY HILL STALWART
Retirement of Coun Edward Cain

Unlike most men who retire, Coun Edwrd Cain, 11 Burns Street, Wheatley Hill, will not be able to sit back and relax when he completes his last shift as checkweighman at Wheatley Hill colliery next Friday after a working career of more than 52 years. Though his working days at the colliery will be over, Coun Cain will still be leading a full public life.

But that's the way he wants it. "I could not bear to be idle," he confessed to me (writes Norman Passfield). From the earliest days of his working career Coun Cain, who celebrated his 66th birthday this month, has been actively associated with virtually every organisation in Wheatley Hill, where he has lived for half a century.

Victimised

It has not always been easy going. Because of his activities as a trade union official during the 1926 strike, he was victimised. He was unable to get a job at any of the local collieries and spent four years on the dole. At that time he was chairman of Wheatley Hill miners' lodge and after such a long spell out of work he was eventually glad to obtain employment as a roadman.

After a few weeks sweeping the roads he was appointed a clerk in a local Ministry of labour office and after three years in this capacity was able to return to Wheatley Hill colliery in 1934 on his election as checkweighman. Elected checkweighman with him was Mr William Lawther – now Sir William – the two men bringing the number of checkweighmen at the colliery to four. This number was later reduced to two and in 1948 when one of these, Mr Horace Bradshaw, resigned, Coun Cain was left the sole checkweighman. It is from these duties that he will be retiring next Friday.

It would take a book to record Coun Cain's many public activities. One of the Highlights of his public career was in June 1950, when he was chosen one of a delegation of five who flew to Nigeria, to examine mining conditions there. He spent three months there and on his return received a letter from Mr James Griffiths, then Secretary of State for the Colonies, congratulating him upon his work, particularly in the establishment of a Joint Consultative Committee in Enugu to thrash out labour problems. When Coun Cain flew on this journey it was the first time he had been in an aircraft.

Work For Labour Party

Coun Cain has long been associated with the Labour Party – he was been both secretary of the local Labour Party in Wheatley Hill and chairman of the Easington Divisional Labour Party – and was also in the old Independent Labour Party. He was assistant agent for Mr Jack Lawson – now Lord Lawson of Beamish – in the "khaki" election in 1918 in the South East Durham Division, and acted in a similar capacity for Mr Ramsey MacDonald in the Seam Division five years later. He did much valuable electioneering work and became the personal friend of many men who later achieved considerable fame, including Mr Sidney Webb and Mr Peter Lee.

For years now an engagement diary has hung on the living room wall of Coun Cain's council house home … and rarely has it shown a day without some public engagement for the owner! Often there have been as many as eight in one day. Council meetings, court sittings, trades union delegations, miners" welfare meetings, conferences, meetings of school governors, have all been taken in Coun Cain's stride.

Coun Cain is the present vice-chairman of Castle Eden magistrates – he was elected to the Bench in October 1946 – and for most of the last 20 years has been a member of Easington Rural Council for the Wheatley Hill ward. He also served a short period on Durham County Council after the last war but did not seek re-election at the end of his term of office. For a quarter of a century he has been a governor of Wellfield A J Dawson Grammar School, Wingate, and is the present chairman.

Miners' Welfare

Coun Cain has always taken a particularly keen interest in miners' welfare work. He is secretary of Wheatley Hill Miners' Welfare Committee, and has also served for some years on the No 3 Area Welfare Committee and the Durham Divisional Welfare Committee of the National Coal Board. The lot of the retired miner has always been dear to his heart and he has played a big part in the work of the local Aged Miners' Committee, as well as the Durham County Aged Mineworkers' Committee, on which he still serves.

Until last year, Coun Cain gave valuable service as an official of the local miners' lodge, mostly as chairman and then secretary, since 1920, and never spared any effort to secure better conditions for the men for whom he worked.

"I have enjoyed every minute of my public life, even though it has often meant one mad rush from getting up in the morning until going to bed late at night!" declared Coun Cain. "At times it has been arduous, but I have never counted any sacrifice too great, if I have been able in any way to help my fellow man."

Coun Cain is a member of the Disabled Persons' Unemployment Committee at Hartlepool and Wingate. As well as being a governor of Wellfield Grammar School, he is governor of Wheatley Hill Senior Girls' Modern Secondary School. He is a member of the Eastern Divisional Education Executive Committee, of which he has been chairman, and quite a number of other local committees claim his attention.

Lover Of Music

Despite so many public calls on his spare time, Coun Cain has always found time to foster his love of good music. He is particularly fond of classical music – he has a collection of about 350 gramophone records – and has delighted many local organisations with his recitals. He is a lover of the violin, being quite a capable player, and for some years played in the old Wheatley Hill Amateur Orchestra. A fluent speaker, his services have often been in demand on the public platform, and on the magisterial Bench he is well known for his wise judgment and sound advice.

Born at Seam Harbour, Coun Cain began work at Philadelphia colliery shortly before his 14th birthday as a trapper boy, earning 1s.11/2d a shift of ten hours. Later he worked at Lambton "D" Pit, Houghton, and Shotton before continuing his mining career at Wheatley Hill. When he moved to Shotton Colliery in 1908, Victoria Street was just being built and three years later when he took up residence in Wheatley Hill, one of the colliery streets – Fifteenth Street – was in the course of erection. He went through all the grades of mining – putting, hewing and filling – before his appointment as checkweighman.

Not only will his public duties, music and his liking for a good book help to keep Coun Cain busy during his well-earned retirement, but he will also take a delight in caring for his flower garden at the front and back of his home. "And, of course, I'll be able to take out my year-old grandson for many more walks," he smiled.

Coun Cain is married with an only son, Edward, who lives in Wingate, and a daughter, Mrs Frances Carr, who lives in Wheatley Hill. They share their father's love of good music. Mr Cain junior, is conductor of Wingate Choral Group, of which his sister is one of the 40-odd members.

LUDWORTH MINERS' AIM – PLAYING-FIELD

Some of the young miners of Ludworth have formed a recreation ground committee, the object being to provide playing fields for the children of the village.

Ludworth is a "colliery village without a colliery," for 80 per cent of its adult male population are miners employed at Thornley, Wheatley Hill, Sherburn Hill, or Shotton Collieries. These young men make their weekly contributions to the local welfare funds of the place at which they are employed, and have no facilities in their own village.

Ludworth is also a village without an housing problem. Its population of just over 1,000 are accommodated in 250 houses.

TRIBUTE TO MR T H HOLDER, THORNLEY

Mr Thomas Henry Holder, Clerk to Thornley parish Council for 38 years and a representative of newspapers locally for 51 years, was honoured at a presentation at Thornley on Wednesday. The presentation was made by Coun Mrs Jane Anderson, longest serving councillor, who handed to Mr Holder a wallet of notes from local organisations, councillors, past councillors and friends. Coun James Nicholson was chairman.

Among those paying tribute to Mr Holder were Messrs Hubert Tunney, Christopher Woodward, Duncan Davie, Swinburne Robinson and William Atkin.

Mr Holder, in reply, mentioned that he had missed but two meetings when he was clerk from 1918 to 1956. Among innumerable positions he had held were: secretary to the King George V Jubilee celebrations, secretary of the local Coronation celebrations in 1953, secretary to the Aged Miners' Homes from 1913 to 1926 and then treasurer of this committee from 1926 to 1951, treasurer for 25 years of the Welfare Committee, secretary and treasurer of the Pithead Baths Committee, a member of St Bartholomew's Church Council since its inception and our churchwarden from 1929 to 1946.

Main Speaker

Mr Tunney, a former member of the Parish Council and retired Labour Director for the NCB, Durham Division, was the main speaker. He said that they all recognised how difficult it was to find the words to give honour to one to whom honour was due.

"It is thought by some that, to be great, they must hit headlines," went on Mr Tunney. "That is not so: some of the greatest men we have ever had in this country have never hit the headlines, but they have given a lifetime to community interests. Mr Holder is a truly great man; he always struck me as a man who has taken a pride in his position."

Mr Tunney, after relating the many changes in Thornley over the years, commented: "If every you are committed to build, I hope that someone will see that there is a 'T H Holder Terrace'."

Two old friends of Mr Holder's, both former clerks of Parish Councils, Mr Swinburne Robinson and Mr William Atkin, moved votes of thanks to the speakers.
29 March 1957

THORNLEY PARISH COUNCIL

Something quite different from what was expected to take place in Thornley under the slum clearance programme of Easington rural District Council was revealed at the meeting of Thornley parish council by Coun J Nicholson, chairman. He said the whole of the south side of Thornley east of the colliery would be cleared within eight years with the exception of the public house, the Railway Tavern. The same treatment is to be given to Hartlepool Street North and South with the exception of the six public houses and the property in the Garden Terrace area.

Coun Nicholson said that after the area was cleared he expected that it would be redeveloped and all the families would be housed in Thornley. This programme included Colliery houses and Coopers Terrace.

Coun Mrs J Anderson gave a report of a meeting of the county highway authority with accident prevention offices and members of the parish council at Thornley Club corner considered the most dangerous spot in the village. It was suggested to narrow the road from Ludworth at its approach to the club.

5 April 1957

NEW WHEATLEY HILL CHECKWEIGHMAN

Mr Christopher Hackworth, 12 Durham Street, Wheatley Hill, who has been elected checkweighman at Wheatley Hill colliery from nine candidates, has been employed at the colliery from leaving school at the age of 14.

A single man, Mr Hackworth, who is 33, succeeds Coun Edward Cain, who retired at the weekend after having filled the position since 1934. While following his occupation as a putter in 1946 Mr Hackworth lost his right eye in a pit accident, and since then has been employed as a filler. His father, Mr Thomas Hackworth, was killed by a fall of stone at the colliery in March 1938 at the age of 39.

An uncle of Mr Hackworth, Mr James Mossop (76), now living in retirement at Gateshead, was formerly checkweighman at Wheatley Hill colliery for many years.

Mr Hackworth, who lives with his widowed mother, mrs S J Hackworth, is actively associated with Wheatley Hill workmen's Club, serving on the finance committee.

12 April 1957

WHEATLEY HILL SCOUTS' PROGRESS

Excellent progress had been made both by the Boy Scouts and the Wolf Cubs, reported Scoutmaster Leslie Barker, at the annual meeting of the 2nd Wheatley Hill Group of Scouts, presided over by Dr A P Gray. Cubs had a membership of 40 and there was a long waiting list, and there were no fewer than 63 Scouts in the Troup, which meant that two sessions had to be held. Altogether, added the Scoutmaster, over 140 Cubs, Scouts and Rovers were using the Scout headquarters, in addition to 25 Girl guides.

The secretary, Coun R Watson, reported a 'very favourable and active year," and the financial statement showed a balance in hand of £41.

Offices elected were: Chairman, Mr H Newton; treasurer, Mr W Harker; secretary, Coun R Watson; committee, Mesdames Hind, S Watson, M Watson, Cowan, Dunn, Walker, Richardson, Cook, Andrew, Burnside, Johnson and Rowland. Miss Shutt, Mr and Mrs Nicholson, Messrs Ayre, Aitkin, Armstrong and Booth and Dr A P Gray.

SOCIAL EVENING – Mrs J Ord (secretary) reports that a successful social evening was organised in aid of Wheatley Hill branch of the Guide Dogs for the Blind

Association. Sum of £22 was raised by the effort. The organisation was in the hands of Mrs Ord, mrs J Hargreaves (Chairman) and a strong committee. Winners were: Whist, Mrs Armstrong, Mrs Bramfitt, Mrs Brown, Robson, Mrs C Hargreaves, Mr Amies; dominoes, Mrs Mills, Mr Aitken, Master Wigham. Special prizes were won by Mrs Williamson and Mrs Durham.

MINISTER PRODUCES PLAY – Wheatley Hill Patton Street Methodist Church presented a religious play on Good Friday night to a "full house" in the Miners' Welfare Hall. The play presented was Ronald Cockram's "Shadow of the Eagle" a play in two acts, which was produced by the Rev g L nelson. Following took part: Alf Green, Lily Green, Dorothy Warnes, Betty Craggs, Tom King, William Walton and Anne Winnard, the Rev G L Nelson, Margaret Winnard, Charles Lister and Tom Venables. Passion music was played on records.
26 April 1957

DEATH OF FORMER THORNLEY MAN

The funeral took place last Thursday of Mr John W Bonar, age 53, (formerly of Thornley), who died on Monday at Brampton Cottage Hospital in Cumberland. Service in the Catholic Church was conducted by the Rev Father Bevenot.

Mr Bonar went to Thornley when a boy with his father, Mr John Bonar, who had been appointed headmaster of Thornley St Godric's RC School. He was educated at Ushaw College and at St Mary's, Hammersmith. At the age of 20 Mr Bonar had the distinction of being one of the youngest men to gain an honours degree first class (BA) in Latin and Greek at London University.

His first teaching appointment was at Jarrow, followed by 17 years at Gosforth Grammar School as music teacher. He went to Brampton in 1947, where he taught Latin at the White House School, and in his last year history and geography. His interest in music continued in Brampton, where he played in the school orchestra and gave violin and piano lessons to pupils at the school.

Chief mourners were his brothers, Messrs Charles, Thomas and Arthur Bonar, who live at Thornley and Haswell.

THORNLEY WIN FINE CUP TIE
Shotton Beaten in 12 Goal Game

One of the most thrilling games in local football for more than 25 years was seen at Thornley on Friday in the semi-final of the MacDonald Bowl competition. The home side, Thornley CW, defeated Shotton CW by 8-4.

Thornley were 4-3 up at the interval and later romped home to an easy win, Shotton being fortunate to escape so easily at the end. Play opened out at a terrific rate and the ball seemed to flash from goal to goal in seconds. Shotton goal nearly came to grief when Dave Carr caught a rebound from Stobbs and smashed the ball past the bewildered Stokoe, only to see it hit the upright.

Cairns was next to be dangerous when one of his centres was caught by the former Chelsea and Hartlepools player, Richardson, who banged it into a crowded goalmouth. Hall kicked off the line to save the dangerous situation.

When Weston went near for Shotton, Laverick gathered the ball at the second attempt. Shotton, however, were first to score when fine work by Ross on the left ended in a goal by Douglass. Thornley equalised when Carr, fed by Richardson, shot a wonderful goal.

In another minute Thornley were ahead when Brown chipped a centre by Cairns into the net. Then away came the home team again when Stobbs fastened on to a clearance by a troubled defence and slammed the ball into the back of the net.

3-3 Score

Elvin netted a second goal for Shotton and a minute later it was 3-3 when Passmore escaped the clutches of Greener for the first time. Before the centre Carr ended a brilliant first half for Thornley with their fourth goal. It was a fine brand of football, well pleasing the 1,500 spectators.

Thornley started off the second period in goal-hungry mood and first Carr and then Pickering rounded off good approach work by Richardson to make it 6-3, Thornley half-backs. Stobbs, Greener and Langley, were playing exceedingly well.

Denis Brown had an admirable game in this period and some of his footwork has the class of "the old maestro." It was Brown who made it seven with a picture goal from a Carr centre and then Langley dribbled his way through a tiring defence for the either. Shotton fought back for their fourth goal through Weston.

3 May 1957

"WORM'S EYE VIEW"
Comedy At Wheatley Hill

Memories – happy and otherwise – of their war time days in the Royal Air Force must have been revived by ex-airmen attending Wheatley Hill Amateur Dramatic Society's production of R F Delderfield's three-act comedy, "Worm's Eye View," in the Welfare Hall, Wheatley Hill. The show, which ended on Saturday night after a successful four night's run, drew capacity audiences who, at times, virtually rocked with laughter at the antics of the airmen billeted with a hard-hearted skinflint of a landlady.

As Mrs Bounty, the landlady, Evelyn Kenny, a seasoned player, brought plenty of punch into the play. Her 200-word-a-minute recital of the rules of the billet – "don't do this and don't do that!" – was a humorous treat in itself. And she received excellent support from her husband, portrayed by Don Willan. It's only a pity that Mr County vanished from the scene at the end of the first act – he was "desperate," he told the airmen billeted at his home from the daily whip-lashing tongue of his wife

Unqualified Success

From the moment he stepped on to the stage, the down- trodden, lugubrious, hen-pecked husband, Don was an unqualified success … and it was good to see his return in the last scene after he had been "missing" from the whole of Act II.

As Porter one of the boisterous newly-arrived recruits to the billet, Les Barker got hundreds of laughs. He fitted the role like a glove and his Cockney wit often had the audience in convulsions – he played no small part in the show and helped it to run along smoothly and at times riotously! His fellow recruit, Taffy the Welshman, was also well portrayed by William Craggs … it was rather a difficult part, calling for a strong Welsh accent, but William made the most of it.

As Mark, the corporal in charge of the billet, and Bella, the landlady's daughter, Ken Dowson and Elizabeth Punshon brought a tender love interest to the play. Both in humorous and serious vein they showed excellent talent. Elizabeth was particularly charming, sweet and modest, but when roused she had a lashing tongue and her ambitious, supercilious stepbrother received the full force of this when he attempted to break up her love affair with the corporal.

The "Villain"

Charles Lister, as Sidney Spooner, the step-brother, was the "villain of the piece." So ably did he play his part that we really thought it served him right when he got that delicious looking "black eye" from the corporal in the scene which was a complete riot … ending with poor Taffy putting his foot in the quivering jelly! Praiseworthy performances also came from Minnie Galloway, as Thelma, Mrs Bounty's saucy, hip-wiggling made – Porter and the audience always followed her with a roving eye – and Les Dryden, as the Duke, the flirt of an airman awaiting aircrew training.

Tom King as Pop, a 1914-18 airman who had re-enlisted in the second World War, showed a fatherly interest in all the airmen … and in the blossoming love affair of Mark and Bella. He gave a sympathetic performance and won his way into the hearts of the audience. Frank Bowes, as the commanding Officer of the Unit, had only a brief role in the last scene but filled it quite well.

Altogether it was a show which gave a novel slant on Service life and the cast, well chosen and well directed by Mrs Vera Fairclough, of Easington Village, gave a most polished performance. Mr Rob Horner was responsible for the sound effects and Mr Cyril Raffell for the lighting and stage managers were Mrs Nora Abbs and Mrs Ivy Scott.

REVELRY AT WHEATLEY HILL
Children's Sports Were Successful

Sponsored by Wheatley Hill Colliery Federation Board, sports day at the Peter Lee Girls' Modern School playing fields provided a real spirit of revelry on Saturday. Workers at Wheatly Hill had paid a levy of twopence for several weeks to help raise a fund of £400 to meet the costs of the event.

The sports were arranged by Mr A W Wharrier (chairman), Coun J Cowie (secretary), Mr C W Venables (assistant secretary), Mr J Hedley (treasurer) and a strong committee. The sports organiser was Mr E Ward, assisted by members of schools' teaching staffs.

Main awards went to: four miles race, Fred Bartram, junior, Baldersera Challenge Cup; outstanding girl, Irene Young, cup presented by DDSS Club; outstanding boy,

Stan Metcalfe, cup presented by Thornley Colliery Federation Board and medal given by Wheatley Hill Workmen's Club.

Proceedings started with a fancy-dress parade through the village, with Wheatley Hill Colliery Band heading the procession. Judges for fancy-dress events were Mrs G McLean, Miss A I Hutchinson and the Rev Gordon G Graham, the Vicar.

Fancy dress winners were: Comic, David White and Robet Ryan, Jennie Henderson, Michael Phenney. Original, Margaret Parnell and George Hedley, Terence Burke, Doreen Mason. Fancy, Maureen Phenney, Gavin and Jennifer Stott, Jeffrey Collingwood. Specials, David Jordan, Margaret Galley, Valerie Golden, Denis Burke.

Adults: comic, R Armstrong and E Evans; fancy, Jack Brown.

Presentations

Cups and awards were handed over by Mr G Richardson, Manager of Wheatley Hill Colliery, and Mrs Richardson.

Mr A Wharrier commented in his speech: "It is a long time since a May Day parade and sports were held in our village. Today we have caught something of the spirit of the days before the war."

Mr Wharrier said that the response had been so good from the people of Wheatley Hill that he had no doubt that the May Day celebrations would be repeated.

10 May 1957

SCHOOLS' FOOTBALL PROBE
Into Events At Wheatley Hill

Mr John Errington, Secretary of Durham County Schools' Football Association of North Road, Chester-le-Street, has communicated the result of an inquiry into publicity in the national press to one of the County Cup semi-finals at Wheatley Hill.

Mr Errington has issued the following statement:

"An inquiry was held by the cup competitions committee into certain complaints made by Darlington Grammar School after the playing of the County Cup semi-final tie between that school and Wheatley Hill Modern School at Wheatley Hill on Monday, April 8, the home team won by one goal to nil, scored by E Porter.

"The committee found, after due examination of all the evidence submitted that the Darlington Grammar School has grounds for complaints against (a) the pitch which was unfenced: (b) the markings which were unsatisfactory: and (c) the light since darkness fell early on the evening in question.

CLOSE WIN FOR WHEATLEY HILL

Wheatley Hill kept up their 100 per cent league when they entertained Silksworth on Saturday, but it was a near thing! After dismissing the visitors for 65, the "Hill" had seven wickets down for 42, but "skipper" Jack martin played a careful innings and his contribution of 21 helped to make the scores level at the fall of the eighth wicket. The last pair were together when the Silksworth score was beaten. Martin hit four boundaries.

SILKSWORTH: 65

WHEATLEY HILL: G Allison c G Page b Teare 11, R Taylor c Laws b Anderson 11, E C Simpson b Teare 6, B Winter b Teare 0, D Chisholm run out 5, A Fishwick lbw b Teare 0, J K Martin lbe b Johnson 21, H Simpson b Anderson 8, W E Simpson not out 4, G L Nelson c Orr b Johnson 0, J Wright not out: extras 1. Total (for nine wickets) 67.

Visiting Silksworth 11, Wheatley Hill 11 figured in a drawn game, replying to Silksworth's 125 for nine with 52 for five. T Graham took bowling honours for the "Hill," with three wickets for only 12 runs. Bobby Patterson had three for 24 and Forster two for 31. Graham was also top batsman with 18 runs and Barlow next with 12.

NEW COUNCIL CHAIRMAN – At the annual meeting of Wingate Parish Council Coun J Fenwick (Wheatley Hill) was elected chairman in succession to Coun J H Charlton and Coun M W Carter (Deaf Hill) vice-chairman. Coun P Unsworth was elected delegate to the annual conference of the Burial and Cremation Authorities at Hastings (September 3 to 5), Coun J H Charlton to the annual conference of Public Lighting Engineers at Torquay (September 17 to 20) and Coun A Bishop (Wheatley Hill) to the annual conference of Parish Councils at Westminster (October 3 to 4).

SCOUTS' EFFORT – Fifty-eight Boy Scouts and 40 Wolf Cubs who took part in the recent Bob-a-Job Week organised locally by the 1st Wheatley Hill Troop of Boy Scouts, raised the magnificent sum of £71. The Scouts alone raised £45 – more than double last year's figure – and the Cubs £26. Scoutmaster L Barker and Assistant Scoutmaster W Mowbray thank all those who found so many "jobs" to keep the boys busy.

CIVIL DEFENCE CUP – County Coun E Colgan on Saturday presented the W H B Cotton Civil Defence Cup to Thornley Colliery rescue team, winners for the second successive year. Thornley team: Messrs F Bradley, senior (leader), F Bradley, junior, F Carter, L Mitchell, N Fort, N Mayne, M Convery, T Bullick and K Lonsdale. Thirty-one teams competed. Thornley met Sedgefield Rural Council in the final.

GOLDEN WEDDING – Mr and Mrs George E Graham, Aged Miners' Cottages, Thornley, celebrated their golden wedding on Saturday. They were married at St Saviour's Church, Shotton, by the Rev E Fenton. Mr Graham is now 74. He retired from work as a deputy overman at Thornley Colliery in 1949. Mrs Graham is 69 years old. Three daughters with their husbands, six grand-daughters, two grandsons and three great-grandsons, saw this grand old couple cut the cake that has been made to meet the gret occasion.

MOTHER'S CLUB – it was visitors' night when Mrs E Powell presided over the meeting of Wheatley Hill Mothers' Club in Welfare Hall. The visitors were present from Wingate, Thornley and Peterlee Mothers' Clubs. Business details were read by the secretary, Mrs I Snowdon. Refreshments were provided by the Wheatley Hill Club. A competition for a cake on behalf of the Wheatley Hill Aged Miners' Fund realised £3.15s.9d. Prize winners were Mrs Raine and Mrs Gilchrist. Games and dancing were enjoyed by the large company. Mrs E Powell was MC
24 May 1957

THORNLEY PARISH COUNCIL
Election of Chairman

At the annual meeting of Thornley parish Council, Councillor Alfred Bushby, 4 Garden Terrace, Thornley, was elected chairman. Councillor James Nicholson, retiring chairman, thanked the members for his pleasant year of office. Councillor James Hoban was elected vice-chairman.

Councillor Bushby has long taken an active interest in the affairs of the village, and is chairman of Thornley Colliery Mechanics' Lodge and a member of the county executive. He was a founder-member of Thornley Colliery Mining Federation Board and holds several other important appointments. In his duties as chairman he will lead the negotiations with NE Electricity Board when they take over the public network from the NCB for the supply of electrical energy.

The council decided to take no action in regard to a complaint by Mr G Eley, farmer, as to damage to his crops following the erection of a roadside seat on the footpath between the council school and Fat Close Farm. Mr Eley said that at least one acre of his crop had been damaged each year.

A request is to be made to land agent, NCB, to complete the repair of a stile at the council school, Thornley. At present cattle gain access to the main road.

Shadforth and Haswell parish councils are to be asked to have footpaths across Shotton moors and Hare Hill Farm made accessible to the public.

Traffic Congestion

The council is concerned about traffic congestion during shopping hours near the Villas, Thornley, and the County Surveyor is to be asked for a report.

MOTOR-CYCLE'S "EXCESSIVE SPEED"

"You certainly had a joy-ride!" said the Chairman (Coun C H Wreford) to a 17-year-old Wheatley Hill youth, William Ord, 22 Liddell Terrace, who was alleged to have driven a motor-cycle belonging to a friend at a reckless speed through the streets of Wheatley Hill at 10 pm on April 5. he was chased by a patrol office.

Ord, who pleaded "Guilty" to dangerous driving, was fined £3 and had his licence endorsed. He was also fined £1 for using a motor-cycle not fitted with two foot-rests for the passenger, and £1 for carrying an unlicensed passenger on the pillion, and his passenger, Charles E Crick (21), 51 Dalton Terrace, Wheatley Hill, who wrote pleading "Guilty" to aiding and abetting Ord to commit these two offences, was fined £5.

The motor-cycle, said Chief Insp J McGill, belonged to Crick, who had bought it only that day. Both Ord and Crick were learner drivers, and Ord was teaching the other man to drive.

In court, Ord said the machine had not been running right. He repaired it and "went up the road" for a ride with Crick on the pillion – he thought there was nothing wrong with this. When he was told the police car was following them he became scared "and did away," and once he had started he "daren't stop."

AID FOR OVER 60'S – The sum of £25.4s was raised for the funds of Wheatley Hill Over-60 Club as a result of a successful "hostess" social evening in the Welfare Hall, organised by the ladies' committee. Arrangements were made by the secretary, Mrs R Richardson.

WAGES OFFER REJECTED – After hearing a report from their delegate, Mr J Cain, on the new wages offer for certain sections of the mining industry, Wheatley Hill miners' lodge at a meeting presided over by Mr A D Wharrier, unanimously voted against acceptance of the offer.

LODGE OFFICIALS – At the annual nomination meeting of Wheatley Hill miners' lodge, the delegate, Mr jack Cain, was the only official opposed. Mr H Bradshaw, junior, was nominated for this position in addition to Mr Cain and balloting for this and the various committees associated with the lodge will take place next week. Officials returned unopposed were: Chairman, Mr A D Wharrier; correspondence secretary, Mr C W Venables; financial secretary, Mr J Hedley; treasurer, Mr T Taylorson; compensation secretary, Mr M Alderton; auditors, Messrs T and G Buxton.
31 May 1957

LUDWORTH MAN'S FUNERAL AT THORNLEY
Funeral took place on Wednesday of Mr Peter Gavaghan, Barnard Avenue, Ludworth. The body was received into Thornley RC Church on Tuesday and following Requiem Mass said by the Rev father McNeill interment took place at Thornley.

Mr Gavaghan was born in Ireland but came to this country as a young man and found work as a farm labourer at Castle Eden. He later worked at West Stanley Colliery and Wheatley Hill Colliery, where he was seriously injured in 1928. He had not worked since. He is survived by his wife and two sons.

CYCLING TESTS AT THORNLEY
Coun Mrs J Anderson, organising secretary of Thornley Road Safety Committee, was well satisfied when 30 children turned up at Thornley Colliery Welfare Football Ground to be tested for cycling proficiency. PC J L Jackson was the test master.

Peter Luke, J Burgin, J Armstrong, Joan Armstrong, Colin Bullock, Margaret Luke, Andrew Bonar, James Garnham, David Horner, Ann Green, John Ramshaw, Tonly Hunt, Norman Gordon, Pauline Adams, Peter Millington, Marjorie Anderson, William Thompson, Wilfred "Gordon, Carole Bullock and Valerie Wright received the highest marks.

7 June 1957

WHEATLEY HILL UNDER-MANAGER'S MBE

Awarded the MBE in yesterday's Birthday Honours List was Mr Frederick Simpson, of West House, Wheatley Hill, under-manager at Wheatley Hill colliery for the past 19 years. Mr Simpson, who is 58 and unmarried, has spent all his mining career at Wheatley Hill colliery. He started as a datal worker at the age of 14 and went through all the various grades of mining. He was fore-overman for 12 years before his appointment as under-manager.

Mr Simpson has served on the colliery consultative committee since its formation during the war years and has been a member of Wheatley Hill Colliery Welfare Committee since 1926. He is also a Welfare trustee and served on the local pit-head baths and canteen committees before the Coal Board took over.

Other Interests

Mr Simpson has always played an active part in the social and sporting life of the village. For 30 years he has been a trustee of the Wheatley Hill Boys Scouts' Association, and for many years vice-president of the local cricket club. He is a trustee of Castle Eden Golf Club, where he has been a playing member for 24 years, and tennis and badminton have also claimed his interest. Throughout the last war he served as an office in the Wheatley Hill Home Guard being a platoon commander in the 22nd Battalion. His father, Mr Robert Simpson, who was an official at the colliery, died in 1946.

14 June 1957

MOTHERS' CLUB – Mrs E Stephenson presided at meeting of Thornley Mothers' Club. There was a good attendance and Mrs Nancy Mason (Secretary) gave business details. Evening outing for mothers is booked for July 4 to South Shields. It was agreed that members' children should be taken for a day's outing to Seaton Carew, one Saturday in August. Competition prizes were awarded to Mrs M Hodgson and Mrs E Robson.

CIVIL DEFENCE – Thornley Colliery Civil Defence rescue team who represented the county in the rally at Newcastle on Saturday, have for the second year in succession won the shield. Thornley team, who are also members of Easington Rural Council Civil Defence are Mr F Bradley, (leader), Mr F Bradley, junior, Mr F Carter, Mr L Mithcell, Mr N Fort, Mr N Mayne, Mr K Lonsdale and Mr S Laird. This team will compete at Washington in the NCB Divisional contest.

BRITISH LEGION WOMEN – Thornley section held a social evening in Thornley Miners' Welfare Institute. Mr J Toy entertained with music and songs and others taking part were Mrs Barras, Mrs Mitchell and Mrs S Redshaw. Prize winners were Mesdames R Cook, Allen, Anderson, Bell, Clough, Cullen, Foster, Hodgson, Howe, Liddle, Musgrave, Raine, C Raine, S Redshaw, Wright and Simms. Best wishes were extended to Mrs Brewster (president) who has been in failing health for some time.
28 June 1957

THORNLEY PARISH AFFAIRS

The chairman, Councillor A Bushby, Councillor J Nicholson and the clerk, Mr M Fleming, are to meet Haswell and Shadforth Parish Council regarding footpaths in the three parishes.

The deplorable state of the allotment gardens was voiced by Councillor Mrs E Bosomworth. It was agreed to draw up new tenancy agreements.

A reply by the United Automobile Services Ltd to a request for a direct bus service from Thornley to Crimdon park was discussed. Mr D S Deacon, traffic manager, said the service was operated during the summer months on Sundays which is normally the best day of the week as far as Crimdon is concerned and it ran during the three peak years 1947-49. Despite this, however, the amount of traffic conveyed did not justify the setting aside of a special bus and crew for this work and they were compelled to discontinue the service.

Councillor J Nicholson said this question was being taken up by Easington RDC who had asked for Mr Shinwell's assistance.
5 July 1957

VETERANS' TRIP – Retired members of Wheatley Hill Discharged and Demobilised Soldiers' and Sailors' Club and their wives, and widows of retired members, spent an enjoyable day at South Shields on Saturday for their annual outing. The men received £1 each pocket money and the women 10s, and in addition each tripper was given 5s meal expenses. The party was taken in six coaches, with members of the committee in charge, and arrangements were made by Messrs C Curry (chairman), W Hackworth (secretary) and R Burnip (Treasurer).
12 July 1957

CLUB COMMITTEE – As a result of a ballot at Wheatley Hill workingmen's Club the following were elected to the committee from 30 nominations: Messrs T Neilson, S Metcalfe, R Armstrong, R cook, R Trotter and S Hastings. Messrs J Maddison, J Gibson and A Poole were elected scrutineers.

VETERANS' TRIP – Each tripper was given 7s.6d pocket money when 300 retired miners at Wheatley Hill colliery and their wives and widows over 55 were taken to Redcar for their outing on Tuesday by Wheatley Hill Aged Miners' Committee. The party, which was in charge of officials and committee of the Aged Miners' fund, was conveyed in a fleet of nine motor-coaches. Arrangements were made by the secretary, Coun J Cowie, and treasurer, Mr J Hedley.

THEIR BIG DAY

Mr J Gair, secretary of Wheatley Hill Colliery Band, announces that tomorrow will be a big day for four Wheatley Hill boys. When the band leaves Wheatley Hill to lead the colliery banner and miners to Durham Gala four juveniles will be playing in public for the first time.

Mr Gair said: "It is the first time for more than eight years that schoolboys will be playing alongside their seniors. The boys are Robert Booth (11), Keith Almond (12), Edward Newby (12) and my own son, Jonathan Gair (10). To play at Durham Miners' Gala is a first experience the lads won't forget in a hurry."

The boys have been taught to play their instruments by the assistant bandmaster, Mr Arthur Donaldson. He has coached them on Wednesday evenings and Sunday mornings for some months.

There is another unusual feature to record. The bandmaster's sister, Miss Olive Strong, of Blackhall, will be the only lady playing in the band. She plays the soprano cornet. The band will be under the leadership of Mr Harold Strong.

LEGION WOMEN – Mrs Slater presided at meeting of Thornley British Legion Women's Section. Business details were given by Mrs P E Morgan (secretary). A "bring-and-buy" sale was held to help branch funds. Special prize was won by Mrs Heard and other winners were Mrs E Ferguson and Mrs B Musgrave. Annual outing was to Penrith, Carlisle and Hexham. Social evening followed the meeting.

"BIG MEETING" morning in Thornley always draws a good number of early morning spectators. In 1870 Durham Miners' Association had 22 lodges and Thornley lodge was second with a membership of 230. There are over 1000 members. In 1871 at the first gala, Thornley miners' banner decorated the platform. Every year since Thornley lodge have attended. This year, Mr Fred Peart MP, a Thornley man, will be one of the chief speakers. A familiar figure with the banner each year is Mr Jos Straughan, a 70 year old retired miner who lost a leg in the first war. He has attended every gala for over 50 years, marching the full route with the help of his crutches. Banner carriers are: Messrs J H Straughan, A Wallace, M Kirk, T George, J McCoy, W Holmes, W Curry (jun), and J H Davis with six reserves. Banner carriers each receive £3, first and second reserves each £1.10s and third, fourth, fifth and sixth 10s each.

THORNLEY TEST MATCHES

St Chad's Square, Thornley, the scene of many a tough game has been the place for a series of test matches for the lads of St Bede's, St Cuthbert's, St Chad's, St Aiden's, Laurel and Kenton. The enthusiasm in this series was fired by the sportsmanlike efforts of Coun Jimmy Nicholson, chief patron, himself an old cricketer and footballer who has presented to the winning team of players one of the eight small cups that he won in his football days.

The tests are by no means comparable to the scene at Lords but, at least they draw a crowd, and each night the tenants on the surrounding estate walk to the garden gate free of entertainment tax to watch the prowess of these youthful cricketers.

The only thing the field can claim in comparison to the pitches of Eton and rugby is that it has some rough grass surrounding the pitch which lends a bit of colour to the battlefield.

The turf, the pitch, and the gear, are only incidentals; there are no autographed Patsy Hendron willows in sight. Easington Rural Council provide free of charge the wickets in the shape of ash bin lids which are supported at the back with two bricks and serve in the dual capacity of stopping the ball dead and notifying the crowd in dinner gong echoes that the batsman has "had it".

When Nicholson comes from his house with the scorebook under his arm they know field must be cleared for action, and the odd half-brick and the old bicycle tyre are thrown clear. When Jimmy raises his hand the game is away. Little Bobby, a spin bowler sends the ball along, and little Jacky returns to the pavilion the first of the many "ducks" of the night's game.

19 July 1957

COUNTY SCHOOL'S FOOTBALL

Congratulating entrants in the County competitions, Mr Errington especially thanked Wheatley Hill Modern School since they were involved in "a most distressing incident" following their semi-final tie with Darlington Grammar School. The incident, he said, might have affected their play in later games, but had instead appeared to act as a fillip.

They deservedly won in the final against Durham Grammar School by two goals to one, the goals scored by H Brierley and D Metcalfe, the game was played on the Welfare ground, Thornley. The team players: H Brierley, W Cook, G Crawford, B Harvey, J Hunter, J Lloyd, C Maughan, D Metcalfe, E Porter, E Wilkinson and J Wilkinson. The much maligned spectators at Wheatley Hill proved their good sportsmanship by patronising to the full the later games staged in that area," he said.

"The National Press," said Mr Errington, "has well-earned our condemnation for its one-sided publicity, on hearsay, of the incident without waiting for confirmation of the facts." Statements by two parents of boys who had played in that match were used.

Successful Season

Mr Errington described the past season as a most successful one. From a playing point of view standards of play had continued to be most satisfactory, the games played had provided some really high standards in football. An end of season team photograph includes, D Abbs, J Peacock and M Tinkler. They replaced the cup winners, G Crawford, E Porter, E Wilkinson, who had left school at the end of term. Permission by Durham School's FA allowed these three players to play in the final.

Wheatley Hill Secondary Modern School 1957

MAY DAY RECKONING – The financial statement issued by the Wheatley Hill May Day Celebrations' Committee shows that the income of £383.1s.4d included £380 from workmen's contributions at the colliery. The sum of £264 was spent on 3s bags of fruit and sweets for 1,760 children in the area on May Day, and £100 on prizes for the children's sports, races and the fancy and comic dress parade. After all expenses had been met a balance of £11.15s.5d remained. The officials in charge were Mr A Wharrier (chairman), Coun J Cowie (secretary) and Mr J Hedley (treasurer).

OCTOGENARIAN HONOURED – Oldest member of Wheatley Hill Church Street Methodist Sisterhood, Mrs Elizabeth Turnbull, who today celebrates her 80th birthday, was entertained to tea by her fellow-members at the meeting on Monday. A birthday cake, provided by members, was cut, and best wishes for many more years of happiness and good health were extended to Mrs Turnbull by the Rev G L Nelson. The meeting, which preceded the tea, was presided over by Mrs E Parnham, and an address was given by Mrs Brown, wife of the Rev Leonard Brown, Peterlee. Mrs Mason was soloist, and Mrs Venables pianist.

OVER-60 CLUB – To mark her birthday and wedding anniversary, a club member, Mrs J Walton presented a gift to the oldest member of Wheatley Hill Over 60-Club, 87 year old Mrs Ann Jackson, at the meeting on Tuesday. Mr C Raffell presided and birthday greetings were extended to Mesdames J Walton, J Westgarth, E Hird, M Woodhead, J Andrewatha, T Gair and Martin, and Mr G Musgrave. A "go-as-you-please" entertainment was by the following: Mesdames W Dixon, E Brownless, R Richardson and E Amies, and Messrs C Raffell, W Kipling, J R Charlton and T H Vincent. Winners of the "lucky" prizes were Mesdames J Robinson, T Hird, W Bell, t Collingwood, J Sutherland, R Bowes, J Hoban, W turnbull, H Lowe and J Walton, and Mr J Iveson.

26 July 1957

CLUB COMMITTEE – As a result of the half-yearly ballot at Wheatley Hill Discharged and Demobilised Soldiers' and Sailors' Club, the following were elected to the committee from 26 nominations: Messrs A Carr, R Hackworth jun, T Christopher, G Hedley, G Curry and J Humes.

UNDER CANVAS – Scholars and teachers said "Good-bye" for six weeks on Friday, but not at Wheatley Hill Boys' Modern school. A party of 36 of the senior boys and members of the staff have travelled to Barnard Castle on a camping holiday. For a week they will live under canvas. Teachers accompanying the boys are mr Arthur Harris, head teacher, and Messrs E Ward, A Stabler, A Jones, J Etherington and G Potts. Bowes Museum, High Force and Egglestone Abbey would be visited. Conducted tours have also been arranged for a glove and leather factory and the Glaxo baby food factory.

2 August 1957

THORNLEY PARISH COUNCIL
Complaints Regarding Street Games

Councillor Frank A Walker, who was co-opted on to the Council in place of Mrs Margaret Hobbs (resigned) was welcomed by Councillor a Bushby.

A letter from Mr Frank McCarroll, 33 Ruskin Crescent, Thornley, asking the Council if anything could be done to stop the playing of football and cricket in certain streets was read. Mr McCarroll said that when he approached the boys about going to the recreation ground he was told that the ground was not fit to play on, and until the Parish Council made it fit they would play in the street.

The Clerk was instructed to consult County Councillor J Andrews with a view to having the schools playing field open for the use of the children of Gore Hall Estate.

Straying Cows

A question of cows straying into the council allotments gardens and destroying leeks prepared for the annual shows was raised by Councillor A Bushby who said that he had received a complaint from a gardener who was a big price-winner not only in local shows but in national contests. He had a number of his prize onions destroyed. Other people had their leeks destroyed. It was a big blow to a man who took pride in his work to see his year's labour wiped out through the negligence of some other person. The clerk was instructed to take this matter up with the owners of the cattle.

76

The very dangerous state of the roadway leading from Hartlepool Street to Coopers Terrace, especially in front of the Police station, was brought to the notice of the Council by Councillor Robert Slater who said the big pot holes in the road made it a danger to even horse-drawn traffic.

DEATH OF MR DUNLAVEY
Peter Lee's Nephew

Many mourners and friends were present at the Requiem Mass and funeral of Mr James Dunlavey, age 67, of Thornlaw, Thornley, who died during the week at his home. A nephew of the later Peter Lee, he was born at South Shields, the third son of a family of 18. His mother was sister to Peter Lee. During the first world war he saw service in France with the RAMC and there contracted trench fever from which he never recovered, and which incapacitated him for many years.

He leaves a widow, three sons and two daughters. His three sons and his son-in-law were underbearers at the funeral.

9 August 1957

FEWER ACCIDENTS RECORDED
Improvement At Wheatley Hill

Since "Keep Left" bollards had been erected near Vincent's Corner, Wheatley Hill, the risk of accidents had been considerably reduced, said Coun N Cook at Wingate Parish Council meeting on Monday, presided over by Coun J Fenwick. "I think they are a big improvement," went on Coun Cook. They help to slow up the traffic and make drivers much more careful. There's been only one smash since they were put there!"

Coun Cook made his comments after a letter had been read from the County Surveyor asking the Council for its observations on the new lay-out at the corner.

It was agreed to write the Surveyor saying that the Council was quite satisfied with the improvement made. At the same time the Surveyor is to be asked if it is possible to erect guard-rails at each side o the road. "If this were done," said the Chairman, "it would compel people to use the pedestrian crossing as in towns."

Condition of Bus Shelters

At the moment two new bus shelters built near Wheatley Hill Colliery offices were not much use when it was raining, said Coun Cook. The rain "teemed in" and people got just as wet inside as outside. "You would have thought the Rural Council would have completed the job once they started it," added Coun Cook.

16 August 1957

DEATH OF MRS FOORD, WHEATLEY HILL

The death occurred at her home of Mrs Margaret Foord (75), 14 Wingate Lane, Wheatley Hill. She is survived by her husband, Mr George Foord, a son and three daughters. Her death ends a marriage partnership of 46 years all spent in Thornley and Wheatley Hill.

Mr Foord is well known as a keen judge and rabbit breeder, specialising in the Dutch variety. He is a member of the Executive Committee of the United Kingdom Dutch Rabbit Club, president of the North East Counties Dutch Rabbit Club and president of the Sedgefield Fanciers' Society. Mrs Foord accompanied her husband at shows all over the British Isles.

Mrs Foord was born in the Houghton-le-Spring area. When she married at the age of 29, Mr and Mrs Foord moved to Thornley to take charge of the Barrel and Grapes Inn, better known as the Half Way House.

She was very interested in the affairs of her village, a member of Wheatley Hill WI and All Saints' Church and Mothers' Union.

Funeral service in All Saints' Church yesterday was conducted by the Rev G G Graham. Cremation followed at Sunderland.

MINING OFFICIAL KILLED
In Harvey Seam of Thornley Colliery

Only a fortnight back at work from his annual holiday which he spent at Great Yarmouth with his wife, Mr Edward Hall (48), 30 Station Road, Shotton Colliery, who recently took up a new appointment in No 3 Area of the Durham Divisional Coal Board as a coal-cutting machine demonstrator, was killed in an accident in the Harvey seam at Thornley colliery on Friday afternoon. Repair work was being carried out on the flight coal-cutting machine when it is understood, it began to move and Hall was trapped. He was killed instantly.

Mr Hall was esteemed at Shotton, when he spent practically the whole of his life. He was employed at the colliery there from leaving school, and eventually became a deputy, then an official. Before taking up his new job as coal-cutting machine demonstrator about three months ago, he was employed as master shifter for a number of years. "He was extremely happy in his new job, liking it very much," a relative told our reporter.

Widow's Elder Son

Mr Hall, elder son of a 79 year old widow, Mrs Dorothy Hall, 17 Aged Miners' Homes, Shotton is survived by his wife, Olive, and an only daughter, Doreen. His daughter will be 18 on Monday – the same day that her father would have celebrated his 49th birthday.

Mr Hall was a member of the Shotton Colliery rescue team and, like his fellow members, gave yeoman service during the Easington pit disaster six years ago. For many years he was actively associated with Shotton CW football club. He was club secretary in the 1948-9 season when, for the first time, they won the Wearside League Challenge Cup. He served as secretary for three seasons after a long term as a member of the Committee.

As a tribute to Mr Hall's memory, players and officials of both Shotton CW and Blackhall CW football teams observed a minute's silence before the start of their Wearside League Challenge Cup match at Blackhall Welfare Park on Saturday.

MINERS' LEVY INCREASE – F Richardson presided at a special meeting of Wheatley Hill Miners' Welfare members at the weekend, when, because of increasing expenses to be met by the Welfare Committee, it was agreed to increase the miners' weekly levy by twopence per full member and a penny per half member. The new levy will be 5d for full members and 21/2d for half members. Coun E Cain, who has served on the Welfare Committee for the past 32 years, resigned as secretary, a position he has filled for the last 15 years, and Coun J Cowie was elected his successor.

6 September 1957

BACK TO AMERICA
After A Visit To Wheatley Hill

A former Wheatley Hill couple, who returned to that village two years ago for a few months' holiday from the United States but extended their stay because of illness in the family, set sail again at the weekend for America where, in their own words, they are to "continue where they left off."

The couple, 37 year old Mr Edward Grosvenor and his wife Mary, were married at Thornley in 1949 and spent the first three years of their married life at Wheatley Hill before emigrating to Canada early in 1952. they settled in Toronto, where Mr Grosvenor soon obtained lucrative employment as a bricklayer, but three years later they moved to Detroit, in Michigan. The reason they left Canada for the United States, Mrs Grosvenor told our reporter, was because of even better prospects for her husband's trade than there were in Canada. "Though," she added, "my husband never lost a day's work in Canada."

Six Months' in Detroit

After six months in Detroit, the couple returned to this county for their first holiday since emigrating. This was in October 1955. they stayed with Mrs Grosvenor's parents, Mr and Mrs Michael Hagan, at Wheatley Hill, and later at Peterlee. Mr Hagan was taken ill and so his daughter and son-in-law decided to extend their stay here. Last December, only seven weeks after moving to Peterlee, Mr Hagan died at the age of 57.

Mr Grosvenor, in the meantime, found employment as a bricklayer with a Stockton contractor and was working until a week before leaving this country again. "We like America very much," said Mrs Grosvenor, "and are looking forward to settling down there again, but the prospects of earning money are so good that it likely won't be long before we are back again in Durham for another holiday." Mrs Grosvenor had been in Canada only a year after first emigrating when she flew home for her sister's wedding at Thornley.

Young Man From Ludworth

When they reach Detroit, the couple are staying for a while with a young man from Ludworth, Mr George Williams, who emigrated shortly after they did. Later they hope to travel further afield to California and Mr Grosvenor, whose father, Mr Edward Grosvenor, lives at 16 West Street, Shotton Colliery, has ambitions of setting up in his own contracting business.

Before emigrating in 1952, Mr Grosvenor was a bricklayer in Newton Aycliffe. Mrs Grosvenor's grandfather was an American. Her widowed mother lives at 60 Basingstoke Road, Peterlee.

20 September 1957

INQUEST ON SHOTTON OFFICIAL

Crushed Between Machine and PropTwo witnesses at a Thornley inquest last Thursday night on a mining official who was killed instantly when crushed between a coal-cutting machine and a prop when the machine unexpectedly lurched forward four-and-a-half yards agreed, in answer to Mr D Davie, HM Inspector of Mines, that the possibility of the machine moving forward in such a fashion was "a new hazard" as far as machine-mining was concerned.

The inquest was on Edward Hall, (48), married with one daughter, of 30 Station Road, Shotton Colliery. The jury returned a verdict of "Accidental death." Hall, a power-loader demonstrator, who was a member of the No 3 Area, NCB, mechanisation power-loading team, had been helping to repair the machine which had broken down earlier in the day at Thornley colliery.

Did Not Realise Danger

William James Jobes, 43 Thornlaw North, Thornley, said when he went to work at the South busty winning face at 11 am he found the machine had broken down and only about seven yards of coal had been cut. He remained with the power-loading team, helping them to fit a new jib, and by 2.30 pm the job was completed. After the machine had been tried, he was with members of the team when they were discussing how the machine should be moved into its working position.

"I picked up a wooden chock," continued Jobes, "and threw it on to the 'goaf' side of the conveyor to get the cutter back to the cutting position again. The chock, however, struck a prop and was deflected on to the moving conveyor chain. I jumped over the conveyor to rap 'hold' and then heard some men shout. I then saw the cutter had been carried down by the loose chock which, in some way, had become wedged under the machine."

Replying to Mr W Ginghorn (representing the Coal Board), Jobes said he was about three yards from the conveyor when he three the chock – in a flash he rapped hold after this to stop the conveyor chain. In reply to Mr J Varley, assistant Regional Officer for the NUM Colliery Officials' and Staffs' Association, he said he did not realise the danger of throwing the chock until it moved the coal-cutting machine.

Engineer George Gilroy, 8 Newark Close, Peterlee, a member of the power-loading team, said that the face where the accident occurred was 95 yards long. The conveyor chain, he explained, was laid the full length of the face, which was cut by the machine sliding on top of the conveyor. While they worked on the broken machine it was stationary in its normal position on the conveyor, but the conveyor chain was being run intermittently to carry the small amount of coal which was being produced at the other end of the face. "We did no consider the running of the conveyor chain to be of any danger," he added, "or we would have asked for it to be stopped.

A "New Hazard"

After the machine had been repaired, witness continued they were preparing to take it up towards the butt end of the coal when he was startled to see the machine lurch forward "as if it had switched itself on in some way."

"I dived for the control switch," said Gilroy, "but found there was no power and it was still out of gear. The machine travelled about 41/2 yards, then stopped, and then I saw Hall had been crushed between the jib and the props as the machine had been propelled forwards."

Afterwards, added Gilroy, he saw a six inch wooden chock wedged beneath the body of the machine. "I came to the conclusion that in some manner it had been carried down on the conveyor," Gilroy said, "and became wedged under the machine, which was carried forward by the moving conveyor chain."

Replying to Mr Davie, witness agreed it was a new hazard in mining which they would have to try and counter.

Mr Davie: I appreciate it is easy to be wise after the event but, looking back, is it not correct to say that the machine could have been moved in many ways, apart from something being thrown? - No.

Mr Davie: Supposing a tool, such as a hammer or axe, had been dropped on the moving chain and carried down on to the cutter, would the cutter have moved in the same manner? – Yes, if the tool had fallen in a certain way.

Mr Davie: And a stone could have fallen and caused the same mishap? – Yes, this could have happened.

Purely An Accident

Thomas Wilkinson, 39 School Square, Thornley, who was the deputy-overman in charge of the back shift in the seam, said that the machine was something quite new to the pit. He, too, agreed with Mr Davie, that the possibility of the machine moving in such a fashion was a new hazard as far as mining was concerned.

Hall, said Dr John Gray, died of severe crushing injuries. He received a fracture of the spine, fractured ribs and other injuries and death must have been instantaneous.

There was no doubt, said Mr Davie, addressing the jury, that the new machine appeared to be "a bit of a hazard." It was purely an accident that had occurred. "And

81

I have no doubt," he added, "that in future when men are working on the machine they will keep a lot clearer from it than they did on this occasion."

Sympathy with the deceased's relatives was expressed by the Coroner, Mr Davie, Mr Kinghorn, Mr Varley, Mr Owens (representing the Deputies' Association) and Sgt Moore (representing the police).

27 September 1957

DIED AT BROADMOOR – George Wilson (63), formerly a miner, Shakespeare Street, Wheatley Hill, died at Broadmoor on Saturday. Wilson, at Durham Assizes in November 1933, was found guilty but insane on a charge of murdering his wife, Annie Wilson.

LIBRARY ISSUES – From Wheatley Hill branch of the Durham County Library last month, 1,943 books were issued as follows: Fiction, 1,422; non-fiction, 395; juvenile, 126. The average daily issue was 162 and 20.3 per cent of the total issues were non-fictional.

DIED AT BLACKPOOL – Well-known in Wheatley Hill, where she had lived for 42 years, Mrs Mary Annie Powell (60), 7 Wordsworth Avenue, died on Tuesday in Blackpool Victoria Hopsital, following two operations in which she lost her right leg and her left hand. Mrs Powell and her husband, Nichol, a miner at Wheatley Hill colliery, left home on September 7 for a fortnight's holiday at Blackpool, but during the second week Mrs Powell was taken ill and removed to hospital, where she had since lain. Mrs Powell, a life-long Methodist, was actively associated with Church Street Methodist Church, at Wheatley Hill, and was formerly a member of the Sisterhood. She is survived by an only son, Mr George Howie Kent, and three daughters. Her eldest daughter, Miss Peggy Kent is a nurse at a Blackpool Maternity Hospital. Her two other daughters are Mrs Dorothy Mitchell, of station Town; and Miss Marjorie Kent.

18 October 1957

HAPPY HOLIDAY IN CANADA
Wheatley Hill Widow Returns Home

After the most wonderful holiday of her life … shortly afterwards joined him at his camp in Canada. The couple are now stationed at Penhold, near Red Deer, in Alberta.

In The Rockies

"My daughter loves Canada and would not dream of coming back to England," said Mrs Cowan. Three-and-a-half years ago she came back here for a holiday with her son and daughter, who are now aged six and ten, respectively, but the climate here affected her health and she shortened her stay from 12 to seven weeks.

Whenever Mrs McHarg's husband Bill – a Flight Sergeant in the Candian RAF – had any free time at the camp he got out his car and took Mrs Cowan to "see the sights." Three weeks of his leave were also spent taking Mrs Cowan through some of Canada"s most beautiful country.

Highlights of Mrs Cowan's visit were a thrilling trip through the Canadian Rockies – "they're certainly everything they are made out to be," she said – and an exciting week at the annual Calgary "Stampede was a Wild West show on a scale I would scarcely have believed possible had I not seen it for myself!" said Mrs Cowan. Indians and cowboys invaded Calgary from all over the country and put on the most spectacular show day after day for a week.

One of Mrs Cowan's many souvenirs is a snapshot of herself with one of the Indian chiefs.

Visited Us

The beautiful scenery through the Rockies had to be seen to be believed, said Mrs Cowan. She and her son-in-law and daughter camped there several nights. The scenery, she said, was "simply breath-taking" … and it was nothing uncommon to see bears strolling around. "They were all right as long as you did not touch them," she said.

Thousands of miles were covered by Mrs Cowan – she visited many of the big towns in Canada and crossed into the United States. Everything was "spic and span" in the self-service stores and she was impressed by the high standard of hygiene in the shops … it was higher than in this country.

People she had spoken to from this country all, without exception, said they had never regretted emigrating. Some of them said it was rather "tough going" during the first year but after that, when they were settled in lucrative employment, they had forged ahead by leaps and bounds and thought Canada brimful of opportunity. "There certainly seems plenty of scope there, especially for young people who are not afraid of hard work and do not expect life to be a bed of roses!" said Mrs Cowan, summing up Canada's prospects.

Mrs Cowan, whose family helped her considerably with the cost of her passage – she has seven daughters and five sons – left this country in May on the "Empress of Britain" and her return voyage this month was on the "Empress of England."

Met Mrs M Lupson

When she reached Montreal on the outward journey she joined the train for Toronto, where she was met by a friend of her daughter's, Mrs Madge Lupson, who emigrated ten years ago. Mrs Lupson, like Mrs Cowan's daughter Mary, married a Canadian airman in this country shortly after the war. Mrs Lupson is a daughter of Mr and Mrs R O'Connor, who recently moved from Wheatley Hill to Thornley.

Mrs Cowan's sight-seeing began in Toronto for she spent a week with the Lupsons before making the long rail journey across Canada to Alberta in the special sight-seeing "dome" train. She spent three nights and four days on the train and as it roared its way westwards through Canada an ever-changing vista of scenery unfolded before her delighted gaze.

The rail coaches were spotlessly clean – "vastly different" from those she had travelled in this country, said Mrs Cowan. "I never quite realised how dirty many of the trains are in this country until I travelled on the Canadian railway," she added.

On her voyage to and from Montreal, Mrs Cowan was accompanied by two other Durham Country women – Mrs Kitty Blake, sub-postmistress at Station Town Post Office and Mrs Martha Barron, of Durham. Mrs Blake visited her two married daughters in Toronto, and Mrs Barron, a daughter in Frankfort.

COLLIERY WATCHMAN
Wheatley Hill Retirement of Mr T E Turner

On reaching his 65th birthday Mr Thomas E Turner, 9 Darlington Street, Wheatley Hill (who has been employed as watchman at Wheatley Hill colliery for nearly 30 years, has retired from work. Mr Turner started work on the screens at the colliery on his 14th birthday, but later lost his right hand in an accident in the engineering room, and for 17 years was out of work until he was appointed watchman.

His First Day

Mr Turner was living at Hesleden when he began his career at the colliery, and vividly recalls his first day at work. "It was the day after the explosion at Wingate colliery when 24 mines lost their lives," he told our reporter this week. "I had finished my very first shift at Wheatley Hill colliery and as I was walking back home to Hesleden – there was no transport in those days! – I was stopped many a time and asked if I had been in the explosion. I was thankful to be able to say I hadn't."

Mr turner received 1s.1d a shift when he started work and when he was about 17 was transferred to the colliery winding-engine room as an engine cleaner. He continued to work there until May 1911, when his hand was crushed in the winding-engine, and he had to have it amputated. He spent three weeks in hospital and in another three weeks his arm was healed.

No other job was found for Mr Turner after his accident, and for 17 years he was "on compensation." He did not allow the loss of his limb, however, to handicap him. He took up carpentry as a hobby and many beautiful pieces of furniture, including a radiogram, which he made himself, though having the use of only one hand, still adorn his home. They serve to illustrate his determination to overcome his physical handicap.

In 1928, after his long spell of unemployment, Mr Turner was appointed colliery watchman and filled this position until his retirement.

WHEATLEY HILL LEGION'S NEW HQ

After being moved about "from pillar to post" during the past few years, Wheatley Hill Women's Section of the British Legion have at last been able to obtain their own headquarters. They have bought an old army Cadet hut on a site behind the village's Front Street, and the members are now hard at work with soap and water and "elbow grease" to make the interior of the building almost like new.

A number of improvements are to be made – new windows have already been fitted and the floor repaired – and the section, which has a membership approaching 100, hopes to move into their new headquarters in time for their Christmas party.

"We have never had a headquarters of our own," the secretary, Mrs E A Stainsby, reports, "although some years ago, in conjunction with the men's section, which does not now function, we raised a lot of money and bought a site. A concrete foundation was laid on the site, but because of the expense involved we were unable to make any progress with the building. The concrete foundation is still their today!"

During the past year the section has held its meetings in the local Discharged and Demobilised Soldiers" and Sailors" Club, and previously they met in the Welfare Hall and in a building in the now demolished Wolmerhausen Street. "Once we are installed in our new headquarters we hope to be able to extend our activities considerably," said Mrs Stainsby.

NEW WAR MEMORIAL AT THORNLEY

The Thornley War Memorial Committee are hoping to make an early start with the erection of the new memorial, to take the place of the old memorial, destroyed by fire in 1944. It commemorated the men lost in the first world war, and carried the names of men who resided in Thornley and those who had worked at Thornley Colliery but lived elsewhere. Fortunately this list of 132 men had been copied from the memorial by the Rev W Alan Lathaen, now Vicar of South Westoe, some time before the memorial was destroyed.

The list of 23 men, all of Thornley, who were lost in the second world war, is to be posted up in the village so that the public can inspect it and point out any omissions or corrections required.

The new memorial, which is three-sided with panels for the names, is to be placed on the cleared site of the old Literary Institute, and will face the main highway. Although the fund is not yet large enough to cover the decorative garden work, the Committee have decided to erect the memorial in the hope that the public will, after seeing the actual memorial, make a combined effort to raise the sum required to complete the committee's scheme. A design of the new memorial is on exhibition in the village.

NEW VICAR – In the presence of a large congregation of parishioners and visitors, including his wife and two children, the Rev Phillip Geoffrey Mold, was instituted to the Vicarage of St Bartholomew, Thornley, on Monday. The institution ceremony was performed by the Bishop of Jarrow and the induction ceremony by the Archdeacon of Durham. Mr Mold is the eighth Vicar since the parish was formed in 1840.

25 October 1957

SALE OF WORK
Wheatley Hill Church Effort
As part of their patronal festival members of All Saints' Church, Wheatley Hill, held a successful sale of work on Saturday. A sum of about £270 was raised.

The Vicar (the Rev G G Graham) opened the sale in the presence of 200 people. He said, "The main objective of the effort is to add to the amenities of our church at Wheatley Hill. At the present time choir and servers are cramped for room. We have decided to build a new vestry and we trust this sale will do much to help us to that end."

8 November 1957

REMEMBRANCE DAY PARADES
Thornley Colliery Silver Prize Band, under Mr E Kitto, headed the parade through the village. Taking part were members of the British Legion (standard bearer Mr R Slater), Legion women (standard bearer Mrs H Slater), Thornley Parish Council, Easington Rural Council, Thornley Colliery Mining Federation Board, Thornley Workingmen's Club, Thornley Mothers' Club, Thornley Boy Scouts and Wingate Naval Reserve.

The service in St Bartholomew's church, was conducted by the Rev Geoffrey Mold, who also preached the sermon. He was assisted by he Rev G R Ireland (Methodist minister) and Captain William Pointon, of Shotton Salvation Army Corps. Mr Wilfred Jones, secretary of the British Legion, recited the Exhortation. "Last Post" was sounded by Mr H Moore and Mr E Kitto.

Wreaths were laid by Dr A P Gray and Mrs H Brewster (British Legion), Coun A Bushby (Thornley Parish Council), Mr E Carter (Thornley Mining Federation), Mr f A Walker (Thornley Labour Party), Mrs Peart (Thornley Labour Women) and Mr J Nicholson (Thornley Club).

WHEATLEY HILL
All Saints' Church, Wheatley Hill, was filled for the annual service. The parade was attended by many local organisations including Wheatley Hill Women's Section of the British Legion, 1st Scout Company, DSS Club, Workmen's Club, Women's Institute and Sherburn Hill Cooperative Society. The service was conducted by the Vicar (the Rev G g Graham) and the address was given by the Rev G L Nelson. After the service the parade reformed and wended its way to the Cenotaph in the Welfare Park. At the Memorial Clock prayers were said and wreaths were laid on the Cenotaph. "Last Post" and "Reveille" were sounded.

THORNLEY PARISH COUNCIL
At the meeting of Thornley Parish Council the Clerk (Mr Martin Fleming) was instructed to write to the County Planning Officer, asking for trees and shrubs to be planted on the "dead" pit-heaps between Thornley and Wheatley Hill.

The halfpenny increase on bus fares was criticised by Coun J R Bosomworth. He said the G and B Service, United and Durham District Services had all put up the fares to threepence, and the Northern General transport were only charging two-pence for the same journey. He said it was a "burning shame" that old-age pension-ers should have to pay threepence from the Colliery Inn to the doctor's surgery, a distance of 500 yards. The Clerk was instructed to make a strong protest against the increase.

The Chairman (Coun A Bushby) presented Coun J Nicholson with the silver lapel badge of the National Blood transfusion Service in recognition of 25 donations of blood.

15 November 1957

WHEATLEY HILL SOLDIER HONOURED

When the passing-out parade of the 45th intake of National Service recruits took place recently at Cowley Barracks, Oxford headquarters of the Oxfordshire and Buckinghamshire Light Infantry, the medal for the best recruit was presented to pri-vate Peter Carr (21), younger son of Mr John Carr and the late Mrs Carr, 28 Quet-law Road, Wheately Hill.

Before being called up for National Service three months ago, Private Carr was em-ployed as a bricklayer. He has played football in the Army.

HOMING SOCIETY – There was a very good display of old and young birds at the Thornley District Homing Society show in Thornley Club. The judge was Mr S Poulson, of Wheatley Hill. First prize-winners were R Bowes and Son and Tunstall and Orton.

TRAGIC DISCOVERY – The body of Mr William Waite (63) 67 Shinwell Cres-cent, Thornley, was recovered from a pool of water near Thornley slag heaps at the end of the village on Sunday evening. Mr Waite had been missing from home since November 10.

WHEATLEY HILL CHURCH FUNCTION

Members of Wheatley Hill Church Street Methodist Sisterhood raised over £40 last week end. On Friday they organised a jumble sale which realised £10. On Saturday afternoon there was an attendance of 100 in the Welfare Hall for a Christmas gift Fayre. Everything on the stalls was given by Sisterhood and church members. The organising secretary was Mrs P H Gailey, senior, and treasurer, Mrs A Ord.

Mrs E Parnham presided and introduced Mrs W G McLean, who opened the Fayre. She was presented with a bouquet by little Gorgon Lambert.

ELECTRICITY CHANGEOVER AT THORNLEY

Thornley Parish Council met representatives of the North Eastern Electricity Board and heard from Mr P H Algar, Wear Sub-Area representative, a detailed account of the work that would take place to change the public lighting system from the NCB to the NEEB network. The cost would be £2,913.

Mr A E Bowers, district engineer, replying to questions from members on the supply of current to private consumers, stated that all consumers must have their installation tested and send in the approved form before a supply of energy was given. He also stated that consumers would have a choice in the way they wished to pay their accounts.

29 November 1957

INQUEST AT THORNLEY
Miner Found Drowned

Fourteen days after a 63-year-old Thornley miner left home "in a cheerful frame of mind," saying he was going to chapel, his body was recovered from a stream not far from his home. The Coroner, Mr T V Devey, was told this at an inquest in Thornley police station last Thursday, on the miner Robert William Waite, 67 Shinwell Crescent, Thornley. A verdict of "Found drowned" was recorded.

Some years ago, a son, John William Waite, 13 Coleridge Avenue, West Hartlepool told the Coroner his father was admitted to Shotley Bridge Hospital with suspected pneumoconiosis and since then had not been in good health. In May 1955 he injured his leg at work and was off work for some time. He became very depressed and in June that year attempted to take his life. Subsequently he became a voluntary patient in Winterton Hospital for four months. "Since then," witness added, "his bodily health has been moderate but he was been quite cheerful."

At Easter this year Waite contracted pneumonia and was off work several months. When he went back to work he complained that it was too heavy for him and this worried him. In September Waite's son continued, his father contracted Asian 'flue and this appeared to leave him very depressed. He had not worked since.

Missing From Home

"On Sunday November 10," witness went on, "my father left home at 5.40 pm, stating his intention of going to chapel. He seemed to be in a cheerful frame of mind and had eaten his meals during the day. He did not return and was reported to the police as missing from home.

PC J Stokoe said about 2.45 pm, on Sunday, November 24, as a result of certain information, he went to the "Gassy Gutter," about half a mile east of the Thornley to Wheatley Hill road. There he saw Waite's body lying on its back at the bottom of the stream. Nearby the officer found articles of clothing similar to that worn by the deceased when he was reported missing, also a diary bearing Waite's name.

Replying to the Coroner, PC Stokoe said there were no marks of violence on the body.

Dr Arthur Todd said that death was due to asphyxia by drowning. Waite, he said was a patient of his. Two years ago he appeared to be very depressed. "But I had not noticed this recently," the doctor added.

COUNTY'S BEST POLICE CADETS
From Wheatley Hill, Crook and Consett
The Durham County police authority were anxious "to recognise and encourage consistently good work among the cadets," declared the chairman of the authority, Ald J W Foster, when, at Castle Eden Court on Saturday, he made presentations to the three best police cadets attending courses at technical colleges in the county during the past year.

The recipients were Cadet Clive Brown (18), Castle Eden Division; Cadet Harold Birbeck (17), Bishop Auckland Division, and Cadet Norman Walker (17), Consett Division.

Cadet Brown, who lives at Kenmor, Quilstile Road, Wheatley Hill, was presented with a shaving kit. Cadet Birbeck, of 4 Jobson Terrace, Wooley PO, near Crook, with a fountain-pen and pencil, and Cadet Walker, of 1 Morley Street, Consett, with a writing set.

Technical College Attendance
An integral part of recruitment to the Durham County police Force was the admission and training of cadets, said Ald Foster. Part of their training consisted of studying certain subjects at a technical college.

"Their attendance, homework, examination results and the teachers' reports enable the principal to tell us the best cadet at his college," the Alderman added, "and the police authority have authorised a prize not exceeding £2 to the best cadet at each of the three colleges where cadets attend."

Cadet Brown was the best cadet at Billingham Technical College, Cadet Birbeck the best at Bishop Auckland Technical College, and Cadet Walker the best at Hebburn Technical College. "We wish them all very well in their careers," said Ald Foster.
6 December 1957

CLUB TREAT – Members of the management of Wheatley Hill colliery and local members of Easington Rural Council were among the guests at the annual party on Wednesday night, organised by Wheatley Hill Discharged and Demobilised Soldiers' and Sailors" Club for retired members and their wives. About sixty old folk were seated to a knife-and-fork tea and later entertainment was by a concert party from Sherburn Hill. The club chairman, Mr C Curry, presided, and welcomed the guests, and seasonal greetings were extended by Mr F Simpson, undermanager at Wheatley Hill colliery. Each retired member received a Christmas gift of £1 and his wife 10s. Arrangements were made by the secretary, Mr W Hackworth, and treasurer, Mr R Burnip.
13 December 1957

"GOLDEN DAY" AT WHEATLEY HILL
Mr and Mrs T D Collingwood

Mr and Mrs Thomas D Collingwood, 15 Ryan Terrace, Wheatley Hill, were married in Holy Trinity Church, Wingate, on December 21 1907. Tomorrow the couple celebrate their golden wedding.

"We have had a happy 50 years of married life," said Mrs Collingwood. "that does not mean that we have had a bed of roses. Both of us have had our ups and downs. I had a spinal accident resulting from a fall which has curtailed my activities. Tom was three times gassed in the first war. But all through, we have stood by one another. My advice to young couples starting out on married life is to trust one another implicitly, have no secrets, and share one another's burdens."

Mr Thomas Collingwood, in his 72nd year, was born at Blyth. He came to Wingate when he was 11 months old and began work at 12 as a trapper boy at the Grange colliery.

He had a brother in the Wingate Pit explosion of 1906 and got out safely. After 16 years at the colliery, Mr Collingwood changed his job. He joined the County Constabulary and started his police career at Stockton.

His Military Service

Mr Collingwood volunteered for active service in 1914. He went to France and served with the No 225 Field Company Royal Engineers. He was awarded the Military Medal for great skill and courage in blowing up enemy gun emplacements. He was mentioned in Military Despatches. Although gassed three times Mr Collingwood was not invalided out of the forces till the war was over. Combing back to "civvy street" he went back to police duties and served at Felling, served 17 years at Wheatley Hill and retired at Hetton-le-Hole in 1939 at the age of 55.

Asked about the highlights of his career he said, "In 1937, while serving at Hetton, I was chosen to do duty at the Coronation of the late King George VI. It was a great experience. I did duty on no less than five occasions when some member of the Royal Family visited the North East."

Went To Foresty

Following his retirement from the Force, Mr Collingwood did forestry work for two years, providing Wheatley Hill with timber for pit props. He also worked at Aycliffe ROF. During his retirement, gardening and bowls have been his hobbies. He has played for Wheatley Hill Welfare and the local Over-60 club teams.

Mrs Collingwood (nee Martha Ord) was born at West Stanley and came to Station Town as a child. She married her husband when she was 19. She is now 70.

The couple are members of the Wheatley Hill Over-60 Club. Mrs Collingwood is a talented comedienne and has entertained fellow members at the concerts. Mr and Mrs Collingwood have two daughters, Mrs Margaret Foster (Trimdon station) and Mrs Martha Walker (Wheatley Hill). There are two grandchildren.

Mr Collingwood, just recovering from a serious illness, is now confined to the house by a severe attack of sciatica. For this reason their daughters are making a small

family celebration party on Sunday, at their parents' home. The golden wedding cake has been made and decorated by Mrs Foster.
20 December 1957

FIFTY YEARS MARRIED
Mr and Mrs G Poulson, Wheatley Hill

Tomorrow, Mr and Mrs George Poulson, 60 Peter Lee Cottages, Wheatley Hill, celebrate their golden wedding. They were married in St Saviour's Church, Shotton Colliery by the Rev R Fenton.

Mr and mrs Poulson will have their family with them in their home for tomorrow's party – four married daughters and a married son and eight grandchildren. Both bridesmaids are still living – Mrs Georgina Close at Shotton and Mr Poulson's sister, Mrs Turner of West Stanley.

Mr Poulson was born at Whitburn and started work as a trapper boy at 13 for a shilling a day. After two years there, his family came to Wheatley Hill. He has lived there for 59 years. At the colliery he worked as putter, hewer and stoneman for 51 years. He retired at 66.

Mr Poulson's father was a great friend of Peter Lee. "It was my father who got Peter work at Wheatley Hill," said Mr Poulson. "He had a meal at our house the day he got work at this colliery. The Wheatley Hill of today with its modern housing estates, its good roads and community facilities and amenities is a grand tribute to the tireless efforts and labours of public-spirited men who have served the village during the last half century.

Keen Gardener

Mr Poulson served as treasurer for six and a half years for the Wheatley Hill Constitutional Club. But his real hobby – or labour of love – has been connected with horticulture. His services as judge are in great demand throughout the county. He is also a noted leek grower.

Mrs Poulson was born at Haswell Moor and spent most of her girlhood at Shotton. "Young married women today cannot realise the hard life we lived 50-60 years ago," she said. "I remember in my young days we had to carry every drop of water from the well a quarter of a mile away. Washing day was a real hard day's work. The water had to be boiled in large pans on the fire. The wash tub and the poss-stick were out tools. The big iron mangle with its hand-turned wheel provided us with plenty of exercise. We baked bread, pies, teacakes and cakes at home. It really meant that in those days we had very little leisure time. Looking after the family was a fulltime job."

Mr Poulson agreed with his wife that leisure was the great boon that has come to workers of both sexes. "With the men in those days it was the same. With many of us it was a case of work at the pit and bed. Now a man has time to develop hobbies and cultural interests."

Mr Poulson's only son, Mr George Poulson of Wordsworth Avenue, is a society steward of Wheatley Hill Church Street Methodist church.

27 December 1957

1958

WHEATLEY HILL SCOUTS - During Christmastide, the 2nd Wheatley Hill Troop of Boy Scouts paid their usual Yuletide visit to the children's ward of Durham County Hospital, which they "adopted" some years ago, and distributed gifts to 15 young people. With Scoutmaster Leslie Barker in charge, they entertained the patients and toured the other wards in the hospital cheering old and young alike with their songs and jokes.

The Christmas gifts were bought from the proceeds of carol singing. Scouters, Rovers and senior Scouts went carol singing in Wheatley Hill for four nights and raised a record sum of £32.10s. They are to discuss with the Matron what to buy for the use of the children's ward with the money remaining after the purchase of the Christmas gifts. The Matron is to attend the Scouts annual reunion on 11 January.
3 January 1958

YOUNG CORNET PLAYER
Started Playing for Thornley Band at 9

One of the most enthusiastic members of Thornley Colliery Silver Prize Band is 13 year old James Wilfred Beddell, son of Mr and Mrs James W Beddell, 79 High Street, Thornley. He started playing in the band at nine years of age under the leadership of the Bandmaster, Mr Edward Kitto.

Wilfred plays the cornet and he entered three competitions for cornet solo. The results were first, runner-up and first. In his first contest Wilfred was placed first and was awarded a silver plaque on an ebony surround. At Durham in June he was runner-up and lost the cup by one point. Back at Durham again in December, he was placed first and gained a silver medal. He gained his first medal when playing with the Thornley Band when they won at Easington two years ago. He was then 11.

Wilfred's father, Mr James Beddell, told our correspondent, "It is not surprising that the lad is interested in the band and the cornet in particular. On both sides of the family we have players who have favoured the cornet. His grandfather, Mr R Fenwick of Cassop, was a cornet player of note and his uncle, Mr Thomas Beddell of Thornley, played the same instrument".

MINER INJURED - Caught by a fall of coal in the Hutton seam at Wheatley Hill colliery about midway through his shift on Tuesday, a 21 year old coal hewer, Sidney Humes, youngest son of Mr and Mrs C Stainsby, 13 Handel Terrace, Wheatley Hill, was taken to Durham County Hospital, suffering from severe spinal injuries.
10 January 1958

WHEATLEY HILL RETIREMENT
Mr R S Chisholm's 51 Years In Mining

After a mining career of 51 years, most of which has been spent at Wheatley Hill colliery as an official, Mr Robert Stoker Chisholm, The Bungalow, Cemetery Road, Wheatley Hill, retired from work on Wednesday on reaching his 65th birthday. For the past 31 years Mr Chisholm has been fore-overman at the colliery, where he was held in the highest esteem by management and workmen alike.

Born at Haswell, Mr Chisholm began work at Wardley colliery on his 14th birthday, as a trapper-boy. His first pay, he recalled in an interview with our reporter, was 8s.7d for eight shifts. He became a driver lad, and then an off-takes lad - nowadays known as a rope-changer.

Seen Many Changes

Mr Chisholm continued his mining career at Wheatley Hill colliery when he moved there in January 1912. He was shot firing in 1919 and the following year took up new duties as a deputy. In 1922 he was appointed master-shifter and three years later, back overman, then in 1927 was made fore-overman, which position he has filled until his retirement.

Mr Chisholm has seen many changes at the colliery and counts himself fortunate that he has never been involved in any major accidents. "Conditions are vastly improved from the days when I first went down the pit - and it is good to see them getting better and better as each year passes", he said.

Mr Chisholm has served on the colliery Consultative Committee since the nationalisation of the mining industry and has been a member of the local Welfare Committee since 1922. For the past 19 years he has been chairman of Wheatley Hill branch of the Colliery Officials' Union and has often been delegate for the branch at meetings in Newcastle.

Early in 1918, Mr Chisholm joined the Army - he served in the 19th DLI known as "The Bantams", and spent some months abroad. His sergeant, he recalled, was Bert Hobson, who was Sunderland FC's right-back. From 1926 to 1946, Mr Chisholm was a Special Constable and he holds a long-service medal.

In his younger days Mr Chisholm was a well known sportsman. He played football and hockey for several local clubs and for some years was a referee in the Palatine League - a well known football combination in Durham County. For 25 years he has been a member of the Hartlepool St Helen's Lodge of Freemasons, one of the oldest lodges in South East Durham.

Methodists

Both Mr Chisholm and his wife have had a long association with the Patton Street Methodist Church, Wheatley Hill. Ten years ago their only daughter, Mary, gave up a promising teaching career to become a Methodist missionary in Western Nigeria. Later she married another missionary, Mr John Boshier, a Bachelor of Science, and both are still on missionary work in Ibadan. Mr Boshier is a tutor at the Wesley College in Ibadan. The couple have been married nearly five years and have two young children. They returned to Nigeria only in October after a six month furlough in this country.

Mr Chisholm is now looking forward to his well earned retirement. "What with gardening, walking and reading, there'll be plenty to occupy my time - then there's always the television to help to fill in my leisure hours"! he said. That both he and his wife may enjoy good health to enjoy a long and happy retirement, is the sincere wish of their many friends throughout the area.

SCOUTS' REUNION - The Matron of Durham Hospital, Miss Harding, and Sister Sutton, were among the guests at the annual reunion of the 2nd Wheatley Hill Troop of Rovers, Scouts and Clubs in the Welfare Hall on Saturday night. Some years ago the Troop "adopted" the children's ward of the hospital and at the reunion the Matron expressed thanks to the Scouts for the many "good turns" they had done for the young patients. Also among the guests were Mr F Richardson (manager of Wheatley Hill colliery) and Mrs Richardson, Mr Fred Simpson (under manager), Miss E Simpson and Mr and Mrs T Johnson. A welcome was extended by Dr A P Gray, a member of the Scouts' Committee, and after supper the Scouts and Rovers gave an excellent entertainment, including sketches and songs. Scoutmaster Leslie Barker was in charge and the accompanist was Tony Carr. The Scouts and Cubs each received a gift of sweets and chocolate and the evening ended with a camp-fire "singsong".

17 January 1958

PARTY - Mrs F Snowdon, chairman and local organiser of the Thornley branch of the Guide Dogs for the Blind Association, reports that members held a successful party in the Club Hall, when over 100 attended. The evening was given over to party games and dancing, music was provided by Mr Jackie Toye, Thornley's blind accordionist. Many prizes were given for competition and "spot" dancing. Mrs Snowdon intimated that the object of the branch is to provide a trained guide dog, which now costs £260. Mrs Snowdon (chairman), Mrs D Wright (treasurer) and Mrs E Hindson (secretary), 42 Dunelm Road, Thornley, will be glad to accept gifts or to advise in the organisation of efforts.

WHEATLEY HILL LABOUR PARTY SURPRISE - By the narrow margin of one vote, Coun Edward Cain, who has served on Easington Rural Council since 1934, with the exception of two years he spent on Durham County Council, was surprisingly beaten as candidate for the forthcoming Rural Council elections, when Wheatley Hill Ward Labour Party made their final choice of candidates.

Two of the sitting members, Couns J Johnson and J Cowie, were again chosen as candidates and the third candidate chosen in place of Coun Cain was Mr Ronald Hughes, who is employed at Thornley Colliery.

The following candidates were chosen for the Wheatley Hill Ward of Wingate Parish Council: Couns A Bishop, N Cook, J Fenwick and R Watson (sitting members), Mr C Hackworth and Mr T Forster.

CLUB OFFICIALS - Mr James Quinn, the chairman of Thornley Working Men's Club and Institute, has been re-elected. Mr Sidney White was returned as secretary and Mr William Walls treasurer. There were 25 candidates for the four seats on the committee, Messrs D Gott, A Espinal, W Weatheral and W Hammond. Mr J Fragelly and Mr C Heale are the doormen.

THORNLEY WI - There was a good attendance at the opening meeting of the year. Mrs D Swinburne presided and business details were read by the secretary Mrs A L Miller. A display of woollen rugs made by members was the centre of interest. Throughout the year members will take part in a series, "I know what I like". The first contributor was Mrs D Lang. Following tradition, the evening was given over to "bag" whist and dominoes. Each player received a prize out of the bag, those with the highest scores taking the first choice of prize.

24 January 1958

MRS PEART TO LEAVE THORNLEY

The decision of Mrs F M Peart to retire from public work and to leave Thornley for the Lake District will end the story of the life of the Pearts in Thornley.

Her late husband, County Coun E F Peart, teacher, sportsman, politician, soldier, was appointed headmaster of Thornley Council School, in July 1929, and brought his wife and family from Crook where he had held a similar position. From the moment he came to Thornley he made an impact on the political life of the village.

Mrs Peart's oldest son, Fred, came to Thornley with the family. He was born in Crook in 1914, and was educated at Wolsingham Grammar School and at Henry Smiths, Hartlepool. He took his B.Sc, at Durham University. Like his father he had an imposing personality and was elected MP for Workington in 1945.

Harry, Mrs Peart's youngest son, joined the Labour Party as a boy and took an active part in the youth section of the Division. He was educated at Durham University and at Freckleton Training College. He was a keen athlete. He now lives in Sunderland and is games master at Ryhope Grammar School. He has been selected to contest the Roker Ward in the next elections.

Mrs Peart has many interests in life apart from politics and as an evening school teacher of handicrafts she should never be idle. She is interested in drama and poetry.

A Presentation

Thornley Labour Party have presented her with a wrought-iron electric table lamp. Coun Mrs H Slater, chairman of the women's section, in handing over the gift wished her many years of happy retirement and hoped the present would be to her "a real Aladdin lamp". Tributes were also paid by County Coun J Andrews, ex-Coun J Williams, Couns J Nicholson and F A Walker. Happy entertainment followed.

LOCAL FOOTBALL
Blackhall Crash at Thornley

Thornley CW strengthened their position at the top of the Wearside League with a 4-1 home victory over Blackhall CW on Saturday, but the game was not so one-sided as the score would suggest. The "Hall", who were first to find the net after only nine minutes, had equally as much of the play as their opponents in the first half and fully deserved to be on level terms at the half-way stage. Later Thornley were more accurate in their finishing and, quicker to take their chances, they rammed in three goals without reply.

Conditions were far from conducive to good football. The pitch was covered with melting snow and eventually the referee decided to play only 35 minutes each way. It was Morley, their inside left, who gave Blackhall their early lead, but near the interval his counterpart, Bower, equalised. Both goals had their share of escapes. Murray and Presho went tantalisingly close to scoring for Thornley, while Ray Brown, making his debut as leader of the visitors' attack, fired inches over the bar from a perfect pass by Barry Ward.

Goals by Murray and Presho in the first quarter of an hour after the resumption put Thornley in front, and Murray, always a dangerous left winger, added another shortly afterwards. Blackhall were unable to recover from these shattering blows and though they were triers throughout, they found the opposition too strong in the second half. Brown showed distinct promise at centre forward but because of the atrocious playing conditions, it was difficult to make any real assessment of his worth. Frank Seddon played soundly in defence at centre half.

31 January 1958

WHEATLEY HILL NEWSAGENTS LONG SERVICE - Mr Jack Hodgson, Front Street, Wheatley Hill, who has been in business in the village as a newsagent since 1916, was re-elected secretary of Durham branch of the National Federation of Newsagents for the 38th year in succession, at the annual meeting on Tuesday. Mr Hodgson has been associated with the selling of newspapers since he left school at the age of 12, first as a newsboy, then as assistant in a newsagent's shop, and finally in his own business.

As well as being re-elected secretary, Mr Hodgson was chosen delegate to attend the newsagents' conference in Weston-Super-Mare in June. Other elections were: president Mr H Bousfield (Easington Lane); vice-president, Mr T Raine (Esh Winning); treasurer, Mr J W Metcalfe (Cornsay); District Council delegates, Messrs H Bousfield, J Hodgson, T Raine and R Taylor (Peterlee). Mr Bousfield was again nominated to serve on the National Council.

Arrangements were made for the annual dinner-dance to be held in Durham on March 5th.

7 February 1958

BIG STONE FELL FROM ROOF
Inquest on Wheatley Hill Miner

So big was a stone which fell from the roof of the canch and killed a coal filler at Wheatley Hill colliery on Tuesday 11th, that it took more than five men to move it, it was revealed at the inquest at Thornley Police Station on Wednesday.

The inquest was on William Edward Evans, 3 Gable Terrace, Wheatley Hill, who would have celebrated his 31st birthday yesterday. The jury returned a verdict of "accidental death". Dr A Gray said that death was due to a fracture of the skull and laceration of the brain and must have been instantaneous.

Thorough Examination

The deputy in charge of the district where Evans was working, John Booth, 8 Luke Terrace, Wheatley Hill, said that after firing two shots he found the place in a safe condition and "securely timbered". There were no cracks in the roof. Witness left that part of the district but later was told there had been an accident.

Replying to Mr D Davie, HM Inspector of Mines, Booth said he made a thorough examination of the district after firing the shots and was quite satisfied about the condition of the coal face.

George Edward Croft, a hoist braker, 40 Gowland Terrace, Wheatley Hill, said about 9.40 am he was braking the hoist at the East Main "gate" and Evans was working about a foot away from him. Evans was laughing and appeared to be in very good health. He was kneeling down under the "lip" of the canch with his head facing towards the coal. "I received a signal to start the hauler and started to haul", continued the witness. "I then heard a click and a thud. I looked in the direction of the noise and saw Evans still in a kneeling position but I could only see the lower part of his back and head. He was buried under a big stone which had fallen from the roof of the canch".

Help was summoned. "It took more than five men to move the stone", added Croft.

Well Timbered

It was quite apparent, said the Coroner, Mr T V Devey, to the jury, that the place was well timbered where the stone fell. "As far as I can see it was purely an accident", he added.

Sympathy with the deceased's relatives was expressed by the Coroner, Mr W Kinghorn (on behalf of the National Coal Board and colliery management), Mr J Crawford (on behalf of the Durham County Deputies' Association), Mr M Alderton (on behalf of Wheatley Hill Miners' Lodge) and Sergeant W Woore (on behalf of the police).

Mr Evans had lived in Wheatley Hill all his life and had been employed at the colliery since leaving school. He is survived by his wife and two daughters, Lynn (5) and Marion (2). He was the only son of Mr and Mrs William E Evans, 92 Wordsworth Avenue, Wheatley Hill. Funeral is to take place at Wheatley Hill cemetery tomorrow (Saturday) following a service in Patton Street Methodist Church.

WHEATLEY HILL FUNERAL DELAYED TWO DAYS

Snow blocked roads between Wheatley Hill and Sunderland on Saturday, caused the postponement of the funeral of an old standard of Wheatley Hill, Mr Phillip Brown (74), 10 Aged Miners' Homes, until Monday. Relatives, including a number from Wrexham, where Mr Brown spent his younger days, had arrived for the funeral on Saturday. When it was found that the hearse and coaches would not be able to get through to the crematorium at Sunderland the funeral service was postponed until Monday and the relatives remained in Wheatley Hill over the weekend.

Mr Brown, whose death occurred with tragic suddenness - he had been out in the village the day before he died - came to Durham County from Wrexham more than 40 years ago. He was employed at Wheatley Hill colliery, where he retired at 65, and was particularly well known in the village for a spare time taxi business which he carried on for 34 years until two years ago.

Mr Brown was a lifelong supporter of Wrexham Football Club and often during the winter months made the long journey there to watch his favourite team. He was a shareholder in the club and in his younger days "scouted" for players. He was a member of Wheatley Hill Over 60 Club.

Mr Brown, whose wife died a year ago, is survived by a daughter and two sons. Cremation at Sunderland on Monday followed a service in All Saints' Church, Wheatley Hill, conducted by the Reverend Gordon G Graham (Vicar).

A MEMORY OF '91
When Thornley Miners Went to Jail

The statement by Mr Alexander Bell, the grand old ex-miner of Dixon Estate, Shotton, who recently celebrated his 100th birthday, that "he was jailed for 14 days for his sympathies with the Silksworth miners at the time of their evictions", suggests that Alex may be the only survivor of the 77 Thornley coal hewers who were charged at Castle Eden Police Court on 14 March 1891 (and convicted) for absenting themselves from work on 21 and 23 February 1891. That was when the Silksworth miners and their families were being evicted from their homes.

Thornley coal hewers were fined 4s.6d each and asked to pay 10s. damages which they refused to do. Judgement summonses were granted against them on 23 April and 14 days in jail was the order. To prove that the convicted men were able to pay, a statement of the last two fortnights' wages was submitted to the Bench. The wages of Alexander Bell were: 26 March for ten shifts, £2.11s 4d; 10 April, for nine shifts, £2.7s.0d.

In Batches of Ten

The convicted men went to jail in batches of ten and as one batch came out the miners' lodge, with band and banner, escorted them back to the village.

A local poet put many verses to music and the words were printed and sold in the "Thornley Songster", entitled "The Imprisoned Thornley Miners".

One verse goes:

It was a treat to see them going away
From Castle Eden on that day,
Though going to jail they were blithe and gay -
The men from Thornley Colliery.

The music sounded clear and sweet.
The banner waved a perfect treat,
And everyone brought plenty to eat.
Away from Thornley Colliery.

Perhaps Mr Bell will remember some of the young men who went into "jug" with him, John Brown, Lawrence and John Burn (father and son), Hugh McCoy, Hugh Murray, Michael Thornton, John William Potts, John Woodhead, Edward Lewis Snr, Edward Lewis Jnr and John Winn.

SCOUT'S PARTY - The 3rd Thornley Scout Group held its annual party and fancy dress parade in Thornley Bow Street Methodist Sunday School. Mr A L Miller, Group Scoutmaster, presided. The fancy dress prize was won by Scout David Horner. Scoutmaster J Dunnett made the following awards: three all-round cords to Patrol Leader K Johnson, seconds to Scouts D Abbs and D Horner and a first class badge to Scout P Luke. The entertainment was provided by members of the Group. Tea was provided with a cake baked by Mrs Turnbull.

CHURCH AIDS MISSIONS - Mr Kenneth Hetherington, Overseas Missions organising secretary for Thornley Waterloo Street Methodist Church, announces that members have raised a total of £182.12s.7d. This is a record income. Of this amount Sunday School scholars collected £158.14s.2d for JMA. Mr Hetherington paid a special tribute to two JMA collectors for outstanding achievements. June Gratton (12) broke all church records by collecting £30, another fine achievement was that of nine year old Peter Lambert, who collected £22.18s.8d.

THORNLEY WI - Mrs D Swinburn presided. Silent tribute was paid to the memory of Mrs Watson, a member for many years. Mrs A L Miller (secretary) gave business details. Mrs A Winter was appointed delegate to the Spring Council meeting at Seaburn. Mrs F Bradley gave an interesting report on the Produce Guild conference. The item of interest given by Mrs J Thornton was entitled "Men are better looking than women". Mrs J Embleton, headmistress of the new Trimdon Village County Infants' School, was speaker. The competition was "Book Titles" and was won by Mrs M Baldasera. The social half hour was an adaptation of the W Pickles' programme "Have-a-Go". Taking part were Mesdames A Greave, E Davies, M Seager, F Bradley junior, S Woodward, W Potts, S Bosomworth, D Lang, E Emmerson, R E Gratton and A Winter.
14 February 1958

BACK TO WHEATLEY HILL
"War Bride" Returns from New Zealand

Twelve years after going to New Zealand as a "war bride", a former assistant in Wheatley Hill miners' canteen has returned to her parents' home in Wheatley Hill to spend a six month holiday … and with her she has brought a glowing account of her new life in a new country.

She is Mrs May Hall who, accompanied by her two children, Sandra (6½) and Christopher (4), is staying with her parents, Mr and Mrs Robert Richardson, at 21 Patton Crescent.

"It's grand being able to come back to Wheatley Hill to see all my family again", Mrs Hall told our reporter this week, "but I don't think I could settle in this country again. Life is wonderful in New Zealand. From the very moment I first set foot in that country I settled down and have found the people wonderfully kind and helpful. They soon made me feel at home and I have made many fine friends".

Whirlwind Courtship

Mrs Hall's husband, Lindsay, has been unable to accompany her on this trip. "He is too busy looking after the farm" smiled Mrs Hall. The couple have a 76 acre dairy farm, Mr Hall taking it over on the death of his father three years ago. In 1954, not long before his death, Mr Hall's father, who was a local town Coun and prominently associated with many public bodies, was, together with his wife, presented to Queen Elizabeth when she toured New Zealand.

Mrs Hall's marriage two days before VJ day in August 1945, was the sequel to a whirlwind three month courtship. She met her husband, who was serving in the New Zealand Navy, at a local dance in Wheatley Hill. Three months after they were married Mr Hall returned to New Zealand and was demobilised, and shortly afterwards - in March 1946 - Mrs Hall set out to join him in New Zealand. She celebrated her 21st birthday on the voyage.

The couple live at Te Awamutu, near Hamilton, on North Island. "We are about four miles out of town", said Mrs Hall, "but there's always plenty going on to occupy our leisure hours". Mrs Hall is a member of the Methodist Church and the Young Mothers' Club and never finds time hanging on her hands.

As near as she could say from the short time she has been back home in Wheatley Hill, said Mrs Hall, the cost of living in the two countries appeared just about the same. Clothes were cheaper in this country but some of the foodstuffs were dearer.

The New Zealand climate was "wonderful" - "we never see any snow", said Mrs Hall - and their was plenty of employment. "It's a great country for young people, and offers plenty of prospects", added Mrs Hall. Girls leaving school at about 16 or 17 could earn £12 a week in some factories, she said, and even in a milk bar an assistant could earn £8 a week at the start.

While she is here Mrs Hall, who worked for four years in Wheatley Hill canteen before her marriage, will have a busy time visiting all her family - she has five sisters and three brothers - and friends, and showing her two young children many of the beauty spots in the county. One of her brothers will be missing from the reunion. He is her oldest brother, Jonathan, who has been in South Africa for the past 15 years.

When Mrs Hall's boat docked in Southampton earlier this month, an affectionate welcome awaited her from her mother, who has been secretary of Wheatley Hill Over 60 Club since its inception, and one of her sisters, Mrs G Gribbens. Since she went to New Zealand, Mrs Hall has been sent the "Durham Chronicle" regularly each week. "I look forward eagerly to its arrival - it's the best link I have with my home village!" she declared.

28 February 1958

WHEATLEY HILL TRAGEDY
Girl Trapped in Blazing Shop

Four joiners made a gallant attempt on Monday to quell a fire that resulted in a 20 year old Wheatley Hill girl losing her life.

The girl was Miss Grace Ashford, daughter of Mr and Mrs Jonathan Ashford, 9 Wordsworth Avenue, Wheatley Hill. She was trapped alone in the back shop when fire broke out in the branch of the 60 Minute Cleaners, Front Street, Wheatley Hill, where she was employed.

Firemen eventually carried the girl from the shop after fighting their way through the flames, but attempts at artificial respiration were unsuccessful.

Sixty Minute Cleaners
Wheatley Hill Front Street

Valiant Efforts

The alarm was raised by some boys who dashed into a shop opposite owned by 25 year old joiner Mr Tony Carr, 4 Durham Street, Wheatley Hill. Mr Carr said after the fire: "I rushed across the road and opened the door but realised that the blaze was too big for me to do anything". Mr Carr ran back to his shop and telephoned for the fire brigade then went with his three assistants to fight the flames with small hand operated fire extinguishers.

His three assistants were his brother, Jack, Mr Norman Fawcett and Mr Billy Carr.

A big crowd gathered outside the shop and Mr Carr realised that the windows might be blown out of the shop at any moment. He flung a piece of ice through the plate glass windows and the others threw their extinguishers through the window. "I thought that the crowd might get showered by flying glass", explained Mr Carr.

Wheatley Hill unit of Durham County Fire Brigade were soon at the scene, quickly followed by the Peterlee unit.

They managed to fight their way to the back shop where the girl had been trapped and carried her to a nearby house.

Extensive Damage

Firemen and police applied artificial respiration but their efforts were in vain.

The fire spread quickly to the front shop where extensive damage was done. Lines of suits, coats and other clothing that had been cleaned and were awaiting collection were destroyed. Only the metal hooks of the coat hangers were left dangling from the racks. The ground floor was completely gutted.

Although the fire spread to upstairs rooms the damage was limited. Firemen soon got the blaze under control and prevented it from spreading to shops on either side.

The fire lasted only about 30 minutes. The cause is being investigated.

DIED IN AUSTRALIA - Mrs Agnes Adams, 4 Second Street, Wheatley Hill, has been notified of the death of her brother, William, who emigrated to Australia in 1925. Mr Hoole was second son of a family of 21 children. He worked at Thornley Colliery from leaving school until 1914 when he went into the Forces. He received the DCM in France and on returning home was presented with a gold watch. Mr Hoole married Miss Mary Johnson of Choppington, who nursed him in hospital and she went to Australia with him where she died 20 years ago. Mrs Adams, Mr Thomas Hoole, Wheatley Hill; Mrs Rachel Sims, Wingate and Mrs Clara Dunning, Thornley, the youngest, are the only survivors of the family.

14 March 1958

BOXING SONS AT THORNLEY

Ronald Harvey, one of Thornley's "Five Fighting Harvey Brothers", was married last Saturday to Miss Maureen Blair, at Haswell. He is one of the five boxing sons of Mr and Mrs J E Harvey, Hillsyde Crescent, and he is a semi-finalist in the NCB Boxing championships at lightweight. He is due to appear in the final a week tomorrow.

Another brother, John, was with Ronald, Durham District novice champion of 1956. Brother Kenneth turned professional after a distinguished amateur career, being amateur youth champion of 1955, North East and Durham District champion. He also fought for the ABA at his weight at Middlesbrough. Since turning professional, he had won his five contests on a knock out.

All the brothers have been trained by that well known popular ex-champion, Pat "Boy" Gorman.

CATHOLIC CLUB - At the annual ballot of Thornley Catholic Club for officials and committee, Mr Pat Ellward, the chairman, was defeated by Mr John Regan. Mr Jim English, the secretary, was re-elected, and Mr Tom McCoy returned unopposed as treasurer. Committee comprises Messrs W A Barron, D Bell, G Dryden, G Graney, J Hoban, M Hoban, T Lennox, H McCoy, E Morrow and S Regan.

CATHOLIC'S DEATH - Following Requiem Mass in the Church of the Sacred Heart and English Martyrs, Thornley, said by the Rev Father H McNeill, interment took place of Mr Michael Rowley (72), 96 Dunelm Road, Thornley. Mr Rowley, born at Castle Eden, worked at Whitburn and Wheatley Hill collieries. In 1914 he joined the Forces and served in the Middle East and in France, where he was wounded and confined to hospital for a long period. At the end of the war he resumed his employment at Wheatley Hill and worked there until he was transferred to Thornley, where he retired. He married Helen, second daughter of Mr John Lee, brother of Mr Peter Lee. He is survived by his wife and two married sons, Tom and Leslie.

THORNLEY FUNERAL OF MISS GRACE ASHFORD

A large congregation filled St Bartholomew's Church, Thornley, on Saturday, for the funeral of Miss Grace Ashford (20), daughter of Mr and Mrs J Ashford, 9 Wordsworth Avenue, Wheatley Hill. The service was conducted by the Vicar of Wheatley Hill (the Rev G Gordon Graham). Interment followed at Thornley cemetery.

Miss Ashford was the victim of a fire tragedy. She was trapped alone when fire broke out in a shop in Front Street, Wheatley Hill. Miss Ashford was a communicant at All Saints' Church, Wheatley Hill.

Miss Ashford's grandmother, Mrs M A Ashford (90), West Hartlepool, and her grandfather Mr J W Lawson (85), of Hetton-le-Hole, could not attend the funeral.

21 March 1958

POURED PETROL INTO HEATER
Tragic Death of Wheatley Hill Girl

Mr T V Devey sat with a jury at the inquest on Tuesday on Grace Ashford (20), of 9 Wordsworth Avenue, Wheatley Hill, who lost her life in a fire which gutted the Wheatley Hill branch of Sixty Minute Cleaners Ltd in Front Street on Monday, March 10th.

The manageress, Mrs Jean J Stewart, 93 North Road East, Wingate, said she gave the boy ?/3d. and asked him to fetch a gallon of paraffin from the Co-operative Garage. She was positive, she declared, answering the Coroner, Mr T V Devey, that she told the boy to get paraffin.

Heater Burst into Flames

The boy, Joseph H Raffell, 26 Wordsworth Avenue, Wheatley Hill, told the Coroner he was just as positive that he was asked to get half a gallon of petrol. "I didn't know what she wanted it for", he added. When he returned to the shop with the petrol Mrs Stewart was just serving and he gave the can to Grace, who carried it into the back shop. He saw the girl bending over a heater which was standing on the floor. She emptied the can of petrol into the container at the bottom of the heater.

"As I watched her", continued Raffell, " I saw the can catch the heater and the heater burst into flames. The flames shot into Grace's face and I saw the side of her hair burning. She turned around and ran into a doorway on the left side at the back of the shop. I shouted to her to come out but she shouted "No". As the girl ran away she dropped the can of petrol and the flames spread across the back shop.

Dr A P Gray said the girl had received severe burns to her face and legs, but her overall was not burned at all. She died from shock as a result of burns, and asphyxia. The jury returned a verdict of "accidental death".

A brother of the dead girl, Thomas H Ashford, Queen Street, Thornley, said his sister had worked at the shop for about two years.

Never Bought Petrol from the Shop

Mrs Stewart, in answer to the Coroner, said they were not in the habit of pouring paraffin into the heater when it was lit. They had put paraffin in when the heater was warm.

Answering Mr A N Levinson, appearing for Miss Ashford's relatives, Mrs Stewart said they had had the heater about 12 months and it was filled about three times a week. They did not use a funnel and, replying to the Coroner, witness admitted that the can did not have a "mouth" to it. Never at any time, said Mrs Stewart, had she bought any petrol for the shop.

"If you are going to use this heater again, let me give you some advice", the Coroner told Mrs Stewart. "First of all, get a proper paraffin container and a funnel - and don't fill heaters when they are hot. It is a dangerous thing to do".

Dr Gray, replying to Mr Levinson, said he did not think the girl would live long after her burns.

The boy Raffell said he did not know whether the heater was already lit when he saw Grace emptying the can of petrol into it.

When the shop became full of flames, the boy continued, he picked up the petrol can to throw it out of the shop but it was so hot he had to drop it.

Boy Asked for Petrol

Seventeen year old Ronald Watson, apprentice motor mechanic, 4 Cemetery Road, Wheatley Hill, who served Raffell with half a gallon of petrol, said that that was what the boy had asked for.

Replying to the Coroner, Watson said that the shop had often bought paraffin at the garage, but he never remembered them getting petrol before.

Anthony Carr, 4 Durham Street, Wheatley Hill, timber merchant, told the Coroner how he dashed to the shop and tried to enter the front door. The flames and smoke kept him back and he dialled 999 for help. He found the whole of the back premises "a mass of flames".

Carr, commented the corone, deserved every credit for what he had done. "You seem to have done all you could", said the Coroner.

Work of the Fire Brigade

Fireman Harold F Horner, 15 Institute Street, Wheatley Hill, said that within seven minutes of the arrival of the brigade at the shop they got a girl out. They found the body in a small room at the back of the building.

From the evidence, said the Coroner, addressing the jury, they had heard Mrs Stewart say she had asked the boy to get paraffin but the boy said he had been asked to get petrol. "I think you will agree with me it was a stupid thing, first of all to try and fill the heater from that type of can, and secondly, it is a foolish trick for anyone to fill a paraffin heater when it is lit, as I assume this would be. We have this poor girl burned to death through it. There is no-one you can blame criminally for it in any way".

Sympathy with the dead girl's parents was expressed by the Coroner, the foreman of the jury, Mr J H Pattison, and Sergeant Woore (on behalf of the police).

DEATH OF A MILITARY MEDALIST
Mr John Lamb, Wheatley Hill

At an inquest at Thornley on Tuesday on a retired miners' checkweighman, Mr John Lamb (68), 8 Byron Street, Wheatley Hill, who was found dead on his bedroom floor on Sunday morning, Dr G H Wallace said death was due to coronary thrombosis, and the Coroner, Mr T V Devey, recorded a verdict of "natural causes" in accordance with this evidence.

Mrs Elizabeth A Scott said Mr Lamb, her brother, had lived with her for 46 years. He was a single man. In 1916 he was wounded in the left arm while serving in the army in France, and since then had been in receipt of a war disability pension. His health had been quite good and it was only two weeks before his death that he complained of having a slight cold.

Replying to the Coroner, Dr Wallace said he did not think Mr Lamb's war wound had had anything to do with his death.

Following a service at "The Rest" on Wednesday, conducted by the Rev G L Nelson, Mr Lamb was buried at Wheatley Hill cemetery.

Mr Lamb's mining career was interrupted when he joined the Scottish Rifles during the 1914-18 war. He was wounded twice - in the battles of Loos and The Somme - and for his bravery on the field of battle was awarded the Military Medal in 1916.

For some time he was unable to work because of his wounds, but in 1930 was appointed miners' checkweighman at Thornley Colliery, which position he filled until his retirement three years ago. Mr Lamb was held in high esteem by a wide circle of friends.

28 March 1958

WHEATLEY HILL DRAMA GROUP - After a series of misfortunes which have prevented them from presenting a play during the winter session for the first time since the Society was formed, Wheatley Hill Amateur Dramatic Society are hoping to be "first in the field" with their production in September of a new three-act comedy, "Doctor in the House" (by Richard Gordon).

The play, with Mrs Vera Fairclough, of Easington, as producer is to be presented in Wheatley Hill Welfare Hall for the four nights, September 17th to 20th.

During the session just ending the Society had hoped to present the drama, "The Gioconda Smile". Illness among both the players and the producer, and other setbacks resulted in the play being postponed on several occasions. Eventually it was decided to abandon it altogether. "There seemed to be a jinx on us", said an official of the Society this week.

4 April 1958

EASTER PLAY - Members of Wheatley Hill Patton Street Methodist Church gave John Drinkwater's Easter play, "A Man's House", in the Welfare Hall. It was produced by the Rev G L Nelson. The acting was reverently done and reached a high standard. Parts were played by Tom King, Dorothy Warnes, William Walton, Joseph Scrafton, Jean Hays, Rev G L Nelson, Jack Robson, Maurice Lang, Brian Cairns, Charles Lister, Wilfred Warnes, Tom Venables, Lawrence Williams, Elizabeth Turner and Margaret Winnard. Mr W Harker was stage manager and Mr J Robson was in charge of lighting and effects.
11 April 1958

WINGATE PARISH COUNCIL - Wingate Parish Council members were told at a meeting on Monday that the takeover by the North Eastern Electricity Board of the electricity supply from the National Coal Board at Wingate was expected to be completed by mid summer.

Coun N Cook declared that the lighting in Wheatley Hill where the Electricity Board had already taken over, was worse than it had ever been when maintained by the National Coal Board.

Mr P H Algar, a representative of the Board, promised to investigate this complaint and also to look into the matter when Coun J D Higgins reported that lights in Wingate Front Street between the cinema and the railway crossing were out for two or three days "every so often".
18 April 1958

DARTS PRESENTATIONS - Most of the 12 clubs in the Wingate and District Darts League were represented at a social function in the New Tavern Inn, Wheatley Hill, on Monday night, when a new silver challenge cup was presented to the league by Mr G Brydon, on behalf of Messrs J Nimmo and Son Ltd. The cup was won by the New Tavern team, league champions with 16 victories out of 22 games, and was presented to the team captain, Mr T Linsley, by Mr Brydon. A cup was also presented to the runners-up, Hesleden Conservative Club, who won 13 of their 22 games. The league secretary, Mr Wedgewood, presented a miniature silver cup to Mr J Robinson, a member of the New Tavern team, who had the highest individual score of 180. The New Tavern team were runners-up last year, but have twice previously been league champions. After the presentations, local talent provided entertainment.

"A SERIOUS CHARGE" AT THORNLEY

Once again Thornley Drama Group have produced a hit. Their production of "A Serious Charge" (by Phillip King) received a wonderful ovation from old age pensioners, who were made welcome at a free showing on Monday night.

Producer Bert Martin's interpretation of this moving drama of our day and age has a touch of genius. Joseph Ferguson, in the leading role of Howard Phillips, vicar of Bellington, is both inspired and inspiring by the noble lines he quotes. He is ably supported by such well known players as Eva Martin, who plays well the part of his mother, Mrs Phillips, who is not the "orthodox" conception of a vicar's mother; Dorothy Burlison as Eva Browning, their maid, and James Bewick as the village schoolmaster.

New Members of the group astounded everyone with their talent. Jean Walker gives a touching portrayal of the tragic role of Mary Williams, a young unmarried girl about to have a baby, while Elizabeth Green is most convincing as Hester Byfield, a pathetic and frustrated spinster. Derek Ord is magnificent in the role of Larry Thompson, a despicable, evil minded youth who brings trouble and sorrow to all he meets.

Supporting in minor roles are Alan Lincoln and David Gott.

The set carries stage manager Harry Hetherington's inimitable touch, and the lighting is by Arthur Clark. Members of the group thank all who have assisted in this production.

The play will be given again tonight.

CRICKET CLUB - At the annual meeting of Thornley Colliery Welfare Cricket Club the balance sheet showed that at the beginning of the season the credit balance was £8.14s and at the end of the year it had risen to £136.10s. Officers elected: Mr Arthur Welsh, president; Mr William Straughan, chairman; Mr Robert Patterson, secretary; Mr James R Taylor, treasurer. The delegate to the North East Durham League is Mr William Wilson, captain, Mr Robert Patterson and vice-captain, Mr David Straughan.

BOB-A-JOB WEEK - In the recent bob-a-job week organised by the Scout movement, a member of the 2nd Wheatley Hill Troop must surely have created a county record, if not a national one. He is Patrol Leader Ivison, who collected no less a sum than £6.2s.6d. Altogether 40 Scouts and 40 Wolf Cubs took part in the effort at Wheatley Hill and raised a total of £66. The Scouts alone raised £43 and the Cubs £23. Scoutmaster Leslie Barker and Cubmaster Alfred Watson were in charge.

THORNLEY - RETIRED - Mr Billy Goodchild, 65 year old boiler minder at Thornley Colliery, has retired. At 14 he began work at the old Beehive Coke Ovens at Trimdon Grange. There he learned how to load and draw the ovens by hand. In the first world war be saw service as a stoker. When he returned to the Grange he got the job of loading and clearing the new ovens with the mechanical rammer until 1930 when the pit closed down. He then joined Ropner's Navy and for four years was a stoker. He left the sea in 1934 and took up work as a fireman at Thornley Colliery. He continued there as a stoker until he was made boiler minder 10 years ago. He also took on the unofficial job of rat catcher in the colliery yard which was infested. He trained four or five stray cats who had their home in the donkey house to kill the rats and bring them back. He fed the cats with milk and fish.

LEGION WOMEN - An enjoyable evening was spent by members of Thornley British Legion Women's Section at an exhibition of films on travel in Britain by the United Automobile Services, under the direction of Mr Jackson, Area Traffic Superintendent. Mrs H Slater presided and business was conducted by Mrs P E Morgan (secretary). Competition was won by Mrs E Harker. Members are to have annual outing to Bridlington.

ELECTRICITY - The North Eastern Electricity Board has taken over the first batch of consumers from the National Coal Board in Thornley Parish.
2 May 1958

FUN AT WHEATLEY HILL

Continuing their efforts to restore the traditional spirit of May Day, the workmen of Wheatley Hill Colliery arranged a day of festivities on Saturday. The organisation was carried out by a strong committee, representing all organisations and interests in the village, with Mr A D Wharrier (chairman), Coun J Cowie (secretary) and Mr J Hedley (treasurer). The workmen of Wheatley Hill colliery accepted a weekly levy, and £340 was spent on the day's festivities.

A parade, headed by Wheatley Hill Colliery Prize Band (conductor, Mr H Strong) moved from Patton Street to Wheatley Hill Peterlee Girls' Modern School playing fields. The children were in colourful fancy dress. Over 2000 people watched the parade and sports. Each child on entering the field received a parcel of fruit and chocolate to the value of half a crown, and each child who competed in the fancy dress parade and the racing events received a consolation prize. Events causing most interest were the men's four mile race and the ladies' scrambles.

Results

four mile race, Raymond Clish, David Young, Benny Thubron; ladies' scramble (under 30), Mrs O'Connor, Mrs Milroy, Mrs Goyns; two scrambles (over 30), Mrs J Young, Mrs Carr, Mrs Aitken, Mrs Pyle, Mrs Williams, Mrs Stephenson.

Fancy dress events were judged by Miss A I Hutchinson, Mrs J Wallace and Coun Edward Cain. Winners: fancy dress, Gavin Stott, Ann Curry, Hazel Rowbotham and Ann Galley (tie); comic dress, Carol Carr, Geoffrey Collingwood, Gordon Tempest; original dress, Derek Lang, Jennifer Stott and Rosaline Beddell (tie), Jessie Kirby.

George Wright received £1 for "spotting" Coun Cain, who was the "mystery man".

Whist, Dancing

The day's celebrations culminated in a well supported whist drive and dance in the Welfare Hall. Thanking the people of Wheatley Hill, the secretary (Coun J Cowie) said: "My committee desire to thank all organisations of the village for the help they have given in making this venture a success. It is our aim to capture the spirit and carefree happiness that characterised May Day before the war years. We want to prove that television, radio and films are not making us lazy. On an occasion such as this it is good to know that we can work together, play together and entertain ourselves by our own activities within our own community".

Mesdames M Brain and C Charlton were MCs for whist and Mr B Aitken was MC for the dance.

Whist winners were: Mrs A R Clogg, Mrs R A Brown, Mrs J Merrington, Mr E Hall, Mr A Petterson and Mr E Cowan. Dominoes: Mrs Dinsdale, Mr S Wilson and Mrs Mills. Prizes were presented by Mrs E Richardson, a member of the committee.
9 May 1958

HUSBAND AND WIFE DIE SAME DAY
Well known couple in SE Durham

Mourners gathering at Wheatley Hill on Wednesday for the funeral of Mrs Mary Ann Taylor (75), 7 Greenhills Terrace, were shocked to learn that earlier that day Mrs Taylor's husband, Robert, had died in Sedgefield General Hospital. A sister of Mrs Taylor, Mrs Hannah Harper, who was 66, died only last Saturday at Ringwood, Hampshire, five months after her husband's death. Mrs Harper spent most of her younger days at Wingate.

Mrs Taylor died in Stockton and Thornaby Hospital on Friday - the day before her sister's death. On Easter Monday, Mr and Mrs Taylor were both taken to Sedgefield General Hospital, but later Mrs Taylor was transferred to Stockton Hospital. It was, incidentally, 53 years gone Easter Monday that the couple were married at Houghton-le-Spring Wesleyan Methodist Church.

Mrs Taylor and her husband had lived in Wheatley Hill for 37 years. Mrs Taylor had a long association with Patton Street Methodist Church and with the Women's Institute. Throughout her life she devoted much of her time to working voluntarily for various charitable organisations.

Both Mr and Mrs Taylor had been members of Wheatley Hill Over 60 Club since its inception. Mrs Taylor formerly played in the Wheatley Hill ladies' bowls team and was a member of the Women's Own at Patton Street Church.

Served at Etaples

Mr Taylor became a fully qualified ambulance man. Shortly after the outbreak of the 1914-18 war, he was one of two members chosen from Hetton Ambulance Brigade to work in the St John Ambulance Hospital at Etaples, in France. After two and a half years' service there he moved into the fighting line and was badly wounded in the lungs shortly before the end of the war.

Because of his war wound, Mr Taylor gave up his career as a miner and became one of the pioneers of a local bus company running a service between Thornley railway station and the nearby pit villages. Eventually, a bigger company took over and Mr Taylor became an Inspector for the G and B Bus Company, filling this position for 20 years until his retirement ten years ago.

Mr Taylor was well known as a cricketer in the Hetton area in his younger days. He played for Hetton Lyons and captained the side which won the mid Durham League in 1911. He was a founder of the Tennis Club and later played in the Wheatley Hill Welfare bowls team. Mr Taylor was a member and Past Master of the Caradoc Lodge of Freemasons at Castle Eden for 27 years.

The funeral service for Mrs Taylor, conducted in Patton Street Church by the Rev George L Nelson, was followed by cremation at Sunderland.

Most of the organisations that Mrs Taylor was connected with were represented at the funeral.

16 May 1958

(It appears that the heading of this article may be incorrect, as Mr Taylor died on the day of his wife's funeral)

WHEATLEY HILL - Music Success - Two Thornley brothers, reports Mr Ernest Goyns, organist of Wheatley Hill Church Street Methodist Church, have gained successes in the musical world. Recently John and Michael Heslop, Hillsyde Crescent, Thornley, went to Sunderland for the Grade IV pianoforte examination of the Associated Board of the Royal Schools of Music.

LODGE SECRETARY - Mr William Dowding, secretary of Thornley Miners' Lodge, has resigned through ill health. He has been succeeded by Mr Ronald Hughes, a 36 year old filler at Thornley Colliery, who served with the Royal Scots Fusiliers in France, Holland and Germany in the last war. In 1953 he won an NUM scholarship, which gave him two year's residential tuition at Ruskin College, Oxford, where he took his diploma in economics and political science. He was one of the three Couns returned to Easington Council by Wheatley Hill ward of Wingate Parish.

30 May 1958

THORNLEY WELFARE RECEIVE TROPHY

Representatives of village organisations, players, committee, friends and relations attended the presentation of the Wearside League Cup in Thornley Welfare Institute to Fred Richardson, captain of Thornley CW, by Mr Ted Green, chairman of the Welfare Committee.

Mr Richard Lewis, club chairman, presided, and Coun A Bushby, chairman of Thornley Miners' Federation Board, presented cup trophies to the following players: F Richardson, G Lewthwaite, Terry Murray, George Rees, Bobby Bell, Wilf Miller, R Presho, G Greener, Austin Almina, A Fishwick, Denny Brown, Leo Harding.

Mr J Quinn, chairman of Thornley Workmen's Club, presented the league trophies to the same players. Mr W Henderson, secretary of the Welfare Committee, handed cup and league trophies to Mr J R Bosomworth, secretary of the football club.

Mr Henderson congratulated the players on their successful year and thanked Mr Bosomworth for the tremendous amount of hard work he had put in.

Mr Charles Lamb, vice chairman of the club and Headmaster of Thornley Junior Primary School, appealed to players to help the local schoolboy footballers, who, he said, looked to local celebrities more than they did to English League stars.

Mr Lamb said it was surprising what influence local players had on the boys - and how they tried to imitate their ideal players. That was why he did not like to hear players using bad language and swearing on the field.

Ladies' committee, providing a fine meal, were thanked by Mr Bosomworth and Mr Lewis.

LEGION HALL OPENED

Saturday was a big day for members of the Women's Section of the British Legion at Wheatley Hill when their new headquarters were opened. Mrs I Carter (secretary) reports that the section was formed 28 years ago. Since then they have had no premises of their own. A year ago, a hut used as Cadets' Headquarters was secured and £200 has been spent on converting the premises into an attractive hall which has been decorated inside and out. It is well heated and lighted. Linoleum covers the floor and four members have made curtains. Officials mainly responsible were Mrs J Tyson (president), Mrs S Eddy (vice president), Mrs M Brain (chairman), Mrs I Carter (secretary), Mrs A E Stainsby (treasurer) and a strong committee.

The opening ceremony was attended by 100 members. The Rev G L Nelson introduced Mrs Jane Tyson, 81 year old president, who was a founder member, to perform the ceremony. She said: "This is a great day for the Women's Section of the British Legion in Wheatley Hill. We have been in existence for 28 years. For us, the opening of this hall represents a dream come true. I hope these comfortable premises will attract more members to our cause". Mrs Tyson also paid tribute to Mrs Hedger, the county secretary, who was unable to attend. She had done a great deal to help the Wheatley Hill section with this project. The new hall will be known as Hedger House in recognition of her services. Mrs M Brain (chairman) presented Mrs Tyson and Mrs S Eddy (vice president) with sprays of carnations. Tea was provided for members and served by committee members - Mesdames D Bishop, M Kime, E Bradley, W Bowes, M Knowles, M Taylor, E Richarsdon, R Maughan, F Court, E Telford and D Jackson.
6 June 1958

THORNLEY FOOTBALL "ANNUAL"

Mr Edward Luke was elected president of Thornley CW Football Club at the annual meeting. Other elections resulted: chairman, Mr R Lewis; secretary, Mr J R Bosomworth; treasurer, Mr G Armstrong; financial secretary, Mr G Pattison; assistant secretary, Mr J Dobbin; assistant treasurer, Mr J Potts; vice chairman, Mr W Headley; committee, Messrs R Richardson, J Luke, R Luke, J Hutchinson, A Redshaw, N Mains, N Howe, J Lennox.

Mr Lewis, chairman, said they could look back on the season with a certain amount of pride. The good relationship between the officials and committee reflected itself in the players, who had done well. He thanked all who had assisted.

Mr Bosomworth recalled that this was the second year in which they had won the league cup, and they were also runners up in the league. He paid special tribute to the ladies' committee, who had given such valuable support during the season.

Mr Bosomworth revealed that they were also to run a junior football team next season - the first time since 1936 that junior football had been considered seriously in the district. The junior club will have all support available from the parent club.

For the junior section, the following were elected: president, Mr E Carter, chairman of Thornley Miners' Lodge; chairman, Mr D Willan; secretary, Mr J R

Greener; treasurer, Mr J Foster; committee, Messrs N Garswood, G Pattison, T Hall, A Barker.

OLD SCOUTS' EFFORT AT WHEATLEY HILL

The first effort organised by Wheatley Hill Old Scouts' Association since its formation eighteen months ago - a field day and garden fete - was a huge success on Saturday. Held in the Peterlee Girls' Modern School field, the effort attracted a large crowd, and the varied programme spiced with humorous events, reflected the hard work put in by the old Scouts.

The programme began with a comic football match between the Rovers and the old Scouts. The players all wore comic dress and anything but the rules of football were observed. Nobody was interested in the result of the match and, for the record, nobody knew either.

A display of ju-jitsu was given by the Vane Tempest Judo Club from Durham, under the leadership of Mr Patterson, and side shows, amusements, competitions and sports were in the charge of the old Scouts. Mr S Saxby won the senior section of the archery tournament and Mr W Humes the junior, and the senior darts competition was won by Mr R Rogers. Refreshments were served and the "hot dog" stall was well patronised.

At night a carnival dance was held in the Welfare Hall, with music by Mr Pratt's Band. MCs were Scoutmaster Leslie Barker and Mr B Aitken and entertainment was provided by the Rovers' Skiffle Group.

Officials responsible for the arrangements were Messrs J Armstrong (chairman), R Watson (secretary) and J Raffell (treasurer). Proceeds of the day's effort were for local Scout headquarters funds.

"We were quite pleased with the result of this, our first effort on the village and it will certainly be the forerunner of many more functions", said Mr Watson at the end of the day.

13 June 1958

VISITOR FROM AMERICA - In the first world war Miss Alice Barker, daughter of the late Mr and Mrs Joseph Barker, of Wheatley Hill, served her country in the WAACs, and was stationed at Marske. Units of the American Air Force were also stationed there. Among them was Mr Eddie Allen. The couple met and romance followed. The war ended and both secured their discharge in 1919, Eddie returning to America. This did not end their romance. Later in the year Miss Barker went to the States and the couple were married in New York. They set up home in Tacoma, Washington State, Mrs Allen was then 19. After 17 years, in 1936, she spent a holiday in this country. Now after a lapse of 22 years, she is spending six weeks' holiday at the home of her sister, Mrs A Forster, 2 Luke Terrace, Wheatley Hill. The couple have one son, Eddie, who is with his father in his plumbing business; two daughters Mrs Isobel Standish and Mrs Dorothy Herbert. All live in Tacoma. "We have nine grandchildren" said Mrs Allen, "but not a grandaughter among them. All are fine boys".

20 June 1958

FREEMASON'S FUNERAL AT WHEATLEY HILL

Masonic, Methodist and business communities were well represented on Monday at the funeral service in Wheatley Hill Church Street Methodist Church of Mr Maurice Nixon (55), 10 Gable Terrace, Wheatley Hill. It was conducted by the superintendent minister (the Rev G H Ireland) and the resident minister (the Reverend G L Nelson). Mr Goyns was at the organ.

Mr Nixon was born at Marske but spent most of his life at Wheatley Hill. At the age of 16 he had to leave Grammar School owing to his father's ill health and go into the family grocery business. He has directed this ever since. Mr Nixon was a prominent Freemason. He was a member of Rowland Burdon Lodge which meets at Castle Eden. At the time of his death he was an officer of that lodge.

He was a well known Methodist and had a lifelong membership with Wheatley Hill Church Street Church. He was a trustee and served the board as treasurer for many years.

Youth work, however, was Mr Nixon's forte. He was treasurer of the Sunday School for more than 30 years. He also served as treasurer of the church youth club. Since 1941 he was treasurer of Thornley Circuit Youth Council, and had much to do with establishing the Circuit Youth Eisteddfod. Mr Nixon was associated with Mr Jack Harrison, JP, in founding the original Wheatley Hill Youth Fellowship.

WHEATLEY HILL HOMING - Principal results of Wheatley Hill Homing Society's race from Welwyn Garden City were: Frost Brothers 1336.4 (trainer, 1d, 2d, 3d). Heal and Sons, 1332.7 (1d, 2d, 3d, 6d, 1s, ladies' special and nomination); Lowther Brothers and Dinsdale, 1331.6 (6d, 1s); Frost Brothers 1325.1 (2s.6d); Dodds Brothers 1319.9; Lowther and Dinsdale, 1319.1 (5s).

WIN FOR WHEATLEY HILL

Most of the runs came from their three opening batsmen when Wheatley Hill defeated Harraton CW by 44 runs at home on Saturday. The "Hill's" opening pair, Brian Winter and Harold Simpson, put on 51 before they were separated and the score climbed to 108 before the fourth wicket fell. The "tail enders", however, fared badly, the innings closing at 121.

Bobby Patterson, who went to the crease at the fall of the first wicket, was top scorer with 39, which included seven boundaries. Winter scored only one run less before being run out and Simpson's contribution was 19. For the visitors, N Mitchell took four wickets for 37.

Mitchell, who opened with Scott for Harraton, was his side's top scorer with 20. His colleagues found runs difficult to get against the accurate bowling of Fred Iddon, who took six wickets for 33 in 13 overs, and they were all back in the pavilion for 77.

Eric Simpson took three wickets for 24 and the other wicket fell to M Fleming for 15 runs.

Wheatley Hill: B Winter run out 38, H Simpson c Young b Dean 19, R Patterson b Young 39, G Carr b Mitchell 2, G Harrison c Dean b Mitchell 7, T Hall c Williams b Mitchell 3, E C Simpson run out 10, W Marshall b Young 0, F Iddon run out 0. J Nicholson not out 0, M Fleming b Mitchell 0, extras 3 - total 121.

Harraton CW, 77.

27 June 1958

FIRE FIGHTING TESTS
Wheatley Hill Colliery's Success

Competing against six other colliery teams from the area, Wheatley Hill won the annual underground fire fighting competition organised by No 3 Area (South East Durham) of the Durham Divisional Coal Board, for the fourth time in five years - on the other occasion they were runners-up. The competition, with tests for both underground and surface fire fighting, was staged in the grounds of The Castle, Castle Eden, No 3 Area headquarters. It attracted many officials from the eight collieries in the area. Deaf Hill Colliery was the only one which did not compete in the surface test, and Shotton the only one which did not take part in the underground test.

The winning Wheatley Hill team comprised Messrs T W Ayre (captain), A Carr, A C Watson and E W Snowdon, with Mr W Gibson reserve. They completed the test in 88.5 seconds, and the runners-up, Thornley, took 99.7 seconds. The Thornley team consisted of Messrs W Davies (captain), R Gratton, J Gill and T Wilkinson, with Mr J E Horner reserve.

Wingate Colliery were third with a time of 121 seconds, and other placings were: 4, Horden, 126.5 seconds; 5, Deaf Hill, 128.5 Seconds; 6, Blackhall, 190.5 seconds; 7, Easington, 252 seconds.

Blackhall Won Surface Test

For the first time since the competition was inaugurated five years ago, a team from Blackhall Colliery won the surface fire fighting test with a time of 78 seconds. The actual test was completed in 71 seconds, but seven seconds were added as a "penalty" for mistakes. The team, trained by Mr W J Hart, fire officer at the colliery, consisted of Messrs R Bradley (captain), E Topping, G Jefferson and R Westland.

Thornley were also runners-up in this test, taking only half a second longer than Blackhall. The team consisted of Messrs S Ord (captain), H Watson, J McCoy, D Scott and L Hodgson (reserve). Horden Colliery were third, with a time of 79 seconds, and the other placings were: 4, Wheatley Hill, 81 seconds; 5, Easington, 89.3 seconds; 6, Shotton, 101.8 seconds; 7, Wingate, 103.5 seconds.

The prize for the best individual in the underground test was won by Mr Charles Edward Carr of Deaf Hill, with Mr Jack Wylie, Easington, runner-up. Mr Leslie Barker, Wheatley Hill, won the prize for the best individual in the surface test, with Mr William Johnson, Shotton Colliery, runner-up.

The adjudicators were Superintendent J J Smith and assistant Station Officer G Rafter, from the Houghton-le-Spring Fire and Rescue Brigade, and Station Officer J Richardson, from the Crook Rescue Brigade. The timekeeper was Mr J Gilliland, Civil Defence and Fire Officer for No 2 Area of the Durham Divisional Coal Board.

"All Very Keen"

In both tests, said Superintendent Smith, summing up the efforts of the competitors, the teams had had quite complicated tasks to carry out, but they had worked extremely hard and done very well. They had all been very keen, and it was this keenness, actually, which led to many "penalties". "They got so keen", added the Superintendent, "that mistakes were made and valuable seconds lost. It is evident, however, that a lot of time and practice has been put in, and I must congratulate the competitors on their performances".

The prizes were presented by the area general manager, Mr L C Timms, who had returned home from holiday barely two hours before. He felt, he said, it was his duty to come straight to the tests to give the competitors what encouragement he could, for fire fighting training was an important part of colliery life. It was "heartening" to know that in the past ten years 1,500 mineworkers in the area had received basic training in fire fighting.

"There have been occasions", went on Mr Timms, "when these trained men have dealt very quickly and efficiently with outbreaks which might otherwise have had most serious results - notably at Easington, when there was a belt conveyor fire and at Blackhall, where fire broke out under the cut on the coal face. The services of these men have come in very useful not only to themselves but also to their workmates and the Coal Board, and we hope they will keep up their good work".

Rescue Section

Mr Timms thanked all those who had taken part in the tests, the adjudicators and officials responsible for arranging the competition. He also presented the prizes to the winners of the Civil Defence competitions held in the area earlier.

Thornley Colliery team, comprising Messrs F Bradley Sen (captain), F Bradley Jnr, F Carter, N Fort, L Mitchell, M Convery, N Maynes, K Lonsdale and D Swallow (reserve), won the rescue section of the competition, and Horden were runners-up. The wardens' section was won by Wheatley Hill team, comprising Messrs T W Ayre (captain), L Barker, R G Horner, F Horner and A Appleby, with Shotton Colliery runners-up.

Arrangements for the fire fighting competition were efficiently carried out by the area safety engineer, Mr E Gascoigne, assisted by the area Civil Defence and Fire Fighting Officer, Mr W Barnfather, Peterlee.

The wining teams in the fire fighting and Civil Defence sections will represent the area in the Durham Divisional competitions to be held later.

4 July 1958

OFF TO CAMP - Under the staggered holiday scheme for pit holidays, Wheatley Hill schools will be closed for the next fortnight. Mr A Harris, head teacher of

Wheatley Hill Boys' Modern school, and the following members of his staff will devote a week of their holiday in taking 36 boys to camp at Hexham: Messrs E H Ward, J Etherington, A Stabler, T Holder, K Charlton, J Lane and R Cherry. Games and camp sing-songs will be organised, and educational visits have been arranged to Corbridge, Dilston Castle and Hexham Abbey.
11 July 1958

WHEATLEY HILL MINERS' LODGE

The following officials of Wheatley Hill Miners' Lodge have been returned unopposed: chairman, Mr A Wharrier; treasurer, Mr T Taylorson; delegate, Mr H Bradshaw; card marker, Mr H Peacock; financial secretary, Mr J Hedley; pit inspector, Mr E Jones; colliery house committee, Messrs J Cain and H Bradshaw. Mr C W Venables died soon after being elected secretary; Mr T Knowles is carrying on pro tem.

Elected by ballot: auditors, Messrs J Cain and T Buxton, lodge committee: Messrs J J Burnside, M Cain, R Cook, J Gair, C Hackworth, M Telford, E Jones, E Peacock, W Rotheray, H Syson and G Henderson; welfare committee: T Buxton, M Alderton, J Hedley and W Rotheray; death fund committee: Messrs R Cook, C Hackworth and H Peacock. Pit Consultative committee: Messrs H Syson and Bradshaw; band committee: Messrs R Teasdale, M Cain, S Mitchison and H Peacock; aged miners' committee: M Alderton, M Telford, H Bradshaw, T Taylorson, J Hedley, G Henderson, C Hackworth and E Jones.

WHEATLEY HILL "GOLDEN"
Mr and Mrs James Rowbotham

Mr and Mrs James Rowbotham, 73 and 71 respectively, 2 Jack Lawson Terrace, Wheatley Hill, celebrated their golden wedding on Friday. They were married in St Bartholomew's, Thornley, in 1908. Mr and Mrs Rowbotham received congratulatory cards and greetings telegrams from their three sons and six daughters.

Mr Rowbotham was born in Shildon, spent some time at Haswell Plough but has lived 61 years in Wheatley Hill. He started work at 13 as a trapper boy at Wheatley Hill colliery and spent most of his working career there. During the last war he worked at Aycliffe and Haverton Hill shipyard. He retired at 65.

In the 1914-18 war Mr Rowbotham joined the 2nd East Yorkshire Regiment. He saw service in the Gallipoli campaign, Egypt and from 1916 he was in France and came through his war service without a scratch. He is a member of Wheatley Hill Discharged Soldiers' and Sailors' Club.

Asked what has impressed him most during his years in Wheatley Hill, Mr Rowbotham replied, "The change in the village itself. When I came here it was a place of long streets of grey, drab miners' houses. Sanitation was very primitive and the main road through the village was only poor. Behind the streets of houses there were no roads at all. In winter we ploughed through mud and clay. There was no direct road to Thornley. Today we have a completely new village. Roads and houses are a pleasure to see. Living conditions are much improved".

Over 60 Club Members

Mrs Rowbotham, formerly Miss Ellen Greener, was born in Trimdon Colliery. She too compared life in Wheatley Hill with living in the early part of the century. "Young people today", she said "cannot have any conception of the struggle people had in those days. To us who knew them they were the bad old days. For our men, it was work and bed. They had long hours to work for little money".

Mr and Mrs Rowbotham enjoy good health and are members of Wheatley Hill Over 60 Club. On behalf of the club, Mrs R Richardson (secretary) visited their home and presented the couple with a bouquet.

Mr Rowbotham said that the introduction of the Over 60 Club movement had made a big difference to the lives of retired people. He said, "The weekly meeting with their light entertainment, gives us something to look forward to; a night of our own which brings friendship and joy to many people who otherwise would be lonely and perhaps friendless".

Mr Rowbotham fills his time gardening and visiting his club.

CLUB COMMITTEE - Members of Wheatley Hill Workmen's Club held a ballot to fill six places on the management committee. There were 24 nominations for the six places. Following were declared elected: Messrs A Bishop, J Harper, T Harper, G Henderson, J Maratty and M Cain.

OVER 60 CLUB ENTERTAINS - Although Wheatley Hill Over 60 Club has closed down for the two weeks pit holidays, members of the concert party remain on duty. Last week they journeyed to Framwellgate Moor to entertain the Over 60 Club of that village. Mr W Williams (entertainments secretary) was compere, Mrs M Williams was pianist. Taking part were Mesdames I Richardson, T E Turner, M Carr, E Kitto, M Woodhead, A M Hewitt, J Harper, B Robinson, A Oswald, M Dixon; Messrs T E Turner, G R Charlton, T Simpson and I Hodgson.

18 July 1958

WHEATLEY HILL "GOLDEN"
Mr and Mrs J Williams Celebrate

On Friday, Mr and Mrs Joseph Williams attained their golden wedding anniversary. The couple were married in Haswell Church.

Recalling her wedding day, Mrs Williams, who is 70, said, "I was 20 at the time. There were no motor cars or taxi cabs to take us to the church. Joe and me were taken in a horse drawn cab. I got just as much thrill out of it as a ride in the smartest car of today".

Mrs Williams was born in Leasingthorne. She enjoys reasonably good health and does most of her own work although her daughters give her a hand. She recalled the hard times which obtained in the early part of the century. She said "We set up house at Shotton. Joe hadn't £3 a fortnight. Everything was certainly much cheaper than it is today, but there was a lot less money and it was often a struggle to make ends meet".

Mrs Williams is a founder member of Wheatley Hill Over 60 Club and is a regular attender.

56 Years in Mining

Mr Williams was born at Tudhoe. He started work at Tudhoe Colliery when he was 12. Retiring at 68 he gave 56 years to the mining industry. He spent a number of years at Shotton Colliery and has been over 30 years at Wheatley Hill. He was transferred from Wheatley Hill to Blackhall Colliery, where he finished his working career.

Being in a reserved occupation did not appeal to Mr Williams and he volunteered for military service in the first world war. He joined the Royal Artillery and saw service in France.

Although Mr Williams has officially finished work, he will not be entirely idle. For three days a week to goes to Wheatley Hill Miners' Welfare Hall. There he acts as steward in the Billiards room. He finds relaxation as a member of Wheatley Hill Constitutional Club and the Discharged Soldiers and Sailors Club.

The couple held a celebration party at their home, 19 Shinwell Terrace, Wheatley Hill. It was attended by their two sons, four daughters, seven grandchildren and other relatives and friends. Among the guests was the bridesmaid of 50 years ago, Mrs Mary Hughes, Mr Williams' sister. For the second time within seven days Mrs R Richardson, secretary of Wheatley Hill Over 60 Club, called at the home of one of its members and presented the couple with a bouquet of carnations and expressed the congratulations of the club on the occasion of their golden wedding.

THORNLEY MINERS' LODGE had a large number of followers to Durham Miners' Gala, led by Thornley Colliery Silver Prize Band conducted by Mr Edward Kitto. The band again played at the service in the cathedral. On arrival home the band and banner were met at the Halfway House, Thornley, by Mr Alex McColl, undermanager of Thornley Colliery, and Mr John Williams, deputy industrial relations officer to No 3 Area Durham Division. They took the poles of the banner and carried it through the main street to the Miners' Welfare Hall.

TO THE GALA - Although Wheatley Hill Colliery miners were on holiday, many returned a day earlier to attend the gala at Durham. Headed by their own colliery band, the lodge banner was carried by Messrs R Stark, W Patterson, R Hogg, M Owens, J Frost and W Hills, with Messrs A Venables and C Bramfitt as reserves. Each man received £3. Mr Edward Cain, a lodge official for many years, attended his 50th gala last year with the Wheatley Hill miners. This year was his first "Big Meeting" as a retired miner. He has only missed two of the last 53 galas. Once he was in hospital and once he was in South Africa.

GOLD MEDAL CHARMIAN
Empire Games Win for Thornley Diver

County Durham's own Charmian Welsh, the 21 year old girl from Thornley, who ranks with the best women divers in the world, won a great honour for her country when she carried off the Gold Medal in the final of the women's springboard at the Commonwealth Games at Cardiff, on Monday.

Giving a wonderfully consistent performance Charmian, who represented Britain in the Olympic Games of 1952 and 1956, held off a strong challenge from Canada's Irene MacDonald, who was considered favourite. The narrow points margin of 118.81 to 117.01 which gave Charmian the victory, illustrates how exacting and close the divers and judges had to be.

First English Swim Win

it was a breathtaking finish in which the Canadian girl, who was third in the 1956 Olympics, scored nearly 17 points in her last dive. But Charmian had clinched the win with some perfect diving before, and what a roar of applause she got when the result was announced. It was in fact, the first time that "Land of Hope and Glory" - signifying the English win - had been heard at the Empire Pool, so strong has been the Commonwealth opposition.

The evening had a champagne success about it for Charmian, for her mother had some good news. Mrs Winifred Welsh watched her daughter's success with Charmian's sister Hillary, but before the all out effort from her daughter, she told her of her success in final examinations to become a schoolteacher.

It was a weight lifted from Charmian's mind on being told of the exams' success, and it served to make her give an exhilarating performance. Charmian has been a student at Sunderland Training College.

Local Support

Two men at Cardiff for the Commonwealth Games shared Charmian's joy. One is Coun Norman Sarsfield, chairman of the ASA committee and coach to Durham City Swimming Club, who has had so much to do with Charmian's success during the last few years. Coun Sarsfield was appointed an umpire for the British Empire Games, and will be technical adviser and coach to the Great Britain team at Budapest for the European championships next month.

Mr Bill Morley, secretary of Durham City Swimming Club, is also at Cardiff for the Games, and if he was successful in getting tickets for the diving competitions a party of boys from Whinney Hill School, Durham, of whom he is in charge, would see Charmian win.

25 July 1958

PRESENTATION - When Thornley RC Infants' School broke up last week for the summer holidays an association between Miss M B Kevany and the school was ended. Miss Kevany retires after 40 years on the staff of Thornley St Godric's Infant School - the last 12 as headmistress. She succeeded Miss O'Hara, who was head teacher. The two live together in Dunelm Road, Thornley, and shortly they return to their native country, Ireland. Miss Kevany had as her assistant teacher, Mrs Wilson, who has been appointed head in succession to Miss Kevany. Parting gifts handed to Miss Kevany were a spiritual bouquet, a travelling clock, a fountain pen and pencil set and a leather writing case. The presentations were made by three children - Marjorie Armstrong, Patricia Hoban and Gerard Kenny.

1 August 1958

LEAVING THORNLEY - The third bench from the front on the epistle side of the high altar in Thornley Catholic Church has been occupied for over 40 years by Miss Brigid O'Hara and Miss Mary Kevany. But now they are both leaving Thornley to retire in their native Sligo. These two teachers have prepared thousands of children for their first Communion and Confirmation. During the last week, many people of the parish have paid tribute to their services. Miss O'Hara was for over 40 years head teacher of St Godric's RC School, and she was succeeded by Miss Kevany, who held the position for 12 years.

WHEATLEY HILL HEAD TEACHER RETIRES

When the dismissal bell sounded on Friday afternoon, in Wheatley Hill County Junior Mixed School, it meant the close of a teaching career, which began in 1914, for the head teacher, Mr John Wesley Willan, 81 North Road East, Wingate.

Mr Willan became a pupil teacher at Medomsley Edge Council School in 1914. In 1916 he went to Westminster Training College but before his course was completed he joined up with the West Yorkshires in the 1914-18 world war. On his discharge he completed his training at Westminster and was appointed to the staff of the Oxhill County Junior School. Mr Willan was appointed to his first headship at Causey Row in 1935, and in 1944 became headmaster of Wheatley Hill County Junior Mixed School. In a teaching association with Durham County of over 40 years, Mr Willan has served 23 years as a head teacher. At Wheatley Hill he is respected by parents and loved by his scholars.

Mr Willan's wife was a school teacher. His married son, Mr Donald Willan, of Easington, is on the teaching staff of Thornley County Junior School, and his daughter, Mrs Margaret Alderson, of Peterlee, is a trained teacher.

Mr Willan is a member of the Wingate North Road Methodist Church and has been a local preacher for 40 years.

Staff and scholars acknowledged their appreciation of Mr Willan's service in Wheatley Hill by making presentations to him and his wife.

County Coun J Andrews presided. Former members of staff present were Miss A I Hutchinson, Miss E Moon, Mrs J Cookson and Mrs F Alderson.

The scholars presented Mr Willan with a portable radio. Two children, Frank Parkin and Margaret Powell, made the presentation speeches. Margaret Gair presented Mrs Willan with a bouquet of carnations. William Million, captain of the school football team, asked Mr Willan to accept a medal won by the team in competitive football. After the children left, members of the staff and school workers paid their tribute to Mr Willan.

Mr T W Nightingale, County Inspector of Schools, said Mr Willan had performed his task of work and now he has the "rest of the day to himself". His school had been marked by a happy family fellowship.

Mr Alec Wright, deputy head teacher, spoke in appreciative terms of Mr Willan's 14 years' headship at Wheatley Hill. On behalf of members of the staff and friends, he presented Mr and Mrs Willan with a picnic set in case and a travelling rug.

In his reply of thanks, Mr Willan said that his term at Wheatley Hill had been a very happy one because of the loyal service and co-operation of staff and colleagues in the work.

8 August 1958

RETIREMENT OF MR C WOODWARD
First Aid Instructor at Thornley Colliery

A forty years partnership was severed when Mr Christopher Woodward left his little office in the pit yard at Thornley which he has shared with Mr Jim Orange, the safety officer. Kit Woodward, as he is known to everyone at the colliery, began work at Eldon Colliery at the age of 14 in 1907. Through a severe accident to his right hand while he was putting he became interested in first aid and joined Eldon Lane Club first aid class. He obtained his medallion, and became captain of the club team which won the Dr Thorpe Shield and medals.

Three months after moving to Thornley in 1914 he became instructor to the colliery first aid class and only three officials then held first aid certificates. It was here that he first met Mr Orange and their partnership in first aid, rescue, fire fighting and safety has continued ever since.

In the first world war Mr Woodward joined the Royal Navy and on his return to the colliery he was made deputy overman and a teamster of the Colliery Rescue Brigade under Houghton Colliery Rescue Brigade and chief ambulance attendant at the colliery.

Each year he has added a label to his medallion and in 1937 was made a Serving Brother of the Order of St John. He also became a member of Thornley Parish Council and ARP instructor for Easington RDC in Thornley parish. In 1953 he was appointed Training Officer at the colliery and also instructor to Durham County Education Committee for first aid at evening classes. Other outside duties were chairman and delegate of his local trade union lodge and a member of the Miners' Welfare Committee.

29 August 1958

MAN WHO FOUGHT ON THE SOMME
Dies at Wheatley Hill

The death has taken place of Mr Thomas Smith (78), 19 Lynn Terrace, Wheatley Hill, widower of Mrs Margaret J Smith who died three years ago. He is survived by three sons and five daughters. Born at Houghall, Mr Smith started work in the mines in

Brandon area when he was 10. After travelling round he came to Wheatley Hill 62 years ago.

Mr Smith served in the first World War with the East Yorkshire Regiment. In France, he fought in the battles of the Somme and the Marne, also at Ypres. He was severely wounded and his left arm became seriously disabled.

After being discharged through wounds, Mr Smith returned to Wheatley Hill pit. He served as checkweighman for 16 years and retired when he was 70.

In his younger days he played football in the Brandon area. He joined a Wheatley Hill RAOB Lodge when he came to the village.

He had been a member of the Wheatley Hill Workmen's Club since it came into being and was a member of the management committee for many years.

JOHN HORAN'S MEMORY

At Thornley Victory celebrations after the 1914-18 war, the committee presented an inscribed gold watch to each of the men of the parish and workmen at the colliery who had distinguished themselves on the battlefield. One of these men, Mr John Horan, now in retirement with the Little Sisters of Charity, Sunderland, has celebrated the 40th anniversary of the deed of valour that gained him the DCM. The citation of the action says:

"At Vauix Wood on 2 September, 1918, he was acting as stretcher bearer and attended the wounded under heavy fire, with fine disregard of his own safety. On reaching the objective, finding the flank of his platoon exposed, he took a rifle and, single handed, attacked a machine gun, dispersing the crew and capturing the gun which he brought into our lines. He then went and brought in a wounded man whom he had observed lying out in the open".

One of the Little Sisters visiting Thornley last week said, "Well that is just like John".

12 September 1958

OFF TO SOUTH AFRICA
Wheatley Hill Aged Couple's Adventure

A Wheatley Hill couple approaching their seventies, who have been actively associated with Wheatley Hill Over 60 Club since its formation four years ago, set sail this week for a six month holiday at the home of their eldest son in Natal, South Africa. They are Mr Robert Richardson and his wife Isabel, 21 Patton Crescent, whose 44 year old son Jonathan married a South African girl towards the end of the last war and has lived there since he was demobilised from the army in 1946.

"We are quite looking forward to the trip", Mrs Richardson, who has been secretary of the Over 60 Club throughout its existence, told our reporter before leaving this country. "We have never been out of the country before and it is a real thrill to think we are going to see our son again for the first time since the war ended". Their son was wounded while serving with the army in the Middle East. It was while he lay in hospital in South Africa that he met his future wife, Iris. She was among a group of friendly people from that country who frequently visited the hospital to cheer up the patients. The couple were married in Durban in 1943 and they have a seven year old son.

Mines Manager in Natal

Before the war Jonathan was employed as a miner at Wheatley Hill colliery. He has since pursued his mining studies and been so successful that now he is a mines manager in Natal.

His father, who will be 70 next March, is a native of Felling. He began work at North Biddick colliery when he was 12½ but shortly afterwards moved to Wheatley Hill, where he continued his mining career until his retirement at 65.

Among the family Mr and Mrs Richardson left behind them when they set sail on Wednesday on the Athlone Castle, was their second youngest daughter, Mrs May Hall, who, with her young son and daughter, has been staying with them on a holiday from New Zealand since February. Mrs Hall who lives in North Island - she went there after marrying a New Zealand sailor at the end of the last war - had expected returning to New Zealand about two months ago, but there was an unexpected delay in her boat. She is now setting sail next month.

Altogether Mr and Mrs Richardson have a family of six daughters and three sons.

Mrs Richardson, who is 67, was married when she was 19, "Our 48th wedding anniversary is in November", she said, "and so I expect we will be having an extra special celebration in South Africa".

AMATEURS' SUCCESS - Members of Wheatley Hill Amateur Dramatic Society scored another success on Wednesday night when, before an appreciative "house" in Wheatley Hill Welfare Hall, they presented the three act comedy, "Doctor in the House" (by Richard Gordon and Ted Willis), which has just been released to amateurs. The story deals with the experiences of three medical students over a period of four years and from the opening curtain the players brought out the best from the many humorous situations. As the medical students, Don Willan, Charles Lister and Les Dryden were an instant success, and they received excellent support from Les Barker, in the comedy role of the hospital porter, newcomer Ken Best, as the burly bad tempered surgeon, Minnie Galloway, Jean Willan, Alice Winter and Elizabeth Punshon. The producer was Mrs Vera Fairclough, of Easington Village, and the stage managers were Mrs Nora Abbs and Ivy Scott. The play was repeated last night and further performances are to be given tonight and tomorrow night.

CHANGES - The Good Intent Inn, Thornley, has been closed after 100 years' service in the village. The Hippodrome, the oldest picture house in the village, has closed its doors because of lack of support. It was built in 1912 by Scully Brothers, and opened for pictures and variety. The business of Messrs Walter Willsons, which was opened in Hartlepool Street in 1894, has been transferred to The Villas, Thornley.

124

MALCOLM GALLOWAY - 17 year old son of Mr and Mrs David Galloway, Dunelm Road, Thornley, has gained a national scholarship in mathematics and a Durham County major scholarship. During his holidays Malcolm, who is a pianist and organist and a member of the National Youth Orchestra, appeared on ITV. Malcolm will spend another year at A J Dawson Grammar School and hopes he may be admitted to Cambridge or Oxford. His ambition is to be an industrial mathematician.

ARMY ABSENTEES - Two soldiers, whose homes are in Thornley, were remanded in custody to await a military escort when, at Castle Eden on Tuesday, they were charged with being Army absentees. They were Edward Laverick (19), 6 St Bede's Crescent, Thornley and George Hardy (21), 17 Kenton Crescent, Thornley. They were arrested the previous day, said Chief Inspector M Reed. Laverick, who was serving in the Royal Northumberland Fusiliers, had been absent from his unit in Germany since 24 July, said the Chief Inspector, and Hardy, who was also stationed in Germany, had been absent from his RASC unit since 14 August.

19 September 1958

DIED IN AUSTRALIA - The death has occurred in Australia of Mr Charles St Julien, who emigrated from Wheatley Hill in 1924. He was born at South Shields and moved with his father and family to work at Thornley Colliery shortly after the opening of No 2 Pit in 1911. Mr St Julien was employed as deputy overman at the colliery until 1914, when he joined the Forces and served in France with the Green Howards. He resumed at the colliery after the war. He was married shortly after landing in Australia to a Durham City girl and they have three children. During the 1939-45 war he served with the Australian Army. His brother Mr Walter St Julien, 130 Thornlaw, Thornley, has received word from his sister-in-law that Mr St Julien was cremated with full military honours.

FIRE FIGHTING UNITS
COLLIERY TEAMS COMPETE AT WASHINGTON

All over the Durham coalfield, collieries can claim an upsurge in the efficiency of their civil defence and fire fighting units. In an all out attempt to conquer whatever hazards may arise in the industry, teams and individuals are being trained to a peak never before attained.

Just how far advanced this training is, and the effectiveness with which these teams can carry it out, was evident on Saturday. Outstanding units from each of the six areas in the Durham Division, competing in the annual finals, gave a stirring practical demonstration of both surface and underground work.

These "precision squads", men with alert minds and strong hands, were judged by every move they made. Yet, even under the careful observation of experienced officers of the county Civil Defence Department and Fire Brigade, they scarcely faulted as they went through the various stages of each test with swiftness, confidence and fixed concentration.

The milling crowd of miners and their families who visited the picturesque Dame Margaret Hall grounds at Washington, were generous in their applause as each test time was announced. The results bore out the enthusiasm of the competitors, the time spent in preparation of the different events and the work put in by the 100 or more qualified instructors.

Dr Reid's Encouraging Words

"If this standard can be improved upon, and it will be done only by constant training coupled with the type of enthusiasm I have seen this afternoon - we will be well on the way to reaching perfection in these two services".

This view, shared by most people present, was expressed by Dr W Reid, chairman of the Durham Division, in an address at the completion of the tests.

He previously remarked: "In a big industry like ours, we have got to take steps to ensure we are ready to deal with these situations as they come along. We have got to be well equipped. There is no doubt that the competitive spirit could not be better in our mines and, if it is maintained and encouraged, the industry should be in capable hands.

Teenage as well as older competitors, are showing an increasing interest in both fire fighting and civil defence, and a fair proportion of the 3000 men trained during the year were comparative youngsters. This, too, is a sound reason why Durham coalmining officials must be feeling pleased with the results attained.

A High Standard

It is generally accepted that the facilities afforded these teams, and the efficiency with which they are run, has never been so high. Collieries throughout the county have never been so effectively manned and the overall standard of these teams and individuals is now at its peak. And the aim of the division is that the achievements so far reached should be improved even more by next year".

Brigadier P Kirkup, chairman of the Divisional Competition Committee, presided at the presentation of awards by Mrs Reid. He thanked the judges for their co-operation; Crookhall Colliery Band (conducted by Mr J J Stobbs) for supplying light music; and the areas taking part for displaying their undoubted worth.

Among colliery officials in attendance were Mr M D Eddington (carbonisation director), Mr N F Nattrass (industrial relations director) and area general managers and members of the Divisional Board.

No 3 Area's Success

The Divisional Challenge Shield for Civil Defence was won by No 3 Area, represented by Thornley and Wheatley Hill collieries. Winners of the Divisional Challenge Shields for Fire Fighting were No 5 Area, which included collieries from Roddymoor, Beamish Mary and Esh. The shields were received by Mr W Barnfather (civil defence) and Mr M Welch (fire fighting).

All the tests were closely contested but Thornley Colliery, in the civil defence rescue section test, had one of the most convincing wins of the day. Their team, comprising Messrs F Bradley senior and junior, L Mitchell, N Convery, F Carter, N

Mayne, N Fort, K Lonsdale and D Swallow (reserve), was well ahead on points of their nearest rivals, Philadelphia Building Department and Chopwell Colliery.

Langley Park Colliery were winners of the closely fought warden section test. The team included Messrs R Atkinson, W Rose, W Clegg, R Thompson and T Clayton. South Hetton and Wheatley Hill collieries were second and third respectively.

Roddymoor Colliery Among the Winners

In the fire fighting section, Roddymoor Colliery - represented by Messrs T Holmes, D Nattrass, C Goodwin, E Boughey, and D Norman (reserve) - won first place from Hylton and Blackhall Collieries.

Wheatley Hill Colliery completed the underground team test in under two minutes to win from Beamish Mary and Washington Glebe collieries. The winning team consisted of Messrs T W Ayre, A C Watson, E W Snowdon, A Carr and W Gibson (reserve).

A Bowburn man, W Carruthers, was an impressive winner of the surface individual test, with D Nattrass (Roddymoor) and G Greenwood (Seaham) second and third respectively.

The underground individual test winner was M Curran, Esh Colliery. Second and third places were secured by J Melvin (Hylton) and C E Carr (Deaf Hill).

FULFILMENT OF A DREAM
New Ludworth Legion Headquarters Opened

Mr James Armstrong, the hardworking treasurer of Ludworth branch of the British Legion, heaved a sigh of relief and satisfaction on Saturday. He had witnessed the realisation of a dream, cherished since 1946, that the Legion at Ludworth should have new headquarters.

Mr Norman Dodds, County chairman, cut the tape at the entrance and formally declared open the Ludworth British Legion Memorial Hall and Headquarters.

For two years a handful of enthusiasts had laboured - often without much encouragement from the villagers - laying cement foundations, erecting walls and fixing the roofing, finally painting and decorating the interior. The building had been an Army hut, and was erected on a site which had been a heap of rubble.

The finished product reflects credit on all concerned - the men who had worked actively on the building and the womenfolk who had encouraged them. When Mr Dodds opened the hall he was supported by the following members: Mr A Winter, chairman; Mr J Ditchburn, secretary; Mr James Armstrong, Mr John Armstrong, Mr H Hodgson, Mr D Aitchinson, Mr T Thompson and Mr J Champley. The women members present were Mrs Thompson (the only woman member qualified to be a member of the men's section by reason of her war service with the ATS), Mesdames J Armstrong, A Winter, John Armstrong, M Hogg, Cowan, Oswald, Gibson, Champley and Ditchburn

For the Welfare of all

Mr Dodds expressed pleasure at being invited by the people of Ludworth to open their new headquarters. By doing so, he was only carrying out the object and principles of the organisation the British Legion stands for. Not only did the Legion look after the benefit side, not only did they look after the interests of the orphans, but they had to look to the social side to keep comradeship and fellowship, and they had to have a home where they could supply these things.

By the opening of the new headquarters established by the sacrifices of the handful of workmen who had erected this hall from a mere shambles an opportunity had been made. He hoped the people of Ludworth would use the hall for the benefits of ex-servicemen and others. The British Legion existed for the benefit of all, and the Legion was interested in the welfare of all.

Mr Winter thanked all who had worked at the hall. The building was only a dream in 1946. Money came in slowly until after they had got the men back from the second world war. Thanks to Mr Armstrong's determination, the hall had been built, and the speaker hoped that the hall would be a memorial to those who helped to build.

Felt Proud

Mr Dodds said it made him very proud, and made him wish there were more workers in the British Legion like the Ludworth members.

Ludworth branch had had a difficult time a few years ago, but these difficulties had been overcome and the members had given the rest of the county a fine example. He urged the community to take advantage of the facilities offered.

Mrs Morgan spoke on behalf of the women's section. She hoped old and young would work in unity, and wished the branch many prosperous years. Mrs Slater, of Thornley, referred to her interest in the progress of the Ludworth branch.

The proceedings ended with a social evening in the assembly hall.

26 September 1958

HARVEST FESTIVAL SERVICES were held in Wheatley Hill Patton Street Methodist Church. On Saturday a social evening organised by the choir was well attended. Organising secretary was Mrs D Warnes. Musical items were given by Mrs P Warnes, Mrs A Walker, Mr W Warnes, Mr T Venables and Miss L Craggs. Mrs D Venables was at the organ. Supper was served by choir members. A programme of games and competitions was organised by Messrs T Venables, T King and W Luke. On Sunday the preacher was the Rev Howard Harrison, of Glasgow, who entered the ministry from Church Street church.

MINER INJURED - Making satisfactory progress in Sedgefield General Hospital this week is a 36 year old miner, Jonathan Gair, 19 Burns Avenue, Wheatley Hill, who received multiple injuries last week when caught by a fall of stone while following his employment at Trimdon Grange colliery. In addition to about eight broken ribs, Mr Gair had his ankle, collar bone and shoulder broken and received a laceration to his leg. Formerly secretary of Wheatley Hill Colliery Band, Mr Gair is compensation secretary for Trimdon Grange miners' lodge and treasurer of Trimdon branch of the Northumberland and Durham Miners' Permanent Relief Fund. He has been employed at Trimdon Grange Colliery for the past nine years. The accident occurred on the eve of his 36th birthday.

3 October 1958

PRESENTATION AT THORNLEY

A reception was given by officials and committee of Station Town, Seaham and Horden Co-operative Society to employees of Thornley Hartlepool Street branch to mark the retirement of Mr Robert Slater. Mr John Worth, manager of the branch, presented Mr Slaater with a chiming clock, a gift of employee and staff of the branch.

Mr William Cessford (president), who represented the Board of management at the function, congratulated Mr Slater on his long and faithful service to the Society.

Mr Worth said Mr Slater had served the Society for 48 years and had been employed by Thornley branch as an outside salesman with a horse-drawn vehicle.

Mr Alan Ord, Dry Goods Department manager and Mr Rober Garbutt, representing the employees, also congratulated Mr Slater and wishes him many happy years of retirement.

Mr J W Brown, chief executive officer and Mr J L Brown, secretary of the Society, apologised for their absence.

THORNLEY PARISH COUNCIL

Thornley Parish Council are to send a letter to the No 3 Area secretary of Durham Division of the National Coal Board asking that immediate steps be taken to repair and clean a portion of the public footpath which is now enclosed by a coal tipping site.

Coun F A Walker, who raised the complaint, said the NCB representatives who had been granted this site by the County Planning Authority on condition that the amenities of the footpath were not disturbed are allowing 6 ton motor lorries to run backwards and forwards across it.

Coun James Nicholson stated that in many cases the street lighting was worse now than when it was supplied by the NCB. He also stated that many consumers living in council houses could not take advantage of some of the electrical equipment because the Board was not yet in a position to take the extra load. The Clerk (Mr Martin Fleming) was instructed to write to the Electricity Board asking them to undertake this work before the winter months come in.

Coun Miss Annie Griffiths asked the council to support the application of people of Dunelm Road for a letterbox with a larger opening so that people had not to twist photographs and greetings cards to get them through the aperture or had to wait until the collector called to clear the box. The Council agreed to support the request.

PETERLEE'S FIRST BOXING PROGRAMME

Edenhill Community Centre Hall, Peterlee, was filled to capacity on Friday night for the first boxing tournament to be held in the new town. Held under ABA rules, it was organised by the Durham County Association of Boys' Clubs in co-operation with the Peterlee Community Association, as a postponed feature of the town's "Festival

Fortnight" programme. The tournament was originally arranged for last month but, owing to unavoidable circumstances, had to be postponed.

"We are quite satisfied with the success of this first show and it is likely to be the forerunner of many more", Mr J J Harrison, warden of the Community Centre, told our reporter. "We had the assistance of many people in organising the tournament and are most grateful to them for their willing help".

The well known boxing brothers from Thornley, Ron and Len Harvey, both won their contests, as well as another talented "local", Kevin Jones of Easington, who has won considerable renown in National Coal Board contests.

Ron Harvey beat K Thompson (Gladstone St YC Darlington) at 10st 7lb and his brother Len beat J Etherington, of Murton, at 11st. Kevin Jones beat J Robinson, of Redheugh, at 11st 8lb.

BROWNIE PACK FORMED - With Mrs R Watson, wife of Coun R Watson, in charge, a Brownie pack was formed at Wheatley Hill on Tuesday. Eighteen young girls have joined the pack, and three "sixes" are to be formed. Mrs Watson, who has been captain of the 1st Wheatley Hill Company of Girl Guides for two years, will be assisted in the running of the pack by Miss Marjorie Thubron, a company leader in the Guides. The Brownies will meet every Tuesday night.

17 October 1958

FUNERAL OF MR J COLBY, THORNLEY

The death has taken place in Winterton Hospital of Mr Joseph Colby, Aged 63, licensee of the Thornley Colliery Inn. Mrs Colby has been a patient in Winterton for several months. Mr Colby carried on the business of the Inn himself. Last week he was also admitted to hospital.

Mr Colby was born at Framwellgate Moor and removed to Burnhope with his family when a boy where he began work in the pit after leaving school. He served with the forces in Ireland in the 1914 war. Mr Colby was one of the professionals who played for Ludworth FC in the Victory League. He had also played for Thornley and Wheatley Hill teams and was a playing member of Wheatley Hill Cricket Club.

He married in 1918 Miss Beatrice Howe only daughter of Mr Tom Howe. In 1924 the couple took the licence of the Spearman's Arms, Thornley, and in 1930 they transferred to the Thornley Colliery Inn.

Mrs Colby, who was transferred from Winterton Hospital, two days before her husband died, to Emlington near Middlesbrough, and is still confined to bed, has been allowed to return home for a few days.

The Funeral

There were many friends and relatives at the Requiem Mass in the Church of the English Martyrs, Thornley, celebrated by Father H McNeill.

Interment took place at Wheatley Hill Cemetery and four licensees were bearers - Messrs Norman Hitch, Dunn Cow Inn; Mr James Rutter, Station Hotel; Mr Stanley Skinner, Thornley; and Mr Tom Welsh.
24 October 1958

WHEATLEYHILL WELFARE HALL
EXTENSION OPENED

When he officially opened a new dining hall extension to Wheatley Hill Welfare Hall on Tuesday night Mr Edward Cain, JP, who, for many years was actively associated with the Wheatley Hill Colliery Welfare Committee, said to the gathering of committee members and friends: "When you look around this beautiful hall I think you will all agree that the time and money put into it has been well worth while".

Though they had some fine Welfare facilities in the village, said Mr E Cain, for many years he had cherished two dreams and he hoped that one day they would come true. One was for a swimming pool to be built in the Welfare grounds, as he believed every boy and girl should be taught to swim, and the other was for a kiddies' paddling pool. "The future depends upon you and upon the life of the colliery", continued Mr Cain, "and I hope there is sufficient life in the colliery to bring about the realisation of these two dreams".

It had been a hard, "uphill struggle" in the early days of the Welfare Scheme at Wheatley Hill, said Mr Cain, referring to the 1926 strike and the "hungry thirties", when Welfare levies were suspended. They had been grateful to the colliery management at that time for their help in meeting the cost of repairs and other expenses associated with the scheme.

Presentation

As a token of appreciation of the excellent service Mr Cain had given to the Welfare Committee - he was secretary for many years until his recent retirement and had also served on the No 3 Area Welfare Committee and the Durham Divisional Coal Board Welfare Committee - he was presented with a case of long playing classical gramophone records by the chairman of the committee, Mr F Richardson (Manager of Wheatley Hill colliery).

Mr Richardson spoke in appreciative terms of Mr Cain's loyal service and said that the Welfare Committee would always be grateful to him for his excellent work. Mr Fred Simpson, undermanager at the colliery, and a member of the Welfare Committee, also paid tribute to Mr Cain's services. He was pleased Teddy Cain had been invited to open the new dining hall, for he could think of no-one more worthy of the honour. Good wishes to Mr Cain were also extended by another member of the committee, County Coun J Andrew.

THORNLEY PARISH COUNCIL

A protest signed by all the tenants of South Street, Thornley, was read at Thornley Parish Council meeting objecting to a scrap yard on a vacant space adjacent to South Street and directly at the front entrance to Waterloo Street Methodist Church. This objection was supported by Coun Nicholson, who was chairman, and Coun A Walker, both members of Easington Rural Council.

Coun Nicholson said this vacant space was caused by the demolition of Waterloo Street under slum clearance and the land was considered unfit for new buildings. Thornley Council said that under the changing circumstances re-housing could be done here. The County Planning Authority, said Coun Nicholson decided that this spot should be laid out as a green belt with trees and shrubs and now they have a scrap yard to be filled with broken cars and pots and pans. The Council decided to ask the County Planning Officer and the Engineer and Surveyor of Easington Rural Council to meet them on the spot.

The Council decided to ask Easington Rural Council to send out their rat catcher to investigate a complaint raised by Coun Mrs J Anderson about the now closed Hippodrome being infested with rats.

WI BIRTHDAY PARTY - In the Welfare Hall, Wheatley Hill WI celebrated its 28th birthday with a party. Mrs R Ord presided and Mrs A Armstrong (secretary) read the business details. The report of the Autumn Council meeting was submitted by Mrs Ord, who attended as a delegate. At a knife and fork supper 157 members were welcomed by the president. A programme of dancing was organised. Music was provided by Mrs R Hodgson and Mr R Clarke (piano accordion). Prizewinners were Mesdames H Briarley, M Moore, J Wallace, W Craggs and E Inchcliffe.

PIGEON FANCIER'S SUCCESS - Mr J Bradley of Bradley Partners, Thornley, sent eight birds to the Birmingham show and they gained seven awards, first, second, fourth, special reserve, two commended and one highly commended.

RE-OPENING SERVICE - Thornley Bow Street Methodist church was filled on Sunday evening when the church was re-opened after painting and decorating, done by the voluntary labour of the men of the society. Service was conducted by the Rev Reginald Hancock, and took the form of a Communion service. The choir sang an anthem, under their conductor Mr Arthur Curry, with Mr Malcolm Galloway at the organ. Mrs A L Miller (Trust secretary and representing the women of the church) read the epistle and Mr James Plant (representing the men workers) read the Gospel passages. An address was given by Mr Hancock.

7 November 1958

WOMEN'S LEGION

A year of excellent progress was reported at the annual meeting of Wheatley Hill women's section of the British Legion, presided over by Mrs M Brain. Fourteen new members had joined during the year the secretary, Mrs I Carter, revealed and with the opening of a new hall as their headquarters at the beginning of the year, they had been able to widen considerably the scope of their activities. It was the first time the section had had their own headquarters - previously they had rented other buildings - and it had resulted in a revival of interest in the work of the Legion, said Mrs Carter. The Section's oldest member, 81 year old Mrs P Tyson, was re-elected president for the ensuing year, and another old member, Mrs Eddy, was re-elected vice president. Other elections were: chairman, Mrs M Brain; vice chairman, Mrs D Bishop; treasurer, Mrs E A Stainsby; assistant treasurer, Mrs R Maughan; secretary, Mrs I Carter; assistant secretary, Mrs W Bowes; committee, Mesdames M Kime, E Bradley, F Court, M Forster, M Taylor, A Fenny and E Jones; standard bearer, Mrs M Brain; assistant Mrs E Bradley. Thanks to the scrutineers for their services were expressed by Mrs B Robinson. Mrs Parsley was appointed Poppy Day organiser.

REMEMBRANCE DAY

Anglicans and Methodists shared in a Remembrance Day service in All Saints' Church, Wheatley Hill. It was conducted by the Vicar (The Rev G G Graham) and the Methodist minister (the Rev D L Nelson). The church was filled. Before the service a parade, headed by Wheatley Hill Colliery band, assembled at Patton Street. The band was conducted by Mr H Strong. Local representatives of Easington Rural Council attended with members of Wingate Parish Council. Wheatley Hill local organisations represented included the Women's Section of the British Legion (standard bearer, Mrs M Brain), Army Cadets, Discharged Soldiers' and Sailors' Club, Scouts, Rovers, Women's Institute, Over 60 Club, Sherburn Hill Co-operative Society, Workmen's Club, Fire Brigade, St John Ambulance Brigade and Police.

After the service the parade reformed and moved off towards the Welfare Park. A halt was made in Front Street beneath the clock, which is a memorial to the dead of the second world war. At the Cenotaph in the Park, the first world war memorial, wreaths were laid by the organisations represented. Mr J Robinson was parade marshal.

WHEATLEY HILL COMPLAINT
No Lighting on Waste Land

Concerned about a large stretch of waste land leading to Lynn Terrace, Wheatley Hill, being without public lighting, a resident Mr Norman Jordison, 14 Lynn Terrace, wrote to Easington Rural Council and Mr C F Grey, MP, on the matter.

Both letters were forwarded to Wingate Parish Council and were read to the members by their Clerk, Mr J Harper, on Monday, but they decided to take no action, since Lynn Terrace is in Shadforth Parish.

"It is not our responsibility to provide lighting for people not in our parish" said Coun J H Charlton. "They once had the opportunity to come into this parish but they turned it down".

In his letter, Mr Jordison complained that there was a demolition area about a quarter of a mile square "right in front of these houses" which was "absolutely unlit". It was dangerous where old property had been pulled down and pavements uplifted, and there were no lights to show the way over the uneven ground. "Anything could happen these dark nights", added Mr Jordison.

Shadforth Council's Refusal

133

There had been previous complaints about the same matter, said the Clerk, and at that time the council had offered Shadforth Parish the use of four electric light poles to illuminate the approach to Lynn Terrace. Shadforth had been asked to meet the cost of energy and maintenance, since Lynn Terrace was in their parish, but had refused, saying it was not their responsibility since part of the approach road was in the Wingate Parish. North of "The Beck", the Clerk explained, was the responsibility of Shadforth Parish, but south of "The Beck" was Wingate's responsibility - in that area, however, there were no houses.

FUNERAL OF MR P J MITCHELL, WHEATLEY HILL

Funeral took place on Tuesday of Mr Philip John Mitchell (73), 28 South View, Wheatley Hill. Service at All Saints' Church was conducted by Rev G G Graham, Mrs C English was at the organ.

Mr Mitchell is survived by his wife Mrs Mary Ann Mitchell and an only daughter, Mrs A J Surman, well known locally as a member of Hartlepool's Operatic Society and a soprano soloist. The couple had been married 52 years.

Mr Mitchell was born in Truro, Cornwall, and until he was 21 he worked in the tin mines in that county. He moved to Wheatley Hill in 1906 and obtained work as a stoneman at Wheatley Hill colliery and continued in that capacity until he retired at 67. In his younger days he was associated with the local RAOB Lodge. At his death he was a member of the Wheatley Hill Workmen's Club and Constitutional Club. He had been a member of Wheatley Hill Over 60 Club since its inception four years ago. He served in the Royal Navy in the 1914-18 war, mostly in Eastern waters on the "Prince Edward". Interment took place at Wheatley Hill cemetery.

14 November 1958

THORNLEY VICAR'S IMPRESSIONS

The Rev Philip Geoffrey Mold was instituted to the Vicarage of St Bartholomew, Thornley, a year ago. In the current issue of his parish magazine he gives his impressions of his first year in the North.

"My first and greatest impression", stated Mr Mold, "is what a kind, warm-hearted, helpful and generous set of people you are here in the North. My second is how much you value your church and its ministration.

"The third impression is not quite so pleasant. Thornley is (as one can expect a colliery to be) a dirty place, but there is also much untidiness and waste land. Why are the streets left so untidy and so much litter, rubbish and unsightly ruin tolerated And mud! For the first time in my life I had to acquire wellingtons to get to and from church and around the parish".

Other impressions of Mr Mold were the amazing size of leeks, the unique Miners' Gala Day in Durham and the slow march with the Thornley banner into and again after the service out of the crowded Durham Cathedral.

NURSES IN THORNLEY COLLIERY

Ten student nurses from Dryburn Hospital, Misses Holmes, Keenan, Gallagher, French, Earwaker, Pullen, Mitchell and Messrs Victor Olnwate, a Nigerian student, and M Storey, with Sister tutor, Miss Dalrymple-Smith in charge, visited Thornley Colliery on Wednesday. The party were welcomed at the medical centre by Mr Arthur Welsh, manager, and Sister Mrs L Green, who is in charge of the centre. The party was conducted underground to see the working on a new 160 yard face with a height of 3 feet 6 inches. They also visited Shadforth district and were conveyed the two mile journey on the manriding haulage.

The visit to the colliery is part of the training of the nurses. Sister Green had a cup of tea prepared for the party when they arrived at the surface after their three hour adventure.

THORNLEY - Members of St Bartholomew's Church, Thornley, will hold their first Christmas Fayre in Thornley Miners' Welfare Hall tomorrow. It will be opened by Mr T H Holder. The Fayre takes the place of the Garden Fete that has been held for many years, and is the Rev Philip Geoffrey Mold's first effort in the parish.

28 November 1958

ANOTHER YEAR OF
ACADEMIC SUCCESSES

During the past year 13 pupils had broken their contracts by leaving school prematurely, the headmaster Mr George Carr, revealed at the Speech Day of Wellfield A J Dawson Grammar School on Wednesday.

Though there was evidence of a keener desire on the part of a greater number of pupils to take a fuller advantage of their educational opportunities, they were still admitting too many who, for reasons other than lack of native ability, were unwilling to submit to the loss of a small part of their freedom in order to win that prize which most enlightened people regarded as being so well worth winning - a trained mind and a well balanced outlook on life.

"It is an ever recurring source of disappointment to my colleagues and me to see, all too frequently, pupils of considerable promise growing restless and eventually joining the ranks of those against whose names in the admission register there eventually appears the entry, 'Premature Withdrawal'", said Mr Carr.

State Scholarship

The school had enjoyed another excellent year of academic successes. One pupil, Malcolm Galloway, Thornley, was awarded a State Scholarship in mathematics. This was particularly meritorious since it was achieved at the end of his sixth year at school. Another pupil, Brian Wilson, of Wheatley Hill, gained a British Petroleum Scholarship, and both he and Malcolm were successful in three advanced level subjects in the GCE examination.

Altogether, said Mr Carr, 16 pupils qualified for a County University Major Scholarship, while 21 gained one or more passes in the GCE advanced level exam. Two distinctions were gained. Ninety six pupils passed their GCE at ordinary level,

70 per cent of them gaining four or more passes. Of the 96, 47 returned to school to continue their studies.

Turning to the field of sport, Mr Carr said that two girls, Valerie Goldsbrough and Enid Poulson, were selected to play for the county second hockey eleven. Last season four senior boys had county rugby trials as well as six under 15s, and two of these, H Wilkinson and Murray, played for the under 15 county team. Three seniors, Rawshaw, Storey and Alan Humphrey, represented the school in the county grammar schools soccer eleven, and Humphrey gained three international caps with the National Association of Boys' Clubs. In gymnastics the second team were runners up in the county championship competition.

"It can now be claimed for the Grammar Schools", said the headmaster, "that their curriculum is sufficiently wide to provide training for any occupation, and the more successful the child and is the more advanced examinations he takes at school, the higher the point from which he begins the next stage of his preparation for the career chosen. Our objective must always be to provide the most comprehensive training to the highest standard possible for the greatest number of children admitted each year".

The modern generation, said Mr Carr, was laying itself open to criticism in respect of standards of behaviour. A trained mind should exercise great restraint on the conduct of its possessor at all times.

Coun J J Noone, chairman of the governors, presided and the prizes were presented by Mr William Reid, Chairman of the Northern Division, National Coal Board.

MR FENWICK MILBURN (51), 84 High Street, Thornley, a shift worker in the Hutton Seam at Thornley Colliery, collapsed and died at work. Mr Milburn began work at Shotton Colliery in 1921 and transferred to Thornley in 1922. For many years he was employed as a face driller but in 1949 through a breakdown in health he had to take up light work. The Coroner has been notified. Mr Milburn is survived by his wife and son.

LEGION WOMEN - Mrs E Clark presided at a meeting of Thornley British Legion Women's Section. The meeting was opened with the silent tribute and there were 70 members present. In the absence of Mrs P E Morgan (secretary) the duties were performed by Mrs B Musgrave. Mrs H Slater (sick visitor) gave her reports. The gift prize was won by Mrs M Charlton. Following the business members were entertained to a film show.

MOTHERS' CLUB - Thornley Mothers' Club concert party gave an excellent concert in aid of Wheatley Hill All Saints Church building fund. Mrs Nancy Mason was compere and Mr Jackie Toye, Thornley's blind pianist, was accompanist. Artistes taking part were Mesdames E Wilson, M Featonby, J Robson, J Peacock, M

Chapman, A Longstaffe, M Hughes, F Lowther, D Pluck, M Mitchell. The Mothers' Club was thanked by the Vicar of Wheatley Hill. Reverend G Gordon Graham.

5 December 1958

POPPY DAY - Mrs M E Parsley, organiser for Wheatley Hill British Legion's Poppy Day effort, reports that income was £132.10s.4d.

12 December 1958

OLD SCOUTS' REUNION - The founder of Wheatley Hill Troop of Boy Scouts, Mr R Cowperthwaite, of Stockton, was among the guests at the annual reunion dinner of the Wheatley Hill Old Scouts' Association at the Garden House Inn, Durham, on Saturday night. Mr Cowperthwaite, who is president of the Association, extended seasonable greetings to the Old Scouts and wished them success in all their efforts during the forthcoming year. A report of the year's activities was given by the secretary, Coun Ralph Watson, who appealed for more Old Scouts to join the Association. With Scoutmaster Les Barker as MC, the Wheatley Hill Rovers "Skiffle Group" entertained. Taking part were George Watson, Tony Carr, Walter Saxby and Colin Thackeray. Solos were sung by Messrs W Turnbull and R Hargreaves, and the accompanist was Mr Carr.

OVER 60 CLUB PARTY - The Vicar of Wheatley Hill, Rev G G Graham, and the resident Methodist Minister, Reverend G L Nelson, were among the guests when Wheatley Hill Over 60 Club held their annual Christmas party on Tuesday. The guests also included County Coun and Mrs J Andrew, and officials of Wheatley Hill Workmen's Club. About 320 members were seated to an excellent tea and each received a Christmas gift of 7s.6d., the money being distributed by the club treasurer, Mr T E Turner. Birthday greetings were extended to Mesdames H Lee, Heslop, M Fenwick, E English, S Gribbens and K Fletcher. Enjoyable entertainment was provided by Mr Sid Chapman's band and concert party from Bishop Auckland, and they were thanked by Mr T H Vincent, supported by the entertainments secretary, Mr W Williams. The guests were welcomed by the club vice chairman, Mrs E Amies, and arrangements were made by the officials and committee.

"DILLY" RETIRES AT THORNLEY

Many a housewife in the Easington Rural District Council's area has been regaled with the singing of Mr William Walton, better known as "Dilly", 21 St Aidan's Crescent, Thornley, as he has been going out to his duties as maintenance plumber for the authority for the last 25 years.

"Dilly" is 65 years of age on Boxing Day, but is retiring before that as he is due to receive a few days' holiday. Born in Cooper's Terrace, Thornley, he was the second son of Mr W Walton, head mason as Thornley Colliery, who helped to build the Thornley and Wheatley Hill Collieries chimneys.

"Dilly" began work in the blacksmith's shops at Thornley Colliery in 1907 and was transferred to Ludworth Colliery when it reopened in 1914. It was during the depression in 1926 that he began work with the plumbing department of the rural council.

"Dilly" though not a Bing Crosby nor a Ras Prince Monolulu, often sang at his work and, during his break time, could always be relied on to tip a favourite or outsider for the day's racing.

19 December 1958

1959

BACK TO WHEATLEY HILL
After nearly two years in Nigeria

It was a happy Christmas reunion for a Wheatley Hill widow, Mrs Elizabeth Bradley, 110 Wordsworth Avenue, when her younger daughter, Mrs Betty Wood, arrived with her soldier husband and baby daughter from Nigeria, just in time for the Yuletide celebrations.

Mrs Wood's husband, Sgt Tom Wood, who is serving as a "regular" in the Royal Corps of Signals, was posted to Lagos, in Nigeria, 22 months ago, and was followed there by his wife and five month old baby Lesley. Lesley will be two in February.

Sgt Wood, only son of Mr and Mrs H Wood, 15 Newholme Estate, Station Town, has been in the army for five years. He was formerly a miner at Fishburn Colliery.

"Red Hot"

Mrs Wood told our reporter it had been a "wonderful experience" spending nearly two years in Nigeria. "It gets red hot, but the heat never bothered me at all," she said. "When it rains, it certainly does rain, but often heavy rain is quickly followed by pleasant sunshine."

Christmas–time was the peak of the hot season and, said Mrs Wood, it "took some time getting used to" a year ago when she saw shops in Lagos filled with Christmas toys, with the sun blazing hot outside. "Somehow or other, it did not seem like Christmas," she said.

The cost of living in Nigeria was much higher than in this country, Mrs Wood found. She could spend £13 a week on food alone for herself, husband and baby. The best butter cost 6s 3d a pound and meat was "terribly expensive." Clothes, too, cost much more than in this country, and so did children's toys.

"Sunday Did The Chores"

Apart from cooking, Mrs Wood had no household chores – they were all efficiently carried out by an African "steward" in the employ of the Army. "Our's was called "Sunday" and he was quite a good chap – very honest and clean," she said. "Sunday" would also have done the cooking if required, but Mrs Wood preferred doing her own. He did the weekly "wash" however!

Mrs Wood, whose father, Mr Robert Bradley, died seven years ago, flew here with her husband and baby for there Christmas leave. At the end of his leave her husband is being posted to Torquay. "And so, although we will miss the sunshine of Africa, we are looking forward to plenty of sun in the south of England during the summer months," said Mrs Wood.

ESCAPED DEATH THREE TIMES
Thornley man dies at age of 82

A man who had several narrow escapes during his mining career and yet lived until he was 82 has died in hospital. He is Mr George Lamb, 37 St Aidan's Terrace, Thornley, who began work at the colliery after leaving school. While coal-hewing he was severely injured by a fall of roof.

In 1919, while carrying out the duties of assistant onsetter, he was drawn up the shaft by an ascending cage which had caught hold of some of his clothing. He was released at the next level. After starting light work in the pit in 1937 as "a waiter-on" at the main shaft he was caught by a descending cage and knocked into the sump. He was saved by a water bucket he was using. The cage came to rest upon it.

2 January 1959

SCOUTS' ANNUAL REUNION
A Wheatley Hill Function

It was their "silver jubilee" when the 2nd Wheatley Hill Group of Boy Scouts held their annual reunion in the Welfare Hall on Saturday, for it was 25 years ago that the group was formed. Two of the original members of the group committee, Mrs S Watson and Mrs Hind, were among those present, and the guests included Miss Harding, Matron of Durham County Hospital, Sister Sutton, of the Children's Ward at the hospital, Mr F Simpson (under manager at Wheatley Hill Colliery) and his sister, Miss E Simpson, Dr A P Gray and Mrs Lindsay.

Dr Gray, who has taken an active interest in the work of the group for many years, said Scouting had played a big part in developing the character of many of the young boys and men of Wheatley Hill. Scouting was a great movement and he hoped it would long continue to flourish in the village.

Birthday Cake

During an excellent supper served by the group committee, a birthday cake made by Mrs S Watson and iced by Mrs Lindsay, was cut by Mrs Watson, who extended seasonable greetings to all the Rovers, Scouts and Cubs. She hoped that the group would enjoy the same measure of success during the next 25 years as in the past quarter of a century.

Mr Simpson proposed the toast to the group, and Miss Harding thanked all those associated with the group for the pleasure they had given to the young patients of Durham County Hospital. The group had "adopted" the children's ward some years ago and since then had paid periodical visits and brought sunshine into the lives of the young patients with their many "good deeds."

After supper the guests were entertained to a camp fire "sing song" and musical items were by senior the Scouts "Skiffle Group." Sweets were given to all the scouts and cubs, and games and competitions were enjoyed.

Arrangements were made by Coun R Watson (secretary) and Mr A Newton (chairman), assisted by the various leaders. Committee members helping included

Mesdames M Watson, Walker, Andrew, Burnside, Cowan, Cook, Dunn, Rowland, Johnson, Nicholson and Hind and Miss Shutt. Entertainment was under the direction of Scoutmaster Les Barker.

16 January 1959

DEATH OF MRS BOSOMWORTH
A life of public service

By the death of Mrs Bessie Bosomworth at her home, 4 Moor View, Thornley has lost one of its ardent social workers. She was born at Sherburn Hill, daughter of Mr Nichol Thornton, one time president of Sherburn Hill Cooperative Society. After her marriage in 1913 Mrs Bosomworth came to live in Thornley where her husband was a blacksmith. As a girl at Wheatley Hill, Mrs Bosomworth was a Sunday School pupil of Mr Peter Lee, and became one of his ardent supporters. Among the many who visited her home were Mr and Mrs Sidney Webb, Mr J Ramsay MacDonald, Miss I MacDonald and Mr and Mrs Emanuel Shinwell.

She began raising funds for Durham County Hospital in 1926, and continued with street collections, concerts, whist drives and dances until the hospital was taken over under the National Health Act. She took part in the street collections herself and raised over £2000. She organised since 1925 the Dr Barnardo's Homes flag day. During both world wars she organised Red Cross collections.

First Woman Councillor

In 1931 she was elected as the first woman councillor to Thornley Parish Council and while on the council formed, with the assistance of Mr Peter Lee, the Thornley Child Welfare, becoming its first chairman. She had been 3 times chairman of Thornley Parish Council, a governor of A J Dawson's Grammar School, manager of the Girls school at Wheatley Hill, and a member of Durham County Library Advisory Sub-committee. She took an active part in the Thornley Literary and Debating Society and was a life long Methodist of Thornley Bow Street Church. At the time of her death Mrs Bosomworth was a senior member of Thornley Parish Council, and entertainments secretary of the Thornley Over-60 Club. Her eldest son, Mr J R Bosomworth, is junior member of the Parish Council. Her husband, Mr Robert Bosomworth, was for some years a member of the Parish Council. He was also secretary of Thornley Workingmen's Club and secretary of the Thornley Lodge of the Durham Colliery Mechanics' Association. Mrs Bosomworth leaves two sons, 3 daughters and her husband.

30 January 1959

A DAY OUT - Fifty members and their wives took part in the first annual dinner of the Thornley Lodge of the Colliery Officials' Association. The party visited a pantomime at Newcastle and had dinner and a reception the at Turks' Head Hotel. The guests were five retired officials and their wives. Entertainment was by local artists from Thornley and district; Mr Jackie Toye, blind musician; Mr Bill Parker, Mr Ronnie Oswald, Mr Reggie Dixon, Mr Ernest Peachy and Mr Albert Dove. The organising committee were Messrss Tom Bower, Bert Hodgson, Joe Oswald, under-

ground officials; George Bennett, William Wilson, clerical staff; William Slater, retired official, with Wilf Armstrong as secretary.
30 January 1959

WHEATLEY HILL WI - Mrs R Ord presided at the monthly meeting on Tuesday and welcomed ten new members. The secretary, Mrs Milne, read the County Letter and business items, and Mrs A Bishop gave the Item of Interest, "The meaning of a smile." Mrs A Armstrong is to attend a course at Denman College and she was also chosen as the delegate to the annual London conference. An interesting account of her holiday in Norway, where she visited the home of a member of the institute's "link" Institute, was given by Mrs R Harker, Shotton Colliery, who was thanked by the president. The competition for guessing the contents of ten bottles by smelling them, was won by Mrs Garbut, and Mrs Atkinson and Mrs R Horner won the "lucky" prizes. During the social half-hour the folk dancing team, under the leadership of Miss A Hutchinson, gave a display. Tea hostesses were Mesdames Dodds, Kenny, Tarren, Todd and Hutchinson.

WOMENS BOWLERS' AWARDS – Representatives of all ten clubs in the North-Eastern Ladies' Bowling League, and the league president, Mrs K Ansell (Owton Lodge Club), were among the guests at the annual presentation social evening in Wheatley Hill Welfare Hall, organized by Wheatley Hill Ladies' Bowling Club. Trophies and prizes won by members of the Wheatley Hill club last season were presented by Mrs MacLean, wife of Dr W |MacLean, who was introduced by the club preside, Mrs S Hodson. The recipients were: Championship Club Mrs Edna Hall; runner-up, Mrs A Ord; William Jones Cup, Mrs E Hall; runner up, Mrs S Hodson; Festival Bowl, Mrs A Ord; runner up, Mrs S Hodson; Festival Bowl, Mrs A Ord; runner-up, Mrs E Hall. On behalf of the club members, Miss A Hutchinson (vice-president) thanked Mrs MacLean and presented her with a bouquet. Congratulations to the winners and best wishes to the club for its future success were extended by the League President. About 165 were seated to supper, and whist and dancing were enjoyed, with the club secretary, Mrs E Hall as MC. Whist prizes were won byt Mesdames E Kent, L Sanderson, M Smith, E Martin and A Haddock and Mr T Simpson. Music for dancing was supplied by Mr J Clancey and partner, West Cornforth.
6 February 1959

THORNLEY COUPLE MARRIED 50 YEARS
Mr and Mrs George Jordan, who live in an aged miner's home, 32 Greenwood Cottages, Thornley, celebrated their golden wedding on Friday. They were married at Houghton Register Office.

Mr Jordan, who is 73, and his wife 69, were both born in Thornley. They have two married daughters, three grandchildren and one great-grandchild.

Mr Jordan began work at Wheatley Hill Colliery when he was 14, and continued there until he was 16, when he moved to Trimdon Quarries. After a year there he transferred to Thornley Colliery, where he began hand putting in the Low Main Seam.

During the 1914-18 war Mr Jordan served in France and Italy with the 14th and 20th Durhams. He was severely wounded at Ypres and lay many months in hospital.

Their two daughters, who live in Thornley, married two miners, Mr William Davies, overman at the colliery, and Mr Robert Grieves, a stoneman.

A family celebration was held at the little aged miners' bungalow on Saturday.

Mr and Mrs Jordan cut the cake supplied by their daughter Mrs Grieves.

MINE MANAGER'S CERTIFICATE FOR WHEATLEY HILL MAN

Within a period of six months a Wheatley Hill man, who has been employed at Wheatley Hill colliery since leaving school at 14-for the last six years as Safety Officer- has qualified for both his second-class (under manager's) and first-class (mine manager's) certificates.

He is Mr Stanley Poulson (36), 5 Weardale Street, a well-known figure in the county fire-fighting circles as well as in the mining industry. Mr Poulson qualified for his second-class certificate last May, then in November sat the Mining Qualifications Board examination at Sunderland for his first-class certificate of competency. News of his success in this latter examination has just reached him.

Mr Poulson began work at Wheatley Hill colliery as a datal hand then went through all the grades of underground mining, eventually gaining his deputy's certificate. He was a deputy for six years before his appointment as Safety Officer in 1953.

In Charge Of Fire Brigade

For the past 14 years Mr Poulson has been officer-in-charge of the Wheatley Hill Retained Fire Brigade, consisting entirely of part time firemen, and during this time the Brigade has won many honours, both locally, in the county and nationally. One of their most notable successes was in 1956 when, at Dorking, they were presented with a trophy as winners of a national fireman's "quiz" competition. Mr Poulson was awarded the Queens Coronation Medal in 1953

Mr Poulson holds the Home Office Instructor's Certificate in Civil Defence and recently was presented with a silver medal on completing ten years service as a member of the Wheatley Hill Colliery Fire and Rescue brigade. He has coached teams from the colliery in firefighting and Civil Defence and seen them win a number of Coal Board competitions.

Mr Poulson's studies for his mine manager's certificate have all been undertaken in his spare time and he has received the congratulations of both officials and workmen at the Colliery on his well earned success. He is married, with an only baby son born last New Years Eve.

13 February 1959

WHEATLEY HILL GOLDEN WEDDING DATE
Husband has Special pocket to accommodate monkey

"Jack the sailor" is the friendly nickname by which he is known among all the villagers..."the man with the monkey" is how all the children affectionately think of one of Wheatley Hill's best known characters, Mr John Pattison Brown, of 49 Liddell Terrace who celebrated his golden wedding on Tuesday.

"Everybody knows me and my monkey", smiled Mr Brown, when our reporter called to congratulate him and his wife on their golden anniversary day. Mr Brown, fondling his pet monkey was soon reminiscing on his days in the navy and how he came to keep the monkey as a pet.

"It's better than a watchdog in the house, cheaper to keep and you don't have to buy a licence for it," said Mr Brown, with a twinkle in his eye. For years now he has had a pet monkey and that means an extra job for his wife every time he gets a new suit, "She has to sew an extra large pocket in the inside of my jacket so that I can carry my monkey around with me," said Mr Brown.

He has had his present pet, "Minnie" for the last 12 months. He never goes out without her. "I love walking," said Mr Brown, "and often cover seven or eight miles a day. Minnie always goes with me-she runs behind me, and then when she gets tired I put her in my inside pocket."

Love To Watch

All the children nearby love to watch Minnie's antic, Mr Brown has built a special shed and playground for her in his back garden, and they often bring the animal sweetmeats and tit bits. "Minnie's as tame a creature as you would find anywhere but, at the same time she would not let a stranger come anywhere near the back door," said Mr Brown.

Mr and Mrs Brown married at Easington on February 17 1909, and all their married life has been spent at Wheatley Hill. Mr Brown will be 79 next month, only a few days after his wife, whose maiden name was Annie Smiles, celebrates her 67 birthday.

Mr Brown has had a colourful life, both at home and at sea. He was only ten when his father died and two years later he went to sea as a cabin boy. "But I got more kicks than dinner- they nearly starved me to death and I got knocked about a bit- and so when I was 13 I ran away from the ship in Spain and returned back to this country on a coal boat."

At Back Prince

When he got back here, Mr Brown began work at the Back Prince Pit at Wardley, near Gateshead, but the "call of the sea" was still there and after a few months he left the pit and went back to sea again, this time as an officer's servant. "Flunkey," was the name they called him at sea." I had a much better life this time," said Mr Brown.

In 1896 Mr Brown joined the navy and served throughout the Boer War. Later, he served in the "Mad Muller's expedition" in Somaliland, but in 1908 he again took up mining- as a hand putter at Wheatley Hill Colliery. With the exception of again serving in the navy during the 1914-18 war, he continued to work at the colliery until his retirement in1948.

During that war Mr Brown was in the Royal Naval division of the land forces and for some time served as Chief Engineer on decoy boats which were used to deceive German submarines. He was again in uniform in the last war-this time as a member of the local Home Guard. He was one of the founders of Wingate branch of the Royal Navy Old Comrades Association in 1937 and was its first chairman.

Carnival Winner

Mr Brown was formerly a well known competitor at carnivals throughout Durham County. As "King Zulu," he won 168 first prizes in different carnival parades and has also been a prizewinner in other "costumes." As recently as last May Day he was first prizewinner at a fancy dress parade in Wheatley Hill.

Mrs Brown was born at Hetton but was only a girl of six when she came to Wheatley Hill. She was actively associated with the Patton Street Methodist Church in her younger days and sang in the choir. Both she and her husband had been members of Wheatley Hill Over -60 Club since its inception, and Mrs Brown served on the committee for two years.

The couple, who enjoy good health, have a family of three daughters and one son, ten grandchildren and four great grandchildren. Their only son Peter lives in Station Town, while two of their daughters, Mrs Ella Wilkes and Mrs Nancy Swan, live at Shotton Colliery, and the other, Mrs Hilda Bowes, at Wheatley Hill.

20 February 1959

PIGEON FANCIER'S DEATH AT WHEATLEY HILL

The death has taken place after a long illness of Mr Cuthbert Lowther, (65), 2 Third Street, Wheatley Hill. He is survived by his wife, two sons, four daughters and 14 grandchildren. Born at Thornley, he has lived all his life there and at Wheatley Hill. He started work at Thornley Colliery and spent 41 years there, retiring seven years ago owing to ill health. Mr Lowther served four and a half years in the First World War in the Northumberland Fusiliers. He spent most of his service in Italy and France.

He was member of Thornley Workmen's Club and Wheatley Hill Constitutional Club. In his younger days he played football for Thornley. His great interest was pigeon breeding. Well known in bird racing circles, with his son he won many cups and much prize money

NEW ORGANIST FOR WHEATLEY HILL

Rev G Gordon Graham, vicar of All Saints' Church, Wheatley Hill, announces that he has appointed Mr A T Tufnell, Easington Colliery, as church organist. He succeeds Mr John Atkinson who was organist for more than 40 years. Mr Atkinson died some months ago.

Mr Tufnell not only comes of a church family but a family with high traditions of church service. Mr Tufnell's father has been organist at Easington Colliery for many years. As Mr Tufnell is already working in the area, Wheatley Hill Parishioners are hoping that he is starting a long association with the church. Mr Graham expressed thanks to Mrs C English, who has helped and rendered good service over the last year,. She has been appointed assistant organist.

WHEATLEY HILL GOLDEN WEDDING

Mr and Mrs John Richardson 14 Quetlaw Road, Wheatley Hill, were married on February 20, 1909 in the little Mission Church, at Horden, by the Rev J B Bott. On Friday they held a family golden wedding party. Their two married daughters, Mrs Irene Orchard of Wheatley Hill, and Mrs Doris Grange of London, together with their only son, Mr Tom Richardson of Glasgow, were present.

Mrs Richardson said "We have had a very happy married life. Money has never been plentiful, but a good family, lots of real friends and reasonably good health spell happiness for any couple."

Mr Richardson was born at Thornley. He started work when he was 13 at Ludworth Colliery on the wagons. The pit closed after four years and Mr Richardson transferred to Thornley Colliery where he went under ground. For most of the 47 years he worked there it was as a stoneman.

Mr Richardson, who is 74, became a member of Thornley Workingmen's Club In 1906. When he went to live in Wheatley Hill in 1915 he joined Wheatley Hill Club. His wife, who was born at Cassop, 71 years ago, was one of a family of 11. She cleans her own aged miner's cottage and does her own cooking and baking.

She is a communicant member of All Saints Church, Wheatley Hill and has been a member of the Mothers Union for 40 years. At one time she was a member of Wheatley Hill W I. She is a regular attender at the local Over 60 Club. She commented "I think the Over 60 Club is an ideal movement. They provide bright entertainment and company of our own generation. This relieves the sameness of life and must relieve a great deal of loneliness."

Wheatley Hill Over-60 Club officials sent Mr and Mrs Richardson a bouquet of flowers to mark their anniversary.

27 February 1959

STRAY CATS AT THORNLEY
Complaint to Parish Council

At Wednesday's meeting of the Parish Council it was decided to write to the RSPCA asking then to investigate the question of the number of stray cats that are running around the village

Coun Mrs E Joicey, who brought the complaint, said that during the last few weeks she had taken into her home three or four homeless cats and fed them. Another kitten had been brought in by one of the family. "It is a disgrace," said Mrs Joicey, "to see those poor animals running about just wanting protection. If people don't want the poor things, why don't they have them destroyed instead of allowing them to wander around to starve or be killed with buses?"

More Cremations

Coun A Bushby asked the Council to consider the provision of the disposal of the ashes in the burial ground of persons of the parish who had been cremated. He stated that during the past year or so, cremations had increased in Thornley and that it was causing a big loss in the burial account.

"If the present trend increases there is going to be only one section of the ground going to be used for burial and in proportion to the population this means only 4 or 5 internments each year," said Coun Bushby.

He said that if the Council provided a portion of ground suitably laid out as a small garden of remembrance, it may encourage the relatives of the deceased to have the ashes interred in their own village. The clerk was instructed to ask other Councils for information.

Street Lighting

Coun Miss A Griffiths, complaining of the public lighting from Thornley police station to East Lea Estate said: "For the last week those lights have only been on for an hour each night and nearly 500 yards of roadway was unlit.

Coun James Nicholson said his attention had been called to these lights and the man who reported them said that if you had kicked pole 91, the lights would come on.

"I kicked the pole and the lights came on and stopped on for about five minutes," said Coun Nicholson.

6 March 1959

WHEATLEY HILL MOTHERS CLUB TEN YEARS OLD

There were 109 members and guests of Wheatley Hill Mothers' Club in the Welfare Hall for the 10th birthday party of the club. Mrs E Powell presided. Among the guests were Miss S Boyes, who was founder president of Wheatley Hill Mothers' Club. Miss Boyes was for some years a Health Visitor in the area.

After supper games and dancing were organised. Music was provided by Mr Clarke and Mrs Hodgson.

The following officers were re-elected: President, Mrs E Powell; secretary, Mrs I Snowdon; treasurer, Mrs V Hodgson; Management committee, the officials together with Mesdames Allison, Ferry, Fulcher, Hargreaves, Tunstall, Wigham, Craggs, Starkey and H Smith.

FEWER BURIALS AT THORNLEY

Because people are no longer using the burial ground preferring instead cremations in nearby cities, Thornley Parish Council is alarmed, and they estimate a loss of £300 in revenue over the past year in respect of the burial account.

Clerk of the Council, Mr Martin Fleming, says the present 7d burial rate may be increased. "We have had a regular rate of 48 burials a year in the council's ground, and from that figure, income amounted to £300 a year, which included burial fees and erection of monuments," said Mr Fleming.

147

He added that it cost about £500 a year for maintenance of the ground." There has been a definite drop in burials and it reflects a new trend towards cremation."

The decrease in revenue presents another problem to the Council. In 1934 Thornley Parish Council burial ground was established, and as a long term policy, the Council borrowed £2000 from the Public Works Loan Board in 1957, towards reclaiming and improving portions of the ground. A drop in income means finding the money elsewhere, hence the possibility of the rate increase.

A proposal to solve the problem was made by Coun A Bushby at the last meeting. He suggests a section of the burial ground be used as a Garden of Remembrance where ashes could be scattered. Coun Bushby said of cremations: "If the present trend increases, there is going to be only one section of the ground used for burials. In proportion to the population, this means only four or five interments a year.

AMATEURS' SUCCESS AT WHEATLEY HILL

Members of Wheatley Hill Amateur Dramatic Society maintained their high reputation for good acting with a polished performance of the three-act comedy "Sailor Beware" (by Philip King and Falkland Cary) before a packed audience in the Welfare Hall, Wheatley Hill, on Wednesday night.

The play, full of humorous situations, has only recently been released for armature production.

Filling, perhaps, the most exacting role of mother-in-law. Emma Hornett, Eva Wharrior, a long standing member of the group, who now lives in Horden, gave faultless performance, and she received excellent support from the rest of the cast, namely, Don Willan, as her husband; Les Barker, as Albert Tufnell, the prospective bridegroom on leave from the navy; Les Dryden, as his Scottish pal; Elizabeth Punshon, as the prospective bride; newcomer Ann McBriar, as the bridesmaid; Minnie Galloway as the fussy Aunt Edie; Tom King, as the helpful vicar, and Evelyn Kenny, as the nosey neighbour, Mrs Lack.

The producer was Mrs Vera Faiclough, of Easington. Mrs Nora Abbs and Mrs Ivy Scott were stage managers, and Mr C Raffell was responsible for the lighting and special effects. The play was repeated last night, and further performances are to be given tonight and tomorrow night.

13 March 1959

THORNLEY MAN'S FUNERAL
Mr W Fleming's many activities

The body of Mr William Fleming, aged 84, if 1 Coopers Terrace, Thornley, the home of his daughter, Mrs J G Makepiece, was received into the church of the English Martyrs, Thornley, the previous evening to the Requiem Mass, celebrated by the Rev Father H McNeill. The service at the burial ground was conducted by Rev Fr P Smith.

Mr Fleming who has been in good health up to a few weeks ago, died in Sedgefield General Hospital. He was born in Murton where his father and mother Mr and Mrs Michael Fleming had settled after leaving County Mayo, Ireland.

148

The family of five brothers and one sister left Murton and went to Thornley after the Seaham Explosion in 1880. In 1883, a year before the Colliery Putt Pay at Thornley, his elder brother John had severe spinal injuries which made him a permanent cripple for life and unable to walk except with the aid of two sticks, he overcame his handicap.

Mr Fleming's elder brother Martin was killed in the same seam as his brother was injured a few months afterwards. Another brother, Michael who went to into the Lancashire Coalfield was fatally injured in the mine in Burnley in 1907.

SHOTTON BOXER SHINES

Maurice Cullen, Shotton Colliery, boxing for Horden NCB Boxing Club, fought and outpointed Joe Jacobs, a Manchester coloured boy, at Barnoldswick, Manchester in a lightweight contest. Cullen gave one of the best performances seen in the amateur ring for some time. Jacobs is an international, and has represented his country on numerous occasions.

The decision of the judges was unanimous, and everyone believes that Cullen is almost sure to receive international recognition soon. The bout was a real thriller, with Cullen having the coloured boy in trouble on several occasions.

The crowd acclaimed the decision at the end of a fine contest. Halifax Police BC members have invited Cullen to appear at one of their tournaments in the near future.

THORNLEY MINERS WELFARE INSTITUTE

Over 150 attended the silver jubilee of the opening of Thornley Child Welfare Clinic, Mrs E Clark Presiding.

Mrs Clark paid tribute to the doctors, staff and voluntary workers who had contributed to the work of the clinic over 25 years. She mentioned Mrs Todd, Mrs Scott, and Mrs. Roper with Mrs I Johnson, who was secretary for many years, and Mrs Anderson who still held the post of treasurer after 21 years service.

Mrs A Todd cut the birthday cake and was the recipient of a spray of flowers. The cake was presented by Mrs Jane Anderson, treasurer of the County Welfare Committee for 12 years. She and her 28 year old son Thomas (now living in London) were the first to be registered at the clinic 25 years ago.

Children and their mothers were entertained to a film show by P C Jackson, accident prevention officer.

27 March 1959

FAMOUS PUTT PAY
THE DAY WHEN THORNLEY MINERS WAITED IN VAIN

Many people have read of the Thornley Colliery "putt pay" of 1884, but most of them have only a vague idea of what it was all about. A local historian has prepared the following account:

"In 1894 coals were selling at 4s.8.07d per ton and the Durham miners were advocating an alteration in the sliding scale agreement. Two collieries, Thornley and Ludworth were at sea with cargoes of Hartlepool Wallsend and Thornley Wallsend coal.

"It was Friday 4 April 1884 and the pitmen were assembled at Thornley Colliery pay-office to draw their fortnightly wages when the news leaked out that the company had gone bankrupt. This was the second time that the original coal company had experienced financial difficulties, for in 1870 wages of workmen had been withheld and half the amount paid,

At the time of this sad news only Thornley Colliery was working. Wheatley Hill and Ludworth in the same group, were temporarily suspended. Only the Low Main seam was in full operation and the hewers, putters, drivers and stonemen, a total of 633, were divided in Inkerman, Gare Hall, Easy Way, Prospect and Speculation districts. The average output per hewer daily was 3.5 tons, the average earnings 5s.5¾d (county average 4s 8.97d per day or shift) and average shifts worked were 8½d.

Financial Crash

"Mr J A Ramsay, the colliery viewer, and Mr W Balderston, the cashier, were unaware, up to the moment of the financial crash, that the colliery's wages cheque sent to the Bank had been refused. They soon realised that something was wrong when they saw an angry mob of wild pitmen bearing down upon them, and they were obliged to lock themselves in the office and ask for police assistance.

Mr Jim Boland, the men's checkweighman and chairman of Thornley Miners Lodge, despatched an urgent message to Mr William Crawford, general secretary of the Durham Miners' Association, for advice and assistance.

Police Sgt Sampson, who was called to the uproar and who saw men threatening officials and gathering tools and missiles to attack the colliery premises, made a special appeal to the division for assistance.

State Of Revolt

Mr John Wilson, an agent for the Durham Miners' Association, arrived and found the whole of the village in a state of revolt. Fifty policemen, under Supt Scott and insp Todd, of Hartlepool's, had previously marched into the village and dispersed the angry crowds from the colliery premises with drawn truncheons.

A local magistrate, the Rev W Mayor, agreed to the Riot Act being read and this was done by Insp Todd in the presence of all the men and many women in the Market Place.

"Mr Wilson, with a deputation from the men, waited on| Mr Ramsay to work out some scheme to assist the men and their families, many of whom were penniless. Mr Wilson returned to the men, who gave him an hostile reception. Before leaving for Durham to put the case before an emergency committee, he promised to return to Thornley the following day for a further meeting.

Light Interlude

Mr Wilson returned to Thornley the following day (a Saturday) and a large meeting of the men was held in a nearby field. In his History of the Durham miners, Mr Wilson writes that a pigeon match was being held at the time and his audience seemed to be more concerned watching the heavens.

Mr Wilson writes that he was in one of his most eloquent moments when a pigeon was spotted and a loud voice from the crowd shouted 'Haad thee hand lad, until the blue cock comes in.' All eyes went to the bird, the hero of the hour, which dropped like an arrow from a bow straight into the ducket. The voice shouted 'Thee can gan on noo it's landed.'

A short time afterwards Mr Ramsay, who had been put in charge of collieries, sold the colliery 'tanky', proceeds from which he intended to distribute to help the distress. When an engine from the NER arrived, however, men, women and children pulled up the railway lines, impounding both engines. The NER were obliged to send out a repair gang before they could recover their engine from the unofficial pound.

Centenarian'S Memories

Two hewers, the Bells, were first cavils in the Prospect district, Alex, now aged 101, and living with relations at Dixon Estate, Shotton Colliery, can still recall some of the incidents. He remembers some of his 'marras' in the Prospect - Hughie Murray, Harry McGreavery, English and Fleming, the two Listers and father and son Rook, cavilled next to him.

Alex remembers well the bills of sale being put up in the village and the drift of families to other collieries. He says that Thornley seemed dead after the pit closed and he remembers the Union men paying out the wages a year later.

The colliery reopened two years after it had closed down and the men again began to assemble on Friday's for pay. Even now, if there is a delay at the start of payment, some wag remarks, 'I doubt it's gannen be a putt pay'.

RETIREMENT OF WHEATLEY HILL OFFICIAL

After 22 years' service as fore-overman at Wheatley Hill colliery, which has meant him, week in and week out, setting out for work at half past one in the morning, Mr Ralph Watson Hagan can at last enjoy "a long lie-in." For Mr Hagan, who lives at 2 Weardale Street, Wheatley Hill, has retired from work after a mining career of 51 years, virtually all of which has been spent underground. "And all the time I have known him I can truthfully say he has never once been late for work," his wife said when our reporter called at their home this week.

Longest Serving Official

Mr Hagan does not retire officially until his 65th birthday, which he celebrates on Sunday, but he has already said "goodbye" to the pit for he is now enjoying a holiday which was due to him. Setting out for work so early every morning soon became a matter of routine for Mr Hagan when he was appointed fore-overman in 1936. "I have always liked my work and have never lost a shift, apart from illness, but now I am going to relax and take it easy", he said "And I'll now have much more time to devote to my wife, who has not been in the best of health during recent years."

Mr Hagan was the colliery's longest-serving official for he has filled an official position since his appointment, as master shifter in 1922. Later, he was back overman for ten years before his appointment as fore-overman. He enjoys excellent health and has not missed a single shift through illness in the last six years of his mining career.

A native of South Shields, Mr Hagan started work at the age of 14 at St Hilda's Colliery as a pick carrier, earning 7s a week and working a daily ten hour shift. After only a few weeks on the surface at this job, he went underground as a trapper-boy, and then was a driver and datal worker. He moved to Wingate Colliery when he was 16 and shortly after going there was pony-putting.

Six Grandchildren

In 1913, when he was 19, Mr Hagan again changed his place of employment, going to Deaf Hill colliery as a coal hewer. Six years later he qualified as a deputy. He was at Deaf Hill when water broke through in 1919 and the pit was laid idle.

"I then left for Wheatley Hill where I have worked ever since," said Mr Hagan. He first served under the colliery manager, Mr Mathew Barrass, as a shot-firer but after 18 months was appointed master shifter.

Mr Hagan is married, with a family of two sons and one daughter. He also has six grandchildren, one of whom, 21 year old William Hagan has followed "the call to sea" serving as a mess-room attendant on the liner the Queen Mary.

Mr Hagan's two sons, William and Ralph, both work at Wheatley Hill colliery, the former as a filler and the latter as a coal cutter. His daughter, Mrs Edna Dodsworth, lives at Shotton Colliery, and her husband, Albert, is also a miner.

10 April 1959

WOMEN'S SUPERIORITY IN THORNLEY COUNCIL
But Newcomer, Mrs Ivy Walker, Is More Worried About Housing

Mrs Ivy Walker, good–looking newcomer to Thornley Parish Council, carries with her – when she attends her first meeting a week on Tuesday – the key to female superiority over the male. Her appearance will give the ladies of Thornley a majority of one over the men at the council meeting.

Demolition Problems

But nobody at Thornley – least of all Mrs Walker – seems to worry about that; in fact Mrs Walker is more worried about the demolition of houses soon near where she lives.

Her husband Mr Frank Walker, chairman of Thornley Workmen's Club, is also on the Parish Council and is the Thornley representative on Easington Rural District Council. So it is he who will have to spearhead representation on behalf of the people of Thornley who are shortly to be moved from their homes.

Building is not allowed on any great scale in the same area as where demolitions are to start again and it seems obvious that some of the people already in Thornley might have to move out.

Mrs Walker starts her new public work at a considerable disadvantage in one respect. She believes (and it is to be hoped that this was not meant to be her secret) that the time of Parish Councils generally is rapidly drawing to a close.

"The powers of the Parish Councils" she says" have been taken away more and more through the years and there is very little that they can do now."

Bloodless Battle

The Battle of Thornley for women's numerical superiority in the Parish Council has been a bloodless one; in fact there has not really been any battle. For, as one stalwart put it: "The men could not care less who is on the Parish Council and the women have been brought in because there is no one else interested."

Turn to Mr Martin Fleming, Clerk to the Parish Council. He comments; "I believe that Thornley is the only council where women have a majority."

"I must say that it has worked very well; the women might be not so good as the men, in council, but, outside, their work is every bit as good, if not better."

"Women's observation is superior and they often bring matters before the council which have been overlooked by the men. They are not as eloquent but what they have to say is often right to the point.

As Good As Others

"I should think that the business of Thornley Parish Council is carried out every bit as well as in councils where the men have the majority."

Mr Fleming agreed that possibly the apathy of local people had enabled the women – many of whom are already enthusiastic members of local organisations – to take over control. The men had the difficulty of shift–working to contend with and that caused many of them to lose interest.

Another member of the council told our representative that Coun Jim Hoban, of Shinwell Crescent, was an excellent chairman in the circumstances. "Women", he said, "are not very inclined to obey the Standing Orders of meetings, and Jim Hoban allows them just the latitude necessary to enable them to have their say while at the same time the meeting is proceeding in satisfactory fashion."

Four From 44

Mr Frank Walker, also representative on Easington RDC for Thornley, seemed to regard questions about the majority of one for the women as superfluous. But he pointed to Easington RDC as a council at almost the other extreme for there are only four women among the 44 members.

Our representative might have been mistaken, but there seemed to be a gleam of satisfaction in Mr Walker's eye as he recorded this fact.

Asked about his wife joining him on the parish council, Mr Walker did not seam to think that it would make much difference so far as he was concerned, but he commented; "She has a mind of her own and we will certainly not be voting the same way as each other automatically."

Mrs Walker – she and her husband were in charge of a public house at Thornley until comparatively recently – also said that she had a mind of her own. Though she had little knowledge of the inner activities of Thornley Parish Council, she and her husband had always been ardent Socialists.

She herself had been to a school at Keswick, while her husband had always been a prominent trade unionist.

Mrs Walker, mother of four children, the youngest a toddler and the eldest at Grammar School, believes that a women's work at home comes first in every respect, but she also believes that women need outside interests.

"I always wish I had had my family earlier in life" she added, "for I would then have been able to take more interest in outdoor activities than I do at the present."

LUDWORTH PLAYING FIELDS

The annual meeting of the Ludworth Sports and Recreation Fund was held in the Village Hall, Ludworth, on Saturday morning when Mr J T White presided over a good attendance. The financial report showed an increased balance of £357.9s.7d. The treasurer, Mr J R Greener, pointed out that during the year, children's equipment which had been installed had cost £718.14s.10d to purchase and erect. Considerable progress in other matters was reported and the secretary, Mr W Maddison, reported upon the previous committee meeting which had been attended by Mr Tom Scollen, Divisional Welfare Officer of the NCB, and MR J B Twemlow, director of the Durham County Community Service Council.

The next project was to be the laying out of a football pitch on the site adjoining the children's playground and Mr Myers had been instructed to provide an estimate for this work. Mr Scollen had promised to help in any way possible this matter.

The committee referred to the assistance given by Mr A Welsh, manager of Thornley Colliery in the activities of the association.

Officers re–elected were: Chairman; Mr White, Secretary; Mr Maddison, and Treasurer, Mr Greener.

24 April 1959

THORNLEY PEOPLE FACE SPECTRE OF PLAN
"Southerners" Have Life of Suspense As They Wait

To live on the south side of Hartlepool Street, Thornley is to live in suspense.

In more than half a dozen streets residents are living with the specter of a Plan above their heads which they believe clearly indicates that their homes must be pulled down to fit into a more comprehensive PLAN. And on top of the waiting and worrying many of them believe they must leave Thornley for good.

Information Is Needed

People are naturally suspicious about something they cannot see or understand, and in Chapel, Vine and South Streets in Thornley, you can meet the folk who are doing all the worrying. They have heard about the talk of the Town Map circulating in the council chambers of the local authorities. They have thought about the planners in other parts of the county making drawing board decisions about the future of their homes. But it has all been hard to understand – and even more difficult to get definite information.

Take Mrs N Johnson for example. She and her husband have lived as owner – tenants in South Street for the past 12 years. Five years ago she heard a whisper about slum clearance which might affect their home, so she put on her hat and coat one day

154

and visited the offices of the local authority. "An official told me the houses where I lived had five years of life," she said.

Since then Mrs Johnson has been in two minds about decorating and improving the property. Her neat, clean house is proof that a lot of money and work have been spent on it. But now she is a worried woman." We eat in the dark waiting for what is going to happen. I would put a new fireplace in, but what's the use? Papering and painting too, is being held back."

An additional worry to them is that Mr Johnson retires in two years time. "There is talk of people being moved to Peterlee, but we would lose a lot of money if that happened. Now we just pay rates for the house, but council house rents are high and we will only have our pension," said Mrs Johnson.

Echoing her words was neighbour, Mrs D Ord, whose husband works at the local colliery. "I certainly don't want to move to Peterlee," she said. Not knowing is also unsettling. "If only we knew what was going to happen, or get a definite answer to our queries," she said.

Demolition Topic

Demolition of housing has been the topic in Thornley for some time but no one appears to have the problem in perspective. Few have even heard of the Town Map which affects Easington RDC area. It began in 1954 when the County Council supplied the district council with their observations of a draft of the map. They were very wide proposals but were accepted by the district council.

Consultations followed between the two authorities and the stage being reached now is that before the draft is submitted to the Ministry of Housing and Local Government, it must go before the district council. That has not yet happened, but when it does, the district council can put their observations to the County Council who, however, are not bound by them.

The county authority is not bound to accept the recommendations of the district council. The difficulties that are anticipated in Thornley's case embrace the areas designated for possible slum clearance. The Town Map will show whether land may be used for development or redevelopment – such as pulling old houses down and rebuilding more. If land is not allocated for development then it will not be developed. Land allocation is the hub of the problem. If none is available for housing then it could mean that people will have to move elsewhere.

Before the Ministry finally accept the Town Map however, affected parties, either local authorities or individuals, will be able to air any grievances in the form of an enquiry.

75 Houses Affected

Now back to Thornley. There are roughly 75 houses south of the main road, which cuts through the main shopping centre that will most likely be demolished. People in that district do not want to move, say, to Peterlee where it is rumoured they will be offered alternative housing. One of the obvious reasons is that travelling to and from work would be more inconvenient – especially to the men working at Deaf Hill

Colliery. The district council have tried to buy land for housing, such as several acres on the recreation ground, but it had been earmarked by the planning authority. One villager summed it all up; "It is a big problem that is facing us" he said.

Problem or not it is one that will be settled in the near future and one which will create quite a controversy. Village folk do not easily give up their homes in which they have lived all their lives and they would certainly resent having to leave Thornley altogether. But among all the confusion and doubt, there are at least two people who fully support the proposals for the demolition of houses.

Terry Cullen and his wife moved into a house in South Street shortly after they married six years ago – and it has been six years of misery for them. Because of the poor state of the house, repairs and decoration have become a nightmare for them as owner–tenants. "I am 100 per cent behind the planning authority if they intend to pull these houses down, and I am quite prepared to live in Peterlee" said Mr Cullen.

FUTURE OF SOUTH EAST DURHAM COLLIERIES
Manpower to be Cut by 300

Addressing miners from the four collieries in "B" Group of No 3 Area (South–East Durham) of the Durham Divisional Coal Board – Wheatley Hill, Wingate, Deaf Hill and Thornley – in Wheatley Hill Welfare Hall on Saturday morning. Mr L G Timms, the area general manager, said he was not trying to "gloss over" the serious position in the coal industry today. "I cannot see into the future and I cannot make guarantees," he added, referring to the future of the collieries. "All we can do today is discuss these matters and see if, together, we can do anything to alleviate the serious position.

Two of the Collieries in the group, said the group manager, Mr C R Knaggs, presiding at the meeting, which was attended by about 200 workmen, had asked for the meeting to be held to hear what the future had to offer in the coal industry in the area, and it was felt by the area officials it would be just as well to have a joint meeting of all four collieries in the group. "Wingate are perhaps more concerned than any other colliery in the group, because, geologically, they are not quite so good," added Mr Knaggs.

"All In It Together"

Mr Timms said that he thought it a good thing that they could get together in such a fashion "to try to iron out these difficulties. "We are all in this boat together, officials and men," he added. "If anything goes wrong with the coal industry we will all suffer alike." There was, generally, a recession in the world coal trade. Similar recessions had been faced before the last war, but there was a difference between this recession and previous ones – now, the coal industry was faced with fierce competition from other sources of power – oil chiefly, nuclear energy and natural gas, "And", added Mr Timms, "we have increasing competition from other foreign countries for the export markets." We used to export 75m tons of coal, but last year only 4m tons went abroad. "And we shall be lucky if we sell 1m tons abroad this year," said Mr Timms.

"Last year continued Mr Timms, 11m extra tons of coal were stocked at the pits in the country. At the present moment in No 3 Area they had on stock 400,000 tons of coal out of an annual area output of 3½m tons. "From these figures," said Mr Timms," you will see that we have lying on the ground about six weeks supply of coal."

"If the mining industry was to exist we would have to start and make it pay in competition with oil and gas. And this is going to be a difficult job," said Mr Timms. We would have to get the coal more cheaply than at present. "What we are trying to do, with your help, in this area, is to improve the efficiency of each pit," said Mr Timms.

Last year the output per man shift in the No 3 Area was 21.8 cwt. In January this year this had been increased to 23.8 cwt, in February to 24.1 cwt, and in March to 24.9 cwt. These figures compared with the country average figure of 26 cwt. We have nothing to crow about," went on Mr Timms, "but we are slowly improving. We have got to keep on improving as time goes on."

"In the area the administrative staff was being cut by five per cent this year", said Mr Timms. Already in the country the Coal Board had closed, or were closing 36 uneconomic pits. "We do not, if we can help it, want to close down any of our nine pits in this area," he said. "We want to struggle together to keep every pit going. It may be beyond our control but this is what we want to do if at all possible." Manpower was being transferred from the worst economic pits in the area to the most economic. At the moment they were transferring men from Shotton Colliery to other pits – manpower at this colliery may run down to such an extent that it may become a single – shift pit.

"Somehow or other we have to get less coal more efficiently," went on the area manager. "That is always a very hard job to do. It is much easier to get it more efficiently by increasing output than by decreasing output. The switch from uneconomic two shift system to one–shift systems is possible. Some of these unpalatable things will have to be adopted."

"They were trying their best in the area to avoid extreme suffering which would result from closures", said Mr Timms. Manpower this year would be run down by 300 in the area – this would be their contribution to the Divisional total of 5000. They would continue to recruit juveniles into the industry, but not adults. "Everybody," added Mr Timms "agrees that this is the proper policy to pursue. As long as we possibly can we will do this."

Right Not To Reduce Price

They were endeavouring to cut down man power by 300 without redundancies. "I cannot guarantee there will be no redundancies," said Mr Timms. "The position is getting far too serious for anyone to give guarantees. The only salvation I can see is for us to become so efficient in our pits that we can again command a place in the world."

Regarding the stock-piling of coal, Durham was being hit worse than any other county because it was so "tied up" with gas and coke. They were now trying wherever possible to get into the steam coal market.

It had often been asked, because of the present state of the industry, why the Coal Board did not reduce the price of coal. "It would be easy to drop the price but you would never get it back," said Mr Timms. "I think the Coal Board is right not to drop the price – they are trying to protect us."

When, during the general discussion which followed Mr Timms's talk, one miner asked the area general manager if he thought that a five per cent cut in the administrative staff was big enough, Mr. Timms replied, "Let us be fair about this. There have been no dismissals at your level, nor any redundancies. We hope to reduce the manpower by 300 this year without any redundancy - at the same time we hope to reduce the staff by not replacing people who leave. When you talk about the axe, we don't want to chop off anybody if we can help it. So far we have chopped off nobody at any level." Mr Knaggs pointed out that the proposed reduction of 300 in manpower represented 2.3 per cent of the total workmen employed in the area - this was less than half of the percentage cut proposed this year for the administrative staff.

Among other area officials attending the meeting were Mr A Ford (area production manager) and the four local colliery managers, Messrss F Richardson (Wheatley Hill), S Bainbridge (Deaf Hill), A Welsh (Thornley) and D Hesler (Wingate).

WAR MEMORIAL WORKERS
AT THORNLEY

A new coffee stall, opened in Hartlepool Street, Thornley, by women members of the village organisations, for the purpose of raising £60 required to complete the newly-erected war memorial, has been so successful that the ladies are to carry on for some time.

The women, organised by Mrs Jane Anderson, treasurer of Thornley War Memorial Committee, acquired some closed business premises in the shopping centre, cleaned them up and fitted them with the necessary equipment for making and serving coffee. Local trades people supplied them with milk, meat for sandwiches and home-made cakes.

Helpers are from the Women's Institute, Mother's Club, Over-60 club, Catholic Women's League and British Legion. They have worked for over 15 years raising funds for a memorial to the men who gave their lives in the world wars. The first memorial was destroyed by fire in 1944.

1 May 1959

THORNLEY AREA
Anonymous Gift

Thornley War Memorial Coffee Stall, run by Mrs J Anderson, treasurer of the War Memorial Committee, and a band of lady helpers from village organisations, this week realised £6. Mrs Anderson states she is quite satisfied with the sale of cups of coffee and the donations of people who are trying to help. She said she was very grateful to one aged lady pensioner who came to the stall and made a present of £3 to the fund, £1 each for the two sons that were lost in the 1914–18 War, and £1 as her personall contribution.

SAFETY OFFICER

Mr Harold Todd, 42 East Lea, Thornley, a 42-year-old deputy overman, of Blackhall Colliery, succeeds to the position of Safety Officer at Thornley Colliery, made vacant by the retirement of Mr James Orange. Mr Todd, previous to his employment at Blackhall Colliery, where he was employed for 11 years, was for five years employed as a deputy overman at Wheatley Hill Colliery. He has been a member of the Houghton Colliery Fire and Rescue Brigade for 11 years and was engaged in rescue operations at Easington and Horden Collieries.

8 May 1959

PROPOSED EXTENSION OF COAL STOCKING SITE

Wingate Parish Council agreed in "principle" at their meeting on Monday to a proposed extension of a coal – stocking site in their parish at Wheatley Hill for coal from Thornley Colliery. In a letter accompanying a plan of proposed the extension, the County Planning Officer, Mr W A Geenty, said that two public rights of way would be affected and would like to hear the Councils comments on the proposal.

Protective Measures

"I shall obtain an undertaking from the National Coal Board" the letter continued," that there will be as little interference as possible with the public rights of way, and impose a condition that any damage to the footpath caused by coal–stocking operations shall be made good by that Coal Board. I should be glad to know if these protective measures will satisfy your Council."

Useless Swamp Land

Coun T Forster said he did not like the site which had been chosen – it was practically opposite the Roman Catholic School – but Coun J H Charlton said the Council should give careful consideration to the matter. "It is only useless swamp land they want to take," added Coun Charlton., "and the Coal Board must stock coal to keep people employed. I would not like to support anything which would stop coal-stocking or, on the other hand, which would stock coal on good arable land. Sites are now very difficult to get."

Too Close To School

Coun Forster replied that he was not objecting to the stockpiling of coal – he was in full agreement with this – but he thought the suggested site was too close to the school and to a path frequently used by workmen.

The Clerk, Mr J Harper, said that ultimately the Education Committee would be consulted about the site and they would undoubtedly safeguard the school. Regarding the path, an "adequate width of land" could be left at each side and the council could suggest that the minimum number of crossings be made. The Clerk was instructed to ask the County Planning Officer to bear these matters in mind when considering the extension plan.

Old Folk Worried

Since the electricity "change over" from the National Coal Board to the North-Eastern Electricity Board a year past March, the meters had not been read at Wheatley Hill, where householders were paying 2s or 3s a fortnight for their electricity, said Coun N Cook. As a result many people, especially the old folk, were "getting worried."

"Some of them may find at the end of the year that their account amounts to more than they have paid fortnightly, and it is this which is worrying them," added Coun Cook. "I think it is about time the men were coming to read the meters." It was agreed to write to the Electricity Board on the matter.

Conference Delegates

When the delegate for the Public Lighting Engineers' three-day conference at Aberdeen in September was being discussed, the Clerk pointed out that Coun N Cook, Wheatley Hill, was next on the rota drawn up by the council for attending conferences. Coun Cook, however, said he had no wish to attend the conference, adding, "I never believe in spending rate-payers' money that way."

The chairman, Coun M W Carter, refused to listen to any further comment from Coun Cook but said to him, "You are entitled to your opinion, but you are in the minority." Coun D Wood was chosen in Coun Cook's place.

Coun A Bishop and Wheatley Hill cemetery superintendent are also to attend the annual conference of the Burial and Cremation authorities at Llandudno in September.

A WAR MEMORIAL - paying tribute to Thornley's sacrifice in two world wars will be dedicated next Saturday; the memorial is being built on the site of the old Literary Institute. The money has been raised by public subscription over the past 10 or 12 years. Work has been going on about three weeks and when it is finished the site should be very pleasant. The memorial will be fronted by lawns and flower beds with several seats.

Our picture shows Bill Smith and Arthur Wilson, both of Durham, at work on the memorial.

15 May 1959

THORNLEY MEMORIAL

Mr W Bovill, who did fine service as secretary of the Thornley branch of the British Legion over a long period, writes about the new Thornley war memorial as follows:- "Had it not been for the former Vicar of Thornley the Rev W A Lathaen, the names of the fallen would not have been known. I wish to state quite definitely that that statement is not true. The names were in records of the Thornley branch of the British Legion." It is generally believed that the list was copied from the memorial by Mr Lathaen. As Mr Bovill does not say that the Legion made the copy it would seem that Mr Lathaen supplied them with a copy.

22 May 1959

UNVEILING OF THORNLEY WAR MEMORIAL

One of the most impressive ceremonies that has taken place in the mining village of Thornley was witnessed on Saturday at the unveiling and dedication of the new War Memorial which replaces the first World War memorial that was destroyed when the Miners' Welfare Institute was destroyed by fire in 1944.

The new memorial has cost £1000, raised by subscriptions, whist drives and collections. It was designed by Mr Dennis Dunlop of Durham, and it is made of Dunhouse stone from Staindrop. A freestanding wall-type memorial 45 feet wide, with centre section bearing inscription panels and bold raised cross, wreath shelf courtyard, the wings are built in random sized blocks, the central portion bearing 158 names in two panels being finely worked. The monument is in a spacious arc giving a splendid opportunity for a fine layout,

Preceding the ceremony Thornley Colliery Silver Prize Band, conducted by Mr Edward Kitto, headed the procession, through the village, of 500 men, women and children, composed of many branches of British Legion men and women bearing their standards, a posse of special constables, members of the Naval Association, Memorial Committee, Parish Council, Mothers' Club, Women's Institute, Civil Defence, Boy Scouts, St Bartholomew's Church, Bow Street and Waterloo Street Methodists, Salvation Army, Catholic Women's League and war veterans of the Boer and 1914-18 War.

Unveiled by Mr T H Holder

The service was conducted by Rev P G Mold. Vicar of Thornley, and the unveiling was conducted by Mr T H Holder, secretary of the War Memorial Committee, and the dedication by the Rev W A Lathaen, deputy assistant chaplain general (TA) Northern Command. Assisting were the Rev R Hancock, Methodist Minister and Captain R Stock, of the Salvation Army. Mr J H Pattison was chairman.

Wreaths were placed on the memorial by Mr James Hoban, Thornley Parish Council: Dr A P Gray, British Legion men, Mrs H Brewster, British Legion women: Mr T Woodward. St Bartholomew's Church: Mr I P Martin, Bow Street Methodists: Mr W Henderson, MBE, Thornley Mining Federation Board: Mrs A Todd, Women's Institute; Mr F A Walker, Thornley Workingmen's Club; Mr H Hoole and two schoolchildren, Barry Gott and Greta Beddell, of Thornley Junior Primary School.

29 May 1959

Thornley War Memorial

WHEATLEY HILL POSTMASTER RETIRES

Mr Albert Ernest Knight has for the last 27 years been postmaster at Wheatley Hill. Mr Knight's retirement breaks a period of 54 years family service, for his father, the late Mr Ernest Albert Knight, was also postmaster for 27 years.

Mr Knight lives with his widowed mother, Mrs Mary Isobel Knight. He served in the postal section of the RAF in the 1939-45 war. While he was away his mother, then over 70, ran the post office. In January Mr Knight was honoured by his fellow postmasters and appointed president of the Durham County Branch of the Sub-Postmasters Federation.

Mr Knight paid tribute to his parents. "I am grateful to my father and mother for the example of high public service they set before me. It was their hard work that made it possible for me to take over the Wheatley Hill Post Office."

Commenting on his future plans, Mr Knight said, "So far as my mother, who is now 88, and I are concerned, it will be a case of where my caravan has rested." We are both keen caravanners and enjoy the life immensely. For some time we shall be by the sea at South Shields."

Mr Knight's successor in Wheatley Hill is Mr G White, of Middleton Tyas.

2000 CHILDREN ENTERTAINED AT WHEATLEY HILL SPORTS

A twopence-a- week levy paid all year round by all sections of workmen at Wheatley Hill Colliery gave 2000 children, practically all of them from Wheatley Hill, a memorial day of "feast and fun" in the village on Saturday.

The occasion was the second annual sports day organised by the Wheatley Hill Mineworkers Federation Board and once again it was favoured by warm sunshine and clear blue skies. Every child in the village up to school leaving age received a bag of chocolate and fruit valued half-a-crown, and similar gifts were presented to children from neighbouring villages whose fathers work at Wheatley Hill Colliery.

Parade Through Village

"We are most grateful to all those who helped to make the day an outstanding success," the secretary, Coun J Cowie, told our reporter afterwards, "especially the women-folk, who had no mean task distributing so many bags of fruit and chocolate. Thanks to their cooperation the distribution was carried out smoothly and efficiently and it was a real treat to see the happy faces of all the youngsters."

The programme began with a fancy and comic dress parade through the village, headed by Wheatley Hill Colliery Band, under the conductorship of Mr Norman Straughan, and the Wheatley Hill miners' lodge banner. The banner carriers, who all gave their services free, were County Coun J Andrews, Coun C Hackworth and Messrss G Burnside, H Bradshaw, Mr Telford and M Cain.

A large number of children entered the parade which, in charge of Mr W Rothery, set off from Patton Street and proceeded to the school football field, where it was judged by the wives of two local doctors, Mrs W G Maclean and Mrs J Wallace.

Prize winners were as follows: Fancy Dress: 1, Glenda Barker; 2, Alan Stephen-son; 3, Margaret Symons. Original dress: 1, Valerie Wilson; 2 Barry Fulcher; 3, (tie)

Dorothy Collingwood and Barbara Galley. Comic dress: 1, Christine Carr; 2, (tie), Jennie Henderson and Margaret Powell; 3, Carol Carr. Adults: Mr and Mrs J Lamb and Mrs I Hammond (The Sheik and his wives).

An attractive programme of sports was in charge of Mr G Burnside and as well three prizes being awarded in every race, consolation prizes were presented to all the other children taking part.

Women Helpers

For the second year running 19 year old Ray Clish, who plays cricket for Castle Eden, was presented with the Baldersera Cup as winner of the adults' four-mile race. David Young was runner up, Peter Mason third, and Messrss M Anderson and M Carr fourth and fifth respectively.

The women who assisted in the distribution of the bags of fruit and chocolate were Mesdames Harper, Storey, Richardson, T E Turner, Hodgson, Bowes, Brain, Taylor, Bradley, Parkin, Wharrier and Jordan and Miss B Galley.

Altogether the treat cost in the region of £340, and the officials in charge of arrangements, who were supported by a strong representative committee, were Mr A D Wharrier, (chairman), Coun J Cowie (secretary) and Mr J Hedley (treasurer). The day's programme ended with a whist drive and dance in the Welfare Hall.

5 June 1959

THORNLEY FOOTBALL CELEBRATION

Mr Ray Middleton, JP, Manager of Hartlepool's United football club, presented trophies to the players and secretary of Thornley Colliery Welfare FC at a reception in the Miners Welfare Institute to celebrate the winning of the Monkwearmouth Charity Cup. Chairman of the club, Mr R Lewis, presided.

Arrangements were made by Mr J R Bosomworth, secretary. Tea and refreshments were provided by the ladies' committee.

Miss Valerie Bosomworth, daughter of the secretary, presented Mrs Middleton with a bouquet.

Receiving trophies were G Outhwaite, F Iddon, E Myres, J Elcoat, G Greener, T Parkin, R Presho, T Horner, F Richardson, F Wyman, D Miller and the secretary.

12 June 1959

Owing to the industrial dispute by the Press, there is a gap of two months in the newspapers.

THORNLEY RC SCHOOL PRESENTATION

The Rev Dr McNeill, a manager, presented the prizes at Thornley St Godric's mixed school speech day at the end of the summer term, and Father Smith and Messrs Brown and Hagan also spoke.

Mr J Finnerty, Headmaster, said that the religious and government reports on the school reflected great credit on the staff and children. He went on, "This year I am celebrating my jubilee as headmaster of the school. I may say that I have taught most of the parents of the children now in my charge. Today a fine spirit permeates the whole school."

Speaking of his 25 years' service, Mr Finnerty said that eight of the old pupils had gained degrees and two boys and three girls had entered religious orders.

Dr McNeil presented a cheque and a smoker's outfit to Mr Finnerty in appreciation of his 25 years as headmaster. Mr Finnerty presented the Rev Mark Hoban with a gift of books to mark his ordination; Mr Hoban was a former St Godric's scholar.

Mr D Doyle, who has left for a teaching appointment in the south, received a leaving gift.

14 August 1959

WHEATLEY HILL COUPLE BACK FROM SOUTH AFRICA

Newly returned from South Africa after an eight-month holiday there with their eldest son and his wife, a Wheatley Hill couple, Mr and Mrs Robert Richardson, Patton Crescent, describe the visit as "the most wonderful holiday of their life."

"We soon got used to living in a part of the country where there were few white people and we had the time of our lives". Mrs Richardson, who is in her 70th year, told our reporter, "Our eyes were opened where the natives were concerned. We saw Indians, Zulus and Basutos and had not realised before the conditions in which they live. They work hard for next to nothing, and on the whole we found them to be quite nice people. I brought back some lovely dresses made by the wives of the black people - they were highly skilled with the needle, and splendid workers."

Mr Richardson, who is 70 and a retired miner at Wheatley Hill Colliery, and his wife stayed with their eldest son JonathAn at Dannhauser, in Natal. It was while he lay wounded in a South African hospital during the 1939-45 war that Jonathan met his future wife, a South African girl. They were married in 1942 and they have a nine-year-old son Robert, who saw his grandparents for the first time, Jonathan formerly miner at Wheatley Hill, is now one of the managers of a coal mine in Natal.

Cheap Fruit

"Meat eggs and fruit were much cheaper than in this country - especially fruit. Pineapples were only a halfpenny each", said Mrs Richardson, "and you could take away as many bananas as you could carry for half a crown." Oranges were "dirt cheap." We got a three-foot sack packed with them for 5s," added Mrs Richardson.

Institute Meeting

Mrs Richardson, who was a founder-member of Wheatley Hill Over-60 Club and was secretary until going away, attended the Women's Institute meetings in the South African town where she stayed and was presented with a silver spoon to bring back home. During her holiday she met a couple from Easington Colliery a Mr and Mrs Turnbull, who have lived in South Africa since the end of the war. Mr Turnbull's mother, Mrs Rogan, lives in Northumberland Street, Horden.

During the day it was very hot all the time Mr and Mrs Richardson were in Africa. "But often we had thunder and lightning during the night," said Mrs Richardson.

"There is no twilight, and with it being pitch dark out of doors we generally went to bed early - much earlier than at home.

Their six week voyage to and from South Africa was on the Athlone Castle. They had just stepped off this liner on their return to England when one of their grandsons, 21-year-old William Hagan, got on board. "But, unfortunately, we never met him," they said. William, who lives at Wheatley Hill, had just switched jobs as an engineer from the Queen Mary.

RIVER WEAR HERO WANTED NO FUSS
Friend Gave Shy Rescuers' Name To Police

Mr Jack Andrews, a 31-year-old local government officer and son of County Coun John Andrews, of Luke Terrace, Wheatley Hill, wanted no fuss after he had saved a four-year-old South Shields girl from drowning in the Wear at lunchtime on Wednesday.

But Jack's friend and working colleague, Alan Charlton, Station Road, Shotton, felt his courage should be recognised - and he gave his name to the police. As a result Jack's action has been reported to the Royal Humane Society.

Jack Andrews was enjoying a spot of lunch-time sunbathing when he heard cries of alarm from the riverside. Jack tore of his jacket and dashed into the river when he saw a little girl floating face downwards towards midstream from St Cuthbert's landing stage.

Left Without Giving Name

Jack brought the girl, who was unconscious, to the river bank, and then he had a hot bath in the public baths while Alan Charlton got him a change of clothing. Then ha left without giving his name or address.

Jack returned to his desk at 15 Old Elvet - minus 10s in silver which he lost from his pocket when he leaped into the water.

Jack did not see the girl's mother, who has three other children and had brought her daughter to Durham on a bus trip. She searched for Jack after her daughter had been taken to Dryburn Hospital, but even the police were unable to help her.

The little girl whom Jack Andrews rescued, Sheila Leahy, is now at home recovering from her experience.

LEFT FOR THORNLEY – The third chapter in the "Book of Ruth" closed last week at Wheatley Hill Colliery, when Mr William Ruth (46), 14 Stockton Street, Wheatley Hill, left to take up his appointment as head blacksmith at Thornley Colliery. For over 70 years the Ruths have been blacksmiths at Wheatley Hill Colliery - Matt, Jim, and Bill, father, son and grandson - giving an aggregate service of 112 Years.
21 August 1959

GARDENING SUCCESS – Seventy-year-old Mr William Poulson, a retired miner, of 1 Fred Peart Square, Wheatley Hill, won first prize and a cup for the best council house garden the village, in the annual competition organised among their tenants by

Easington Rural Council. Mr Poulson, whose hollyhocks and gladioli stand higher than himself in his flower packed front garden, retired five years ago after a mining career of 53 years.

VETERANS BOWLERS SUCCESS – The annual Mrs McLean pairs tournament organised among veteran members of Wheatley Hill Welfare Bowls Club was won this year by Messrss J Hodgson and W Kendall. Runners up were Messrss T Chaytor and W Snowdon, and third prize was won by Messrss T Lang and T Phillips and the fourth by Messrss O Warnes and C Raffell. The prizes were presented by Mrs McLean wife of Dr W G McLean, and on behalf of the veteran bowlers Mr J Thornton presented her with a bouquet and thanked her for her interest in the club.

4 September 1959

OUTSTANDING YEAR FOR THORNLEY CATHOLICS

In the Roman Catholic parish of Thornley this year may prove to be the most notable since the parish was formed in 1850.

Last June Mr James Finnerty, headmaster of St Godric's School, celebrated his silver jubilee. At a reception in his honour Mr Finnerty, reviewing his 25 years headship, said he was proud of his school record. Amongst his pupils were numbered priests, nuns, doctors, solicitors and many other executives.

On July 19 Mr Mark Hoban, eldest son of Mr and Mrs William Hoban, 2 Emmerson Square, Thornley, was raised to the order of priesthood at Ushaw College. Father Hoban, a former pupil of St Godric's, is the first parishioner to be ordained at Ushaw. At a reception the Rev Father H McNeill, parish priest, presented him with a cheque for £150 from the parishioners.

Father Columbo Adamson, another pupil at St Godric's, was ordained at Mill Hill, London, as a foreign missionary

Dr McNeill's Jubilee

On September 20, 1909, the present school, built on the side of the highway between Thornley and Wheatley Hill, was opened. The ceremony was performed by Canon Rooney of Darlington, in the presence of a large congregation. The priest-in- charge was the Rev Father W Toner, and the headmaster and infants' mistress was Mr John Bonar and Miss Mary Burke respectively.

The Rev Hugh McNeill, parish priest, will in October celebrate the silver jubilee of his ordination to the priesthood. Dr McNeill, who has been in the parish since 1952, was raised to the priesthood at the English College, Rome, on 28 October, 1934. He was educated at the St Cuthbert's Grammar School, Newcastle, Ushaw College and English College, Rome.

To close a happy year Dr McNeill has undertaken a course of reconstruction at St Godric's School which will cost £9000. Preparations are under way to honour Dr McNeill on his anniversary.

MAGISTRATE'S TALKS – Talk on the work of the magistrates' court and juvenile delinquency was given by Mr Edward Cain, deputy chairman of Castle Eden Magistrates' Bench at a meeting of Wheatley Hill Mothers Club on Wednesday.

BOWLS CHAMPION – Mr George Carr won the Wheatley Hill Welfare Bowls Championship Cup on Saturday, when he defeated Mr J Steel by 21 shots to 17 in the final. Mr Carr was captain of Wheatley Hill's senior cricket team during the season just ended.

HOLIDAY IN BELGIUM – Twenty-three pupils of Wheatley Hill Boy's Modern School had many interesting adventures to relate to their schoolfellows abut their holiday in Belgium when they returned to school on Monday. The party, in charge of the headmaster, Mr A Harris, returned home last Friday after an enjoyable eight day holiday at Blankenberg, on the Belgium Coast. It is the fifth year running that Mr Harris has organised such a holiday in Belgium. "The weather was excellent and we all spent a wonderful time", commented the headmaster this week. "The boys were no trouble at all."

11 September 1959

SOMETHING THE STATES HAVE NOT GOT
Reflections on a Holiday at Wheatley Hill

Mrs Jane Ward Taylor, of 527 Smith Street, Benton, Illinois, has just spent six months' holiday in England with her nephew and niece, Mr and Mrs James Martin, 4 Darlington Street, Wheatley Hill. This was the home of her parents, the late Mr and Mrs George and Dorothy Kent.

Mrs Taylor said, "This has been the most wonderful holiday of my life. I wanted to come home again and visit my family. I was last here in 1920. My family in America made the trip possible to celebrate my 70th birthday."

She went to America with her first husband, Mr Isaiah Ward, who at that time, 1914, was a miner at Horden. Promotion came to him in the State of Illinois and at the time of his death he was a mines inspector.

Found a Staunch Friend

When her husband died, Mrs Taylor found a staunch friend in Mr Marshall Taylor, who emigrated from Horden at the same time.

The couple were later married. Mr Taylor died 6 years ago. Mrs Taylor said, "I have had my ups and downs in the States. Twice I have been widowed but in spite of that, America has been kind to me and my family. My son Arthur is a mine manager, my daughter Clair is a sales representative in Chicago and Dorothy is a medical receptionist. But for all that, England to me is tops.

In her journeys through her native county, Mrs Taylor has found time to visit her relatives - Mr and Mrs John Ward, Mrs Dobbin, Mr Ben Bowes, Wheatley Hill (the brothers and sisters-in-law), Mrs J Everett, Cleadon and Mrs M Saint, Washington (her sisters) and her niece and nephew, Mr and Mrs Ward, Sedgefield. She was conveyed by Mr and Mrs Ward to Southampton by car yesterday and will sail on SS United States.

Early Memories of SE Durham

Recalling her early years in this county, Mrs Taylor said in an interview: "I remember Wheatley Hill as an isolated village. There was no road to Thornley save by a muddy field path which was nigh impossible in the depth of a bad winter. The new road linking the villages must be a great help to local people. I am also agreeably surprised at the number of 'buses which can be caught and the number of towns which can be reached from Wheatley Hill with little trouble. Your 'bus conductors are wonderful. I have been impressed with their courtesy and helpfulness wherever I have travelled."

Mrs Taylor was surprised that the local pit was still being worked. She said, "I thought it would have been worked out long ago. In America the pits are worked out long before 50 or 100 years."

Commenting on housing and home conditions Mrs Taylor expressed her great pleasure. "In my days at Wheatley Hill I remember the poor houses which housed the miner. I recall how hard women had to work in the home.

Water From Tap

Water was carried in from taps in the street and then boiled on the kitchen fire. The wash tub and the old possing-stick made washing day the hardest of the week. Then I recall the old steel and brass fenders and the gleaming fire-irons which were often the pride of the Durham miner's wife.

Mrs Taylor was impressed with our English health and medical services. "Here you really have something the Americans have not got. I am amazed that the doctors services, hospitals, pre and post natal care of children and your care of old people are provided for you by the State. In America we have no State facilities. If we want a doctor, or have to go into hospital or want our children's health checking, we have to pay and all are dear items. It has been known that people have had to mortgage their homes to provide money for hospitalisation.

Your health services are something of which you can be justly proud and something for which Americans envy you."

No Such Thing in the States

Mrs Taylor was impressed by the aged miners' homes and the bungalows for old people. She said that there was no such scheme in the States.

During her stay she visited the Wheatley Hill Over-60 Club. "This is a grand movement," she said. "It solves the problem of leisure for the old people and must reduce loneliness among the members."

Mrs Taylor is a active member of Benton Missionary Church. She is also a voluntary worker in hospitals. She said: "I am Sunshine Lady in these hospitals for old people. We write letters, read their mail for them and bring them various oddments from the canteen and wheel them down there in their chairs if they are well enough. As well as this service for the aged we also help the young married couples

168

with children. In order to help these couples to get out together, several of us do babysitting. We believe this makes life easier for the young people.

Smooth Marriages

"We regard this as piece of social service that makes marriage run more smoothly."

Mrs Taylor is an active member of the American Legion Auxiliary and is a member of the Rebecca Lodge, a religious organisation.

Mrs Taylor was visibly moved as she said, "I am glad my family made it possible for me to visit my own people and old home. People have been wonderfully kind. I am grateful to everyone and will take home with me many happy memories of what will possibly be my last visit to England.

LUDWORTH MAN RETIRES – Mr Joseph Cherry of Ludworth, who has been treasurer of Thornley Miners Lodge for 14 years, took his last payment of union contributions from the Thornley Miners on Friday. Mr Cherry retired from the Colliery some months ago but retained the position of treasurer of the lodge until his successor was elected.

He started work at Thornley Colliery in 1908 and one of the incidents he recalls was the "Boys' strike" in 1910 when putters and drivers refused to go down the pit. Mr Cherry says "I turned out to work not knowing of the trouble, but the older lads shouted me back from the lamp cabin to go home."

One of the duties of the treasurer of the lodge is to take union money each fortnight. Thornley Lodge still takes the money "over the desk". This method was instituted in the early days of the association when fortnightly pays were in operation, and it was at the desk that Mr Cherry retained the goodwill of the men who kept him in the position for 14 years.

THORNLEY MINER KILLED IN ROAD ACCIDENT – At the weekend a 34-year-old Thornley miner had a pair of leeks "stamped" in his back garden as a preliminary to them being entered in the annual leek show at the Queens Head Hotel, Thornley, next weekend. But the miner, Thomas Walker, who would have celebrated his 35th birthday in December, will not be at the show to see what prize his leeks won... he was killed in a road accident while returning home on his motor-cycle combination after visiting another show – the county show at Murton – on Saturday night.

Keen Leek Grower

"Tom was a member of the Queen's Head Hotel Leek Club," one of his brothers told our reporter at the week-end. "He was a keen leek grower and his leeks will still be exhibited in our show."

Mr Walker, who lived at 11 St Cuthbert's Road, Thornley, was the only person on the combination when the accident occurred, on the South Hetton to Haswell road, with two motor-vans. One of these vans, driven by John Edwards, 13 Lansbury Crescent, Haswell, was following him along the road, and the other, driven by

Richard Lawes, 8 Polygrane Road, Sunderland, was approaching from the direction of Haswell. The van drivers both escaped injury in the collision, but the two women passengers in the van driven by Lawes – his wife and another Sunderland woman, Mrs Ivy Barton – were taken to Leeholme Hospital, Easington but were discharged after treatment for minor injuries. The combination was wrecked and the vans were damaged.

Always Careful Driver

Mr Walker had been to the show at Murton, where his wife's parents live, and on his way back home had, it is understood, given a lift as far as Easington Lane to his brother-in law, John Robert Lawson, of Francis Street, Hetton. It was shortly after his brother-in-law had got off the machine that the accident occurred about 10.20pm.

Employed as a face worker at Thornley Colliery, Mr Walker leaves a widow, who is expecting another child, and three young daughters – Shirley, who will be five next month, Margaret Ann, who will be four on Christmas Day and Norah, who is two years of age. "He was always a careful driver," his widow, Mrs Nora Walker, told our reporter. "The children and I have gone all over with him – as far away as Liverpool and Blackpool – and he has always driven extremely carefully."

Mr Walker was one of a family of six - five brothers and a sister

18 September 1959

THORNLEY CATHOLIC SCHOOL JUBILEE

Fifty years ago, Thornley St Godric's Roman Catholic School, Built on the side of the Thornley to Wheatley Hill road, was opened by Canon Rooney, of Darlington, in the presence of a large congregation. It was designed to accommodate 240 pupils in six large class rooms with wide windows, centrally heated, with washbasins and separate domestic offices and boys' and girls' playgrounds.

It took the place of St Godric's of Hartlepool Street, Thornley, a large limestone structure that had served the community for 50 years. The old school was situated in an overcrowded mining area with long rows of low cottages bounded on all sides by public houses. Its playground was the unmade streets between the rows of dwellings and its water supply the street tap. In one large class 160 scholars were instructed in reading, writing and arithmetic. Their writing material, slates and slate pencils, with a lump of rag or coat sleeves to wipe their slates clean. For 3d a week his boys and girls were taught to become eligible for employment.

Mr John Bonar was the last headmaster of the old school, and the first of the new. He was followed by Mr Isaac Taylor, Mr Robert Smith and the present Head, Mr James Finnety, who has just celebrated his 25th anniversary.

WHEATLEY HILL MAN'S HEROISM

An heroic deed in his earlier years which resulted in him visiting Buckingham Palace to be decorated by the late King George V, is recalled by the death of Mr George

William Lofthouse, 75-year-old retired miner, of 15 Aged Miners' Homes, Wheatley Hill.

It was in recognition of his courageous action in descending a deep quarry and trying to save the life of a fellow workman overcome by gas, that Mr Lofthouse was presented with the Edward Medal of the Second Class. He also received a framed certificate and £20 from the Carnegie Hero Fund Trust and a parchment recording his heroism.

On August 4, 1914 – the day war broke out – blasting operations were in progress at the bottom of a 21 ft deep pit at Wingate Quarry, the parchment records. The morning shift had fired three charges of gunpowder (between 30 and 40 pounds) and later when a workman was lowered down in a "kibble" or tub, he was overcome by fumes. His mate at the top shouted for assistance and Mr Lofthouse, who was working some distance away, immediately ran to the pit and descended be a rope to attempt a rescue. He managed to get hold of the workman and signalled to be raised to the top in the "kibble." Both men fell out as the "kibble" was being hauled up.

Workmen at the top swung the "kibble" about to clear away the fumes and eventually both men were brought out unconscious. Artificial respiration was applied but the man Mr Lofthouse had attempted to save – a Mr George Hayes – could not be revived. It was two hours before Mr Lofthouse himself recovered consciousness.

"Mr Lofthouse was experienced in the use of explosives and knew the danger of descending into the fumes," the citation ends. "His action was therefore extremely courageous." Mr Lofthouse's health was so affected that he was unable to return to work for about six months.

25 September 1959

MR AND MRS POTTS LEAVE THORNLEY

A popular couple in Thornley for the last 20 years, Mr and Mrs John Wilfred Potts, left Thornley last week to make their home at West Hartlepool, where Mr Potts was appointed to a headship at West View Junior Mixed School a short while ago. Mr Potts has been on the staff of Thornley Mixed School for 20 years. He has been organist at Thornley Waterloo Street Methodist Church for many years, where his father has been choir-master. His grandfather Mr John William Potts was for many years chairman of Thornley Parish Council.

Mrs Potts, a native of Trimdon, has been a very enthusiastic member of Thornley Women's Institute. Two years ago she presented the case of the WI on the destructive action of the atomic fall-out and its effect on future generations in the Albert Hall, London. She has been a regular collector in the village for any worthy charity.

Both Mr and Mrs Potts have been associated with various drama groups in the village, taking parts in plays, presenting them and organising them.

23 October 1959

DEATH OF MRS SARAH J BARNETT

Thornley Bow Street Methodist Church was full for the funeral service, conducted by the Rev Reginald Hancock, of Mrs Sarah Jane Barnett (Rosie), wife of Mr John Henry Barnett, Hartlepool Street, Thornley.

Mrs Barnett (65) spent most of her life in Thornley. She was born in Scotland and spent a few years in Wales with her father and then removed with her mother's brother, Police Sergeant Mathew Cox (who was transferred from West Hartlepool) to Thornley in 1901.

Mrs Barnett was one of the most loved women in Thornley. Although heavily handicapped by paralysis she has been, by the help of her husband or sons, able to meet all the people of the village on the public seat in Hartlepool Street near her home. Here she sat every day listening to their trials and troubles.

Mr and Mrs Barnett bought the business of Mr Thomas Henry Ashford about 32 years ago, and they now employ four sons and one grandson. Mrs Barnett was a life long Methodist and a member of Bow Street Sisterhood.

30 October 1959

VISITORS FROM AUSTRALIA AT THORNLEY

Mr and Mrs J Scott, Fenroyd, Thornley, are accommodating two visitors from Australia who emigrated in 1926. They are Mr and Mrs W H Tilley, 79 First Street, Weston, New South Wales – Mr Scott's sister and Mrs Scott's brother.

Mr Tilley, who was born in Haswell, worked at South Hetton, Ludworth and Tursdale. In Australia he has been employed in the coal mines in which he found the seams to be 20ft thick and less arduous to work than the seams in Durham.

Both Mr and Mrs Tilley have noticed the tremendous changes that have taken place since they left, especially the demolition of the old colliery houses and the rebuilding of a new village.

– The colliery town in which Mr Tilley lives has a large population of people from Northumberland and Durham. It has the name of "Geordie Town". In the local team for some years Jimmy Mordue, nephew of Jackie Mordue, of Sunderland fame, and Billy Davison, of Sacriston, have played.

Now retired at 60 years of age with a pension of £40 a month, Mr Tilley recalls an amusing incident which took off some of the home sickness when he arrived. The last shift he worked at Ludworth Colliery he was lowered down the shaft by Mr Fred Hutchinson, brakesman, the first shift he worked at Weston Colliery he was again let down by the same man!

THEY WANT THORNLEY TIDIED UP

Mrs D Swinburne, chairman of Thornley Women's Institute, Mrs A Todd, Mrs T Lincoln and Mrs A Clark attended Thornley Parish Council meeting to discuss the cleaning and tidying up of the village. They were welcomed by Coun J Nicholson.

Mrs Swinburne said the members of the WI were deeply concerned with the dilapidated state of the village. Houses were pulled down in 1939, but stones and bricks and rubbish still remained on the sites. The Woman's Institute are compiling a history of the village and there is little doubt that this period will be the most sordid in its records.

Mrs A Todd and Mrs Clark dealt with the question of litter lying about the main road and footpaths and gutters of the main street, especially at the 'bus-stops and in the Market Place after tradesmen had left.

. Mrs Lincoln asked why all the lights were on one side of the street, and why they cannot have some more and better lights.

Coun Walker gave the position of the clearance of slum sites from the point of view of the Council, who were, said Coun Walker, "blocked, frustrated and power-less" against the county plan.

Coun Nicholson, dealing with the electricity supply and distribution, said last year the Council had expended £3,396 on the renewal of plant; they had also expend-ed nearly £1,000 on current consumption. He also stated that the extra fittings and lights which were going to be installed would cost another £640. A penny rate gives £110.

Coun A Bushby said in his opinion members of the WI should come along to the annual meeting of the Council and see how the money is expended.

The Council decided to fall in line with the suggestion of Mrs Swinburne and take part in the Tidy Village Competition for 1960.

A letter received from Mr F Parkin, secretary of No 3 Area NCB, stated that the complaint of the filthy condition of Thornley- Wheatley Hill footpath owing to the tipping of coal, which had appeared in the Press, was attended to immediately. The Council decided to send a copy of Mr Parkin's letter to Mr Williams, who brought the complaint foreword.

THORNLEY FUNERAL OF SALVATIONIST
Captain E Stock, of Shotton officiated at the Salvation Army Citadel, Thornley at the funeral of Mrs Alice Dunning (76) St Bede Crescent, Thornley, who collapsed and died while having breakfast at Winterton Hospital.

Mrs Dunning was born in Wigan. She went to live in Thornley district about 60 years ago. A life long Salvationist, she was one of the few regular members left of the old Thornley Corps.

Her late husband, M Jonathan Dunning, was one of the old soldiers of the 1914 – 18 war of Thornley who gained the Military Medal and received an inscribed gold watch from the War Distinctions Committee.

Mrs Dunning leaves three sons and two daughters, 21 grand children and two great-grandchildren.
6 November 1959

REMEMBRANCE
SHADFORTH AND LUDWORTH
At both the Parish Church at Shadforth and the Mission Church at Ludworth, there was fitting observance of Remembrance Day. The Rector (the Rev A R L prentice) conducted a Requiem Eucharist at both churches. Ludworth British Legion's open-air

service at the War Memorial at the east end of Front Street was well attended. The procession through the main street was led by Legion members headed by the branch president. Mr A Winter and standard bearer, Mrs Thompson. The service was conducted by the parochial reader, Mr T Johnson, who gave the address.

13 November 1959

WHEATLEY HILL GOLDEN WEDDING

A retired Wheatley Hill colliery official, who had a narrow escape from death when he was trapped beneath a big fall of stone at the colliery more than 40 years ago, celebrated his golden wedding on Tuesday. "To look at me today you would not think I had been so near to death," the official, Mr Nicholas Smithson, 24 Peterlee Cottages, Wheatley Hill, told our reporter, who called to offer congratulations.

Mr Smithson enjoys quite good health, but his wife, whose maiden name was Dorothy Ann Gutcher, has been in poor health for the past four years. It was when he was working as a master shifter at Wheatley Hill Colliery during the 1914 – 18 war that Mr Smithson received severe injuries to his back when pinned to the ground by the fall of stone.

"Twenty eight tubs of stone had to be shifted before I was freed, and it was perhaps the fact that two big slabs of stone formed a sort of bridge over me that I was not killed," said Mr Smithson.

Deputy at Thornley

Born at Shildon, Mr Smithson began work at Middridge Colliery shortly before his 13th birthday, earning 10½d a shift of ten hours as a trapper boy. When he was 16 he went to Wheatley Hill and was employed there for 21 years, mostly as deputy overman and master shifter, before transferring to Thornley Colliery.

Apart from a short period on stone work, Mr Smithson was a deputy overman for 26 years at Thornley until his retirement nine years ago after a mining career of 52 years. In another pit accident Mr Smithson lost one of his toes.

Mrs Smithson was born at Hetton-le-Hole, but has lived in Wheatley Hill since she was seven. Both she and her husband have been actively associated with All Saints Church, Wheatley Hill, all their married life. Mrs Smithson was formerly a member of the Mothers' Union, but her recent ill health has prevented her from continuing her membership. Her husband has been a sidesman at the church for many years. Mrs Smithson has also been a member of the local branch of the Women's Institute for many years.

Over-60 Club Members

The couple are both members of Wheatley Hill Over-60 Club. I have enjoyed every minute of since I joined," said Mr Smithson. Since his wife's illness Mr Smithson has helped considerably with the housework. "Pottering about the house and in the garden keeps me pretty well occupied," he said.

Mr and Mrs Smithson, who were married in St Bartholomew's Parish Church, Thornley, have two married daughters, Mrs Jane Judson, of Bromsgrove, near Birmingham, and Mrs Ethel Shepherd, of Blackpool, and two grandchildren.

On their golden wedding day the couple received many beautiful cards and presents as well as several bouquets. Their elder daughter, Mrs Judson, made them a two-tier "golden wedding" cake. She brought it with her on a recent visit, and the cake is to be cut at a quiet family party on Sunday.

WED 50 YEARS, MR STRAGHAN MAKES WIFE'S BREAKFAST

Mr and Mrs Joseph Straughan, of 8 Aged Miners Cottages, Thornley, celebrated their golden wedding anniversary last week.

At the time of their wedding Jos Straughan, as he is known, was a young coal hewer at Thornley Colliery and Ada his bride was keeping house for her father Bill Gildar, a blacksmith at Richardson Westgarths, West Hartlepool.

At the outbreak of war in 1914 Mr Straughan enlisted and while serving in France at Armentieres his right leg was blown off below the knee.

Two Shillings a day

On her husbands' discharge from the service, Mrs Straughan was obliged to go out to work to supplement the small pension they got, and some occasions, says Mrs Straughan "I worked from 8 o'clock in the morning until 5 o'clock at night for 2s a day, possing, scrubbing, mangling and ironing.

Mr and Mrs Straughan have three sons and one daughter, 12 grandchildren and one greatgrandchild. Two of her sons are blacksmiths at Thornley Colliery and their second son, Malcolm, during the last war was a sergeant in the 51st division of the Gordon Highlanders.

Mr and Mrs Straughan are happy in their Aged Miners' Cottage. Ada is now 73 and Joe is 71, but Jos gets up early each morning and makes Ada's breakfast before she goes to Mass every morning. Inside the house he hops about on his one leg, but outside he is a familiar figure on his two crutches. He has only missed one Durham Big Meeting since 1918 and he marches with the band and banner the full mile and a quarter route in Thornley and in Durham from the bus stop to the Race Course.

Mrs Straughan has been a member of the Women's Institute for 34 years and at their last meeting she was presented with a large bouquet of carnations on the occasion of her jubilee. She was also a pioneer member of Thornley British Legion Women's Section 34 years ago.

Fifty guests were present on Saturday in the Catholic Club, Thornley.

Their daughter and son-in law, Mr and Mrs J Duddy, and the six grandchildren were not at the party but they sent their wedding gifts, a golden half sovereign of Edward VII, dated 1902, ornamented, to be carried on Jos's watch chain, and a cameo set in gold for Ada.

20 November 1959

THORNLEY HEALTH VISITOR'S FIND

Miss Margaret Tunney, a County Council health visitor, of Theodore Cottage, Thornley, visited many countries during and after the last war as a nursing sister. She was attached to a hospital in Jerusalem and while sightseeing at Ascension Tower near the hill of Kopas in 1945 she picked up a small coin a little larger than a sixpenny piece.

Last week, Miss Tunney who has mementoes of her travels once again came across her little coin. She asked her brother-in-law, Mr Leslie Rowley, a group surveyor at Easington Colliery, if he would send it to the British Museum asking them to accept it if they found it to have a special significance.

Mr Rowley has received a reply thanking him for the offer and asking him for the name of the young lady who found it. The letter explains that the coin is a 20 nummia piece of the Bysantine Emperor Tiberious Constantine and his wife Anastasia dated in the fifth year of his reign A D 578. It was minted at Thessalonica. Although we have similar specimens, says Mr John Walker, Keeper of the Department of Coins and Medals, we are very glad to accept your offer because it is clearer than the ones we have.

20 November 1959

PROMISING STUDENT OF THORNLEY

The trustees of the Miners' Welfare Scholarship and Student Exhibition scheme have awarded 18-year-old Malcolm Galloway a non-recurring scholarship for an honours degree course in mathematics at the Imperial College of Science and Technology at London University.

Malcolm is the eldest son of Mr and Mrs David Galloway, 55 Dunelm Road, Thornley. At Wellfeild A J Grammar School, Wingate, he demonstrated he was a student of great ability. At the age of 15 he took ten subjects in GCE and did well in all He was successful in Advanced Level subjects and was awarded a State scholarship at 17.

Music has always appealed to Malcolm. He was organist at Thornley Bow Methodist Church for four years. He is also an accomplished player of the viola and was a member of the National Youth Orchestra. Since going to London University in September he has become a member of the Collage Orchestra and pianist of a University Drama Group.

Macolm is grandson of the late Mr David Galloway, of Quarrington Hill, who preached in Thornley Methodist Circuit Plan till he was 84. His father is a miner.

27 November 1959

NCB BRASS BAND CONTEST

Mr H Nattrass, OBE, of the Durham Divisional Coal Board Welfare Organisation, presided over a brass band contest in the Mainsforth Miner's Welfare Hall, Ferryhill.

He paid tribute to the Dean and Chapter Colliery Ambulance Brigade, who had won the Grand Prior's Trophy. It was his ambition to see one of the brass bands from the Durham coalfield bring back the senior prize from the National Brass Band competition in London.

In section D eight bands from Dawdon, Deaf Hill, Fishburn, Handen Hold, Hylton, Lumley, Mainsforth and and Ryhope collieries took part.

Results were: 1, Handen Hold, 168 points; 2, Mainsforth, 167 points; 3, Dawdon, 165 points.

In section B four bands took part from Boldon, Brancepeth, Thornley and Wheatley Hill collieries.

The winners were Wheatley Hill with 178 points, Thornley Colliery (175) were second, and Boldon Colliery (173) were third.

Mr L Davies, of Manchester, was the adjudicator, and Mr G H Braithwaite, general manager No 4 Area, presented the prizes.
27 November 1959

AWARD TO SAFETY OFFICER – Harold Todd, 42 East Lea, Thornley, has received from the National Coal Board an engraved silver emblem in recognition of ten years service with the Mining Rescue Brigade. Mr Todd, 42-year-old Safety Officer at Thornley Colliery, already has the Boards bronze emblem for five years service. He took part in rescue work at Easington Colliery in March, 1951, when 83 lives were lost, and also at Hordon Colliery in Maech1953.
27 November 1959

WHEATLEY HILL BL POPPY DAY

Mrs M E Parsley, Poppy day organizer for Wheatley Hill women's section of the British Legion, reports that the effort realized £115 15s 9d. This total included £6 19s 3d special efforts within the legion section;£5 from the Remembrance day collection in the Parish Church; and £1 donation from Wheatley Hill RAOB Lodge.

Mrs Parsley had some straight forward comments to make on the result. She said "£115 15s 9d appears to be a worthy figure on the surface. But that figure represents a decrease on last year of £17. This does not mean that the public of Wheatley Hill is less generous than last year. Our difficulty was that we could not get all the collectors we required. Last year we had 25 collectors. This year we could only muster 18. I hope that by another year more may realize their responsibility and that enough collectors will volunteer for this necessary service.
11 December 1959

WHEATLEY HILL GOLDEN WEDDING
Memories of 2s.6d A Week

How times have changed since the beginning of the century was vividly illustrated by a 68-year-old Wheatley Hill housewife, Mrs Rose Hannah Lang, who on Monday celebrated her golden wedding.

When she left school, Mrs Lang recalled in an interview with our reporter, she went straight into domestic service as a nursemaid at West Hartlepool, and was paid the "princely" sum of 2s 6d a week.

"And we knew what work was in those days," said Mrs Lang. "It was hard graft all the time. I could only get back home to Wheatley Hill once every three months from where I worked, because I just did not have the money." Later Mrs Lang worked as a cook-general and earned 7s a week. "That was considered a good wage in those days," she said.

Out to Earn

Mrs Lang was the eldest of a family of 12. "As soon as we were old enough we had to go out and earn our living," she said.

Mrs Lang, whose maiden name was Firmstone, and her husband Thomas, who is 72, live in a cosy prefabricated bungalow at 9 Taylorson Crescent. She enjoys quite good health, being able to do all her own housework, but her husband is just recovering from a serious illness.

"I am feeling much better know," he said.

A native of Walker, Mr Lang began work in the shipyards there as a steam hammer – driver after passing a "Labour" examination at school. When he was 15½, however, he left the shipyards and took up a mining career at Wheatley Hill. Later he was employed at Shotton, but from his marriage worked at Thornley Colliery until his retirement about six years ago. "I have done practically every type of job down the pit and finished on datal work," he said.

Mrs Lang was born at Brandon, but was only two years old when she went to Wheatley Hill with her parents- they lived in Quarry Street, now demolished, which was only a stone's throw from where she now lives.

Over 60 Club Members

Both Mr and Mrs Lang have been members of Wheatley Hill Over-60 Club since its inception, and Mr Lang has served on the committee, Mr Lang has also been actively associated with Wheatley Hill Welfare Bowls Club for many Years, he was secretary one year, and when working at Thornley took an active interest in the affairs of the local miners' lodge, serving both on the committee and as auditor.

A life long Methodist, Mrs Lang has had a long association with Patton Street Methodist Church in the village and is a member of the Women's Own.

The couple, who were married at Easington, have three sons and a daughter, and eight grandchildren. Their daughter, Mrs Nora Phillipo, lives in Colchester. Their eldest son, Donald, lives in Thornley, while Harold recently moved to Luton, where he has taken up new employment in a car factory, and Maurice lives in Wheatley Hill.

As a surprise golden wedding gift from their family, Mr and Mrs Lang received a 17-inch television set. "It was a wonderful surprise," they said, "and already it has given us many hours of pleasure."

A family celebration party was held at the couple's home on Monday. The couple have been readers of the "Durham Chronicle" practically all their married life.

11 December 1959

WOMEN BOWLERS' AWARDS – For the second successive year, Mrs E Hall, secretary of Wheatley Hill Ladies' Bowl Club, has won the club's Championship Cup, and she was presented with the trophy at the annual prize-giving social evening in the Welfare Hall, Wheatley Hill, last week. Mrs E Atkinson was runner-up. Mrs Hall also won the Festival Bowl, with Mrs A Ord runner-up, while Mrs Ord won the William Jones Cup, with Mrs Hall runner-up. The trophies and prizes were presented by Mrs W G MacLean of Wheatley Hill, who was introduced by the club chairman, Mrs J Hodson. Officials of the North East Ladies' Bowling League were among the guests.

CLUB EFFORT – Organised by the officials and committee of Wheatley Hill Over-60 Club, a social evening was held in the Welfare Hall to raise funds for the Christmas party and annual trip. Messrss C Raffell and T Simpson were MCs for whist, and Mr J Steele was MC for dominoes. Prizewinners were: Whist, Miss E Simpson, Mrs R Gregory, Mrs V Fairless, Mrs R Ord, M Walker and Mrs Newby; dominoes, Mrs M Carter, Mrs L Mason, Mr A Collingwood and Mr J Bradshaw. Mr H Bellas officiated as steward for the dancing, music for which w\as supplied by Mr J Pratt's Band.

11 December 1959

WORKMEN'S CLUB PARTY – Each retired member of Wheatley Hill Workmen's Club received a Christmas gift of £1 at the annual Christmas party in the club's concert hall. About 300 retired members and their wives, and widows over 60 were seated to an excellent "high tea" and afterwards were entertained by the "Racketeers" concert party from Darlington. Mr W Henderson, the club chairman, presided and the old folk were welcomed by the club secretary, Mr B Aitken.

CLUB "TREAT" – About 140 retired members of Wheatley Hill Discharged and Demobilised Soldiers and Sailors' Club, and their wives, were entertained to the annual party at the club headquarters, They were welcomed by the chairman of the club, Mr G Reay, who also presided at an excellent concert given after a knife-and-fork tea by a Middlesbrough party. On behalf of the guests, Mr F Simpson, under-manager at Wheatley Hill Colliery, and Mr E Cain, thanked the club management committee for their generosity and extended seasonal greetings to all the old folk. Each married couple received a Christmas gift of 30s, and each retired widower £1. Mr H Syson, secretary was responsible for the arrangements, together with the treasurer, Mr R Burnip.

18 December 1959

OLD SCOUTS DINNER – The importance of Scouting in building character and providing young people with a useful outlet for their leisure, was stressed by one of the founders of the Wheatley Hill Scout movement, Mr R Cowperthwaite, at the fourth annual dinner of Wheatley Hill Old Scouts Association in The Three Tuns Hotel, Durham, on Saturday. Forty-five members were present and they and their guests were welcomed by the chairman, Mr J Armstrong. The Wheatley Hill Group of Scouts had long flourished, said Mr Cowperthwaite, and members of 25 years ago were still giving valuable help to the present Group and encouraging it in its activities. The Association pledged its help in rebuilding the present Scout headquarters. Entertainment was by members of the Scout Group, with Mr J Cain accompanist. Arrangements were made by Coun R Watson.

18 December 1959

PARISH COUCIL WAS NOT CONSULTED
Complaints by Wingate Representatives To RDC

When a councilor reported to Wingate Parish council on Monday that, though the council had not been informed in any way, approval had been given by Easington Rural Council to a big timber yard close to Front Street, Wheatley Hill, and that already a brick building had gone up, other councillors declared that they could at least have been "told about the matter."

"The parish council should have been brought more into the picture when an important proposal like this was being considered," said the chairman, Coun J H Charlton. "After all, we are in much closer contact with the people of the villages."

"The other authorities had "by-passed" the parish council", said Coun J Carr. "It would only have been courteous for them to let us know what was happening," he added. "We might as well not be here if we are not to be told about such thing".

Tidy Villages

Even if the parish council could not have stopped the scheme for the timber yard, at least they could have been invited to give their observations, said Coun Charlton. Another councillor said there was much talk these days about "tidy villages" but surely a timber yard adjoining the main street of a village would certainly not make it look "very tidy."

After the chairman had said they were "quite perturbed" about the matter, the clerk (Mr J Harper) was instructed to write to Easington RDC and the County Planning Officer, complaining that no consultations had taken place with the parish council before approval had been given for the timber yard.

18 December 1959

WHEATLEY HILL HORSEKEEPER FOR 40 YEARS

Mr Thomas Robson, 32 Luke Terrace, Wheatley Hill, has retired from work at Wheatley Hill Colliery after giving 51 years to the industry. Mr Robson, a widower, has one son, Thomas, who works underground at Thornley Colliery.

Mr Robson, born at Hesleden, started work on the 'belts' at the local colliery. In 1914 he volunteered for military service and served with the 5th Durham Light Infantry. He came through some of the toughest fighting of the First World War. After demobilisaion he returned to Wheatley Hill Colliery and had a short spell coal leading. He then went down the pit as horsekeeper. He held this post for 40 years.

Mr Robson said, "When I became horse keeper in 1919 we had 96 ponies to look after. There were six of us for the job. Today we only have 25 and three to look after them. The falling numbers are due to mechanisations below ground. But however much machinery and mechanical haulage is introduced there will always be places where the pit pony is needed. Today at Wheatley Hill they are used in the North West and South West Districts.

Better Conditions

Mr Robson said, "Many changes have come into the pits for the better conditions of the miners. I am glad to say that better conditions have come for the ponies. When I started as horse keeper 40 years ago it was no unusual thing for them to be kept working two or three shifts continuously. Now they can only be worked one shift at a time and must be rested in the stables. They have a statutory 48 hour week."

Mr Robson recalls the long uninspiring streets of drab grey miners cottages. He went on "I recall where there were no decent roads and in winter the backs of the houses were simply quagmires and the women had a job to keep their houses clean. Conditions at the colliery and in the village itself were changed largely through the efforts of men like Jack Morgan and Peter Lee."

Mr Robson is a member of Wheatley Hill Constitutional Club and has been a member of the Workmen's Club since it was opened.

18 December 1959

KILLED IN A COLLISION

Conflicting evidence about whether the driver of a motor-cycle combination overtook a van before being in collision with an approaching van was heard at the inquest at Castle Eden on Friday on the driver of the combination, Thomas Walker (35) a miner, of 11, St Cuthbert's Road, Thornley, who was killed instantly. Walker, who was a married man with a young family, died of a fractured skull and other multiple injuries, said Dr Alexandre Mackenzie.

The jury returned a verdict of "accidental death."

The accident occurred on Saturday night, September 12, on the Haswell to South Hetton road. Shortly before the accident Walker had stopped at Easington Lane to drop off his brother-in-law, John Robert Lawson, Francis Street, Hetton-le hole, whom he had given a "lift" forom Murton.

The Coroner, Mr T V Devey, addressing the jury, said it seemed to him that the "main point" about the accident was that both the motor-cycle combination and the oncoming van were travelling too close to the white line when they collided.

25 December 1959

1960

WHEATLEY HILL RETIREMENT

After a mining career of 51 years, most of which has been spent at Wheatley Hill Colliery, Mr James Robert Gill, 20 Byron Street, Wheatley Hill, who was 65 in October, has retired from work.

"I've done practically every kind of job down the pit, except deputy work, and have had quite a few 'bits of bumps' but have never been involved in any serious accident, thank goodness.

Mr Gill was born at West Hartlepool. He began work at Wheatley Hill colliery when he was 14 as a lamp-carrier and then a trapper- boy and was paid a 1s per ten-hour shift. For a short time he worked at Thornley and Shotton collieries and during the 1914-18 war he served in the Royal Field Artillery. He was severely wounded in 1916 in the Battle of the Somme but made a good recovery and went back "into the line" again.

For most of his mining career Mr Gill was employed as a stone-man and it was in this capacity that he retired. His only son, James Robert, is a deputy at Thornley colliery, and his only daughter, Mrs Patricia Draycott, lives at Billingham.

Mr Gill and his wife, who is very nimble with her fingers- she has knitted some beautiful garments, and artificial flowers she makes as a hobby are as near the "real thing" as anything in the shops- have four grandchildren. Mr Gill has had a long association with Wheatley Hill Workmen's Club and has served on the committee on a number of occasions.

1 January 1960

WI PARTY

The children of members of Ludworth W I were entertained to a party in the Village Hall, where the Institute president welcomed the small guests. Tea was provided and each child received a gift of fruit. After tea a performance of the pantomime, The Sleeping Beauty, was given by the children of the Waterloo Street Methodist Church, Thornley.

HIGHER AWARDS FOR FANCIERS

Mr John Bradley and Mr George Hutchinson, East Veiw, Thornley, whose entry gained the highly recommended card in the class for cocks Y B, flown 75 miles or over, at the International Show if Racing Pigeons in London last month, have been notified of a revision of the awards. This follows the original first prize winner being disqualified because of an infringement of his Homing Union rules. As a result, the Thornley pair now receive the very highly commended card in the one-place- higher re-arrangement of the class awards.

8 **January 1960**

THORNLEY GIRL COLLECTS £41 FOR MISSIONS

Mr Kenneth Hetherington, Overseas Missions organising secretary of Thornley Waterloo Street Methodist Church, reports that £160 14s 8d has been raised by the church last year. Maureen Carter, a Juvenile Missionary Association collector, has raised the highest amount for a juvenile in the history of the church. She collected £41 8s 8d. Peter Lambert collected over £27.

Mr Hetherington intimates that a good deal of the credit for the church's fine effort must go to Mr Peter Gowland, J M A secretary. Under his leadership, Sunday School scholars have raised £132 18s 4d   80 per cent of the total income.

Bronze medals and bars were awarded to the following J M A collectors for sums of £5 or over; Maureen Carter, Peter Lambert, Denise Elliot, Audrey Parkin, Elaine Day, Joyce Hubbard, Margaret Wilson, and Margaret Holmes.

Other J M A collectors were Melvyn Mains, Robert Walls, Mary Luke, June Musgrave, Trevor Fisher, Lawrence Slater and Maureen Porter.

BANDSMEN IN MOURNING
Death of Mr E Mordica Wheatley Hill

The death took place suddenly at his home of Mr Edward Mordica (49), 5 Seventh Street Wheatley Hill. He returned from his shift at Thornley colliery on Wednesday night and had supper. He collapsed at the foot of the stairs and died later. He is survived by his wife, Mrs Alice Mordica and two unmarried sons Eddie and Alan.

Mr Mordica was born at Coxhoe and started work at Bowburn colliery at 14. He went to work at Thornley colliery 22 years ago. An accident caused him to leave underground mining and work in the lamp cabin and later in the dry-cleaner. Ten years ago, he and his wife moved to Wheatley Hill so that their son Eddie, who was a polio victim might get to school without the difficulty of travelling down from Thornley.

The passion of Mr Mordica's life was brass band music. He played the G Trombone.

In Band At 15

He made an early start and plated in Coxhoe band at the age of 15. At various times in his career he has played for Blackhall, Horden, Thornley and Wheatley Hill. He played in the Albert Hall, London, with the Blackhall band and has played in London with the Wheatley Hill band. His younger son Alan played with his father in the latter band.

MR Mordica had two spells as secretary for the Wheatley Hill band covering about ten years. He was also secretary of the Thornley band for some time.

As a schoolboy he played for Coxhoe school in the Kelloe League and took a big interest in sport in the village.

THORNLEY PRESENTATION TO EX-MINER

Tribute was paid to Mr Joseph Cherry (65), Barnard Avenue, Ludworth, who has held the position of treasurer of Thornley Miners' Lodge for 22 years and a similar position in Thornley Mining Federation Board for eight years. At a reception at Thornley on Saterday, Mr George Bennett, chairman of Thornley Mining federation Board, presided.

Mr J R Greener and Mr Sam Greener, two of the youngest members of the Federation Board, presented Mr Cherry with a chiming clock and a wrist watch. Mr E Carter, chairman of Thornley Miners' Lodge and secretaryof the Federation Board, said that during Mr Cherry's term of office a consolidation of all the funds contributed to by the workmen of the colliery had taken place and Mr Cherry had been responsible for £250,000. Each year since the change sums of £2,000 had been contributed to the old folk's Christmas Treat, and summer outings, over £800, to a children's sport day, and £300 to sports clubs.

Entertainment was given by Mr Sandywell, Mr Oswald, Mr Parker, Mr Dove and Me Webb, Mr Dalton, landlord of the hotel was thanked for his services. Refreshment were provided by Mr and Mrs Carter.

15 January 1960

LOCOMOTIVE STRUCK CAR
Miraculous escape at Wheatley Hill

Four members of the teaching profession, including a married couple, were among the six people in a car which was stuck by a National Coal Board locomotive on a single–line railway crossing at Wheatley Hill on Tuesday morning, but although the car, with the two front buffers of the locomotive stuck through its nearside windows, was carried 20 yards along the line, no-one was seriously injured.

"If ever I have seen a miracle I have seen one today," the shunter on the locomotive, William Bolam Harrison (44), 3 Fourteenth Street, Wheatley Hill, told our reporter later. It was certainly a miracle that no-one was killed, he said.

Only one of the passengers in the car, Mrs Jean Gargett, 28 North Road East, Wingate, was taken to hospital. She suffered from shock and facial injuries. The others all suffered from cuts and bruises and shock but after attention in the Wheatley Hill colliery ambulance room from Dr A P Gray, were allowed to return home. The nearside of the car was wrecked.

Buffers Through Car Windows

The car, which had come from the direction of Thornley railway crossing, was travelling up a bank towards the Wheatley Hill crossing which is near a bend close to the colliery yard. It was driven by William Strong (35), 7 Northumberland Place

184

Peterlee, a lecturer at Durham Technical College. Accompanying him were his wife Margaret, and their six-year-old daughter Susan, whom he had intended dropping off about 200 yards further along the road at Wheatley Hill Infants' School, where Mrs Strong is a teacher.

Also in the car in addition to Mrs Gargett, who lectures at the same college as Mr Strong, were Miss Elizabeth Moon, 96 Acre Rigg Road, Peterlee, a teacher at Wheatley hill Infants' School, and Ralph Hughes (27), a miner, 61 Laybourne Place, Peterlee.

The driver of the locomotive, Thomas Holmes (52), 11 York Street, Wheatley Hill, had just left the colliery yard with his load of wagons on the mile journey to the central coal-washery at the neighbouring colliery at Thornley when the accident occurred.

The railway line crosses one of the roads leading into Wheatley Hill and before reaching the road, said Mr Holmes, he had stopped his engine in accordance with procedure, to make sure the way was clear. He started to cross after being given the signal to proceed.

"The next thing I knew the car was on the line and the buffers of my engine went straight through its windows and pushed it along the line." added Mr Holmes, who pulled up as quickly as possible.

Held In A Firm Grip

The shunter, Mr Harrison, said he saw no traffic on the road after he jumped off the locomotive and so he waved on the driver of the locomotive. "He blew his whistle and drove on then, in a flash, the car was in front of the locomotive and was pushed along," added Mr Harrison.

Mr Harrison and a plate-layer, David Scott of Johnson Estate, Wheatley Hill, who had been keeping watch at the bottom side of the line and jumped clear when the car approached, ran to the car to give assistance to its occupants.

"The side was smashed in," said Mr Harrison," but with the exception of one woman, whose face was covered in blood, they were all able to walk away from the car. They appeared to be badly shaken, however."

In the circumstances it was perhaps fortunate, said a senior police officer, that the buffers had gone through the car windows. "This probably prevented the car from turning over in the path of the locomotive," he added. "The buffers held the car upright in a firm grip and pushed it along."

The road was blocked for about 80 minutes after the accident until a breakdown lorry towed away the car and the locomotive was able to clear the crossing.

22 January 1960

SOME COSTS OF BUILDING IN THE 1830s
Thornley scrap book turns back pages of the past

Mr Sammy Edwards, a 74-year-old ex-miner of 6 Shinwell Crescent, Thornley, owns an interesting scrap book. Torn and disfigured in some places, it would not command a place on a book shelf, but it was the treasured possession of his late wife, an heirloom from her great grandfather and her first effort to make a scrap book.

As a girl at home one day, Mrs Edwards discovered in a cupboard an old accounts book. It had been the property of her great grandfather, Thomas Dunlop, a builder and contractor. It was just the thing for her cuttings, pictures and cartoons from newspapers and magazines.

Years afterwards, long after she had married Mr Edwards, the scrap book came to light again, bringing back memories of early days. But a cartoon had peeled a little from one of the pages. The writings and figures of a century ago could be seen, shedding light on the early history of some of our colliery villages.

Thomas and Robert Dunlop were building masons when many of the local collieries in East Durham were sunk, and their work includes churches, miners cottages, public houses and school buildings.

Cost Of A Church

The first entry to be exposed dated February 8, 1831, was an estimate for building a church at Hetton. The sum was £551- drains extra! Money received for building the church was £100 from Sir Mathews Bank, Newcastle, December 28, 1831; £185 from Thomas Wood, Hetton, June 12, 1832; and by cheque on Messrs. Backhouse Co. Bank, Sunderland, £397 7s 10d.

A memorandum of January 1 1833, shows the estimated cost of building 44 houses at South Hetton for Thomas Wood, Hetton, was £1,760.

A public house was built at South Hetton in 1833 on the order of Mr George Livingstone. Cost was £180, and the account was settled in full on October 24, 1833.

Houses In Thornley

The first mention of building houses in Thornley is 1833: Six houses at Thornley New Winning for Thornley Coal Co.; houses finished, labour to mason work, ovens, bars, pot, and leading marle lime, bricks, and water, and painting and glazing, at £22.10s per house, £135."

Account was by cheque on Chaytors Bank, Durham, £100. on September 7, and by cash £35, on account from Thomas Wood, agent of Thornley Coal Co.

In 1834 Mr Dunlop let houses for rent in Thornley to: mason Harling Corner; blacksmith, John Waugh: countryman, Michael Mitchinson; and joiner, John Jackson; each two rooms and loft at £5.10s per year. One single room and loft was let to Thornley Coal Co at 33 10s per year. Bartholomew Potter had a butchers' shop for £8 per year from Candlemass. In 1836 Thornley Coal Co. rented seven double houses with loft at £4.10s per year and one single at £3.10s.

To balance the account for building 55 houses in Thornley in 1836 Thornley Coal Co paid Mr Dunlop the sum of £1,242 in 1837, in which year another contract was made to build eight single houses in Thornley next to the stables at £20 each; three single in Quarry Row at £25 each and School Room Building at £132.

29 January 1960

MBE LINK WITH THORNLEY

The induction on Wednesday of the Rev. William Alan Lathaen as Vicar of St Andrew's, Roker, recalls to the Thornley people that when he was vicar of that parish he was appointed a member of the British Empire for his work as a chaplain in a German prison camp in the last war. It was soon after the outbreak of the war that he went to France as a padre, and it was also soon after he got there that he was taken prisoner. His family and parishioners spent several weeks of anxiety, being without further news than that he was "missing."

Towards the end of the war, when some men in his camp were being repatriated, he also was offered repatriation, but chose to stay until the last of the men under his care were sent home. At one of the supper parties they gave to men on leave or discharged, the Thornley War Committee presented Mr Lathaen with a special gift, as they did with other men who had gained honours. After the war he resumed his work at Thornley, staying there until he was transferred to the much larger parish of St Michael, South Westoe, from where he has gone to Roker. He visited Thornley last year to dedicate the new memorial. His wife served in the A T S in the last war. At Roker Mr Lathaen succeeds the Rev. J Maxloe How, another former Thornley vicar.

THORNLEY TO PROTEST OVER "BLACKOUT"

Thornley Parish Council this week decided to send a strong letter of protest to the North Eastern Electricty Board regarding the service in maintenance of the public lighting, during this last week. For four successive nights Thornley had been in a state of blackout in different sections of the village.

The only lighting at the East End of the parish was a newly erected sign on the Working Men's Club. Various members of the council stated they had sent in fault cards to the Board, but no immediate action was taken. Coun. F A Walker, said that if each member of the Council had 150 cards each they could have used them up within a week under the system of inspection operating in the Parish. The Council also instructed the clerk to ask for adjustment charges for the period of the blackout.

Town Map

In reply to an application to Mr W A Geenty, Durham County Planning Officer, for an exhibition of a portion of the Easington Town Map applicable to Thornley. Mr Geenty replied that Mr Gill of his department would be willing to meet and discuss the matter with the council, so that he could have a plan prepared for display showing the effects of the Town map proposals on the village.

The council decided to accept me Geenty's offer and also to ask his advice and that of Mr Kelly, the legal adviser of Easington rural Council upon an offer made by Spearman's Trust to convey to the council a stretch of land from High Street to Coopers Terrace adjacent to St Bartholomew's Church and School Square.

The Council asked the Spearman's Trust to make a gift to the parish of this land in 1951 so that it could be cleaned up and developed.

Strayng Cattle

Complaints of cattle straying in the allotment gardens was brought forward by Coun. F A Walker, and the council instructed the clerk to write to the farmers concerned warning them of not fencing the animals in. Miss A Griffiths, reported that she had received complaints of household refuse being tipped near the bridge on the Thornley-Wheatley Hill road.

Coun. James Nicholson, chairman, stated that it was very little good people complaining to councillors or the parish council because they had the remedy in their own hands by reporting the people who were committing the nuisance to the police at once.

5 February 1960

WHEATLEY HILL DRAMA GROUP DISBANDS

"We never closed," famous wartime slogan of the London Windmill Theatre might well be applied to Wheatley Hill Drama Group during the past 17 years, But now, after having entertained thousands of people in Wheatley Hill and the surrounding area with some really high standard productions, the group has decided to disband.

The decision was reached at a meeting of the members this week because of the lack of acting members. The group was formed during the difficult war years- as far back as 1943- but they did not allow the blackout to upset their plans and twice a year since its formation they have successfully presented a new play. The members have been able to turn their hand with equal success to both comedy and drama and they deservedly built up a sound reputation for good acting.

Reluctance

"It was only with considerable reluctance that we decided to disband," one of the founder members, Mrs Minnie Galloway, told our reporter on Wednesday.

"But we were faced with no other choice since we have not sufficient acting members to put on a show." Only two other founder members and players have remained with the Group throughout the 17 years, they are Mrs Ivy Scott and Mrs Eva Warrier, who now lives at Horden.

Mrs Vera Fairclough, of Easington Village, has been the group's producer all the time. She, too, has been compelled to resign because of pressure of charitable work. "We have had a struggle to keep the flag flying for the past 18 months," she said. "We appealed for more members but there was no response."

Mrs Fairclough said she considered the group "the most outstanding of its kind" in the county both for the length of time it has existed and the packed audiences it has entertained.

Large Audiences

Every production- right up to the last one of Sailor Beware, last April – has attracted an audience of between 800 and 1,000 on the four nights it has been presented.

"In a way it is heart-breaking for we have done a lot of good work and have a faithful following of supporters," said Mrs Fairclough. The group's costliest production was Shaw's Pygmalion about five years ago. The costumes alone cost£100 for that play, but the group still made a profit of £5.

With the group disbanding, the members have decided unanimously to send a cheque for £150, the last of their funds to the World Refugee Organisation on behalf of the people of Wheatley Hill.

19 February 1960

THANKSGIVING AT LUDWORTH
Villagers rallied round their church

After two years and three months, the end of a task of faith and devotion by church people of Ludworth has been rewarded. This was to raise more than £700 for the repairs to their Mission Church of St. Andrew.

Anxiety was felt in 1957 about the state of the building and an inspection by the Diocesan architect, Mr D McIntyre, revealed that urgent repairs were needed to the roof and supporting beams.

When the issue was placed before the Ludworth congregation the church members pledged themselves to raise funds and a short while ago it was possible to meet the cost of the repairs. A new roof for the vestry and the north side of the naïve was carried out; the shoring timbers supporting the roof were spliced and capped; work was carried out to the bell tower; and new guttering and spouting placed in position.

The money needed to meet the cost has been raised chiefly by weekly visits to the members and friends living in the village and devoted ladies who did the canvassing kept up their task throughout the long period from November1957, to the beginning of February.

The Parochial Council expressed their appreciation of the work of the Ludworth people and joined in a service of thanksgiving in the Mission Church on Tuesday.

Generous Service

In addition to raising the money the good people of Ludworth worked for their church in other directions. For instance, after the naïve repairs had been completed the male members put on a coating of creosote on the outside of the entire building (which is a wooden erection built in 1902) and in other ways improved its appearance.

The thanksgiving service was conducted by the Rector, the Rev. A R L Prentice, assisted by the parochial reader, Mr T T Johnson. Mrs B York was organist,

and the hymns were sung from a new issue of Hymns A and M (Revised) which the Church Council has provided for the Church. The Rector gave an appropriate address.
26 February 1960

THORNLEY MINER RETIRES

Mr William Brereton, of 30 Dunelm Road Thornley, who has retired from work at Thornley Colliery, was born in Staffordshire. The family moved to Castle Eden in 1910 and Mr Brereton's first day down the Thornley pit was a "nightmare." He could not understand the Durham dialect!

He and his father walked night and morning to and from the pit to Castle Eden and did this for three years before removing to Wheatley Hill.

In 1914 he enlisted in the Royal Dublin Fusiliers. On April 25 1919 he was in Gallipoli and in September the same year he was wounded in the knee and invalided back to England. After his recovery he was sent back to his depot and to France in June 1916 for the battle of the Somme. Later he was transferred to the 50th Division (Northumberland) as a Lewis gunner. He was one of the gunners under Sgt. Jack Downie who won the VC, DCM, MM , the Croix de Guerre (French) and the Golde Medal (Russian), in a single encounter.

Mr Brereton returned to the pits in 1919, and took an active part in trade union work and social work in the parish. He has been a member of Thornley Miners' Lodge Committee, secretary of Thornley Colliery Pit Canteen, Chairman of Thornley Parish Council, and has also represented Thornley on Easington Rural District Council.

After25 years at stone work Mr Brereton was injured. For the last few years he has been employed in light work underground.
4 March 1960

WHEATLEY HILL COLLIERY ENGINEER RETIRES

Mr J Robson presided over a social function in the Nimmo Hotel, Wheatley Hill, the purpose of which was to make a presentation to Mr John Wallace, 1 Gowland Terrace, Wheatley Hill, who has been colliery engineer at the local pit since 1948. On behalf of the officials and staff, Mr F Richardson presented Mr Wallace with a Westminster chiming clock.

Mr Richardson said, "This is a unique presentation in that every department is represented and four out of five collieries in the Group are represented here. It is not often that happens. Mr Wallace has been an ideal engineer, devoted to his job and giving the highest service."

Mr Wallace replied, "The cooperation and loyalty I have always received at Wheatley Hill has made the last 12 years one of the happiest periods of my life."

Entertainment was provided by Messrs L Barker, J Turnbull, C Thackeray and J Watson.

Served In France

Mr Wallace was born in Stanhope and spent his early years in the Dales. He was educated at Stanhope and Frosterley. His first job was in the shops of the Harehope Mining and Quarrying Company. As the 1914-18 war started they went into liquidation.

Mr Wallace was a member of the Territorials and with the outbreak of the war he was drafted into the 6th D L I regiment and served from 1914-18 with the 50th Division in France as a sergeant and rose to be Regimental Sergeant Major.

Mr Wallace's connection with colliery life started in1927. He was an official at Cornsay Colliery till 1945.

It was during the second war that Mr Wallace formed the Home Guard organisation at Cornsay Colliery. He commanded E Company till the cessation of hostilities.

For three years Mr Wallace was in charge of underground haulage at Horden Colliery. From Horden he came to Wheatley Hill in1948.

Mr and Mrs Wallace hope to take up residence in Peterlee at an early date.

THORNLEY FIRST-AIDERS

Mr John Ellis, class teacher and secretary to Thornley Colliery Ambulance and First-Aid Class, has received notification that all students who took the recent examination have been successful.

First year students were: T E Dent, J Turner, F Lock, J White, T W Robson, N Fort, J E Hughes, Jas Hughes.

Students who were re-examined were: B Murray, J T Hedley, B Cooke, A Fleetham, N Osbaldestin, D Parker, R Smith, H Todd, J W L Convery, Jos Harvey, W Bates, R L Major, J F Thompson, J R Gill, J Ellis, G Dockerty, R W Conway, G M Peel, R Grainger, A Terry, T Robson and T Parsons.

Dr A Todd, of Thornley was lecturer, and Dr A P Gray, of Wheatley Hill examiner.

Mr Ellis announces that a new rule comes into operation for the year 1961 with regard to re-examinations. In the past it has only been first year certificate holders who were re-examined but in future all holders of medallions and labels held for three years or more must be re-examined.

11 March 1960

DEATH OF MISS M E OSWALD OF THORNLEY
Worked On Farm Till She Was 70

The funeral of Miss Mary Ellen Oswald, who died at her home, 14 Vine Street, Thornley, took place on Saturday in St Bartholomew's Church. The service was conducted by the Rev P G Mould.

Miss Oswald, who was 85, was a native of Thornley and was one of the first children born in Coopers Terrace. She attended the newly erected Board School in

Thornley and on leaving she went to Gore Hall Farm, where she was employed in all sorts of farm work until she was 70 years of age.

She lived alone in her small house in Vine Street, the only house in the village that had not a supply of electricity.

18 March 1960

APPOINTMENT

Mr Thomas Robinson (40), a bachelor living with his parents at 82 Shinwell Crescent, Thornley, has been appointed traffic manager at the surface of Thornley Colliery. The vacancy was caused by the retirement of Mr Norman Parker, who held the position for 36 years. Mr Robinson began work on the surface at Thornley in 1935, and for a short period worked on the heap-stead. He was transferred to the traffic office, at which he has worked since with the exception of six years with the Forces from 1939 to 1945.

THORNLEY GOLDEN WEDDING

Mr and Mrs William Dawson, landlord and landlady at the Railway Taver, Thornley, were married at St Bartholomew's Church, Thornley, on March 1910, by the Rev William Hodgson. Mr and Mrs Dawson have held the licence of the Tavern for 28 years. It is a typical industrial inn of the early 19th century.

Mrs Dawson at 70 is still a young, good-looking woman, neatly and modestly dressed. Born in Thornley she is the oldest of four girls and one boy of Mr and Mrs Robert Youll. The Youll family settled in Thornley shortly after the colliery was sunk in1835. Her cousin was Lieut John Scott Youll, V C who was killed at the end of 1918.

Mr Dawson, better known as Ginger, is one of the best known men in the county, and familiar with every course in the country. He is a fearless big-hearted humorist with a great live of children. His sporting activities included boxing, whippet breeding and coursing, quoits and fives, foot handicaps and flat racing. He still recalls some of the old sporting characters of the early part of the century - Jackie Besford, George Scott, Pompey King, and his two friends Tommy Lancaster, and Tommy Sharp.

Mr and Mrs Dawson held a family reception in their little pub, with sons, daughters, grandchildren and great-grandchildren, bridesmaid and best man of 1910 (Mr and Mrs Abe Dawson), Bill's brother and Mrs Dawson's sister and Bill's grandson who celebrates his 21st birthday.

25 March 1960

THORNLEY'S TRIBUTE TO CHARMIAN WELSH
No More Competitive Diving For Olympic Star

The "champion of champions" was the description given to Thornley's internationally-known diving champion, 22 year-old Miss Charmian Welsh, daughter of the local colliery manager, when, at a social gathering of representatives of all sections of workmen at Thornley Colliery, she was presented with a number of gifts to mark her splendid achievements, in Thornley Miners' Welfare Hall on Saturday afternoon.

Despite all the "glory and honour" she had brought, not only to the village of Thornley but to the county and the country, Charmian, declared Mr Edward Carter secretary of the Thornley Mining Federation Board, had not changed. She was the same "shy unassuming girl," and there was no "bigheadedness" whatever about her.

Monster Trophy

Thornley, said Mr Carter, who on behalf of all the workmen at the colliery, presented Charmian with a monster-size silver cup, had always prided itself on "raising champions," and that day they were honouring the champion of all champions for her magnificent achievements in the world of swimming and diving.

The cup Charmian received is inscribed, "Presented by the Thornley Mining Federation Board to mark the achievement of Charmian Welsh, British Empire High-diving and Springboard Diving Chanpion, 1958." The trophy, in turn, is for a ladies' national one-meter diving championship.

Mr G Bennett, chairman of Thornley Mining Federation Board, presided at Saturday's function, and also presented a record-player to Charmian on behalf of the colliery workmen. Mr Fred Bradley, chairman of the local Welfare Committee, presented her with a rifle- Charmian is now a keen member of the Houghton Small-bore rifle Club- and Mr W Henderson, secretary of the Welfare Committee, presented her with a telescope.

The presentations from the Welfare Committee, said Mr Bradley, were in acknowledgment of Charmian's outstanding performances in the water. "I have known her almost since the day she was born," said Mr Bradley, "and followed her career and successes with ardent and prolonged interest. It is nice to know that success has in no way affected her. She still remains the same quiet, rather shy and unassuming young lady I have always known.

"These successes in her chosen sport were not come by easily-they had to be worked for very hard indeed. But she was undeterred by hard work, and overcoming many difficulties, injuries, illness and other things, she carried on and eventually made the grade."

"Gross Information"

Charmian's mother, Mrs Ena Welsh, who was among the guests, together with Charmian's younger sister, Hilary, and twin brothers, Peter and Arthur, said that afternoon was not only a celebration, but from Charmian's point of view it was her "farewell" to competitive diving. She will not be diving any more except for the fun of the game," added Mrs Welsh.

The reasons for this, said Mrs Welsh, were "not very far to seek." Since 1955-the year in which Charmian's projected visit to America to dive and train was cancelled by her parents because of "gross mis-information supplied to us"- things had got tougher and tougher, declared Mrs Welsh

"And you will all know from Press reports in 1959 just how bad things became." Added Mrs Welsh.

Mrs Welsh said she was referring to the rescinding of the Mothersdale Trophy without hearing Charmian's side of the story at all, and events which followed, including especially Charmian being denied diving training facilities at the Durham City Baths.

Mrs Welsh went on, "In the end thinking it over carefully, we came to the conclusion that it was just not any longer possible to continue. Charmian did not come to that decision readily or easily, but only after weeks and months of reflection. It caused her a good deal of pain, naturally, because everything in her life has been geared to diving."

They were grateful to certain people last year, said Mrs Welsh- to the Durham City Council, for instance, for confirming her right to use the City Baths, and also to certain members of the Press who did what they could to bring the baths controversy into prominence.

"We offer our thanks also to Thornley as a whole for the backing the people gave her-a backing which was not offered her by her own swimming area."

Thanks were also due to the Dawdon Swimming Club, where her daughter had been able to practice diving as and when she pleased.

Charmian, said Mr Welsh had gained every diving honour possible, except an Olympic title. She held a record number of national titles.

"I Will Never Forget"

In a final word, Mrs Welsh said she was not willing that Charmian should withdraw from diving, especially in this pre- Olympic year, as though she were the culprit, without making it clear publicly that the responsibility for her withdrawal was not her daughter's.

Expressing her deep gratitude for the gifts she had received that day. Charmian also thanked the people of Thornley "for their wonderful support." "I will never forget what you have all done for me." she added.

After the presentation, Charmian confirmed, in an interview with our reporter, that in the future she would be diving "purely for pleasure." She did not intend, she said, to take part in any more national or international diving competitions.

8 April 1960

LABOUR OF LOVE AT WHEATLEY HILL
Volunteers rebuilding H Q of Scouts and Guides

While most people were rushing off to the sea or country to enjoy the sunshine over the Easter holiday, a group of young men, and middle-aged ones, too, were putting on work clothes and overalls to start a real "labour of love" at a dilapidated old building in Wheatley Hill, the headquarters of the local Boy Scouts and Girl Guides.

They were members of the Wheatley Hill Old Scouts' Association and when I visited the headquarters on Wednesday (writes Norman Passfield) many of them

194

were still hard at work, pulling the building down bit by bit, then re-building it with pre-cast concrete slabs. They were making excellent progress.

"We started to pull the old wooden walls down on Good Friday morning," one of them, 30-year- old Allen Lambert, who lives in the village, told me, "and we soon had plenty of help. We expect the new building to be completed by the week-end, then everything put ship-shape inside within another two weeks after that."

"It will be the speediest Scout building ever erected." Smiled another 30-year-old former Scouter, Thomas Howe, who lives in Peterlee, where he moved form Wheatley Hill three years ago.

Gave Up A Week

Both Mr Lambert, who is employed by Easington Rural Council and Mr Howe, who works at Grantham Airport, near West Hartlepool, have sacrificed a week of their annual holiday to do all the brickwork. They are the only two "full-time" men on the job, the rest, most of them acting as labourers, come straight down to the building, situated behind the village's Front Street, at the end of their shift as miners at the local colliery or their day's work as shop assistants, insurance agents and the like.

Although, about 30 old Scouts are giving voluntarily of their time to erect practically a new building. Only the old foundations and the roof will be incorporated into the new headquarters.

The men have had valuable technical advice, and help, from Bill Harker, foreman joiner at Wheatley Hill colliery, and a local builder, Tony Carr himself an old Scout, has loaned them some wood and materials.

"Everybody is pulling together grand, it shows a fine team spirit," commented Mr Howe, "I only wish we had the same sort of spirit in the new town of Peterlee where I live. There, very little is being done for the young people."

Most of the old Scouts already have sons in the cubs or Scouts, or youngsters whom they hope will one day join the movement. "Wheatley Hill has long been noted for its keen interest in the Scout movement," said one of them. "Some families have had three, four and five lads members of the local Scout Troop."

It was no easy task the old Scouts set themselves. They have acted in a wholly unorthodox manner by starting to re-build from the roof downwards!

Bit By Bit

"We started at the gable ends," said Mr Howe. "We took each gable end down bit by bit, shoring up as we went along, and then built sections of concrete slabs bit by bit." By Wednesday the gable ends had been renewed with the slabs and the men were busy working along one side of the building. New windows are being fitted and there's no doubt that by their voluntary labour the old Scouts have saved a considerable sum of money.

The money for the slabs and other materials they are using was raised by various social functions and "field days," and the local Parents' Committee have also given considerable financial assistance. Coun Ralph Watson, secretary of the Old Scouts Association, first suggested everybody pooling their ideas and labour to put up a really first-class building, and the enthusiastic support he has received is ample proof of the interest the old Scouts have in the new generation of Cubs and Scouts.

The two "full-time" men have been at work about 8 30 every morning this week - Easter Monday included, and have kept at it until half-past five at night. Then other old Scouts, straight after a meal at the end of their ordinary day's work, have rushed to the building to work all night in preparation for the two brick-layers resuming their task next morning.

The building is 61 ft long and 21 ft wide. When completed it will stand as a worthy monument to self-sacrifice on the part of lovers of the Scout Movement eager for the younger generation to have a pleasant, airy and permanent building to enjoy their Scouting activities.

22 April 1960

Volunteer Workers from Wheatley Hill Old Scouts' Association

THORNLEY HAS SITES FOR BUILDING

Thornley Parish Council decided to accept the recommendations of a sub-committee and have bus shelters erected at the two bus stops west of the Catholic Church. It was also recommended to have a cantilever shelter erected at the south side bus stop in the Villas, and remove the bus stop from Thornlaw Post Office to a spot adjacent to St Bartholomew's Church Hall, at the west of High Street North.

In the discussion that took place on the question of the Council's objection to the town map, the clerk, Mr Martin Fleming, stated that the objection submitted by Easington Rural District Council, which had been circulated to all parish councils, was a well thought out document. It proved without doubt, in dealing with the build up of the new town of Peterlee, that it was unnecessary to remove any of the displaced families to complete the building programme.

He believed the Minister would accept the statement as a fact, and all Thornley Parish Council should do, was to prove to the Minister that there were available sites in the parish for building.

Coun F A Walker agreed with the clerk that Easington had presented a good case, "but," said Coun Walker, "do not let us rest on our laurels. The planners will do

anything to justify the town map. It is unfortunate that the Queen has chosen this time to visit Peterlee, because there is no doubt the people concerned will take the opportunity to exploit every avenue to bring the grandeur of the town to the whole of the country, while we will be blotted out with their flood of publicity.
29 April 1960

WHEATLEY HILL MAN HONOURED

A well-known figure in the Co-operative movement in East Durham area, Mr Septimus Woodward, of Allenwood, Gable Terrace, Wheatley hill, who has been traffic manager for the Sherburn Hill Co-operative Society for the past 26 years, has been elected chairman of the National Co-operative Traffic Managers' Association. He will be inducted into the chair when the Association holds its annual conference at Blackpool on May 24.

Mr Woodward has been associated with the Co-operative movement for the past 38 years. When he left school he became an apprentice engineer at Thornley colliery but later he left the mine and in 1922 took up new employment as an apprentice with the Haswell Co-operative Society until his appointment in 1934 as traffic manager with Sherburn Hill Co-operative Society.

Mr Woodward has been vice-chairman of the Northern section of the Traffic Managers' Association for the past three years and he is also secretary of the Sherburn Hill branch of the Association. He is married with an only daughter, who at present is living in Singapore, where her husband is a school teacher.
6 May 1960

MARRIED FOR HALF A CENTURY
Mr and Mrs Thompson, of Wheatley Hill

It will be "gold" and "silver" combined tomorrow when Mr and Mrs George Thompson, 4 Byron Street, Wheatley Hill, celebrate their golden wedding with a party in the Welfare Hall in the village. Later this month one of their three daughters, Mrs Ena Hateley, and her husband Wilfred, will complete 25 years of married life and so they are bringing forward their celebration to coincide with their parents' golden wedding.

"We thought it would be nice to have a joint celebration seeing that both anniversaries are so close together," Mrs Thompson, whose maiden name was Hannah Saunders, told our reporter on Wednesday. Mrs Thompson is 72 but looks much younger than her years. She enjoys good health and does all her own housework, keeping a spic-and-span council house home.

Ten Hours Daily For 1s.1d

Mr Thompson, who celebrated his 70th birthday last Saturday was born at Willington. He started work at Wheatley Hill colliery" on the belts" when he was 12 years of age, being paid 10½ an eleven hour shift.

"Conditions in the mining industry have certainly changed for the better since those hard working days and it's a good job too, for they could not have been much worse," said Mr Thompson.

After only a month at Wheatley Hill, Mr Thompson transferred to the neighbouring colliery at Thornley where, in turn, he was lamp carrier, trapper boy, helper up and hand putter. There he worked ten hours a day for 1s 1d. Later he was at Chilton colliery for a short period but in 1908 returned to Wheatley Hill colliery, where he remained until he retired at 65 after a mining career of 53 years. "I have done practically every kind of job down the pit and was a deputy for a few years," said Mr Thompson.

Both Mr and Mrs Thompson have been members of Wheatley Hill Over-60 Club for the past three years. The couple were married at Shadforth Parish Church on May 14 1910. While working down the pit in 1943 Mr Thompson was involved in a serious accident and lay in hospital for many weeks, but he made quite a good recovery, though he has to "take things easy."

"Golden" And "Silver" Cakes

Mrs Thompson was born at Castle Eden bur was only seven when she went to Wheatley Hill and she has lived there ever since. She was one of a family of ten children, of whom eight are still alive. She was formerly actively associated with Wheatley Hill Women's Institute and the Mothers Union of all Saints' Church.

Mr and Mrs Thompson have a family of three daughters, all married, and six grandchildren. One of Mrs Thompson's brothers, Tom Saunders, emigrated to America 32 years ago. He was a blacksmith at Shotton colliery before emigrating and is now employed in a bank at Chicago. He and his wife visited this country only a year ago for a three-week holiday and their only daughter, an air hostess, who was married last Saturday hope to visit her relatives here in the near future.

Mrs Thompson has baked both a golden wedding cake and a silver wedding cake for tomorrow's party and quite a number of close relatives of the couple are expected to be present, their daughter, Mrs Hateley, who is celebrating her silver wedding, lives in Sandwick Terrace.

American Visitor

Mrs Elizabeth Harbron, of San Francisco, U S A, has spent the last few weeks with her sister and her husband, Mr and Mrs A Williamson, Jack Lawson Terrace, Wheatley Hill. On her way North she broke her journey at Birmingham to visit her son, Mr Robert Harbron. She returned to Birmingham on Monday and she goes back to the States on June 1. Mrs Harbron lived at Wheatley Hill and on leaving school chose nursing as her career. She did part of her training at Hartlepools and later at London. Her husband, Mr Robert Harbron, served in the 1914-18 war and was killed in the Dardenelles campaign. In 1918, Mrs Harbron emigrated to Canada and took up a nursing post at Montreal, and then at Toronto. She next worked in a New York hospital and then took another appointment in Canada at Vancouver. She retired two years ago as a matron of a hospital in San Francisco. With her sister, Mrs Williamson, she has visited the Wheatley Hill Over-60 Club and the local Mothers' Club Mrs

Harbron's final words were "I have had a wonderful holiday in England. It was grand seeing my son and other relatives. I have thoroughly enjoyed my stay in Wheatley Hill. People have been wonderfully kind.

COLLAPSED AT COLLIERY

The funeral took place on Tuesday of Mr Thomas (Tot) Armstrong (53), 4 First Street, Wheatley Hill. He collapsed and died as he was walking out by after finishing his shift at Thornley Colliery on Thursday evening. He is survived by his widow, Mrs Ethel Armstrong, nine daughters and two sons. One of his daughters, Mrs J A Hague, lives in Ontario, Canada.

A service in All Saints' Church, Wheatley Hill, was conducted by the Vicar, the Rev G G Graham. Cremation followed at Sunderland. Mr Armstrong was born at Thornley, and lived in Wheatley Hill since he was 19. He started work at Thornley Colliery. He was employed as a stoneman, and worked there till his death.

He was a member of Wheatley Hill Workmen's Club for many years.

PHOTOGRAPHY CLUB

A new Photography Club for amateurs interested in the art of the camera has been formed at Wheatley Hill, with Mr D Griffiths, 7 Stevens Terrace, as secretary. Mr B Henderson has been elected chairman of the club, and Mr S Oswald treasurer. At the request of the club an evening class in photography, under the auspieces of the Durham County Education Committee, has been organised with Mr H Holder as tutor. The class is being held on Tuesday evenings (7-9pm) in Wheatley Hill Boys' Modern School. Enrolment fees for the course of eleven weeks are 10s for adults,7s 6d for young people between 18 and 20, and 3s for young people between 15 and 17.
13 May 1960

BIG GATHERING IN SE DURHAM

Postponed from the previous week to avoid clashing with the FA Cup final, the May Day demonstration organised by Easington Divisional Labour Party at Wheatley Hill and Thornley on Saturday was favoured with sunshine. Many people lined the streets to watch the parade of colliery bands, miners' lodges with their banners, and women's sections of the Labour Party, with their green and white banners.

The parade with Mr Emanuel Shinwell, MP at its head together with Division-al Labour Party officials and Thornley miners' lodge officials, assembled in Front Street Wheatley Hill, and marched the mile-long journey to Thornley Miners' Wel-fare Hall, where the speech-making took place. Thornley Colliery Band, conducted by Mr E Kitto, led the parade, which also included Shotton Colliery, Wheatley Hill, Murton, Wingate, Horden and Peterlee women's sections of the Labour Party with their banners, and Thornley, Wheatley Hill, Murton, Blackhall, Wingate, Horden, Easington and Shotton miners' lodges, with their bands and banners. South Hetton and Deaf Hill miners' lodges were also represented.

Mr Jack Dormand of Haswell chairman of the Divisional Labour Party, presided in the Welfare Hall, when the speakers were Mr Shinwell and Coun Mrs B E Mann JP, a member of West Hartlepool Town Council.

May Day Parade at Wheatley Hill and Thornley

Municipal Elections

Referring to the results of the municipal elections, Mr Shinwell said it was no use pretending they were not a serious setback for the Labour Party, but two facts had to be borne in mind.

The first was that a political party must accept defeats in a reasonable spirit just as it rejoiced when it gained victories.

"let us not forget," he added," that the Tory party in 1945 suffered a graver defeat than any experienced by the Labour Party yet it recovered in spite of the fact that no attempt was made by the Tory leaders to water down Conservative principles."

"These disputes in the Labour Party," went on Mr Shinwell. "derive from honest and sincere convictions and instead of concealing them it is better to expose them before the public and to thrash them out in the hope of reaching a rational conclusion. What the municipal defeats mean for the Labour Party is that we must stand by our principles and, at the same time, work harder than ever before in order to recover the support we have lost. That means creating more enthusiasm among the rank and file. And the leaders of the Labour Party have got to understand that you cannot create enthusiasm among your active supporters by modifying your policy or pretending that you are not Socialists. The sooner this is understood, the better it will be for the whole of the Labour movement.

RESCUED FROM DROWNING
Young Men's Gallantry Recognised

Mr Jack Andrew, a 22-year- old local government officer, wanted no fuss after he saved a four-year-old South Shields girl from drowning in the Wear last August. He returned to work without giving his name and address, but a colleague thought that his courage should be recognised and he informed the police.

The rescue was recalled at Durham Magistrate Court on Monday when Mr Andrew, of Luke Terrace, Wheatley Hill, and Douglas McClelland (34), of East Boldon Road Cleadon, received testimonials from the Royal Humane Society.

The chairman of the magistrates, Ald Mrs H H Rushford, told the men, "I am sure that everyone here today is filled with admiration at the thought of what you did. We are very proud that Durham men came forward to prevent a tragedy."

During Lunch-Time Break

Chief Inspector Richard Lander told the court that Mr Andrew was spending his lunchtime break on the riverside when he heard screams and a cry, "get that bairn out of the water"! He jumped to his feet and saw a child floating face downwards towards the centre of the river and into the currents. Immediately he swam out and rescued the child at a point where the depth of the river was 10 to 12 feet.

Mr McClelland, who was standing some distance away, had heard shouting and realised that someone was in trouble. He ran to the riverside, took the child from Mr Andrew when he swam ashore and applied artificial respiration for about two minutes before the child recovered and began to ask for her mother.

The Chief Inspector commended both men for the promptitude with which they acted.

20 May 1916

FLEW FROM CANADA TO ATTEND MOTHER'S FUNERAL

The death took place in hospital of Mrs Sarah Ellen Kilbourn (69), of 24 Granville Terrace, Wheatley Hill. She is survived by her husband, Mr Robert Kilbourn and a married daughter, Mrs G Mather.

Mrs Mather received word of her mother's death on Saturday afternoon at Ajax, Ontario, Canada. There was only one way to be in time for her mother's funeral – to fly. She booked a seat on the plane and arrived at Wheatley Hill on Monday evening.

Mrs Kilbourn was born at Esh Winning and went to Wheatley Hill when a child. She was communicant member of the Wheatley Hill All Saints' Church and for many years an active member of the Mothers' Union. She was also a member of Wheatley Hill Over-60 Club

The funeral service on Wednesday at All Saints' Church was conducted by the Vicar (the rev G G Graham) cremation followed at Sunderland.

27 May 1960

ROYAL VISIT TO COUNTY REMEMBERED

The sunshine visit of the Queen and the Duke of Edinburgh will be The Event in the lives of many County Durham folk for years to come.

Long after the Queen had completed her tour of Peterlee, Durham City and Newton Aycliffe, children, housewives, shoppers, ordinary folk and notabilities were talking about how lovely the Queen looked and of the Duke's witty little asides, when he spoke to those he met on tour.The Dean of Durham on Saturday described the Royal visit to the cathedral as the great event of the past 12 months.

The Royal Party en route for Durham travelling through Wheatley Hill

The excitement had all died down. The Queen and the Duke of Edinburgh in their new transparent-hooded Royal rolls were leaving the Peterlee Town centre for Passfield Way on their last "port of call" in the new town on Friday morning, and the hot sun still blazed down from a clear blue sky.

One Peterlee resident stood in Surtees Road overlooking the whole of the Town Centre, the shops, both churches and the Technical College, with the picturesque Castle Eden Dene in the background. He turned to another Peterlee man who had just drawn up in his car to admire the same breathtaking view.

"It's been a wonderful day," said the first resident.

"It has indeed," the other replied. "We've a town to be proud of and a gracious Queen to be thankful for. We'll never forget this historic day in the young life of the town!"

Thoughts like these must have been running through all Peterlee's 12,000 inhabitants on Friday. It was a Royal visit which will never be forgotten. The Queen and Duke charmed everyone wherever they went from the moment of their arrival at the red-carpeted marquee in the Town Centre to when they visited the home of a Peterlee family in Avon Road prior to continuing their tour in Durham City.

Gala day

The weather was perfect, everyone was in a happy holiday mood and it was undoubtedly a real "Gala day" in Peterlee's history, one which will have none but the pleasantest memories for years to come.

The Royal couple seemed nearly to go out of their way to make everybody feel "at ease" when they spoke to them and the bronzed Duke with his ready wit and infectious smile, seemed to be enjoying himself immensely. Nervousness on the part of those presented to him was quickly dispelled by his jocular remarks.

"They were the nicest couple I have ever met in my life," Mr Jack Harrison, Warden at the Eden Hill Community Centre, said afterwards. "From the moment they both shook hands with me I felt completely at ease. They were very interested in all the activities going on at the Community Centre and did not seem at all in a hurry to leave.

The Duke was still only halfway along the line of 14 people presented at the Centre, headquarters of the Peterlee Community Association, when the Queen had already shaken hands with everyone and was on her way inside the hall to sign the visitors' book. The Duke followed her into the hall and added his signature, with a pen lent by Mr Ernest Bostwick, treasurer of the Association, and the couple also signed an enlarged photograph of themselves.

Still Talking

As they returned to the forecourt of the Community Centre the Duke was still talking animatedly with Mr Harrison and PC Jimmy Jackson, chairman of the Association, who had also been presented to him, and as she left the Queen shook PC Jackson's hand once more.

Father John V Burns, Peterlee's Roman Catholic priest, who was first presented to the Royal visitors at the Community Centre, was happy to be able to tell them that only the day before, he had heard the glad news that this month a start is to be made on the first Roman Catholic school in the town.

"The Queen told me she knew we did not have a Roman Catholic Church," said Father Burns, "and asked me when we were going to get one. I told her that I hoped we would as soon as the school was built."

The Duke, added Father burns, appeared "quite astonished" when told that of the 1,500 Roman Catholic parishioners in the town nearly half were under 15.

There were cheering crowds and flag-waving children wherever the Royal couple went and all those who lined the Royal route had an exceptionally good view of the distinguished visitors. Quite a number of householders sat in groups on the grass verges in front of their homes waiting for the Queen and Duke to pass, and while they waited patiently many of the enjoyed a cup of coffee or tea.

The crowds, perhaps, were not quite so big as expected, but Peterlee is not the easiest of places to get to by half-past nine in the morning from the surrounding colliery villages and this, seemingly, kept down the numbers. But for those who visited the town it was "nice and comfortable," and though crush barriers had been erected where the biggest crowds were anticipated, there was never any danger of overcrowding.

Planned early

Two young married Hesleden women were so keen to have a "grandstand" view that they slept at a friend's home, in the town and then were up bright and early to take their places at the crush barrier near the arrival point for the Queen. They were Mrs Elsie Stainson, 14 West Terrace, who was accompanied by her six-year-old son John, and Mrs Sheila garner, 17 Single Burdon Street, who had her 20-month-old son Clive with her.

"We were the first here at half-past five on this side of the road," they said, "but at the other side four people had already arrived."

Mrs Stainson, who is an aunt of George Bowes the well-known bantamweight in the boxing world said they got "drenched" in a short but heavy shower early on. "We were glad to see the sun come out later and the splendid view we had of the Queen and Duke was worth all our trouble," she smiled.

Thirteen-year-old Jacqueline Owens, a miner's daughter, of 36 Robson Avenue, will certainly never forget the Royal visit. Jacqueline was the lucky schoolgirl chosen to present the Queen with a bouquet.

She did it most charmingly, "Oh, I thought the Queen was really lovely," she exclaimed afterwards. Jacqueline had been fighting a cold all week but her mother had "dosed" her well and though she still had a "sniff" as she got dressed in her new white tricel shirt-waister, with three-quarter length sleeves, she felt pretty well on top form for the bouquet-presenting ceremony.

Many times during the Queen's tour of Peterlee Jacqueline's remark, "I thought the Queen was really lovely ," was repeated. The Queen's radiance matched the sunshine and before she left the new town she and the Duke had won a place in everyone's heart. Their visit brought a warmth and friendliness to the town which will never be forgotten.

THORNLEY COUPLE'S "GOLDEN"

Mr and Mrs Joseph Hogg, of 8 St Cuthbert's Square, Thornley, celebrated their golden wedding last week. Since their marriage the couple have resided in Thornley. They have two sons and five daughters, 16 grandchildren and six great grandchildren. Mrs Hogg was born in Thornley and she attended St Godric's catholic School.

Mr Hogg was born at Shotton and removed to Trimdon with his family when a schoolboy. He began work as a pick carrier at Trimdon Colliery when he was 13 at 1s.3d a shift of 11 hours. The family again removed to Thornley and Mr Hogg worked as a putter at Thornley Colliery.

During the 1914-18 war, he saw service with 11th Batt DLI and was wounded four times, being discharged in1919. He resumed his work underground at Thornley Colliery and worked as a coal hewer until 1931 when he was obliged to seek work on the surface owing to war injuries. He worked on the surface as a platelayer and as a boiler fireman until he retired three years ago.

At the celebration party all the family were present with the exception of one daughter who is living in London, Mrs Hogg's bridesmaid Miss Mary Hamilton who is 84, lives in Sunderland.

WHEATLEY HILL MAN'S DEATH IN AUSTRALIA

Mr Sid Taylor, of 12 Wandsworth Road, Newcastle, received new recently that his brother Harold, had died in a Fremantle (Western Australia) hospital.

Mr Harold Taylor was well known in Wheatley Hill. He served in the Royal Field Artillery during the 1914-18 war and was awarded theMilitary Medal for bravery in the field. On his demobilisation the people of Wheatley Hill presented him with a watch. He was interested in the trade union movement, being a member of Wheatley Hill lodge of the DMA.

In 1926 together with his wife and their children, two twin sons and one daughter, he emigrated to Australia, where he trained as a dairy farmer under a Government scheme. All went well for Harold Taylor until the slump of the 30s.

Later he became an electric welder with a well-known Perth firm. In 1953 he came home on a six months' holiday to see his 88-year-old mother. He met many old friends and went to Durham Miners' Gals. He retired in 1959. He was buried beside his wife, who died in 1939, at Barrakatta cemetery.

3 June 1960

WHEATLEY HILL MINER'S SUCCESS

For the third year running a young Wheatley Hill miner has won an essay competition organised by the Durham Area NUM, in connection with the National Council of Labour Colleges. He is 19-year-old Frank Russell Harper, son of Mrs R Harper and the late Mr T Harper, 6 Darlington Street, and his success earns him a week's holiday at the Labour College at Cloughton Bay, Scarborough. He goes there on June 11.

Mr Harper, formerly a pupil at Wellfield A J Dawson Grammar School, Wingate, is employed on the training face at Wheatley Hill Colliery. A year ago he was elected to the committee of the miners' lodge and, it is believed, was the youngest miner in the county to fill such a position.

His two previous essay successes also gave him the chance of attending a week's school at the Labour College at Cloughton Bay.

10 June 1960

WHEATLEY HILL

FINANCIAL SECRETARY - Mr J Hedley has been re-elected financial secretary, unopposed of Wheatley Hill miners lodge for the ensuing year.

MINERS' BALLOT – As a result of the annual ballot of Wheatley Hill Miners' Lodge, Mr Thomas Knowles was re-elected secretary. He polled 267 votes against the 159 of his opponent, Mr A Wharrier. Mr H Bradshaw was also re-elected chairman, defeating County Coun J Andrew by 303 votes to 121. Others elected by ballot were, Delegate, Coun C Hackworth; card-maker, Mr S Mitchison; band committee, Messrs G Burnside, R Teasdale, M Cain and S Mitchison; welfare committee. Messrs J Hedley, C Hackworth, T Buxton and W Rotheray; lodge committee, Messrs G Burnside, W Rotheray, S Mitchison, J Foster, R Hunter, R Teasdale, M Cain, T

Ellward, G Henderson, J Gair, E Jones and M Telford; Aged Miners' committee, Messrs C Hackworth, E Jones, H Bradshaw, G Henderson, J Hedley, R Cook, G Burnside and M Telford. Mr R Cook was re-elected treasurer, unopposed, Mr M Alderton compensation secretary, and Messrs T Buxton and J Cain auditors.

17 June 1960

SCOUT RALLY AT WHEATLEY HILL

There was a large crowd at Nanny's Wood, Wheatley Hill, on Saturday, to attend a Scout and Cub Rally organised by the Castle Eden and Easington District. The rally, which was meant as a challenge to initiative, owed much to the inspiration of Assistant District Comissioner, Alan Hall, of Peterlee. Five and fifty Scouters representing Thornley, Wheatley hill, Horden, Easinton, Blackhall, Peterlee, Heselden, Trimdon, Fishburn, Fleming Field and Castle Eden attended.

Cubs competition took the form of a programme of Olympic Games, while the Scouts tackled a stiffer programme, patrol camp site and a bridge building competition. Judges were Group Scoutmaster Farne and Scoutmaster Davison, of Seaham. The Cub Competition Trophy was won by the 4th Horden Pack with 23 points, Trimdon were runners-up with 11 points, followed by Thornley with 10.

The patrol camp site competition was fairly close. Camping Trophy was awarded to the 4th Horden Troop with 87 points, Hesleden were runners-up with 82 and Wheatley Hill were third with79.

Bridge making competition was won by Thornley with 42 points, 1st Peterlee Troop was second with 40 and Easington were third with 36. Placings for the District Trophy for the highest combined scores in the competitions were, 1, Thornley; 2, Wheatley Hill; 3, Easington, Horden and Fleming Field.

DEATH SEVERS 53 YEARS' LINK AT WHEATLEY HILL

The funeral took place on Wednesday of Mr James Rowbotham (75), 2 Jack Lawson Terrace Wheatley Hill. Many friends attended a service in Wheatley Hill Church Street Methodist church, conducted by Rev E P Lucas of Wingate.

Mr Rowbotham is survived by his wife, Mrs Ellen Rowbotham, three sons, six daughters and 22 grandchildren.

The couple had been married 53 years. Mr Rowbotham was born in The Boyne, in the Bishop Auckland district. He came to Wheatley Hill 61 years ago. He chose mining as a career and started at Wheatley Hill pit. Ill health curtailed his working life. Mr Rowbotham served in the First World War with the East Yorkshire regiment. From 1914-1918 he saw fighting in Egypt, the Dardenelles and France and came through without a scratch.

He was a founder member of the Wheatley Hill Workmen's Club and was a member of the Wheatley Hill Discharged Soldiers and Sailors Club.

24 June 1960

FIFTY YEARS A MINEWORKER
Mr Joseph Hays retires on 1 July

Mr Joseph Hays, of South View, Ludworth, assistant mechanical engineer at Thornley Colliery, retires on July 1 under the NCB age limit.

He was initiated into the hazards of the pit with his christening. The ceremony took place by the side of his father's coffin in a little colliery house at Station Town when he was 3 weeks old. His father had been killed at Station Town Colliery. Mr Hays still has a memento of that event, his father's hand made hand hammer, initialled HHCC, Hutton Henry Coal Co. The youngest of 5 orphans, brought up by their mother on her little savings in the Co-operative Store, Mr Hays began work at 14 as an apprentice fitter at Wingate Grange Colliery in 1909. He spent two years with the Royal Flying Corps, in the 1914-18 war and saw service in France. After the war he worked for some time as a fitter and turner at Armstrong-Whitworths, Newcastle, before removing to Thornley in 1920.

First Aluminium Coal Tubs

In his early days at Thornley he worked on the first aluminium coal tubs that were produced in the country and put into service at the colliery, he also saw the complete centralisation of coal drawing from all seams to one shaft. While at Thornley one of Mr Hays' brothers was fatally injured at Wingate Grange Colliery.

In 1924 Mr Hays was transferred to Ludworth Colliery to assist Mr Atkin, the resident engineer, in the resinking and widening of the Hutton seam shaft from the main coal to the Hutton seam. One of Mr Hays' first jobs in the shaft here was the removal of the beam and attachments for the spear pump that had been installed when the pit opened in 1850. two accidents that will always be remembered by Mr Hays while sinking was the fatal accident of Mr Atkin, the engineer's brother who fell from the kibble while he and Mr Hays were descending and the breaking of the spur wheel of the old jack engine while he was descending in the same kibble.

The engineman lost control and the kibble descended the shaft at a tremendous speed. It was only Mr Hays' calmness and knowledge of the shaft that saved his life. He jumped to the side buttons and safety. He remained in the shaft for some hours until help came.

Resident Engineer At Ludworth

Mr Hays was appointed resident engineer at Ludworth in 1934. He saw the complete demolition of the old colliery village under slum clearance. The only house left was the one he still occupies.

When men-riding was stopped at Ludworth Colliery and men transferred to Thornley 10 years ago, Mr Hays went back to Thornley Colliery as assistant engineer and has been so until his retirement. A popular fellow, a practical joker and tale-spinner, with an abundance of tall stories he will be long remembered and will leave the colliery with the best wishes of all his friends

1 July 1960

WHEATLEY HILL SCOUTS' GOOD TURN
For Durham County Hospital

Some time ago the 1st Wheatley Hill Scouts adopted the children's ward of Durham County Hospital. By various efforts they have provided money for purchasing toys, equipment and treats of various kinds for child patients in Durham.

The latest act of generosity on the part of the Scouts and Cubs of Wheatley Hill has been to present two garden shelters. The presentation was made by Group Scoutmaster Les Barker, Scoutmaster Colin Thackeray, Assistant Scoutmaster R Woodward, Cub master W Saxby and Coun R Watson (sectetary). The shelters were received by the Matron, Miss M C Harding.

Group Scoutmaster Les Barker said "As a troop we enjoy doing what we can for the children in Durham County Hospital. We feel it brings them a little pleasure when it is most needed. It also works the other way, for it gives our lads something to work for and gives them an interest in other people."

Mr Barker said that Wheatley Hill Scouts and Cubs had given £300 in various gifts to the children's ward.

OUTING

Annual outing for the aged of Wheatley Hill Workmen's Club took place on Saturday. About 400 retired members and their waves and widows of club members went to South Shields. Each received a gift of £2 and free meals for the day. Arrangements were in the hands of Mr T Henderson (chairman) B Aitkin (secretary) and J Dunn (treasurer) and committee.

SCOUTS' FIELD DAY

In sunny weather 400 people enjoyed a successful field day organised by Wheatley Hill Old Scouts' Association. The organising secretary was Coun Ralph Watson, assisted by Group Scoutmaster Les Barker and a strong committee. A slow bicycle race for children resulted: 1,David White. 2 Robert Urwin. 3 George Wright. 4 Thomas Urwin. In charge of sideshows, treasure hunt and other events were, Messrs J Pyle, L Hetherington, B Lindsey, A Watson, R Hargreaves, J Raffell, C Thackeray, C Raffell, J Armstrong, F Alderson, J Carter, and R Woodward. Refreshments were served by Mesdames R Watson, L Barker, E Thackeray, B Andrews, G Burnside, J Cowan, E Cook and J Nichloson.

300 AT OVER-60 CLUB

There was an attendance of 300 at meeting of Wheatley Hill Over-60 Club, and Mr C Raffell presided. Secretary duties were undertaken by Mrs E Richardson. Birthday greetings were sung to Mrs Jefferson and Mrs Frampton and Mr Gutcher. Entertainment was provided by Dean Bank Over-60 Club concert party. Mrs E Potts compere and Messrs B Copley and J Dodds were accompanists. Those taking part were Mesdames A Hope, L Fleetham, E Rothery, B Foster and M G Harle; Messrs J

Garforth, B Foster, W Hayes, R Copley, G Carey and J Dodds. The party presented two of the Wheatley hill club's oldest members with bouquets. Mrs E Shutt and Mrs J Tyson, both over 80. Competition winners were Mesdames A Murray, L brown, E Amies, A Rowbotham, J Hicks, M Hutler, N Hodgson, I Storey, E Henley, A Bowes and H Colvine; Messrs T Simpson, T Phillips and B Bowes. Special prizes for club funds realised £3 16s 6d and were won by Mrs Allison and Mrs Williamson.

FUNERAL OF WHEATLEY HILL PERSONALITY

The funeral took place on Thursday of a well-known Wheatley Hill personality. He was Mr Owen Rowland (66), 10 Peter Lee Cottages, Wheatley Hill. The service was conducted by Rev G L Nelson (Methodist minister) at Sunderland Crematorium.

Mr Rowland leaves a widow, Mrs Elizabeth Rowland, and a married son. The couple have been married 43 years.

Born at Houghton-le-Spring, he started work in that area when he was 14. Most of his working life was spent at Wheatley Hill colliery as a putter and coal hewer. He did light work for the last few years before his retirement.

Mr Rowland was a craftsman and expert in making artificial flowers. His hobby was making model houses with match boxes. He was a member of Wheatley Hill Workmen's Club and was a former member of the local Over-60 Club.

1 July 1960

THORNLEY
Miner fatally injured

The death has occurred in Durham County Hospital of Mr John Walker (60), 45 Ruskin Crescent, Thornley. Mr Walker, who was employed as a datal hand at Thornley Colliery, received injuries while at work on Monday 4th. He was admitted to hospital but died the same evening. He was born in Thornley and was well known throughout the district as a popular sportsman. He played for some years with Thornley and Hartlepools united and was also a good sprinter. Mr Walker is survived by his wife, three daughters and two sons.

SUCCESSFUL CHILDREN'S DAY AT THORNLEY

It was children's day in Thornley on Saturday and the programme set by thr Thornley Colliery Sports Club attracted thousands of spectators to the third annual sports day held on the CW Sports Field.

A procession through the main street of the village to the sports field, was headed by Sunderland and District Pipe Band in full Highland dress. Also on parade were Thornley Colliery Silver Prize Band (conductor, Mr E Kitto), jazz bands of the Hartlepoop Jazz Band Association, children in fancy dress, tableaux, pit ponies, and adults in fancy dress.

A baby show in Thornley Miners' Welfare Institute attracted 31 entries. The judges were Sister Lily Green, Thornley Colliery Medical Centre and Mrs Irene Harding, former health worker.

The winning babies were, boys, 1 John Baker, 2 Christopher Hancock, 3 Kenneth Bentham; girls, 1 Valerie J Robson, 2 Dawn Momenon, 3 Christine Bonar, 4 (consolation prize) Susan Hutchinson.

Challenge cups were presented to the winners, by Miss Charmian Welsh and Mr J L Timms, General Manager, No3 Area NCB.

The pit ponies were judged by Mr Frank Butters, head horse-keeper of No3 Area NCB. The first prize of £5, and challenge cup was won by Sherburn Hill. Second were Thornley, third Wingate, and fourth Wheatley Hill. The challenge cup was presented by Mr Joseph Cherry, retired treasurer of Thornley Miners' Lodge.

Over 100 children entered the competition for fancy dress, and they were judged by Mesdames A McCall, A Woodward, F Bradley Junr. The prize-winners were, Eilena Watson, Miss Sunderland, and Maxine Slater.

Five tableaux were judged by Messrs W Bovil, J Storey, W Hetherington, and prizes were won by 1,Thornley Women's Institute, 2 Thornley Mother's Club, 3 Thornley Over-60 Club.

8 July 1960

Childrens Day at Thornley

SPORTS DAY AT WHEATLEY HILL

More than 100 children took part in a fancy and comic dress parade at Wheatley Hill on Saturday in connection with the fourth annual sports day organised by the Wheatley Hill Colliery Federation Board. "It was the most colourful procession we have had yet and more children than ever took part," the secretary, Mr A D Wharrier, told our reporter. The four-mile race for adults also attracted a record entry of 34. The parade which was headed by Wheatley Hill Colliery Band and the local miners' lodge banner and officials, was marshalled in Patton Street by Mr Mark Alderton, and proceeded through the village to the Senior Girls' School playing field where judging took place.

The sun shone throughout the parade but later a heavy shower of rain interrupted the sports programme and the remainder of the sports were held on Monday.

On the playing field bags of fruit and chocolate valued 3s were presented to 1,800 children, "Every child, no matter whether or not his or her father worked at the colliery, received a bag," Mr Wharrier said "and children outside Wheatley Hill whose fathers are employed at the colliery, also received bags and qualified to take part in the sports."

The fancy dress parade was judged by the resident Methodist minister, Rev G L Nelson, and his wife, and Miss J McLean, daughter of Dr and Mrs W G McLean, of Wheatley Hill.

Prizewinners

Children: Fancy dress: 1 Pamela Mather, 2 Hazel Hedley, 3 Julia Grady. Comic dress: 1 William Jobes, 2 Maureen Powell, 3 Barbara Galley. Original dress: 1 George and Pamela Hedley, 2 Miss M Broughton and Miss J Croft, 3 Miss Dowsey and Miss Anthony.

Adults: Comic dress: Messrs C Evans and G Hewitson. Original: Mrs R Hammond and Mrs G Hall. A half-crown savings stamp was presented to every child in the parade not among the principal prizewinners.

The winners of the adults' four mile race were; 1 Mr A Connell, 2 Mr B Thubron, 3 Mr Ray Clish. Miss Barbara Galley won the special prize for discovering and correctly challenging "Miss Sports Day Lady."

In charge of the sports were Messrs B Aitkin and D Clish, and a treasure hunt and sideshows were organised by Wheatley Hill Boy Scouts. County Coun John Andrew was chairman of the organising committee, Mr Wharrier secretary and Mr J Hedley treasurer.

The cost of the sports day was met by a weekly twopenny levy paid all year round by all classes of workmen at Wheatley Hill Colliery, together with a number of donations from local tradesmen and others not employed at the colliery. A ladies committee representative of all the village organisations was responsible for the distribution of the bags of fruit and chocolate.

WHEATLEY HILL PAIR TOO GOOD FOR HARRATON

Wheatley Hill gained a convincing seven wickets victory over Harraton CW in their Durham Coast league (Division1) game at Wheatley Hill on Saturday.

The home side can thank their bowlers, Leslie and Iddon, for their victory, for they skittled out Harraton for a mere 41. Leslie took six for 21 and Iddon four for18.

Only two of Herraton's batsmen, Hunter and Mawson, reached double figures, both were bowled by Leslie.

For Harraton, King took all three Wheatley Hill wickets for22 runs.

Scores: Harraton: F Hunter b Leslie12, T Southern c Fishwick b Iddon1, G Mawson b Leslie 0, N Mitchell b Leslie 6, D Dean c Harrison b Iddon 5, B Mawson b Leslie

13, E Scott c Leslie b Iddon1, F Humble c and b Leslie 0, W King B Leslie 0, E Jones not out 0: extras 2 total 41.

Leslie 6-21, Iddon 4-18.

Wheatley Hill: A Carter not out 19, T Simpson c Dean b King 0, E C Simpson lbw b King 17, D Leslie c Mawson b King 5, A Fishwick not out 1. total (3wickets) 42.

King 3-22, Colpitts 0-10, Dean 0-10.

MINER'S WIFE WINS £750 - OR A CAR

A Wheatley Hill miner's wife, who for 15 years has regularly submitted an entry in a weekly competition run by a national Sunday newspaper, had her first win at the weekend, and it was a really big one.

The woman, Mrs Isabella Routledge (45), of 14 Eighth Street, has won outright, subject to a re scrutiny, the first prize of £750 or a new Ford Anglia de-luxe car, including a heater, plus 1,000 miles of free petrol, a complete summer wardrobe valued £75 and £50 holiday spending money.

Asked if she would take the £750 cash or the car, Mrs Routledge said, "I haven't made up my mind yet. We have never had a car and it would be nice to have one, but the money would also come in most useful."

WHEATLEY HILL WILL REMEMBERS DR MACLEAN

Wheatley Hill's well-known and esteemed "family doctor," Dr William Gordon MacLean, who had been in practice in the village for the past 30 years, died in Dryburn Hospital on Sunday after a fortnight's illness. Dr Maclean, who had not enjoyed the best of health for the last year or so, was 57.

Dr MacLean, who lived at Valdigarth, Front Street, studied medicine at Glasgow University. He graduated there as a Bachelor of Medicine (MB) and Bachelor of chemistry (ChB) and then underwent a special gynaecological course at the Rotunda Hospital Dublin.

For a short time after qualifying as a doctor, Dr MacLean was in practice with his father, Dr James MacLean, in Glasgow, but he moved to Wheat-

Dr W G MacLean

ley Hill 30 years ago and took over the practice of his uncle Dr George Russell, on the latter's death.

The Navy

Dr MacLean was in the Royal Navy Volunteer Reserve for some years and was called up on the outbreak of the 1939-45 War. He served throughout the war and held the rank of Lieutenant-Commander on his demobilisation.

Until three years ago, Dr MacLean was a part-time anaesthetist at the Durham group of hospitals. He was president of the Constitutional Club in Wheatley Hill and for some years was president of the local branch of the local British Legion, Men's branch, which is now defunct.

Dr MacLean, whose death is sadly mourned by the whole village, is survived by his wife and a son and a daughter. His son James is training as a male nurse at Sedgefield General hospital and his daughter Josephine is a secretary tat Ludworth.

AWARDS TO BRAVE THORNLEY MINERS

Mr R Kellett, Shotton and District Mines Inspector, and Mr L C Timms, general manager, No 3 Area, NCB, with five Thornley Colliery miners to whom they presented gold watches and meritorious service certificates and cheques at a ceremony on Tuesday in Thornley Miners' Welfare Hall to mark their prompt action which probably prevented a serious accident at the pit.

The men were, Mr James O'Connor, of 49 Gloucester Terrace, Haswell Plough, Mr Robert G White, 130 Barnard Avenue, Ludworth, Mr Ralph Woodward jun. 19 Byron Street, Wheatley Hill, Mr Laurence Crangle, 18 Kent Terrace, Haswell Plough, and Mr Dennis Elliott, 53 St Aidan's Crescent, Thornley.

The incident occurred last month, when Mr Elliott, a shotfirer, saw a sheet of flame on the coalface after he had fired several shots. He switched off the electric current and ran to warn Mr White and Mr Woodward.

Certificate Presented by the
DURHAM DIVISION
of the National Coal Board
to
Dennis Elliott

for meritorious service in that on the 1st East Face, County Busty Seam, at Thornley Colliery on 17th June, 1960, he did conduct himself in an exemplary manner. The immediate and effective steps he took to contain the dangers arising from the ignition of gas were in accordance with the highest traditions of the Mining Industry.

Certificate presented to Dennis Elliott of Thornley in recognition of his quick thinking in avoiding a possible explosion in the pit

Together they returned to the coalface and finding no gas present, Mr Woodward and Mr Elliott used fire extinguishers before spraying the area with a hose from a cutting machine.

Meanwhile, Mr White went to warn workmen nearby, a precautionary measure, which was also taken by Mr Crangle and Mr O'Connor.

Mr Kellett presented the men with gold watches on behalf of Thornley Colliery Federation Board, and Mr Timms presented meritorious service certificates and £10 cheques on behalf of the Durham Divisional Board.

Mr Kellett was thanked by Mr E Carter, chairman of Thornley Miner's Lodge and Coun R Hughes, secretary. Mr C R Knaggs, No 3 group agent thanked Mr Timms and was supported by Mr Gascoigne, area safety officer.

Mr George Bennett, chairman of the Federation Board presided.

22 July 1960

MOURNERS PAY TRIBUTE TO DR MACLEAN AT WHEATLEY HILL

All Saints' Church, Wheatley Hill, was well filled for the funeral service of Dr William Gordon MacLean.

It was conducted by the Vicar, Rev G G Graham. The choir was in charge of Mrs C English, who was at the organ.

Mourners were representative of the whole of the village life of Wheatley Hill, including many who were the doctor's patients. The Vicar, in his address, said, "It is only right for so many of you to want to pay your last tributes today. To many of you, Dr MacLean was guide, counsellor and friend and also your medical adviser. Cremation followed at Birtley.

29 July 1960

"EASINGTON HAS FINEST BEAUTIES IN BRITAIN"
Said Mr Shinwell at Crimdon Lido

An eighteen-year-old radiantly happy brunette, Miss Sally Fleetham, of 5 Eight Street, Wheatley Hill, chosen "Miss Crimdon 1960" when the annual beauty queen contest organised by Mr Roy Isherwood, entertainments manager at Easington Rural Council's holiday lido at Crimdon was staged in picturesque Crimdon Dene on Monday, later told our reporter she was "thrilled to bits" at her success. It was the first time she had ever entered the contest, she said, and she could scarcely believe her good fortune in winning the coveted Miss Crimdon title.

Three times the value of the prize given during recent years, Sally, with the white silken "Miss Crimdon" sash placed over her shoulders by Mrs Shinwell wife of Mr Emanuel Shinwell M P for Easington was also presented with a bouquet.

Among the happy holiday crowd, estimated at 50,000, watching the judging of the contest by Mr and Mrs Shinwell, were Sally's parents, Mr and Mrs Alfred Fleetham, her father is a deputy at Thornley colliery, and her 13-year-old brother Thomas. Her younger sister, Kathryn, was the only member of the family missing, she was away on holiday. "And my boyfriend was also there from Haswell," smiled Sally.

For the past two years Sally who wore a lemon cotton dress when she paraded with twelve other village "beauty queens" from all parts of Easington Rural areas for judging on the bandstand, has been employed as a clerk at West Hartlepool branch of

Martin's Bank Ltd. Before that she attended West Hartlepool St Joseph's Convent Grammar School.

"Miss Wingate" Was Second

The second prize of £10, and a bouquet, was won by another attractive 18-year-old brunette, Miss Kathleen Martindale, youngest daughter of Mr and Mrs Frederick Martindale, 6 Partridge Terrace, Wingate. Miss Martindale who is unemployed, won the "Miss Wingate" title three years ago but on that occasion was not among the three principal prize-winners at Crimdon.

A 15-year-old shop assistant, Miss Margaret Jones, 47 Station Road, Easington Colliery, who was still at school when she won the "Miss Easington" title at a local dance, won the third prize of £5 in the final. She too, was presented with a bouquet and there were happy smiles all round when she and the two other winners, after receiving warm congratulations from their competitors, faced a battery of cameras.

A fresh looking Mr Shinwell beaming at the vast crowd thronging the Dene, said, "We have done our best. Among any of the young ladies here could have taken a first prize. You bring us up here every year and in deciding who is to be Miss Crimdon we try to be as impartial and objective as we can, but it is always difficult! I think we have the finest beauties in this part of the county than in any part of the United Kingdom!"

Critics Found Their Answer

Mr Shinwell reminded the visitors that it was 23 years since Easington Rural Council had started this annual beauty contest. "It was in 1937," he said," and I am also reminded that I am now in the 26th year of my representation in Parliament of the Easington constituency."

When the beauty contest was started 23 years ago, said Mr Shinwell, there was a great deal of criticism.

"But," he went on, "you have the answer to such criticism here today in this great and glorious concourse of ordinary men and women and their families, who have come to enjoy themselves at one of the finest beauty spots in the United Kingdom."

Five-year-old Ann Isherwood daughter of the entertainments manager, presented Mrs Shinwell with a bouquet before the judging took place, and a warm welcome to both Mr and Mrs Shinwell was extended by Coun J B Davison, of Murton, chairman of Easington Rural Council, Coun Davison was introduced by the chairman of the Parks Committee, Coun A Foster, of Easington, who, in turn, was introduced by Mr Isherwood.

It was the council's intention said Coun Davison, to put Crimdon to the fore-front where seaside resorts were concerned. "We aim to offer you more and better facicities," he added," and hope to compare favourably with all the other resorts in the North- East."

After the judging and presentations, the beauty queens, together with the runners-up for each village title, were entertained to tea in a large marquee nearby.

5 August 1960

90TH BIRTHDAY AT CARAVAN RALLY

Ninety on Saturday, That is the achievement of Mrs Mary Knight, now of "no fixed abode," but formerly of the Post Office, Granville Terrace, Wheatley Hill.

Of the few people who reach the ripe old age of 90, most are content to sit in a chair by the fire and are glad to be centred on one place. Not so Mrs Knight. When her son, Albert Knight retired from Wheatley Hill Post Office last summer, they solved all housing problems by making their home in a caravan. Mrs Knight is as keen as her son on caravan travel. They have travelled as far as the South Coast and Mrs Knight has thoroughly enjoyed travelling from place to place.

For Mrs Knight today, there will be no quiet cup of tea to celebrate her 90th birthday. She will be at Pooley Bridge for a Caravan Rally near Lake Ullswater. She and her son Albert left Castle Eden yesterday morning. Interviewed, Mrs Knight said, "I thoroughly enjoy my caravan life. On Saturday at Pooley Bridge we shall meet many friends we have made since attending these rallies. There is a real fellowship of the road. Caravanning at 90 has its attractions. There is always a change of scene."

Mrs Knight lived many years in Wheatley Hill. She became a well-known figure, helping her husband, the late Mr Ernest Knight, in his Post Office.

When her son Albert succeeded his father, she continued to help in the business.

When Mrs knight should have been enjoying a well earned retirement, the war came along. Although over 70 Mrs Knight carried on the Post Office when Albert was called to the RAF. She carried on throughout the war years.

5 August 1960

LEGION BIRTHDAY PARTY

There were 101 members at the 35th birthday party of Thornley British Legion women. Mrs J Clark presided and welcomed guests and asked them to join the branch and take part in the good work of the Legion. Following the tea, the birthday cake was cut by Mrs R Brewster (president). During the entertainment given by the Horner Sisters, Mrs J Robson and members of the Thornley Over-60 Club, Mrs Clark presented Mrs Barras with a present for knitting the most squares in a blanket presented to the World Refugee Fund. Prizes given by the section and Mrs E Archer in aid of the branch funds, were won by Mesdames V Templeton, J Anderson and S Parker. Music was provided by Mr Jackie Toye.

BIRTHDAY RECALLS FOOTLIGHT DAYS TO THORNLEY MAN

Many of the ex-service men of the First World War must have got a happy surprise and recalled happy memories when they heard that Bransby Williams, that character of characters of the stage had celebrated his 90th birthday on August 14.

Bransby did much in the hospitals and theatres of London for the lads in hospital blues. His portrayals and his talks, brought hope and courage to men shattered in body and mind, but to none more than Private John Dempsey of The King's Liverpool Rifles.

Jack Dempsey or Little Jackie, as he is better known, is a retired council bricklayer, living with his son-in-law and daughter Mr and Mrs John Regan, 91 Thornlaw, Thornley. At 71, Little Jackie can still play the piano, sing a canny song and spin the tale like a professional entertainer and drink a pint of beer.

Life And Soul

Before going into the army in 1914, Jackie was the life and soul of the many parties he attended. In the trenches at Ypres he kept up the moral until he got blown up and was sent to blighty with a shattered left arm and hand.

He was convalescent for many months in Edmunton Hospital London, before he was discharged. When he recovered he began to entertain the sisters and nurses and soldiers.

Although handicapped with a bandaged left hand, he played the piano. A typical Geordie, Jackie put across Blaydon Races, Keep your feet still Geordie Hinney, and Our Nan's Amazer. His fame spread and he was invited to outside parties.

He was selected to appear at the Prince of Wales Theatre in a first class charity programme which starred Bransby Williams, Etty King, Daisy Dorma, Little Tich and Little Jackie.

That night as he stood in the wings, he heard Bransby bring that massive audience to a deathly silence. Only the rustle of straw, the slow tick of the stage clock, and the long drawn sigh of the great character actor could be heard though the building.

The prince of comedians, little Tich followed Bransby, and he just turned the deathly silence to a yell.

When Little Jackie got in front of the footlights he was shaking in his shoes, but one solitary voice caught his ear, "Gan on Jackie lad" gie us "fish and chips." Jackie did, he got an encore and sang Blaydon Races. He got a tobacco pouch from Bransby and a fountain pen from Little Tich. Now when Jack Dempsey sits down at the piano with a pint on the top and his pipe filled ready to sing Our Nans Amazer he thinks of the old Master Bransby.

26 August 1960

EFFORT FOR BLIND

The committee of Wheatley Hill branch of the Guide Dogs for the Blind Association have been hard at work all this week preparing for a garden party to be held tomorrow in the grounds of Wheatley House, Wheatley Hill, by kind permission of Mr F Richardson (manager of Wheatley Hill Colliery) and his wife. Mrs Richardson will perform the opening ceremony at 2 pm and a varied programme includes displays by the local Boy Scouts and a gymnastic team from the Senior Boys' School. The Scouts will also be in charge of side - shows, competitions and a balloon race. Many prizes are being awarded and the winner of the balloon race is to receive a petite-point dressing table set. The balloons are being sold at a shilling each and the buyer of the

217

one travelling the furthest will receive the prize. "We hope this effort, which is in aid of branch funds, will be well supported," says the secretary, Mrs Charlton. "We only have a small committee but they have devoted many hours of their time to arranging a bumper programme."

CLUB PROFIT

Mr G Reay presided at the half-yearly meeting of Wheatley Hill Discharged and Demobilised Sailors' and soldiers' Social Club and Institute, when a profit of £808 16s 11d on the half-year's working was reported. Refreshment sales during the six months amounted to £7,935. Membership was reported as 337. From 21 nominations the following were elected by ballot to the committee for the ensuing year: Messrs N Dougherty, J Bradshaw, W Peacock, A Cain, P Leck and J Piercy.

2 September 1960

GUIDE DOGS FOR BLIND

Fine support at Wheatley Hill

The large crowd attending a garden fete at Wheatley Hill on Saturday, organised by Wheatley Hill branch of the Guide Dogs for the Blind Association, found an excellently arranged programme of attractions. The programme included a display of gymnastics by pupils of Wheatley Hill senior boys' school, and there were many side-shows and competitions in the charge of Wheatley Hill Troop of Boy Scouts.

Scoutmaster Leslie Barker and Messrs Colin Thackeray and F Richardson were also in charge of a balloon race. The balloons were sold for a shilling each, and each was flown into the air with a label attached requesting the finder to return it with details where it had been picked up. A prize will go to the buyer of the balloon found to have travelled the farthest distance.

At Weardale House

The fete was held in the grounds of Weardale House, by permission of the manager of Wheatley Hill colliery, Mr F Richardson, and his wife. The chairman of the branch, Mrs E Cowan, presided at the opening ceremony, which was performed by Mrs Richardson. Mrs Richardson was presented with a box of chocolates by Mrs Cowan.

Taking part in the gymnastic display were, Gordon Walls, Thomas Turnbull, John race, Geoffrey Day, John O'Sullivan, Thomas Routledge, John Harvey, Leslie Barker, James Stogdale, Barry Hammond, John Fishwick and John Bradshaw.

Various stalls, including a bring-and-buy, flowers, vegetables, ice cream, handkerchief and confectionery, were in the charge of the officials and committee of the branch, namely Mesdames E Cowan (chairman), C Charlton (secretary), Lowther (treasurer), Ord, Robinson, Walton, Foster, Ramage, Booth, Walker and Wilson, assisted by Mesdames Hodgson, G Charlton, L Hughes, Dinsdale, Gibson, Dodds, and Hastings.

Winners of the ladies ankle competition, judged by Messrs L Barker, C Thakeray and F Richardson, were 1, Mrs J Wilson; 2, Mrs P Walker; 3, Mrs T Ramage.

Master M Booth won the treasure hunt, and Mrs Neasham the guessing the doll's name competition.

As a result of the fete, £75 was raised for branch funds. "We have already raised £500 to buy two guide dogs and are now well on the way to having sufficient money for a third," the secretary, Mrs C Charlton, said. "We are most grateful to all those who supported the fete, including local tradesmen who so generously provided many of the prizes."

9 September 1960

CEMETERY KERBSTONES AT WHEATLEY HILL

Wingate Parish Council, at their meeting at Wheatley Hill on Monday presided over by Coun A Bishop agreed to accept responsibility for the removal of kerbstones around graves in their cemetery at Wheatley Hill and to meet the cost, where relatives requested this be done.

Previously, said the Clerk, Mr John Harper, the council had had no set policy on this matter, but kerbstones around graves meant extra work to keep the cemetery tidy. Shears had to be used to cut the grass around the graves, whereas if there were no kerbstones, the large electric mower would be able to make a clean sweep past the headstones.

"Every kerbstone in our cemetery," added the Clerk, "is an obstruction to efficient maintenance, and if people wished to have them removed, the cemetery superintendent assures us it would be quite a simple job and there would be no possibility of damage to the headstones.

To Keep Cemetery Tidier

He had read recently in the Press, said the Clerk, that other councils had agreed, where they had the consent of the people concerned, to remove kerbstones in an effort to keep their cemeteries tidier.

There was no doubt, said Coun J H Charlton, that the removal of kerbstones would result in the graves being better maintained and would eventually help to make the cemetery similar to the of a lawn-type burial ground. Some churchyards were a veritable wilderness but if people realised how much easier it would be to keep them tidy were there no kerbstones, they would be quick to give their consent for their removal, added Coun Charlton.

The proposal to pay for the cosy of the removal of the kerbstones where they had the consent of the people concerned, was proposed by Coun R Watson and seconded by Coun C Hackworth.

Replying to the council's request for an additional early morning bus to Durham from the Wingate area, the Gillett Bros. Motor Services wrote they were applying to the Traffic Commissioners for an additional run to leave Station Town at 7 am for Durham. This would be an extension of the present Thornley to Durham service.

The Council welcomed this news, though Coun J Carr said there would likely be an objection from another company operating along the same route.

"We seem to be like a shuttlecock between two companies," said Coun Charlton, "but I hope we land on the right side of the net!"

A WHEATLEY HILL FOOTPATH

Following a request for the footpath between Wheatley Hill road-ends and Old Wingate to be put into better order, the County Surveyor wrote that the matter had been discussed with representatives of the National Coal Board. It was the intention of the County Council to collect stones from local quarries and for the tenant farmers to spread them and fill in the potholes.

"This department will then roll the path, and consolidate the letter added. "After this work has been done I trust there will be no further complaint."

WHEATLEY HILL COUPLE TO EMIGRATE TO AUSTRALIA
Expect To Get Jobs Soon After Arrival

With the spirit of adventure in their blood, a young Wheatley Hill couple, who were married only nine months ago on Boxing Day, are setting sail for Australia tomorrow on the Fairsea.

"For months before we were married we talked of emigrating to Australia, especially as we had heard what splendid opportunities that country offered," Mr Alan Heslop told our reporter this week. "But it was not until after our wedding at Wheatley Hill that we finally signed the emigration papers to go."

For the past week or so Mr Heslop and his 22-year-old wife Dorothy have been living with his wife's parents, Mr and Mrs Harold Howarth, Wheatley Terrace, Wheatley Hill. Before that they lived at West Farm, Old Shotton.

First real home

"But with thoughts of emigrating in our minds there were lots of things we had not bought for our home," said Mrs Heslop. "Our first real home will be set up in Australia."

Mrs Heslop has been teaching at Wingate Secondary Modern School for the past two years. A former pupil of Wellfield A J Dawson grammar School, she began teaching after training at a college in London. Mr Heslop who is 27, is the only son of Mr and Mrs Norman Heslop 12 Ridding Court, Esh Winning.

For the past six months Mr Heslop has been employed as a fitter at Wheatley Hill colliery, but before that he worked at Hedley Hope colliery until it closed down and then Langley Park colliery

Neither he nor his wife have a job fixed up in Australia, but they don't expect having long to wait. They hope to follow the same occupations they have been engaged in here.

A furnished flat, however awaits them at the small town of Balgownie, New South Wales. It has been fixed up for them by a friend of Mrs Heslop's parents, Mrs Margaret Simpson, who herself emigrated to Australia many years ago from the Shotton area. "We are very thankful for this," said Mr Heslop. "I don't we'll be long before we are working."

Mr Heslop lived in Esh Winning practically all his life until his marriage. For the past seven years he has been actively associated with the Durham Ice Speed Skating Club. He has been secretary for three years and is a former captain of the speed team. He has been county quarter-mile champion twice and county half-mile champion once, and he was the winner of an open ice-speed skating event at Nottingham.

The present state of the mining industry had been one of the reasons why he and his wife had decided to emigrate, said Mr Heslop. He is a maintenance fitter and, he said, there appeared to be many good openings for his trade "down under." "Then, of course, there is the spirit of adventure, going to a new country and meeting new people." He said.

The couple, to whom their many friends extend best wishes for their future success and happiness, are due to dock in Sydney on October 22.

When will they return to England for a holiday? "Well, I suppose as soon as we have got nicely settled down and saved plenty of money." Said Mrs Heslop, with a smile.

CULLEN TO MEET
TOP FIGHTERS

Maurice Cullen gave a superb performance against Tom Tiger of Leicester, at Wolverhampton Town Hall, where he won every round against a rugged tear-away fighter. Cullen's left hand worked like a well-oiled piston, and Tiger had no answer to it. Cullen showed the Midland fans why he is such a big attraction at National Sporting Club, London.

Cullen has been booked to meet Phil McGrath, Halifax, on September 20. McGrath has topped the bill at many northern towns, and the N S C think he will give Cullen a good fight.

The programme for Cullen is a busy one, in October: when he will meet an old opponent, none other than Scotland's Jimmy Gibson, the idol of many television viewers. This fight is eagerly awaited by Northern boxing fans, for many think Gibson side-stepped Cullen. They will be able to see these boys in action at Middlesbrough, at Farrer Street Stadium on October 10.

MAURICE CULLEN
No. 1 LIGHTWEIGHT CONTENDER
Manager:- TERRY CULLEN
Telephone Thornley 349

Busy Programme Ahead

The demand for Cullen's services are growing, for he will make the return trip to Carlisle Covered Market on 28 October, where he fought Pat Loughran of Belfast, a selected opponent by the British Board of Boxing. For the record Cullen knocked out Loughran in the third round of their scheduled eight round bout.

His opponent will be Dave Stone, who fought Darkie Hughes in an eliminator for the lightweight title. Many will remember this gruelling fight, for Stone was narrowly out-pointed by Hughes of Cardiff, for the fight was televised.

Dave Stone has represented his country and fans are asking why was Cullen not chosen to represent England? This will give those who are wondering the opporutnity to see Cullen against an international boxer.

11 September 1960

PHOTOGRAPHY AT WHEATLEY HILL
Fine Send-Off In First Exhibition

Some excellent exhibits were on view when the Wheatley Hill and District Photographic Society, formed only in April this year, staged its first annual photography exhibition in the music room of the Nimmo Hotel.

The exhibition attracted no fewer than 65 entries from amateur photographers in Wheatley Hill and the surrounding villages and afterwards the secretary, Mr d Griffiths, of Wheatley Hill, said that the officials were delighted with such a fine response. "The standard of photography was quite high," he said, "and with such a good send off for our first exhibition, we are hoping for even better things in the future. The photographs were judges by Mr H Holder, of Coxhoe who is instructor at the photography evening class in Wheatley Hill modern boys' school.

Prizewinners

Portraiture: 1 Mr W Hudson, Moore Terrace, Shotton Colliery; 2 Mr W Tarn, 38 Cemetery Road East, Wheatley Hill; 3 Mr Thomas Heron, 9 Thornley Road, Wheatley Hill.

Landscapes: Mr J Gutcher, 101 Wordsworth Avenue, Wheatley Hill; 2 and 3 Mr W Tarn.

Flash and children: 1 Mr T Heron; 2 and 3 Mr W Hudson.

Holidays: 1 and 2 Mr R Gratton, Craiglaw, Cemetery Road East, Wheatley Hill; 3 Mr W Hudson.

Since the Society's formation the membership has steadily increased from a dozen to the present 30, "We are still increasing in numbers week by week," Mr Griffiths told our reporter. "We will be glad to welcome new members any time."

When the next exhibition is held, Mr Griffiths added, it was hoped to inaugurate an open class for entries from the public.

RETIREMENT OF WHEATLEY HILL MAN OF MANY PARTS

A Wheatley Hill miner, who was awarded the Military Medal for gallantry on the field of battle during the 1914-18 war, has retired from work at Wheatley Hill colliery after a mining career of nearly 53 years, all spent at the same colliery.

He is Mr William Simpson, 9 Fifteenth Street, who has just celebrated his 65th birthday. Though he was often "in the thick of the fighting," Mr Simpson went right through the war "without a scratch," he told our reporter this week.

"Then shortly after I resumed work at the colliery after being demobilised I broke my leg in a pit accident," he said with an ironic smile.

Mr Simpson was born at Wheatley Hill and has never lived out of the village. He was only 12½ years of age when he began work on the screens and was paid at the rate of a shilling a ten-hour shift. When he was 14 he went down the pit as a trapper-boy and then was a lamp-carrier.

After serving throughput the 1914-18 war as a sergeant in the 9th Yorkshire Regiment, Mr Simpson resumed his mining career as a putter. As well as the accident in which he broke a leg, he was also involved in another serious accident in 1934. This time both his legs were broken and when he returned to work he was employed on surface duties. He went back down the pit again as a stone-man, but in 1940, still feeling the effects of his accident, he returned to the surface and since then has been employed in the powder magazine house.

FORMER NORTHERN LEAGUE PLAYER

When Mr Simpson returned to civilian life after the war, the villagers of Wheatley Hill presented him with a gold watch and a Bible in recognition of him winning the Military Medal.

In his younger days Mr Simpson was a well-known local footballer. He played at centre half for Wheatley Hill Athletic, and later spent a season with Willington in the Northern League. When he broke his leg shortly after the war, however, this ended his football career. For three years running he played for his army divisional football team during the war.

Mr Simpson is married with three daughters, Mrs Doreen Owen, has been in Brazil for the past five years, her husband, Roland is manager of a gold mine there. His second daughter, Mrs Sheila Taylor, and her husband, William are steward and stewardess of Cassop Workmen's Club, and his youngest daughter, Mrs Patricia Terrington, lives in London where her husband, Ronnie, is a sergeant in the Metropolitan Police. Mr and Mrs Simpson also have three grandchildren.

23 September 1960

WHEATLEY HILL'S CHAMPION LEEK-GROWER

A 69-year-old retired Wheatley Hill miner, Mr William Curry, well-known in the area for his prolific successes at local shows, once again proved himself a champion leek-grower at the weekend

Not only did the leeks he entered in the annual show at Wheatley Hill constitutional Club win the principal three prizes, but his leeks also won second prize at the Thornley Workmen's Club show.

In addition to these successes, Mr Curry, who will be 70 next April, won second and third prizes for intermediate leeks at the Thornley show, and prizes for other vegetables at the two Wheatley Hill shows. At the Wheatley Hill Workmen's Club show he won first prize for long carrots and round potatoes.

What Mr Curry does not know about leeks is not worth knowing, for he has been a master of the art since 1928. "In the first competition I entered that year," he told me, "I won a sideboard with the best pair of leeks in the show 'over the beck' at Wheatley Hill. Next year I again carried off first prize, this time it was a wardrobe, and I have been winning prizes ever since."

Two years ago, however, Mr Curry failed for first time to win a principal prize, but it was no fault of his own! That year he had no fewer than 88 leeks stolen out of his jars and he could not get any more prepared in time foe the shows. "It was a bitter blow to me, that!" he said.

Mr Curry says that he has no secret for successful leek-growing. "Good manure, that's the head gardener," he said, with a twinkle in his eye. "But," he added mysteriously, "There is an art in growing a prize-winning leek."

30 September 1960

COLLAPSED IN THE MINE
Funeral of Mr George Dryden

The funeral took place of Mr George Dryden (55), of 6 Thornlaw North, Thornley, who collapsed and died at Wheatley Hill Colliery on Friday. Mr Dryden who had been doing light work at the shaft bottom had one of his legs amputated through an injury while coal-cutting 14 years ago.

He was a native of Quarrington Hill and began work at Kelloe Colliery. He removed to Wheatley Hill some 30 years ago. He settled in Thornley after his marriage.

His body was received into the church of the English Martyrs previous to Requiem Mass said by Fr H McNeill and interment was at Thornley Cemetery, Fr P Smith officiating.

Mr Dryden and his family have been enthusiastic workers for the RC Church. He was one of the founder members of the Catholic Club.

14 October 1960

PLAYGROUND SOLD FOR SLUM CLEARANCE AT THORNLEY

Thornley Parish Council agreed to allow a piece of the land now used as a children; recreation ground to be sold on terms agreed upon by the District Valuer. Coun A F Walker, chairman, said that Easington Rural District Council, of which he is a member, required this portion of land to start the first phase of their slum clearance programme.

Coun Mrs J Anderson, who moved that the land be sold to the district council, said the first concern of this council is to see that people are housed in their village and that there are many open spaces where the children's recreation equipment can be transferred.

In a letter to the council, Messrs Sparks and Blake, solicitors of Crewkerne, Somerset, stated that they had now completed the sale of the Spearman's Estate to the National Coal Board and have been able to prepare the necessary deed to convey to the council, Church Street, as a gift to the parish. This piece of land is a wide open space 30yards wide by 120 yards long lying south of St Bartholomew's Church, it had been promised to the councils by the trustees of the estate some years ago. The council agreed to ask Mr Kelly the legal adviser of Easington Rural District Council to examine the deed and advise them on the terms.

Coun Miss A Griffiths complained of the footpath running between heaps of coal on the colliery tipping site at the east end of the village being flooded. She said it was in a disgraceful condition and she had seen two workmen travelling to Wheatley Hill who had climbed up on top of the coal heaps to get to the roadway. She said the heavy downpour of rain had made channels in the side of the heaps and just collected at the bottom making the footpath impassable. The clerk was instructed to inform Mr F Parkin the No 3 Area Secretary of the NCB of the problem.

Coun J R Bosomworth also complained to the council about some fencing wire, which had been broken in many places and then tied around the supporting posts, the ends of the wire left sticking out at the side of the footpath thus tearing the clothes of passers by.

These wire ends sticking, out said Coun Bosomworth, can be a real danger to little children if they penetrate an eye or cut the face. He said the fencing was practically a new job but it was pulled to pieces by the children jumping upon the wire. The council decided to ask the owners of the land to have the wire removed.

THORNLEY GOLDEN WEDDING

Mr and Mrs Thomas Tunney 17 Aged Miners' Homes, Thornley, celebrated their golden wedding on Saturday. They were married at West Cornforth R C Church, by the Rev Father P J Sheehan. Bridesmaid was Miss Rosie Kilgallen (now Mrs Mark McDonnell of Thornley) and best man Mr Tunney's brother William (now in USA).

Mrs Tunney, formerly Miss Julia McDonnell, was born at Hartlepool in 1887. Mr Tunney is also 73 and was born in Kelloe. He worked in the pits for 53 years and as a deputy overman for 42 years at Thornley Colliery.

Mr and Mrs Tunney will hold the first party celebration with their son-in-law and youngest daughter Mr and Mrs W Curry, at their home in Watford, where they are spending a holiday. They will also hold a small reception at home when they return with their son, Mr and Mrs John Tunney, of Middlesbrough, and their son-in-law and daughter, Mr and Mrs J Carr, of Thornley.

WHEATLEY HILL COUPLE WED 50 YEARS

Two founder members of Wheatley Hill Over-60 Club, Mr and Mrs Robert Richardson, 47 Johnson Estate, Wheatley Hill, tomorrow celebrate their golden wedding, and to mark the occasion they are holding a family party in the new council bungalow they moved into six months ago.

Mrs Richardson, whose maiden name was Isabel Cowie, played a major part in launching the Over 60 Club, which has gone on from success to success since its formation seven years ago. Mrs Richardson was its first secretary, and continued to fill this position, putting in much hard work to ensure the success of the club, until about two years ago, when she and her husband went to South Africa to spend an eight-month holiday with their eldest son. She has had the satisfaction of seeing the club increase in numbers year by year, until now the membership is well over300 and she is still a member of the concert party.

Mr Richardson, who is 71, was born at Heworth Lane, near felling, and was only 12½ when he began work at North Biddick Colliery, "I was a driver-lad, earning a shilling a ten-hour shift," he told our reporter this week, "but was there only a few months before moving to Wheatley Hill.

53 Years In Mining

Mr Richardson continued his mining career at Wheatley Hill Colliery, where he has done most jobs underground, until his retirement six years ago, after a mining career of nearly 53 years. "Fortunately," he said "I have never been involved in any accidents of a serious nature."

In his younger days Mr Richardson was a well known figure at local wedding receptions, entertaining the guests on his "melodian." He has always been fond of music, and only recently bought himself a new piano-accordion.

Both Mr and Mrs Richardson enjoy good health and Mrs Richardson, who is 69 does all her own housework. She has often freely given of her help to voluntary committees in the village. During the last war she worked three years in munitions, and she was formerly associated with the local women's section of the British Legion.

The couple, who formerly lived in Darlington Street, Wheatley Hill, for 34 years, have had a family of 12. They now have living six daughters and three sons and 15 grandchildren.

Their eldest son Jonathan is in South Africa, and they have two daughters, Mrs May Hall and Mrs Alice Hagan, in New Zealand. Another son, Robert, is serving in the Royal Navy.

Good wishes are extended to the couple for many more happy years together, by their many friends in he area.

28 October 1960

PROBLEMS AT THORNLEY

Councillor James Hoban asked at Thornley Parish Council "What is the good of this land to us?" He was referring to a piece of land given to the council by the trustees of the Spearmans Estate,

Coun Alfred Bushby said: "We can make use of the land in several ways, but I think our first duty is to try and make a decent road to the parish church. In the weather which we have experience these last few weeks, people going and returning from church over the shoe tops in mud."

Coun Miss Annie Griffiths, supporting the idea of a roadway, said, "we had promised the church council to do all we can to help in making a better approach to the church and that was three years ago."

Coun James Nicholson said: "I expect we are not going to make any plans on this plot of ground that will conflict with the county plan for this spot and expend money needlessly."

Coun F A Walker, chairman, said the best thing the council could do was to get an estimate of the cost of the footpath from High Street and Coopers Terrace to the church entrance. This was agreed to.

In "No Man's Land

Another problem faced the council when Coun James Nicholson asked if anything could be done to have a bare lifeless tree standing alone on "no man's land" removed or cut down. The tree said Coun Nicholson, is a playground for children who climb to the top. Some of the branches are rotten. We cannot get anyone to say who the land belongs to.

The clerk, Mr Martin Flemming, was instructed to ask the landowners surrounding this section to supply a drawing of their boundary.

A Danger Point

A dangerous spot at the entrance to Greenwood Cottage from St Chad's Square was reported by Miss A Griffiths. The lighting in this district was said to be very poor.

Coun Bushby thought more lighting units were needed. The clerk was instructed to take the complaints up with the officials concerned.

PRESENTATION

To mark his retirement as night shift overman at Thornley Colliery, which he has held for 24 years, Mr Bertie Hodgson, of Thornley, has been presented with a cigarette case and lighter by underground officials. Mr Hodgson spent 52 years at the colliery.

LEGION WOMEN

Mrs E Clark presided at meeting of Thornley British legion Women's Section and 50 members were present.

Business details were presented by Miss Nellie Redshaw, secretary, and the financial statement by Mrs E Middleton. Prizes were won by Mesdames N Harle and E Johnson. At the annual meeting officials were elected as follows: Mesdames E Clark, N Redshaw and E Middleton, chairman, secretary and treasurer respectively; Mesdames H Brewster and S Parker, president and vice-president; Mrs H Slater vice-chairman and standard bearer. Others elected were: sick visitors, Wheatley hill, Mesdames A Hird and P E Morgan. Thornley, Mesdames S Redshaw and E Middleton, Committee: Mesdames B Musgrave, H Thompson, E P Morgan D Wright, V

Templeton, E Peaceful, Ena Ferguson, L Gordon and M Barrass. Mrs Clark congratulated the secretary and treasurer on the efficient way they had carried out their duties, and also thanked members for the splendid contributions. The branch had contributed to the county handicrafts exhibition, to the refugee fund with presents of blankets, to the RSPCA and to Queens Mead rest Home.

11 November 1960

THORNLEY ROYAL MARINE'S DREAM COMES TRUE

Sitting listening to the stories of the sea, watching the white masted sailing ships, pass by and the rough waves smash upon the foreshore; built up in young Frances Drake the burning desire to be a man of war, and now today Sir Frances Drake and his exploits with the Armada are legend.

It would be difficult to number the young men whose boyhood dreams inspired them in later life, but there are still stories of adventure and daring that were absorbed in the dreams of childhood.

Ellis Mather, youngest son of Mr and Mrs Ellis Mather of 72 East Lea, Thornley, would sit spellbound in front of the television set watching the march past of troops at the Remembrance Sunday parade. He developed that burning desires to take part in the solemn ceremony, but his desire was to march with the Royal Marines.

Last weekend Ellis Mather of 41st Commandos of Royal Marines marched with his own unit in that parade, he was one of the men chosen, for duty for the Lord Mayor's show on Saturday and the Armistice service.

Sitting watching the march past at 72 East Lea, Thornley were Mr and Mrs Mather proud to think their youngest boy made his dream come true.

NEW SOCIAL CLUB FOR THORNLEY

Thornley Colliery officials after many months have received planning permission for the conversion of a dwelling house into a social club.

The members formed their committee 18 months ago and appointed Messrs J Hedley,G Bennett, and T Weatherall, as chairman, secretary and treasurer respectively and they were entrusted to expedite the opening of the club. Unfortunately things have been difficult because of the future development planned for the village.

Mr George Bennett now states that work will immediately start and he hopes that members will be having refreshments in their own club within a few weeks.

The house they have acquired is situated in the Villas, Thornley, and for many years has been the home of the colliery engineer. It is spacious and has garden and lawn on the south and cellars under the house. It will now be the third social club in the village.

18 November 1960

HORSEKEEPER RETIRES AT THORNLEY

With the exception of two years spent with the Royal Artillery during the 1914-18 war, Mr Albert Thomas, of 104 Thornlaw North, Thornley, who retired from work as a horsekeeper at Thornley Colliery, has completed 51 years' service in the pits.

Mr Thomas commenced work at Wingate Grange Colliery in 1909, and was driving and putting before going into the army. He resumed his employment on demobilisation and worked at Wingate Colliery until the 1921 strike and in that year he got married.

For the first six months of their married life Mr and Mrs Thomas had only one pay packet of £3 3s, because Mr Thomas did not get a start after the strike, Eventually Mr Thomas got work at Thornley Colliery towards the end of 1921 and worked as a horsekeeper until his retirement.

His wife, Mrs Edith Thomas, is a native of Thornley, and her grandfather, Mr James Carter, was for many years farm bailiff on the Thornley Estate. He worked under three coal companies, Thornley Coal Co., the Original Hartlepool Coal Co., and the Weardale Iron and Coal Co. He lived at Thornley Hall Farm and died at Cassop at the age of 86.

When Mr Thomas began horsekeeping there was something like 300 horses underground to look after. Today, says Mr Thomas, there are about 30 and of course the job is a lot better.

Mr Thomas has always been interested in local boxing and can recall the fights of now old Johnny Gorman and his son Pat, Charlie Curry, Gunner Raine and many of the local lads.

25 November 1960

"GOLDEN DAY" AT THORNLEY
Hutchinson family celebration

Mr and Mrs Joseph Hutchinson, of 90, Dunelm Road, Thornley, celebrated their golden wedding on Saturday. They were married in the Primitive Methodist Church, Thornley, by the Rev William Gelley.

The celebration party was held in the schoolroom of the chapel where they were married. The cake was made by the youngest daughter, Miss Betsy Hutchinson, and was iced by her sister, Mrs Norman Garswood. Two of the guests at the wedding were present at the celebration party. Mrs R Willie of Peterlee who was bridesmaid, and Miss Joanna Wilkinson. Mr Hutchinson, a retired miner, was born at Trimdon. His father, Mr Joseph Hutchinson, was a native of Newcastle and he was the youngest of four brothers who held prominent positions on Tyneside. The elder brother, Humphrey, at one time landlord of the Sportsmen's Arms, Carville, was a foreman erector on the Swing Bridge across the Tyne. Mr Christopher Hutchinson was chief sports reporter on a Newcastle newspaper and Thomas Hutchinson was a chief reporter at Newcastle.

Mr Hutchinson began work at Thornley Colliery in 1905. He worked also at Bowburn and Kelloe and retired from Thornley in 1955 after completing 52 years in the pits. He served with four other brothers in the 1914-18 war, and was wounded in 1917 and discharged.

Mrs Hutchinson was born in Thornley and lived for many years in Coopers Terrace before removing to Dunelm Road 38 years ago. She was a founder member of Thornley Over 60 Club.

MARRIED AT WHEATLEY HILL

November 5 was a disappointing day for Miss Rita Banks, youngest daughter of Mr and Mrs John Banks, 75 Wordsworth Avenue, Wheatley hill. She had all arrangements made to marry Mr Rex James Davies, Glen View, Lower Milk Wall, Coleford, Gloucester. Unfortunately, as her bridegroom was leaving Osnabruck in Germany for his wedding, Corporal Davies who is in the Regular Army had a motoring accident. He received minor injuries and shock and so the wedding had to be postponed.

The wedding took place in Wheatley Hill Patton Street Methodist Church, with Rev G L Nelson officiating. Mr Wm Luke was at the organ. The bride, given away by her father, was also in military service in Germany and was nursing in the British Military hospital in Munster. She was attired in a full-length gown of white brocade with circular veil surmounted by a coronet of pearls. She carried a bouquet of pink roses.

Miss Joyce Davies, Coleford (sister of the bridegroom) and Miss Pauline Lofthouse (bride's niece) were bridesmaids. They wore dresses of turquoise brocade with white flowered headdresses and carried bouquets of white carnations. The bride's nephew, Neville Cain, was page. Best man was groom's brother, Robert.

The bride had a gold sovereign tucked in her shoe. As she left the church she received a lucky horseshoe from her niece Sandra Cain, After a honeymoon at St Austel the couple will return to Germany.

MRS E HALL'S SUCCESSES

Mrs Edna Hall, secretary of Wheatley Hill Women's Bowls Club won all three trophies in last season's singles tournaments, and last night she was presented with them at the club's evening in the Welfare Hall. Mrs Hall won both the Championship Cup and the festival Bowl for the second year running. Mrs J Hodgson, chairman of the club, presided, and the cups and prizes were presented to the following, by Mrs Lucille Haddock. Championship Cup Mrs Hall, runner up Mrs E Atkinson, William Jones Cup, Mrs Hall, runner up Mrs D Snowden, Festival Bowl Mrs Hall, runner up Mrs E Atkinson. Representatives of the North Eastern Women's Bowling League, in which Wheatley Hill club competes were among the guests.

2 December 1960

HONOUR FOR WHEATLEY HILL SCHOOL

Wheatley Hill Boys' Modern School brought honour to South-East Durham when they competed in the Durham County Schools' Gymnastic Championship at Billingham Technical College. Mr Arthur Harris reports that his boys were placed first in Grade 1 section. Wheatley Hill were awarded the Joseph Championship Cup. The team representing Wheatley Hill was Eric Weatherell (captian), Barry Hammond, Robert Walls, Alan Peters, James Stogdale and Leslie Barker.

A member of the Wheatley Hill team, Barry Hammond, came out top in the individual events. He gained the title of Durham County Junior Gymnastic Champion and was presented with the Vickerstaffe Cup.

Eric Wetherell, the Wheatley Hill captain, was placed third in the individual events. Cups, trophies, and certificates were presented by County Coun Coxon.

The Wheatley Hill team were trained by the school's PE specialists, Mr N Norton and Mrs K Charlton.

9 December 1960

CHRISTMAS GIFTS

From the Wheatley Hill Aged Miners' Treat Fund, retired workmen at Wheatley Hill colliery and their wives, and widows over 55, are to receive Christmas gifts of 10s each. The distribution is to take place from the Wheatley Hill Old Men's Hostel tomorrow (Saturday). Officials of the fund will be in charge.

CHOIR WEEKEND

A successful choir weekend was celebrated at Wheatley Hill Church Street Methodist Church. There were good congregations. On Saturday evening a concert was held in the church. The programme was provided by the Circle Singers, of Spennymoor (accompanist and conductor Mr J Prest). Mr Alan Straughan presided. Supper was served by members of the church and choir. The services on Sunday were conducted by Mr I Atkinson, of Seaton Delaval, Mrs R Ord was at the organ.

CHRISTMAS CHEER

Over 300 old aged pensioners, their wives, and widows of members were remembered by the patrons of Wheatley Hill Workmen's Club and Institute. There were entertained to their annual tea and musical entertainment. The guests were welcomed by Mr W Henderson, club chairman. A knife and fork tea was enjoyed. Local artists entertained. Each person present received a gift of £1 from the club treasurer, Mr J Dunn. All the arrangements were in the hands of the secretary, Mr B Aitken, and a strong committee.

JUMBLE SALE

As a result of a jumble sale on Friday organised by the 2nd Wheatley Hill group of Boy Scouts, the sum of £8 5s was raised for Scout funds. The Group secretary, Coun R Watson, announces that the Scouts, as in past years, are going carol singing in the area, commencing tonight (Friday). Group Scoutmaster Leslie Barker will be in charge, anyone wishing to help is invited to join the group of singers. The money collected will be used to provide gifts for the children's ward of Durham County Hospital, which the Scouts "adopted" some years ago. "Already we have spent about £300 on equipment for the ward and other gifts since we adopted the ward," Coun R Ward told our reported this week.

Scouts' Re-union

Thirty-seven "old Scouts" attended the fourth annual re-union dinner and social evening and social evening of the Wheatley Hill Old Scouts' Association in the King's head Hotel, Easington Village, on Saturday night. Group Scoutmaster Leslie Barker presided, and a minute's silence was observed in memory of an old Scout, Mr John Armstrong, of Thornley, who had died suddenly the previous day. Coun Ralph Watson secretary of the Wheatley Hill group of Scouts, congratulated the old Scouts on the excellent "job of work" they die earlier this year in devoting all their spare time to re-building the Scout headquarters. It was well worthwhile work for it helped to keep the youth of the village "off the streets." Entertainment was provided by Mr T Howe (comedian), and Messrs J Pyle and W Turnbull (soloists), and the pianists were Messrs W Walker and Tony Carr.

16 December1960

NEW OFFICIALS CLUB FOR THORNLEY

Over 200 members and guests were entertained on Saturday 17th, when the Thornley Colliery Officials' Club was opened by Mr L C Timms, General Manager of No 3 Area, NCB Mr Timms congratulated the official and committee on the reorganisation and furnishing of the premises in so short a time and said that it was 125 years since the colliery began and they had waited a long time for an officials' club.

Mr Arthur Welsh, jun., presided, and drew the first pints of ale, which were distributed to old retired members. Mr Amos Robinson, 86-year-old retired deputy overman, who had spent over 60 years underground, made history when he received his pint, as he received a similar gift over 60years ago when the first social club was opened in Thornley.

Mr Welsh also presided at the reception given to the guests, who included his 82-years-old father, late colliery manager of Thornley, who was the last under private enterprise and first under nationalisation; Mr Duncan Davie, H M Inspector on Mines, Rev Phillip G Mould, Vicar of Thornley, Mr D Hesler, manager, Wingate Colliery, Mr J Galley, manager East Hetton, Colliery, Mr T Mackeay, manager Ryhope, Mr P Galley, ex-cashier, Wheatley Hill, Mr J W Bell, general manager Station Town, Seaham and Horden Co-op Society, Mr W J Reay, clerk of Shadforth Parish Council, Messrs A Bushby (chairman), E Carter (secretary), W Thompson(treasurer), Thornley Mining Federation Board, Mr F Bradley (chairman), Thornley Miners' Welfare Committee.

The club is situated at a central point in the village. It was the former residence of the colliery engineers.

Credit is due to Messrs J Hedley (chairman), G Bennett (secretary) and T Weatherall (treasurer) for their efforts to open the new premises before Christmas and New Year.

23 December1960

GIRL GUIDES ENTERTAINED

At the annual party of the 1st Wheatley Hill Company of Girls Guides and Brownies held at the Scout headquarters on Wednesday, about 50 girls were entertained. Tea was served and games and competitions were organised by Guide Captain Mrs R Watson, assisted by the patrol leaders.

CAROL SINGING

The sum of £19, was raised by Wheatley Hill Troop of Boy Scouts as a result of carol singing in the village during the festive season. Tonight they will be out singing again, this being their final "performance." The money collected is to be used to buy gifts for the children's ward of Durham County Hospital, which the Troop "adopted" some years ago.

EXTRA DAY

Workmen at Wheatley Hill colliery had an "extra day" holiday at Christmas. Though neighbouring collieries returned to work on Tuesday, the Wheatley Hill miners did not start until Wednesday. They were given Tuesday holiday because their fortnight's holiday last year included August Bank Holiday Monday. "It made a nice long week-end break," said one of the miners on Wednesday.

SUNDAY SCHOOLS PARTIES

About 90 senior scholars and 60 juniors were entertained, respectively, at the annual Sunday School parties at Church Street Methodist Church, Wheatley Hill. For the seniors there were gamed and competitions, and ice-cream and jelly were served. The juniors were provided with tea and each received a gift from Santa Claus (Mr E Hutchinson), as well as an apple and orange. Messrs V Swift (Sunday School secretary) and P H Galley, junior (treasurer) were in charge of the arrangements.

AID FOR GUIDE DOGS

More that £22 was raised for funds of Wheatley Hill branch of the Guide Dogs for the Blind Association as a result of a recent successful social evening in the Welfare Hall. In a special competition organised to replace a balloon race held earlier at a garden fete, the first prize of a dressing table set, was won by Mr George Graves. Mrs R Connor won second prize. In the balloon race a prize was to have gone to buyer of the balloon found to have travelled the greatest distance. No balloons, however, were returned, and so the special competition was organised. The secretary, Mrs G Charlton, was responsible for the arrangements. The annual party of the branch is to be held on January 7.

FUNERAL OF BUTCHER

A large company gathered in All Saints Church, Wheatley Hill, for the Funeral of Mr Robert Henderson, (57) 2 Co-operative Villas, Wheatley Hill. He died suddenly after attending Sedgefield Auction Mart. His wife, Jennie died suddenly only seven months ago. He is survived by a married daughter, a daughter and two sons. Mr Henderson became foreman and then for 13 years manager of Wheatley Hill Co-operative Society butchering department and 18 months ago was appointed manager and buyer for Sherburn Hill Co-operative Society.

FIRE FIGHTING CONTEST

Under the greater safety campaign at Thornley Colliery the annual fire-fighting competition was won by a team of underground workers; Marice Kirk, coal cutter, Ray Briggs, stoneman, Tom Robson, face trainee, William Convery, assistant ventilation officer. The individual competition was won by Alan Straughan, pipe fitter. The judge was Mr Wilfred Barnfather, No 3 Area Civil Defence and Fire Fighting Officer, and arrangements were made by Mr Harold Todd, Colliery Safety Officer.

PRIZES PRESENTED

Before the annual party at Thornley RC St Godric's Mixed School, the usual Christmas concert was held Rev Father Smith presented prizes to: John McDonnell, James Dunn, Hubert Tunney, Lorretta Shutt, Kathleen Nuttall, Brian McDonnell, James Wilson, Christine Callaghan, Margaret English, Peter Connelly, William Waistell, Kevin Boulger, Stephen Gilling, Margaret Ellward, Patrica Hoban, Joan Luke, John Regan, John Morton, Doreen English, Patrica Drydon.   Good   conduct: Valerie Tatters and Ann Luke.
30 December 1960

1961

A CAR CRASH NEAR WHEATLEY HILL

A Wheatley Hill motorist, Joseph Collins, of Broadmeadows, Durham Road, had a narrow escape from serious injury in the early hours of New Year's Day when his car skidded across the road, mounted a slight embankment and came to rest upside down in a nearby wood. Collins, who was the only person in the car, was taken to Hartlepools Hospital, suffering from shock, lacerations to his head and bruises, but was allowed to return home after treatment.

The accident occurred about 2.45am on the main road between the Fir Tree, Wingate and Wheatley Hill.

Seeing the car in the wood with its wheels in the air, another motorist, James Gibson, 71 Luke Terrace, Wheatley Hill, stopped and, with passers-by, gave assistance to Collins.

While Gibson's car was parked at the side of the road, however, another motorist travelling from the direction of Wingate, collided with it. This motorist, Norman Harrison (28), Shinwell Crescent, Thornley, was also taken to Hartlepools Hospital, but was allowed home after treatment for shock and slight head injuries. Damage was done to both cars.

WHEATLEY HILL BOY'S RAF PROGRESS

Among outstanding boy entrants who completed their training recently at No 4 School of Technical Training, RAF Station, St Athan, Glamorgan, and who received Air Ministry prizes, was Sergeant Boy Entrant Robert Turnbull (18) of 18 Jack Lawson Terrace, Wheatley Hill, County Durham.

Born at Wheatley Hill and educated at Shotton Secondary Modern School, Robert joined the RAF in June, 1959. He was awarded an Air Ministry prize for gaining second place in educational examinations.

The Reviewing Officer at the passing-out was Air Vice-Marshal J G Davis, CB, OBE, MA, Air Officer Commanding No 1 Bomber Group.

6 January 1961

FORMER THORNLEY SAFETY OFFICER'S FUNERAL

The Rev R Hancock, officiated in Bow Street Methodist Church, Thornley, and at the Crematorium, Durham for the funeral service of Mr James Orange (66), who died suddenly at his home, 18 Dunelm Road, Thornley, on New Year's Eve.

Mr Orange retired from his employment as Safety Officer at Thornley Colliery in April 1959, under the age limit. He was born at Wheatley Hill, and commenced work at Thornley Colliery in 1908. He worked for a short period on the surface before going underground, where he was a driver, putter and shot firer before he enlisted in the Grenadier Guards in 1916 and served in France. On his return he worked as a stoneman and deputy overman, and took his second class mine manager's certificate in 1921 and worked as foreshift overman until he was appointed Safety Officer in 1953.

Secretary 40 Years

Mr Orange became secretary of Thornley Colliery Ambulance Class in 1918 and held the position for 40 years. He was also secretary of Durham, Cleveland and Westmorland Ambulance League for six years and 27 years as a member of Houghton Fire and Rescue Brigade. In first aid he held a medallion and 37 labels and in 1937 the Duke of Connaught invested him as a Serving Brother of the Order of St John and in 1950 at Glasgow he became an Officer Brother.

Among the mourners was Mr Christopher Woodward, a retired training officer, who first met Mr Orange at an ambulance class in 1918 and put in an aggregate service together in class and at the colliery of nearly 90 years. Mr Orange is survived by his wife and a married son.

13 January 1961

POINTS VERDICT FOR CULLEN

Maurice Cullen, the promising Shotton lightweight had one of the hardest bouts in his short but successful professional career when he gained a narrow points decision over Phil McGrath (Halifax) at Middlesbrough.

They had previously been paired to meet at the White City in London some time ago, but McGrath had to call off with a damaged hand.

Cullen proved himself the more polished boxer and he made good use of his whip-lash left. McGrath was a tough proposition when it came to in-fighting, and handed out some heavy body punishment which troubled Cullen in the later stages of the fight.

During the first six rounds McGrath was always trying to carry the fight to his opponent, but Cullen kept himself out of trouble and boxed cleverly at long range.

McGrath was always strong and dangerous and even when he suffered a badly cut eye in one bout of hard in-fighting, early in the seventh round, he was still in a tigerish mood. For the remainder of the seventh and also in the final round, the Halifax man was most dangerous and was bent on a knock-out in spite of his handicap.

He frequently cornered Cullen on the ropes and handed out some heavy body punishment but the Shotton boxer was just too clever for him and, although Cullen knew he had been in a fight before the end, he was worth the decision on points.

20 January 1961

THORNLEY FUNERAL OF MR A ROBINSON

The Rev R Hancock conducted the funeral service in Bow Street Methodist Church, Thornley, of Mr Amos Robinson (85), who died at his home, 31 Aged Miners' Homes, Thornley. Mr Robinson was a native of Spennymoor, and began work at Haswell Colliery when he was 12. He moved to Thornley when Haswell Colliery closed in 1896 and worked as a hewer.

He joined Kitchener's Army in 1914 with his 18-year-old son. They served together with the 37th Siege Battery in Egypt and France for four years. He resumed work at Thornley and worked until his retirement in 1948 completing 61 years in the pits and 34 years as deputy overman, a position held at retirement.

Mr Robinson was a playing member of the old Thornley Colliery Band and was present at the opening of the first county aged miners' homes at Haswell Moor. He was a founder member of Thornley Workingmen's Club, which was formed in 1900. He was also an honorary member of Thornley Catholic Club.

GREATER SAFETY CAMPAIGN
COMPETITON AT THORNLEY

Another effort to popularise the Greater Safety Campaign at the colliery was made by Thornley ambulance students in a competition in the Welfare Institute. Teams were made up of two senior members and two juniors, with one reserve. Individual competition was in senior and junior sections. The adjudicator was Dr John Gray. Prizes of saving stamps were awarded from the managers' safety fund. Team winners were:

1   W Routledge Senior
    T Robson, Senior
    R Errington, Junior
    D Robson, Junior
    W R Simons, Reserve
2   W D Docherty, Senior
    D Barker, Senior
    T Mason, Junior
    R P Luck, Junior
    B Walker, Reserve

Individual prizewinners: W Routledge, T Robson and D Barker and W G Docherty tied for third place. Juniors R Errington, T Mason, D Robson. A 2ft model of a human skeleton, also from the managers' fund, was on exhibition.

VARIED CAREER OF THORNLEY'S AULD MATT

Mr Mathew Joseph Wilson, Auld Matt as he is known to all the bairns of the recreation ground, of 7 Nelson Street, Thornley, celebrated his 80th birthday last week. He was born in the old Kings Head Inn, Albert Street, Thornley on 20 January 1871 while his father, Mr John Wilson, was licensee.

He attended school at St Godric's, Hartlepool Street, when the children paid 2d a week school fees or a certificate from the relieving officer, and also the Board School at Wheatley Hill where the fees were 6d per week.

When he was 16, the Kings Head was one of the four public houses in Thornley that lost its licence and his father took over the tenancy of White House Farm.

BARMAN AND POT BOY

He worked for a short time as barman and pot boy at the Nimmo Hotel, Wheatley Hill, before he attended the hirings at Stockton and was employed on a farm in Stokesley. After many hirings and work at different farms Mr Wilson got work at Thornley Colliery as a horseman, and worked at White House in the evenings. He spent 35 years at Thornley Colliery before he retired in 1945 and had been employed as a pit heap erector, general labourer, fireman and engine driver.

Grand memory

Mr Wilson has a grand memory. He recalls the three shifts strike in 1910 when the young miners kicked the ballot boxes through the street. He also remembers the yearly visit of the Estate Agent to the Half Way House when all the tenant farmers paid the yearly dues and many had to be taken home on the farm cart.

Since he retired Auld Matt was taken a special interest in the children's recreation ground near his home and can be seen with his grandchildren at the mountain glide and swings when the weather is fair.

Mr Wilson has four married sons and three married daughters and lives in his own house with a single daughter, Miss Mary Wilson, who is employed in Thornley Post Officer.

LUDWORTH LEGION PARTY (PHOTO)

Upwards of 80 persons, all over 60 years of age, residents of Ludworth, were guests last week of Ludworth branch of the British Legion.

The event was a repeat of a similar one held last year, and in welcoming the guests, Mr A Winter, chairman of the branch, said that the members would try to make the event an annual one. It was the second year the treat had been held and the members would try to carry on. He thanked the committee for the hard work which had been put in.

An excellent meal was served, and at the end a cake, made by Mrs Winter and decorated by Mrs Kelly, was formally cut by the oldest couple present, Mr and Mrs Lumsden. Wine was served and the loyal toast given. Mr and Mrs Lumsden were presented with a gift by the chairman.

Concert

After the tables had been cleared a concert was given by Mr Ernest Peachey and his party of entertainers. The party consisted of Mr J Toye, Mr Ernest Peachey, his son, Miss Elizabeth Peachey and Mrs Chapman. There were also games and dancing.

The arrangements were efficiently carried out by a strong band of Legion members. Mrs J Champley (president), Mr A Winter (chairman), Mr J Ditchburn (secretary), Mr James Armstrong (treasurer), Mrs N Armstrong (vice-chairman of the management committee), Mesdames Winter, Gibson, E Armstrong, Hogg, Leathers, Cowan, L Hammond and S Oswald with Messrs John Armstrong, H Hodgson and D Atkinson.

The cost of the treat was defrayed entirely by the British Legion Branch.

27 January 1961

THORNLEY MAN DIES IN AUSTRALIA

Mr Thomas Bonar, of Linden Lea, Thornley, has been informed that the last of four elder brothers, Mr Edward Bonar, has died at his home in Adelaide, Australia. He emigrated from this country in 1928. He was then 19 and was employed as a putter at Wheatley Hill Colliery. Mr Bonar was the third of six sons of the late Mr John Bonar, who was for many years headmaster of St Godrics RC School, Thornley. He leaves a widow, one son and one daughter.

Chief Officer Joseph Bonar was lost at sea during the last war. The eldest son, Mr John Bonar, a grammar school master in Northumberland, died three years ago and Mr Charles Bonar, the second son, a painter for Easington Council, collapsed and died suddenly last year.

Mr Thomas Bonar is assistant engineer at Thornley Colliery and his youngest brother, Arthur, who had two legs amputated in a coal cutter accident some years ago, is employed as a machinist at the colliery.

FORMER WHEATLEY HILL MAN DIED IN YORKSHIRE

Formerly cleansing superintendent to Easington Rural Council for five years until resigning five years ago on taking up a new appointment with an oil company, Mr John William Moore, who formerly lived at Wheatley Hill, has died at his home in Leeds. Mr Moore, who was 48, moved to Leeds from Peterlee only three years ago.

When he left school Mr Moore, who spent his younger days in the Easington area, began employment with Easington Rural Council and was in the Health Department 23 years before his promotion as cleansing superintendent. For some five years, while living in Wheatley Hill, he was in partnership in a newsagent's business with his brother-in-law, Mr R W Bell, who is the present newsagent.

Cricket was Mr Moore's favourite sport, and he played for both Easington and Wheatley Hill for many seasons, being their opening bat. He was actively associated with the Wheatley Hill Area Labour Party, and for some years represented the Wheatley Hill Ward on Wingate Parish Council.

Mr Moore began employment with Shell Mex Ltd when he resigned as cleansing superintendent to the Council. He lived in Peterlee for about three years, and while there was an active member of the local Methodist Church.

Mr Moore, who is survived by his wife and a 20-year-old daughter, who is a school teacher, was cremated at Lawnswood, Leeds on Tuesday.

3 February 1961

NEW CLOTHING FACTORY FOR WHEATLEY HILL

A former Wheatley Hill dance hall, later used as a furniture showroom, is being converted into a clothing factory.

The Embassy Hall has been equipped with sewing machines, cutting tables and other machinery and will open on 20 February with a few machinists.

The company behind the new venture, Cosmit Manufacturing Co of Binchester, near Bishop Auckland, expects the labour force eventually to be about 125.

Coun George Cosgrove, principal of the company, said yesterday that Wheatley Hill had its unemployment problems and many people were at present having to travel to jobs at Darlington, Durham, the Hartlepools and Sunderland.

Handful At Start

"We expect to start with a handful of machinists and a small number of experienced operators from the Binchester factory", said Coun Cosgrove. "We also hope to recruit a number of machinists in the area who have been 'out-workers' for the Binchester factory for some time".

Pyjamas will be the first garments produced at the factory and later probably shirts.

Coun Cosgrove said work prospects for the Wheatley Hill factory, which has a floor space of about 10,000 square feet, were very good. Expansion at the Binchester factory was impossible and the company had been finding it difficult to get the work done.

MRS E CLARK - presiding at Thornley British Legion Women's Section welcomed back Miss Nellie Redshaw, secretary, who had been absent through illness, who presented the minutes and correspondence, which were confirmed by Mesdames Hird and Peacock. The meeting is to send representatives to the Group meeting in Sedgefield on 21 March. Mrs E Middleton, treasurer, presented the monthly financial statement which was approved by Mesdames S Redshaw and M Aitken. Mr and Mrs Slater, Poppy Day organisers, reported that Poppy Day effort had raised £87, a slight increase on last year. They thanked all concerned. The prize was won by Mrs C Walker and raffle for sports, by Mrs M Barrass.

MINER RETIRES – Mr Mark Brain, who began work at Mainsforth Colliery when he was 12-year-old in 1908, retires this weekend as an underground worker at Thornley Colliery. Mr Brain removed with his family to the newly-built colliery houses at High Wheatley Hill and started work at Thornley Colliery as a driver in 1910. He has worked underground as a driver, putter, coal hewer, face canch, back by canch and datal worker completing 53 years' service. Mr Brain at one time took an active part in the affairs of Thornley Miners' Lodge and for many years he was assistant financial secretary taking the members contributions each fortnight at the Old Plough Inn, Haswell. Mr Brain lives with his wife in a colliery house near the one his family entered 50 years ago.

THE DEATH has taken place at his home, 14 Kenton Crescent, Thornley, of Mr John Adamson (83), who has been ill for some time. Mr Adamson, who was a bachelor, lived with his niece and her husband, Mr and Mrs J Dawson. He retired from work as a blacksmith's striker at Thornley Colliery in 1943. Mr Adamson was born at Castle Eden, removing to Thornley after the pit closed in 1893. He worked at Thornley Colliery brickyard as a boy and was employed for some years on an engine, lifting clay from the pits. He was employed as a haulier from the beginning of the construction on the 169ft pit chimney at Thornley Colliery, which was started in August 1899 and finished in March 1900. He was also employed on the Wheatley Hill chimney. Mr Adamson was a playing member of the old cricket club of Thornley which was dissolved in 1914.

WHEATLEY HILL MAN SPENT LIFE IN THE MINES

Mr Edward Edwards (72), 59 Jack Lawson Terrace, Wheatley Hill, was interred on Wednesday, in Wheatley Hill Cemetery, following a service in Wheatley Hill Church Street Methodist Church, conducted by the Rev R Hancock of Thornley, Mrs R Ord was at the organ.

Mr Edwards is survived by his wife, Mrs Hannah Mary Edwards, two sons and one daughter. Born at Station Town, he moved to Wheatley Hill 60 years ago when he was 12. He chose mining as a career and spent all his working life of 53 years at Wheatley Hill Colliery, where he was known as a conscientious worker.

Mr Edwards was keenly interested in the workmens' club movement. In his younger days he was a member of the Wheatley Hill Club. He then transferred his membership to Thornley. A keen sportsman, Mr Edwards was no mean performer at billiards, snooker and darts. He played competitive billiards and snooker with the Wheatley Hill Club team.

Mr Edwards was a member of Wheatley Hill Over-60 Club and since its inception, he has often entertained members.

The Over-60 Club was represented by officials and members at the service.

10 February 1961

THORNLEY FOLK FACE MOVE TO PETERLEE
Most Want to Stay

Many families in Thornley face a move to Peterlee within the next few years and most do not want to go. "What has Peterlee to offer, that we haven't" said Mr M Fleming, Clerk to the Thornley Parish Council. Over 300 people will be affected, 111 of whom are living in colliery houses which stretch from the High Street to the Police Station and School Square.

"We have land available in Thornley to re-house everybody. In the last 30 years 700 Council houses have been built and we are going to build a lot more in the next few years to take the people who are at present living on the North side of the village", continued Mr Fleming. "The rents in Peterlee are far higher than in Thornley. A three bedroomed house in Thornley costs 32s a week whereas it is 10s more in Peterlee".

Roots Here

"The general feeling among the miners is that they have their roots in Thornley. Why should they move to a strange new town and cut themselves off from all their friends and connections in the village? It is not fair to expect the older people to move. They are too set in their ways to move", said Mr Fleming.

The village cannot offer the green verges of Peterlee but there are the colliery playing fields. There are facilities for dancing, the workmen's club, and the younger people have a good 'bus service to Sunderland and Durham if they wish to have anything further in the way of entertainment.

241

"This is not a dying village. The pit is expected to last for at least another 40 years and it employs 1400 people. There are quite adequate facilities for shopping and we plan to build a new shopping centre. In fact, when the last census was taken, only two people on the south side of the village wanted to move to Peterlee", continued Mr Fleming.

"The organisations and churches in the village are thriving. The Roman Catholic Church has a membership of 1300, the Methodist 600 and the Church of England 800, as well as a big Sunday School. There are three clubs in the village, the Catholic, the Workingmen's and the Officials' Club. For the women there is a Women's Institute, a Mothers' Club and a Labour Women's Society and a number of other organisations connected with the church".

"The children will not gain by a move to Peterlee", said Mr Fleming. "Some will have further to travel, as those under the age of 11 go to the Council and Catholic Schools and over 11 to Wheatley Hill."

"You know, it is a funny thing how people retain their link with Thornley. Some travel long distances to the Workmen's Club or to come and see their relatives in the village. We have a community spirit built round the mine which would be impossible in Peterlee and we will fight to stay here", said Mr Fleming.

FORMER LUDWORTH COUPLE BEREAVED

The death has occurred in Cyprus of Chief Technician Wilfred Campbell of the Royal Air Force. He was 34 years of age, married for four years and had a son. At the time of his death his wife, Pat, was in this country where she had come to arrange for their son's education. On being told of her husband's death, Mrs Campbell arranged to fly back to Cyprus for the funeral at Akrotiki.

Mr Campbell was eldest son of Mr and Mrs Charles Campbell, formerly of Ludworth, and now of 1 Ramside View, Carrville. He was educated at Ludworth School and the A J Dawson Grammar School, Wellfield. On leaving school he enlisted as an apprentice craftsman in the RAF and had served 17 years. He was in Germany for 3½ years and for the last two years in Cyprus. He was the eldest of three sons.

Mr Campbell Snr was a popular official in Durham County football circles. He was chairman of Houghton and District League, secretary of Thornley Aged Miners' Cup competition and secretary of Ludworth Juniors.

Mrs Campbell, while living at Ludworth, was a faithful church-woman and member of Shadforth Mothers' Union.

Their many friends in the Ludworth and Thornley district extend deepest sympathy to Mr Campbell's widow and only son and his parents.

THORNLEY COUNCIL IN LADY C PROTEST

Thornley Parish Council last week agreed, following a report by councillors, F A Walker, chairman, Mrs J Anderson and the clerk, Mr Martin Fleming, on a meeting of representatives of Durham County Council, Easington Rural District and No 3 Area

NCB to the suggestion of Messrs W Oswald, Group Engineer and W N Fleming, Estate Agent NCB, for an extension of tipping facilities in the Hilly, near Durham Road and White House Farm, which includes the public footpath that runs from the colliery on the north to Durham Road on the south. At the present the footbath is flooded in the hollows, the additional tipping will fill in all the hollows, making the footpath a level road from north to south.

A letter was received from Sparks and Blake, solicitors of Crewkerne, Somerset, enclosing the title deed of a parcel of land known as Church Street. It was the last remaining piece of land of the 1760 acre estate held by the trustees of the Spearman Estate and it is their gift to the Parish Council. The council is to thank the trustees and also pay the necessary conveyance fees.

The Council also decided to protest to the County Association of Parish Councils about the lectures given to week end school held for parish councillors at Lambton Residential College. They thought the subject of the novel Lady Chatterley's Lover did not bear on the work of a parish council.

THORNLEY HEADSTONE IS REMINDER OF PIT DISASTER IN 1871

A headstone in Thornley churchyard erected by the miners, of Thornley, Wheatley Hill and Ludworth Collieries to the memory of five fellow workmen who lost their lives in an inundation at Wheatley Hill Colliery on 19 January 1871, recalls the 90th anniversary of the verdict of the Coroner's court held at Wingate Grange on 8 February 1871.

Wheatley Hill Colliery was sunk in 1869, by the old Hartlepool Coal Company, and the main coal seam in No 1 shaft was proved on 4 March 1870. The coal was 4ft 2in thick and of good quality.

At the time of the accident only 27 of the cottages, built by Hirst and Sons of Sunderland, were occupied, 23 more were in the course of construction.

Difficult Sinking

Sinking in No 2 shaft had proved difficult. Sand, water, faulty tubbing and inability to get sinkers, held up the work. Death had already claimed two sinkers in this shaft which was so necessary to the ventilation and working of coal in No 1 Pit. To hasten the ventilation and working of the main coal, a drift was projected into the old Thornley workings, the men from Thornley working a similar drift to meet it.

At the time of the accident there were 13 coal hewers, five putters, three helpers-up, with deputies, drivers and others in the Wheatley Hill Pit, and the drift had advanced some 400 yards, leaving an estimated distance of 27 yards to meet the Thornley drift which had been driven 500 yards. A drift was also made from No 1 shaft to underneath No 2 and boring in this shaft was put down to relieve the accumulation of water.

The inquest which had been adjourned at the request of Mr William Crawford, agent to the Durham Miners, was upon the bodies of James Hall, 42; John Ball, 30;

Robert Smith, 28; John Walker, 21 and George Cooper, 13 who were killed in the main coal seam on 19 January.

The newly-formed Durham Miners' Association was represented by Mr William Crawford, agent, Mr Arthur Cairns, secretary, who was also checkweighman at Thornley Colliery and Mr Kewney, solicitor, North Shields.

The verdict was that the men were killed by a burst of water in Wheatley Hill Pit through the gross negligence of three officials. The Coroner committed all three for trial at the Assizes on a charge of manslaughter.

The Verdict

The verdict had far-reaching results. It opened a decade of strikes, lock-outs, evictions and the building of long rows of miners' cottages in Wheatley Hill. It stabilised the position of William Crawford, and the sacking of Arthur Cairns. It caused the resignation of Mr William Spencer. His position was filled by Phillip Cooper, one of the founder members of the Durham Coal Owners Association.

Another tablet was added to the little memorial standing in the old churchyard. It was in memory of late fellow workmen who lost their lives by an explosion of gas in Wheatley Hill mine on 26 September 1876; George Dixon Robson, 34; James Kelly Atack, 24; Thomas Quinn, 22 and William Edward Johns Abram, 16.

LAWN MOWER TYPE OF CEMETERY
Wheatley Hill Scheme Brings Appreciation

In an effort to improve the appearance of their cemetery at Wheatley Hill, Wingate Parish Council recently agreed to remove, at their own expense, but only with the consent of the relatives concerned, kerb-stones surrounding graves. This, they pointed out at the time, could eventually lead to a lawn-type cemetery and would have a much tidier and neater appearance.

Appreciation of their efforts was expressed in a letter to the council on Monday from Mrs L Cutter of Sunderland. She had recently visited her brother's grave in the cemetery, she said, and found that the removal of the kerb-stones and concrete had been carried out to her complete satisfaction. She wished to thank the council for doing such a tidy job.

The Clerk, Mr John Harper, said that if more people would agree to the removal of the kerb-stones it would certainly improve the appearance of the cemetery, but at the same time, he emphasised, the council were in no way trying to force relatives consent for their removal.

There were many graves, said the Clerk, which received no attention at all. If the relatives would only spare a few moments to call at the cemetery and sign the agreement forms, for the removal of the kerb-stones, it would be appreciated by the council. Many graves, of course, were maintained in a tidy condition and they caused no problem.

17 February 1961

HALF CENTURY PARTNERSHIP: WHEATLEY HILL CELEBRATION

Mr and Mrs John Hutler of 7 Fred Peart Square, Wheatley Hill, celebrated their golden wedding with a family party. The couple were married at Easington Register Office. Mrs Hutler smiled as she said, "Fifty years ago the journey from Wheatley Hill to Easington was quite an adventure. There were no cars or 'buses then. We had to hire a horse-drawn cab. It was just as big a thrill to me as the same journey by car would be to the modern bride. In those days joys and pleasures were of the simple variety and often of our own making".

Mr Hutler, who is 72, was born at Hetton-le-Hole. A month before he was 12 he began work at a Hetton-le-Hole brick yard. He said, "I worked from six in the morning till five at night, and worked eleven shifts a fortnight for a shilling a day".

After working there for eight months he was taken to Lumley Sixth Pit. There he worked as a driver till he was 14 when he moved to Wheatley Hill Colliery. In 1914 he enlisted with the 7th Yorkshire Light Infantry but was returned to essential work in the mines after six months. He remained at Wheatley Hill Colliery until 1939.

At the age of 51, Mr Hutler decided to do his bit. He said, "I had three sons in the Navy so off I went to enlist with the 76th Pioneer Corps. I know I told a lie to get in. I said I was 45. Our mob was in the embarkation from Dunkirk. I reckon we were extremely lucky. We got away on 5 June, after spending 24 hours on the beaches.

"After landing in England, I went to Troutbridge in Wiltshire. I was luckier than my son. He was taken prisoner by the Japs and died in a prisoner-of-war camp in Sumatra".

After Dunkirk, Mr Hutler applied for something lighter. He found the pace of competing with younger men a bit too trying. He was transferred to the blue cap police and assigned to guard duties in this country. At one time he was on duty on Lord Melford's estate near Newmarket.

After serving for four years Mr Hutler returned to the pits and was transferred to Blackhall where he retired at 65. Mr Hutler was an accomplished billiards player. He played for the Wheatley Hill Institute when the team operated in the Trimdon and District Billiards League. He owns a gold medal for winning a league billiards competition.

Started Work at 6am

Mrs Margaret Jane Hutler, who is 70, does all her own work. She was born at Middlesbrough and came to Shotton when she was 14. Before her marriage at 20 Mrs Hutler worked as a domestic help at various farm houses.

"It was hard work", she said. "I started work at six in the morning and finished often after five. For this work I got my meals and 2s.6d a week. If that was not sweated labour I don't know what is".

Mrs Hutler said, "When we were married my husband brought in 25s a week. It was a struggle. With a growing family – we had three sons and five daughters – it was a job to make both ends meet. We went through at least three strikes which took all our reserves. It was a blessing that the soup kitchens were organised. That meant that the children at least were fed".

Mr and Mrs Hutler have a crippled daughter, Margaret, who has spent several years in the Leazes Hospital, Wolsingham. "Every Sunday", said Mr Hutler, "my· wife makes the journey to Wolsingham to see her". Mrs Hutler has been a member of the Wheatley Hill Over-60 Club since its formation. The Club presented the couple with a bouquet.

3 March 1961

THORNLEY BOXING RECORD: 2 NATIONAL SEMI FINALISTS: 4 NOVICE CHAMPIONS

Although Thornley Boxing Club has only been in its new gym for four months, two national semi-finalists and four divisional novice champions hail from the club. With the support of local pitmen, the Federated Board and Thornley Colliery manager, Mr A Welch, the club has grown from strength to strength and none can rival its superiority among Durham Welfare Clubs.

Mr Henry Hubbard (colliery training officer), Mr William Williamson (ex-professional) and Kenny Harvey (ex-professional) have a promising school of young boxers under their wing. Everyone is keen to compete in local boxing tournaments, but unfortunately they are unable to do so.

"The first thing we need is a ring," said Mr Hubbard, "then we can join the ABA and arrange tournaments with other clubs".

The Federated Board have already supplied the Club with gloves and other accessories and it is hoped that they may help to buy a ring.

The Club meets every Tuesday, Thursday and Sunday in the Band Hall, Thornley. Mr Hubbard envisages a club in Thornley where boxing, weight-lifting, first aid and other such hobbies may be pursued. He believes that the onus of paying for the upkeep of such a club should not be on the youths. "Boys will lose interest if they are tied by subscriptions", he commented.

He catches the boys when they·first come to the Colliery and finds that many are interested in attending the Club. "It keeps them off the streets", he said. There was a lack of facilities in Thornley and many boys went to Horden for their training, but when the Club was allowed the use of the band hall they agreed to return to Thornley. Since then the Club has thrived and now has about 25 members. On any of the practice nights the hall is full of boxers.

National semi-finalists are Len Harvey and Ronnie Harvey, while Divisional novice champions are Brian Hardy, Joe Harvey, Harry Morton and Norman Armstrong. Whenever boxing is the topic of talk in the area, the Harvey name is bound to crop up. There are five brothers whose achievements make the name Thornley well-known in CISWO and ABA boxing circles.

Thirty Trophies

The Harvey brothers have won over 30 trophies and a host of prizes between them. Kenny Harvey was a runner-up in the National ABA tournament a few years ago and is a professional. The family's second professional (retired) is John Harvey, who fought 14 fights and only lost two. Ronnie is divisional champion and will take part in the national semi-finals this year. He was narrowly beaten in the finals last year.

Len will take part in the semi-finals, too, this year. He has had 14 fights and only lost one, which was a "special" and not for any championship. Joseph Harvey is the youngster of the family at 17, but he, too, is beginning to make a name for himself. Divisional Novice champion this year, he is a bright prospect for future NCB finals.

Not content to let her brothers bring home the trophies, sister Joan has taken three medals for sprinting. Does their mother mind having so many hard-fisted sons? Not a bit! "I'm proud of my sons", she says, "and I'm sure they could furnish the house if they wanted".

10 March 1961

THORNLEY'S NONAGENARIAN

"Old soldiers never die", says Ned Fryer, and Ned should know because he celebrates his 90th birthday this week.

Born in Eccleston, Lancashire, on Monday, 13 March 1871, he began work in the pits at 13. He enlisted in the East Lancashires at 18. At the time he was hand-putting at the colliery. For 10 years he served in India and at the outbreak of the South African War he was transferred with his unit to fight the Boers.

At the end of 16 years regular service, Ned went on to the reserve and returned to the pits, first in Lancashire, and then in Scotland and Yorkshire before walking into Durham where he settled in Thornley in 1910. He was recalled back to his regiment on 6 August 1914, at the outbreak of the First World War and served in France, Belgium and Germany until the end of hostilities. He returned to civilian life after 20 years regular service without a scratch.

Shortly after his return to the pit, Ned suffered an injury to his right knee and shortly after his return to work a pit pony damaged his left thigh.

Ned's birthday party was held at the home of Mr and Mrs D Holden of School Square, Thornley. The cake was made by Mrs Holden and Mr Holden and his three sons made their contributions. One of the principle guests was Mrs Alice Gibson, landlady of the Colliery Inn, where Ned goes each day for his regular pint and drop of rum.

Ned can recall the revolt of the tribesmen on the North West Frontier and also the celebrations of the Queen's jubilee, the Siege of Ladysmith, Mafeking and Kimberley and the Coronation Celebrations of King Edward VII.

DOG FANCIER'S SUCCESSES - A Wheatley Hill Pekingese exhibitor, Mr T W Hogan, had several successes in the North of England Toy Dog Society's first show of the year at Middlesbrough on Saturday. He gained first prizes in three Peke classes and a first for the AV toy puppy. These successes resulted in the award of the Wilton Grange Cup for the best peke novice; the Sundila Cup for the best peke puppy and the Duncorry Cup for the best opposite sex.

PENSIONERS ENTERTAINED – The manager and his wife, Mr and Mrs R Pettler, were in charge of the arrangements when about sixty pensioner patrons of the Coronation Inn, Wheatley Hill, and their wives were entertained to an excellent supper and concert at the Inn recently. Mr E Cain, JP, deputy chairman of Castle Eden Magistrates, and his wife were among the guests, and thanks to Mr and Mrs Pettler for their kindly interest in the old folk were expressed by Mr Cain. Miss Maureen Pettler, only daughter of Mr and Mrs Pettler, was hostess for the evening and her brother, Mr R Pettler, was among those who entertained. The entertainment was given by a concert party from West Hartlepool. Mr R Armstrong compered the programme and the accompanist was Mr Ernest Evans. It was the first such party organised for the old folk and they were unstinting in their praise to Mr and Mrs Pettler for such an enjoyable evening.
17 March 1961

WHEATLEY HILL OLD SCOUTS PLAN FOR JUNE FIELD DAY
Plans for various activities this year, including social evenings, dinners and the annual Field Day on 24 June, were made at the annual meeting of the Wheatley Hill Old Scouts' Association. It is hoped to provide heating for the Scout Headquarters and pay for further improvements as a result of the Field Day.

Several new members were enrolled, making a total membership of 52. Mr Selwyn Fawcett, chairman of the Durham County BP Scout Guild, and Mr J M Knutson, secretary, spoke on the constitution of the Guild and its work in the county.

The financial statement, presented by the Treasurer, Mr J Raffell, showed a total income for the year of £470.6s.4d and expenditure of £366.10s.4d, leaving a balance in hand of £103.16s.

The election of officers for the ensuing year resulted as follows: Chairman, Mr J Armstrong; Secretary, Coun Ralph Watson; Treasurer, Mr E Snowdon; Auditors, Messrs L Barker and C Thackeray; Committee, Messrs T Alderson, W Gibson, W Saxby, G Watson, B Aitken, A Watson, A Carr and T Carr.

It was reported that the cost to the Association for the new Scout Headquarters was £183. All the labour was done voluntarily by the members.
24 March 1961

LONG WAITING LIST FOR WHEATLEY HILL OVER-60's
So many old people are wanting to join Wheatley Hill Over-60 Club that there is now a long waiting list, the secretary, Mrs E Richardson, revealed at the annual meeting of the club, presided over by Mr C Raffell.

Membership was 362, said Mrs Richardson in her annual review of the year's work, but at the moment they had to restrict it to this number because of lack of accommodation. There was a waiting-list of more than 40 members and these would be absorbed at the earliest possible opportunity.

Eighteen members had died during the year, said Mrs Richardson, and a similar number had resigned from membership, but 20 new members had been enrolled. Four couples had celebrated their golden wedding during the year, namely Mr and Mrs W Greenwell, Mr and Mrs R Richardson, Mr and Mrs J Hutler and Mr and Mrs N Smithson.

Not a single meeting had passed throughout the year without there being a concert party to provide entertainment. Mrs Richardson revealed. There had been 44 visiting concert parties and on six occasions the club's own concert party had entertained.

Eggs For Winterton

Mrs Richardson thanked the members for their loyal support during the year and various local organisations and others who had helped the club in many ways. The treasurer, Mr I Hodgson, presented a satisfactory financial statement.

It was agreed to hold the annual outing at South Shields, but the date has yet to be arranged.

Birthday greetings were sung to Mr J P Brown and Mr E Kitto. Mr and Mrs B Bowes judged the dyed egg competition, the winners of which were 1, Mrs E Hodgson; 2, Mr B Murray; 3, Mrs E Hodgson.

All the dyed eggs and fresh eggs brought by the members, totalling about 250, were afterwards taken to Winterton Hospital, Sedgefield. Winners of the special prizes were Mrs L Ward and Mrs E Carter.

Officers Elected

The following officers were elected for the ensuing year: Chairman, Mr G Farrar; Vice-Chairman, Mrs E Amies; Treasurer, Mr I Hodgson; Secretary and Entertainments Secretary, Mrs E Richardson, 10 Wordsworth Avenue, Wheatley Hill; Committee, Mesdames B Carter, J Harper, A Oswald, B Robinson, B Storey and L Turner and Messrs M Mahoney, W Poulson, T Peel, A Patterson, C Raffell and T Taylorson; Auditors Messrs N Cook and H Lee.

7 April 1961

THORNLEY FLAGSTONES A DANGER POINT

Coun Miss A Griffiths, at a meeting of Thornley Parish Council, raised the question of a woman who had hurt both legs by falling over a raised flagstone on the footpath of the highway in Ruskin Crescent, Thornley.

Miss Griffiths said this was the third complaint she had brought, of elderly people being injured on these footpaths during the last three months, with no attempt being made to remedy the position.

Coun James Nicholson said, "many of the people who make complaints about roads and footpaths think we are doing nothing to help, but, we were told last year, by the County Highway Authority, that money was to be made available for this work to be done at an early date".

Snare To The Unwary

"Every sub road and every footpath in the parish needs repair. They are a public danger; unwary travellers on the East Lea Roads need safety belts to keep them in their vehicles, and children are thrown from small tricycles onto the roadways". The Council agreed to complain to the District Highway Surveyor.

Councillors F A Walker, chairman, and J Nicholson, members of Easington RDC agreed to take up a complaint, brought by Coun Douglas Gott, about over filled ashbins and ashes lying about the footpaths of the houses in St Bede's Crescent.

Coun Gott said there was a regularity in cleansing and the clearing of bins twice a week, but the system had been changed and for the worse.

Coun J R Bosomworth asked the Council if anything could be done to stop double deck 'buses using the roadway at the top of School Square and breaking up the roadway. Coun Bosomworth said the road was not a public road in the sense that it was built to carry the weight of these big 'buses who were making pot holes, which filled with rain and slush in wet weather. The clerk Mr M Fleming is to write to the company concerned to ask them to instruct drivers not to use this route.

21 April 1961

MORE LAURELS FOR WHEATLEY HILL FIREMEN

For the second time in five years a team of firemen from Wheatley Hill unit of the Durham County Fire Brigade have won the annual inter-brigade quiz competition organised by the Chief Fire Officer's Association in conjunction with the Fire Research and Training Trust.

The competition was open to retained firemen from all parts of Great Britain, and Wheatley Hill, after winning the Durham County section, won the semi-final at Leeds. They journeyed to Dorking for the final on Saturday, and there competed against teams representing Lancashire County Fire Brigade, the Derbyshire Fire Service and Wiltshire Fire Brigade.

The Wheatley Hill team collected 38 points out of a possible 45. Lancashire were runners-up with 33 points. The winning team was captained by Sub-Officer H F Horner and the other members were Leading Fireman P E Whynn and Firemen A C Appleby, L Barker and T W Ayre. The team was coached by the Station Officer, Mr Stan Poulson, who accompanied the team to Dorking.

The team are all employed by the National Coal Board at Wheatley Hill Colliery. As well as being presented with the same trophy which they won in 1956, the team received prizes of £5 each.

WHEATLEY HILL GOLDEN WEDDING HUSBAND WAS 50 YEARS IN LOCAL MINE

Both in good health, a well-known Wheatley Hill couple, Mr and Mrs William Poulson, who have spent all their married life in the village, celebrated their golden wedding recently. They were married at Thornley Parish Church and they now live at 1 Fred Peart Square.

Born at Marsden, Mr Poulson who is 72, began work at Wheatley Hill Colliery at the age of 12, earning a shilling a ten-hour shift as a trapper-boy. All his mining career was spent at this colliery until his retirement at 65, and he did virtually every kind of job down the pit, including putting, hewing and stonework. He was a maintenance worker when he retired.

Mr Poulson, who has certificates from both the National Coal Board and the Durham Area NUM, to mark half a century in the mines, was formerly actively associated with a number of committees in the village. He served for many years on the committee of Wheatley Hill branch of the Northumberland and Durham Miners' Permanent Relief Fund and was also on the band committee, Welfare Committee and the committee of the Wheatley Hill Colliery Hospital and Ambulance Fund.

Both Mr Poulson and his wife formerly played bowls as members of the Wheatley Hill Bowls' Club. They are keen members of the local Over-60 Club, where Mr Poulson served on the committee.

During the 1914-18 war, Mr Poulson served for two years in the 5th DLI, and he was an ARP warden throughout the last war. He was one of the first members of the Rescue Brigade when it was formed at Wheatley Hill Colliery in 1912.

Mrs Poulson, who is 69, was born at Wheatley Hill but lived in a number of other villages before her marriage. Her maiden name was Ethel Pickering. Before her marriage, she was employed in the dress-making department of Thornley branch of Scott's Ltd for four years.

Best Kept Garden

Most of Mr Poulson's spare time is spent in the beautiful garden surrounding his bungalow home. Two years ago he won the Easington Rural Council cup for the best-kept council house garden in Wheatley Hill and on other occasions he has been placed second and third. "Keeping a nice garden is hard work, but it is good exercise and it helps to keep me in good health", Mr Poulson told our reporter, who called to congratulate him and his wife on Wednesday.

Mr Poulson organises a pensioners' trip from the village to Blackpool every year. They spend a week there in the early season – 43 pensioners are joining this year's trip in June.

The couple have a family of three daughters and one son, ten grandchildren and two great-grandchildren.

28 April 1961

RECORD OUTPUT AT THORNLEY COLLIERY

Last week's output of 11,007 tons at Thornley Colliery, one of the nine in No 3 Area (South-East Durham), Durham Division, NCB, was the highest ever produced since coal-drawing operations began at the pit. It exceeded the target figure by 3007 tons.

Easington colliery also had another good week, producing 6139 tons more than its target, and the other target-breakers were Horden, Sherburn Hill and Deaf Hill. The area's total output of 98,570 tons was 6270 above the combined target.

Individual outputs , with targets in brackets, were: Horden, 24,102 (22,750); Easington, 23,139 (17,000); Blackhall, 14,623 (15,500); Thornley, 11,007 (8000); Shotton, 6831 (7000); Sherburn Hill, 7263 (7250); Wheatley Hill, 5507 (6000); Wingate, 2028 (4800); Deaf Hill, 4070 (4000).

5 May 1961

THORNLEY NONAGENARIAN

Mrs Margaret Ord, who lives with her widowed daughter, Mrs Annie Smith, 13 Asquith Street, Thornley, celebrated her 90th birthday on Monday. She was born in 2 Swinburne Street, Thornley. The Rev P G Mold, Vicar of St Bartholomew's, Thornley, administered Holy Communion. Mrs Ord said she thought it was a good way to begin a happy birthday.

Although there are two persons in the village older than Mrs Ord she claims she is the oldest native with the longest family ties in the village. Her father, Mr Bill Ainsley, was born in Nelson Street, Thornley, and her grandfather, Mr Mark Ainsley settled in the village when the colliery was being sunk in 1833.

Swinburne Street at the time was a long row of 25 low limestone cottages lying 100 yards west of the colliery. They were cottages built by Mr John Gully the British boxer, when he was a partner in the Thornley Coal Co. Each contained a large kitchen with doorways at back and front, a 12 paned window a little to the left or right of the door with a wooden shutter that covered the window at night, a large brick fireplace set on the middle wall with round oven and set pot at either side. A small pantry was attached on the outside door at the back. The attic was accessible from the kitchen by a loose ladder.

Fire Of 1875 Recalled

Mrs Ord at 90 has a very clear memory, and she speaks of events which happened 70 and 85 years ago as if they took place yesterday. She related the story of the fire that took place at the colliery on 7 May 1875, which destroyed all the surface heapstead and engines. The pit was closed down for nearly a year and the damage was estimated at over £35,000. Her father, who was a brakesman at the Low Main Winding Engine, was overcome with the fumes which affected him and died within a year of the incident.

Mrs Ord likes to talk of her school days. She started at the little colliery school near the police station, the children were taught by an old school master called Dickie Wilson and his sister. She remembered well when the new Board School was opened by Mr William Mayor, the Vicar and Chairman of the board.

At the new school a fee of 3d per week was charged to each pupil. Children whose parents were on the parish took a note from the parish man. Mrs Ord recalls

252

on one occasion after her father died and the family felt hardship she paid her fees with a little silver threepenny bit which had been made into a pair of earrings for her!

Another incident which impressed Mrs Ord while she was still at school was the boiler explosion which took place at the colliery on 18 June 1878. The report was heard all over the village and people rushed to the pit head. Four men were killed.

Nine Great-Grandchildren

Mrs Ord has been twice married. Her first husband, Mr Dave Morriss, was a deputy overman at Thornley Colliery for many years and died in 1914. She had five daughters of the marriage. Her second husband, Mr Ned Ord, worked for many years as farm bailiff at Thornley Hall Farm and as a canch man at Trimdon Quarries. He died in 1936. Mrs Ord has seven grandchildren and nine great grandchildren.

Mrs Ord in her neat little bed sitting-room is happy when she is busy knitting or sewing. She has many visitors and some of her old friends still call her Maggie Ainsley.

19 May 1961

THORNLEY MAN CHAIRED ON HIS RETIRMENET

Mr William Robinson, 1 St Chad's Square, Thornley, retired from work as a labourer in the fitting department of the engineering works at Thornley Colliery, at the weekend.

Mr Robinson has worked at the colliery, except for four years in the Army in 1914, for 51 years. He began as a driver underground in 1910, and he was pony putting before he enlisted.

He served in France with the Bantams and was badly wounded on the Somme. After the war he was unable to follow his ordinary work underground and he was placed on the surface where he has worked since.

The opinion of the fitters and mechanics of Mr Robinson's service was expressed when he was carried bodily the full length of the shop, in front of all the men, by Gene Tunney and Babe Stoackley the two heavy weights, and placed on a pedestal and presented by Rocky Hutchinson with a wallet and notes contributed by the men as a parting gift.

Appreciation of Mr Robinson's grand sense of humour, his gift of winning every argument and his great command of language, which he acquired when he served with the bantams, was expressed by all who were present to wish him a happy retirement.

26 May 1961

OLD SOLDIER CELEBRATES GOLDEN WEDDING

Mr and Mrs Harry Cowton, Dunelm Road, Thornley, celebrated their golden wedding on Saturday. Mr Cowton who is 73 and Mrs Cowton 69, were married on 3 June 1911, at St Bartholomew's Church, Thornley, by the Rev E Coltier Biggs.

Mr Cowton who is a native of the Yorkshire Dales, removed to the Durham coalfield in 1908. He was employed underground at Horden, Wheatley Hill and Thornley before he retired through ill health ten years ago. He served with the Green Howards in Asia and France during the First World War and was decorated with the MM in 1916. While in France he met Pte Vernal Crossley of Lincolnshire and a lifelong friendship developed. Mr and Mrs Crossley were guests at the party on Saturday.

Mrs Cowton was born at Wheatley Hill. Her parents, Mr and Mrs C Gibson, were well known business people in the fish trade for many years. Mr and Mrs Cowton have two married daughters living in Wiltshire and Lancashire and one married son, Mr Fred Cowton, general surface foreman at Wingate Grange Colliery.

9 June 1961

NEW CHAIRMAN of Thornley Parish Council, Mr J R Bosomworth, is a 40-year-old plumber employed by Easington Rural Council. He has been a member of the Parish Council for six years. His mother, Mrs Bessie Bosomworth, was the first woman in Thornley to sit on the Council. She had over 20 years' service when she died two years ago. His father, Mr Robert Bosomworth, was a member of the council from 1924 to 1927. Mr Bosomworth is secretary of Thornley Colliery Welfare Club. He served in the RAF during the last war. While in North Africa he organised a very successful Geordie Club which raised many pounds which were forwarded to the Dean of Durham for distribution to aged people. Mr Bosomworth is an active trade unionist. He was founder member of Easington branch of the Plumber's Trade Union; he held the position of treasurer of the branch two years and has held the post of secretary for six years.

16 June 1961

FUN AND GAMES AT WHEATLEY HILL
Many Entries for Children's Fancy Dress

Though the weather had not looked too promising in the morning, the sun showed its welcome face just at the right moment when the annual sports day at Wheatley Hill on Saturday, organised by the Wheatley Hill Colliery Workmen's Federation Board, opened with a colourful procession through the village, headed by the local Colliery Prize Band. From then onwards the sun never returned behind the clouds and villagers in their hundreds, both young and old, joined in the packed programme of events and enjoyed themselves to the full.

Crowds lined the route of the procession, which included the Sunderland and District Pipe Band and the Silksworth Juvenile and Hartlepool Juvenile Jazz Bands, as well as the local miners' lodge banner, and there was a steady stream of people into the Peterlee Girls' School field, where the judging took place and the sports were held.

It was perhaps the most successful sports day ever held in the village – the children's fancy dress parade certainly attracted the biggest-ever entry. More than 200 children in all kinds of fancy costume and ranging from toddlers of three to boys and girls of 15, took part in the parade and the judges must never before have been faced with such a difficult task to name the winners.

But though there were only nine major prizes to be won – three for each section – not a single child was disappointed, for every one of those not among the prize-winners received a half-crown consolation prize.

"There were so many excellent entries and it was clearly evident that both the children and their parents had worked so hard at their original, fancy and comic dresses", Coun A D Wharrier, the organising secretary, told our reporter, "that we decided on the spot to give every one of them a consolation prize. None of them knew we were going to do this, but they turned up in big numbers just the same, and we were delighted to see such a splendid response – it helped to make the monster procession one of the most colourful ever".

The parade was judged by the resident Methodist minister, the Rev G L Nelson and his wife; Mr F Richardson, manager of Wheatley Hill colliery, and his wife; Dr and Mrs Wallace and Mrs L Hutchinson and Mrs Wallace.

The Winners

Fancy dress: 1 Kathleen Quinn (Queen of Hearts); 2 and 3 (tie), Maureen Maughan (Hawaiian girl) and George and Pauline Hedley (Turkish Delight).

Comic Dress: 1 Joan Cowell and Eva Burrell (Andy Capp and Flo); 2 Marjorie Armstrong (clown); 3 Susan Carr (Worth Nine Guineas an Ounce).

Original Dress: 1 Ellen and Margaret Dobbin (waitresses); 2 Eileen Carr and Margaret Powell (Road Safety); 3 Colin Hall (Zulu).

The prize for the best tableau was won by Wheatley Hill Mother' Club, with nine children dressed to represent nursery rhymes. The children were: Eric and Ian Starkie, Carol White, Janice Lowther, Patricia Jones, John Hodgson, Robert Hodgson, Christine Harper and Joyce Smith.

The second prize went to Wheatley Hill Women's Section of the British Legion with a Poppy Day tableau and the third to Mr E W Collingwood's entry, depicting the Dairy Queen and her attendants.

Winner of the Silver Challenge Cup and first prize of £3 in the adults four-mile race, which attracted a record entry of 45, was Mr B Thubron, who completed the course in 27 minutes. Mr A Connell, who was half a minute behind, won second prize, and Mr T Hoban was third and Mr D Poole fourth. Those not among the four main prize winners received consolation awards of 5s each.

An innovation this year was a pit pony contest, judged by three retired horse-keepers at Wheatley Hill colliery, Messrs B Ward, R Simpson and T Robson. The winner, Tom, a 16-year-old pony from Easington colliery, was shown by Mr E Robinson. This "veteran of the mines" has won more than 60 first prizes in all parts of the county. The second prize went to Pompey, from Blackhall Colliery, which was shown by Mr T Flackerty. Third was Major of Wingate, shown by Mr C Horn and fourth, Major, of Wheatley Hill, in charge of Mr A Poole.

During the afternoon every child in the village up to school-leaving age was given a three-shilling bag of chocolate, and the gigantic task in distributing these to nearly 2000 children was efficiently handled by women members of various organisations in the village.

Hunt For "Mystery Man"

Messrs D Clish and B Aitken were in charge of the sports programme, and the parade marshal was Mr M Alderton. Throughout the afternoon Wheatley Hill Boy Scouts were in charge of side-stalls and shows.

Another attraction was "Hunt for Mr Sports Day", who was described on the official programme as a "well-known workman at Wheatley Hill Colliery aged between 40 and 65". Mr Horace Bradshaw filled this role and he was eventually tracked down by Miss Errington, who received the prize of £2.

The officials in charge of the day's programme were Mr H Bradshaw (chairman), Coun A D Wharrier (secretary) and Mr J Hedley (treasurer), and valuable assistance was given by members of the committee, who spared no effort to make the day one of the most memorable in the post-war social life of the community.

THORNLEY MAN CAN RECALL GOLD AND SILVER PAY

Mr Redvers Brandling, of Dunelm Road, Thornley, who has been cashier at Thornley Colliery since 1949, has retired after 46 years' service in the coal industry.

Mr Brandling is a native of Thornley and began work in the office at 15, when Mr A J Curry was manager, and Mr William Laidler cashier. He received 7s.6d per week.

Mr Brandling married Miss Janet Simpson, eldest daughter of Mr J T Simpson, who was for many years chief engineer for the Weardale Steel, Coal and Coke Company and was killed during the 1921 strike trying to stop a runaway horse and trap.

When Mr Brandling started in the office all wages were paid each fortnight in gold and silver, sovereigns and half sovereigns, crowns, half crowns and florins, the cashier paid out all workmen, surface and underground in little over one hour.

Mr Brandling spent four years as cashier at Deaf Hill Colliery before his appointment to Thornley, ten years ago. He took an active part in the social life of the village. He was for some years treasurer of Thornley Miners' Welfare; secretary of St Bartholomew's Church Council; a member of the committee of Station Town, Seaham and Horden Co-operative Society and a member of No 6 District Council Northern Section of Co-operative Union.

THORNLEY MOTHERS' CLUB 10TH BIRTHDAY

Members of Thornley Mothers' Club held their tenth birthday party in the Workmen's Club hall. Mrs Johnson presided and welcomed 150 members and visitors, among whom were the matron of Earl's House Children's Hospital, Miss H Appleton; Mr J Toye, the club's pianist; Mr A L Miller and Mr and Mrs J Plant, representing Thornley Bow Street Methodist Church.

The club's president, Mrs Johnson cut the birthday cake which had been baked and iced by Mrs J Anderson. She congratulated the club on attaining its tenth birthday.

Mrs Johnson presented the Matron of Earls House with a cheque for £15. This gift is to meet the cost of two outings to the seaside for the children, who are deprived of normal home life. Miss Appleton thanked the club for its generous gift and the interest in Earls House displayed by members over the years.

The club also remembered the children of its own village. Miss Johnson presented a cheque to Mr Miller for the use of the Thornley Methodist Boys' Brigade.

Mrs M Hobbs then presented Mrs I Johnson with a bouquet and thanked her for her ten years presidency of the club.

Members were entertained with a programme on the new electric organ. Vocal numbers were contributed by Mesdames M Hobbs, E Wilson, M Hughes, J Robson, A Longstaff, L Jones and Mr J Toye.

Special prizes were donated by Mesdames M Archer, E Turner, M Hobbs, M Dinning and a tray made by spastic children. They were won by Mesdames M Day, L Hughes, J Taylor, M Slater and M Hodgson.

Arrangements were made by the organising secretary, Mrs N Mason.

23 June 1961

WHEATLEY HILL OFFICIAL'S RETIREMENT

After a mining career of half a century, all of which has been spent at Wheatley Hill Colliery, Mr Thomas Poulson, 6 Thirteenth Street, Wheatley Hill, has retired from work.

Mr Poulson recently celebrated his 64th birthday and he has gone into early retirement on medical advice. He has not been able to follow his employment since June last year, when he fractured his left leg in an accident at the colliery.

Born at Whitburn, Mr Poulson was only five years old when he moved with his parents to Wheatley Hill, where he has since lived. He began work at the colliery there when he was 14, earning 11s a week as a driver-lad. Later he was hand-putting, and began coal-hewing when he was 23. Three years later, Mr Poulson took up deputy work and for the past 23 years has been an official – for most of this time he has been back shift overman.

For some 20 years Mr Poulson was a member of the colliery's underground rescue team. Two notable rescue operations in which he took part were at Deaf Hill Colliery shortly before the last war when two men lost their lives when fire broke out, and at Thornley 12 years ago when water broke through into the pit workings and three miners were drowned.

Mr Poulson is married, with a son and daughter, both married, and three grandchildren. His son, Thomas, is a police-constable stationed at Hutton Henry, in the Castle Eden Police Division, and his daughter, Mrs Margaret Condren lives at Peterlee.

SCOUTS FIELD DAY AT WHEATLEY HILL

Wheatley Hill BP Scouts Guild held their annual Field Day on the Girls' Modern School playing field on Saturday afternoon. The event was organised by the secretary, Coun Ralph Watson assisted by a strong committee. A crowd of 300 enjoyed an entertaining afternoon, and £70 was raised for local funds.

Highlight was the appearance of St Luke's Amateur Wrestling team, who put on some interesting bouts.

In charge of the side-shows were Messrs L Barker, W Gibson, J Horrocks, C Thackeray, W Saxby, C Hinds, S Snowden, W Walker, D Orchard, W Smart, A Watson, L Craggs, T Meachin, F Horner, A Carr, F Willett, A Hildrew, N Waugh and L Etherington.

Tea was served by the members of the ladies' committee – Mesdames M Watson, H Dunn, G Barker, E Thackeray, E Cowen and M Nicholson and Miss E Shutt.

Wheatley Hill Annual Sports Day June 1961
Local Teacher Mr Fred Alderson in foreground

VICTORY FOR WHEATLEY HILL

Playing a big part in Wheatley Hill's home win over Boldon on Saturday, in Division 1 of the Durham Coast League, was their professional, Derek Leslie. Wheatley Hill were all out for 82, but Leslie was in excellent form with the ball, taking seven wickets for only 20 runs in Boldon's dismissal for 53.

Half the Wheatley Hill wickets were down for only 29 runs, but Alan Fishwick made the final score more respectable with 33 runs. Leslie was the only other double-figure batsman, with 13. For the visitors, Braydon took three wickets for 12. Leonard four for 35, and Mason three for 31.

One of the Boldon batsmen was run out and the other two wickets fell to Fleming for 26 runs. Scores:

Wheatley Hill: A Carter lbw b Mason 7, D Alderton c Stockdale b Leonard 8, D Leslie c Braydon b Leonard 13, G Harrison b Leonard 2, T Cowie b Mason 2, A Fishwick b Braydon 33, G Battye b Leonard 0, G Carr b Mason 5, F Ashford not out 2, J Squires c Leonard b Braydon 2, M Fleming b Braydon 4; extras 4. Total 81.
Boldon: 53
30 June 1961

258

GAY PROCESSION AT THORNLEY

Hundreds of people on Saturday watched the biggest procession seen in Thornley since the Colliery Sports Fund inaugurated the sports day three years ago. The highlight was the parade of six juvenile jazz bands. "They made it the best procession we have had yet", said the fund secretary, Mr Ed Carter.

Though the bands did not compete against each other they added to the colour of the day. They were well supported by 122 youngsters in fancy dress and several tableaux.

The day's entertainment cost the fund between £700 and £800. The money was raised by miners employed at the colliery, who contribute sixpence a week. At the time there is a balance of about £2000.

Later in the afternoon, demonstrations were given by the Sunderland and District Pipe Band and by the Peterlee and District Caledonian Society, who gave a display of Highland dancing.

A collection for the Thornley Aged Mineworkers Home Committee raised more than £40.

Prizes for the sports were presented by Mr and Mrs R Kellett. Mr Kellett is No 3 area safety officer with the NCB.

Twenty-three handicapped children each received a special prize. They were given a 30s gift voucher which they were asked to exchange at a post office for two 15s savings certificates.

List Of Awards

Best dressed house: 1 Mrs Mitchell, 58 High street; 2 Mrs Crisp, 64 High Street; 3 Mrs Quinn, 60 High Street.

Tableaux: 1 Mothers' Club; 2 British Legion; 3 Over-60 Club; 4 Women's Institute.

Champion Pit Pony No 3 Area: 1 Tom of Easington; 2 Pompy of Blackhall; 3 Salty of Horden.

Cleanest Pit Pony No 3 Area B Group: 1 Tiny of Thornley; 2 Rodger of Shotton; 3 Major of Wingate

Trophy for the best drum major: Lorna Scott of The Ashington Gay Geordies

Trophy for the best band major: Dorothy Queen of Stakeford and Guidepost High Fliers.

Pet class for handicapped children: 1 Ann Robinson (dog); 2 E Coldwell (rabbit); 3 Ann Hardy (rabbit); 4 Thelma Dobbin (bird).

Open Pet class for children: 1 Graham Walker (dog); 2 Susan Hill (cavy); 3 Allan Day (rabbit); 4 Freda Mellington (bird).

Fancy Dress

Adults Original: 1 Mr G Copeland; 2 Mrs M Crisp; 3 Mr Hook and Ptnr.

Adults Comic: 1 Mr Hook and Ptnr; 2 Mrs M Crisp; 3 Mr G Copeland.

Children 5-7 years Original: 1 S Heslop; 2 B Tilley; 3 J Luke.

Comic: C Craggs.

8-10 years Original: 1 A Buck; 2 F Millington; 3 R Bentham.
Comic: 1 A Morton; 2 V Jones; 3 L Saunders.
11-15 years Original: 1 P Millington; 2 L Turner; 3 C Dowson.
Comic: 1 R Thorner; 2 C Mossop; 3 W Walker.
J Bennett won the go-as-you-please competition for the A Baldasera Memorial Cup.

Field Events

Boys 5-6 years: 1 J G Adams; 2 J Watson; 3 A Jones.
6-7 years: 1 D Pattison; 2 W Fradgley; 3 T Winter.
7-8 years: 1 T Wilson; 2 W Youll; 3 D J Cockburn.
8-9 years: 1 D Ord; 2 D Embleton; 3 D Parker.
9-10 years: 1 D Spence; 2 P Pattison; 3 R Nicholson.
10-11 years: 1 A Dower; 2 D Still; 3 J Walls.
11-12 years: 1 B Parker; 2 T Moore; 3 J Walton.
12-13 years: 1 I Bradley; 2 C Frampton; 3 R Gallant.
13-14 years: 1 W Walker; 2 P Templeton; 3 J Peachey.
14-15 years and over: 1 P T Wilkinson; 2 E Dewer; 3 G Southeran.
Girls: 5-6 years: 1 M McDonnell; 2 L Parker; 3 M Hughes.
6-8 years: 1 M Walker; 2 E O Gilday; 3 J Dawson.
8-9 years: 1 Z Walker; 2 D Errington,; 3 P Nicholson.
9-10 years: 1 L Walker; 2 H Bowman; 3 A Rutherford.

10-11 years: 1 M Day; 3 A Stephenson. *(no mention of a 2nd place in newspaper)*
11-12 years: 1 M A Parker; 2 I Marshall; 3 E Worthington.
12-13 years: 1 A Moyle; 2 A Bennett; 3 D Sunley.
13-14 years: 1 F Fox; 2 P Jones; 3 J Thompson.
14-15 years and over: 1 M White; 2 S Walls; 3 F Hutchinson.

EXTENSIONS TO THORNLEY CLUB
MP was Behind the Bar

Mr Emanuel Shinwell, MP for Easington, had the first one on the house when he opened the newly-reconstructed Thornley and District Workingmen's Club in Hartlepool Street at the weekend.

He had postponed an engagement with the BBC to perform the opening ceremony in his constituency. His performance in drawing the first pint, giving it a good top and drinking it off with a smack of his lips was highly satisfactory to the hundreds of members who watched.

More than 200 guests were afterwards entertained to high tea in the new ballroom when Coun F A Walker, chairman of the club, presided.

Mr Shinwell was supported by Mr Sid Lavers, chairman of the Federation Breweries, and Mr Arthur Welsh, Thornley Colliery manager, whose speeches were conveyed by loud speaker to all the members and visitors who filled the club to capacity for the occasion.

Cost Nearly £20,000

The cost of the reconstruction is nearly £20,000 and the club has been assisted by the Federation Breweries and the Co-operative Society, who did all the building and furnishing alterations.

The first workingmen's club was formed in Thornley 70 year ago in an old limestone building across the street from the present structure. The old portion of the present building was formerly a doctor's house and was acquired in 1900. An addition was made in 1921 when a dance hall and billiard room was added. These extra buildings retained the old Victorian service arrangements.

The club can now cater for all classes of members and their wives and families. There is a quiet reading room, a large lounge and spacious bar. The concert hall with buffet is fitted with loud speaker arrangements and all furniture blends with the floor coverings.

Secretary's Efforts

Much credit for the reconstruction is due to the efforts of Coun James Nicholson, the club secretary, who has spent much time in getting the building underway and seeking advice to make the new premises worthy of the expenditure.

Although the members have put up with a great deal of discomfort during the last six months they will be repaid many times in the new club.

The guests included Mr Arhur Welsh, Thornley Colliery Manager; Mr Robert Blythe, secretaryof the Durham Club and Institute Union; Mr James Anthony Kelly, president of the Durham Area NUM; Coun Edward Cain, JP; Mr Edward Carter, chairman of Thornley Miners' Lodge; Mr Ronald Hughes, secretary; Coun Michael Purcell, secretary of Horden Labour Club; Coun and Mrs Arthur Langthorne, chairman of Crimdon Parks Committee; Mr Roy Isherwood, manager; Mr Sid Lavers, chairman of Federation Breweries; Mr Jack Barlow of Federation Breweries; Mr J Kemp of Easington Workingmen's Club and representatives of many district clubs and organisations.

7 July 1961

Mr Shinwell behind the bar at Thornley Workingmens Club

THORNLEY CW FORGE AHEAD

With a convincing win over Bartram's Sports Club at Whitburn, Thornley CW increased their lead in the league to eight points above their opponents, who, with Ericssons, are their nearest rivals.

Fine bowling by A Brierley and D Iddon – 4-26 and 3-26 respectively – had the Sunderland side all out for 76, and the Welfare passed this total for the loss of only six wickets. Straughan and Gratton formed a resolute partnership, which took the score up to 50, and A Brierley was equally successful with the bat, contributing 20.

Bartram's SC: 76 (Hall 31)

Thornley CW: Straughan b Thompson 24, Greener b White 5, H Brierley b Rudkin 3, Gratton run out 20, Iddon b Thompson 0, A Brierley b White 20, Dent not out 3, Thubron not out 1; extras 1 – total (6 wkts) 77.

LEAGUE TABLE

	P	W	D	L	Pts
Thornley CW	7	6	0	1	18
Bartram's SC	6	3	1	2	10
Ericssons SC	6	3	1	2	10
Hazard Colliery	5	3	0	2	9
Morrison Busty CW	4	0	1	3	1
Alexandre	6	0	1	5	1

GARDEN PARTY – Organised by Wheatley Hill branch of the Guide Dogs for the Blind Association, a successful garden party was held in the grounds of Weardale House, Wheatley Hill, by kind permission of Mr F Richardson, manager of Wheatley Hill Colliery. Mr Richardson officially opened the fete and the programme included games, competitions and side-shows, and a gymnastic display by a team of boys from Wheatley Hill Senior Boys' School. Wheatley Hill Boy Scouts were in charge of the sideshows and stalls. Refreshments were served by the branch committee and other helpers. Winners of the lucky programme prizes were Mrs L Bromilow and Mrs A Burnside, and other competition winners were Mrs M Symons and Mr S Mills. Mrs Hope, of Shotton Colliery, won the treasure hunt and was also the winner of a cake given for another special competition. A balloon race was organised but the winner of this will not be know until later. As a result of the effort the sum of £59.18s.4d was raised. Secretarial duties were carried out by Mrs H Charlton.
21 July 1961

MINER RETIRES – After completing 51½ years service, in a variety of capacities in several pits in the county, Mr James Turnbull of 19 St Bede Crescent, Thornley, has retired under the age limit. Born at New Herrington in 1896, Mr Turnbull began work on the screens at 13½ and worked for a year before going underground to be employed at many datal jobs. He served in France and Belgium during the 1914-1918 War. On his return to the pits he was employed as a coal cutter at Sherburn Hill and as a puller up at Ryhope Colliery before removing to Thornley where he was employed as a hewer and datal hand until his retirement.

SCHOOL CAMP – Wheatley Hill Boys' Modern School headmaster, Mr A Harris and members of his staff, Messrs E Ward, J Etherington, R Walker, A Jones and A Potts, are sharing with 40 boys a week's holiday under canvas at Haltwhistle. After school on Friday the party were conveyed, with their equipment, by road to their destination. Outdoor activities, exploration of the countryside and games will be the order of the day. Mr Harris intimated that it was intended to give the boys experience of light-weight camping as outlined in the Duke of Edinburgh's Award Scheme. Asked why he was in favour of staff and pupils camping together the headmaster said, "I think it is a good thing. It brings staff and the boys together in a different relationship. The community life shared by the boys is a good training in character building".

4 August 1961

POPULAR BOXING COACH

An act of "lease lend" done in the best of faith, but terminated so abruptly as caused some consternation for the RAF authorities in South Cerney, Gloucestershire, and all because they lent out a Geordie as coach to a Boxing Club.

Three months ago a committee, with Major R B Freeman as president, formed the Amateur Boxing Club and asked the RAF for assistance. The RAF loaned the club equipment and also Sgt Ernest Curry as a coach. The club now has 45 members with some promising young boxers.

Sgt Curry, an apprentice blacksmith at Thornley Colliery before he joined up, is the youngest son of Mr and Mrs William Curry, of Wheatley Hill, and one of the five fighting brothers. He won the Northern Division of the NCB Novice Competition at St James's Hall, Newcastle in 1951 and 1952. He got his county colours of Boys' Clubs when he was 15½.

Sgt Curry has spent two nights each week away from the Sgts' Mess to be with the boys and he was appointed on to the committee, under Mr Peter Sheppard, an ex-amateur champion as chairman, and the club has gone with leaps and bounds.

Now the lease-lend has ended, the RAF are to withdraw Sgt Curry – they want him for a special mission in Aden. He is to leave the lads of Cirencester and they are up in arms. They have already recognised Sgt Curry's valuable service with two engraved tankards, and they have petitioned the RAF authorities to allow him to stay, and they are to make a last-minute appeal, with the help of Lord Bathurst and Mr W I Croome, chairman of the Cirencester Magistrates, to keep the Geordie coach at home.

11 August 1961

MINERS ON HOLIDAY – This weekend will see a big exodus from Wheatley Hill for the start of the annual miners' holiday. Only a few maintenance workers will remain on duty at the colliery after today (Friday). Quite a number of the miners and their families are going away for at least one week of their fortnight's holiday, with Blackpool, Scarborough, London, the Isle of Man and Great Yarmouth all popular venues. Some will be touring various parts of the British Isles in their own cars.

NEW WELFARE GROUNDSMAN – From 26 applications, Mr James William Hine (45), who has held a similar position with the National Coal Board in Yorkshire for the past two and a half years, has been appointed groundsman caretaker of Wheatley Hill Welfare Park, in succession to Mr Walter Myers, who had taken a new position at Sedgefield General Hospital. Mr Hine, who is married with five children, has been groundsman for the NCB at Allerton-Bywater, near Castleford. All his working career has been spent on similar duties, with the care of bowling greens, tennis courts and cricket pitches prominent among his duties. He has been employed in Yorkshire since 1946. Mr Hine and his family arrived at Wheatley Hill this week to take up residence in the groundsman's house in the Welfare Park grounds and he will begin his new duties on Monday.

LEAGUE CHAMPIONSHIP FOR THORNLEY CW

With their convincing win over Bartram's Sports Club on Saturday, Thornley CW assured themselves of the NE Durham League championship for the first time since they joined the league in 1951.

In the ten matches played they have only once been defeated, and much of the credit for their success can be attributed to the splendid bowling of A Brierley.

Against Bartram's, he captured four wickets for 12 runs and with E Gratton (3-10) succeeded in dismissing the visitors for only 44 runs.

Gratton, opening bat, set the foundation of Thornley's victory, carrying his bat for 63, but for this contribution the Welfare would have been in trouble for the last four batsmen failed to add to the total of 78. Best for Bartrams was W White who returned 6-37.

Scores:

Thornley CW: D Straughan b White, 2, E Gratton not out 63, H Brierley b Thompson 0, A Brierley b White 5, G Abbs b White 2, B Thubron b Thompson 5, T E Dent b White 1, T G Allen b Thompson 0, J Mangles b White 0, R Dawson b White 0, E Fulcher b Tansey 0, extras 0 – total 78.

Bartram's SC: 40

Thornley qualify for the £10 talent award, but the runners-up award of £5 still remains to be settled.

18 August 1961

Thornley CW - League Champions 1961

THORNLEY LEGION WOMEN'S 36TH BIRTHDAY PARTY

Mrs E Clark presided at the 36th annual birthday party of the Thornley British Legion Women, held in Thornley Miners' Welfare Institute. She welcomed members and guests who included Mrs W Hedger, county secretary, Mrs M Dixon, county treasurer and Mrs L Armstrong, the group representative, Mrs H Brewster, branch president and Mrs S Parker, vice-president and Miss Nellie Redshaw, secretary. Members were entertained to a high tea, and a full tea was sent to all sick members.

Mrs Ledger and Mrs Dixon addressed the members and invited them to take a more active interest in the county affairs and gain some of the trophies that were available in the various sections.

Mrs Brewster cut the cake and she was congratulated by Mrs Armstrong for the good work she had done for the ex-service men and for the interest she was still showing in the branch.

Mrs Clark, on behalf of the members, wished Mrs Harriet Thompson a pleasant air trip and a happy holiday in Canada, where she is to spend six months with her son, his wife and her grandchild. The evening ended with singing and dancing and prizes were won my Mesdames Walls, a cake; Stephenson, a shopping bag; and S Parker, a pair of towels.

"DESERTED VILLAGE"

In common with the Sherburn district and Thornley, the village of Ludworth is affected by the holiday season as applied to Sherburn Hill and Thornley Collieries. Since the male population of the village is employed at the two pits named, the village is more or less deserted.

On Saturday three 'bus loads of holiday makers departed for Blackpool; during the week a number of day excursions are taking place.

As is the custom, August is regarded as a holiday month by the Women's Institutes; consequently all three WI's Ludworth, Shadforth and Sherburn Hill are suspending their monthly activities.

25 August 1961

BRAVERY AWARD FOR WHEATLEY HILL PC

A County Durham policeman who rescued a ten-year-old boy from a dangerous cliff top at Blackhall Rocks last May has been awarded a testimonial on parchment by the Royal Humane Society.

He is PC Joseph Carr, aged 40, of 40 Cemetery Road East, Wheatley Hill.

The boy was bird-nesting with others on the cliff top at Crimdon camping site, Sawmills, when he got stuck on a 1ft wide ledge above a 60ft drop.

His friends gave the alarm, and PC Carr arrived. He sent Mr George Lennard, a miner, of 291 New Row, Wingate, for a rope.

Meanwhile the policeman went down onto the ledge to support the boy. To get to the ledge he had to climb down a 40ft gradual slope covered with grass and then a steeper 50ft slope covered with wet and slippery clay.

Mr Lennard lowered the rope, and the boy was hauled to safety.

BOWLS WINNER AT WHEATLEY HILL

A large crowd say Mr J W Burrell win the Moore Cup, which is put up for annual competition by the Wheatley Hill Welfare Bowls Club. He defeated Mr J Steel in a close game. This is the sixth occasion on which Mr Burrell has carried off the Moore Cup.

The cup was presented to the victor by Mr C Raffell. Congratulating Mr Burrell, he said, "The residents of Wheatley Hill are proud to have a bowls player of your standing and ability in the village. Not only have you won this cup for the sixth time, you have also won the Club Championship Cup for the fifth time. This is undoubtedly a worthy achievement. Your prowess has become known outside the club. You won the NC Singles competition for the County. We are glad Wheatley Hill can claim the miners' champion for this county".

8 September 1961

SUCCESSFUL RUN BY WHEATLEY HILL BAND

At the beginning of this year, Mr J Rutter, a well known principal cornetist took over the baton of Wheatley Hill Colliery Band. During the last ten weeks the resident conductor has steered his band through a highly successful run of competition playing. The band has won the major prizes at the following band contests, winning four cups, six first prizes and a second prize: Deaf Hill Sports Day 1st prize (selection); Spennymoor Show, 1st prize (march), 1st prize (selection); Easington Lane Sports Show, 1st prize (march), 1st prize (selection); Wolsingham Show, 2nd prize (march), 1st prize (selection).

Mr Rutter, who was at one time a member of the Munn and Felton's Shoe Works Band in Kettering, told our correspondent. "The adjudicators have commented on the rich tone of the band and the excellent quality of the players, especially in supporting the individual soloists. They have indicated that the band was well controlled with good tempo and rhythm".

The secretary of the band had this to say, "While we have had a most successful run this summer we are competing under strength. Twenty-four players are recognised as the correct combination for competitive work. In view of the fact that the band has competed with a strength of 18 players, the success is most commendable".

The bandmaster, Mr Rutter, or the secretary, Mr J Beresford, 2 Office Street, Wheatley Hill, will be pleased to welcome additional playing strength to the band.

WHEATLEY HILL "GOLDEN"

Two of Wheatley Hill's well known residents celebrated their golden wedding on Saturday. On 9 September, 1911, Mr and Mrs William S Hedley, 13 Gable Terrace, Wheatley Hill, were married in Haswell Methodist Church.

Born at Gateshead, Mr Hedley moved to New Washington when he was five. His father had a butcher's business there. Owing to his father's death at 36, his mother sold the business to Mr Brewis and Mr Hedley became his butcher's boy when he was 13. After three years he took a post with Mr Ford of Gateshead. When he was 19 he became a butcher in the business of Mr Ashford of Thornley.

Mr Hedley commented on conditions in those days. "Butcher's today have a much better time than we did, both as regards conditions of work and wages. I worked for Mr Ashford from six in the morning till 11 at night and I received 10s a week wages. I am glad conditions have improved for the younger men".

Own Business

After serving four years with Mr Ashford, Mr Hedley was appointed branch butchering manager at Trimdon Colliery for the Station Town Co-operative Society. Mr Hedley has always had the ambition to build his own business. He took the first step towards its fulfilment when in 1920 he took over Mr Ashford's business in Wheatley Hill.

So successful did Mr Hedley build and work that today his four sons are all in the business. Mr Hedley retired in February owing to ill health after being a butcher for 60 years. He is 73.

He is a Freemason and is a member of the Rowland Burdon Lodge. Two of his sons are in the same Lodge.

During the Second World War Mr Hedley served his calling in an administrative capacity. He was Deputy Meat Agent for the Ministry of Food for the Easington and Hetton area. For the past 12 years he has graded cattle at Castle Eden, Haswell and Stockton marts.

Four Great-Grandchildren

Mrs Hedley was born at Kelloe. When her father, Mr Simon Henderson, got work at Thornley she came to Gullock Street in Wheatley Hill. Later she moved to Swinburn

Street, Thornley. The family were Methodists and her father was choirmaster both at Kelloe and Thornley ex-Wesleyan churches.

The couple have four sons, three daughters, 20 grandchildren and four great grandchildren.

Mrs Hedley said, "In spite of having to look after a large family, I found time to help in the shop. I baked pies and pasties to help to expand the business".

Mrs Hedley has been a Women's Institute member for many years. Mr and Mrs Hedley are members of the Wheatley Hill Over 60 Club and on Saturday they received a bouquet of carnations from the Club. Owing to Mr Hedley's health it was agreed not to subject him to the strain and excitement of a large family party. Mrs Hedley said, " We spent the day quietly at home. Our family dropped in to see us during the day. Flowers and bouquets turned out home into a bower of beauty".

15 September 1961

GOLDEN DAY FOR THORNLEY COUPLE

A 72-year-old couple, who have lived all their married life in Thornley, yet were both born and married in Sunderland on 16 September, 1911, celebrated their golden wedding on Saturday with a party of over 40 relatives in St Bartholomew's Church Hall.

The party was given to the couple, Mr and Mrs A J Wallace, 23 Dunelm Road, Thornley, by their two married daughters, Mrs T Ward and Mrs J H Foster. The only guest present at the party who was at the wedding in St Ignatius Church, Sunderland, fifty years ago was Mrs Eliza Jobes, 62-year-old sister of Mr Wallace.

While at school in Sunderland Mr Wallace made his name as a schoolboy footballer, and although he did not reach international fame like his elder brother, Charlie Wallace of Aston Villa, in the days of Buchan and Mordue of Sunderland, he holds many medals and trophies. He also played for Horden and Wheatley Hill Church.

Mr Wallace worked at Thornley Colliery, as an onsetter, for 30 years with the exception of four years he spent with the Anglesey Royal Engineers' during the First World War. He was severely injured in a cage accident in 1940.

Mrs Wallace has been an active worker for St Bartholomew's Church and a member of the Mothers' Union since coming to the parish. The couple have four grandchildren.

WHEATLEY HILL CONSTITUTIONAL CLUB

There were 28 stands of leeks at the second annual show organised by the Leek Club of the Wheatley Hill Constitutional Club, and prize money totalled £650. The judge was Mr W Myers of Sedgefield.

The secretary of the club, Mr C W Rose, won the first prize, and Mr J Bradshaw was second. J Scott was awarded third prize and other principal winners, in order of merit, were Messrs J Cowan, S Scott, G Bowes, J Jordan, W Curry, W Cowan, J Dodds, T Sweeting, G Curry, N Lowther, T Foster, J Orchard and C Frampton.

Winners of the vegetable classes were: Round beet: 1 W Curry; 2 G Curry; 3 S Hedley. Short carrots: J Cowan. Long carrots: 1 J Jordan; 2 T Foster; 3 E Lowther.

Parsnips: 1 E Lowther; 2 R Foster; 3 T Foster. Round potatoes: G Curry. Kidney potatoes: J Orchard. Cauliflowers: 1 S Hedley; 2 W Curry; 3 J Dodds. Tomatoes: 1 C W Rose; 2 S Hedley; 3 R Foster. Onions: 1 G Bowes; 2 C Frampton; 3 J Orchard. Celery: 1 E Lowther; 2 T Foster; 3 S Hedley.

Bunch of flowers: G Dodds

The officials in charge of the arrangements were Messrs J Orchard (chairman), C W Rose (secretary) and C Frampton (treasurer).

22 September 1961

DURHAM NCB CIVIL DEFENCE AND FIRE-FIGHTING FINALS

Durham miners demonstrated how efficient they are in Civil Defence and firefighting at the Training Centre at Washington on Saturday when the finals of the divisional competitions were held.

Teams and individuals representing the various areas in the Durham Division of the NCB took part in six events, and there were challenge trophies as well as individual prizes to be won.

No 5 Area won the Divisional Challenge Shield for Civil Defence, and No 3 Area the shield for firefighting.

The speed and efficiency with which the tests were tackled impressed the many spectators, who also had the opportunity of seeing a Civil Defence demonstration arranged by the Durham County Training Headquarters of the Civil Defence Corps.

Mrs N F Nattrass, wife of the Industrial Relations Director of the Durham Division, presented the trophies and prizes. She was introduced by Mr R S McLaren, Production Director, and thanked by Mr W M Crooks, deputy chairman of the Durham Division. She received a bouquet from Mr M Welsh, who himself received gifts from the Area Civil Defence and Safety Officers, on his retirement as Civil Defence Officer for No 5 Area.

Comments on the competitions were made by the adjudicators, Mr R Martin (Warden Section), Mr W Parker (Rescue Section) and Mr H Twist (Firefighting Section).

The increasing emphasis put by the NCB on the importance of industrial Civil Defence was given in the announcement that among the Board's employees are 57 qualified instructors and about 3000 men trained or under training.

In the Civil Defence competition colliery teams from Boldon, Seaham, Thornley, Tursdale Workshops, Langley Park, Marley Hill, Washington Glebe, Dawdon, Easington and Addison took part.

Represented in the firefighting competitions were Hylton, South Hetton, Wheatley Hill, Trimdon Grange, Pit House, Marley Hill, Eppleton, Bowburn, Handen Hold and Fenhall Drift.

Crookhall Colliery Band, conducted by J J Stobbs, played selections during the afternoon.

Results

Rescue Section: 1 and Rescue Cup, Langley Park (G Yates, J Boyle, A Sinclair, J Yates, S Martin, J Agar, B Leighton, G Cartmell, J Wigham reserve); 2 Thornley (F Bradley, T Mitchell, F Carter, K Lonsdale, T Bullock, M Convery, W Convery, N Fort, T Armstrong reserve); 3 Boldon (J Wilson, C Young, G Dawes, F Bell, A Marshall, C Goss, R Baldridge, J Ellison, J Nixon reserve).

Warden Section: 1 and Warden's Cup, Dawdon (A Thompson, D Lacey, L Welch, R Gadd, I Storey); 2 Langley Park (R Atkinson, W Rose, W Clegg, L Morland, R Thompson); 3 Easington (F Ranson, N Burnhope, R Kell, P Lamb, T Harle).

Firefighting: Surface team: 1 Hylton (A Wilkinson, B Adey, E Atkinson, W Robertson, S Sopp reserve); 2 Wheatley Hill (R Horner, L Barker, A Appleby, M Dunn, T Smythe reserve); 3 Pit House (M Graham, T Wood, J Chance, R Hall, A Wilson reserve). Individual: 1 L Barker, Wheatley Hill; 2 A Hallam, Waterhouses; 3 H Blenkiron, South Hetton. Underground team: 1 Wheatley Hill (T Ayre, A Watson, W Gibson, J Cowan, J Poole reserve); 2 Handen Hold (G Robson, W Burridge, R Lockey, G Smith, J Wailes reserve); 3 Hylton (G Solomon, R Smith, F Wall, A Raine, H Rawlings reserve). Individual: 1 A Robson, Boldon; 2 P Ellis, Fishburn; 2 J Hall, Easington.

Wheatley Hill Fire Fighting Team
In NCB Civil Defence & Fire Fighting Finals

THORNLEY CLUB

When the three days' display of leeks, vegetables and flowers closed at Thornley Workingmen's Club some several thousands of visitors had seen one of the best exhibitions in the village for many years.

The newly-reconstructed and decorated dance room lent itself admirably for the display of gladioli, dahlias, chrysanthemums, roses, carrots and parsnips and the deep green flags and white buttons of the giant leeks and the array of prizes costing £1200.

The chief prizes for leeks went to Mr Stan Brass, a local farmer who has won several shows in the district, Mr Sam Hargreaves, 73-year-old retired checkweighman, who lost a leg in the First World War and Mr Jim Abbs, a colliery blacksmith.

270

Others included J R Greener, H Brierly, J Bellwood, W Smith, H Hoole, G Greener, W Curry and B Foster.

Other awards: Blanch leeks: 1 S Brass; 2 E Luke; 3 E Luke. Intermediate leeks: 1 J Abbs; 2 H Brierly; 3 D Greener. Onions: 1 and 2 S Brass; 3 E Luke. Celery (pink): 1 S Brass; 2 J Abbs; 3 R Lewis. Celery (white): 1 S Brass; 2 B Foster.

Parsnips: 1 and 2 J Abbs; 3 R Lewis. Carrots (shorthorn): 1 S Brass; 2 S Hargreaves; 3 E Luke. Carrots (long): 1 S Brass; 2 and 3 R Lewis. Potatoes (kidney): 1 and 2 J Bellwood; 3 S Brass.

GOLDEN DAY CELEBRATION AWAY FOR WHEATLEY HILL COUPLE

When Mr and Mrs John Hodson, 10 South View, Wheatley Hill, went on holiday, they had more than the annual visit to their two sons, John and Charles in view. For at John's home in Dunscroft, near Doncaster, the couple celebrated their golden wedding. They were married in Haswell Primitive Methodist Chapel in 1911. "We were brought up in that little chapel", said Mrs Hodson. "In fact we went three times a Sunday in our younger days. I remember the minister that married us. He was Rev Tom Dale".

Mrs Hodson said that her bridesmaid, a Miss Lily Cass of West Hartlepool, was still alive but was in Australia. Mr Hodson is 72 and was born at Trimdon Colliery, where his father worked in the pit long since closed. He started work at Wheatley Hill colliery and worked there 52 years. He passed through all the grades of mining, became a deputy and retired at 65 as a shot firer.

Mr Hodson has nothing but praise for the progress he has seen during his lifetime. He said, "I remember the long rows of colliery houses, primitive sanitary conditions and the muddy paths that existed instead of roads. Now we have well planned Council house estates and good roads. We can get to Thornley in a few minutes. These improvements are reflected in the better health of children". Mr Hodson went on, "One of the most beneficial changes that has affected the miner's living conditions was the introduction of pithead baths in 1939. I always said that the muck and dust of our calling should be left where it belonged – the pit. Bathing at the pit made our homes cleaner and certainly made the work of our womenfolk much easier. The young people now cannot understand what it was like for a family of three or four men to have to bath in a tin bath in the kitchen and the water to be boiled on the only fire in the house. These conditions have gone. The progress that has come to our village was due to the courage and devotion of men like Peter Lee and John Dickinson and the continued efforts of their successors".

Keen Bowls Player

Mr Hodson devoted a good deal of his spare time to the affairs of the Bristol and West of England Friendly Society, and was branch secretary for many years. His service was recognised when he was elected to the General Council and then to the national executive. He was honoured by being elected national Chairman of the society. Mr Hodson was a founder member of Wheatley Hill Welfare Bowls Club in 1930 and its chairman. He is a player of ability and last year won the Moore Memorial Cup.

Mrs Sarah Hodson is 70 and was born at Wheatley Hill. With the exception of a short time spent at Springwell she has lived in the village all her life. Interested in child health she has been a member of the Child Welfare Committee for many years and for some time acted as its treasurer. She was also a founder of the Wheatley Hill Women's Labour Party. Recalling her wedding day, Mrs Hodson said, "We went to Newcastle for our honeymoon. There was no week or fortnight for us. We only had a weekend. We went by train from Thornley station. It was quite an adventure, a train ride in those days".

Like her husband, Mrs Hodson is a bowls player. She was a founder member of Wheatley Hill Welfare Ladies' Bowls Club. "I haven't been among the cup winners yet", Mrs Hodson smiled. "I have been runner-up on more than one occasion". Both are members of the Wheatley Hill Over-60 Club and have been so since its inception eight years ago.

The celebration party in Dunscroft was attended by their two sons, their wives and six grandchildren. Both sons have followed in father's footsteps and have chosen mining as a career. They went to the Doncaster coalfield 20 years ago. The couple received a bouquet from members of the Over-60 Club. It was presented by the secretary, Mrs M E Richardson.

29 September 1961

NEAR MISS FOR WHEATLEY HILL SHOP

A load of 60ft long iron rails just missed crashing through the plate glass window of a hardware shop, at a busy road junction in Wheatley Hill last Thursday, but tore a hole in the woodwork above, when an articulated National Coal Board lorry failed to negotiate a traffic island.

The rails were resting on a trestle on the 50ft long trailer which had travelled down Cemetery Road. As the driver was turning right at the island, to go along the village's main street, the protruding rails caught a lamp standard and were dragged to the edge of the trestle.

They struck the name-board above the corner shop of R Vincent and Son and damaged spouting at the Constitutional Club next door. The rails were prevented from falling off the vehicle by six iron chains holding them to the trestle.

Miss Margaret Raine, who was working behind the counter of the shop with another woman, Mrs A Humble, told our reporter later, "We saw the lorry coming round the bend, then suddenly heard the crash and saw that the rails had struck the shop about a foot above the window".

The lorry and trailer blocked the road for about an hour and police had to divert traffic until the arrival of a crane to move the rails.

The driver of the lorry, Betram Brown (50) of 48 Tees Crescent, Spennymoor, who was on his way to deliver the load at Wheatley Hill colliery, was unhurt.

THE BALDASERA FAMILY

When the Baldasera family removed from the little bungalow adjacent to the RC Church, Thornley, the Catholic community in the village lost zealous church workers.

The Baldasera family for over 50 years have played an active part in the welfare of the Church in Thornley and none more so than Mrs Rosaria Baldasera, the mother, who goes with her son, Dr Joseph Baldasera, to their new home in Sunderland.

Mrs Baldasera, born in Italy, removed to Thornley at the outbreak of the First World War after her marriage to the late Mr Angelo Baldasera, a thriving ice-cream manufacturer in the Thornley district, who had four small children from his first marriage.

Mrs Baldasera, who has had four children, has attended Mass daily at the Church of the English Martyrs and is an active member of the Catholic Women's League. Her only daughter, Rosaria, is in the teaching order of the Little Sisters at Oak Lea Convent, Sunderland, and her youngest son, Dr Joseph Baldasera was educated at Corby Hall, Sunderland, Ushaw College and King's College, Newcastle. He takes up a senior appointment with the Sunderland Hospital Board.

To mark her service to the Catholic Women's League members of Thornley branch presented Mrs Baldasera with an inscribed brooch brought specially from Lourdes.

WHEATLEY HILL WORKMEN'S CLUB

Prizes amounting to £600 were awarded at the annual show of Wheatley Hill Workmen's Club Leek Club at the weekend. The show, which attracted 25 stands, was judged by Mr S Poulson, Wheatley Hill.

With a pair of leeks measuring 86.20 cubic inches. Mr A Atkinson won the first prize, and the chairman of the show, Mr A Bramfitt, was second. Next, in order of merit were Messrs J Nattrass, R Cook, A Bishop, E Almond, S Owens, W Curry, M Bailes, M Telford.

Winners of the other classes were: Kidney potatoes: 1 J Raffell; 2 and 3 W Curry. Round potatoes: 1 and 2 J Raffell; 3 A Bishop. Onions: 1 W Foster; 2 and 3 J Nattrass. Long beet: 1 and 2 W Curry; 3 A Bishop. Intermediate leeks: 1 J Nattrass; 2 R Cook; 3 J Raffell. Globe beet: 1 C Soppitt; 2 R Waite; 3 M Telford. Pink celery: 1 and 2 J Raffell; 3 R Waite. White celery: 1 W Newell; 2 and 3 R Cook. Short carrots: 1, 2 and 3 R Cook. Long carrots: 1 W Curry; 2 A Bishop; 3 J Raffell. Cauliflowers: 1 W Foster; 2 R Waite; 3 J Telford. Parsnips: 1 J Raffell; 2 W Curry; 3 J Raffell. Bunch of flowers: 1 J Nattrass; 2 M Telford; 3 W Foster.

Coun A Bishop was secretary and treasurer for the show and Mr A Bramfitt chairman.

SHERBURN HILL CO-OPERATIVE SOCIETY RETIREMENT

Mr John Brady, assistant secretary of Sherburn Hill Co-operative Society since 1955, retired last weekend on reaching retirement age. To mark their appreciation members of the office staff presented Mr Brady with an electric razor.

Mr Brady had worked for the society since he was 15½ years of age. He was born at Shadforth and lived with his parents, Mr and Mrs James Brady, in the village, and afterwards at Church Villas, Shadforth.

When he was engaged by the Co-operative Society his first post was office boy at the Wheatley Hill branch in 1912. This branch had then just been opened and the membership was drawn from Thornley, Cassop, Quarrington Hill, all transferred from Shotton to make up the Wheatley Hill branch; Mr Matthew Lee was the first branch manager. Mr J Wilkinson, from Sherburn branch, was chief clerk at Wheatley Hill to be followed by Mr James Hutchinson.

From 1916 to 1919 Mr Brady served in the RFA and saw service abroad. On his demobilisation he returned to Wheatley Hill but in February 1922, was moved to Shotton, staying there until 1934. On the absorption of Haswell Society by Sherburn Hill Society, Mr Brady was transferred to Easington where he remained until 1955 when he took up the post he has just relinquished. Altogether he has served under the following secretaries: Mr T N Robson, Mr J R Williamson, Mr J Hutchinson and Mr G H Gibbon.

An interesting fact regarding the Wheatley Hill branch is that when Mr Brady began there the membership was in the neighbourhood of 1000. It has now grown to over 5000.

Asked how he proposed to spend his leisure time, Mr Brady intimated that it would be devoted to his garden and to long walks. He is interested in football and a faithful follower of the Sherburn Wednesday Club.

23 GOALS AT WHEATLEY HILL

Twenty-three goals were seen at two football matches at Wheatley Hill on Saturday.

Wheatley Hill Mechanics who, the previous Saturday drew 2-2 with Horden Casuals, trounced Hartlepool Wanderers 12-1 in the Division II of the Hartlepools and District League, while Wheatley Hill Workmen's Club had a runaway 10-0 victory over Wingate Constitutional Club in the newly-formed Durham County Club Union League.

6 October 1961

CULLEN TO MEET GRACIA

An important date for Maurice Cullen, the Shotton lightweight boxer, will be Monday, 13 November when he steps into the Newcastle ring of boxing promoter Joe Shepherd to meet Guy Gracia, the French Algerian.

Gracia has twice defeated the reigning British lightweight champion, Dave Charnley, and also beaten many British lightweights.

The British Boxing Board of Control is keenly interested in the rise of Cullen as challenger to Dave Charnley, and as the fight will be televised it will prove first-class entertainment to many boxing fans in the North-East.

20 October 1961

NEW POST FOR MURTON LIBRARIAN

Mr W H Hume, branch librarian at Murton, has been appointed to take charge of Wingate, Thornley and Wheatley Hill branches.

The appointment means that Murton readers will find lighter books, not normally available through the students' service, a little easier to obtain. Now the stocks at the four branches can be tapped to meet any requests.

Book issues over the last six months have shown a rapid increase over the corresponding period of last year. "What this increase (4000) may prove, is debatable", says Mr Hume. "But it could be that television is losing some of its support and that discriminating people are reverting to the medium over which they have a greater control".

This is confirmed by the fact that the increase is largely in adult fiction. The number of books issued over the six months was 45,398.

27 October 1961

WHEATLEY HILL MINER-MUSICIAN

The funeral took place last week of Mr Ernest Evans (60), of 19 Wordsworth Avenue, Wheatley Hill. Service was conducted by the Rev E P Lucas in Wheatley Hill Patton Street Methodist Church. Mr Evans is survived by his wife, Elizabeth, two sons, two daughters and eight grandchildren.

Born in Wigan, Mr Evans came to Wheatley Hill with his parents when he was two. He spent 58 years in Wheatley Hill and worked at the local colliery and Blackhall Colliery. He played football in his younger days, a half-back of no mean ability, for Wheatley Hill, Deaf Hill and Trimdon St Mary's.

But it was as a musician that Mr Evans was best known. For many years he was a member of Wheatley Hill Colliery Band and played First Cornet. The piano was his first love. He was one of the last piano players to appear in the county as accompanist to the silent films. He played in picture houses at Thornley, Wheatley Hill, Wingate and finally at Shotton, and at many concerts for charity. He was a member of Wheatley Hill Club for over 40 years.

3 November 1961

CHRISTMAS FAYRE AT WHEATLEY HILL

Everything on the well-laden stalls were given by the members and friends of the Wheatley Hill Church Street Methodist Church Sisterhood, when the annual Christmas "Fayre", organised by the Sisterhood, was held in Wheatley Hill Welfare Hall on Saturday afternoon.

The Sisterhood president, Mrs L Mason, presided at the opening ceremony, which was performed by Mrs A Wigham, of Wellfield, Wingate. 5-year-old Glynis Dunn presented a bouquet to Mrs Wigham and thanks were expressed by Mrs Mason. As a result of the effort nearly £40 was raised for Sisterhood funds.

Refreshments were served by Mesdames Howarth, Hamilton and Kirk, and the stallholders were: Gifts – Mesdames A Lambert, Calvert, Lang and Austin; Shilling Parcels – Mrs Howarth and Mrs Hodgson; Home Made Cakes – Mrs Milne; White

Elephant – Mrs O Warnes; Sweets – Miss Ann Galley; Christmas Cards – Miss Barbara Galley; Bran Tub – Mrs G Poulson; Ice Cream – Mrs Hughes.

Mrs R Ord and Miss Bessie Galley were in charge of the treasure hunt, which was won by Miss Elizabeth Barron.

As the Sisterhood secretary, Mrs P H Galley, was indisposed, the duties of both secretary and treasurer were carried out by Mrs R Ord.

IN MEMORY OF THE FALLEN
Dedication Ceremony at Thornley

A dedication ceremony in Thornley Parish Church was conducted by the Vicar (Rev P G Mold) who was assisted by Rev G Johnson, Methodist Minister and Capt J L Stock, of the Salvation Army.

A Book of Remembrance and cabinet stand were dedicated to the memory of 135 men of Thornley and Thornley Colliery who fell in the 1914-18 War and the 24 men, all of Thornley, who fell in the 19349-45 War.

The book is bound in red morocco leather with the names of the fallen in letters of gold. The cabinet and stand are of oak. They are the gifts of a retired couple, Mr and Mrs Rowland Brewster, 23 Thornlaw, Thornley.

Following the hymns and address by the Vicar, Dr A P Gray, president of Thornley British Legion, made the presentation on behalf of Mr and Mrs Brewster and called upon Mr William Bovil, Chairman, to unveil them saying, "I present unto you this Book of Remembrance and cabinet to be kept in this Parish Church as a perpetual memorial to those who gave their lives in both World Wars".

The Vicar said, "I accept on behalf of the Church and heartily thank you and the donors for these worthy presents which I now dedicate".

The lesson was read by Capt Stock and the prayer recited by Mr Johnson. Last Post was sounded by Mr Edward Kitto, bandmaster of Thornley Colliery Band.

Mr and Mrs Rowland Brewster have been well known in Thornley for over 40 years, Mrs Brewster as a county midwife, a parish councillor and president of the British Legion women's section, and her husband in civil defence, a blood donor who has given 90 pints of blood, and a chapel chorister. He is a permanent cripple through a motor crash 30 years ago.

They have given the money for a lasting and worthy tribute to many of the boys Mrs Brewster delivered and the many friends they made and lost in both Wars.

BRIGADE PARENTS NIGHT – The 1st Thornley Boys' Brigade Parents' Night was held in Thornley Bow Street Methodist Church Sunday School. A large audience was welcomed by Captain J Plant. Parade and inspection were taken by Mr J Murray; recruit drill by Sgt J Oswald; senior drill by Lieut K Hetherington and the Brigade Band by Mr E Kitto and Lieut K Hetherington. Lieut A Potts trained a team who gave a gymnastic display and an exhibition of dribbling through skittles was given by L/Cpl E Dower and Pte J Wilkinson. There was keen competition in a programme of the games. Tea and refreshments were served by the ladies. Mrs Murray, dressed in Boys' Brigade uniform, presented certificates and badges to Brigade members and a statuette to the best boy, L/Cpl William Crisp.

10 November 1961

WHEATLEY HILL DEPUTY RETIRES

After a mining career of 51 years, practically all of which has been spent at Wheatley Hill colliery, Mr Thomas Todd, of 17 Handel Terrace, Wheatley Hill, has retired on reaching his 65th birthday.

A native of Kelloe, Mr Todd began work at Tursdale colliery, when he was 14, earning 1s.4½d a shift. "My first job was working on the screens and my shift a ten-hour one, but shortly afterwards I went down the pit and worked an eight-hour shift".

Started In 1911

Mr Todd transferred to Thrislington colliery, after only a short time at Tursdale, and in 1911 began work at Wheatley Hill colliery, where he remained until his retirement, being one of the colliery's longest-serving deputies.

At Wheatley Hill, Mr Todd went through all grades of pit work including driving, putting and hewing. He was also a stone-man for a time, but for the past 36 years served as a deputy. During recent years he was spare overman.

Mr Todd was involved in a fairly serious accident before his marriage, but since then has suffered little injury. "I have been pretty fortunate where accidents down the pit are concerned", he said. For about eight years he was secretary of Wheatley Hill Lodge of the Durham County Colliery Deputies' Association.

Favourite Hobby

Now that he has retired, Mr Todd said, he will be able to devote more time to his favourite hobby of gardening. "I have always been fond of gardening – especially growing flowers – and have always had a greenhouse", he said.

Chrysanthemum growing is Mr Todd's speciality but, though he produces some fine specimens year after year, he has never entered them in shows. "I have grown them purely for the satisfaction I get out of it", he said. And he gave our reporter a surprise by taking him into his greenhouse in the back garden of his home and showing him several beautiful green chrysanthemums.

Mr Todd is married, with two daughters and four grandchildren. His elder daughter, Mrs Hilda Harper, lives in Wheatley Hill and his other daughter, Mrs Mildred Stewart, at Bedlington.

REMEMBRANCE DAY PARADES
THORNLEY

The remembrance day service in Thornley took place at the war memorial and was conducted by the vicar, the Rev P G Mold, assisted by Rev G Johnson, Methodist Minister and Capt Stock of the Salvation Army.

The procession to the memorial from Dunelm Road was led by Thornley Colliery band, under Mr E Kitto, and included Dr A P Gray, president of the British Legion; the branch standard bearers, Mr and Mrs R Slater, and ex-servicemen of both wars: Mr J Carr, chairman of Thornley Colliery Mining Federation Board; Coun J R Bosomworth, chairman of Thornley Parish Council; Mesdames G M Bromilow and E Middleton, British Legion; M W Salter and N Mason, Thornley Mothers' Club; the Boys' Brigade under Lieuts J Plant and Speckman and the Girl Guides under Miss I Stainthorpe. Hymn singing was led by the band and the Last Post was sounded by Mr H Hood (cornet) and wreaths were placed on the memorial by the officials of each organisation.

WHEATLEY HILL

At Wheatley Hill the parade was headed by the Colliery Band. Easington RDC and Wingate Parish Councils were represented. The British Legion (Women's Section), Wheatley Hill WI, Fire Service, Discharged Soldiers, Sailors and Airmen's Club, Scouts, Workmen's and Constitutional Clubs and Mothers' Club took part in the parade.

All Saints Church was packed to capacity and the service was conducted by the Vicar, Rev G G Graham. Address was given by the Rev G L Nelson, entitled Peace through Prayer. Mr A E Tuffnell was at the organ.

After the service the procession re-formed and marched to the War Memorial clock on the Boys' School, a memorial to the dead of World War II. Prayers were said and then the parade moved to the Cenotaph for a short service, where wreaths from all organisations in the village were laid.

CULLEN JABS HIS WAY TO POINTS WIN

Maurice Cullen, the stylish Shotton Colliery lightweight boxer, took a step nearer to a title fight when at St James' Hall, Newcastle, on Monday, he gained a points decision over the French-Algerian, Guy Gracia, in a ten-round contest.

Cullen, 24 years old, is now rated as No 2 challenger for Dave Charnley's title. Of his 19 bouts the Shotton lad has only lost one to, Spike McCormack, and since then that decision has been reversed. He has also beaten such well-known boxers as Dave Stone, of Battersea and John McNally.

It is interesting to note that Guy Gracia, a veteran of some 200 bouts, has beaten Charnley, the British champion, twice and has also fought and beaten Sammy MacCarthy and Willie Lloyd.

AT THE ANNUAL MEETING – of Thornley Colliery Mining Federation Board, Mr J Carr, of the Colliery Officials' Association, was elected chairman. Mr E Carter, who has been secretary to the board for some years, did not seek re-election and Mr S Greener, of the Miners' Lodge, was elected. Mr W Thompson, of the Mechanics' Lodge, who held the post of treasurer, was unopposed. Mr Carter is to continue as secretary to the Aged Miners' homes fund. The 20 members of the committee are composed of eight miners, three mechanics, three officials, three deputies and three enginemen who are elected by their Lodges.

17 November 1961

TESTIMONIAL FOR BRAVE POLICEMAN
Played part in cliff rescue of Wingate boy

It was one of the bravest deeds he had heard of for a very long time, said the chairman, Mr E Chicken, at Castle Eden magistrates' court on Saturday, when he presented a testimonial on parchment from the Royal Humane Society to PC Joseph Carr, of Wheatley Hill, for the part he played in the rescue of a 10-year-old Wingate boy trapped 40 feet down a 150ft cliff at Crimdon on 15 May.

The boy, David Robinson of 40 Dawson Road, Wingate, was at the Crimdon caravan site at 6.30pm with two friends, Denis Tait (10) of 65 Tenth Street, Blackhall and Joseph William Younger (13) of 12 Manor Close, Trimdon Village, when they decided to go to see a bird's nest down the cliff side, said Supt M Reed.

Robinson was followed down the cliff by Younger, but Younger, after climbing about six feet down, realised it was too dangerous because of the difficulty he was having in keeping his feet on the slippery slope.

He shouted to Robinson to return, but Robinson continued his way down the cliff and when he was about 40 feet down, found himself in difficulties. He shouted to his friends above that he could not find the nest and said he could not climb back up the cliff.

Fastened Rope Around Boy

Younger told Tait to go to a nearby caravan for help and the first people he saw were PC Carr and Mr George Lennard of 391 New Row, Wingate.

The two men rushed to the top of the cliff but could not see Robinson because of the position he was in. Mr Lennard was sent for a rope by PC Carr, who started to climb down the cliff to try and reach the boy.

Mr Lennard also climbed down to a ledge just above where PC Carr had reached the boy, said Supt Reed. He lowered the rope and PC Carr fastened it round the boy and then climbed back towards Mr Lennard. The two men then hauled the boy to safety.

Apart from shock, the boy was unharmed and was able to go home, little the worse for his alarming experience.

The upper half of the cliff was very steep, said Supt Reed, and then there was a sheer drop to the rock-covered beach below. One false step, by either Robinson or PC Carr, when they were perched precariously on the narrow ledge might have had serious consequences.

In presenting the parchment to PC Carr, a married man with four children, Mr Chicken said that recently a lot had been heard about the alleged poor relations between the police and the general public. But a rescue of this sort proved once again how ready a constable was to go to anyone's help. Whenever any member of the general public was in trouble, a policeman was always the first person they thought of sending for.

"Brave Deed Very Well Done"

PC Joe Carr (centre)
With Sgt Yates (left) &
Chief Constable Arthur Puckering

PC Carr had gone straight down the dangerous cliff side to the boy's rescue. As well as giving the boy confidence, he had made sure he did not fall to the beach below and had given all the help he could.

"This is one of the bravest deeds I have heard of for a very long time", added Mr Chicken. "I know that particular cliff side very well. When Constable Carr went to this boy's rescue they both could have been involved in a fatal accident. Fortunately the rescue was successful. We would like to commend PC Carr very sincerely indeed – the parchment will always remind him of a very brave deed very well done."

The Bench, said Mr Chicken, wished PC Carr many more useful years in the police service.

PC Carr, who is 40, formerly worked as a deputy at Trimdon Grange Colliery. He joined the West Riding Police 12 years ago, when he left the pits, and served there for three years. He then transferred to the Durham County Constabulary and has served in the Thornley section of the Castle Eden Police Division - first at Thornleyand latterly at Wheatley Hill, for the past nine years. He lives at 40 Cemetery Road East, Wheatley Hill

LEGION WOMEN – Mrs J Clark presided at a meeting of Thornley British Legion Women's Section. Mrs G M Bromilow, secretary, gave business details. Reports from sick visitors were received, and Miss N Redshaw and Mrs H Simpson gave a report on the sale of the work done by ex-Servicemen. Mrs H Brewster, president, thanked the members who had attended the service in the parish church to take part in the dedication of the Book of Remembrance she had presented to the Legion. Members were entertained by a film show given by a firm of flour manufacturers. Prizes given by Mesdames Bromilow and Langley were won by Mesdames Brewster and Worthington and other prizes by Mesdames Simpson and Harper.

MR ROBERT YOULL of Wheatley Hill, one of ten men who took the examination of the Worshipful Company of Farriers last week.
1 December 1961

LUDWORTH SCHOOL PRIZE DAY AND CONCERT

In the Ludworth Junior Mixed and Infants' School on Wednesday afternoon and evening an entertainment was given by the school children. Both performances were well attended but the afternoon one had special significance because of the presentation of school prizes.

The managers of the school, Messrs D Thornton, J T White and J T Hedley were present, and Mr White, chairman of the managers, presented the prizes as follows:

Infants I class: Margaret Ditchburn (progress), Norman Deluce (physical education), Howard Carr (initiative and good manners).

Infants II class: Ann Whittle (initiative and helpfulness), Janet Lee (good manners), David Hughff (physical education).

Junior I class: Norman Ewens (history, geography and nature), George Ditchburn (general knowledge), Jacqueline Sunley (progress and neatness), Gordon Teasdale (writing), Keith Parsons (physical education).

Junior II class: Margaret Maddison (singing), Enid Dixon (politeness), Raymond Deluce (drama) and John Hartley (effort and neatness).

Snow White

The headmaster, Mr R Simpson, presided. The entertainment was two plays, with carols.

Snow White and the Seven Dwarfs had the following cast: Susan Armstrong, Margaret Maddison, Stella Winter, Thomas Bennett, William Widdowfield, Raymond Deluce, Colin Stoves, George Marley, Harry White, David Hughff, Kevin Brown and Norman Deluce.

A Nativity play, Bethlehem is Here was reverently presented by Susan Wilson, David Embleton, David Youll, George Ditchburn, Glyn Hutchinson, Robert Milburn, Dennis Morgan, Joseph Atkinson, Susan White and Linda Raine.

The Infant Choir were: Lynette Todd, Winifred Johnston, Janet Lee, Ann Whittle, George Marley, Kevin Brown, David Hughff, Janet Peachey, Ann Hooker, Margaret Ditchburn, Ellen Geddes, Norman Deluce and Niall Webster.

The Junior Choir were: Kenneth Bradshaw, John Howarth, David Youll, Dennis Morgan, John Hartley, David Embleton, Glyn Hutchinson, Reuben Whittle, George Ditchburn, William Youll, Jean Dunn, Joyce Morrow, Stella Winter, Christine Winter, Margaret Maddison, Susan Armstrong, Patricia Sunley, Ann Vasey, Susan Wilson, Linda Raine, Susan White, Pauline Smith, Christine Peachey, Dorothy Hughff, Norma Ewens, Margaret Whittle and Dorothy Hughff.

The recorded voices of the Infant and Junior Choirs were introduced by Stella Winter.

Members of the school teaching staff were responsible for the production of the entertainment, these were: Mrs E Wilson, Mrs E A Walton, Miss J Morgan and Mr J Madgin with the headmaster. The proceeds are for the school Christmas party.

Coun G Smith, chairman of the Shadforth Parish Council, was present at the evening performance, also the Rev A R L Prentice, Rector of Shadforth.

281

THORNLEY FUNERAL OF COLLIERY SURVEYOR

The funeral service of Mr Stanley Edwin Smith (40), Office Villas, Thornley, head surveyor of B Group of Collieries in No 3 Area of NCB, was held in St Bartholomew's Church, Thornley, conducted by the Vicar (the Rev P G Mold).

Mr Smith was born in Thornley, only son of Mr and Mrs Charles Smith, Dunelm Road. His father was chief clerk at Thornley Colliery.

A month ago, Mr Smith attended the funeral service of Mr John Leslie Rowley (41) head surveyor of Easington Colliery. They served their apprenticeship together with Weardale group of collieries at Thornley, Wheatley Hill and Wingate.

Mr Smith was a very popular sportsman in the village. He was a founder member of Thornley Cricket Club, and played for them for many seasons. Like his father and grandfather he had the shooting rights of Thornley Estate, a privilege they held for over 60 years.

Mr Smith leaves a wife and two children, both at school.

WHEATLEY HILL CHURCH BAZAAR RAISED £270

The Christmas bazaar of All Saints Church, Wheatley Hill, was opened by the Vicar, the Rev G G Graham. It was held on Saturday in the Church Hall and was well supported. The effort realised £270 for church funds.

Stallholders were Mesdames Atkinson, Alderton, Woodward, Richardson, Purvis, Kelly, Longstaffe, Holmes, Weightman, Smith, Lincoln, Jordan, Stark, Morgan, Walker, Halliwell, Robson, Howe, Craggs, Bellas, Thomas, Thompson, Bell, Poulson, Sweeting, Raffell, McBriar, Dinsdale; the Misses Towell, J Raffell; Messrs Alderton, Waite and Dinsdale. Mr G Sayers acted as doorkeeper.

In the evening the Vicar welcomed about 100 guests to a social evening. Mr C Raffell was MC for whist and Mrs E Kelly was in charge of dominoes.

Prize winners were: whist – ladies – Mrs Towler, Mrs White, Mrs Parker, Mrs Robson, Mr J T Robinson, Mr M Hall. Dominoes – Mrs Jones, Miss Robinson, Mrs Lincoln.

Mrs E Kelly was MC for dancing.

WORKMEN'S CLUB PARTY – The oldest guest, Mr John Snowdon, who is in his mid-eighties, cut the Christmas cake at the annual party organised by Wheatley Hill Workmen's Club for retired club members and their wives and widows over 60. About 300 old folk were entertained and among the guests were Mr F Simpson, under-manager at Wheatley Hill Colliery, Mr Stan Hale, Durham County secretary of the Club and Institute Union, and Mr Sid Lavers, chairman of the Northern Federation Breweries, who all extended Yuletide greetings to the old folk. Greetings were also read from the club secretary, Mr B Aitken, who was unable to be present through indisposition. An excellent tea was served and each guest received a £1 Christmas gift. Mr Peter McCarron entertained with selections on the electric organ, and other entertainers were Mr Colin Murray (Middlesbrough), Mr G Lyons (Stanley), Mr G

Hepton (Hetton-le-Hole) and Miss Irene Waters (Stockton). Mr W Henderson, chairman of the club, presided and thanked the concert party.

OVER-60 CLUB PARTY – When the Christmas party of Wheatley Hill Over-60 Club was held in the Workmen's Club concert hall on Tuesday, a warm welcome was extended to about 350 members by the chairman, Mr George Farrar, and each received a Christmas gift of 15s. Seasonable greetings were extended by the Vicar of Wheatley Hill, Rev George Gordon Graham. An excellent knife-and-fork tea was served and during the evening many gifts were distributed, including 28 which had been personally collected by County Coun John Andrews. Coun and Mrs Andrews, who were among the guests, also sent baskets of fruit to 11 sick members and wished them a speedy recovery from their illness. Birthday greetings were sung to Mesdames M Fenwick, E Bailes and M Aitken and Mr J Robinson. An excellent entertainment was given by the Blackhall Excelsior Road Show concert party, with Mr Joe Fishwick compere and Mrs N Jordan accompanist, and Mr Peter McCarron entertained on the club's electric organ. Arrangements were made by the secretary, Mrs E Richardson, who wishes to thank all those who contributed towards the success of the party with gifts and donations.
15 December 1961

CHRISTMAS GIFTS - The annual "pay-out" from the Wheatley Hill Aged Miners' Treat Fund is to take place between 1 and 3pm from the local Aged Miners' Hostel tomorrow (Saturday), and this year the recipients – retired miners and their wives and widows over 55 – will find that their Christmas gifts have been increased from 10s to £1. "The committee have worked splendidly throughout the year and it is as a result of the many special efforts held from time to time that we are able this year to pay out gifts of £1", the secretary, Coun C Hackworth, told our reporter this week. Altogether about 500 old folk will benefit. In charge of the distribution will be the chairman and treasurer of the committee, Coun M Telford and Mr J Hedley, in addition to Coun Hackworth.

CHEAP BEER - For the two weeks commencing Christmas Eve – from 24 December to 6 January – the 800 members of Wheatley Hill Workmen's Club will be able to buy their beer at a reduced price, as a holiday concession. Fourpence a pint will be knocked off all draught and bottled beer during this period. Workmen were "full steam ahead" at the club this week putting the finishing touches to extensive alterations to the club bar and lounges, which are being completely modernised.

MP OPENS CHRISTMAS FAYRE AT THORNLEY
A Christmas Fayre, arranged by Thornley Bow Street, Thornley Waterloo Street, Cassop, Haswell and Haswell Plough Methodist Churches on Saturday, was very successful. It was well supported. Mrs J Plant was organising secretary and Mrs E

Gratton treasurer. The effort realised £118.12s.4d in aid of Thornley Manse Trust Board.

The event took place on Thornley Waterloo Street premises. The Rev G Johnson presided, and the MP for Durham, Mr C F Grey, was opener. He was presented with a buttonhole by Carol Ann Johnson.

Stallholders were Thornley Bow Street (draperies), Mesdames B Appleby, I Henderson, M Galloway and E Thornton; (children's gifts), Mrs G Speckman and Coun Miss A Griffiths; (sweets and preserves), Mesdames M Harrison, J Wigham and Miss I Smart. Cassop (cakes), Mesdames A Newton, M Horner, W Ezart, T Long, the Misses D Stokoe and G Fenwick. Thornley Waterloo Street (bathroom requisites), the Misses J Gratton, M Carter, J Maines and A Booth; (gifts), Mesdames E Pattison, G Jordison, A V Turner and G Hetherington; (pound stall), Messrs T Robinson and R Hedley. Haswell and Haswell Plough (household goods), Mesdames A Stoker, R Belton and the Misses K Meek and J Park.

Tableau

The men organised a tableau with Santa Clause and Aladdin's Cave. The grotto was built by Messrs A L Miller, T Lincoln, I P Martin, J Plant, J Hedley and I Jones. Those taking part were E Robinson, A Lincoln, E Plant, G Thornton, C Davies, K Jackson, W Crisp, E Galloway and P Galloway.

Refreshments were served by Mesdames E Gratton, M Hedley, J Bott, B Booth, M Wilson, M Atkinson, M E Ruth, J Bullock and E Hinchcliffe. Door-keepers were Messrs. J Pattison and G Hetherington.

WHEATLEY HILL CLUB TEAM

Wheatley Hill Workmen's Club football team enjoyed a 4-2 away win over Seaham York House in the Durham County Club Union League on Saturday. One of their goals was scored by a Seaham player in attempting to clear the ball, and the other scorers were Harvey, Moir and Wood. For the second week running Keith Jackson, the Wheatley Hill goalkeeper, saved a penalty.

Tomorrow, Wheatley Hill entertain Hetton Comrades Club with the following team: Jackson, Harry Hepple, Battye, Richardson, Young, Nichols, Ainscough, Harvey, Moir, Wood, O'Connor. Reserves: Hugh Hepple, Cook, Raffell.

22 December 1961

1962

A THORNLEY LINK WITH OLD CRAFT IS SEVERED

The funeral took place yesterday of Mr Thomas Waller, 83, of 6 Ruskin Crescent, Thornley, who died in hospital at the weekend.

Mr Waller was one of the best known characters in Thornley where he was born. For over 60 years he was the only village blacksmith in the district, and in the days when horses were the chief motive power and transport for farmers and tradesmen, his anvil in Bow Street could be heard from early morning until late at night.

The village forge was the meeting place of the schoolboys who competed to blow the bellows.

The service in St Barthlolomew's Church and at Thornley Cemetery was conducted by the Rev P G Mold. Mr Waller leaves a wife. four sons and two daughters.

5 January 1962

Mr Thomas Waller of Thornley

RECORD RECEIPTS – Though beer – both draught and bottled – was reduced by four pence a pint at Wheatley Hill Workmen's Club during Christmas week the week's receipts of £1453.8s.5d set up a new record for the club, it was revealed this week. During the last few months extensive alterations have been taking place in the club's main bar and lounge and they were completed just in time for the Christmas holiday. The lounges now have a gay, attractive look – they have been re-furnished throughout and new floor coverings, lighting and wallpaper have all helped to complete the club's modernisations plans.

CLUB BALLOT – This weekend will see keen balloting at Wheatley Hill Workmen's Club for the annual election of officers and committee, as all the principal positions are being contested – chairman, secretary, treasurer and door-man – and there are no fewer than 43 nominations for six vacancies on the committee. But the number of nominations for the committee is not a record. A committee member told our reporter on Wednesday that on one occasion there were as many as fifty. Mr J Dunn is retiring as treasurer after 28 years unbroken service and there are five nominations to fill the position, namely Messrs C Hackworth, S Hastings, J Maddison, W Wood and L Young. The chairman, Mr W Henderson and secretary Mr B Aitken are both opposed.

12 January 1962

WHEATLEY HILL SCOUTS VISIT HOSPITAL

On Sunday the senior members of the second Wheatley Hill Group Scouts paid their New Year visit to Durham County Hospital and entertained the young people in the children's ward, which they "adopted" some years ago.

As well as singing Scout songs and the latest "hits", the visitors also took part in a "request" programme. The girl's special requests were sung by Ray Turnbull and George Watson and each child in the ward was presented with sweets and chocolate.

The scouts then toured some of the men's wards and entertained patients with singing and musical items. Individual items were given by Mr G Watson, Scoutmaster, C Thackeray and Mr R Turnbull to accompaniment of guitar music provided by the Group Scoutmaster, Mr Les Barker.

Refreshments for the scouts were provided by the matron, Miss Harding, who, together with Sister Sutton and Sister Lee, accompanied the scouts on their tour of the wards. Taking part in the entertainment, in addition to those already mentioned, were cubmaster W Saxby and Messrs R Woodward, T White, D Orchard, S Saxby, W Kellett, A Watson, A Lambert and R Watson.

Another visit is to be paid by the scouts to the children's ward later in the year to hand over a gift for the use of the whole ward. This will be bought from the £26.14s.6d raised by carol-singing in Wheatley Hill at Christmastime.

CLUB ELECTIONS – There was a record ballot and competition was keen when the half-yearly elections took place at Wheatley Hill Workmen's Social Club and Institute at the weekend. Mr William Henderson was re-elected chairman. He polled 259 votes against the 164 votes of Mr J Bradley and 25 of Mr P Atherton. Mr B Aitken was re-elected secretary, defeating Mr T White by 263 votes to 185, and Mr T Wilson was re-elected door-man with 290 votes against the 158 votes of Mr J Gill. There were five nominations for the position of treasurer to succeed Mr J Dunn, who has retired after 28 years' unbroken service. Mr J Maddison was elected with 146 votes. His closest challenger was Coun C Hackworth, who polled 140 votes. From 43 nominations the following were elected to the committee: Messrs H Maratty, Snr, J Andrew, Snr, R Bradley, M Telford, W Gibson and W Hackworth.

CLUB ELECTIONS – In the annual ballot at Wheatley Hill Discharged and Demobilised Soldiers' and Sailors' Club, Mr G Reay was elected chairman. Mr Reay, a former chairman of the club, regained the position by defeating the retiring chairman, Mr B Miller by 12 votes. The voting was: Mr Reay, 61; Mr Miller, 49; Mr W Peacock, 23. Mr R Burnip was re-elected treasurer, defeating Mr R Jones by 99 votes to 32, and Mr H Syson was re-elected secretary, unopposed, and Mr R Dodds door-man. From 16 nominations Messrs A Cain, J Gair, P Leck, N Dougherty, C Williams, Jnr, and R Syson were elected to the committee.

19 January 1962

MR E KITTO, the retiring bandmaster of Thornley Silver Prize band, tells us that he was appointed deputy bandmaster to Spennymoor Salvation Army in 1910; was transferred to Thornley Salvation Army in July 1914 and appointed bandmaster in January 1915; military service began in the last year of the 1914-18 war (he was previously exempt because of mine work); resumed activities with Thornley Salvation Army Band until 1920, when he resigned, and was appointed instructor and conductor of Thornley Colliery Band in September, 1921. Previous conductors were Mr H Moore and Mr T Cowan. The band carried off 221 prizes during the time that he was the conductor.

26 Janaury 1962

CATHOLICS of Wheatley Hill who have been zealous workers for English Martyrs Church, Thornley, for many years are to have a church of their own. The Rev Father H McNeill, parish priest in charge of Thornley, stated that the new church without furnishings will cost £30,000. The church is to be erected on land purchased some years ago near Wheatley Hill Miners' Welfare grounds. Mass on Sundays and Holy days for Wheatley Hill members has been held in St Godric's School on the Thornley-Wheatley Hill road. The membership of the parish in 1961 was 1300 and about 400 live in Wheatley Hill.

9 February 1962

40 YEARS SERVICE AS THORNLEY BANDMASTER

In a trip down Memory Lane when he recalled some of the highlights of his 40 years' service as bandmaster of Thornley Colliery Silver Prize Band, at a presentation tea organised in his honour on Saturday by Thornley Colliery Federation Board, Mr Edward G T Kitto – familiarly known as Teddy Kitto among the older bandsmen in the county – proved himself a fluent story-teller. He had many stories – gay, happy and humorous – to tell of his record-breaking association with the band, and his listeners, who included members of his band, workmen's representatives and bandsmen from further afield who had come to pay him tribute on his retirement, were thrilled with the band's success story.

On one occasion before the last war, recalled Mr Kitto, who will celebrate his 70th birthday next month, the band went to London to take part in the Crystal Palace contest for the senior shield. But as well as taking part in the contest in their spruce uniforms, they took the stage in two dance halls – in their pit clothes!

The occasion was 1933 and that year the band were placed fourth in the contest. "We were engaged while we were down in London to play in two big halls between the dances and we turned out, at special request, in our pit clothes", recalled Mr Kitto. "That is something I will never forget! We were a roaring success".

Won 221 Trophies and Prizes

During another visit to Crystal Palace they were drawn No 21 out of 28 bands. "We had travelled down to London through the night", said Mr Kitto, "and we were all very tired, the youngest ones especially. They were so tired, in fact, that they were sitting asleep beside their instruments just before it was our turn to take part in the

287

contest". But the young bandsmen did not let the band down – they also finished fourth that year.

Altogether, said Mr Kitto, the Band had won 221 trophies and prizes under his baton. He was very proud, he said, to have been associated with such a fine combination, for it had certainly made its presence felt, not only in the county but in the country.

Presiding at the presentation ceremony, Mr J Carr, chairman of the Federation Board, said that the village of Thornley was very proud of their bandmaster. He had given loyal and faithful service over a long period and they wished him the best of health and happiness in his retirement from active band work.

Among the apologies received from a number of people unable to be present that day, said Mr Carr, was one from Mr Norman F Nattrass, of the Durham Divisional Coal Board.

Presentation of TV Set

Mr Nattrass wrote that he had known Mr Kitto for many years in the band world. "And", he added, "I have always had a great admiration for his capabilities and enthusiasm, particularly among the young bandsmen". Nothing ever discouraged Mr Kitto, said Mr Nattrass, and he was always ready to help those taking up music for the first time.

His services as bandmaster at Thornley would be greatly missed. In extending kind regards and best wishes to Mr Kitto for a happy retirement, Mr Nattrass added, "I sincerely hope he will still put in an appearance at the various contests held in the county".

On behalf of the Federation Board, Mr Edward Carter, who is chairman of the local miners' lodge, presented Mr Kitto with a 19-inch television set, complete with a year's licence, and added his best wishes for the future.

"I have known him since I was a boy and no tribute I can pay to him today can be too high," said Mr Carter. Mr Kitto was "every inch a bandsman", said Mr Carter. He had been untiring in his efforts to make the band one of the best in the county.

Mr Carter then examined each letter of the bandmaster's surname and said it could truly be said to represent his qualities – K for knowledgeable, I for intelligent, T for tolerance, T for teaching ability and O for his keen observation.

Mr Kitto's observant qualities could detect in an instant a good bandsman when he saw one. "If he said a lad was going to make a first-class bandsman, you could depend upon it he was right", said Mr Carter.

Thornley's Debt to Mr Kitto

On behalf of the band, an old member and former secretary, Mr Joseph Oswald, presented Mr Kitto with a gold wrist watch, while the present band secretary, Mr C Ryan, presented Mrs Kitto with a handbag and pair of gloves.

The interest and enthusiasm Mrs Kitto had also revealed, where the colliery band was concerned, would never be forgotten, said Mr Ryan. "We can never repay her and these gifts are just a small token from the band lads to say 'Thank you' to her", added Mr Ryan.

Mr A Welsh, manager of Thornley colliery, in proposing thanks on behalf of the guests and the National Coal Board, said that Mr Kitto had devoted the greater part of his life to giving pleasure to others through his music. "And it is wonderful to see the cheerful smile that is always on his face", added Mr Welsh.

Thornley undoubtedly owed Mr Kitto a lot – in fact, more than they could ever repay. "His band has always been tip-top", said Mr Welsh. Mr Kitto's work as a miner had also been of the highest standard. "He was the sort of man who, when you asked him to do a job, you knew for a certainty it was going to be done properly", said Mr Welsh.

Tributes to Mr Kitto's fine service were also paid by Mr A Woodward (electrical engineer at the colliery), Mr R Hughes (vice-chairman of the Federation Board), Mr J Hedley, ex-Chief Inspector N Piper of Sunderland (conductor of Sunderland Police Band) and Mr Cecil Peacock of Easington (chairman of the Durham County Brass Band League).

Has Grandson in the Band

Mr Kitto, said Mr Piper, had brought "an element of culture" to the mining village. He had gained the high respect of everyone, not only because of his music ability, but because of his impeccable character. "We owe him a very deep debt of gratitude, not only here but throughout the county", added Mr Piper.

In returning thanks for the good wishes extended to him, Mr Kitto, after recalling some of the band's outstanding successes, said it had been his one ambition to have a good band in Thornley. The band had been well supported by the Colliery Federation, and this had meant a lot.

There were some splendid players in the band and if they all, including the youngest members, continued to pull their weight there was no reason why it should not always remain one of the best in the county. "I hope, in fact, that they will go on to accomplish even greater successes," added Mr Kitto.

At the function, the arrangements for which were efficiently made by the Federation Board secretary, Mr S G Greener, Mr Kitto's family of two sons and their wives and his six grandchildren were among the guests.

Mr Kitto's sons, Edward and Gordon, both play in the Thornley Band, as well as one of his grandsons – 12-year-old Gordon Kitto, who is a cornetist.

NEW CEMETERY SUPERINTENDENT

From a short list of six, Mr R A Pemberton, of Cemetery Lodge, Northallerton, has been appointed superintendent and grave-digger at Wheatley Hill cemetery, in succession to Mr G Griffiths who, after filling the position for two-and-a-half-years, has taken up a new appointment with Peterlee Parish Council. Mr Pemberton was appointed by Wingate Parish Council at their meeting on Monday night. Originally there were 36 applicants for the post.

16 February 1962

LUDWORTH TO LIMA

Mr and Mrs Victor R Bunting with their only son, Peter, left Ludworth on Monday to return to their home in Miraflores, Lima in Peru after spending a six months vacation with Mrs Bunting's mother, Mrs Lister, and her sister, Martha, at 37 Barnard Avenue, Ludworth.

Mrs Bunting, formerly Bella Lister, was born at Ludworth and while an assistant nurse at York County Hospital she decided to go overseas to serve in the British General Hospital at Blankenburg in Belgium. There she met her future husband, Mr Bunting, who was wounded and became a patient in the hospital. They were married just a month after D-Day in Belgium.

After the war Mr Bunting obtained a post with the United Nations Organisation and spent six years in Geneva. He served five years in Turkey and then went to Peru. Their son, Peter, had his early education in this country but later joined his parents abroad and is now in a boarding school at Miraflores.

Mrs Bunting maintained her association with the Church of England and in Turkey was a member of the Mothers' Union. The incumbent of the parish was the Rev Keen, a former student at Bede College, Durham, who was delighted to find members of his congregation included a family with such close connections with Durham. Mrs Bunting's father died some years ago and a short time ago she lost by death her brother, Robert, at Thornley. Mr Bunting was born at Haywards Heath and after leaving college he enlisted in the RAF.

THREE TITLES FOR THORNLEY FAMILY AT DURHAM NCB BOXING CHAMPIONSHIPS

One of the county's most successful boxing families, the Harveys, of Thornley, dominated the Durham Division NCB championships and walked off with one – TWO – THREE titles! And each was won inside the distance!

Part of the championships were watched by Lord Robens (Chairman of the National Coal Board), who received a big ovation when introduced to the crowd. A party of Durham Division NCB officials was headed by Dr W Reid (chairman) and with them at the ringside was Mr Sam Watson, secretary of the Durham Miners' Association.

Prizes were presented to the winning boxers by Mr N F Nattrass, Industrial Relations Director for the Durham Division.

Two Brothers Watched

The three brothers who will go with the Divisional team to Edinburgh on 13 April for the national semi-finals are 28-year-old John Harvey, a coal face trainee; Len Harvey (21), a fire prevention man; and Joe Harvey (18), a datal hand. Watching them smash their way to success in the divisional finals at Durham Technical College last week were another two brothers, Ken (23) – a retired professional – and Ronnie (26), who collected a divisional title last year.

Probably the best of the three brothers' performances was that by Joe Harvey, who got up from the canvas to take the welterweight crown by knocking out W Stocks (Horden), a tough and rugged opponent, in the second round.

Len, who was defending his light-middleweight title, made it "two-up" for the family with a first round victory over Tommy Graham (Brandon), who was counted out under a new ABA rule, after the bell had signalled the end of the round.

Finally John took the light-welterweight title (won last year by brother Joe) by battering R Herron (Brandon) into submission in the second round.

Other Title Winners

Other title-winners were featherweight Jeff Williams (Easington), who beat Eddie Ginty (Burnopfield) on points; and the very competent Len Simpson (Beamish Mary), who disposed of R Kennedy (Mainsforth) in their light-heavyweight match with a shattering body punch in the second round.

The remaining divisional titles, all won on a walk-over, went to the following: Bantam, H Hall (Sherburn Hill): Lightweight, C Henderson (Shotton): Middleweight, John Short (Coundon).

The undoubted highlight of the evening's boxing feast was the Stocks-Harvey clash, in which the tables were dramatically turned during a tremendously hard fought first round.

On The Canvas

It was a tough, no-quarter scrap from the first bell and spectators winced as both men got home with solid blows to the head and body. Harvey, with his fast and accurate left, was just getting the measure of his man when a powerful swinging right by Stocks stopped him dead in his tracks.

Seeing his opportunity, the fair-headed Stocks was onto him like a tiger and another powerhouse right made Harvey buckle at the knees and sag to the canvas. Regaining his feet, the Thornley man cleverly gained precious breathing space by moving in close to his opponent and by the end of the round had recovered his poise.

Harvey took the fight straight to his man in the second round and a crunching right-hand felled Stocks. Now it was the Thornley man who sensed the kill and Stocks went down again for another count of eight. Battered and bemused, he struggled to his feet but there was no escape and yet another right to the head laid him low. Although Stocks struggled to his knees and looked capable of beating the count, he was too dazed to appreciate what was happening and he failed to rise in time.

New ABA Rule

The ending of the Len Harvey-Graham bout came as a surprise to many spectators unaware of the new ABA rule whereby it is no longer possible for a boxer to be saved by the bell in the first or second rounds.

A perfect right to the solar plexus dropped Graham in agony and he was still on his knees with the count at "eight", when the bell signalled the end of the round. Mr Tommy Todd, of Ashington, however, continued the count to "ten" and indicated that Graham was out, then crossed to the ringside and explained to officials that Harvey was the winner and that the bell should not have gone.

This was the first time that Mr Todd had invoked the new rule and at the interval he was congratulated on his decision by Lord Robens, who told him with smile, "It's a good job you had read the rules".

The most courageous display of the evening was that by R Herron (Brandon), who took on the third of the Harvey brothers.

Floored Three Times

Herron had fought earlier in the evening and gained what was to many a surprising points-decision over D Kirkbride (Hylton), who did more of the forcing and had his man in trouble on the ropes more than once. In the second round Herron was warned about his chopping blows to the head and in the last he was put on the canvas, partly due to a slip.

Almost from the first bell in his final against Harvey, Herron was in serious trouble and was floored three times. In the second round, it was apparent that only one result was possible. Herron could not live in the same ring with the Thornley man and three times he struggled to his feet after being mercilessly clobbered about the head. A push sent the weakened boxer down once more, but with a somewhat pathetic smile he struggled gamely up to face his tormentor. It was not for long, however, and this time when he crashed to the canvas the referee stepped in and indicated that it was all over.

Skilful Ringcraft

Slightly harder and more accurate punching by Len Simpson carried him to victory with a second round KO against Kennedy, who was also capable of making his opponent wince with his powerful rights to the body.

In the second round, however, Simpson battered him to the floor with a volley of right and left hooks and after another bout of savage in-fighting the Mainsforth man was glad to hold on. Simpson pushed him off and then blasted him under the heart with a cannonball right hand that put Kennedy down for the full count.

In the featherweight championship Jeff Williams had to summon up all his ringcraft to master Eddie Ginty, a skilful southpaw. It was the Burnopfield man who forced the early pace and Williamson needed to use the ring to keep clear of real trouble, but the fight was by no means one-sided and a sizzling right put the southpaw down for a count of eight.

Williams continued to keep the fight at a distance in the second round and Ginty found him an elusive opponent. On the few occasions he did manage to force him to the ropes, Williams slipped punches cleverly and with great adroitness manoeuvred an exchange of positions.

In the last round Ginty countered a right to the head with a left-hook which caught Williams off-balance and made him stagger. Ginty followed up into a corner and caught his man with a hard left which clearly shook him, but Williams shrugged off the effects and got home with a good right to the side of the head. Two more rights to the jaw had Ginty wobbling at the knees, but he refused to go down.

Other Bouts

Several special contests completed the bill and in these H Hall (Sherburn Hill) beat R Moore (South Pelaw Welfare); Terry Coulson (Langley Park) beat A Henderson (8th DLI); Trooper Fowler (Dragoon Guards) beat P Richardson (South Church); Tpr W Bain (Dragoon Guards) beat M Bartholomew (Horden); and E Jackson (South Church) beat E Harper (8th DLI).

9 March 1962

CATHOLIC CLUB In a ballot for officials and committee of Thornley Catholic Club, Mr John Regan, chairman, and Mr John Williams, secretary, were unopposed. Committee: Messrs J Barron, R Bell, T Corbett, B Connelly, M Hopkins, E Morrow, M McCoy, M O'Brien, W Scott, T Smythe. Scrutineers were: Messrs D Bell and W Graney.

16 March 1962

MR P S COOK'S DEATH LOSS TO THORNLEY

Business people of the village and local farmers attended the funeral service in St Bartholomew's Church, Thornley, of Mr Stanley Cook (71), who died at his home, Corner House, Hartlepool Street, Thornley.

Born in Thornley, Mr Cook began work with W L Liddle, grocers, drapers and shipping agents, in Corner House, where Mr Cook and his family have made their home for the last 20 years.

At the outbreak of war in 1914 Mr Cook enlisted in the Royal Artillery and served four years in France. In 1920 Mr Cook took over the old-established business of his uncle, Mr George Cook, fruiterer. He and his son Philip have occupied the present business premises for the last 20 years.

Mr Cook was a lifelong member of Thornley Parish Church, a vice-president of Thornley British Legion and a popular supporter of many village organisations. His daughter, Mrs Ralph Scott, a widow is on the teaching staff of Shotton Infants' School.

30 March 1962

MR PETER HERBERT GALLEY

The village has lost one of its best known figures by the death of Mr Peter Herbert Galley (69), of Granville Terrace, Wheatley Hill. He is survived by his wife, Mrs Maria Galley, a married son and a daughter, well known business people in Wheatley Hill.

Mr Galley was born at Sunnyside, near Tow Law, and came to Wheatley Hill as a child.

He started work at Wheatley Hill colliery at 13, and worked there for 52 years, retiring four years ago. His first job was as messenger boy for 10s a fortnight. He soon became assistant weigh-clerk. At 18 he was promoted to bill clerk, at a weekly wage of 25s. Further promotion came when he was appointed head clerk. Four years before his retirement he succeeded Mr John White as colliery cashier.

Mr Galley had a distinguished career in the First World War. He enlisted in the Grenadier Guards and served in France. Mr Galley was wounded in the battle of Ypres, and was awarded the MM for gallantry. To mark the occasion the villagers of Wheatley Hill presented him with a gold watch.

Under Five Managers

During his long mining career of 52 years, Mr Galley served under five managers at the colliery.

He became a founder member of the Wheatley Hill men's section of the British Legion, now defunct. He served on the Wheatley Hill Welfare Committee. In his younger days he was a keen hockey player.

Mr Galley was widely respected in Masonic circles. He was a member of the craft for 38 years, and a member of the Fawcett Lodge, Seaham Harbour, and since 1931 of Caradoc Lodge, Castle Eden. He was granted Provincial Honours in the Provincial Grand Lodge of Durham.

The funeral took place on Tuesday. Wheatley Hill Church Street Methodist Church was filled by representatives of the Masonic Church (?) *should this be Lodge?* and business communities. The service was conducted by the Rev G L Nelson and Mrs R Ord was at the organ Cremation followed at Sunderland. Four members of the Caradoc Lodge acted as bearers: Bros W Spinks, A Bradley, A Elliott and T Houghton. *(The original article lists all mourners at Mr Galley's funeral)*
6 April 1962

THORNLEY MAY GET 'BUS ROUTE DIVERSION: COUNCIL MOVE

Thornley Parish Council is to ask representatives of the four 'bus companies operating in the parish to meet representatives of the county council, Easington Rural District and the parish, to discuss the possibility of a diverted service at specified times from the present route by the Villas to a new route via Coopers Terrace and Gore Hall Estate.

Coun James Nicholson, Thornley representative on Easington Rural Council, who raised the question said this problem was considered some years ago and the council were unable to get the support of the county highway authority.

Since then the roadway has been renewed and the highway authority are now satisfied that the roadways are quite suitable for 'bus traffic.

Car Park Suggestion

Sup Maurice Reed , of the Castle Eden Divisional Police, in a letter to the council in reply to the complaint on the behaviour of car owners attending dances in Thornley Miners' Welfare, said he could find only one resident in that neighbourhood who had any complaint after the police dance referred to. Local officers had been instructed to deal appropriately with people who misbehave when leaving functions at Thornley Miners' Institute.

He felt that the provision of a proper car park at Thornley would reduce the annoyance complained about.

The council decided to try and procure a piece of land formerly an old goods station yard for the purpose and to ask Sup Reed for his help.

VETERAN OF 1914-18 WAR
Varied Life Ends at Thornley

A man who claimed that he came through the First World War without a scratch, Mr John F Whitehead, aged 73, formerly of Aged Miners' Homes, Thornley, has died at the home of his son-in-law and daughter, Mr and Mrs W Roberts, 31 Luke Street, Trimdon Station. Cremation took place at Sunderland following the funeral service in Bow Street Methodist Church at which the Rev G Johnson officiated. Mr Whitehead is survived by a son and two daughters, one of whom, Mrs A M Hoeckstra, lives in Holland. Mrs Mary Whitehead died last June.

Mr Whitehead was born in Kendal, and spent his childhood at Normanton. He entered the postal service in his youth and went to Thornley as postman when he was 19.

He left the postal service for Thornley Colliery where he remained some years. Later he became a full-time bookmaker. Mr Whitehead finished his working career with a spell at Thornley Colliery.

He served in the First World Wear with the East Yorkshire Regiment. He saw service in Egypt, the Dardanelles and France.

Skilled Musician

Mr Whitehead, in his younger days, was a keen amateur cyclist, winning many events. With his brother, he became a noted dog breeder. Bull terriers were his speciality.

Music was included in the skills of this versatile man. For many years he played the piccolo and flute in the orchestra at the Hippodrome, Thornley. He organised and was leader of a dance band.

13 April 1962

WHEATLEY HILL COUPLE MARK GOLDEN WEDDING

A well known Wheatley Hill couple, Mr and Mrs George William Dixon, 76 Luke Terrace, who recently celebrated their golden wedding, have spent nearly all their married life in the village, where they are held in the highest esteem. They were married at Easington and lived for a short time at Thornley and Shotton before moving into a colliery house at Wheatley Hill.

Born at South Church, near Bishop Auckland, Mr Dixon, who is 73, began work at Auckland Park colliery at 13. "My first job was working in the lamp-cabin for nine shillings a week", he told our reporter.

Two years later Mr Dixon went underground at Black Boy colliery a short distance away and they worked at Shildon Bank colliery before continuing his mining career at Wheatley Hill colliery in 1911. He remained at Wheatley Hill colliery, where for most of the time he was a hewer, until ill-health compelled him to finish work 18 years ago.

Was Treasurer

Only last year, Mr Dixon retired as treasurer of Wheatley Hill branch of he Northumberland and Durham miners' Permanent Relief Fund after 27 years' unbroken service.

He was also secretary and treasurer of the Wheatley Hill Colliery Checkweigh Fund, for 12 years, and he has served on the committee of several clubs in the village.

In his younger days Mr Dixon was a well-known local footballer. For a time he played at left half for Bishop Auckland.

Mr Dixon's wife, whose maiden name was Margaret Burnip, is 69. She was born at Haswell. Both she and her husband are actively associated with Wheatley Hill Over 60 Club, and at present Mrs Dixon is a member of the committee. Mrs Dixon is also a member of the Patton Street Methodist Church and the Sisterhood.

Mr and Mrs Dixon both enjoy fairly good health. "I was in hospital for three months three years ago, but am keeping much better now", said Mrs Dixon.

The couple have two sons, three daughters and three grand children.

20 April 1962

WHEATLEY HILL PLAYGROUND CAUSES ADULT ANXIETY

A proposed new playground for children has some adults on the Johnson Estate, Wheatley Hill, worried. The playground is to be built behind their houses, and they are afraid that the children will make too much noise and will trample into their back gardens.

Mrs Elsie Atkinson, who is 55, and whose house is one of those backing onto the playground site, told the Chronicle: "There are going to be umpteen complaints". She is afraid that the gardens would be over-run by children retrieving balls, and also hints that her husband's new greenhouse might suffer damage.

I'm not against the children having somewhere to play, but they definitely want a high mesh round the playground", she said.

Miners Displeased

Mrs Freda Ryan, who is 32, said: "My husband is not too pleased. He's a miner and gets most of his sleep during the day. But I don't mind myself – I've children of my own. They must have somewhere to play".

Another woman whose husband is a miner said that he didn't mind as he slept in the front bedroom. "It's mainly the big ones who make the noise", she added.

The playground site is a triangular piece of waste ground about 100 yards long on either side and 50 yards wide at the base. Except for a narrow opening it is entirely surrounded by ten houses and 13 old people's bungalows.

Some people are worried that the noise may disturb the old age pensioners in the bungalows. But none of the pensioners seem at all concerned.

Mrs Mary Alderton (66) who has 11 grandchildren, said: "There's not going to be a lot of noise. It's not all the time – they have to go to bed. There's lots of children round here and they have to play somewhere".

And 75-year-old grandmother, Mrs Ethel Harker said, "They played there all last summer and we sat outside and watched them".

Gardens Offer

Several pensioners said they would be glad to give up half their gardens, which were too big for them to manage in any case, to make the playground bigger.

Wingate Parish Councillor, Mr Ralph Watson of Cemetery Road, Wheatley Hill, said that the new playground, on which it was planned to spend £100, would not be started until details had been approved at the next Parish Council meeting in a week's time.

The playground would cater for children up to the age of eight and would be an adventure playground, with pipes, a log cabin, stepping stones and old tree trunks. It would be impossible to put a mesh round due to the high cost.

"We consider the new playground will be a benefit to the community", said Mr Watson, "and will help keep the youngsters off the roads".

27 April 1962

EX-NAVAL MAN'S DEATH AT WHEATLEY HILL

A Wheatley Hill man who, formerly served for many years in the Royal Navy and went through both World Wars, died at his home on Monday morning.

He was Mr John Burnside (70), of 88 Wordsworth Avenue, who had lived in the village for the greater part of his life. During his long service in the Navy Mr Burnside had visited most parts of the world. He served throughout the 1914-18 war and three years before the last war broke out he re-joined the Navy and remained in the service until being demobilised at the end of hostilities. He helped in the evacuation of Dunkirk, making seven trips across the Channel to bring home members of the Forces.

Baths Attendant

When he left school Mr Burnside began work at Wheatley Hill Colliery and remained there, apart from his service during the 1914-18 war, until he re-joined the Navy. After he was demobilised at the end of the 1939-45 war he went to Thornley Colliery as a baths attendant and remained there until his retirement five years ago.

Mr Burnside was a member of the Wingate Royal Naval Comrades Association.

Mr Burnside, who was well-known and esteemed in Wheatley Hill and the surrounding area, is survived by his wife, two married daughters and a son, who is unmarried, and three grandchildren. A son John was lost at sea in 1940 while serving in the Navy.

Following a service in All Saints' Church, Wheatley Hill, yesterday Mr Burnside was cremated at West Hartlepool. Later his ashes are to be interred at sea.

Among the many floral tributes yesterday was one shaped like an anchor and made up of red, white and blue flowers from his family.

4 May 1962

QUICK THINKING BY WHEATLEY HILL WOMAN

When fire broke out in the detached lock-up paint and wallpaper shop of Messrs Rose Bros, in Front Street, Wheatley Hill, the entire stock of wallpaper was ruined by smoke, and damage was also done to a large quantity of decorating materials, including brushes and tins of paint ... but quick thinking by Mrs Florence Rose, wife of one of the owners, prevented the building being gutted.

Mrs Rose, of 23 Stoker Crescent, Wheatley Hill, was on her way to open up the shop when someone told her it was on fire. "I ran along as fast as I could", she told our reporter later, "and when I got there found the shop full of flames and smoke. But I kept the door locked and got someone to telephone for the Fire Brigade. Later the fire chief said this was the best thing I could do – had I unlocked the door and opened it the fire would have blazed up much more fiercely".

Breathing Apparatus

Wheatley Hill retained unit of the Durham County Fire Brigade had to wear breathing apparatus to enter the shop but they quickly got the blaze under control and prevented more serious damage to the building. The counter was burned, together with woodwork near the large plate-glass window, which was cracked, and the lids burst off a number of tins of paint.

Said Mr Ernest Rose, Mrs Rose's husband, "None of the wallpaper will be of any use, it is so badly scorched, and it was only a few days before that we took delivery of a new supply".

Only half an hour before his wife had gone to the shop, he added, he and his brother Charles, who is in business with him, had been there to collect their decorating materials before setting out on their day's work. When they were there they lit a paraffin stove to warm the building. It is believed that the over-heated stove started the blaze.

11 May 1962

THORNLEY SCOUTS IN LONDON

Two members of the 3rd Thornley Troop of Boy Scouts, Trevor Fisher, of Bow Street, Thornley, and George Hoben (Trimdon Village) have qualified for the Queen's Scout badge.

They went to London by car, accompanied by their Scoutmaster, Mr Donald Miller, a school teacher, and their Group Scoutmaster, Mr A L Miller, and were presented with their certificates at the International Training Camp of the Scouts Association at Gilwell Park by Mr Thurman, Camp Chief, in the presence of the Chief Scout, Sir Charles McLean.

The boys realised something of the size of the movement when they were part of a crowd of 10,000. Group Scoutmaster A L Miller told our correspondent, "I am proud of the lads' achievement. Really I got as much kick out of the awards as the lads themselves. This is the first time such a high award has come to Thornley for over 30 years".

AN ARSON CHARGE – When Andrew Robinson (36), a self-employed handyman of 15 Patton Crescent, Wheatley Hill, faced a charge of arson at a special court at Castle Eden on Tuesday, it was alleged that he set fire to two storage sheds belonging to a Wheatley Hill timber merchant, Mr Tony Carr, at the back of Front Street, Wheatley Hill, and a nearby garage workshop belonging to Mr Thomas Billingham, late at night. He was remanded in custody until yesterday his application for bail being opposed by the police and rejected.

TIMBER MERCHANT'S LOSS – Damage estimated at several hundreds of pounds was done late on Saturday night when fire swept through a range of wooden buildings behind Front Street, Wheatley Hill, belonging to a local timber merchant, Mr Tony Carr. The buildings were used to store lengths of timber and a large quantity of the timber went up in smoke. The buildings were well ablaze when Peterlee Unit of the Durham County Fire Brigade reached the scene and the flames, leaping high in the air, were seen for miles around. It took the firemen half an hour to get the blaze under control and altogether they were at the scene for two-and-a-half hours. They prevented the flames from spreading to other buildings and nearby property. On Sunday, fire officers and the police were investigating the cause of the outbreak.

18 May 1962

WHEATLEY HILL MAN ACCUSED OF ARSON

When Andrew Robinson (36), 15 Patton Crescent, Wheatley Hill, appeared on remand at Castle Eden on Saturday on a charge of arson, it was alleged that he maliciously set fire to two store-sheds belonging to a Wheatley Hill timber merchant, Mr Tony Carr, at the back of Front Street, and to a garage-workshop belonging to Mr Thomas Billingham, also of Wheatley Hill.

The buildings, said Insp C Buchan, prosecuting, were completely destroyed, and damage was estimated at £1000.

The fire, said the inspector, occurred about 11.00pm on 12 May. Following inquiries, Robinson was interviewed by PC Fletcher and Det Con Jackson on 14 May. Robinson, alleged Insp Buchan, had been identified by a witness as being inside the burning shed when the witness discovered the fire.

Robinson denied the offence, but was arrested and had since been in custody, said Insp Buchan, who said he strongly opposed bail because of the serious nature of the charge. Robinson was a single man, living with his widowed mother, the inspector added. Police inquiries were now complete and committal proceedings had been arranged for 4 June.

Mr Richard Reed, appearing for Robinson, applied for bail. Robinson, he said, had all along strongly denied the offence.

Bail was granted in Robinson's own recognisance of £50 and a surety for the same amount, and he was remanded until 4 June.

THORNLEY WOMEN'S INSTITUTE – 37 NOT OUT!

In December 1925, a meeting was called in the old Temperance Hall at Thornley. Ladies of the village and Wheatley Hill were called together to consider forming a Women's Institute. The result was Thornley and Wheatley Hill WI.

Mrs Elliott has the first programme printed. The first officials and committee were Miss Ainscow (president), now 90 and living in Durham, Miss O'Hara (vice-president), for many years headmistress of Thornley RC Infants' School and now living in Ireland; Mrs J A Simpson (secretary); Mrs J T Scott (treasurer); Mesdames Alderslade, Chisholme, E Liddle, T Liddle, Scott, Smithson, White; the Misses Barrass, Dobson and Million. The motto on the front page of the programme was:

"Time cannot stay to make us wise, We must improve it as it flies"

That motto has inspired members over the years. There has been criticism at national and county level that there is a growing tendency to make the Institute a social club. This Institute has always striven for the highest level of social, civic, educational and cultural interests. In every sense it stands for Home and Country, the national motto.

The meetings were held alternately at Thornley Waterloo Street Methodist Hall and Wheatley Hill School.

This arrangement lasted until 1930 when Wheatley Hill formed its own Institute.

Long Serving Officials

Mrs J M Scott, has served the Institute in an official capacity for 32 years. For the first 16 years she was treasurer. This was followed by four years as secretary, then by 12 years in the presidential chair. Mrs Scott is one of the few surviving members who attended the first meeting. Miss Kirk is another.

Mrs Scott said, "When the Institute was formed there was little to interest women in the life of the village. It was a Godsend with its wider horizons, its opportunities for relaxation from the cares of family life and its encouragement of various crafts, among which was Durham quilting.

1 June 1962

MINERS' LODGE – The following officials have been returned unopposed by Wheatley Hill miners' lodge for the ensuing year; chairman, Mr H Bradshaw; treasurer, Mr R Cook; delegate, Coun C Hackworth; financial secretary, Mr J Hedley; compensation secretary, Mr M Alderton; average taker, Mr M Cain; card-marker, Mr S Mitchinson; auditors, Messrs T Buxton and J Cain; pit inspector, Mr N Jones; Death Fund committee, Coun C Hackworth, Mr R Cook and Coun G Burnside; political delegate, Coun M Telford. The secretary, Coun A Wharrier, is being opposed by 21-year-old Mr Frank Harper, who served on the lodge committee when he was only 17. The ballot to fill this position and other committees associated with the lodge began on Wednesday and finishes today. Nominations for the other committees include: Band committee, (four wanted), Messrs S Mitchinson, M Cain, G Burnside, R Teasdale, W Newby and J Foster; Welfare committee (four wanted), Messrs W Rothery, T Buxton, C Hackworth, A O'Connor, G Harper, M Alderton, F Harper and M Cain. There are 17 nominations for eight vacancies on the Aged Miners' Committee, 17 for the lodge committee of twelve, and ten for the Checkweigh Fund committee of six.

ESSAY SUCCESS – As a result of their successes in an essay competition organised by the Durham Area, NUM, two miners at Wheatley Hill Colliery, Coun C Hackworth, who is checkweighman there, and Mr Frank Russell Harper, who is a pony putter, have won scholarships tenable for a week's summer school at Scarborough, commencing 23 June. Coun Hackworth, who lives at 12 Durham Street, Wheatley Hill, wrote an essay on "Industrial Relations". He is delegate for the local Miners' lodge. Mr Harper, son of Mrs Harper and the late Mr T Harper, 6 Darlington Street, Wheatley Hill, wrote an essay on "Peaceful World Co-existence". This is the fifth running year he has been successful in the competition. Mr Harper, who is only 21, is a former member of the local miners' lodge committee, and in this year's ballot, being held this week, he is opposing Coun A Wharrier for the secretaryship.

WHEATLEY HILL MAN ON ARSON CHARGES
For Trial after Court Story of £1200 Damage

When a 36-year-old self-employed handyman, Andrew Robinson, 15 Patton Crescent, Wheatley Hill, was accused of arson at a special court at Castle Eden, it was alleged that the owner of a garage, one of the three buiuldings destroyed in the fire, had seen Robinson in a shed where a pile of shavings was ablaze in the corner.

Robinson, who was accused of maliciously setting fire to two large timber-built sheds belonging to Tony Carr, a timber merchant and joinery manufacturer, of Greenhills Farm, Thornley crossings, and a combined workshop and garage belonging to Thomas Billingham, Halcon House, Front Street, Wheatley Hill, was committed on bail for trial at the next Durham Assizes.

The damage to Mr Carr's property amounted to about £1000, said Mr J A Shaw, prosecuting and Mr Billingham told the presiding magistrate, Mr E Chicken, that he estimated his loss at £200.

The sheds and the garage, said Mr Shaw, were behind Front Street, Wheatley Hill. There was no heating apparatus, electricity or anything of a nature easily inflammable in the sheds, which were used for storage purposes.

Heard a Noise

Mr Billingham went to his garage about 11.00pm on 12 May, continued Mr Shaw, and while walking down the path heard a noise which he thought came from one of the two nearby sheds. He looked through a hole in the window of the shed and saw flames inside and when he looked through another window alleged Mr Shaw, he saw the accused and in the corner a pile of shavings was on fire.

Mr Billingham spoke to Robinson and said he (the accused) had set the shed ablaze, but the accused only mumbled a reply. The fire Brigade was called but when they reached the scene the two sheds and the garage were burned out.

Mr Billingham, said Mr Shaw, did not know the accused by name but later made enquiries and ascertained his name. "There was no apparent reason for this fire", said Mr Shaw. "Nothing of a combustible nature was stored there. This is a clear case of arson where a man has deliberately, for some reason or other, set fire to these premises. When seen by the police, Robinson said he had been drinking and gone straight home whereas, in fact, he had been in this shed".

Mr Billingham said that after be looked through a three-inch gap at the bottom of a partly boarded up saw the fire. He ran round to the other side of the shed and, through another window, saw a heap of wood shavings burning. He saw the accused there and he appeared to be coming out through the window. When he said to the accused, "You have set the shed on fire," the accused made a reply. "But I could not make out what he said", witness added.

Robinson, added Mr Billingham, appeared to be "shocked and surprised". He had apparently had a drink.

Witness returned to the scene after the Fire Brigade had been called. The fire, he said, had spread very quickly to his own garage and to Mr Carr's other shed. "My own workshop and garage were completely burned down, together with tools and other property which I had not been able to get out", he added.

Joined in Dominoes

Mr Billingham said he had seen Robinson several times previously, and at Easter had played with him in a domino handicap at a local hotel, but he did not know his name. Cross-examined by Mr D J Millar, defending, he said he told the police at the time of the fire that he would recognise the man he had seen in the shed if he saw him again.

PC Gordon Fletcher said he interviewed Robinson with Det Con R Jackson, and told him there was reason to believe he was responsible for setting fire to the sheds and garage. Robinson replied, "It's a cock-and-bull story. I was drinking in the Nimmo all night. I came out and went as far as Baldasera's and bought a bar of chocolate and then I went home to bed. My mother can tell you what time I came in".

When charged, he said, "It is ridiculous, that's all".

THORNLEY METHODIST'S DEATH

The death has occurred of Mr Robert Lee (64) 101 Thornlaw North, Thornley. He is survived by his wife, Mrs Sarah Lee, two sons and two daughters. The couple lost a son on active service in the 1939-45 War.

Mr Lee was on his way to a Sunday School anniversary service at Cassop when he was taken suddenly ill and collapsed. He died later in the day. Born at Cassop, Mr Lee started work at 13 at East Hetton Colliery. For many years he worked for the late Mr Caleb B Henderson, a chemist in the Trimdons.

Mr Lee enlisted with the Durham Light Infantry in the 1914-18 War. His active service was of short duration for he was wounded in the leg five weeks after landing in France. During the 1939-45 War he was directed to munitions factory work, first at Aycliffe and then at Haverton Hill. When freed from Ministry of Labour direction, Mr Lee returned to work at East Hetton Colliery, where he was employed at the time of his death.

Mr Lee was a life-long Methodist and an active member of Cassop church. He was a Sunday School worker for 45 years and was for many years treasurer.

He was a class leader, and it was largely through his drive, vision and encouragement that a new Methodist church was built at Cassop two years ago.

Mr Lee had been a local preacher since 1919. Three years ago he received a certificate for 40 years service.

Cassop Methodist Church was filled for the funeral service conducted by Rev G Johnson. Mr J Hinchcliffe was at the organ. Cremation took place at Durham.

IS WHEATLEY HILL MAN THE YOUNGEST LODGE SECRETARY?

Mr Frank Russell Harper, of 6 Darlington Street, Wheatley Hill, who was elected secretary of Wheatley Hill miners' lodge in their annual ballot which ended at the weekend, must be the youngest miner in the county to fill such a position – he is only 21.

Mr Harper, who is employed as a pony putter at the local colliery, defeated Coun A D Wharrier, the retiring secretary, by 305 votes to 155. The new secretary is a former pupil of Wellfield A J Dawson Grammar School. He left at 15 to take up mining as a career and is in his third year as a mining student at the Easington Technical College, Peterlee – twice recently he has given papers on mining to No 3 Area, NCB classes.

Mr Harper has always taken an active interest in union affairs and was only 17 when he was elected to the miners' lodge committee at Wheatley Hill. He is delegate to the Wheatley Hill Labour Party and recently he received word that for the fifth year running, he had won a scholarship to a summer school at Scarborough in an essay competition organised by the Durham Area NUM.

15 June 1962

5000 AT WHEATLEY HILL'S GENEROUS SPORTS DAY

The fifth annual sports day organised by Wheatley Hill Colliery Miners' Federation Board, in conjunction with other organisations in the village, was held in the playing fields of the Wheatley Hill Girls' modern school.

The efforts of Messrs H Bradshaw (chairman), A D Wharrier (organising secretary), J Hedley (treasurer) and Mr C Hackworth (sports secretary) were backed by a strong committee. The support of the village as a whole was evidenced by the fact that 5000 people watched the parade and sports.

A procession through the streets of the village was headed by Wheatley Hill Colliery Prize Band under their conductor, Mr E Rutter. Mr M Alderton acted as parade marshal. Artistically decorated lorries and traps formed attractive tableaux.

Along with children's and adults' fancy dress parade they were judged by Dr and Mrs G H Wallis, Dr L Hutchinson, Mr F Richardson (colliery manager) and Mrs Richardson, and County Coun J Andrew.

Results

Tableau: 1, Wheatley Hill Road Safety Committee; 2, Dairy Queen, Dorothy Collingwood; 3, J T Scott and Sons, Wheatley Hill (The Bride, Violet Jones). **Children's fancy dress: Comic:** 1, Marjorie Armstrong; 2 JeanCarr; 3, John Halsall. **Fancy:** 1, Robert and Susan Atkinson; 2, Moira Gilmore; 3, Pauline Dowson. **Original:** 1, Susan Lawson; 2, James and Kenneth Halsall; 3, Patricia Hoban. **Adults Fancy Dress:** Mr T Taylorson (**comic**), Mr J Brown (**original**), Mrs Hammond (**fancy**). An interesting feature of the programme was a parade of pit ponies. **Result:** 1, Royal (Wheatley Hill); 2, Sally (Horden), 3, Pompy (Shotton); 4, Tiny (Thornley).

A large crown applauded the finish of a gruelling four-mile race. The four first home were: 1, T Hoban; 2, S Jobes; 3, T Cullen; 4, G Barrett.

Prior to the children's sports there was a display of marching to music by the jazz bands from South Shields, Silksworth and Sunderland.

Childrens Sports

Boys' flat race – Five years: 1, I Starkie; 2, C Turner; 3, J Rickard. **Six years:** 1, M Rutherford; 2, J Christopher; 3, A Miller. **Seven years:** 1, F Mitchell; 2, J Youll; 3, J Fishwick. **Eight years:** 1, T Anderson; 2, A Patterson; 3, B Harker. **Nine years:** 1, D Parker; 2, B Venables; 3, R Patterson. **Ten years:** 1, K O'Connor; 2, B Evans; 3, R Watson. **11 years:** 1, B Hackworth; 2, E Evans; 3, D Jones. **12 years:** 1, G Smith; 2, D Jordan; 3, B Young. **13 years;** 1, V Gair; 2, O Dinsdale; 3, E Aitken. **14 years:** 1, R Luke; 2, K Mercer; 3 J Howe.

Boys' Novelty Race: Five years: 1, J Stockdale, 2, I Starkie; 3, G Rowbotham. **Six years:** 1, P Appleby; 2, P Dunn; 3, D Halliwell. **Seven years:** 1, P Carr; 2, J Smith; 3, F Mitchell. **Eight years:** 1, E Starkie; 2, J Hind; 3, B Harker. **Nine years:** 1, G Burke; 2, R Patterson; 3, R Carr. **Ten years:** 1, B Hackworth; 2, D Jones; 3, A Maines. **11 years:** 1, R Watson; 2, B Evans; 3, K O'Connor. **12 years:** 1, J Huntingdon; 2, G Smith; 3 B Young. **13 years:** 1, R Lee; 2, D Meecham; 3, E Marratty. **14 years:** 1, R Luke; 2, J Howe; 3, K Mercer.

Girls' flat race: - five years: 1, M Bartley; 2, S Howe; 3, T Tatters. **Six years:** 1, Linda Parker; 2 S O'Connor; 3, S Kirk. **Seven years:** 1, Jean Carr; 2, P Stobbs; 3, C Million. **Eight years:** 1, D Errington; 2, S Luke; 3, M Luke. **Nine years:** 1, Ann Lofthouse; 2, E Peacock; 3, A Aspinall. **Ten years:** 1, S Patterson; 2, I Burke; 3, S Armstrong. **11 years:** 1, P Hoban; 2, M Armstrong; 3, G Local. **12 years:** 1, K Leck; 2, I Marshall; 3, R Williams. **13 years:** 1, J Bradshaw; 2, M Henderson; 3, V Hammond.

Girls' Novelty Race: Five years: 1, S Howe; 2, E Bromilow; 3, J Gallon. **Six years:** 1, M Luke; 2, P Stobbs; 3, L Parker. **Seven years:** 1, S Foster; 2, N Dunn. **Nine years:** 1, P Robson; 2, F Hardwick; 3, J Sims. **Nine years:** 1, Ann Lofthouse; 2, E Peacock; 3, D Worthington. **Ten years:** 1, S Parsley; 2, Sandra King; 3, J Foster. **11 years:** 1, J Lowther; 2, G Local; 3, Marion Leverton. **12 years:** 1, E Marshall; 2, C Fishwick; 3, I Marshall. **13 years:** 1, M Henderson; 2, E Burrell; 3 V Hammond.

WEAKENED CASUALS CRASHED

Peterlee Casuals fielded only nine players in their NE Durham League game against Thornley CW, and were dismissed for only 18 runs. Iddon captured five wickets for only one run, and A Brierley had four for nine.

Although Roberts performed well in the Casuals attack, taking five wickets for seven runs, Thornley passed their total with five wickets intact. Scores:

Peterlee: Rawcroft b Iddon 0, Clarkson b Brierley 0, Roberts b Iddon 0, Killien b Iddon 1, Green b Brierley 0, Garrigan b Brierley 5, Rawle b Iddon 4, Cudlip not out 0, Trest b Iddon 0, extras 8 – Total 18.

Thornley: Greener b Roberts 0, Dent b Rawle 6, Harrison b Roberts 0, Gair b Roberts 0, Abbs b Roberts 4, Thubron not out 0, A Brierely not out 8, extras 1 – Total (six wkts) 20.

22 June 1962

WHEATLEY HILL'S HAPPY COUPLE

Married in June, 1912, at Spennymoor Parish Church, Mr and Mrs Joseph Soulsby, 15 Aged Miners' Homes, Wheatley Hill, have just celebrated their golden wedding. This was also the 17th wedding anniversary of their married daughter, Mrs Sonia Woodward (Thornley). The couple have another married daughter, Mrs June Alderton of Bexley Heath, Kent.

Mr Soulsby, who is 75, and in perfect health, was born at Tudhoe, and started work as a stocktaker at 13 at the iron works in Spennymoor. "I don't know whether I brought the works bad luck", said Mr Soulsby, "but I had only worked a year there when they closed down".

Never out of Work

Mr Soulsby is proud of the fact that in a working career of 52 years he was never out of work. Mr Soulsby was transferred to Wheatley Hill Colliery where he retired at 65 after giving 51 years to the coal industry.

In the First World War he served with the army for four years. In France, because of his mining experience, Mr Soulsby was transferred to the Royal Engineers, the Tunnellers as they were called. "It was as well I knew something of the job for we had to do a lot of tunnelling in the Vimy Ridge sector", commented Mr Soulsby. While in France he was wounded three times.

Ardent Sportsman

Mr Souslby was keenly interested both in cricket and football and says, "I was pretty handy at both". In one season Tudhoe United FC, with whom he was playing, won four cups. He captained Tudhoe Colliery CC for 20 years. He said it would be a good thing if the village communities took more interest in their local clubs. Since 1945 Mr Soulsby has been groundsman for Wheatley Hill CC.

His wife, Alice, is 69 and a native of Spennymoor. For many years she made clipping and hooky mats. "Joe and I", she said, "Have had a happy married life together in spite of the fact that we would never qualify for the Dunmow Flitch. If young people want the best out of married life my advice to them is to be prepared to give and take and not allow any outside interference". Joe agreed.

Both are members of the Over-60-Club and Mrs M E Richardson, on behalf of the club, presented them with a bouquet of carnations.

(The town of Dunmow in Essex is famous for its four-yearly ritual of the Flitch Trials, in which couples must convince a jury of six local bachelors and six local maidens that they have never wished themselves un-wed for a year and a day. If successful the couple are paraded through the High Street and receive a flitch of bacon).

SOMERSAULTED THREE TIMES AT THORNLEY

Five young men from the Thornley area who were in a car which somersaulted three times before coming to rest on its wheels near a bend in the road at Thornley on Saturday, were all taken to Durham County Hospital suffering from shock and injuries. The car was travelling from Ludworth to Thornley and when it somersaulted near Thornley Welfare Hall one of the young men was thrown out.

The car belonged to 18-year-old Alan Turner, 12 Thornlaw North, Thornley, and it is believed he was driving when the accident happened. He was taken to hospital, with injuries to his head and legs, together with the four other occupants – Terence Hall (17) and his brother Stanley (23) of The Lodge, Haswell; Richard Robinson (17), 13 Sixth Street, Wheatley Hill (head and facial injuries); and Joseph Harvey (19), 18 Hillsyde Crescent, Thornley (minor abrasions and an elbow injury).

The brothers Hall were the only ones detained in hospital and the following day their condition was said to be "fairly comfortable". Terence Hall received leg and head injuries and his brother Stanley injuries to his leg, back and arm.

The sound of the crash brought people quickly to the scene from nearby houses and a garage, and they gave assistance to the injured men until the ambulance arrived. The man thrown out of the car was trapped beneath it for a short time. The car had to be lifted bodily to release him.

29 June 1962

LUDWORTH DIAMOND PAIR HAVE FAMILY REUINION

On 28 June 1902, the wedding took place of Thomas Briggs, of Sherburn Hill and Eleanor Gibson, of Pittington.

A Methodist marriage, it was solemnised in the Wesleyan Chapel in Old Elvet, Durham, in Chapel Passage. So began a happy married life of 60 years.

Thursday was spent very quietly by this unassuming couple but the family had made preparations for a more ambitious celebration at Wheatley Hill, the home of the youngest daughter on Sunday.

Thomas Briggs was born at Quebec on 5 January 1878. He went to school at Quebec but with the removal of his parents (Mr and Mrs John Briggs) to Wingate, he completed his education an early age and went to the mine at Hutton Henry, at 13.

Started at Bank

He started at "bank" at the outset and worked 10½ hours a day for 11d per shift. Later going underground after serving 12 months, he received a rise in pay which amounted to 1s.3d per shift.

Hutton Henry Colliery was declining, and at the age of 18 years, Thomas Briggs left the pit which eventually shut down six months after. After working at New Brancepeth where he was a putter, he started coal hewing at Houghton eventually arriving at Sherburn Hill.

The maiden name of Mrs Briggs was Eleanor Gibson, daughter of Mr and Mrs George Gibson, who lived at High Pittington; she was born on 1 August 1883. Her schooldays were spent at the old Pittington Church of England School, where Mr J B Taylor was schoolmaster. Her young life was spent at home helping her mother with household chores.

House for a Footballer

Mr and Mrs Briggs set up housekeeping in a cottage in the Long Open (later Victoria Street) Low Pittington; then to High Pittington in Elemore Row. An application was made for a colliery house at Littletown, and when the colliery manager heard that Tom Briggs, the footballer, wanted a house, he gave him one at the Long Row, Littletown.

Mr Briggs left Sherburn Hill Colliery for Wheatley Hill; afterwards he returned to the Sherburn group of pits in 1916, starting work as a shotfirer at Sherburn House pit which had been reopened after sinking to the Busty Seam. Then in 1918 he went to Ludworth pit and to live at Ludworth.

Incidentally, Mr Briggs recalled that before going to Wheatley Hill he and his wife set out to walk to the place, and they travelled through Shadforth and Ludworth en route, passing through Ludworth the remark was made by Mr Briggs, "I would not be found dead here".

Sports Lover

In his young days, Mr Briggs was a great lover of sport. He played for Pittington and Littletown football teams. Among his contemporaries were the brothers Tom and Joe Allanton, Jim Silcox, Ernest Wiles, Tom Wilkes, Jim Hall (later of Sherburn Wanderers) and Dick Kendrick.

During the 1926 strike, a branch of the Labour Party was formed at Ludworth and Mr Briggs became the chairman. Both his wife and himself were staunch members of the Labour movement in Ludworth.

After ten years in a colliery house in Shadforth Terrace, Mr and Mrs Briggs removed to a Council house and their present address in 76 Barnard Avenue, Ludworth.

They were both Methodists but the family were all members of the Church of England.

Sunday's celebration would be a noteworthy one with the family. There are four sons and four daughters living; 19 grandchildren and 15 great-grandchildren to facilitate the diamond wedding of Mr and Mrs Briggs.

WHEATLEY HILL STRIKE WAS SHORT LIVED

It was back to work again for the 700 miners at Wheatley Hill colliery on Monday, following a strike which began last Thursday when the coal-fillers in the night shift, dissatisfied with their pay for work on a new coal-face, refused to go down the pit to start their shift.

The rest of the miners in that shift came out in sympathy with them, and the strike was continued on Friday.

The decision to return to work was made at a packed meeting of the miners' lodge in the Welfare Hall on Sunday morning. The meeting, attended by about 350 members, lasted 40 minutes and afterwards the lodge secretary, Coun A D Wharrier, told our reporter it had been a unanimous decision to return to work. Work was resumed in the ten o'clock stonemen's shift on Sunday night.

Dissatisfied

The management, said Coun Wharrier, had agreed, together with the area Labour Relations Officer, Mr O Blackwell, to meet lodge officials and representatives of the fillers and other piece workers to discuss their alleged pay grievances, provided they went back to work.

"And with this promise", said Coun Wharrier, "the men decided to go back – not one member voted against this action". They were now hoping for "an amicable settlement" to the men's grievances, added Coun Wharrier.

It was when the coal-fillers received their pay-notes about 4.00pm last Thursday, that the strike began. They were dissatisfied with their pay and, they said later, when they got no satisfaction from the management, they decided to stop work.

One of the fillers said that since a new coal face had been started in the Low Main seam more than two months ago there had been considerable discontent among the piece-workers over what they were paid. The trouble had kept "brewing up" and came to a head when they got their pay-notes last week and found there was still no improvement.

About 1000 Tons Lost

It is six years since there was a strike at the colliery and that, like this latest one, lasted only a short time. The colliery is one of the smallest of the nine in No 3 Area (South-East Durham), Durham Division, NCB. It has a weekly target of 6000 tons and it is estimated that the strike action resulted in about 1000 tons being lost.

This weekend Coun Wharrier terminates 20 months' service as lodge secretary – he was beaten for the position in a recent ballot by 21-year-old Mr Frank Harper. But he is acting jointly with the new secretary until the present trouble is settled.

The colliery starts its annual fortnight's holiday in three weeks time.

CHOCOLATE FOR NEARLY 2000 CHILDREN AT THORLEY

One of the highlights of the Thornley Colliery Sports Fund's fifth annual sports day to be held on Thornley Colliery Welfare ground tomorrow (Saturday) – at any rate, as far as the children are concerned – will be the presentation of gift bags of chocolate and confectionery to every child in the village up to school-leaving age.

Each bag will contain more than five shillings worth of chocolate and sweets and 1850 children are due to receive them. "Once again we have a big programme arranged, commencing with a procession through the village, and all we want to ensure the success of the day is plenty of sunshine", the secretary, Mr S G Greener, of Wheatley Hill, told our reporter on Wednesday.

The parade, which will start at 1.30pm at the top of Dunelm Road, Thornley, will be headed by the band of the local Boys' Brigade, conducted by Mr J Plant, members of the Thornley Methodist Church Girls' Guildry and Thornley Colliery Band.

Jazz Bands

Jazz bands will also be taking part – eight have entered this competition – and a big entry is expected for the fancy and comic dress for both children and adults. There are three age groups for the children's fancy dress – 5-7 years, 8-10 years and 11-15 years. Prizes will also be awarded for the best tableaux in the parade.

"Altogether", said Mr Greener, "more than £100 will be distributed in prizes".

Sports for infants, juniors and seniors are being organised, and there is a pit pony contest, with £5 and a silver challenge cup going to the cleanest pit pony in the No 3 Area, B Group.

In planning "the big day", the committee have not overlooked physically handicapped children unable to take part in the racing. For them there will be an arts and crafts and handwriting competition, and these entries will be exhibited in Thornley Welfare Hall.

During the afternoon there will be a gymnastic display by the Billingham Synthonia Recreation Club, and when the parade makes its way through the village a collection will be taken in aid of Thornley Aged Miners' Homes.

"Mystery Couple"

A "mystery couple" will be mingling among the large crowds – they are Mr and Mrs Sports Day, and a £5 prize awaits the first person identifying each of them. Mrs Sports Day is described as "a well-known resident of Thornley aged 25 to 50 – she has lovely hair and will be wearing a dress and a smile".

Mr Sports Day is a "well known workman, above the age of 35. He will be wearing a suit of clothes and a smile. He is jovial, a wit and an underground worker". Challengers must be over 15 and members of the Sports Fund.

The money to cover the cost of the sports has been raised by sixpence-a-week levy paid by the workmen at Thornley colliery all the year round.

Officials in charge of the arrangements are: Chairman, Mr J Carr, vice-chairman, Mr R Hughes, secretary, Mr S G Greener, treasurer, Mr William Thompson.

6 July 1962

COLLIERY FAMILY TRADITIONS OF THORNLEY 'DIAMOND' COUPLE

Mr and Mrs Thomas Thompson, 5 The Bungalows, Thornley, celebrated their diamond wedding on Monday. There was a family celebration party at the home of their son-in-law and daughter Mr and Mrs Lawrence White, 128 Barnard Avenue, Ludworth, when two married sons and ten grandchildren met to wish the old couple many more happy years together.

Mr Thompson was born at Murton, where his grandfather Martin Thompson, a colliery sinker, had settled when Murton Colliery was being sunk. Martin Thompson was one of the pioneers of the Durham Miners' Association and a member of the first executive committee in 1869. Mr Thompson's father, who afterwards got employment at Station Town Colliery, was the first lorry man to be employed by

Station Town Co-operative Society when it was formed in 1886. He also became the first branch manager for the society when they opened Thornley branch 64 years ago.

Local Historian

Mrs Thompson was a native of Hetton-le-Hole and removed to Thornley with her parents when she was a schoolgirl. After their marriage at Easington on 9 July 1902, Mr and Mrs Thompson settled in Thornley where Mr Thompson was employed as a miner.

Mrs Thompson is very interested in local history. She is well acquainted with Richard Fynes and John Wilson and knew personally many of the miners' leaders. Her son Mr William Thompson was a member last year of the executive committee of the Durham Colliery Mechanics' Association and is at present treasurer of the Thornley Colliery Federation Board.

MOTHERS' CLUB AT THORNLEY

Mrs M Hobbs presided over a meeting of Thornley Mothers' Club. Business details were read by Mrs I Musgrave (assistant secretary). Arrangements were made for next week's meeting to take the form of an evening trip to Redcar. Entertainment took the form of a social evening shared with guests from Wheatley Hill Mothers' Club. Mrs C Wake was MC for a programme of dancing and games. Music was supplied by Mr E Kitto and Mr J Doyle.

THORNLEY COLLIERY'S WINNERS

Thousands of villagers and visitors lined the 1½ mile route from Half Way House to Thornley Colliery Welfare Sports ground to see the most colourful procession for many years.

The procession marshalled by Mr Jack Carr, chairman of the Colliery's sports fund, Mr Ronnie Hughes, secretary of Thornley Miners' Lodge, were led by Thornley Boys' Brigade Band, Thornley Colliery Band and 8 juvenile jazz bands.

The first sports event of the day was started by Mr J H Taylor, Chief Steward, when he opened the go-as-you-please race for the Baldasera Memorial Cup, over 1½ miles, which was won by S Dower (15).

Other winners were: **The best dressed tableaux**: Thornley Mothers' Club; **Comic dress for children:** Keith Allan, Brian Tilley, Marion Lock and Lillian St Julien.
Original dress: Leslie Gray, Peter Cairns, George Hedley, George Copeland, T Taylorson.
Field Events: Boys: J Ramage, K Brownless, J Youll, R Hogan, J Peachy, R Peachy, A Dower, A Gutcher.
Girls: A McCoy, M Wood, T Bonar, J Wood, A Aspinal, L Walker, V Jones, K Leck, A Moyle, A Bennett.
13 July 1962

FUNERAL OF WHEATLEY HILL CATHOLIC

Requiem Mass was conducted in Thornley RC Church of the English Martyrs on Wednesday for Mr Thomas Lawler (67), 5 Jack Lawson Terrace, Wheatley Hill. Mass was conducted by Dr H McNeil and committal service at Wheatley Hill Cemetery by Father Smith.

Mr Lawler was born at Castle Eden and is survived by a married son and daughter. He started work at Monkwearmouth Colliery but transferred to Wheatley Hill in his early teens, after living a while at Horden. He was a coal hewer at Wheatley Hill. Thirteen years ago he suffered severe head injuries in an accident which cut short his working career at the age of 54.

Mr Lawler served his country in the 1914-18 War and he saw action in France. In the Battle of Mons he was wounded and was awarded the MM for outstanding bravery. He was demobbed with the rank of sergeant.

In the 1939-45 War, he served with the Wheatley Hill branch of the Home Guard with the rank of Sgt Major. He was an active member of Thornley RC Church of the English Martyrs.

20 July 1962

HAPPY TIMES AHEAD FOR WHEATLEY HILL YOUTH
Adventure playground has many attractions

Happy days are being planned by the children of the Johnson Estate area of Wheatley Hill for they have been provided with what they think is a youngsters' paradise – an adventure playground with all the equipment to keep children amused.

The people they have to thank for the playground are Wingate Parish Council, who are financing it, and the Wheatley Hill BP Guild of Old Scouts, who are carrying out voluntary construction work.

The Parish Council decided to construct the children's "Garden of Eden" last September after several people had enquired about the site, which was then just a plot of waste land, overgrown with weeds, where people used to tip rubbish.

Voluntary Work

Old lamp standards, concrete slabs for stepping stones, bricks for a climbing wall, metal grids and other simple materials were obtained and the local BP Guild under the direction of Coun Ralph Watson, of 4 Cemetery Road, Wheatley Hill, began voluntary work on the small site in June this year.

Although the children seem quite pleased with the result of the work, they will be given added satisfaction when swings and seats are installed.

The 'adventure-type' playground as the Parish Council calls it, is designed for children whose ages range from five to nine. It has been constructed at low cost in view of the fact that it has been made from simple, but quite adequate, materials.

Well used

"I have visited the playground several times and it seems to be fairly well used by the Johnson Estate children. It will be an even greater attraction when it is fully completed", Mr J Harper, Clerk to the Wingate Parish Council, told the Durham Chronicle.

Before the playground was built, children had to walk over half a mile and across a busy main road to the nearest recreational facilities. But the new playground will enable them to enjoy themselves virtually on their doorsteps and most important of all, enjoy their fun in safety.

3 August 1962

BEAUTY CROWN AT CRIMDON LIDO
Mr Shinwell Speaks of Difficult Task

It was a happy holiday surprise for 16-year-old Miss Blanche Barker, an attractive brunette, of 14 Patton Crescent, Wheatley Hill, when, as "Miss Wheatley Hill", she won the annual beauty queen contest at Easington Rural Council's holiday lido at Crimdon, near Blackhall, on Monday.

Two years ago Blanche, who is the second youngest of the four daughters of Mr and Mrs Abraham Barker, was runner-up for the "Miss Wheatley Hill" title. "When I won the village title this year", she told our reporter after being presented with the coveted "Miss Crimdon" silken sash as winner of Monday's final, "I little dreamed I would go on to win the contest. It is a wonderful thrill – something I will never forget!"

Blanche's success brought her a prize of £15. Asked what she intended doing with the money, Blanche, who arrived at Crimdon only last Saturday for a fortnight's caravan holiday with some girl friends, said frankly, "I haven't a clue!".

Blanche was one of 13 village beauty queens from all parts of the Easington Rural area, previously chosen at dances, who paraded on the bandstand in Crimdon Dene before a happy, colourful holiday crown estimated at more than 60,000 ... and, as usual, the judges were Mr Emanuel Shinwell, MP for Easington and his wife.

When Miss Barker, who wore a simple dress of pink cotton, with white broderie anglais, was announced as the winner by Mr Roy Isherwood, Crimdon's manager, she was presented with a beautiful bouquet by Mrs Shinwell, who also placed the "Miss Crimdon 1962" sash around her shoulders, and then a light-hearted Mr Shinwell delighted the cheering crown by kissing the winner on the cheek.

Miss Barker is employed by a woollen firm in Darlington.

In his speech to the crowds, Mr Shinwell said, "It is a very difficult problem for my wife and I to choose a winner", he added, "because there are so many beautiful girls and young married women in the Easington area".

Mr Shinwell said he gloried in the existence of Crimdon and he only wished they had more money to spend to develop it further for the benefit of the workers of Durham County and elsewhere.

For an hour before the judging of the beauty queens took place, community singing was enjoyed by the holiday crowd, and entertainment was provided by the Newcastle tenor, Mr Michael Hibberd and Mr Peter McCarron on the electric organ.

After the judging the 13 finalists, together with the runners-up for the village beauty queen titles, were entertained to tea with the other guests and Mr and Mrs Shinwell in an adjoining marquee.

Miss Wheatley Hill, Blanche Barker at Crimdon

WHEATLEY HILL NOTCH SIXTH WIN IN A ROW

It was their sixth victory in a row when Wheatley Hill defeated Washington Colliery Welfare by four wickets at home on Saturday in Division 1 of the Durham Coast League, and their success puts them back among the challengers for the league title.

After dismissing their opponents for 82, the "Hill" got off to a bad start, losing two wickets for only 16 runs, but 23 runs were added before they lost another, and Jack Wright batted confidently for a useful 21. The sixth wicket fell at 64, then Alan Fishwick quickly rattled up 18, which included four boundaries, to take the score to victory with his partner Billy Marshall.

Derek Leslie, their professional, took bowling honours for Wheatley Hill, with three wickets for 14. Eric Simpson had three for 20 and Marshall three for 29. Best of the visiting bowlers was R Johnson, with three for 41, and Davison topped their scores with 23. It was a brilliant catch by Stan Cudlip which dismissed Washington's fifth batsman, Poole, for ten runs.
Details:

WASHINGTON COLLIERY WELFARE:
D Chisholm c Fishwick b Leslie 5, J Oliveer b Leslie 1, C Davison b Simpson 23, M Stearman c Fishwick b Simpson 1, D Poole c Cudlip b Marshall 10, H Grayson c and b Marshall 13, J Smith run out 11, J Martin c Leslie b Marshall 1, A Armstrong c Simpson b Leslie 7, W Plender not out 3, R Johnson b Simpson 2 extras 5 – Total 82.

313

WHEATLEY HILL:

A E B Hill c Stearman b Johnson 6, S Cudlip c Smith b Johnson 8, J Wright b Johnson 21, D Leslie run out 8, F Ashford run out 6, E C Simjpson c Armstrong b Oliver 1, A Fishwick not out 18, W Marshall not out 6; extras 9 – total (6wkts) 83.

Wheatley Hill II made it a winning double for club on Saturday when, in a low-scoring game, they defeated Washington II by 17 runs away from home.

Wheatley Hill were sent back for 70, G Trotter doing most of the damage with five wickets for 32, but they soon got among the wickets when the home team went in to bat. Baker took six for 22 and Washington's last wicket fell at 53. **10 August 1962**

MR G FOORD, 80, DIES AT WHEATLEY HILL

The death has taken place of one of Wheatley Hill's most popular octogenarians, Mr George Foord (80), 14 Wingate Lane. His wife, Mrs Margaret Foord, died five years ago. He is survived by one son and three daughters.

Mr Foord was a Yorkshireman born at Guisborough. With his parents he moved to Shadforth at an early age, where his first job was farming. For some years he was in the licensing trade. After his marriage he became 'mine host' at The Half Way House, or as it was originally called, The Barrel of Grapes Inn. After nine years there he transferred to Thornley Colliery Inn. After three years he moved to Wingate Lane, Wheatley Hill and worked as manager of the lime kilns of Running Waters. He retired at 68.

Noted Rabbit Breeder

During the First World War Mr Foord served with the Royal Engineers in France. He became an expert rabbit breeder and exhibitor, and his name will always be associated with the breeding of a strain of black and blue Dutch rabbit, which has not only achieved prominence in this country, but abroad. After many notable successes as an exhibitor at local, county and national shows, he exported many of his Dutch rabbits to other countries, particularly to the United States. Many Dutch rabbits, carrying off the big prizes in American shows today, have as their ancestors the Dutch rabbits bred in Wheatley Hill by Mr Foord.

Mr Foord was a member of local societies like Wingate and District Club, Sedgefield and Durham. He was a past president of Sedgefield and Durham societies and an honorary member of the United Kingdom Dutch Rabbit Club. As an expert in this breed of exhibit, Mr Foord had been a judge at all the important shows in the country.

Funeral service was held in All Saints Church, Wheatley Hill, conducted by the Rev G G Graham. Cremation followed at Sunderland.
24 August 1962

....AND NOW THERE ARE FOUR IN A THORNLEY STREET

The Station Hotel, Hartlepool Street, Thornley, the largest and latest licensed house in the village, has been closed for the sale of intoxicants and will be closed indefinitely for business.

The officials of the brewery have decided to close the house and not renew the licence which they have held for over 75 years. This is the second closure for this brewery in the same street in five years and reduces the number if licensed houses in the street to four with one working men's club.

There were at one time in the same street, within a distance of 400 yards, nine public houses and one club.

WHEATLEY HILL MAN LOVED HORSES

The death took place suddenly last weekend of Mr Arthur Chorlton (77), of 1 The Avenue, Thornley Road, Wheatley Hill. He was the widower of the late Mrs Mary Chorlton, who died 17 years ago. He is survived by an only daughter, Miss Zena Chorlton.

Mr Chorlton was born at Lymm. Ever since being a boy, horses have been his main interest and hobby. He entered gentleman's service at the age of 14 and was employed in the stables. When coming to County Durham, he was employed as a coachman by Dr Harrison of Sherburn and held the post for ten years. He was then appointed horse-keeper for the Sherburn Hill Co-operative Society. After 27 years with the Society, he retired when he was 65.

With the Pioneers

In the First World War, Mr Chorlton served at Coldstream, in Scotland, with the Pioneer Corps.

A funeral service was conducted in All Saints Church, Wheatley Hill by the Rev G G Graham on Wednesday morning. Cremation followed at Durham

(a full list of mourners is included in the original newspaper article).

FIVE TARGET BREAKERS IN SOUTH-EAST DURHAM

With five of the nine colliers passing their targets last week in No 3 Area (South-East Durham) of the Durham Divisional Coal Board, the total output of 101,365 tons exceeded the combined target by 9065 tons.

Best performance was that of Easington Colliery, which passed its target of 17,000 tons by 7357 tons. Horden, the biggest colliery, produced 4409 tons more than its target figure and the other target breakers were Thornley, Shotton and Deaf Hill.

Individual outputs with targets in brackets were: Horden, 27,159 (22,750); Easington, 24,537 (17,000); Blackhall, 13,225 (15,000); Thornley 9447 (8500); Wheatley Hill, 4779 (6000); Sherburn Hill, 6807 (7250); Shotton, 7089 (7000); Deaf Hill, 4309 (4000); Wingate, 3993 (4800).

WHEATLEY HILL MAN DIES THREE DAYS AFTER GOLDEN WEDDING

All Saints Church, Wheatley Hill was filled on Saturday for the funeral of Mr Samuel Gibson (75), 10 Quilstyle Road, Wheatley Hill. The service was conducted by the Rev G G Graham with Mrs C English at the organ. Cremation followed at Sunderland.

Mr Gibson is survived by his wife, Mrs Mary Ann Gibson, three sons and four daughters. Last weekend, the family quietly celebrated Mr and Mrs Gibson's Golden Wedding. Mr Gibson died three days later.

A Cumbrian by birth, Mr Gibson obtained his first job at Trimdon Grange Colliery, moving to Wheatley Hill just prior to his marriage. He retired from mining at the age of 66 after giving 52 years service to the coal industry. He was a member of Wheatley Hill Workmen's Club for 50 years and was a member of the local Over 60 Club. These two organisations were well represented at the funeral service.

(a full list of mourners is included in the original newspaper article).

31 August 1962

HONOUR FOR WHEATLEY HILL SCHOOL

Wheatley Hill Boys' Modern School brought honour to South-East Durham when they competed in the Durham County Schools' Gymnastic Championships at Billingham Technical College. Mr Arthur Harris reports that his boys were placed first in Grade I section. Wheatley Hill were awarded the Joseph Championship Cup. The team representing Wheatley Hill was Eric Weatherell (captain); Barry Hammond, Robert Walls, Alan Peters, James Stogdale and Leslie Barker.

A member of the Wheatley Hill team, Barry Hammond, came out top in the individual events. He gained the title of Durham County Junior Gymnastic Champion and was presented with the Vickerstaffe Cup.

Eric Weatherell, the Wheatley Hill captain, was placed third in the individual events. Cups, trophies and certificates were presented by County Coun Coxon.

The Wheatley Hill team were trained by the school's PE specialists – Mr N Norton and Mr K Charlton.

THORNLEY'S SWINGS PLEA TO RDC

Thornley Parish Council are to ask Easington Rural District Council for permission to erect swings and other playground equipment on the open space between St Chad's Square and Laurel Crescent and St Aidan's.

Coun James Nicholson, who suggested this approach, said that this estate, the largest in Thornley and owned by the ERDC, was fortunate to have an open space capable of being turned into a playground for the 200 or more children. He also supported the idea of the district council to help in providing some of the equipment.

The council also decided to apply to Pharmaceutical Committee of the County Health Service to have the chemist's shop open in the Villas, to dispense prescriptions, until after surgery hours. Coun James Hoban said he had been told that last Saturday an urgent prescription could not be supplied in Thornley, because the chemist had closed the shop during the doctor's hours.

Coun J R Bosomworth complained about the South Shields Water Company dumping a stack of water mains on the open space near Morris Crescent. He stated that the Easington RDC had just got these open spaces cleared of all the rubbish, trimming the grass which was looking fresh and green, when a load of pipes wrapped in straw and cardboard was being scattered all about the grass. The Council decided to take the matter up with the District Engineer and Surveyor.
14 September 1962

THORNLEY COLLIERY INN
The first leek show in Thornley held at the Colliery Inn attracted a large crowd of visitors. Mr Jack Taylor who was secretary of the club last year, gained the first prize with two leeks of 77.9 cubic inches. Others were: M Mitchinson 65.93, J Jobes 65.55, F Walker 59.96, J Kay, R Smith, J Ollett, A Johnson, T Lennox, Mr Fishwick, J Morton, G Clough, W Johnson, T Barker, W Norrie, W Evans, T Lennox, T Hopkins, M Rain, J Bell, N Handley, K Million, W Williams, J Hogg, J Youll.

WHEATLEY HILL CONSTITUTIONAL CLUB
For the second year running Mr C W Rose, an official of the Wheatley Hill Constitutional Club Leek Club, won first prize for the best pair of leeks at the annual show. Mr Rose was secretary of the club when he carried off the premier prize last year – this year he is treasurer. His leeks measured 111.9 cubic inches.

The second prize went to Mr J Jordan, with leeks measuring 96.8 cubic inches and Mr T Sweeting won third prize with a leek measurement of 85.4 cubic inches.

Other principal winners, in order of merit, were Messrs S Scott, J Scott, R Cook, G Curry, W Franklin, J Langlands, D Parsley, R Forster, W Curry, A Davies, J Orchard, J Dodds.

Wheatley Hill Constitutional Club Leek Show

317

WAS CLUBMAN FOR 50 YEARS

Mr Joseph Dunn, aged 69, of 60 Luke Terrace, Wheatley Hill, who has died, was interred in the local cemetery following a service conducted by the Rev G F Nelson in The Rest. Mr Dunn, a bachelor, had lived in the village all his life. He started work there at the age of 13 and when he had to change his occupation because of eye trouble he became a storekeeper at Newton Aycliffe. His last job was at Peterlee. He retired when he was 65.

Mr Dunn was in the First World War, serving as a signalman in the 7th Green Howards. He saw service in France. He had always been interested in the Working Men's Club movement and was a member of Wheatley Hill Club for 50 years. For 29 years he served as treasurer, relinquishing the office at the beginning of this year. *(a full list of mourners is included in the original newspaper article).*
21 September 1962

LOSS TO THORNLEY CATHOLICS

A well known personality in the Thornley, Wheatley Hill and Kelloe district, Mr Patrick O'Brien (67), has died at his home in High Street, Thornley, after a long illness.

A native of County Mayo, Ireland, Mr O'Brien came to this country when a young man in his teens and found employment in the steel works on Teesside, he was also employed at Garmondsway Quarry, Coxhoe, before he settled in Thornley in 1924.

Mr O'Brien retired from work underground at Thornley Colliery in 1960; he lived for some years at Wheatley Hill, before returning to Thornley. An ardent Roman Catholic he was an active member of the Church of the English Martyrs, Thornley. He was also an old member of Thornley Working Men's Club and Thornley Catholic Club.

Mr O'Brien leaves a widow, three sons and four daughters.

SEVEN FOR WHEATLEY HILL MECHANICS

Ben Harvey, their inside-left, scored a 'hat trick' for Wheatley Hill Mechanics on Saturday when they visited Blackhall Athletic Reserves in Division 2 of the Harlepools and District League and enjoyed an easy 7-1 victory.

The opening exchanges were evenly fought but the Mechanics came more into the picture near the interval and a well-taken goal by Dave Robson, their inside-right, put them in front.

The second half saw the swift-moving Wheatley Hill attack causing plenty of panic in the home defence and they scored six more goals, the Athletic replying with two. Robson got a second goal and the other Wheatley Hills scorers, in addition to hat-trickster Harvey, were Jim Carr, who led the attack, and right half Jim Rowbotham. It was the Mechanics' second win in five games.
28 September 1962

318

WHEATLEY HILL CLUB

With a pair of leeks measuring 63.98 cubic inches, Mr J Nattress won first prize and two specials at the annual leek show in Wheatley Hill Workmen's Club at the weekend, and he was also awarded first prize for intermediate leeks.

The show was judged by Mr S Poulson of Wheatley Hill, and prizes valued at £400 were awarded. Second prize for leeks was won by Mr R Cook, and other winners, in order of merit, were Messrs S Owens, F Burnside, W Foster, A Atkinson, A Hunter, A Evans, T Hodgson, M Bailes, A J Sutherland, Ray Humes, S Smith, W Walker, J Durante, R Waite, T E Greener, G O'Connor and S Maughan. Winners of the other classes were:

Long carrots: 1, A Sutherland; 2, G O'Connor; 3, A Hunter. Short carrots: 1, T Hodgson; 2, A Hunter; 3, W Walker. Cauliflowers: 1 and 2, R Waite; 3, A Evans. Parsnips: 1, A Sutherland; 2, A Hunter; 3, S Smith. Onions: 1, A Hunter; 2, R Cook; 3, W Foster. Round potatoes: 1, 2 and 3, A Hunter. Kidney potatoes: 1, S Maughan; 2, W Walker; 3, W Foster. Pink celery: 1, R Cook; 2, W Forster: 3, G O'Connor. White celery: 1 and 2, A Evans; 3, S Owens. Long beet: 1, W Foster; 2 and 3, G O'Connor. Globe beet: 1, W Walker; 2, S Smith; 3, M Bailes. Intermediate leeks: 1, J Nattress; 2, R Cook; 3, A Atkinson.

Flowers: 1, W Foster; 2, S Owens; 3, R Cook.

Arrangements for the show were made by Mr William Walker (joint secretary and treasurer) and Mr M Bailes (chairman).

5 October 1962

Exhibitors among the prizes at Wheatley Hill Workingmen's Club annual leek, vegetable and flower show—(D A)

Prizewinners at Wheatley Hill Club Leek Show

CHILDREN LOVED HIM

After a service in Wheatley Hill Church Street Methodist Church on Saturday, the remains of Mr Matthew Shevels, 69, of 2 Rock Cottage, Wheatley Hill, were cremated at Sunderland. He leaves a wife and married son. It was while working as a stoneman at Deaf Hill Colliery that Mr Shevels had an accident which cut short his working career at 40.

He was in the Army with the Northumberland Fusiliers in the First World War. He served in France and was wounded. For many years he was secretary of the Wheatley Hill British Legion. He fought for some time to keep the branch going but it ultimately disbanded. Mr Shevels was secretary of the Soldiers' and Sailors' Club in Wheatley Hill for many years.

Mr Shevels was well loved among the children who attended Wheatley Hill county junior mixed and infants' school. During the years he could not follow his normal employment, he assisted his wife, who was caretaker of the infants' school.

CULLEN IN LINE FOR TITLE TILT

Maurice Cullen, of Shotton Colliery, qualified for a fight for Dave Charnley's British lightweight title when he outpointed Johnny Cooke (Bootle) after 12 exciting rounds. This was the final eliminator for the title, and the second time Cullen had out-pointed Cooke.

There could have been very little in it. In fact the referee, Ike Powell of Wales, took a long time to add up his points. He went towards Cooke's corner, then stopped, looked at his card again, walked over and awarded Cullen the decision.

Yet Cooke, in a sensational ninth round, almost became the first to knock out Cullen, who literally wilted under the ferocity and power of Cooke's two-handed attack which he kept up for three minutes. At times Cullen staggered back.

But Cooke did not keep up his attack in the tenth. He began to seek openings instead of creating them by his own skill and this enabled Cullen to come back into the fight.

Cooke came again in the 11th, but, without the former power and, although he did win the last round, he failed to wipe out Cullen's lead, which had been set up with flashing straight lefts and speed.

Cullen looked much more impressive during the first four rounds when he was ready to go forward as willingly as he subsequently went backwards.

Cooke, although more versatile, was too often inactive, but had a great fifth round in which his hooking to head and body had Cullen looking unhappy. But he let Cullen off the hook.

"HAT-TRICK" FOR WHEATLEY HILL WOMAN BOWLER

During the season just ended, Mrs Edna Hall, secretary of Wheatley Hill Welfare Women's Bowls Club, has won all three trophies in singles tournaments organised by the club.

Defeating the club treasurer, Mrs R Ord, in the final, she won the Club Championship Cup for the fifth year running, and she also beat Mrs Ord in the final of the William Jones Cup.

Mrs Hall made it a "hat-trick" of successes when she defeated Mrs E Atkinson in the final of the Festival Bowl competition.

The trophies and prizes are to be presented at a social evening in the Welfare Hall, Wheatley Hill, on 10 November.

WHEATLEY HILL FUNERAL OF MR F D CARR

The funeral took place of Mr Frederick Dennis Carr (69), 3 Stockton Street, Wheatley Hill. His wife, Mrs Barbara Ellen Carr, died four years ago. He is survived by seven sons and two daughters. One of his sons, Mr Teddy Carr, was well known as a footballer with Arsenal and Huddersfield Town and is at present manager of Darlington FC. Another son, Mr John Carr, is fore-overman at Thornley Colliery.

Mr Carr was born at Chilton but spent many years at Ludworth. He went to Wheatley Hill 30 years ago and worked at the one colliery (Wheatley Hill) all his career and retired at 65. He was a member of Wheatley Hill Over-60 Club, Thornley Workmen's Club and Thornley Officials' Club.

A service at Wheatley Hill Patton Street Methodist Church was conducted by Rev G L Nelson, prior to interment in the local cemetery. The Over-60 Club was represented by officials and members.

12 October 1962

WHEATLEY HILL FAMILY SAIL FOR AUSTRALIA
Decision taken because of "worsening position in the mining industry"

This week a Wheatley Hill Family of seven – a 48-year-old miner and his wife and their four sons and daughter – "dug up their roots" in the village where they have spent virtually all their life and set sail for a new life in Australia as emigrants under the Government sponsored scheme.

"For a long time now we have been thinking about emigrating", the miner, Mr Fred Bartram, of 20 Burns Street, told our reporter. "We finally made the decision when we saw the position getting worse in the mining industry locally. Wingate Colliery has just closed down and it seems to me other collieries will soon have to face the same problem of redundancy".

Thirteen months ago Mr Bartram's younger brother, Richard, who is 43, emigrated to Australia from South Shields with his wife and five-year-old daughter Ann. "He is now happily settled in a job in the ICI works in Brisbane", said Mr Bartram, "and has never regretted leaving this country. In fact, in his letters back to us, he says he only wishes he had taken the step sooner to go abroad!"

Waiting list for Jobs

No jobs are fixed up for Mr Bartram and his three sons, whose schooling is over. But they don't expect to be long without employment. "We are quite prepared to do anything", said Mr Bartram, "but it won't be mining if we can help it. Even if we wanted to work down the pits we would probably find it difficult because the emigration officer told us that wages are so high in the coal industry in Australia that there is a waiting-list for jobs."

Mr Bartram and his eldest son Fred, who is 23 and has been employed as a packer at the East Durham Co-operative Dairies, can both drive, and they hope they may be able to get employment as drivers.

The second eldest son, Billy who is 20, has been working at Wheatley Hill colliery as a putter, but the next son David, who is 15, left school only during the ummer and has not yet had a job. The other members of the family are four-year-old Doreen and two-year-old Stephen.

Mr and Mrs Bartram with their family

Mr Bartram's 42-year-old wife Jennie, like the rest of the family, is eagerly looking forward to their new life "down under".

"From what my brother-in-law tells us, everyone is very friendly out there and keen to lend a helping hand", she said.

Mr Bartram said he thought prospects for a young family were "pretty poor" these days in this country. It was with the future of his own family in mind that he decided to emigrate. "I think they will have a much better chance of getting on in Australia", he said, "It is a big step we are taking, but I am sure we can make a success of things".

'All For It'

And what do the two oldest sons, Fred and Billy, think about emigrating? "We are all for it – there's nothing much around here", they said.

Emigration means separation of the family from Mrs Bartram's 70-year-old widowed mother, Mrs Hannah Coldwell, who lives next door to them in Burns Street. But the separation is not expected to last long.

"As soon as we have got nicely settled down in Australia we are hoping my mother will come out and join us", said Mrs Bartram.

Fred, the eldest of the family, expects his sweetheart to follow him out soon. About nine weeks ago he became engaged to 20-year-old Ann Bannister, of Horden, who works at a factory at West Hartlepool. "We plan to get married in Australia", he said.

Billy also has a girlfriend – 18-year-old Betty Marsden of Cassop, "We'll certainly miss the girls", he said.

Mr Bartram, who has another brother, Norman, living at Thornley, was born in Wheatley Hill and has worked as a miner since leaving school. He formerly worked at Thornley and Blackhall collieries, but most of his mining career has been spent at Wheatley Hill as a shot-firer. During the last war he served for six years in the RAF Regiment.

The family, having sold up all their belongings, set sail from Southampton on Monday in the Italian ship, the Castelfeilice. They will be on the water about five weeks before reaching Brisbane.

Before they left Wheatley Hill they were showered with good wishes from their neighbours and friends. "One thing is certain – it won't be our fault if we don't make 'a go' of it", were Mr Bartram's parting words.

9 November 1962

WHEATLEY HILL BOWLS CLUB FUNCTION

The men's and women's sections of Wheatley Hill Welfare Bowls Club "joined forces" on Saturday night at the annual supper and social evening organised for the presentation of trophies and prizes won by the members of both clubs during the past season.

Held in the Welfare Hall, the function was a big success, about 170 members and friends attending. Among the guests were the president and secretary of the North-East Coast Women's Bowling League, Mrs Moul and Mrs Edna Martin. Women's bowling clubs were also represented from Burn Valley, Brinkburn, Hartlepool and Wingate.

In presenting the women's section trophies, Mrs Martin, who is the county women's bowls secretary, congratulated the members on their success and wished "better luck next time" to those not among the winners.

Won Three Trophies

The Wheatley Hill secretary, Mrs Edna Hall, "swept the board" where cup-hunting was concerned, winning all three trophies. The winners were: Championship Cup, Mrs E Hall; runner-up, Mrs R Ord. William Jones Cup, Mrs E Hall; runner-up, Mrs Ord. Festival Bowl, Mrs E Hall; runner-up, Mrs E Atkinson.

Mrs A Carter, chairman of the club, presided at the presentations, and thanks to Mrs Martin were expressed by Mrs Ord, the club treasurer, who also presented her with a bouquet of carnations.

The men's prizegiving was presided over by Mr C Raffell, vice-chairman of the club, and the presentations were made by Mr W Slater, jun. Winners were: Championship Cup, Mr J Burrell; runner-up, Mr G Watson. Robert Moor Cup, Mr G Hughes; runner-up, Mr W Kendall.

After supper whist and dancing were enjoyed. Mrs Hall was MC for whist and with Mr J T Jones, officiated as steward for the dancing. The whist winners were Miss A Richardson, Mrs M Hall (Thornley), Mrs R Ord and Messrs R Dunn, Ostick and T Bullock.

POINTS WIN FOR MAURICE CULLEN

Leading contender for Dave Charnley's British lightweight title, Maurice Cullen, the Shotton boxer, was a good points winner in his ten-round bout with Ben Said (France) in Manchester. Cullen, noted for his classic left lead, this time found an opponent who proved both elusive and aggressive and the Shotton man frequently had to bring a right hook into play. There were plenty of points for Cullen from his accurate straight left, but the Frenchman's ducking and weaving style made him a difficult target. Said made an all-round effort in the final round, but the cool boxing of Cullen nullified.

REMEMBRANCE - The British Legion arranged the Remembrance Day parade at Wheatley Hill when the procession marched through the village headed by Wheatley Hill Silver Prize Band, to All Saints' Church. The service was conducted by the Rev G L Nelson (Methodist minister) and the address was given by the Vicar (the Rev G G Graham). On leaving the church the parade proceeded to the Memorial Clock on the Boys' Modern School in Front Street, a tribute to the fallen of the Second World War. A halt was made and prayers were said. The final act of homage and remembrance was at the Cenotaph in the Welfare Park, where wreaths were laid. Wreaths were laid on behalf of Wheatley Hill British Legion, Constitutional Club, Workmen's Club, Wheatley Hill WI, Soldiers', Sailors' and Airmen's Club, Sherburn Hill Co-operative Society, police, fire services and others. The service and the parade were attended by members of Wingate Parish Council, representatives on the Easington Rural District Council.

16 November 1962

OFFICIALS RETIREMENT

The fine record of having spent the whole of his mining career of nearly 51 years at the same colliery, where he rose to be an official, is held by Mr Bert Alderton, 1 South View, Wheatley Hill, who retired at the week-end.

Mr Alderton will not be 65 until February, and his earlier retirement has come for health reasons. Born at West Hartlepool, he began work at Wheatley Hill Colliery as a trapper-boy when he left school at the age of 14. He was paid at the rate of a shilling an eight-hour shift.

He went through all the grades of pit work underground and eventually became a deputy at the same colliery. He was on deputy work for 28 years, but for the last seven years has been an official, first on salvage work and then as a ventilation officer.

Mr Matthew Barrass was manager of the colliery when Mr Alderton started work and since then he has worked under four different managers. He has seen many changes at the pit - production was much higher when he began his career than it is now.

For 14 years Mr Alderton was a member of the Houghton-le-Spring Fire and Rescue Brigade and recognition of his service was made when he was presented with a silver medal and two diplomas. He assisted in the rescue work when fire broke put at Deaf Hill Colliery and two men lost their lives, and when there was a break-in of water at Thornley Colliery in 1949 and three men were drowned.

Mr Alderton is married, with an only son, Ralph, who lives at Peterlee. His wife is a founder-member of Wheatley Hill Women's Institute. Mr Alderton has no special hobbies. "I haven't had much time for them", he told me this week. "But now that I am retired I am going to enjoy life as much as I can".

THEY WOULD NOT QUIT WHEATLEY HILL WI "FOR THE WORLD"

"I wouldn't for the world ever dream of leaving the Women's Institute", 75-year-old Mrs Edith Harker, who was widowed three years ago, told our East Durham reporter,

Norman Passfield, when he visited the 32nd birthday party of Wheatley Hill Women's Institute recently.

"And neither would I!" chimed another jolly-looking "over-70" member, Mrs Dora Snowdon.

Mrs Harker and Mrs Snowdon, who is 73, have been members of the Institute since its formation and played an active part in the excellent progress it has made. Both formerly sang in the Institute choir, which made quite a name for itself locally.

They are also members of the village's Over-60 club. The club meets every Tuesday night, but once a month these two fresh-looking ladies are missing, that is the night it "clashes" with their Institute meeting.

It is easy to see why these two fine old ladies, and all the other members, do not like to miss their Institute. They are a friendly, happy crowd, the Wheatley Hill women, and a new member does not feel "new" very long, in such a homely atmosphere she is soon made to feel she has been going there for years.

23 November 1962

WHEATLEY HILL MINER RETIRES
He was a Survivor of a Wartime Explosion

A Wheatley Hill miner, who was one of the lucky survivors of an explosion on a ship on which he was serving during the 1914-18 War, has just retired from work after a mining career of 51 years, all of which has been spent at Wheatley Hill Colliery. He is Mr Thomas Taylorson, of 4 Dalton Terrace, who recently celebrated his 65th birthday.

Mr Taylorson was only 17½ when he joined the Royal Navy in 1915 and had been in uniform barely six months when he was involved in the explosion which shattered HMS Natal while it was in a Scottish harbour. About 400 sailors lost their lives.

"The tragedy would have even been worse had the ship been out at sea when the explosion occurred", Mr Taylorson, who enjoys pretty good health, told our reporter this week.

Mr Thomas Taylorson

Many Men Trapped

With it being in dock, some of its 700-odd personnel were on shore when it sank. "I can remember the explosion as though it were yesterday", said Mr Taylorson. "I was down below deck, when the ship suddenly gave a great shudder and the lights went out".

Slowly the ship heeled over. "Everybody who was able, raced to the decks and jumped into the water", said Mr Taylorson. "I lost no time myself in leaving the vessel and was swimming around in the water for about half an hour before being picked up". But many men were trapped and burned to death in the explosion and others were drowned.

Mr Taylorson served in the Navy for four years but that was the only time he was involved in an accident – "if accident it was", he said. Some had called it an act of sabotage.

Miners' Lodge Official

Mr Taylorson was born at West Cornforth but began work at Wheatley Hill colliery when he was 14, as a lamp-carrier underground. He was paid at the rate of 1s.4½d a shift. "We worked ten hours a shift when I first began work, but shortly afterwards the hours were reduced to eight", he said.

A year later Mr Taylorson was pony-putting and then went through the various grades of mining, including hand-putting and hewing. Until eight years ago, when he came to the surface on lighter duties after developing pneumoconiosis, Mr Taylor was a piece-worker for many years.

Until his resignation 4½ years ago – he resigned shortly after the death of his wife – Mr Taylorson gave excellent service to Wheatley Hill Miners' Lodge as its treasurer for 21 years. Shortly after the last war he represented Wheatley Hill on Easington Rural Council for three years.

Mr Taylorson is actively associated with the village's Over-60 Club. He is a member of the committee and, as a member of the concert party for nearly three years, has travelled all over the county with them, entertaining other old people's organisations. "We have a grand concert party", said Mr Taylorson, "and I find real pleasure in going around with them to other Over-60 clubs in the county. It helps to fill in mamy a lonely night for me – we all get a real kick out of it".

Mr Taylorson, who has lived by himself since his wife's death, has always taken a keen interest in local carnivals. He often entertained in the colourful parades before the last war, and during recent years, with village Sports Days having been revived in Wheatley Hill and the neighbouring colliery village of Thornley, he has again "dressed up" and played his part in entertaining the children in the monster processions.

"It is great fun and I think it is a fine thing that these sports days are back with us again", he said.

Three Sons are All Miners

Mr Taylorson has a family of three sons and two daughters. All his sons have followed in his footsteps in the mining industry - the two eldest, Thomas William and Leslie, work at Wheatley Hill colliery and the youngest, Robert, at Trimdon.

WHEATLEY HILL DANCE WITH A PURPOSE

The new Roman Catholic Church at Wheatley Hill, which is in course of construction, is to cost the Wheatley Hill communities about £40,000.

Mr and Mrs J Doyle are earnest workers for the scheme. For the last three months they have organised a weekly old-time dance in the Welfare Hall.

Mr Doyle said, "We hit on this idea as a pleasant way of raising part of the £40,000 needed for our new church. The dances have proved popular and since starting we have pulled in £130. Unfortunately expenses are heavy. The hire of the hall eats a good deal of our takings. Still, we have handed over £30 to the fund. We believe more will come and in time our dances will make a steady contribution to our Church."

THORNLEY PIGEON FANCIERS IN LONDON SHOW

Thornley pigeon fancying partners, Mr J G Bradley and Mr G L Hutchinson, of Fearnleigh, East View, are competing in the biggest racing pigeon show of the year.

They have entered a dozen birds in the British section of an international show of racing pigeons at London's New Horticultural Hall.

The two-day show, which has attracted more than 2,300 exhibits from home and overseas, opens today.

The County Durham partners have won scores of awards in the sport of pigeon racing and showing.

30 November 1962

CO-OP CLERK DIES AT WHEATLEY HILL

The death has taken place suddenly this weekend of Mr Maurice Moore (50), Abbingdon, 28 Sandwick Terrace, Wheatley Hill. He is survived by his wife, Mrs Christine Moore and a daughter, Marjorie.

A service and cremation was conducted at Sunderland by the Rev G L Nelson, Methodist Minister of Wheatley Hill.

Mr Moore was born in the village and was well known as a Co-operative Society employee. He started with the old Haswell Society and for many years has been a clerical worker in the General Manager's office at Sherburn, of the Sherburn Hill Co-operative Society.

Throughout the 1939-45 War, Mr Moore served with the RAF and had the rank of corporal. He saw active service at the invasion of Sicily and Italy. His two hobbies were gardening and motoring. Mr Moore had a full attendance at work for 26 years and has never received sick pay. He recently received a long-service certificate for membership of his union.

The Society was represented by Mr T F Hope (General Manager), Mr H Gibbons (General Secretary), Mr T Cairns (President) and members of the committee.

WHEATLEY HILL CLUB'S GREAT REVIVAL

Due to the untiring efforts of popular secretary, Mr Tommy Cowie and his committee, the Wheatley Hill Club football team are now enjoying a most successful run. Having lost their first six games, the team, under the leadership of Ben Harvey (captain) has now won nine and drawn one of their last ten games, including the first defeat inflicted upon the strong Easington Colliery SC team.

Under the firm guidance of Mr Cowie and his committee, and a great team spirit among the players, the "Hill" can be confident in their forthcoming Sid Lavers League Trophy encounter.

7 December 1962

Wheatley Hill Workingmens Club Football Team

POST OFFICE NEED: With 98 new houses being built at Wingate Lane, the biggest part of the Wheatley Hill population would eventually be living in the "Lane" area, said Coun C Hackworth at Wingate Parish Council meeting on Monday night, when he stressed the need for a new sub-Post Office being provided for the people there. It was decided to write to the area Postmaster asking what prospects there were for a new office.

CONSTITUTIONAL CLUB PARTY – When retired members of Wheatley Hill Constitutional Club were entertained to their annual Christmas party by the management committee, they each received a Christmas "box" of £1 and their wives, who were also guests, received 5s. An excellent knife-and-fork tea was served to about 70 old folk and later they were entertained by Mr W Hill's concert party from Horden. The chairman of the club, Mr R V Peacock, presided, and the money gifts were distributed by the treasurer, Mr J Urwin. After tea each guest received a glass of sherry. Secretarial duties were carried out by Mr J Cowan.

14 December 1962

1963

GREYHOUND AND PUPS DIE IN THORNLEY FIRE

A greyhound, which a week before had a litter of seven puppies, was rescued during the early hours of New Year's Day when fire broke out in a large shed at the back of what was formerly The Good Intent Inn, in Hartlepool Street, Thornley. It had no sooner reached safety however than it dashed back into the blazing building to where its young puppies lay huddled together.

Mr Laverick, the man who had rescued the animal, was unable to re-enter the burning shed because of the intense heat, and the greyhound perished together with all the puppies.

"When we had got the fire out," Sub-officer Stan Poulson, of Wheatley Hill Fire Brigade, which quickly dealt with the outbreak, told our reporter, "we found the greyhound lying dead with all the puppies lying dead around it."

Mr Laverick, who first spotted the fire, had got the greyhound out in the first place before the Fire Brigade reached the scene. He burned his hands in the rescue.

The firemen managed to save a motor-cycle in the shed, but extensive damage was done to the building. The shed, greyhound and puppies were the property of Mr D Burgin, who lives nearby.

CLUB'S RECORD SALES – Though beer was reduced by fourpence a pint to members throughout the week, last week's refreshment sales of £1,600 at Wheatley Hill Workmen's Club set up a new record. "The total was more than double our usual weekly takings," the club secretary, Mr B Aitken, told our reporter this week. The cheap beer concession was also in force all this week.

CLUB PARTY – About 300 retired members and their wives and widows over 60 were entertained to their annual supper and concert in Wheatley Hill Workmen's Club by the club management committee. They were welcomed by the club chairman, Mr W Henderson, and secretary, Mr B Aitken, who extended seasonal good wishes. During supper a Christmas cake was cut by one of the oldest guests, Mr Benjamin Bowes, who is 83. Each guest received a Christmas gift of £2 and an enjoyable entertainment was given by local artistes, with accompaniment provided on the electronic organ by Mr Gordon Brownless.
4 January 1963

DEPUTIES' OFFICERS – Coun R Watson, who presided at the annual meeting of Wheatley Hill lodge of the Durham County Colliery Deputies' Association at the week-end, was re-elected chairman for the ensuing year. Other elections were: secretary, Mr J Henderson; treasurer, Mr J Fishwick; auditor, Mr E Dawes; Aged Miners' committee representative, Coun R Watson; housing committee, Mr A C

Watson; Death Fund committee, Coun R Watson; Federation Board, Messrs A C Watson, J Henderson, J Armstrong and B Aitken; Welfare committee, Mr W Smart.

THORNLEY TEACHER MARRIES – The wedding took place at St Bartholomew's Church, Thornley, of Mr Joseph Michael Griffin, only son of Mr and Mrs Robert Griffin, Kings Langley, Hertfordshire, and Miss Gladys Moody, second daughter of Mr and Mrs John Moody, 34 Hillsyde Crescent Thornley. The Rev P G Mold officiated and Mrs Armstrong was at the organ. The bridegroom is a compositor and the bride has been a teacher at Horden Secondary Modern School.

Given away by her father, the bride was attired in a full-length gown of white Nottingham lace with circular veil and coronet of pearls. She carried a bouquet of cream roses. The bride was attended by her sister, Elizabeth, who wore a dress of cream silk with headdress to match. She carried a bouquet of anemonies. Best man was Mr Norman Ramshaw.

NURSE WEDS AT THORNLEY – Dr H McNeill officiated at the wedding at Thornley RC Church of the English Martyrs of Mr William Elcoat Lincoln, second son of Mr and Mrs Robert Lincoln, 6 Third Street, Wheatley Hill, and Miss Mary Robinson, youngest daughter of Mr and Mrs Jonathon S Robinson, 1 Kenton Crescent, Thornley. The bride has been nursing at the Sedgefield General Hospital for the past eight years.

She was given away by her father and wore a ballerina length gown of brocade with circular veil held in place by a headdress of roses. She carried a prayer book with a spray of red roses. Bridesmaid was Miss Joan Wilson, who wore a dress of flame taffeta with white and carried a prayer book with a spray of cream roses. Duties of best man were carried out by the 'groom's brother, Mr Robert Lincoln.
11 January 1963

CLUB ELECTION – From five nominations, Mr R Armstrong was elected the new chairman of Wheatley Hill Workmen's Club in the half-yearly ballot at the week-end. He succeeds Mr W Henderson, who has retired from the position. Mr B Aitken was re-elected secretary. Mr J Maddison was also re-elected treasurer, and Mr T Wilson was re-elected doorman. From 36 nominations, Messrs J Henderson, J Stark, R Carr, A Poole, M Bailes and J Fishwick were elected to the committee.
18 January 1963

MINERS WARNED: CLEAR YOUR COAL

Miners in South-East Durham are being warned that if they leave loads of coals lying on the roads or pavements outside their homes that they may be liable to prosecution by the police.

Mr L C Timms, Area General Manager for No 3 Area NCB, is now sending a final notice to all Coal Board employees who are supplied with coal and with each load now delivered goes the following message:

"I wrote to you last year pointing out the many cases in the district of loads of coal being left out overnight, sometimes for a number of days, and that the police were likely to take action against future offenders.

Accidents

"Since then there have been two accidents in which motor-cyclists and pillion riders have been injured through having collided with loads of coal left out after dark. I was recently informed by the Divisional Police Superintendent that the position can be tolerated no longer. People who do not remove coal promptly in the future will be prosecuted.

"I hope that in your case this warning is unnecessary, but you will appreciate my concern. Everyone who has coal tipped at his home understands quite clearly the consequences. If they do not remove it without delay they may well be prosecuted for causing an obstruction. Furthermore, they may find that they have caused an accident involving serious injuries."

DRAW – The quarterly safety draw held in the Working Men's Club for workmen who remained accident free at Thornley Colliery was attended by Mr R Kellett, No 3 Area Safety Officer, and Mr H Todd, colliery safety officer. The main prize of a £30 voucher was drawn for Mr B Gilday an apprentice fitter. Winners of £1 premium bonds were: underground, J Wilson, W Hammond, S Walton; surface, B Sunley and W Nicholson.

25 January 1963

DEPUTIES' DINNER – The colliery manager, Mr F Richardson, and his wife, and the undermanager, Mr Fred Simpson, and his sister, Miss E Simpson, were among the guests at the annual dinner-dance in Wheatley Hill Welfare Hall on Saturday night, organised by Wheatley Hill branch of the Durham County Colliery Deputies' Association. Coun R Watson, chairman of the branch, presided, and welcomed about 140 members, with their wives and friends, and after dinner Mr B Aitken was MC for dancing to music by Billy Pratt's Band. Arrangements were carried out by Mr J Henderson, secretary.

1 February 1963

FINE GESTURE BY WHEATLEY HILL SCOUTS

When she was a guest at the annual reunion social evening of the 2nd Wheatley Hill Group of Scouts, Miss Harding, Matron of Durham Hospital, thanked the Scouts for the kindly interest they had taken in the children's ward at the hospital since "adopting" it some years ago.

Then she had a further word of thanks when Group Scoutmaster Les Barker revealed that the Scouts were buying a record-player for the use of the Ward from the proceeds of carol singing at Christmas. Some of the money they raised by carol singing was also spent on sweets and gifts for the young patients during the festive season.

Sister Sutton, of the children's ward, was also a guest at the party, and other guests included the president of the Group, Dr A P Gray, and his wife; Mr F Richardson, manager of Wheatley Hill colliery, and his wife, and Mr Fred Simpson, colliery undermanager, and his sister, Miss E Simpson.

About 100 rovers, scouts and cubs were present and after supper they were entertained to a film show and a programme of games and competitions, with Group Scoutmaster Barker in charge. The supper was provided by the ladies' committee.

8 February 1963

CLUB BALLOT – In the recent ballot for officials and committee of Thornley Working men's Club, Mr F A Walker (chairman) was defeated by Mr W McCarroll who received 197 votes against 156. Mr Thomas Brown (secretary) was unopposed. Mr George W Walls (treasurer), who has held the position for 23 years, received 204 votes against his opponent, Mr W A Kirby, who received 145. For four positions on the committee there were 19 candidates. Those successful were: J Nicholson, 164; S Blakemore, 143; J Willans, 131; D Hardy, 114.

CULLEN IN BRILLIANT FORM

Maurice Cullen, the 25-year-old miner from Shotton, the chief contender for the British lightweight title, brought some of the real old-fashioned craft to town to whip Vic Andreeti (Hoxton) in a brilliant ten-round fight at the Royal Albert Hall.

There was an ovation for Cullen as he completed a most workmanlike job on Andreeti and turned smartly to the referee to have his arm raised as the bell ended the tenth round.

Andreeti turned away in disgust, not so much in disagreement with the verdict, which was perfectly fair, but at his own inability to pin down this Durham schemer for more than a few seconds at a time.

Undue Risk

Some people thought that Cullen, who is due to fight Dave Charnley for the British title, was taking an undue risk in getting mixed up with Andreeti, the No 2 contender, on his own home ground.

But after two tentative rounds, Cullen left no one in the slightest doubt as to his ability to deal with the up-and-coming Londoner. He used sheer speed of foot and almost a sleight of hand to overcome Andreeti, who fell further and further behind as Cullen stepped up the pace in the middle rounds.

In one round alone, the sixth, he threw left hands at Andreeti's face at a rate of one every three seconds, and most of them found a mark. Spirit and determination brought the solid little Londoner back in the fight in the ninth round, but Cullen was on top again in the tenth, and his win was a most impressive one.

15 February 1963

DOYEN OF NEWSAGENTS DIES AT WHEATLEY HILL
Mr John Hodgson gave long service to Federation

A well-known figure in newsagency circles throughout the North-East and especially in the Wheatley Hill area where he had been in business most of his life, Mr John Hodgson, of 10 Granville Terrace, Wheatley Hill, died suddenly at his home last Friday. Mr Hodgson, who was 74, had been actively associated with the National Federation of Retail Newsagents for about half a century – until he resigned four years ago he was secretary of the Durham branch for 38 years.

This long record of service was thought to be a national record and when Mr Hodgson resigned he received a warm letter of appreciation of his work from the national secretary, who wrote: "It is the enthusiastic endeavour on the part of many hundreds of newsagents like your good self which has helped to make the Federation like it is today."

Mr Hodgson served on the North-East District Council, covering an area from Berwick to Whitby, for many years, and he also served on the District Executive. For about ten years he was a member of the National Council of the Federation and during this time was one of the four members elected to serve on the Shropshire Convalescent Home Committee.

A Delivery Boy

Mr Hodgson, who had been in the newsagency business all his life – he started as a delivery boy for a Haswell newsagent, Mr M D Laws, when he was only 12 years of age – took an active part in his own business right up to his death.

Last Thursday night, only a few hours before he was taken suddenly ill and died, he was busy in his shop. "He was folding the Durham Chronicles and arranging them for delivery the following morning," his only son Robert told our reporter, "and seemed to be in his usual health. It was shortly afterwards, during the night, that he was taken ill."

When Mr Hodgson began work as a newspaper lad delivering the papers to a scattered area around Haswell it was a full-time job and he was paid 4s a week. Not only did he deliver newspapers in Haswell, but also in many of the surrounding villages.

Made Many Friends

He made many friends in the area and demonstrated his interest in the newsagency business so strongly that he quickly made progress and as a young man became manager for his employer, but his career was interrupted by the war.

In 1916 Mr Hodgson enlisted in the 2nd DLI and it was shortly after this that his wife opened a newsagent's business in Wheatley Hill and carried on with the work until her husband was demobilised.

Founder Member of Durham Branch

On leaving the Army at the end of hostilities Mr Hodgson returned to his own business and had his shop in the main street of Wheatley Hill ever since. Mr Hodgson was a founder-member of the Durham branch of the Newsagents' Federation and his wife was a founder-member of the Houghton branch, which eventually merged with the Durham branch.

When he first established his business in Wheatley Hill, Mr Hodgson used to recall, a daily newspaper cost only a halfpenny – a sixth of today's price. And the price of the Durham Chronicle was a penny – a quarter of today's price.

Changed Reading Habits

The reading habits of the public had changed considerably since his younger days – and, handling so many newspapers and magazines as Mr Hodgson did, he had adequate proof of this.

In the olden days, Mr Hodgson was fond of recalling, it was rarely indeed that a household took more than one newspaper and only a fraction of the magazines on sale to the public today were available then. Women's magazines especially were in the minority half a century ago.

Mr Hodgson and his wife, who survives him with his son, celebrated their golden wedding two years ago. His son has a garage business in Wheatley Hill.

Although Mr Hodgson resigned as Durham branch secretary of the Newsagents' Federation four years ago, he still continued to take an active interest in the work of the Federation, as a district organiser and District Council representative.

Following a service in All Saints' Church, Wheatley Hill, on Tuesday, conducted by the Rev G G Graham (Vicar of Wheatley Hill), Mr Hodgson was cremated at Durham.

NEW MANAGER AT THORNLEY

A social evening to mark the departure from Thornley Colliery of Mr Arthur Welsh, jun, manager of the colliery, and father of Miss Charmian Welsh, former Olympic diving champion, was held in Thornley Officials' Club on Saturday.

Gift for all the family was presented to Mr. A. Welsh, manager of Thornley Colliery, when he retired after 26 years at the colliery. Mr. E. Carter (left), made the presentation and looking on is the Welsh family.—(D A)

Presiding over a meeting of all underground and surface men, Mr Jack Carr, overman and local chairman of the Colliery Officials' Union, presented to Mr and Mrs Welsh, a record player, case of cutlery and a brandy bowl. He spoke of Mr Welsh's popularity with all employees.

Mr T Mackay, former undermanager at Thornley, and now manager at Ryhope Colliery, said that not every manager could have handled so wisely labour relations during the immediate post-nationalisation period nor maintained production under difficult geological conditions.

Mr Jim Hedley, local Deputies' Association secretary and chairman of the club, presented to Mr and Mrs Welsh a wallet and notes and hoped that they would continue to visit Thornley.

Mr Welsh, accepting the presents, said that he regretted leaving Thornley. He had lived in the village 33 years and for 25 years had been undermanager and manager at the colliery. He was now on specialist duties with NCB Area HQ at Castle Eden, and would shortly take up residence at West Hartlepool. Mr W S Hutton, formerly Sherburn Hill Colliery manager, was now manager at Thornley. Mr Welsh felt sure that management and men would ensure the future of Thornley Colliery by teamwork.

22 February 1963

FIREMEN'S SUCCESS – Wheatley Hill retained unit of the Durham County Fire Brigade, who have won the national retained firemen's "quiz" twice in the last six years – the last time was in 1961 – made a good start in this year's competition when they won the county quiz at the county Brigade headquarters at Framwellgate Moor. Three teams took part – Wheatley Hill, Bishop Auckland and Birtley. The Wheatley Hill team was captained by Sub-Officer H F Horner, and the other members were Firemen A Appleby, L Barker and R Woodward, with Fireman T W Ayre reserve. Wheatley Hill will now compete against the winners of the North Riding of Yorkshire and Northumberland competitions in the regional final at Durham on 8 March.

1 March 1963

CULLEN TO FIGHT FOR TITLE

Maurice Cullen, the Shotton lightweight boxer, and leading contender for the British title, will have his chance at Belle Vue, Manchester, on 22 April, when the longed for meeting between him and the champion Dave Charnley, takes place. The British Boxing Board of Control has accepted the purse offer of Harry Levene and for Charnley it will be a return to the same ring in which he brilliantly knocked out former world title holder Joe Brown last week.

Both boxers are on top of their form. Last month Cullen gave a brilliant display to whip Vic Andreeti of Hoxton, the tough Londoner and No 2 contender, at the Royal Albert Hall. In this ten round fight Cullen used his famous left and speed of footwork to outpoint Andreeti with a dazzling display.

Charnley won the British title as far back as 1957 and has only made one defence and that ended in a 40 seconds knock-out of Darkie Hughes in 1961.

Mr Levene, in announcing the date and venue for the fight, said he felt that this was a fight for the North of England. Even allowing for Charnley's magnificent win over Brown, this contest was going to be a tough one for him. Cullen, he said, probably has the finest left hand in Britain, and he will certainly give Charnley a busy night.

THORNLEY AND SHOTTON CARRY OFF CUPS: BLACKHALL SECOND

"If you have a happy wife you have a happy family and if you have a happy family, then you have a happy pit!" declared Mr J C Robinson, agent to the Durham Area, NUM, when, at a supper-dance in Blackhall Welfare Hall on Monday night, he added his congratulations to Thornley and Shotton collieries, winners of the two principal trophies in the annual No 3 Area (South East Durham) Coal Board safety campaign.

It was because of happy relationships, said Mr Robinson, that he believed that Thornley and Shotton were consistently at the top of the safety competitions. "They must breed happy people at these two pits," he said.

Thornley have won the shield and certificate for the lowest accident rate among the eight collieries in the area every year since the safety competition was introduced five years ago, and they were warmly congratulated on their fine achievement when the shield was presented by Mr R Hughes, secretary of the miners' lodge, by Mr H R Warburton, Staff Director to the Durham Divisional Coal Board.

Blackhall runners-up – A cup and certificate were also presented by Mr Warburton to Mr W R Donaghue, manager of Shotton Colliery, which won the section for the best improvement where accident figures were concerned last year. Blackhall colliery were runners-up in both sections and were presented with certificates – the manager, Mr Walter Everett, received the lowest accident rate certificate on behalf of the colliery, and the miners' lodge secretary, Mr Jack Wilson, the other certificate.
8 March 1963

MINER WAS SAVED FROM DROWNING BY TEENAGER

The mystery of the girl who saved a life and then disappeared was cleared up on Sunday when a Durham miner met 16-year-old Helena Bowes of Ludworth Village.

The miner, 62-year-old Mr Richard Cayslaw, of Annand Road, Durham, has called her "the bravest girl I have ever known" because Helena kept his head above water and saved his life when he fell into a swollen stream and nearly drowned.

Mr Cayslaw was on his way to work at Thornley Colliery but the bus taking him there was stopped by flooding. He decided to cut across some fields through which a swollen stream ran. But he slipped, over-balanced and fell into the water. "I must have been standing too near the edge," he said.

Helena, who had got off the same bus, turned to find Mr Cayslaw in difficulties. "He began to sink into the snow and finally all I could see was his arm waving above his head."

She ran to him, threw herself on the ground and grabbed Mr Cayslaw, at the same time shouting for help. Two boys came to her aid and later Durham County Council men working on flood damage got Mr Cayslaw out of the water.

"They came just in time because I heard Mr Cayslaw say he could not hold on much longer, and neither could I," said Helena.

"If the girl had let go I would have been swept away in the strong current. What a brave girl she was. I will never forget what happened and what she did to save me, said Mr Cayslaw.

THE "THING" AT THORNLEY
Family Frightened by "Floating Shape"

For years a Thornley man was "rather sceptical about a floating shape" which his wife and other members of his family had said they had either seen or felt themselves … then one day he was in the passage of his five-roomed council house when he saw "the thing" himself.

"It was about half-past six in the morning," Mr John Moody, of 34 Hillsyde Crescent, told our reporter this week. "Something black of a shape I can hardly describe confronted me. I saw it distinctly and then it vanished. Before this I had ridiculed the idea of a spirit, but I haven't since."

The "thing" has haunted the Thornley household of five, Mr Moody and his wife, Evelyn, and their three daughters, the youngest of whom is 18, since they first moved into the house, a prefabricated two-storeyed semi-detached, when it was built about 16 years ago. It was so frightening, said Mrs Moody, who seems to have seen more of it than anyone else, that she has felt quite ill about it and has had to receive medical attention.

"Once I was in the bedroom with my sister when we knew at once it was there," said Joyce. "We got out of the room straightaway. It seemed to take every bit of our will-power to get out, even with all the lights on. It is overpowering and very strong when you first realise it is there."

At times it was like a "black shirt floating past you," said Mrs Moody. She added, "It hasn't harmed us, but it has certainly scared us stiff." Sometimes it appeared to be suspended in mid-air. The last time she had actually seen the "thing" was about Christmas time, said Mrs Moody, but she had felt its presence about a fortnight ago. Her terrier was in the kitchen with her on one occasion when this "black shape" appeared, said Mrs Moody. The dog pricked up its ears and looked up. "But the dog did not seem to be affected by it and did not even bark," she added.

Vicar Said Prayer

"It is a terrible sensation when it is there," she said. "When you can't see it, you can feel it, and that is just as bad. I think I must have lost about three stone with the worry of it all."

Recently the Vicar of Thornley, the Rev P J Mold, was called to the house. He said a prayer. "Since then we have felt a little more settled," said Mrs Moody. "We are all hoping we have seen the last of it. It has you a bundle of nerves."

Two of the couple's daughters, Elizabeth, the youngest, and Joyce, the eldest, live at home. The other daughter, Gladys, is married and lives away. Elizabeth has seen the "thing" as well as her parents, and so has her brother-in-law and her boy friend.

"I haven't actually seen it," said Joyce, "but I have felt its presence many a time. It is all very horrible. I used to think it was only a vivid imagination, but when so many of us have either seen or felt it, this cannot be so. It is difficult to describe it but when it makes its visitation you know it is there. Its power seems to reach a peak and then fade away."

The "thing" has visited the house at all times of the day and night.

Awful Sensation

Sometimes the "thing" disappeared for months on end. "I could never have believed it possible there could be anything happening like this," said Mrs Moody. "We went into this house when it was new and I thought a ghost was completely out of the question. But then I saw it for the first time and I felt as if I was just going to die. It was an awful sensation. It would be the happiest day of my life if I knew it had gone forever."

Mr Moody is employed as a medical room attendant at East Hetton Colliery. Asked if he had any intention of moving from the house, he said, "No, we will stick it out. If we moved into another house, it would probably just follow us there. We are not moving."

Quite a number of villagers have heard about the ghost, poltergeist, departed spirit ... or whatever it is. "They have given it all sorts of names," said Joyce. "Some call it Oliver Cromwell. But, believe me, it's no joke."

ON THEIR WAY TO AUSTRALIA
New life for Thornley man and family

For the second time since he left school a former Thornley mineworker is seeking "pastures new" where employment is concerned. This time, however, he is going much further than the 250 miles which took him to London 13 years ago. He is, in fact, off to Australia.

"I never regretted giving up my job as an underground haulage engineman at Thornley colliery to go to London in 1950," the emigrant, Mr Dennis Liddell, told our reporter at the weekend the home of his parents, Mr and Mrs G A Liddell, 20 Shinwell Crescent, Thornley.

With his wife Betty and two-year-old daughter Jacqueline, Mr Liddell spent ten days of his last fortnight in this country with his parents. When he first left Thornley to "try his luck" in the South, said Mr Liddell, it was the best move he ever made. "But, mind you, I went to London prepared to work hard and do my best to further my education," he said.

Photographic Technician

Mr Liddell took up employment in London as a photographic technician with Kodak Ltd, then later became a micro-film operator with the North-West Metropolitan Regional Hospital Board. This work consisted of photographing old records on micro-film and in the course of his duties Mr Liddell visited hospitals within an 80-mile radius of his home.

Later he went back to Kodak and it is with this firm he hopes to get employment when he reaches Melbourne. "There is nothing settled but I feel sure, with the references and introductions given to me from London, I will not be long in getting fixed up with a job," he said.

Mr Liddell is going to Australia with the same determined spirit to make good as when he left Thornley for London. "My wife and I are both prepared to make a 'go' of it," he said, "and I will be quite happy if I fare as well there as I did in the south."

Mr Liddell was married ten years ago – his wife is a Londoner – and the couple have had their own home at Rickmansworth.

Relatives to Follow

Quite a number of their friends from the London area have already emigrated to Australia. "We have had a lot of letters from them and they all speak highly of the country and its prospects," said Mr Liddell.

More friends are following the Liddells to Australia, and in three months' time Mrs Liddell's sister Lesley and her husband David and their two children are also going there under the Government-assisted emigration scheme.

Mrs Liddell said her sister and family had just been told they had passed their medical. "That has made me feel much happier about going out, knowing it won't be long before they will be with us," she added. Her brother-in-law is a builder. When he gets to Australia he is hoping to build houses for both families.

Mrs Liddell is a qualified shorthand teacher – she was formerly an office worker – and has been teaching at evening classes in London four nights a week. She is hoping to do similar work in Australia. Her father lives in Wembley, but her mother died four years ago.

Mr Liddell was born at Thornley and started work at the colliery there when he left school at 14. He looks upon the trip to Australia as a "real adventure". "It is a young country with plenty of opportunities for young people – in this country, I am afraid you are all too often thought too old at 40!" were Mr Liddell's parting words.

22 March 1963

WHEATLEY HILL FATHER AND DAUGHTER

With the election of Mrs R W Carr as the new secretary of Wheatley Hill Women's Section of the Labour Party, father and daughter now hold the same position in the Party in the village, for Mrs Carr's father, Coun E Cain, who is a deputy chairman of Castle Eden magistrates, was recently re-elected secretary of the local Ward Labour Party at its annual meeting.

Mrs Carr has been elected secretary in place of Mrs Thackeray, who has resigned for domestic reasons. Other officers elected by the women's section at the annual meeting were:- Chairman, Mrs J Johnson; vice-chairman, Mrs R Watson; assistant secretary, Mrs E Bradley; literature secretary, Mrs J Pringle; Easington Women's Federation delegate, Mrs B Bowes; Easington Divisional Executive delegate, Mrs R Watson; auditors, Mrs Golightly and Mrs R Dunn.

Mrs J Dodds is to be delegate to the Labour women's national conference at Porthcawl on Monday. Today the section is organising a house-to-house collection in Wheatley Hill in aid of the Freedom from Hunger Campaign.

Other officers elected by the Wheatley Hill Ward Labour Party are:- Chairman, Coun John Andrew; treasurer, Coun A D Wharrier; delegate, Coun J Andrew; auditors, Messrs M Forster and N Cook.

29 March 1963

WHEATLEY HILL TURN TABLES AT HOUGHTON

Wheatley Hill Workmen's Club, beaten 4-1 at home by Houghton Social Club in the early part of the season, obtained their revenge when they visited Houghton on Saturday and won by four clear goals.

Although worthy of their success, the "Hill" were flattered by the margin of their win, for Houghton missed several good chances, and in the second half were without their scheming inside right, Goodhall, who retired with a foot injury.

Cowan opened the scoring and Purvis increased the lead before half-time, when Williams, the home 'keeper, failed to hold the ball and it rolled across the line. Houghton hotly disputed the referee's decision, claiming that the ball had not entered the net. The same two players scored in the second half, in which Houghton, with only ten men, were equal to their opponents. But the reluctance of the forwards to shoot when within range, cost them goals.

RETIREMENT OF POULAR WHEATLEY HILL OFFICIAL

Wheatley Hill Colliery's popular under-manager, Mr Fred Simpson, who retired at the weekend after a mining career of more than half a century, is shortly moving from Wheatley Hill, where he has lived since he was a boy.

But he is going only about a mile away – to Durham Road, Wingate – and from his front window he will still be able to see the colliery where he has seen so many changes during his long career.

"It is something of a wrench to leave the colliery after all those years, but I am not going far and will still be able to keep in touch with my many friends in Wheatley Hill," Mr Simpson, who will be 65 in August, told our reporter on Wednesday.

Mr Simpson, a bachelor, lives with his sister, Miss Ella Simpson, and younger brother, Sidney, who is also a bachelor, at West House, Wheatley Hill. All three will still be together when the move is made to the neighbouring village of Wingate.

Started Work at 14

Born at Haswell, Mr Simpson moved with his family to Wheatley Hill as a boy of seven and began work when he was 14 at Wheatley Hill colliery as a trapper-boy, earning 1s.4d. an eight-hour shift.

At that time, he recalled, about 1,400 men and boys were employed there and they were producing about 12,500 tons of coal a week. Just after the last war about 1,200 were working at the colliery, but there have been two redundancy schemes since then and now manpower has run down to about 800 and the weekly target is 6,000 tons.

Mr Simpson, whose father was an official at the same colliery, went through all the various grades of mining and eventually became a deputy. About three years later – in 1927 – he was appointed a fore-overman and filled this position until being promoted under-manager 25 years ago.

The first manager he served under was Mr J A Simpson (no relation) and since then he has served under three other colliery managers.

Mr Simpson holds a highly esteemed place among the affections of the people of Wheatley Hill, where he has spent such a great part of his life and been actively associated with so many organisations.

He has served on Wheatley Hill Colliery Welfare Committee since its inception in 1927 and is also a trustee, and has also had a long association with the colliery consultative committee – formerly the pit production committee.

He is president of Wheatley Hill Discharged and Demobilised Soldiers' and Sailors' Club and of Wheatley Hill Boy Scouts' Association, and is a vice-present of the local Cricket Club.

Awarded MBE

For 28 years Mr Simpson has been a member of Castle Eden Golf Club and is one of the trustees there. In 1957 he was awarded the MBE for his services to the village in which he lives and his service with the National Coal Board, and travelled to London with his sister to have the honour conferred upon him.

His sister, like Mr Simpson, is a well-known and esteemed figure in Wheatley Hill. She is a loyal member of All Saints' Church and is also associated with the Women's Institute.

Now that he is retired, says Mr Simpson, he will have more time to devote to gardening, one of his favourite pastimes. "The house where I am moving to has quite a big garden and a greenhouse, and so I will find plenty to occupy my time," he added. "I will also be only a short distance from the Golf Club."

In Wheatley Hill Welfare Hall tomorrow night Mr Simpson, at a dinner-dance, is to receive a presentation from all sections of workmen and officials at the local colliery. About 150 are expected to attend the function.

5 April 1963

WHEATLEY HILL PREACHER'S "JUBILEE"

Mr Peter Cairns, sen, 58 Luke Terrace, Wheatley Hill, now 71, has just completed 50 years as a local preacher on Thornley Methodist Circuit plan. It is not simply a case of a man having his name on the plan. He has really taken appointments for half a century.

Mr Cairns told our correspondent, "I was converted in a mission at the Wheatley Hill Church Street Methodist Church which was conducted by the late John Bell, William Bell and John Huggins of Haswell. I soon felt an urge to preach and trained under two old stalwarts of the Thornley Circuit, the late Mr James Wick and Mr Tom Brandling. I was accepted on to Full Plan in 1913."

Born at Sherburn Hill, Mr Cairns moved to Wheatley Hill 61 years ago. He has been a member of Patton Street Methodist Church for 58 years. During that time he has served the church in a number of ways. For 40 years he has been a trustee, and for the last 12 years he has been society steward. He was also a Sunday School teacher and for many years a leader of the church.

As a preacher Mr Cairns has seen the Thornley circuit reformed or re-organised three times. He said, "Preaching, both ministerial and lay, has altered during the last 50 years. In my younger days it was more evangelical in character.

"One great difference between then and now was that preachers expected to get converts. Indeed they were disappointed if they didn't. An appeal was made for decisions at the end of every Sunday evening service."

Mr Cairns worked for 31 years at Wheatley Hill Colliery as a surface worker. He spent 20 years in the employment of Durham County Council as a road lengthsman.

In the 1914-18 war he served with the Royal Army Service Corps. He took a great interest in the Co-operative Movement and for 20 years was president of Sherburn Hill Co-operative Society. During his term of office the society made rapid headway.

Mr and Mrs Cairns have two sons.

WHEATLEY HILL FIREMEN IN QUIZ FINAL

As a result of collecting top marks in the Northern semi-final of the quiz on fire topics organised among part-time firemen throughout the country, Wheatley Hill retained unit of the Durham County Fire Brigade have reached the final for the third time. And when they take part in the final - at Dorking Fire Services' Club on 27 April – they hope to make it a hat-trick of successes, for they were national champions in 1956 and 1961.

Four teams took part in the semi-final, held at Barnsley Fire Brigade Headquarters, and the two top ones, Wheatley Hill and the Bridge of Alan, Scotland, qualified for the final. They will meet the two top teams of the Southern section in the final.

Wheatley Hill were awarded 40 points out of a possible 45 - 4½ more than Bridge of Alan. The Wheatley Hill team was captained by Sub-Officer H F Horner and the other members were Leading Fireman P E Whinn and Fireman L Barker, A Appleby and R Woodward.

PRESENTATION TO RETIRING WHEATLEY HILL COLLIERY UNDER-MANAGER

Many tributes to his loyal service at Wheatley Hill Colliery, where he had spent the whole of his mining career of nearly 50 years, were paid on Saturday night to Mr Fred Simpson, under-manager for the past 25 years, when he was guest of honour at a dinner dance in the Welfare Hall, Wheatley Hill, organised by the colliery officials, shot-firers and deputies.

"Rarely in one man do you find a combination of wit, tact, ability, human understanding and the driving urge for efficiency as we have always found in Mr Simpson," eulogised Mr C R Knaggs, the group agent, who was among the guests.

The function was attended by about 150 officials, and retired officials and their wives and a number of colliery managers formerly associated with Mr Simpson, whose retirement was reported in last week's Durham Chronicle.

So highly esteemed was Mr Simpson, said Coun Ralph Watson, chairman of Wheatley Hill branch of the Durham County Colliery Deputies' Association, that they could have filled a hall three times the size with people who wanted to come to pay him honour. But the numbers, unfortunately, had to be restricted because of lack of accommodation.

Presentation to Mr F Simpson, Undermanager
Back L-R: Tommy Chapman, Billy Vincent, ?, Billy Smart, ?, Anty Worthington, Jack Amies, Hughie Wilson, Jack Kelsey
Front L-R: Billy Carr, Dick Story,Alfie Martin, Ralph Watson, Alf Watson, Billy Walker, Fred Simpson, J Linsey, Mr Million, F Richardson (Colliery Manager), Billy Burnip, Jimmy Beresford, Alf Watson

Unique Occasion

It was a unique occasion because of the unique record of Mr Simpson at the colliery – a record which would take some beating, said Coun Watson. "We all know Mr Simpson, not only as an under-manager but as a friend. He knows all of us here – he has trained us and helped us – and the majority of our fathers also worked under him."

Mr Simpson knew every man and boy who worked at the colliery, said Coun Watson – he was very considerate to them all. He knew their individual strength and capabilities, and many times had been "a read friend indeed".

Mr Simpson had played a big part in social and welfare work in the village, the chairman added, and they were particularly proud of his work for the Scout movement – he had been a trustee of the movement at Wheatley Hill since its inception more than 30 years ago.

In making a presentation to Mr Simpson of a gold wrist watch and bracelet and a transistor radio, on behalf of the officials, shot-firers and deputies, the colliery manager, Mr F Richardson, also paid a warm tribute to his excellent service.

Mr Richardson has been manager for eight years. Throughout that time, he said he had always found Mr Simpson to be an excellent official and one whose character and ability were unsurpassed. He had been a real friend to everyone and his work in the village would never be forgotten.

Fifty Years' Service

Mr Richardson also presented Mr Simpson with a long- service staff certificate from the Durham Division of the National Coal Board recording the under-manager's 50 years' service to the mining industry.

Mr Knaggs said he had had nothing else but loyal service and co-operation from Mr Simpson during his long association with him. "And there has never been a wrong word between us," he said.

In 1950, said Mr Knaggs, the life of the colliery was said to be no more than four to five years, but they had managed to keep it going, and while it was a very tough fight there was "every possibility of some more years yet" for the colliery. Mr Simpson could claim no small part in the continuation of the life of the colliery.

Throughout his career, said Mr Simpson, in expressing thanks for the gifts, he had been greatly helped and encouraged by an excellent staff of officials and deputies - some had worked with him throughout his 25 years as under-manage, and some even longer. He had served under four managers and two group managers and was pleased to say he could always count on the friendship of every one of them.

THE STRANGE STORY OF THORNLEY COLLIERY OFFICIALS' CLUB

Thornley Colliery Officials' Club had failed to register their club within the specified time allowed under the Licensing Act of 1961, Castle Eden magistrates heard on Tuesday, but, said Mr A N Levinson, appearing for the club, "by some freak of circumstances" this fact did not emerge until Wednesday 3 April.

On that date police visited the secretary and told him the club should be closed as it had no authority whatever to be open. The club had since remained closed.

Mr Levinson, who was applying for an occasional licence for Mr William Dawson, licensee of the Railway Tavern, Thornley, to supply intoxicating liquor to the club for Easter weekend from Good Friday to Easter Monday, said the application was being made until the transfer sessions on 23 April when the club could apply for registration. It was a "most unusual application," Mr Levinson admitted.

Mr Levinson also applied for an occasional licence for each weekend until the transfer sessions.

Holiday Weekend Application Granted

After a brief retirement the application was granted for Easter weekend only, from 7.00 to 10.30 pm. Applications for the other weekends would have to be made as they were needed, said the chairman, Coun E Cain.

Apparently, Mr Levinson told the court, the former club secretary had no knowledge of the requirement to apply for a registration certificate for the club under the 1961 Licensing Act.

In the normal course of his duties the new secretary, Mr Dove, lodged his annual return with the Clerk to the Justices on 10 January this year. Nothing further was heard about this until the police visited him almost three months later when they learned that the club had failed to comply with the requirements of the 1961 Act.

Since the police visit last Wednesday, the club had been closed, said Mr Levinson, and the applications before the court that day were for occasional licences for special social occasions.

Arrangements had now been made to put the "club's house in order," said Mr Levinson. The club had held a special meeting and the appropriate forms were now being filled in to apply for registration under the Act.

The members of the club were anxious to keep together until the registration was put right, said Mr Levinson, and that was why they were applying for these occasional licences.

After the court hearing, the club secretary, Mr Albert William Dove, of 16 High Street, Thornley, told our reporter he had succeeded Mr George Bennett as secretary on 5 January. He had no idea, he said, that the club was not properly registered and, as instructed, shortly after taking over as secretary, lodged his annual return with the Clerk to the Justices.

"Flabbergasted"

It was not until last Wednesday, said Mr Dove, who is an overman at Thornley colliery, that he was told the club was not registered. Police called at his home in the afternoon while he was in bed.

"I was flabbergasted when they told me the position," said Mr Dove. He immediately went down to the club and acquainted his fellow officials and members with what had happened. The club did not open that night and it had been shut down since.

Somebody had evidently "slipped up somewhere," said Mr Dove, but now that they were aware of the position they were taking immediate steps to put it right. A general meeting of the members had been held and the position fully explained to them and rules were now being drawn up and an application made for registration.

"In the meantime," said Mr Dove, "we are applying for these occasional licences so that we can keep together at weekends until the club is on a proper legal footing again."

The club was opened just over two years ago. It has a membership of about 300, including 40 retired officials.

12 April 1963

THORNLEY CLUB INSTITUTE'S LEAGUE TEAMS

Thornley visited Pallion, Sunderland, on Saturday seeking to avenge a 6-1 defeat and within five minutes looked like doing just that. In the first minute Harry Morton slipped the ball past the home goalie and four minutes later E Porter crashed a 25-yard rocket into the Pallion net to make the score 2-0.

Unfortunately for Thornley, Pallion's outside left came through after an alleged handling offence and scored a hotly disputed goal. The same player equalised before half-time.

After the interval the game developed into a stern struggle for supremacy and Pallion's tenacity triumphed over Thornley's weekened defence.

Although unlucky not to win, Thornley nevertheless maintained their improvement shown in recent weeks and would probably have gained a point if they had not had to field two reserves.

Dickie Day, who will be remembered for his sterling work for former Thornley soccer teams, has now taken over the position of games secretary at Thornley club and his keenness will no doubt have its effect.

The team to entertain Houghton Glendale next Saturday is Billy Williamson, Johnny Morton, Bob Adams, Ken Hillom, Doug Wetherall, George Soulsby, Laurie Morton, Billy Luke, Ernie Porter, Harry Morton and Tom Dent.

The darts team, comprising of Bob Appleby, Tom Dent, Alf Steel and John Morton won by 709 and look set to carry off the league trophy.

The domino team drew their match 17 all.

WHEATLEY HILL REWARD FOR SAFETY

When the combined draw among accident-free miners at Wheatley Hill and Wingate Grange collieries was held in Wheatley Hill Workmen's Club on Friday night, the first prize of a weekend in London for two people, with all expenses paid, was won by a 20-year-old pony putter, Fred Errington, of 6 Cemetery Road, Wheatley Hill. The prize is valued at £30. More than 700 names went into the draw, including, for the last time, a number from Wingate colliery, where salvage work, following the closure of the colliery last year, is now nearly complete. Mr Errington also won a £1 Premium Bond and other Bond winners, all from Wheatley Hill colliery, were Messrs C Maughan, J M Craggs, R Thompson, A V Buxton and R Hindle. Mr F Richardson, colliery manager, who was introduced by Mr R Armstrong, chairman of the club, presided at the draw. There had been a slight increase in the number of accidents last quarter, said Mr Richardson, and he appealed to miners to take "just that little but extra care" where their own safety and that of others was concerned.

NO LICENCE FOR THORNLEY OFFICIALS' CLUB

Not until 3 April had it been brought to the notice of Thornley Colliery Officials' Club that it was not registered under the 1961 Licensing Act and as a result the club had since been closed, except for Easter week-end, Mr A N Levinson said at Castle Eden court on Tuesday.

Mr Levinson, who was applying for an occasional licence on behalf of Mr William Dawson, licensee of Railway Tavern, Thornley, to supply the club with liquor this week-end – Friday, Saturday and Sunday – said the application was being made to enable the members of the club to keep together socially until their club was properly registered. After a lengthy retirement the magistrates turned down the application.

The club, unfortunately, had not been registered under the new Act, said Mr Levinson and could not carry on without a licence. It had shut down when information was received three weeks ago it was not registered, but an occasional licence for Easter week-end had been granted by the magistrates and so the club had been able to open that week-end.

In January this year, said Mr Levinson, the new club secretary had sent off his annual returns relating to the club, but it was not until 3 April that he was informed that the club, in fact, was not registered and that he would have to apply for a Certificate of Registration.

This application had now been made, said Mr Levinson, and would be heard after 28 days had been allowed for possible objections.

26 April 1963

WHEATLEY HILL CW AIDS NEW YOUTH CLUB

A new youth club formed at Wheatley Hill for young people from the village and surrounding area has got off to an enthusiastic start and to ease its finances in the early stages Wheatley Hill Colliery Welfare Committee have granted the club the use of their tea-room attached to the Welfare Hall for their three nights a week meetings at only a nominal cost.

"We feel there is plenty of scope for such a club for the youth of the area and we are only too happy to help them along," a Welfare official told our reporter.

The Welfare committee are also allowing the new club the use of an old tennis hut which has fallen into disrepair. Windows have been broken and the woodwork damaged but the members of the club plan to renovate and repair it themselves and eventually use it for some of their activities.

How They Meet

The junior section of the club for boys and girls between 11 and 13 meets on Thursday evening from 6.30 to 9.00, and the seniors, those from 14 to 20, meet on Tuesday and Wednesday evenings from 6.30 to 9.30. Junior membership costs 1s and senior, 2s 6d.

This week there was ample evidence of a lively, go-ahead club in the attractive posters on the notice-board. They gave details of a bus outing to the swimming baths at Seaton Carew and threw out a suggestion that teenagers able to play a guitar might be interested in forming a club.

There were also notices about dancing, keep-fit classes and PT, and a list of rules, none of them harsh, showed that the club meant to run on a sound business-like footing.

Members' Committee

There is an adult management committee controlling the club but it also had its own members' committee, who will help to organise various activities and assist in the general running of the club.

The management committee is:- Chairman, County Coun John Andrew; vice-chairman, R G Burnside; secretary, Mr Frank Dunn; treasurer, Mrs V Hodgson; committee, Messrs J Gair, L Gair, R Peacock, T Cowie and A Barker and Mesdames R Peacock, Powell, J N Gare, N Cain, Foster and Burnside.

Joyce Hubbard is chairman of the members' committee, with John Knowles vice-chairman, J Gair secretary and Judith Hodgson treasurer. The committee consists of L Holcroft, G Barker, S Goddam, G Curry, B Armstrong, J Buxton, M Powell and G Gilmore.

The club is to be known as the Wheatley Hill and District Youth Club. There is a well-stocked coffee bar and this will be open for refreshments every club night.

THORNLEY TO BE RID OF 79 HOUSES UNDER SLUM CLEARANCE –
Seventy-nine houses in Thornley are to be pulled down under slum clearance.

The houses are in Nelson Street, Queen Street, Chapel Street, Vine Street, John Street, Martins Buildings, and part of Bow Street. The majority, but not all of the houses in these streets, will be demolished.

The occupants of these houses will be re-housed in Council houses to be built in Thornley. Recently, the deputy clerk of Easington Rural District Council said that the Council had acquired land on which to build new houses, and was likely to start building this year. Re-housing would start next year.
3 May 1963

LUDWORTH BRIDGE HIT BY VANDALS – Mr Thornton presided at the meeting of Shadforth Parish Council held at Ludworth. Arising out of the minutes was the matter of repairs to the footbridge crossing the Ludworth Golf Links. It was reported that since last meeting the bridge had been damaged by vandals so as to be almost beyond repair. The clerk, Mr W N Reay, was directed to ask the surveyor of the Durham Rural District to supply an estimate of the cost to build a new bridge.

THORNLEY – APPRECIATION – Mr Raymond Atherton, Hartlepool Street, Thornley, while working as a caunch-worker at the Tilley sharer face underground at Thornley Colliery injured his wrist when stone fell from the roof. Rapidly losing blood and having no first aid knowledge, Mr Atherton was relieved when Mr William Lee arrived on the scene to locate the pressure point and apply a constrictive bandage to arrest the bleeding, the "bandage" being a neck scarf. Recounting this incident at his Union meeting, Mr Atherton wished his appreciation of Mr Lee's prompt action to be placed on record. Mr Jack Ellis, Thornley Colliery Medical Attendant, who is in charge of a first aid class attended by Mr Lee, has identified himself with this appreciation. This week, Mr Lee, of Brackendale Street, Shotton, will receive from Thornley Branch of the National Union of Mineworkers, a letter of commendation "for his efficient handling of the situation until the deputy-in-charge arrived".

1ST THORNLEY COMPANY of the Boys' Brigade gave a musical play and entertainment, Stranger in Paradise, in the Thornley Bow Street schoolroom. The superintendent minister, the Rev G Johnson, presided. The play was written by Mr Jim Plant, captain of the Brigade and a Trustee of Bow Street Church. The leading roles were excellently interpreted by L/Cpl Colin Davies, Pte Malcom Crisp, Pte Russell Wyatt, L/Cpl Joe Bennett, Staff Sgt Fred Thornton, Sgt William Crisp, Cpl Peter Wilkinson, L/Cpl Eric Dower, L/Cpl Lawrence Slater, Pte Eddie Cutter, Pte Malcolm Scott. Others were Ptes Dennis Wilson, Charles Gott, Leslie Thompson, Graham Walker, Ronald Thompson, Trevor Crisp and Stanley Williamson. The dance ensemble was trained by Miss Eilen Plant and the costumes were made by members of the Parents' Committee. The show was produced by Mrs O Lincoln with Lieut Kenneth Hetherington as musical director. Scenery was designed and painted by Mr A Shutt (Wheatley Hill) and Mr J Plant. Lighting effects were in the hands of the Rev G Johnson, Mr T Lincoln and Mr J Hedley.

WHEATLEY HILL – A fall of stone injured Joseph Holdcroft (52), 22 Institute Street, Wheatley Hill, last week. He was taken to the Durham County Hospital. He was later discharged.
10 May 1963

THORNLEY GOLDEN WEDDING: MINING DAYS RECALLED
Mr and Mrs Robert H Gott, of 36 Greenwood Cottages, Thornley's Aged Miners' Homes, celebrated their 50th wedding anniversary on Friday.

Married in St Bartholomew's Church in May1913, they have lived in Thornley ever since, their family consisting of three daughters, two sons and 18 grandchildren.

Apart from Mr Gott's poor eyesight, the couple enjoy good health and are "quite comfortable" after, as Mrs Gott cheerfully remarks, "two world wars and three major mining strikes".

Mr Gott, 80 next birthday, started work as a "helper-up" at Thornley Colliery six weeks before his 12th birthday in 1895. His first pay, for 106 hours fortnight, was 10s.5d. Retiring 53 years later, Mr Gott had served the local NUM Lodge for more than 30 consecutive years and as Parish Councillor for 15 years. He still likes a trip to Thornley Workmen's Club, which he joined on the first day that the Club opened in 1901.

Sporting Memories
Several "world" champions, Mr Gott reminisces, belonged to Thornley. He remembers John Walker, checkers (draughts) champion, taking six months to complete a championship match because his opponent lived in America; Jacky Bestford and Bill Scott, fives champions; Tom Nicholson, championship pot-share bowling on Seaton Carew Sands; George Wallace, 120 yards sprinter and the famous "miler", pigeon, "Coalie", owned by Mr Gott winning twice in championship "open challenge" races.

349

These races, held in 1927 and 1928, over measured miles at Thornley and Easington for £75 a side, each race, Mr Gott remembers, with remarkable clarity. The figures were 52 seconds to 50 seconds and, one minute two seconds to 58 seconds.

Mining Comparison

Comparing the modern speedy mining techniques, Mr Gott recalls that, in 1906, Thornley New Pit Shaft, the largest in the county at that time, with 40 men to the "cage-deck", was sunk, and coal produced in ten months.

17 May 1963

THORNLEY OFFICIALS' CLUB TO RE-OPEN

After having been closed for the past seven weeks, with the exception for Easter week-end, because of a slip-up in registration procedure, Thornley Colliery Officials' Club is to be re-opened tonight (Friday).

At Castle Eden court on Tuesday, Mr A N Levinson, on behalf of the club, successfully applied for a club registration certificate. Owing to a series of unfortunate circumstances, said Mr Levinson, the club had failed to apply for registration at the proper time under the 1961 Licensing Act.

It was not until 3 April, however, that it came to light that the club was not, in fact, registered. It had to be immediately closed and had remained closed since, with the exception of Easter week-end when a local publican was granted an occasional licence to supply with intoxicating liquor.

The club had now complied with the appropriate rules and regulations or registration. "I understand that no objections have been raised," said Mr Levinson. The registration certificate was granted for one year.

A Setback

After the hearing the club secretary, Mr Albert William Dove, 16 High Street, Thornley, told our reporter it had been quite a set-back to the club to close its doors for seven weeks. The club, formed two-and-a-half years ago, had a membership of 246, and since its closure the members had been "scattered all over".

The "discomfort" the members had had to suffer had been one of the main concerns of the officials. "But now that we are properly registered and can open up again we are hoping to have all our members back with us so that the club will soon be on a sound footing once again," said Mr Dove.

THORNLEY MEN'S LONG SERVICE TO MINING – Mr Tom Richardson and Mr Bob Potts were presented by Mr W S Hutton, Manager of Thornley Colliery, with long service certificates on Saturday. Both men have served the coal industry for 47 years each; Mr Richardson for 30 years as master weighman and Mr Potts for 25 years in the same capacity.

The certificates, framed, and signed by Dr William Reid, Chairman of the Durham Divisional Coal Board, record the Board's warm appreciation for loyal services.

A GOOD FIGHT SAYS MAURICE CULLEN

"I was quite satisfied with the fight – I gained a lot of valuable experience and, in my opinion, the verdict could have gone either way", summed up Maurice Cullen when he returned to his home in Ashbrooke Crescent, Shotton Colliery, after his unsuccessful attempt to win the British lightweight title from Dave Charnley on Monday.

Maurice, an eye-shield covering the swollen, discoloured left eye he got in the fight at Belle Vue, Manchester, smiled, and said, "It's a beauty, isn't it?" Apart from his "black eye" there was nothing to show that Maurice had gone the full 15 rounds with the title-holder.

It was the first fifteen-rounder he had fought and before the fight many "experts" thought that if he went the distance he would win on points. But the verdict went to Charnley, who must have found the Shotton lad a tough handful and a bigger proposition than he had anticipated.

Full praise was given in the national and local Press to Maurice's gallant efforts to win the title, though the majority of the critics agreed that the right winner was named.

Maurice said on Wednesday he hoped to get another chance against Charnley. "I feel I will do better still next time," he said. He and his manager-brother Terry have some new training ideas "up their sleeves" when he gets into full training again.

In the meantime Maurice, after weeks of hard training, is relaxing for a few weeks and there are no plans yet for his next fight.

Last night (Thursday) he and his parents were among the guests invited to the annual dinner of Easington Rural Council at Crimdon Lido and many tributes were paid to the young boxer's fine performance on Monday.

24 May 1963

THORNLEY MAN REMEMBERS

When Mr James R Burn, of Thornlaw, Thornley, now retired, goes on his walks through the fields and woods his mind is constantly revolving round the incidents of those grim days in France and Flanders when, in the 1914-18 War, he was serving with the 20th Battalion the Durham Light Infantry. He often wonders if the hardships the veterans of that war were called to endure are forgotten in the stress of all the exciting events since then.

As he strolls along, a vivid picture of over 40 years ago is recalled of Joe Iveson, now living at Wheatley Hill. "As I was looking at our new position on the eve of Passchendaele a soldier was coming towards me. As he came nearer I recognised a man I had known at home – Joe Iveson, who still lives at Wheatley Hill. We talked about home and about the battle we had come through. Then he asked me if I had ever seen a Prussian guard.

"He took me to a concrete bay and there was the guard, one of our prisoners. The guard smiled at me and pointed to my water bottle. He wanted a drink. Against the wishes of my comrades I took the bottle to him and he had good drink."

Left for dead

Mr Burn survived Paschendaele and all its horrors and he often wonders if the reason he got off so lightly was because he gave that Prussian guard a drink of Water.

Another memory that comes to him is of that moment when their officer in command, Capt Hand, standing in an exposed position on the parapet was shot through the head and killed.

Next day Mr Burn suffered a thigh wound which laid him low. He wondered if he would suffer the same fate as a soldier who was killed on the previous day. But he kept absolutely still and the Germans, apparently thinking he was dead, passed him over and disappeared.

"Having assured myself that they had all gone, I crawled from shell hole to shell hole and eventually reached the British lines and, soon afterwards, a ward in a Nottingham hospital."

THORNLEY WC ENDED THE SEASON IN FINE FASHION

Thornley Workmen's Club ended the football season in sparkling form on Saturday when they defeated Hetton Comrades 7-1. Thornley went ahead in the fifth minute through Brian Porter. Five minutes later the same player put Thornley two up. Hetton reduced the arrears through Tapping but Thornley went further ahead when Ernie Porter hit the crossbar and Harry Morton made no mistake from the rebound.

In the second half Thornley were on top again and Billy Luke cracked in a fourth goal. From then on it was "one way traffic" with Thornley in full cry and Hillam scored the fifth with a brilliant header from Luke's centre. Hetton goalie made some wonderful saves but Thornley scored twice more through Ernie and Brian Porter.

Thornley defence, which includes Billie Williamson (in goal) who takes up life guard duties in the close season at Crimdon Lido, were in command all through the game.

Thornley darts team were successful once again. Bob Appleby scored 140 twice, Tom Dent, Alf Steel and John Morton all went over the "ton" to bring victory by 565 and the season's final record read: Played 30, won 26, lost four. This may mean a play-off for the Darts League trophy with Seaham York House, last season's holders.

Thornley dominoes team lost by the narrow margin 17 to 18.

31 May 1963

THORNLEY TWINS DO WELL IN ROAD SAFETY

There were proud and smiling faces all round after some 20 children had entered the Road Safety Cycling Proficiency Test on Thornley Colliery Welfare Sports Ground, for all 20 who had competed to represent Thornley at Crimdon Dene in the area finals had passed with flying colours.

For young Edgar Galloway it was a special occasion. On his first appearance he gained the full 100 marks, achieving the double for the family, for his elder brother won it some years ago. Edgar's twin brother, Peter, also competed, and got two points less than his brother. Both the twins and Malcolm Crisp, who also received 100 points, and Ian Brown, 98 points, will represent the village at Crimdon Dene.

Other successful competitors were J Day, K Hardy, B Williamson, B Scott, D Jones, J Swan, P Cairns, G Kenny, G Atherton, A Richardson, C Frampton, P Laidler, E Parker, W Murray, D Hammond, C Davies.

The competition was organised by Coun M Slater, chairman of Thornley Parish Council, under the supervision of PC Pearson and his colleagues from the special constabulary.

THORNLEY WOMEN IN TOP COUNCIL POSITIONS

At Thornley Parish Council's annual meeting the longest serving councillor, Mrs Hilda Slater, who has served the Council for 14 years, was elected chairman for the ensuing year; Miss Annie Griffiths, who has never missed a monthly meeting of the Council for nearly nine years, was elected vice-chairman. Miss Griffiths was al elected to the Easington Area Committee of Parish Councils, and, together with Coun James Bennett, was elected Durham County Parish Councils' Representative. Councillors Jim Nicholson and J R Bosomworth are to represent the Parish Council on the Playing Fields Association, of which Coun Bosomworth is already an executive member. Coun Douglas Gott was elected representative to the Library Advisory Committee and Mrs May Slater and Mrs Hilda Slater were elected to the Easington Road Safety Committee.

Public Lighting

Satisfaction was expressed by Coun Nicholson on the Electricity Board's work in lighting the site of the new bungalows in Dunelm Road, but he still wanted to see other black spots attended to.

Bus diversion through Gore Hall Estate. The Council wished to give publicity to the Durham District Services failing to bring this division to the public. Coun Nicholson said the authorities claimed that the road surface would allow an hourly, single deck bus service.

Depositing of Litter

Complaints about the depositing of litter were received and it was decided to inform the public that the depositing of litter was a punishable offence and simply by notifying the local cleansing staff, litter could be disposed of; there was no need for, as one member stated, midnight expeditions with old mattresses

Coun Frank Walker, speaking with Easington Rural Councillor experience, said Thornley was more fortunate with regard to vandalism than other areas and public lighting had not suffered to a great extent but seven roadside seats had been repaired and two totally destroyed seats were too far removed from surveillance to repair.

The offer of roses to plant in the War Memorial garden, by Mr W S Hutton, Manager of Thornley Colliery, was gratefully accepted by the Council and work is to proceed affixing chains and fencing.

Trouble is still being experience by grit choking sinks on the road between Wheatley Hill and Thornley and in Thornlaw South, and Coun Annie Griffiths moved the Highways Department be contacted.

WHEATLEY HILL SCOUTS' DAY HAS RECORD CROWD
Warm sunshine and blue skies attracted a crowd of over 500 to the seventh annual Field Day organised by the Wheatley Hill Group of Boy Scouts. The organising secretary was Coun R Watson, assisted by Group scoutmaster Les Barker (chairman), Mr E Snowdon (treasurer), and a strong committee of the Old Scouts Association. Stalls and sideshows were made by Mr Tony Carr and were painted and decorated by members of the Association. The effort realised over £100 which will be used for the maintenance of Scout Headquarters.

Highlight of the day was a gymnastic display by scholars of Wheatley Hill Boys' Modern School, by permission of the Headmaster, Mr A Harris. The boys were trained by the games master, Mr K Charlton and appeared under the direction of Mr E Ward. Log sawing competition winners were Mr D Orchard and Mr R Turnbull. A log-splitting display was given by Messrs Tony Carr, Norman Watson and William Hedley.

In charge of side-shows were Messrs W Smart, A C Watson, J Horrocks, M Waugh, N Watson, A Lambert, C Thackeray, E Hutchinson, R Elliott, W Taylor, L Craggs, J Craggs, J Henderson, R Hunter, B Aitkin, G Armstrong, Mesdames S Watson, R Rowlands, M Walker, M Nicholson, E Cowan, S Cook, J Hodgson, E Thackeray and Miss Shutt.

Good turn
The Scouts did their proverbial good turn on this day devoted to outdoor pleasure. Some years ago the Wheatley Hill Scout Troop adopted the children's ward of Durham County Hospital. Mrs Collingwood provided transport to bring two children to the Field Day who had been in the hospital for over a year.

Coun Watson wishes to express the thanks of the Old Scouts Association to all who contributed in any way to the seventh annual effort. Boys taking part in the gym display were Keith Foster, Dennis Burke, Peter Martin, Richard Foster, Gerald Smith, Terence Hind, Eric Harper, Sidney Urwin, Robert Gair, Edward Maratty.

14 June 1963

FANCY DRESS PARADE WITH 150 ENTRANTS
Everyone received a prize
It was prizes, prizes all the way when the annual sports day organised by the Wheatley Hill Colliery Federation Board was held in the village on Saturday. Once again the event was favoured with warm sunshine.

Where the prizes were concerned there was not a single disappointment among the youngsters – for there were no losers! More than 150 children took part in the fancy dress parade and although there were only three principal prizes for each section – 15s, 10s and 5s – those not winning one of these all received a half-crown savings stamp.

It was the same in the programme of children's sports. Every child taking part, whether or not among the winners, was presented with a savings stamp.

Monster Procession

The sports day has become one of the most popular attractions in the community life of the village and Saturday's programme, catering for all the village's 2,000 children, got off to a splendid start with a monster procession through the main streets.

When the procession, which was headed by Wheatley Hill Colliery Band, conducted by Mr J Rutter, reached the playing fields of the Peter Lee Girls' Modern School, where the sports were staged, women of the village had a busy time distributing bags of chocolate and sweets. Each bag was valued at 3s and every child in the village received one.

"It was quite a task making up the bags the night before," the organising secretary, Mr J Armstrong, told our reporter. "But everyone worked well and felt fully rewarded when they saw the happy smiles of the youngsters as they received their gifts."

Three jazz bands – from Silksworth, Sunderland and South Shields – took part in the parade and as they swung along in their attractive costumes they added vivid colour to the happy scene.

Demonstration by Police Dogs

The RSPCA's mascot goat, Albert, from Hartlepool, and pit pony, also joined the procession – 14-year-old Annette Ogle led the friendly-looking goat, and 15-year-old George Eddy the pony – and later on the sports field, a police dog demonstration was given by a team from Aycliffe, in charge of Inspector T Cessford.

Every variety of fancy costume was seen in the parade and the judge had no easy task in choosing the principal winners. Tiny tots just turned a year old were even among the competitors, and one of these, 15-month-old Judith Hodgson, dressed as a fairy, carried off a third prize.

The judges were Dr and Mrs G H Wallace, Dr Mrs Hutchinson, Rev G G Graham (Vicar of Wheatey Hill), Mr F Walker (under-manager at Wheatley Hill Colliery) and Mrs Walker, and County Coun and Mrs John Andrew.

Prizewinners

Comic Dress: 1, Barbara Galley (the Belle of St Trinian's); 2, William Stanley ("Miss Wheatley Hill"); 3, Linda Gibson and Denise Raffell (Ug and Og).

Fancy Dress: 1, Jean Forster (Indian Lady); 2, Peter Hoban (Roman warrior); 3, Judith Hodson (Fairy Nuf).

Original Dress: 1, George Rowbotham (White hunter); 2, Pauline Hedley (mermaid); 3, Brian Dinsley (Swiss boy).

Adults: Mrs Lydia Hammond.

The prize for the best decorated tableau was won by Wheatley Hill women's section of the British Legion, with their "Miss World" entry.

The first prize of a silver cup and £5 for the four-mile race for youths and men over 15, was won by James Lee, of Peterlee, a pupil at Wellfield A J Dawson Grammar School. His time was 25 minutes. Second prize went to Eric Dower, and Terry Hoban was third and Sid Jobes fourth.

355

The medal for the smartest drum major on parade with the jazz bands was won by Miss M Brown, a member of the Silksworth band.

Side-shows and stalls were arranged and supervised by Wheatley Hill Old Scouts' Association and women members of the organising committee served refreshments.

Altogether it was a memorably happy day and the organising officials: Messrs H Bradshaw (chairman), J Armstrong (secretary) and J Hedley (treasurer) – together with representatives of women's organisations in the village, who have their whole-hearted support, deserve every credit for making it such a success.

THORNLEY MAN WORTHY DARTS CHAMPION

Mr Robert Appley, of Aycliffe House, Thornley, has collected handsome trophies from darts competitions. While playing for Ludworth Inn darts team he was in the finals of the Durham Advertiser Championship three times 1958, 59, 62; and was in the winning team of the Durham County National Championship (The People) in1959-60.

Playing in the Sherburn Hill District League, Mr Appleby made the highest individual score and was in the winning team three years in succession; he was in the Area Finals of the Nordor Competition in 1961-2.

Latest Successes

For Horden Hotel team, "Bob" has played his party in winning for the second year in succession the Horden and District League Championship and the Pairs Championship; in 1962; the Durham County Championship (Sunday newspaper), and the Nimmo Cup two years (1962 and 1963) in succession.

Working underground at Thornley Colliery, Appleby is a prominent member of Thornley Workmen's Club Darts team who have won the Club Institute Union Trophy. Bob likes gardening and in his spare time likes to pop in at the local for a quiet game of darts!

THORNLEY FUNERAL OF MRS TODD

Members of the Mothers' Union, and the Women's Institute and the general public attended the funeral service in St Bartholomew's Church, Thornley, conducted by the Rev P G Mold, of Mrs Anne Todd, wife of Dr Arthur Todd, Wesley Villas, Thornley.

For over 30 years Mrs Todd has been a well known public worker in the parish. She was for many years an Independent member on Thornley Parish Council, and an active member of the Women's Institute and Mothers' Union.

Her husband is a well known north-east surgeon practising at Dryburn Hospital and a general practitioner at Thornley, Wheatley Hill and Ludworth.

Mrs Todd leaves husband, one son, Dr Alistair Todd, of Dundee, and two married daughters ,Dr Anne Brough of Bromley and Mrs Margaret Hedge of Durham. Cremation was private.

21 June 1963

INJURED MINER WEDS

Mr Robert Bennett, a 30-year-old miner, of 98 Barnard Avenue, Ludworth, went to his wedding at West Ed Methodist Church, Hexham, on Saturday, in a spinal carriage. Miss Rhoda Walls, a 21-year-old shop assistant, of 9 St Chad Square, Thornley, has been told by doctors her bridegroom will never walk again.

Three days before the original date of the wedding – 13 weeks ago – he injured his back in a fall of stone at Wheatley Hill Colliery. Mr John Halliday, who helped rescue him after the accident, was best man on Saturday.

Mr Bennett was taken by ambulance to the wedding from the paraplegic ward of Hexham General Hospital and went back to hospital after the reception. His wife went to the hospital for a few hours before returning home.

She said: "I know what I have to face up to but he is the only man for me." Her husband said: "I am proud of Rhoda for the way she has stood by me."

MMB FINED AT CASTLE EDEN

Defending the Milk Marketing Board at Castle Eden court when the Board was charged with selling, through a Wheatley Hill supplier, a pint bottle of milk containing extraneous matter, "namely, cement", Mr G I Drimmie said that the Board had been supplying milk in the Easington area for the last 16 years. They supplied well over three million bottles a year.

"In those 16 years more than 50 million bottles have come into the area and this is the first time that a complaint has come to the notice of the Board," added Mr Drimmie. The Board was fined £5 after admitting the offence.

On 21 April, said Mr D C Kelly, prosecuting for Easington Rural Council, Ms Margaret Booth, of East View, Wheatley Hill, bought a pint bottle of milk from her usual supplier and it contained some "extraneous black substance". It was not, however, suggested that the substance was injurious to health, said M Kelly.

5 July 1963

GOLDEN WEDDING PARTY AT WHEATLEY HILL

All their family of three sons and four daughters, together with their 23 grandchildren and five great-grandchildren, were at a party in Wheatley Hill Welfare Hall on Saturday which Mr and Mrs Benjamin Murray, of 107 Wordsworth Avenue, Wheatley Hill, arranged for the celebration of their golden wedding. The couple, who had spent all their married life in the village, were the recipients of many good wishes and gifts and a shoal of greetings cards received at their home.

They were married at St Bartholomew's Church, Thornley. Mr Murray, how is 75, was born at Sunderland but was only about six when he moved to Wheatley Hill. He began work at Thornley colliery as a trapper-boy at the age of 13, earning tenpence a ten-hour shift.

"We were paid fortnightly," he told our reporter, "and when I handed over my pay to my mother I got ninepence back for my pocket money."

But the ninepence, he recalled, "went a long way". "In those days you could buy a big bag of fish and chips for twopence and a bottle of lemonade for a penny," he said. "I always used to spend some of my pocket money on these!"

War Service Overseas

Because of nystagmus, Mr Murray gave up mining in 1933 and since then until his retirement ten years ago was employed as a labourer. For a number of years he worked for Easington Rural Council and later did some contracting work at Coxhoe and Billingham.

Because of nystagmus, Mr Murray gave up mining in 1933 and since then until his retirement ten years ago was employed as a labourer. For a number of years he worked for Easington Rural Council and later did some contracting work at Coxhoe and Billingham.

During the 1914-18 war Mr Murray served in the RAMC. Most of his service was abroad – he served in Malta, Egypt, Mesopotamia and the Dardenelles. "I was called up about a year after we were married." He said.

Mrs Murray, whose maiden name was Agnes Green, was born at Ludworth. She and her husband, who enjoy good health, were among the first members to join the local Over-60 Club when it was formed about ten years ago and served on the original committee. Later Mrs Murray was a member of the concert party five years. She was also a founder-member of the Wheatley Hill women's section of the British Legion.

Mrs Murray and her sister, Mrs Mary Jane Venables, who died eight weeks ago, were the first caretakers of the old Miners' Hall in Patton Street, and also worked for some time at the Workmen's Club.

Nowadays Mr Murray fills in a lot of time in his outsize garden. "And I often help my wife with the washing up and do a bit of baby-sitting now and again for the family – don't forget that," he smiled.

THORNLEY CARNIVAL PLEASED BOTH YOUNG AND OLD

Crowds lined Thornley's main streets on Saturday for the procession of silver and jazz bands, pit ponies, tableaux and competitors in fancy dress. The parade was part of Thornley Colliery Mining Federation Board's sixth annual sports day.

Both young and old enjoyed themselves. The old benefited from the proceeds of a street collection which amounted to £60.6s.1d, while over 2,000 packets of sweets were distributed to the children.

There were the usual comic items. A fierce Zulu warrior, really George Copeland, of Shotton, brandished his spears, mock "ban-the-bomb" enthusiasts were lifted bodily into an imitation "Police Kart," and "King Cassius," in the person of Peter Cairns, strode arrogantly along.

Weekly Deduction

The day was made possible by a weekly deduction from the pay packets of Thornley miners together with a lot of hard work by secretary Sam Greener, chairman Ron Hughes, vice-chairman Ned Carter and treasurer Bill Thompson.

Members of the committee and volunteers who helped to organise the event were: Messrs W Cowan, W Wilson, E Wilkinson, R Hughes, S Dower, G Armstrong, B Pattison, W Henderson, J Hedley, G Bennett, J Carr, W Anderson, J Barron, J Sandiwell J Craven, J Nicholson, J Lewis, W Barron, J Craggs, J Foster, R Bullock, W Smith, H Brierly, L Williamson, J Storey, W Hammond, W Kirby, J Durkin, F Walker, J Richardson, J Willans, D Gott, H Robinson, R Spink, J Kirk, A Bushby, L Mitchell, J Taylor, J Burnham, W Moreland, L Hodgson, H Hubbard, H Todd, J Greener, F Watson, R Major, B Foster, G Wetherall, E Robinson, R Briggs, G Lake, G Burnham.

Results

Pit ponies: Cleanest pony in B Group No 3 Area: 1, Royal, Wheatley Hill, led by L Bell; 2, Tosh, Thornley, L Harvey; 3, Pompey, Shotton, R Young.

Durham Division Champion: Ten hands high and under: 1, Salty, Horden, J Haswell. Ten to 11 hands: 1 Pompey, Shotton, R Young. Eleven hands and over: 1, Boxer, Horden, J Haswell. Overall champion: Boxer, Horden, J Haswell. Judges: HM Inspector J Roberts and Area Horsekeeper F Butters.

Fancy dress: eight to ten years: 1, B Musgrove; 2, M Shutt; 3, A Williams. 11 to 13 years: 1, P Cairns; 2, J Burgin; 3, P Hedley. Comic eight to ten years: 1, M Jones. Comic five to seven years: 1, K Allen. Comic 11 to 15 years: joint 1, R Bowes and E Marshall; joint 2, J Routledge and R Mawson; 3, R Luke. Original five to seven years: 1, P Williams; 2, M Slater; 3, C Davison.

Adults: Comic: 1, Mrs M Crisp; 2, P Hunt; 3, M Smith and partner. Fancy: 1, G Copeland; 2, D Burgin; 3, W Pearce. Judges: the Rev and Mrs Mold, Mr and Mrs W Maddison, Mr and Mrs J Luke, Mr and Mrs W Stoker, Mr and Mrs A Woodward, Mr and Mrs F Bradley, Mr and Mrs J Williams, Mr and Mrs T Bonar.

Art competition: Girls: 1, C Coldwell; 2, D Bell; 3, A Hardy. Boys: 1, W Murray; 2, J Morton; 3, J Johnson. Judges: Mr and Mrs C Lamb.

12 July 1963

THORNLEY PARISH COUNCIL CRITICISM OF BUS DIVERSION DELAY

Criticism of a bus company's alleged delays in providing a bus diversion through the Gore Hall Estate was expressed at Thornley Parish Council meeting by Coun Jim Nicholson, a member of Easington RDC.

"This diversion," he said, "is a 'must', relieving as it would, traffic congestion in the Villas and serving a new and expanding part of Thornley. He stressed that he would not cease to press for an improvement, until this great need was fulfilled.

Villas' Traffic Congestion

After a meeting of representatives of the Parish County Council, the Easington RDC and the Chief Constable (Mr A A Muir), the Parish Council approved the introduction of a "No Waiting" Order on the south side of road B1279, between the entrances of the Roman Catholic Church and the Thornley Officials' Club – a distance of 365 yards.

It was said that though the order would not, in itself, solve the congestion problem, if it were reinforced by police supervision and public vigilance, it would tend to alleviate the trouble.

The account for repairing 28 roadside seats was approved.

Wall Improvements

The National Coal Board's Estates' Department said that work would go ahead to improve the appearance of the walls adjoining the main street.

The Council accepted a lease of land for Thornlaw South Children's Playground and there was satisfaction at the erection of the children's swings on the site.

The North East Electricity Board reported work completed on the installation of lighting near the Aged Miners' Homes, and said they intended to install lighting in Dunelm Road and on the Ludworth to Wheatley Hill Road, Thornlaw South, Shinwell Crescent, Ruskin Crescent and Morris Crescent.

Footpath Light

Because of probable alterations in the Villas, the Council decided to investigate the positioning of a light on the footpath linking the Villas.

Councillors J R Bosomworth and J Nicholson reported on the annual meeting of the National Association of Parish Councils.

Mrs Hilda Slater presided over the Thornley Parish Council meeting.

WHEATLEY HILL GOLDEN WEDDING

Mr and Mrs George Curry, 8 Johnson Estate, Wheatley Hill, last eek held a family celebration party to mark their golden wedding. Mrs Norah Hayes (Easington Colliery) was present at the party and was a bridesmaid for the couple. Mrs Ethel Smith (West Cornforth) was the other bridesmaid and is Mr Curry's sister. She was unable to be present through bereavement.

The couple were married in Houghton-le-Spring ex-Wesleyan Methodist Church on 12 July 1913.

Mr Curry was born at Coxhoe. He started work at East Hetton Colliery earning 1s a day on the screens. At 17 he served his time as a colliery bricklayer. After 12 years at East Hetton pit he moved to Hetton Lyons. He came as bricklayer to Wheatley Hill colliery at the end of 1913 and retired at that colliery when he was 66.

During the First World War Mr Curry worked or ton months at his trade with German prisoners of war in Weardale.

For 40 years he was a playing member of Coxhoe and Wheatley Hill Prize Bands, playing the drum. He is one of the few founders of the Wheatley Hill Band now living. He is a member of Wheatley Hill Workmen's Club and the local Discharged Soldiers and Sailors Club.

Mrs Curry was born at Sherburn Hill. She is a Methodist and was active in her younger days in choral work.

Mr ad Mrs Curry have a married son, George, living in London, a bricklayer like his father; and a married daughter, Mrs Jennie Smith, of Peterlee; and two grandchildren. Mrs Smith baked her mother's golden wedding cake.

WHEATLEY HILL MINERS' WELFARE

Steady progress during the past year was reported at the annual meeting of Wheatley Hill Miners' Welfare Committee, presided over by Mr F Richardson, manager of Wheatley Hill colliery.

Mr Richardson was re-elected chairman for the ensuing year, Mr J Pattison secretary and Mr R Moore elected vice-chairman and also delegate to the No 3 Area Welfare Committee.

These officers will comprise the committee, together with Messrs T Buxton, G Harper, J Gair, G Burnside, W Smart, R B Elliott, R Dinsley, J Cowie, W Young, C Hardy, J Robson, W Burns, E Parsley, F Walker, F Cowton, A D Wharrier, H Poole, J W Burrell and H Galley, County Coun J Andrew and the Rev G L Nelson.

It was reported that a new groundsman, Mr Derek Hall, had been engaged for the Welfare grounds with a view to improving the general appearance of the grounds.
26 July 1963

REGIMENTAL HONOUR GUARD AT WHEATLEY HILL WEDDING

A wedding of great interest in school circles took place in Wheatley Hill Church Street Methodist church. Mr John Robson Heron, only son of Mr and Mrs Alexander Heron, 13 Redwing Lane, Norton-on-Tees, was married to Miss Enid Poulson, only daughter of Mr and Mrs George Poulson, 93 Wordsworth Avenue, Wheatley Hill. The Rev G L Nelson officiated and Mrs J Shutt was at the organ.

The bridegroom is a teacher on the staff of the Billingham Campus school and for the past two years the bride has been teaching in Sedgefield Secondary Modern School. The bridegroom is an officer with the No 463 Regiment TA Royal Artillery, West Hartlepool. The Regiment provided a Guard of Honour.

The bride was given in marriage by her father, society steward of the church in which she was married. She was in a full length gown of white satin with bouffant veil and coronet of pearls. She carried orange roses with white carnations.

Miss Dorothy Stavers, and the bride's cousins, the Misses June Rodmell (Wingate) and Carol Charlton (Trimdon Village) were bridesmaids. They wore dresses of pale green satin and carried bouquets of white carnations and sweet peas.

The duties of best man were carried out by Mr Philip H Wood, Royal Military Academy, Sandhurst. Groomsmen were Mr Robert Huey (Whitley Bay) and Mr R Tindle (Chester-le-Street).

WHEATLEY HILL WOMAN WINS COUNTY FINAL

WHEATLEY HILL WOMAN WINS COUNTY FINAL – Mr Edna Hall, secretary of Wheatley Hill Welfare Women's Bowls Club, has won the Durham County EBA women's singles and so, for the second time in nine years, will be taking part in the Wimbledon finals – she last appeared in these in 1954.

In the county final at Sunderland last Thursday Mrs Hall defeated Mrs Bulman, of Roker Park, 21-18, Mrs Bulman will also be competing in the finals at Wimbledon.

WHEN THOMAS SIMPSON of Wheatley Hill, and his Irish bride, Miss Rita McDermott, of Dublin, arrived at the hotel for the reception after their marriage, they were greeted by American screen star Pat Boone, who was staying at the hotel and had been invited to join the reception. Afterwards Pat Boone insisted on being photographed with the happy couple. Photograph shows left to right: Noel McDermott, best man and brother of the bride; Mrs Simpson, Miss Rita McDermott and Pat Boone. Tom Simpson works at Wheatley Hill Colliery as an electrician and plays cricket for Wheatley Hill Cricket Club. The happy couple are to reside in Wheatley Hill after a fortnight's honeymoon in London.

2 August 1963

WATER "BLANKET" WOULD KEEP WHEATLEY HILL MYSTERY AMMUNTION DUMP SAFE

This week, members of a bomb disposal unit from Catterick Camp had discussions with officials of No 3 Area Headquarters of the Durham Divisional Coal Board to try and reach some agreement regarding the level of water to be maintained in a pond at Wheatley Hill, known as "Burns Pond".

The pond is close to the colliery and water is drawn from it by the Coal Board. Recently, however, when the pond was practically drained a considerable quantity of small arms ammunition of varying calibre was found.

Children playing nearby got hold of some of the ammunition and some of them handed it to the local police. The police visited the spot and found that many more rounds of ammunition remained at the bottom of the pond covered in mud.

At once they issued an appeal to anyone with ammunition in their possession from the pond to let them know immediately. "It could be highly dangerous, especially if in the hands of children," a senior Castle Eden Divisional Police officer told our reporter.

Disposal Unit's Aid

The police called in the bomb disposal unit and then helped these men to recover many rounds of ammunition. "More than 1,000 rounds have been recovered so far," said the police spokesman, "but we are continuing our efforts until we are satisfied there is none left." The ammunition was "live," but how it got into the pond remains a mystery.

We have examined our records for years past, but have not come across any ammunition being reported missing," said the police spokesman.

It was felt, he added, that if the water was not allowed to drop below a certain level, this would help to prevent any further danger. The Coal Board were only too eager to co-operate all they possibly could in the matter.

WHEATLEY HILL WEDDING REUNION AFTER 50 YEARS

Their best man and bridesmaid of 50 years ago were among the guests when Mr and Mrs Thomas Armes Burnett, of 31 Peterlee Cottages, Wheatley Hill, celebrated their

Golden Wedding Anniversary at the weekend with a party attended by about 50 relatives and friends.

Their best man was Mrs Burnett's brother, Mr William Bowden, who lives in Wingate, and the bridesmaid was Mrs Evelyn Todd, Mr Burnett's sister, who lives in Blackhall.

Mr and Mrs Burnett, who both enjoy excellent health, have spent practically all their married life in Wheatley Hill. "And they have been 50 very happy years," Mrs Burnett, who is 70, told our reporter. "Wherever we go we like to be together and it is very rarely that one of us goes out alone." The couple always go away for an annual holiday and it is only three weeks ago that they returned from Torquay.

Started at Wingate

Born at Trimdon 71 years ago, Mr Burnett started work at Wingate Colliery as a trapper boy, earning 1s.8½d a ten-hour shift. About 18 months later he transferred to Wheatley Hill Colliery, where he retired six years go after a mining career of more than 50 years. "I have done practically every kind of job down the pit," he said.

Mr Burnett was employed at Wingate Colliery during the explosion of 1906. But he was not at the pit at the time. "The explosion occurred six ours before I was due to start my shift," he said.

Party

Mr and Mrs Burnett were married at Holy Trinity Church, Wingate, on 2 August 1913. They held their party on Sunday at the Station Hotel, Easington Colliery, where their son, William, has been manager for the past six years. Their son and his wife have been in the licensing trade for about 14 years.

Mr Burnett, whose maiden name was Rebecca Bowden, is 70. She does all her own housework and has a happy and contented outlook on life. Her husband, she said, "never minds doing an errand for me." The couple have three grandchildren and one great-grandchild.

9 August 1963

CULLEN AS A LIFEGUARD

Boxer turns lifeguard. That is the story of Maurice Cullen, the Shotton boxer, who is keeping in fighting trim by working as a lifeguard at Crimdon. "I feel better for it," he said, "and it keeps your mind off thinking about boxing all the time."

Maurice said he felt fit enough for another fight and was looking forward to one. He thought his next opponent might be a continental boxer, as he had fought all the leading English boxers in his class.

The job of a lifeguard was a good one. "I can do my training in the morning on the sands," he said.

Mr Roy Isherwood, resort manager, said Cullen's employment was temporary. "He is quite a good swimmer," he said, "and is obviously very fit."

Maurice has not yet had a chance to show his capabilities as a lifeguard by going to the aid of a bather in distress, but he has helped to haul an injured man up the cliffs during his short spell of employment.

16 August 1963

POLICE ESCORT FOR INJURED THORNLEY MINER - A 47-year-old miner, Leslie Proud, of East Lea, Thornley, who received a head injury in an accident at Thornley Colliery on Wednesday, was taken to Durham County Hospital and later transferred to Newcastle General Hospital. He was said yesterday to be "critically ill".

The ambulance taking Mr Proud, who is a deputy overman, to Newcastle was met, by arrangement, at Low Fell by two police cars and escorted through the rush-hour traffic to the General Hospital.

30 August 1963

PRESENTATION AT THORNLEY

Mr W S Hutton, manager of Thornley Colliery, on Saturday night in Thornley Officials' Club, presented wallets and notes from the Officials and Staffs' Association to six colliery officials who retired during the year.

A total of 284 years was represented by Mr Tom Bower (overman), Mr Ned Burnip (foreman platelayer), Mr Wilf Ingram (fire officer), Mr Jos Oswald (head wagonwayman), Mr Bob Potts and Mr Tom Richardson (master weighmen).

Mr Hutton paid tribute to long and loyal service and said that a tinge of regret at losing valuable team members was always associated with retirement presentations.

Mr Arthur Welsh (former manager) and Mr Tom Mackey (former undermanager), both paid tribute to the retiring officials, and Mr Fred Bradley (forman joiner) proposed the toast of They are jolly good fellows.

Mr Potts thanked everyone concerned on behalf of the recipients.

A separate presentation was made to Mr Tom Bower, a founder member of the Officials' Club, by the club chairman, Mr Jim Hedley. Presenting Mr Bower with an eiderdown, Mr Hedley said that the gift as accompanied by respect and affection.

Mr Jack Carr, chairman of Officials' and Staffs' Association, who presided, extended sympathy to Mr George Bennett, former secretary of the Club, and secretary of the Staff's Association, who was prevented from attending by an unfortunate accident.

Club secretary Mr Albert Dove was in charge of the catering arrangements.

THORNLEY PARISH COUNCIL AFFAIRS - Mrs H Slater presided at Thornley Parish Council meeting.

A member explained that he felt that although the no waiting order at present in force in the Villas was a slight improvement, the complete answer was one way traffic. He had proposed that an approach be made from Easington Road Safety Committee to the Minister of Transport to try and alleviate the dangerous traffic problem in this area.

Coun Nicholson pressed for an approach to be made to the police and to the owners of the Ritz Bingo Establishment to deter motorists crossing the footpath.

13 September 1963

RECORD OUTPUT – Last week, ending 13 September, Thornley Colliery produced its record output of 11,036 tons of coal.

COLLIERY OFFICIALS – The following were elected to the committee of the Thornley Officials' Club for the ensuing year: Social members, Messrs W Adams, W Walker, J Hubbard and A Butler; officials' members, Messrs F Locke, W Wilson, B Scott, J Carr, W Parker, W Bowman, E Cutter and E Wilkinson.

20 September 1963

PRODUCE SHOW - When Thornley Workingmen's Club ended their three-day exhibition of leeks, vegetables and flowers some thousands of visitors had examined the produce and prizes gained by the 38 members. Prizes and vouchers valued at over £1,000 were distributed at a special function in the club hall when members and visitors were entertained by The Four Just Men of Newcastle and other local artists. The first prize of the show went to Mr J W Race with his leeks of 1113.1 cubic inches and the second prize to his uncle, Mr D Race, and third to Mr E Luke. Mr D Race also won first prize with intermediate leeks, carrots and celery. The Race Family have been growers of prize leeks for over 50 years and have won hundreds of first prizes. The organisation of the show and celebration was by Messrs H Brierly (chairman) W Kirby (secretary) and L Dobbin.

WHEATLEY HILL CLUB

Total of £400 in prize money was awarded to members of Wheatley Hill Constitutional Club at their annual leek show. J Myers, of Sedgefield, was judge, Mr R Storey was organising secretary.

Dave Race had the most points at Thornley Workingmen's Club leek and produce show. [D A]

Mr J Orchard was the outstanding exhibitor. He obtained five firsts, one second and two third prizes. Mr S Scott proved to be the champion leek grower. Awards:-

Leek Club: 1, S Scott (103 cu ins); 2, W Curry; 3, G Bowes; 4, J Jordan. Best leek in show: S Scott. Intermediate leek: J Jordan. Long beet: 1, R Forster; 2, R Cook; 3, W Curry. Globe beet: 1, R Trotter; 2, R Forster; 3, J Bradshaw. Parsnips: 1 and 2, J Orchard. Onions: 1, J Orchard; 2, R Storey; 3, R Forster. Long carrots: 1, J Orchard; 2, S Scott; 3, J Jordan. Short carrots: 1, C W Rose; 2 and 3, J Fenwick. Celery (white): 1, R Cook; 2, J W Peacock; 3, J Dodds. Celery (pink): 1, C Frampton; 2, R Forster; 3, G Bowes.

365

Tomatoes: 1, R Trotter; 2 and 3, R Forster. Potatoes (round): 1, J Orchard; 2, S Scott; 3, J Jordan. Potatoes (kidney): 1, C Cowie; 2 and 3, J Orchard. Cabbage (white): 1, J Orchard; 2, R Cook, 3, W Curry. Cauliflower: 1, M Rutherford; 2, G Curry; 3, A Bramfitt. Flowers: 1, R Storey; 2, S Scott; 3, A Bramfitt.
27 September 1963

THORNLEY LODGE NUM ELECTION – Chairman, Mr Rich Robson; Lodge committee, Messrs Harry Brierly, Joe Craven, Jim Nicholson, Frank Walker, Jim Sandiwell, J R Barron, Joe Templeton, Ben Jones, JimWillans, Bill Curry. Federation Board members, Messrs Jim Sandiwell, Bill Curry, Jim Willans, Joe Craven, Bill Quinn.
4 October 1963

WHEATLEY HILL FUNERAL OF MRS HUMES
The funeral took place last week of Mrs Rebecca Humes (64), 3 Quilstyle Road, Wheatley Hill. The service was conducted in Wheatley Hill Patton Street Methodist Church, by the Rev G L Nelson. Cremation followed at Sunderland.

Mrs Hume is survived by her husband, Mr William Humes, and four married daughters. She was born in Silksworth but spent over 40 years in Wheatley Hill. About 30 years ago she opened a small general shop in Emily Street (now demolished) and continued her business at premises in Quilstyle Road, serving the public for 24 years.

Mrs Humes was a former member of Wheatley Hill Women's Section of the British Legion. She also had a long association with the Patton Street Methodist Church.
11 October 1963

NEW ERA FOR THORNLEY METHODISM
A service of unity on Tuesday night ended a long chapter of Methodist history in Thornley. It brought to a close the separate existence of the Waterloo Street and Bow Street churches. The service also signified the opening of a new era by the amalgamation of the two churches into one society to be known as Thornley St Stephen's Methodist Church.

Service at the Waterloo Street premises, home of the new society, was conducted by the superintendent minister, the Rev Gordon Johnson, assisted by the Revs G L Nelson, W A Stones and J G Cox. The Rev Kenneth Alton was the visiting preacher. The good wishes of Thornley Circuit were brought by Mr J Craig, circuit steward. The choir, under the leadership of Mr W Potts, sang an anthem with Mrs V Wilson as organist.

Population of 56 in 1851
In 1851 the population of Thornley was 56. In 1820 this agricultural corner of Durham boasted 60 souls – an increase of four in 20 years. But by 1837 there was a

change. The South East Durham coal field was being rapidly developed and Thornley was being pegged out as sites for miners' houses. Wesleyan Methodists coming to Thornley, following coal, with only £19 and great faith, purchased a site for a church.

It is recorded that both men and women carried stones from the quarry to the site. In 1838 the church was completed and the opening ceremony held. The building may not have possessed architectural beauty but it was their own.

The church was accepted into the Durham Wesleyan Circuit, which stretched as far as Chester-le-Street to the North and Shotton to the South. Preachers planned on Sundays had to walk these distances twice and often went straight into the pit when they arrived home.

In 1865 such progress had been made that the premises were inadequate. The church was extended and rebuilt, taking on the shape and dimensions of the present building. Hemmed in by other property the extensions could only go upward. A gallery was put in and the church rebuilt to seat 500.

(With regard to the population figures quoted in this article, readers who are familiar with our publication "The Thornley Census 1851" will know that this figure is inaccurate. Thornley was a thriving community by 1851 as their colliery was almost 15 years old and I believe the reference to 1851 should read 1801 and is a mis-print in the newspaper)

Head of the circuit

It was a proud moment in the history of this church when the Newcastle Conference of 1873 decided that another two circuits should be shaped out of the large Durham circuit. It was decided that Thornley should be the head of one of them.

The new circuit was to consist of Thornley Colliery, Kelloe, Quarrington Hill, Shotton, Wheatley Hill, Cassop and Fishburn. The Rev W E Gardner was the first minister and Thornley became the head of a circuit of 314 members with an income of £164.

When Mr Gardner arrived at Thornley he had to leave his wife and child in Durham for as he records, "there was no accommodation or lodgings to be had". His books were deposited in Wheatley Hill Colliery offices until proper arrangements were made. The manse was finally built and furnished in 1875, at a cost of £1,350.

Surviving serious strikes, lockouts, evictions and the like the church prospered under the leadership of Messrs R Clarke, J Hills, J Fell Smith, R Youll, I Youll and J Clark and Sister Clark, Mrs Robinson, Mrs Sharp, Mr M Cook and Miss Robinson. The membership fluctuated between 25 at its lowest and 117 at its peak.

War Memorial

In 1920 the church decide to install a pipe organ as a memorial to its young men who gave their lives in the 1914-18 war. With Mr R Nicholson as secretary and Mr R Willey as treasurer, the sum of 650 was raised in three years, and the organ was opened on 29 August 1923.

The church has been served by various families over the years. Apart from those already mentioned there were Messrs Robert and Tom Hedley, James Tait Scott and James H C Scott (trust treasurer for many years); Mr Bob Potts (who with two sons and a daughter, all became local preachers); and Mr Joe Pattison, with 60 years association with the church and who has held every office. These and many others have built up the tradition of this great church.

Honourable History

Bow Street Church represented the response to the Primitive Methodist impact in Durham County and has had an honourable history of witness and achievement.

Bow Street records of the early days are scanty. The present building was opened in 1874 and registered for marriages in 1876. The land was purchased in 1869 and conveyed the same year. However the church came into being earlier than 1874 for there is record of a small building in Chapel Street before that time. The minister was the Rev J Fosson.

Bow Street, like its neighbour Waterloo Street, was in a Durham Circuit (Primitive Methodist) and remained there until Thornley was made an independent circuit.

Families who have given yeoman service to Bow Street include Griffiths, Ebdale, Rivers, Vickers, Featonby, Walton, Gaskells, Farrells, Stephenson, Thorntons, Galloway, Fort, Ridley, Archers, Smart, Henderson, Miller, Speckman, Brewster, and the present circuit and society steward, Mr I P Martin.

NEW RC CHURCH FOR WHEATLEY HILL

Next Thursday Roman Catholics in the area will see the fulfilment of a long-cherished dream when a new Roman Catholic Church at Wheatley Hill, work on which started just over a year ago, is officially opened and blessed by the Right Rev Monsignor Provost J J Cunningham, Vicar General of the Hexham and Newcastle Diocese.

Mass in a School

This is the first Roman Catholic Church to be built in the village. Throughout the years the parishioners there have had to travel to the neighbouring village of Thornley for Sunday and mid-week worship, and for marriages, funerals, baptisms and special celebrations.

Only once a week – on a Sunday - have the Wheatley Hill parishioners been able to have Mass in their own village. That was at the local Roman Catholic School, a room of which was converted specially each week for this one Mass. "But for everything else they have had to go to the church at Thornley," the parish priest, Father H McNeill, told our reporter on Wednesday.

It was shortly after Father McNeill arrived as parish priest at Thornley 11 years ago that thoughts began centring around a new church which, with its furnishings and the adjoining presbytery, has cost in the region of £40,000.

The Thornley parish which has been I existence since 1850, includes the smaller villages of Cassop, Ludworth and Shadforth, as well as Thornley and Wheatley Hill. There are about 1,300 parishioners and about 600 of these belong to Wheatley Hill. Father McNeill's curate is Father Michael Sweeney, who came to the parish a few months ago.

Dome Spotlights

Situated close to the Wheatley Hill Welfare grounds, the new church exquisitely combines tradition and modern ideas. The latest designs are embodied in the strip lighting running the entire length of the nave and up the side of the tall windows, and automatic electric heating comes from beneath the floor.

Two spotlights in the dome of the sanctuary highlight this beautiful part of the well-planned church, which includes the baldachino (canopy) and reredos in French walnut and teak, matching the pulpit. The altar is of marble.

The seating for the congregation is made of light oak and walnut,

Wheatley Hill Roman Catholic Church

and a new feature is the combination of the confession boxes in one oak panel. The 14 "Stations of Christ", beautifully carved in oak, have come from Italy. There is a spacious gallery and altogether the church will seat about 350.

About 120 priests from various parts of the diocese have been invited to the opening next Thursday. The first Mass will be said by Monsignor Cunningham, and the sermon will be preached by Canon Edward Avery, parish priest of Seaham Harbour.

FOUND DEAD

Shortly after he had gone down the pit with the back-shift men at Wheatley Hill colliery on Wednesday morning, Mr Harry Strong, who was employed as a ventilation officer, was found dead on one of the travelling roads leading to the coal-face in the East Main District. The facts have been reported to the Coroner. Mr Strong, who was 52, was formerly an official at Wingate colliery. He took up his new post as ventilation officer at Wheatley Hill when Wingate closed own last year. Mr Strong lived at 2 Moor Lane, Wingate, and actively associated with Holy Trinity Church, Wingate, where he had been organist for the past 13 years. He leaves a widow, a son and a daughter.

18 October 1963

WHEATLEY HILL'S NEW RC CHURCH

More than 400, including 73 priests from various parts of the diocese, attended the official opening and dedication of Wheatley Hill's new Roman Catholic church, by the Right Rev Monsignor Provost J J Cunningham, Vicar General of Hexham and Newcastle Diocese.

The church, which has cost more than £40,000, is enclosed in an acre of land with a spacious car park and lawn plots.

The Vicar General, with his retinue, walked round the church sprinkling holy water on the walls, while the priests standing at the entrance to the church chanted a service in Latin.

The Vicar General then opened the doors of the church and headed the procession of priests into the building. Twenty minutes later the church was opened to the public and the first Mass was said by Monsignor Cunningham. The sermon was preached by Canon Edward Avery, of Seaham Habour.

Will Serve 600

The new church will serve the 600 or more Roman Catholics at Wheatley Hill, who previously have had to attend Sunday Mass in a classroom of the RC School between Thornley and Wheatley Hill, and had to travel to Thornley, about one mile away, or all other services and church functions.

Eleven Year Fund

The church is named Our Lady, The Queen. The Parish Priest is the Rev H McNeil and his Curate, the Rev M Sweeney.

It is 113 years since Wheatley Hill was incorporated in the foundation of the Catholic parish of Thornley, and a church building fund was set up by Father McNeil when he came to the parish 11 years ago.

Contemporary in design, the building has strip lighting, automatic electric floor heating, and spotlights in the dome to illuminate the sanctuary.

This is the first RC church to be built at Wheatley Hill.

WHEATLEY HILL MAN'S SAFETY WINDFALL

Mr B Walker, of 7 Eighth Street, Wheatley Hill, a underground worker at Thornley Colliery, won a voucher for £30 and a £1 Premium Bond, at Thornley Colliery's quarterly safety draw.

Mrs Bell, of Ludworth, picked the lucky winners at Thornley's Over-60 club meeting. Mr Harold Todd, safety officer, organised the draw, which was attended by Mr W Hutton, Thornley Colliery Manager, with members of Thornley Miners' Lodge and officials of the Federation Board. Other £1 Premium Bond winners were: Underground workers, Mr M O'Brien, 7 Greenhills Terrace, Wheatley Hill; Mr J

Armstrong, 37 Hillsyde Crescent, Thornley and Mr F Dove, 8 High Street, Thornley. Surface workers, Mr J Maddison, 43 Morris Crescent, Shotton; Mr J W Beddell, 7 High Street, Thornley; Mr K Lonsdale, mechanic, 8 Ninth Street, Wheatley Hill.

WHEATLEY HILL BUTCHER DIES

After a long illness the death occurred on Monday night of a well-known Wheatley Hill butcher, Mr William Soulsby Hedley (75), of 13 Gable Terrace, who had been in the butchering trade all his life. For about 50 years Mr Hedley, who was a familiar figure at cattle markets throughout the North-East, was in business in Front Street, Wheatley Hill, and also had branches at Murton and Blackhall.

Born at Washington, Mr Hedley began work in the butchering trade on Tyneside but when he was 19 moved to Thornley and worked there for a local butcher, Mr Thomas Henry Ashford. Later he bought a business at Wheatley Hill and although he went into semi-retirement about ten years ago he still retained an active interest in the business.

A Freemason, Mr Hedley had been a member of the Rowland Burdon lodge at Castle Eden for about 25 years.

He celebrated his golden wedding two years ago, and he is survived by his wife, four sons and three daughters. His sons, William, Simon, James and Thomas, are all engaged in the family butchering business at Wheatley Hill and Blackhall.

Following a service in Church Street Methodist Church, Wheatley Hill, conducted by the Rev G L Nelson, Mr Hedley was buried at Wheatley Hill cemetery.
1 November 1963

REMEMBRANCE DAY

Wheatley Hill All Saints' Church was filled for the service on Sunday afternoon. The parade, organised by the British Legion, assembled at Patton Street, and headed by Wheatley Hill Colliery Prize Silver Band, marched to the church. The service was conducted by the Vicar (the Rev G G Graham), and the address was given by the Methodist minister (the Rev G L Nelson).

The parade reformed and marched through the main road of the village, halting at the Memorial Clock, placed on the Wheatley Hill Boys' Modern School as a memorial to the fallen of the second world war. Then the procession moved towards the Cenotaph in the Wheatley Hill Welfare Park, when the final act of devotion and dedication took place. Wreaths were placed on the Cenotaph by the following organisations: Wheatley Hill British Legion (Women's Section), Wheatley Hill Women's Institute, Police, Workmen's Club, Constitutional Club, Discharged Soldiers' and Sailors' Club, Sherburn Hill Co-operative Society, 1st Wheatley Hill troop Boy Scouts, and many families.

THORNLEY – A joint service was held in St Bartholomew's Church, Thornley, on Sunday. Dr A P Gray read the "remembrance," the Rev G Johnson of St Stephens, gave an address, and Mrs V Dowson, of the Salvation Army, read the lesson. The Rev P G Mold conducted the service.

Thornley Colliery Band was in attendance and the British Legion's standard-bearer was Mrs Hilda Slater. Wreaths were laid by representatives of parish and rural councillors, clubs and youth organisations. The wreaths were later transferred to the recently renovated war memorial.

15 November 1963

DIED THREE WEEKS AFTER HUSBAND

Three weeks after the funeral of her husband, Mr William Soulsby Hedley, the funeral took place this week of Mrs Emily Hedley (73), 13 Gable Terrace, Wheatley Hill. The couple had been married 52 years.

Mrs Hedley was born at Kelloe and met Mr Hedley when he was a young butcher. After Mr Hedley bought the Wheatley Hill branch of Mr Ashford's butchering business, Mrs Hedley assisted in the early days of the venture.

Mrs Hedley was associated with the Wheatley Hill Church Street Methodist Church. She was for some years a member of Wheatley Hill Over-60 Club and Wheatley Hill Women's Institute.

Mrs Hedley is survived by four sons and three daughters.

Tradespeople and local organisations were well represented at the funeral service conducted in Wheatley Hill Church Street Methodist Church by the Rev G L Nelson. Mrs R Ord was organist. Interment took place at the local cemetery.

22 November 1963

THORNLEY PARISH COUNCIL ACTS ON LIGHTING COMPLAINTS

Complaints were made at Thornley Parish Council regarding unsatisfactory lighting and it was decided to contact the Clerk, when lighting failed so that the supply company could be contacted immediately. Plans from the supply company for alterations and improvements to the lighting system were examined.

Plans from the Easington Rural District Council for the proposed lighting of the 104 houses to be built in Gore Hall were examined and accepted.

Durham County Council's plans of the rights of way were also adopted.

Further Vandalism

Damage to Market Place conveniences was again reported. This damage, although heavy, reported Coun Walker, compared favourably with the rest of Easington District.

Coun Bennett gave a detailed report of the annual meeting of the Durham County Association of Parish Councils.

Coun Redshaw complained again of an uneven stretch of footpath and it was noted for immediate attention. Coun Bosomworth said that damage was being caused by pavement repairers' huts and fires to grass areas in the Council estate.

Councillors Walker and Nicholson explained that apparently an agreement existed between Durham County Council and Easington Rural District Council, that these spaces could be used for siting workmen's huts etc.

Payment Due

Arising from the 1962-3 audit report it was decided to circularise allotment holders to the effect that payment for year ending March 1963 was owed to the Parish Council.

Reference had been made in the Easington Road Safety Committee's minutes that the Durham County Surveyor would be asked for his observations on a proposed roundabout, at the south end of Hartlepool Street, on the site of the demolished Station Hotel.

Renovation to the New Road Bridge was favourably commented upon, although it was pointed out that the Parish Council had received no notification that this work was imminent.

Gore Hall Bus Diversion

Service 37 of the United Bus Company will be diverted through Gore Hall Estate for a three months trial period commencing Sunday 1 December. Mr Mason, United Traffic Manager, has notified the Thornley Parish Council of this diversion. It is felt that it would supply the need for public transport for this area especially in view of the proposed building of an extra 104 houses.

Coun J Nicholson presided.

YOUTH AT THE HELM

Wheatley Hill and District Youth Club, formed eight months ago, has now a membership of 100 and junior membership of 80. The management of the club is under the guidance of an entirely voluntary committee who put in many hours useful work.

Chairman of the adult committee is County Coun Andrew; treasurer, Thornley business woman, Mrs V Hodgson, and secretary, NCB accountant, Mr Frank Dunn. Other members of the committee are Mr and Mrs George Burnside, Mrs W Foster, Mrs J Heale, Mrs E Powell, Mr and Mrs R Peacock, Mrs Carr, Mrs Gair, Mr J Gair and MrA Barker. Part-time paid leaders are Mrs Rosalind Sinclair (junior section) and Mr Colin S Gregg (senior section). The club is also fortunate in having a voluntary leader for both sections in Mr Ernie Curry.

The club has already junior, senior and five-a-side football teams under the supervision of Mr Curry, who spends a lot of his spare time supervising physical training classes at the club, using knowledge gained while sergeant instructor in the RAF.

Apart from normal club activities, dancing, table tennis and the like, the boys have a motor mechanics class, the girls a dress making class and a life saving class is being formed.

At present Mrs R Sinclair is working hard with the juniors, who are busy rehearsing for their pantomime Cinderella, which they will be presenting early in the New Year.

There are separate committees for seniors and juniors. Joyce Hubbard (aged 15) is not only the chairman of the senior committee but is also the Press officer for the members' council of the County Association of Youth Clubs. Other members of the senior committee are secretary, Jonathan Gair; treasurer Judith Hodgson; vice-chairman, John Knowles, with Shirley Godding, Gwyneth Gilmore, John Buxton, Les Holdcroft, Margaret Powell, Billy Armstrong, George Curry and Glenda Barker as other members.

29 November 1963

WHEATLEY HILL MAN, 72, LEADS BUSY LIFE

Few men have led – or for that matter still lead – a busier public life than 72-year-old Coun Edward Cain, of 11 Burns Street, Wheatley Hill, who today celebrates his golden wedding. Throughout his life he has been actively associated with trade union and local government affairs – he has served on both Durham County Council and Easington Rural Council – and since 1946 ha been a magistrate on the Castle Eden Bench, where for the past seven years he has been a deputy chairman.

But despite the busy life he leads- his diary is always full of engagements, although he has passed his three score years and ten – Coun Cain still finds time for relaxation. One of his chief diversions is reading and listening to classical music.

He has a fine collection of 350 records, and has delighted many local organisations with recitals from time to time. Beethoven is his favourite composer, and in the literary world Robbie Burns his favourite poet.

Celebration Party

Coun Cain and his wife, Frances Mary, who, in a different channel, is just as active as her husband – she does all her own housework, is always busy sewing and knitting, a bakes all her own bread – were married at Thornley on 6 December 1913. All their married life has been spent in Wheatley Hill, where they are well known and highly esteemed among a wide circle of friends. Tomorrow they are holding a celebration party in the hall of the local Workmen's Club.

Coun Cain, who was born at Seaham Harbour, started work at the Dolly Pit at Herrington when he was 13. He earned 1s.3d a shift of ten hours. Later he was employed at the D Pit at Lambton and then at Houghton-le-Spring and Shotton before settling in Wheatley Hill in 1911.

Coun Cain continued his mining career at Wheatley Hill Colliery as a filler, but after the 1926 strike was victimised for his trade union and political activities. When work was resumed at the pits after the strike he was unable to return to his mining job – all doors were closed to him in the coalmining world.

Victimised

"I was one of the few men in the county to be victimised for my activities," Coun Cain told our reporter this week. "We were even evicted from our colliery house at Wheatley Hill, but, fortunately, were able to move straight into a Council house in the village."

Coun Cain, however, was successful in obtaining employment as a clerk in the Ministry of Labour offices in Wingate. He spent three and a half years there and also had a spell on the roads as a County Council labourer.

But altogether he was out of work about four years before returning to Wheatley Hill colliery early in 1934 as miners' checkweighman. Elected checkweighman with him was Mr William Lawther – now Sir William – the two men bringing the number of checkweighmen to two, and in 1948 when one of these resigned, Coun Cain was left sole checkweighman and filled this position until he retired early in 1957.

One of the highlights of Coun Cain's trade union career was in June 1950, when he was chosen one of the delegation of five from this country to fly to Enugu, in Nigeria, to examine mining conditions there.

He spent three months there, and on his return received a letter from Mr James Griffiths, then Secretary of State for the Colonies, congratulating his upon his work, particularly for the part he played in the establishment of a Joint Consultative Committee in Enugu to deal with labour problems.

Coun Cain was also abroad in1928, when he was a Durham miners' delegate to the international miners' conference in Poland.

Coun Cain has been actively associated with the Labour movement since joining the Independent Labour Party in 1911. He is still secretary of Wheatley Hill Labour Party. In his younger days he was assistant agent for Mr Jack Lawson (now Lord Lawson of Beamish) in the "khaki" election of 1918 in the South-East Durham Division. Five years later he filled a similar role for Mr Ramsey MacDonald in the Seaham Division.

POPPY DAY APPEAL – Mrs Doris Bishop, Poppy Day Organiser at Wheatley Hill, announces that this year's appeal in the village realised £103.7s.2d for the Earl Haig Fund. This sum consists of the following amounts – Street collections, £48.11s.3d.; church collection, £2.2s. £; sale of wreaths, £29.7s.; car poppies, £14.10s.; Legion efforts, £8.6s.11d.; donation, 10s. The total was an increase of £7 on last year. Mrs Bishop thanks all who assisted her in the effort and the people of Wheatley Hill who gave so generously.
6 December 1963

NEW SUB-POST OFFICE – News of another sub-post office for Wheatley Hill came in a letter from the Head Postmaster at Durham. It is some time ago that the Council urged the need for an additional post office in the village and the Postmaster wrote that, although it was a "marginal case," it had been agreed to provide one.

The new office, however, would have to be sited in the Wingate Lane-Quetlaw Road area, where 98 new council houses were being built, and the Postmaster asked the Council's views on this. It was agreed to reply that the Council had no objection to the office being sited near the new estate. "That certainly seems to be the best place," said the chairman.
13 December 1963

WHEATLEY HILL CLUB TREAT
When Wheatley Hill Discharged and Demobilised Soldiers' and Sailors' Club entertained retired members and their wives to their annual "treat" in the club, among the

guests were officials of the village's two other clubs and representatives from the public-houses.

Other guests included Mr Fred Simpson, retired under-manager at Wheatley Hill Colliery, Mr F Richardson, manager of the colliery, and his wife, Mr F Walker colliery under-manager, and his wife, and Couns J Andrew, E Cain, J Harper and E Wharrier and their wives.

A warm welcome to the old folk and the guests, numbering about 170, was extended by the club chairman, Mr Bert Millar. An excellent knife-and-fork tea was served, following which entertainment was provided by Messrs W Bradley and T Spencer (Blackhall), R Armstrong and W Forster (Wheatley Hill) and W Burrell (Houghton). The accompanist was Mr J Vincent.

As a Christmas gift each retired member of the club received £1 and his wife 10s. Gifts of 10s. each were also made to widows of members who had died during the year.

Arrangements for the party were in the hands of the club chairman, secretary, Mr H Straughan, and treasurer, Mr D Holcroft.

TEA, MONEY AND GIFTS FOR WHEATLEY HILL OVER-60s

When the annual party of Wheatley Hill Over-60 Club was held in the local Workmen's Club concert hall on Tuesday, about 330 were seated to a knife-and-fork tea and among the guests were the Rev G G Graham (Vicar of Wheatley Hill), the Rev G L Nelson (resident Methodist minister) and his wife, and County Coun John Andrew and his wife.

The club chairman, Mrs E Amies, presided, and welcomed the members and extended seasonal greetings.

Each member of the club received a Christmas gift of £1 and during the evening Mr R Keen, as Father Christmas, presented each with gifts of fruit and chocolate. Coun Andrew distributed 30 chickens given by Mr J Ridley of Shotton, and Mr C Waites of Wheatley Hill, and other prizes, given by local tradespeople. Baskets of fruit were sent to sick members unable to attend the party.

An excellent entertainment was given by Mr Alan Shutt's concert party, with Mrs J Shutt pianist, and Mr A Shutt compère. They were thanked by the chairman.

Greetings were read from a former Wheatley Hill couple, Mr and Mrs J Richardson of South Africa, where they returned recently after spending a holiday in the village. Thanking the club for the kindness they showed during their recent visit, they extended best wishes for the future good health and happiness of the members.

Mrs May Davies won a Christmas hamper given by Mr R Gargett, and Miss E Shutt a carton of wine and glasses given by the Constitutional Club.

Thanks to all who had helped to make the party such a huge success and to local people for the support they had given in various ways, were expressed by the secretary, Mrs M E Richardson.

20 December 1963

GIFTS FOR WHEATLEY HILL CLUB VETERANS

The sum of £520 was distributed in gifts of £2 each to retired members of Wheatley Hill Workmen's Club and their wives, and widows, when they were entertained to their annual party in the club's concert hall on Thursday night.

They we given a warm welcome by the club chairman, Mr R Armstrong, and secretary, Mr B Aitken, and greetings were also extended by Mr T Croft of Easington, a member of the Durham County Club union Executive. The cash gifts were handed out by the treasurer, Mr J Maddison.

About 330 guests were seated to an excellent tea, and this was followed by an entertainment by Dorothy Turner, Nancy Rumley, George Oliver, Pat Hardy and Glen Griffin. Musical accompaniment was provided on the electronic organ by Mr L Hudspeth, with Mr T Hargreaves on the drums.

During the tea a Christmas cake was cut by the oldest guest, 84-year-old Mr B Bowes senior, who thanked the club for their splendid hospitality and the generous way in which they always provided for their old members.

27 December 1963

1964

FUNERAL OF THORNLEY FISH MERCHANT - Many relations, friends and business associates attended the funeral of Mr Norman Gowland (62), of Benoni, The Villas, Thornley, who died at his home after a long illness.

For the last 35 years Mr Gowland, had carried on the business of a fish fryer and potato merchant in Thornley and district. In his younger days he played as goalkeeper for Middlesbrough FC. He was a lifelong member of Thornley Working Men's Club and Thornley Colliery Officials' Club.

The service at St Bartholomew's Church and at Thornley Cemetery was conducted by Reverend P C Mold, Vicar.

10 January 1964

WHEATLEY HILL FIGHTING BACK - Wheatley Hill Workmen's Club operating in the CIU League, have had a lean time until recently owing to injuries sustained by key players in the last few weeks, however, they have regained their form and last week with a full strength team they toppled Peterlee WMC from their lofty perch at the head of the table to the tune of 6-2.

Man of the match was inside left Ben Harvey, who hit a fine hat-trick. He was closely followed by goalkeeper Sid Jobes, as Sid improves with every game and last week gave a great exhibition of goalkeeping.

It was also pleasing to see the centre forward, Ray Wood, finding the net again with a couple of rocket-like headers. Wood received a face injury early in the season, but has now made a good recovery.

MR EDWARD FRYER OF THORNLEY DIES - The funeral took place yesterday of Mr Edward Fryer (92), who died at the home of his friends, Mr and Mrs D Holden, of Thornley. A service at St Bartholomew's Church, Thornley and cremation at Durham were conducted by the Reverend P G Mold.

Mr Fryer was a native of Lancashire and had served as a regular soldier in India and South Africa before coming to Thornley in 1904, where he worked in the pits until he was recalled to the Forces at the outbreak of the 1914-18 War. On his discharge in 1919 he returned to Thornley colliery until he retired in 1947. He leaves one daughter and two grandchildren.

WHEATLEY HILL BUSINESSMAN DIES AGED 65 - The funeral took place in All Saints' Church, Wheatley Hill, of Mr Walter Heron (65), 9 Thornley Road, Wheatley Hill. He is survived by his wife, Mrs Elizabeth Ann Heron, two sons and a daughter. The funeral service was conducted by the Reverend G G Graham.

Mr Heron was born at Coxhoe. On leaving school he had one or two posts as errand boy, but eventually went into mining. On his marriage he obtained employment in the grocery department of the Coxhoe and Cornforth Co-operative Society in their Ferryhill branch. After some years at Ferryhill he took his own business at Wheatley Hill. He retired last November.

For more than 20 years Mr Heron has been a member of Wheatley Hill Workmen's Club, which was represented at the funeral by officials and members.

17 January 1964

MINER'S RETIREMENT

After spending the whole of his 51 year mining career at Wheatley Hill Colliery, Mr Michael Cain, who lives in a street of Council houses named after his older brother, retired from work at the weekend.

Mr Cain, who lives at 13 Cain Terrace, Wheatley Hill, celebrated his 65th birthday on Monday. The street was named after Councillor Edward Cain, who is a member of Easington Rural Council and deputy chairman of Castle Eden magistrates.

Born at Southwick, Mr Cain began work at Wheatley Hill colliery when he left school at the age of 14. At first he was a trapper-boy, and then he went through the various grades of mining underground and was hewing for many years. About ten years ago he transferred to datal work.

Like his councillor brother, Mr Cain has always taken an active interest in trade unionism. He has served on the local miners' lodge committee for a long period, and recently completed 25 years' faithful service as average-taker.

Mr Cain has also been keenly interested in the progress of Wheatley Hill Colliery Band and has served on the committee for many years. On a number of occasions, he has been on the committee of Wheatley Hill Workmen's Club. Towards the end of the 1914-18 war he served for eighteen months in the 3rd DLI.

Mr Cain is married, with three sons, who are all married. None of his sons, however, has followed in his footsteps as a miner - one is a plumber, another a store counter assistant and the other a clerk.

BEM FOR FORMER WHEATLEY HILL MAN - Mr William J Lister, a former Wheatley Hill man, son of the late Mr and Mrs George Lister, is to receive the British Empire Medal at Buckingham Palace for his work in connection with the Ministry of Aviation establishment at Boscombe Down, where he is principal photographer. Mr Lister left Wheatley Hill to join the Forces at the age of 18. His wife Eveline (formerly Miss Sanders), is daughter of the horse keeper at Shotton Colliery. They have a family of six. Mr Lister, Aged 64, of Hilltop Way, Paul's Dene Estate, Salisbury, left Durham in 1949.

MINERS' SAFETY DRAW - A surface worker, Mr Walter Ridley, of Wingate, won the major prize of a £30 voucher, exchangeable for household goods, when the quarterly draw among accident-free miners at Wheatley Hill colliery was held in the Welfare Hall on Friday night. The draw took place after two films on Underground safety measures in the mines had been shown By Mr W Stout, No 3 Area Dust Suppression Engineer. The colliery manager Mr F Richardson, presided, and made the draw. Mr Ridley won a £1 Premium Bond in addition to the principal prize, and other Bond winners were Messrs C Crick, C Maughan, W Hicks, R Patterson and N Atkinson.

DELAY POSSIBLE IN NEW WHEATLEY HILL CLINIC - Before a new child welfare clinic is built, Wheatley Hill may find itself for a period without a clinic at all.

Easington Rural District Council is worried about this possibility, as they have learned that the Wheatley Hill Parochial Church Council say that their hall cannot continue to be used as a child welfare centre after March.

However rather than spend £2,000 converting the ground floor of Wheatley School house into a child welfare centre, the County Council has stated that they would rather build new premises.

District councillors have welcomed this proposal, but fear that in view of the time it would take to build new premises, no child welfare facilities may be available in Wheatley Hill after March. They have asked the County Council to proceed as quickly as possible with the building of new premises.

24 January 1964

TRIBUTE TO A NURSE

Many tributes to her work as the village midwife, were paid at a social in Wheatley Hill Welfare Hall to Nurse F Laws, of 8 Burns Street, Wheatley Hill, who recently retired after 26 years' service in this capacity.

During this time Nurse Laws has delivered about 2000 babies in the village and it was a thoughtful gesture on the part of the committee organising the function when they invited Mrs Foster, of Castle Eden, to make a presentation to the nurse, for Mrs Foster was the first baby to be delivered by Nurse Laws when she began her duties as midwife.

The presentation - a china tea set and coffee table - was made on behalf of all the women's organisations in Wheatley Hill. Mrs Foster was introduced by Mrs A Bishop, chairman of Wheatley Hill women's section of the British Legion. A bouquet was presented to Nurse Laws by Mrs Chapman, who was the last mother in Wheatley Hill to be delivered of a baby by the nurse before she retired.

Taken by surprise with the unexpected gift, Nurse Laws was "at a loss for words", but she thanked the organisations for their kindness and generosity and spoke of the many happy years she had spent in Wheatley Hill.

Supper was served, followed by whist, dominoes and dancing, and prizes were won by Mrs Fulcher and Mrs E Jones (whist), Mrs Atkinson (dominoes) and Mesdames Routledge, Champley, Willis and Foster (Special competitions). Mrs G Bowes was in charge of the arrangements.

7 February 1964

"BOMBSHELL"

The news was a "bombshell", said Councillor Mrs D Dodds, when the Clerk read a letter from the head postmaster at Durham saying that a new sub-Post Office was to be opened on April 1st at the premises of Mr J R Sheild, 1 Wingate Lane, Wheatley Hill.

The Wheatley Hill councillors, said Mrs Dodds, had been asked to consider a suitable site for a Post Office to serve the needs of the people in the Wingate Lane area, including the new council housing estate there, but they had not even met yet to discuss the matter. "There is no point in holding a meeting now with the district councillors", she said.

Mrs Dodds and the other Wheatley Hill members, however, agreed that the new Post office as in an ideal position for the new housing estate.

After a previous letter from the head postmaster at West Hartlepool asking the council to consider a change of postal address for Trimdon Station, the council wrote that they thought the opinions of the people living in the area should be sought.

But on Monday night the postmaster wrote that it was considered "impracticable" for the Post Office to invite comments or opinions on the proposal. He added, "The suggested change of address was intended to be of benefit to the area as a whole and would actually be of little advantage to the Post Office". If the Council did not wish to make the change the Post Office would regard the matter as "closed".

NEW BUS SERVICE? - Councillor M W Carter said that people he had talked to about the change of address "did not want it". It was agreed to take no further action in the matter.

After being approached by various people to run their service through the new housing estate at Wheatley Hill, they were making appropriate application to the Traffic Commissioners, the traffic manager of Gillett Bros Bus Company wrote to the council. He added, "I would appreciate any help you can give us to provide a better service for the people o this estate".

Said Mrs Dodds, "The more buses we can get, the better". It was agreed to support the bus company's application.

TWO LONG-SERVICE MINERS AT WHEATLEY HILL RETIRE

Mates for many years as truck-loaders at Wheatley Hill colliery, where they have a record of 100 years' service between them, two miners - one from Wheatley Hill and the other from Station Town - have retired on reaching the age of 65.

They are Mr James Harrower, of 105 Wordsworth Avenue, Wheatley Hill, and Mr Thomas William Hildrew, of 89 Newholme Estate, Station Town.

Mr Harrower, who was born at Shotton Colliery, has spent the whole of his 51 year mining career at the colliery, while his "marra" has worked there nearly 50 years.

"For many years we have worked together as truck-loaders on the surface and we have been very good 'marras'", Mr Harrower told our reporter this week.

Devout Churchman

Mr Harrower has worked on the surface at the colliery from starting at the age of 14 on the screens. He was paid a shilling a ten hour shift, he recalled. "And I had a two mile walk to the colliery every day from Shotton until I was married and then I moved to Wheatley Hill and have lived their ever since," he said.

Mr Harrower did "various jobs" on the pitheap until becoming a truck-loader - filling coal into the trucks off the screens. During the 1914-18 war he served in the King's Own Yorkshire Light Infantry and spent two years in France. He was an ARP Warden in the last war.

A lifelong churchman, Mr Harrower is a member of All Saints' Church, Wheatley Hill, where he has been a sidesman for some years. He is fond of "gardening, reading and television". "They will occupy a lot of my time in my retirement", he said.

Mr Harrower is married with an only son, Cyril James, who is regular airman, serving as a chief technician in the RAF.

Has "Travelled the Road"

A native of Stockton, Mr Hildrew began work as a trapper-boy at Shotton colliery when he was 14, earning 9s.9d a week. He worked nine hours a shift. After only a year at Shotton he transferred to Wheatley Hill colliery, where he worked down the pit until he was 18 and then took up a surface job, which he has since filled.

Mr Hildrew has "travelled the road" all the time he has worked at Wheatley Hill. He has walked there from Trimdon Grange, Wingate and Station Town, where he has lived at various stages of his married life.

"I have always had a long walk to get to work - sometimes as long as six miles", he said. "That was when I was living at Trimdon". He had walked to the pit in all kinds of bad weather during the winter months. "And often it was not very pleasant in the early hours of the morning", he said.

Like his "marra", Mr Hildrew is married with an only son. His son, Derrick, is a miner at Horden colliery.

WOMEN'S LEGION - Forty-eight members were present at the weekly meeting of Wheatley Hill women's section of the British Legion, when the 34th anniversary of the inauguration of the section was celebrated. A welcome was given to Mrs Alderton on her return to the meeting after a long absence. Minutes and correspondence were read by the secretary, Mrs Pringle, and Mrs E Stainsby reported on the area confer-ence. The Legion prize given by Mrs M Foster was won by Mrs Davis, and winners of the special competition prizes were Mesdames Bramfitt, Cain, Pringle, Hughes and Rowbotham. Supper was provided and served by the committee.

SAFETY DRAW WAS AT THORNLEY OVER 60 CLUB - At the quarterly safety draw at Thornley Colliery, the organiser, Mr Harold Todd, Safety Officer at the colliery, had the novel idea of making this quarter's draw at a meeting of the Over 60 Club at Thornley Miners' Welfare Hall.

Chairman of the Thornley Miners' Federation Board, Mr Ron Hughes, introduced the manager of Thornley Colliery, Mr Hutton, to the members of the club, of which 90 per cent are ex-miners, and their wives. Mr Hutton spoke of the need to keep free from accidents both underground and on the surface, and presented premium bonds to the lucky winners. For surface worker M Charlton it was a lucky night for his name came of the hat for a premium bond and then came out a second time for a £30 voucher. Other lucky recipients were:- Underground: E Luke, J Burnip, R Richardson and A Martin. Surface workers: M Charlton and J Pringle. Mechanic: L Mitchell. Mrs Hodgson, a member of the Over 60s made the draw.

14 February 1964

WHEATLEY HILL PANTO SUCCESS

So successful was the pantomime Cinderella, which was presented before a packed audience in Wheatley Hill Welfare Hall by members of the junior section of Wheatley Hill and District Youth Club, that a repeat performance has been arranged for the same hall tomorrow afternoon.

The hall was filled to capacity and more than 100 people had to be turned away. "It was really amazing the number of people who told us afterwards how delighted they were at the variety of talent shown", the club leader, Mrs Rosaline Sinclair, told our reporter.

Fourteen year old Margaret Smith was an outstanding success in the title role of Cinderella and the audience was always sure of plenty of fun when the "Ugly Sisters" - 13 year old David Jordan and 12 year old John Reay - appeared. Leonora Carr was a really charming "Prince Charming" and "hep cat" singer, George Bean, was so popular among the audience that he was encored even after the final bow!

The singing, acting and dancing - as well as the humour provided by the "Ugly Sisters" - all reached a high standard and great credit is due to the organisers for staging such a colourful and talented show.

Other Parts

Leading parts, in addition to those mentioned, were taken by Jennifer Heal, Eileen Worthington, John Taylorson, Denise Raffell, Melvin Abbott, Stewart Carr and Kevin Gilling.

A fine acrobatic turn was given by Raymond Gair and the solo dances of Lynne Mercer were executed gracefully. The other members of the chorus were Ena Symons, Wendy Gribbens, Majorie Dinsley, Jane Hogan, Valerie Hall, Richard Curry, Eric Henderson, Kevin Gardner and Robert Waite.

The show was produced by Mrs Sinclair, and the pianist was Mrs Nancy Robinson. The senior and intermediate club leaders and members of the adult management committee were responsible for the sound effects, scenery, and many of the costumes.

21 February 1964

"SAFETY" CUPS FOR YOUNG
CYCLISTS AT WHEATLEY HILL

At a social evening at Wheatley Hill organised by the village's Road Safety Committee, five boys who gained more than 90 marks out of 100 in the annual cycling proficiency test were presented with miniature cups.

They were Thomas Hodgson who was champion cyclist with 98 marks, Jeffrey Athey and Eric Harper (97 each), Graham Walker (95), and John Hodgson (91).

Certificates and medals were also presented to the following cyclists who passed the test: Colin Atkinson, Eric Harper, Stuart Carr, Brian Harding, Ann Hedley, Valerie Hall, June Inchcliffe, Sheila Parsley, William Hackworth, Edwin Robinson, Graham Walker, John Hodgson, Thomas Hodgson and Alan Frank.

Councillor E Cain presided at the presentations, which were made by PC Gordon Fletcher, of Wheatley Hill, who congratulated the young cyclists on the keen interest they had shown in the test. He hoped they would always take every care on the road and keep their machines in a good state of repair.

Road safety films were shown by PC Fletcher and PC Brown, and refreshments were served by Mrs Slater, Mrs Armstrong and Mrs Hodgson. The secretary of the committee, Mrs Slater, was responsible for the arrangements.

PROUD YOUNG BANDSMAN - Gordon Kitto, of Peterlee, was adjudged Durham County juvenile champion in brass bands in December last, and now he adds to that distinction his success as NCB juvenile champion and received the CISWO challenge cup for cornet playing in the instrumental class on Saturday. He has just been informed that he has been chosen for the national youth brass band of Great Britain at the age of 13. His younger brother, Barry, aged 12, was placed fourth in the juvenile section playing the trombone. He was highly commended. Barry was also placed third in the piano recital class under 14 years.

Both boys are members of Thornley Colliery band conducted by their grandfather, the veteran Mr E G T Kitto.
6 March 1964

AT THE ANNUAL BALLOT for officials and committee of Thornley Catholic Club, Mr John Williams, secretary, was unopposed for 10 seats on the committee. Fifteen members went forward. Those elected were Messrs Edward Hutchinson, 60; Edmund Morrow, 57; Mathew O'Brien, 56; Richard Bell, 55; J Regan, 55; Martin Kenny, 51; Walter Scott, 48; Mathew Hopkins, 44; William Graney, 35; John Ellward, 32. In the balance sheet the sales for the year were: £16,645 which gave a gross profit of £3,533 10s. Entrance fees and subscriptions were: £35 19s. And donations were £1,130. Officials and committee of the club receive no salary or fees.
13 March 1964

LABOUR PARTY'S NEW CANDIDATE

From four nominations, Thornley Area Labour Party have chosen Mr Edward Carter, of Thornley, as their candidate for the forthcoming Durham County Council elections.

About three months ago the party again nominated a Wheatley Hill miner, Councillor John Andrew, who had represented the division, which covers Wheatley Hill and Thornley, on the County Council for the past 11 years, but recently Councillor Andrew resigned from the Council.

The other nominations before the Area Labour Party when Mr Carter was chosen candidate were those of Mr J Cain, Mr John Fenwick and Councillor R Hughes, all of Wheatley Hill. The meeting agreed unanimously to place on record the "untiring work", of Councillor Andrew for the neighbouring villages for Wheatley Hill and Thornley, during his term of office on the County Council.

Mr Carter, the new candidate, is 54. He is a well known figure in Thornley, where he has been actively associated with a number of organisations. He has been employed at Thornley Colliery practically since leaving school, with the exception of five years' war service in the RAF.

He is secretary of Thornley Miners' Welfare Committee, president of Thornley CW Football Club, and is a former chairman of the local miners' lodge.

20 March 1964

WHEATLEY HILL FIRST AID SUCCESSES

The following members of Wheatley Hill Ambulance Class were successful in a recent first aid examination:

Preliminary certificate, Mr B Aitken Jnr.

First year certificates, Messrs P Woodward, J Quinn, E Waitell, B Aitken Snr and W Higham.

Re-examination, Messrs J Cook, R Clarkson, R Maughan, V Hodgson, W Vincent, T Ayre, A C Watson, J Booth, T Christopher, R Howe, E Bell, J R Craggs, T Burnside, N Lonsdale, E Dawes, T Dinsale, A Devine, L Holdcroft, J Tully Snr, A Surman, T Ramage, M Conway, J Tully Jnr, N Osbaldestin, R Foster Jnr, J Pringle, L Taylorson, G Blackett, F Winnard, R Foster Snr, and F Woodhead.

Mr R Wilson was class instructor and the lecturer was Dr G H Wallace. Dr Harland, of Sherburn, was the examiner, and Mr R W Storey class secretary.

3 April 1964

VICAR OF WHEATLEY HILL WED

Wheatley Hill All Saints' Church was filled to capacity for the wedding of its Vicar, the Reverend George Gordon Graham, The Vicarage, Wheatley Hill, only son of the late Mr and Mrs Walter Graham, to Miss Patricia Sheila Puttee, only daughter of Mr and Mrs Reginald E Puttee, Croyde, North Devon.

Before taking Holy Orders Mr Graham studied metallurgy and steel analysis at Sheffield University. He spent ten years as a metallurgist in the steel industry at Sheffield and then responded to the call of the Church. He took his theological training at St Chad's College, Durham. Mr Graham was assistant priest at

Christchurch, Luton and then moved to All Saints' Church, Bakewell, Derbyshire. He went to Wheatley Hill as vicar in 1956.

The bride studied at Hull University and took a degree in botany. She is a tutor in field biology at the Field Centres of Flatford Mill and Ford Castle in Northumberland.

The Service, which was fully choral, with Mr A T Tuffnell at the organ, was conducted by the Very Reverend G W O Addleshaw, Dean of Chester. Nuptial Mass was celebrated by Reverend W H Langford, Vice-Principal of St Chad's College, Durham.

Given away by her father, the bride was attired in a full length gown of white brocade with bouffant veil, held in place with a headdress of white roses. She carried a bouquet of anemones, freesias, irises and tradescantia.

Bridesmaids were the Misses Susan Renshaw and Marguerite Wardle, who wore dresses of blue shot silk and carried bouquets of freesias. Duties of best man were carried out by Dr D S Craig and Messrs M R Puttee, J Wardle and L Graham were ushers.

A reception was held in Wheatley Hill Welfare Hall, after which the couple left on a motoring tour of the South of England.

Wedding of Rev G G Graham & Miss P S Puttee at Wheatley Hill

CELEBRATION PARTY A FORTNIGHT EARLY

Wheatley Hill Couple's 50th Anniversary

Though a well known Wheatley Hill couple, Mr and Mrs George William Hird, of 18 Burns Street, do not complete 50 years of married life until tomorrow they have already held a celebration party to mark their golden wedding - a fortnight ago, on Easter Saturday.

"Easter Saturday was the day on which we were married and so it was rather nice to have our party then", Mr Hird told our reporter this week. "But the chief reason why we held the party a fortnight before the actual anniversary was because our eldest son was visiting us from London - he could not come up later. With him here on holiday, it meant all our family were with us for the celebration".

Mr and Mrs Hird were married in Bishop Auckland United Methodist Church on April 11, 1914. Both were living in Hunwick at the time and they caught the train to Bishop Auckland and then walked to the church for the ceremony. "It was a fine sunny day", Mrs Hird recalled, "but was very frosty".

When she was married Mrs Hird was not 19 until the following September. "Looking back, I do not think it was too young", she said. "It all depends on whom you marry. My husband and I have spent a happily married life and I have no regrets at marrying when I was 18".

Mr Hird, who celebrated his 73rd birthday on Tuesday, was born at Copley. He began work at the Black Boy Pit, Coundon, when he was 13, earning 1s.3d a ten hour shift. His first job was picking stones off the belts.

Does own housework

Later he worked at a number of different collieries in the area, but after the 1921 strike left the mines - he was at Bowden Close at the time - and took up new employment in the cleansing department of Easington Rural Council. He worked for the Council for 36 years until his retirement at 65 and for the last four years of his career was foreman in the cleansing department.

Both Mr and Mrs Hird have been members of Wheatley Hill Over 60 Club for the past three years. "We enjoy going to the meetings", said Mrs Hird, whose maiden name as Mary Studholme Nunn.

Mrs Hird, who is a native of Auckland Park, enjoys excellent health. She does all her own housework, cooking and baking.

When our reporter called at her Council house home she was busy making bread. "I have always baked all my own bread and cakes - there's nothing to beat home-made", she said. Mrs Hird is a former member of Wheatley Hill Women's Institute. She and her husband, who also enjoys good health, have lived in Wheatley Hill 42 years and have occupied their present house 40 years.

They have a family of three sons and two daughters and ten grandchildren. All were at the golden wedding party to extend their personal greetings to the old couple for many more years of good health and happiness.

WHEATLEY HILL MEMORIAL CLOCK

The clock had been a "source of expense and worry" ever since it was erected outside the school wall in Front Street, Wheatley Hill, declared Councillor R C Watson at Monday night's meeting of Wingate Parish Council, when estimates were being considered to carry out repairs to the village's War Memorial clock.

It was certainly a "Hardy Annual", said Councillor J H Charlton. There had always been complaints about the clock - about it never showing the right time and about it starting and stopping at intervals.

But, the Clerk, Mr John Harper, pointed out, they had recently had their biggest run "Free of trouble". "The clock was last repaired in 1958," he said "and since then it has gone quite well up to this last year".

The clock was a war memorial and as such the Council had accepted responsibility for maintaining it.

After considering estimate from the manufacturers the Council agreed to accept one for £95 for a complete overhaul and repair. "It is our responsibility and we have no other choice but see it is repaired", said Councillor Watson, proposing the acceptance of the estimate.

The clock, said the Clerk, would have to be "stripped down" completely and a new dial fitted. Copper will be used in the repair work. The estimate for the work in steel was £10 less. "We might as well have as good a job as possible done", said Councillor Watson.

WHEATLEY HILL COUPLE'S "GOLDEN" CELEBRATION

Formerly well-known throughout the county as a judge at vegetable and flower shows, Mr George Robinson, of 24 Shinwell Terrace, Wheatley Hill, celebrated his golden wedding on Saturday. He and his wife, whose maiden name was Mary Havelock, were married at Easington on April 11, 1914, and have spent all their wedded life in Wheatley Hill.

Mr Robinson has been a keen gardener practically all his life. "But recently I have had to give it up because of my health", he told our reporter this week.

Show Judge

For a number of years he was a regular judge at the Durham Club Union shows and he has visited villages and towns throughout the county to give his expert ruling on flower and vegetable exhibits. He still occasionally acts as a judge at local shows. "But I do not go to as many shows as I used to", he said.

Mr Robinson, who will be 72 in September, was born at Wheatley Hill but as a boy left the village with his parents and started work at Castletown colliery when he was 14.

"My first job was on the pit heap", he recalled, "and I earned ten pence for a shift of 11 hours". After six months he went down the pit and did various jobs, including trapping and driving, before returning to Wheatley Hill seven years later.

He continued as a miner at Wheatley Hill colliery, but ten years before retiring gave up working underground following a bad accident, in which his back was injured in a fall of stone. He then worked as gardener for the colliery manager until his retirement at 65.

Sportsman

Mr Robinson was a well known local footballer in his younger days. He was one of the founders of Wheatley Hill Athletic FC, which competed in a number of leagues, including the Ferryhill and District and Hartlepools and District. He captained the team as full back for about ten years.

He was also a keen billiards player and was a member of the team from Wheatley Hill Workmen's Club which won a number of trophies in county tournaments.

Cheerful Outlook

Mrs Robinson, who will be 70 in August, was born at Framwellgate Moor. Like her husband, she does not enjoy the best of health - she suffers from arthritis - but she has a cheerful outlook on life. "I make the best of things", she said.

One of her weekly pleasures is attending the meeting of the village's Over 60 Club. "A friend always takes me there and I enjoy going very much", she said. She has been a member of the club practically since its inception and she was formerly a member of Wheatley Hill Women's Institute.

Mr and Mrs Robinson have an only daughter, Mrs Edna Nevins who lives at Scarborough, and two grandchildren and two great grandchildren. All were present, together with a number of other relations at a family party at their home on Saturday.

WHEATLEY HILL HAS 81ST SUB-POST OFFICE - A new sub-post office has just opened at Wingate Lane, Wheatley Hill, making the sub-offices in Durham County total 81.
17 April 1964

SAFETY DRAW AT THORNLEY COLLIERY - At the Thornley Colliery Safety draw in the Thornley Miners' Hall, presided over by Mr Hughes, a fitter Mr John Templeton won the £30 voucher and a £1 premium bond.

It was a lucky day for the Templeton family, for his father, an underground worker, Joseph, also received a £1 premium bond from the draw.

Underground workers to receive premium bonds were, Wilf Owens, of Shotton; Robert Richardson of Haswell, Dave Walker, of Thornley. Surface workers: Sam Greener, of Wheatley Hill and William Molyneaux, of Wingate, and John Templeton a fitter as stated came from the Mechanics' Department. All these men are employed at Thornley Colliery.

Mr Hutton, Manager of Thornley Colliery made the draw, organised by Mr Harold Todd, of Thornley, Safety Officer at the colliery.

WHEATLEY HILL CC CALL IT A DAY AFTER 60 YEARS

After being in existence more than 60 years - it is the village's oldest sporting organisation - Wheatley Hill Cricket Club has decided to disband.

The decision, taken at a general meeting of the club at the weekend, means that the club will now have to withdraw from the Durham Coast League where they have competed virtually since its inception.

Just after the last war the club left the Coast League for the Durham County League, but two years later - in 1948 - they rejoined the Coast League, where they have since played and in 1956 won the championship. They have won the Andrew Dixon Cup three times since rejoining the league. This competition is confined to the league's first division clubs.

More expenditure

The weekend meeting was attended by only 17 members out of a possible 96. After the meeting Mr Eric Simpson, secretary of the club for the past ten years, told our reporter the point had been reached where considerable expenditure would have had to be incurred this coming season to bring the field and other facilities up to the required standard.

They had a balance of £100, but it was estimated that more than £500 would be needed and they "just could not carry on", especially with support having fallen off so badly during recent years.

"Over a long period", said Mr Simpson, "the club has attempted to obtain financial backing from various sources but there has been only a poor response". The local Colliery Welfare Committee had helped with certain items of expenditure and two years ago undertook to pay the rent and rates of the ground.

Penalty for apathy

But the Welfare Committee had many commitments of their own, said Mr Simpson, and it was abundantly clear that the cricket club could not expect "substantial aid in the future".

At almost every annual meeting of the cricket club during the past ten years the members' attention had been drawn to the necessity for fund-raising and for everyone to take a fair share of the work.

But these appeals and warnings had been consistently ignored, said Mr Simpson. "And so now the penalty for this apathy has to be paid", he said. Only a few members had borne the burnt of the work.

"We regret very much having to disband, but the choice has been forced upon us", added Mr Simpson.

24 April 1964

SON OF PETER LEE

Mr Harold Lee, the only surviving son of Peter Lee, the former well known Durham miners' leader, after whom the new town of Peterlee was named, died at this home, 36 East View, Wheatley Hill, on Monday at the age of 74.

Unlike his famous father before him, Mr Lee was never in the limelight where trade union and political affairs were concerned, but he was a well known figure in the area and was held in the highest esteem by a wide circle of friends.

In his younger days at Wheatley Hill Colliery, where his father was checkweighman, Mr Lee was secretary for a time of the local branch of the Mechanics' Association and up to his death retained a book presented to him when he was 33 to mark his loyal service.

In Royal and Merchant Navy

The sea was one of the ruling passions of Mr Lee's life. There were few ports in the world he had not visited while in the Royal and Merchant Navy and during the 1914-18 war, while serving in the Royal Navy, he was awarded the DSM for his heroism on HMS Spitfire at Jutland.

Harold Lee with his father, Peter Lee

An account of this action was given by Rudyard Kipling in his book, "Sea Warfare", and Mr Lee is among the naval men mentioned in the book. Mr Lee was also awarded the Medaille Militaire from the French Government.

After the war Mr Lee remained in the Royal Naval Reserve until 1938 - he was an engineer commander - and during the last war he served in the Merchant Navy, where he saw plenty of action.

When he left school Mr Lee started work as an apprentice fitter at Wheatley Hill colliery. Later he went to the Marine School at South Shields and served his time in the dockyards before joining the Merchant Navy before the outbreak of the 1914-18 war.

Methodist

He resumed his work at Wheatley Hill colliery between the two wars and after the last war was in charge of the colliery boilers until his retirement at 65.

Mr Lee had a long association with the Bow Street Methodist Church at Thornley and was one of the trustees there. He was also a founder-member of Wheatley Hill Over 60 Club.

Mr Lee is survived by his wife, two sons, Gilbert and Norman, and a daughter, Mrs Sybil Eltringham, of Cosford. "My father never went into politics - the sea was his life," Mr Gilbert Lee told our reporter. "My grandfather used to tell him that one in the family as enough where politics were concerned".

Mr Lee, who moved to Wheatley Hill from Thornley about 35 years ago, would have celebrated his golden wedding in July next year. His two sisters live in Durham.

Following a service in Patton Street Methodist Church, Wheatley Hill today (Friday), Mr Lee is to be cremated at Durham.

MEMORIES OF DODGER AND NOTTY AT THE "HILL"

So Wheatley Hill CC have followed the example of Littletown and have withdrawn from the Durham Coast League for financial reasons. And another longstanding club has fallen by the wayside through lack of interest.

Time was when Wheatley Hill Cricket Club was a power in East Durham cricket. Their members were enthusiastic and played their cricket in sporting fashion.

The Palmy Days

Perhaps the palmy days were when George Allison was the pro but there were noteworthy exponents before him. Old stagers would recall the slow bowling of "Dodger" Urwin and after him, of "Notty" Oldham. Littletown batsmen who were always at home against fast bowling seemed to be unable to cope with spin, and invariably they fell to the wiles of the bowlers mentioned. Another slow bowler who used to tie up Littletown consistently was Benny Tapping of Hetton Lyons.

Other Stars - Wheatley Hill possessed another outstanding player in J W Huggins, then a schoolteacher in the village who was a member of Durham City CC in their championship year of 1907. When Blackhall Colliery obtained admission to the North Yorkshire and South Durham League, their captain was Tom Elliot who learned his cricket at Wheatley Hill and subsequently captained Littletown in 1926. George Broughton, another Littletown star, was a migrant from the colliery village, and Isaac Patterson was also a Wheatley Hill man. Alan Fishwick, last year's Wheatley Hill captain, graduated with Littletown second team.

1 May 1964

WAS MINE DEPUTY FOR 42 YEARS - Following requiem mass in the Church of Our Lady of the Queen at Wheatley Hill, the interment took place on Saturday of Mr John Gilling, aged 75, of 91 Johnson Estate. Father Sweeney officiated. Mr Gilling a native of Haswell Plough, had spent 52 years in the mining industry starting at Thornley Colliery as an office boy. Later he went to East Hetton Colliery but spent most of his working career at Wheatley Hill where he was a deputy for 42 years. He had been a member of the over 60 club since it began, and was a member of the workmen's club and the Discharged Soldiers and Sailors Club.

He is survived by his wife, Margaret Ellen, to whom he was married 48 years ago, four daughters and three sons.

8 May 1964

WHEATLEY HILL BOYS WERE GUESTS OF THE ARMY

Eighteen boys and their leaders, Mr E Curry and Mr C Gregg, of Wheatley Hill and District Youth Club, were guests of the army at the Light Infantry Brigade Depot, at Shrewsbury, for a weekend.

The boys aged between 13 and 15, went down in an Army mini-bus and cars. The journey was educational for the boys, as some of them had never ventured out of the county before.

On arrival the boys were shown to their billets and given a hot drink and sandwiches.

The following morning they were called at reveille and had breakfast in the soldiers' dining room. After breakfast they had PT and were most impressed by the PT Instructor's patient and instructing manner.

The boys also took part in the obstacle course and fired weapons on the 30 yard range. The range was rather a challenging experience for the boys, as none of them had ever fired live rounds before, but all did exceptionally well.

The programme also consisted of a night exercise and a visit to the regimental museum. The night exercise was an unforgettable experience, with bangs, splashes, guns, water and suspense all adding to a wonderful weekend.

Major Burini, who was the officer in charge of the weekend, was impressed by the boys' enthusiasm and determination, and the boys themselves were full of praise for the Major and his staff's understanding.

Finally what did they think of the Army food? Excellent, and of high standard, with a good variety and plenty of it. On June 5 to 7, a further 12 boys will be going from Wheatley Hill and District Youth Club.

15 May 1964

WHEATLEY HILL DOCUMENTS
123 YEARS OLD, TELL SIMPLE DRAMA

At the beginning of this year we told the story of a 92 year old indenture whereby, as was the custom in those days, an apprentice became "bound" to his employer for a number of years.

The indenture, in a good state of preservation, with every word, both printed and handwritten, legible, is in the possession of Mr and Mrs Robert Lonsdale, 64 Hardwick Street, Blackhall. It related to the apprenticeship as a brass fitter, of Mrs Lonsdale's father, Mr Joseph Watson, and is dated October 5, 1871.

Certainly an old document - and a most interesting one - but this week we learned of an even older indenture in the same remarkable state of preservation and equally as legible.

The indenture, in the hands of Mr and Mrs Mark Alderton, of 63 Wordsworth Avenue, Wheatley Hill, is 123 years old - 31 years older than the Blackhall document.

In 1841

It relates to the "binding" as an apprentice mariner of Mrs Alderton's great grandfather, Mr Thomas Bedford, on February 4, 1841, when he was 16.

Some of the terms of the agreement are similar to those in the indenture held by Mr and Mrs Lonsdale. In it Mr Bedford promised to serve his employer, Mr John Robinson, of Bishop Wearmouth, faithfully for four years ... and the total salary he was to receive for the four years was £35.

In the first year of his apprenticeship he was promised a wage of £7 by his employer, in the second year £7, in the third £10, and the final year £11.

And in return for this Mr Bedford agreed, by his still clearly decipherable signature on the parchment indenture, to "serve his master well and faithfully, his secrets keep, his lawful commands everywhere do and execute, hurt or damage to his said master he will not do, consent to or allow to be done by others, but to the utmost of his power will hinder the same and forthwith his said master thereof warn".

Matrimony was out

The apprentice also agreed not to get married during his four years' apprenticeship, for the indenture continues, "Matrimony during the said term he will not contract, nor from the service of his said master, without his consent at any time absent himself, but as a true and faithful apprentice will demean and behave himself towards his said master, his family, executors and administrators during the said term".

The employer, as his part of the bargain, agreed to "teach, learn and inform the apprentice, or cause him to be taught, learned and informed in the art, trade or business of a mariner or seaman, with the circumstances thereunto belonging".

Meat, drink and lodging

The "master" also agreed to provide the apprentice with "sufficient meat, drink and lodging" and to pay him twelve shillings yearly "in lieu of washing". But the apprentice had to provide himself "with all manner of sea bedding, wearing apparel and other necessaries".

The apprentice bound himself to his employer in the sum of £100. Mr Bedford must have proved himself a capable apprentice in every respect for on the other side of the indenture, are the words in his employer's handwriting - still quite clear - I do hereby certify that Thomas Bedford hath served his apprenticeship out with me as a good and faithfully servant, as witness my hand this 20th day of March, 1845".

The two seals at the bottom of the document alongside the signature of Mr Bedford and his employer are still unbroken - and there is not the slightest crack in either of them.

Not much recalled

Mrs Alderton, whose maiden name was Hilda Bedford, told our reporter she knew little about her great grandfather - the apprentice named in the indenture. "He was obviously a seaman", she said, "but whether he remained at sea all his life or not, I do not know".

The indenture had been handed down from one generation to the next until it came into the hands of her father, who had the same name as the apprentice of so many years ago. Her father, said Mrs Alderton, died eleven years ago at Wheatley Hill at the age of 75. He was a retired miner at the local colliery, and his father before him was a miner at Wingate Colliery.

Only Daughter

The indenture came into Mrs Alderton's possession on the death of her father. She was his only daughter - he had no sons - but her father has a number of relatives in the Wingate area.

Mrs Alderton's husband is a datal worker at Wheatley Hill colliery. He has been compensation secretary to the miners' lodge for the past 14 years and recently was elected to Wingate Parish Council as a representative of the Wheatley Hill ward.
29 May 1964

WHEATLEY HILL COUPLE'S GOLDEN ANNIVERSARY

A well known Wheatley Hill couple, Mr and Mrs Peter Gair, of 27 Henderson Avenue, who have spent all their married life in the village, where they are held in high esteem, celebrated their golden wedding with a family party at their home on Sunday. The couple were married in St Bartholomew's Church, Thornley.

Though Mrs Gair, whose maiden name was Elizabeth Ann Anderson, is in pretty good health, her husband, who is 72, is not so well.

"My legs give me trouble", Mr Gair told our reporter this week. Through working, "so wet" when he was a miner at the local colliery, said Mr Gair, he had developed pains and this stopped him getting about as well as he would like. He has to be wheeled in a chair when he goes out into the village.

Tenpence for ten hours

Born at Spennymoor, Mr Gair began work at Heworth colliery, near Felling, when he was 13½. He was paid at the rate of ten pence a ten hour shift as a trapper boy.

At the age of 16 he moved to Wheatley Hill and continued his mining career at the colliery there, "doing practically every kind of job underground", until he retired at 65½. He went on to the "skip" when he was 56 - that was "really hard work for a man of his age", he said.

Brass band enthusiast

Mr Gair has been keenly interested in brass bands all his life and it was not until he was about 60 that he retired from playing in Wheatley Hill Colliery Band. He was only 13 when he began as a bandsman in Thornley Salvation Army Band.

"I have played a number of instruments, including the tenor and fugal horn", he said, "and when I finished was playing the drums".

Mrs Gair was born at Castle Eden 71 years ago, but has lived in Wheatley Hill practically all her life.

Lifelong Methodist

A lifelong Methodist, she has been a member of the Patton Street Methodist Church in the village for many years and is also associated with the Sisterhood. She has been a member of the village Over 60 Club since its inception.

She does all her own housework, cooking and baking and, in fact, made the cake for her golden wedding party.

Married on the same day as the couple and at the same church was Mr Gair's brother, Mr John Anderson. He is now a widower living in Doncaster.

Mr and Mrs Gair, who have been lifelong readers of the Durham Chronicle, have a family of three sons and two daughters, all married and nine grandchildren and two great grandchildren.

We extend to them best wishes for many more years of happiness and good health together.
5 June 1964

THORNLEY AGED MINERS' HOMES
WERE FOUNDED 50 YEARS AGO

Last Saturday marked the 50th anniversary of the foundation stone laying of aged miners' cottages and a hostel for eight bachelors at Thornley. It was on June 6 1914 that the first 12 free houses were started.

The first Aged Miners' Committee was formed on July 7 1913, with Mr G A Curry, colliery manager, as chairman. Representatives from the miners, mechanics, enginemen and deputies were present. Unlike the county system which was voluntary, Thornley committee decided to levy each member 2d per member each week and half members a 1d and decided to confine the homes only to retired workmen of Thornley colliery. The committee also decided to invite the Reverend E Coltier Biggs, Vicar of Thornley, Reverend Father McDermott, Catholic priest, the Reverend G Rymer, PM Minister, the Reverend G Newall, WM Minister and Mr T Swinburne, landlord of the Robin Hood Inn.

The first buildings of houses and bachelors quarters was done by Mr W Sparrow of Hetton for the price of £1,998. The land had already been bought in 1913 at a cost of £300 per 180 sq ft. The first caretakers to be appointed for the bachelors quarters were Mr and Mrs Ralph Foster and the first tenants for the cottages were Jont Gair, R Bunting, Jos Hall, G Burnham, R Bosomworth, A Coldwell, W Humble, W Lambert, G Jordan, T Lee, T Wilkinson, John Mather. The first inhabitants of the bachelors' quarters were Jas Batty, John Holmes, John Hall, Hugh Blaney, John Champley and John Cummings.
12 June 1964.

MASKED MEN ROB THORNLEY LICENSEE

Extensive enquiries were carried out this week by detectives in the Castle Eden Police Division, following a break-in at The Halfway House, Thornley - a public house near the Wheatley Hill to Durham road - during the early hours of Sunday, but up to Wednesday no arrests had been made.

The licensee, Mrs Irene Robinson, who is a widow, lives alone. About 2.30 am she heard noises from the next bedroom. She found three men, the lower half of their faces covered with handkerchiefs, searching the room.

They demanded to know "where the money was kept." Mrs Robinson, who is 67, told them and they quickly made their getaway with a green handbag containing about £3.

The intruders, believed to be in their early twenties, entered the public house after breaking a front window and they made their escape by the front door.

A description of the men has been circulated by the police. They are said to be of thickset build and were wearing black caps and donkey jackets. Two of them were wearing dark jeans and the other light blue jeans.

Anyone who saw anything suspicious in the neighbourhood is asked to contact the nearest police officer.

19 June 1964

A LOSS TO WHEATLEY HILL
LEGION AND METHODISTS

A well known figure in Methodist and British Legion circles was cremated at Sunderland on Saturday. He was Mr James Robinson (65), 15 South View, Wheatley Hill. Wheatley Hill Church Street Methodist Church was filled for the funeral service, which was conducted by Reverend G L Nelson. Members of Wheatley Hill Women's section of the British Legion formed a guard of honour.

Mr Robinson is survived by his wife, Mrs Isabel Robinson, to whom he was married 43 years, and a son and daughter. With the exception of a few years at Castletown, he spent all of his life in Wheatley Hill. He started work at the local colliery at 14, and was a stoneman for most of his mining career (which lasted for 50 years) at the one colliery. He retired a year ago owing to ill health.

Was severely wounded

Mr Robinson served in the First World War, with the Duke of Wellington's Regiment. He was severely wounded in bitter righting in France. On demobilisation he took a great interest in the British Legion movement. He was a past secretary of the Men's Section, at Wheatley Hill. It was a great disappointment to him when the men's section had to close down through lack of support. He continued to serve the Legion as Welfare Officer to the Hartlepools and District War Pensions Committee, for 18 years, a position he held until just prior to his death.

Mr Robinson was a lifelong Methodist, being a member of Wheatley Hill Church Street Church.

Trustee

He was a trustee of the church for 40 years and in his younger days he was an active worker in the Sunday School and choir.

He was also a keen member of Wheatley Hill Over 60 Club.

26 June 1964

5,000 WATCH WHEATLEY HILL MINERS' SPORTS

Five thousand people watched events at the Wheatley Hill Miners' Federation Board Sports Day on Saturday in Wheatley Hill Girls' Modern School playing field.

A colourful parade started at the Colliery Offices and marched through the village. Parade marshal was Mr John Harper. The Wheatley Hill Colliery Band, under its conductor, Mr J Rutter headed the parade. Also taking part were three Jazz Bands, Sunderland Juveniles, Hylton Castle Hussars and Cleadon Legionnaires.

Some 2,000 children received bags of sweets and chocolate. A substantial surplus of these will be sent to the Children's Wards of Durham County and Dryburn Hospitals. Each competitor in children's events received a 2s.6d savings stamp.

The cost of the Sports Day was £650, raised by a weekly levy on miners' wages. Other popular attractions were sideshows in the charge of members of Wheatley Hill Old Scouts' Association and an RSPCA exhibition.

Judges of events were Police Sergeant and Mrs J Jackson, Dr and Mrs J Wallace, Dr and Mrs Hutchinson, Mr F Richardson (colliery manager), and Mrs Richardson, Mr F Walker (under manager), and Mrs Walker, Reverend and Mrs G L Nelson.

Miners' officials in charge of organisation were Mr H Bradshaw (chairman), Mr W N Gibson (secretary), Mr J Hedley (treasurer), backed by a strong committee. Mr Gibson, organising secretary, paid tribute to the massive help given by the women's organisations of the village and the Wheatley Hill Scouts.

Results - Children's Fancy Dress parade: Original: 1, P Hoban; 2, tie, B Murray and A Clarkson; 3, G Hogan. Fancy: 1, C Atkinson; 2, tie, B Hall and L Evans; 3, tie, A Warnes and I Rowbotham. Comic: 1, L Hall; 2, K Hicks; 3, R Hedley.

Adult, Fancy Dress: 1, Miss D Lee; 2, Miss R Marratty.

Councillor R Watson, who acted as Mr Sports Day went unchallenged till teatime. He was eventually challenged by Mrs J Slack who was awarded the £2 prize. Pit ponies, Best in Show; 1, Boxer of Easington Colliery. Cleanest and Best Groomed: 1, Tiny (Thornley); 2, Salty (Easington); 3, Pompey (Shotton). Four Mile Open Race: 1, J Murray; 2, W Jobes; 3, G Bennett; 4, W Million.

Children's Events - Girls, flat races, 5 years: 1, V Errington; 2, E Cullon; 3, L Dawson. 6 years: L Richardson, S Cain, S Dixon. 7 years: L Tatters, D Stephenson, D Taylor. 8 years: A Tie: L Parker, Joyce Luke, S O'Connor. 9 years: J Carr, M Bulmer, D Curry. 10 years: E Frost, M Luke, Tie A Gilling, B Harker. 11 years: D Errington, A Loftus, P Goynes. 12 years: S Patterson, A Peacock, J Forster. 13 years: C O'Connor, J Rowbotham, D Rushton. 14 years: K Lock, M Maughan, J Luke. 15 years: I V Hammond.

Egg and Spoon Races: 5 years: 1, E Cullon; 2, V Errington; 3, P Telford. 6 years: L Patterson, L Richardson, C Welch. 7 years: J Parkin, L Tatters, P Gilling. 8 years: P Howe, J Whinn, L Harker. 9 years: P Stobbs, M Dunn, C Hodson.

Sack Races: 10 years: 1, S Luke; 2, H Rowbotham; 3, M Luke. 11 years: D Errington, A Loftus, T Bartley. 12 years: E Worthington, A Hedley, S Patterson. 13 years: D Rushton, J Greener, J Rowbotham. 14 years: J Luke, A Million, M Humes.

Boys - Flat Races: 5 years: 1, K Quinn; 2, G Darby; 3, K Vincent. 6 years: G Pattison, J Gutcher, S Chatter. 7 years: M Granet, D Cox, E Starkey. 8 years: Ray Lambert, D Hardy, S Kell. 9 years: F Mitchell, J Hinds, G Tarren.

10 years: A Patterson, E Starkey, M Cain. 11 years: T Bradshaw, D Parker, J Dunn. 12 years: K O'Connor, B Evans, M Potts. 13 years: W Hackworth, T Cain, E Harper. 14 years: M Waistell, J Rushton, R Watson. 15 years: B Aitken, B Young.

Egg and Spoon races: 5 years: 1, M Carr; 2, K Vincent; 3, S Million. 6 years: B Clarkson, G Pace, A Parker. 7 years: J Rickard, J Dawson, F Telford. 8 years: P Dunn, D Million, S Kell. 9 years: J Hinds, D Patterson, F Mitchell.

Sack Races: 10 years: 1, E Starkey, 2, A Patterson; 3, A Dyson. 11 years: B Venables, T Carr, T Anderson. 12 years: B Evans, G Burke, D Evans. 13 years: W Hackworth, E Harper, J Jordon. 14 years: M Waistell, R Hughes, J Rushton. 15 years: B Young, B Aitken.

3 July 1964

CARNIVAL AND SPORTS DAY AT THORNLEY

Over 12,000 people from Thornley and the nearby colliery villages, lined the mile and a half route in brilliant sunshine when Thornley Miners' Sports Committee held their seventh annual Carnival and Sports Day. The police aided by special constables and a patrol car with a loudspeaker, had quite an arduous day in controlling the large crowds, who were in a gay and festive mood.

The parade was headed by the Rose Fletcher Pipe Band from Manchester, who later on the sports field gave a demonstration of marching and Scottish dancing. Also taking part in the Parade were the Thornley Colliery Silver Prize Band (Conductor E Kitto) and the Girls' Brigade and various tableaux, jazz bands, and fancy dress entrants.

The two people who found Mr and Mrs Sports Day were also successful in their quest this year. Mr Sports Day was Mr M Hopkins, a shotfirer at Thornley Colliery, who was successfully challenged by Mr J Onion.

Mrs Sports Day (Mrs D Ord) was successfully challenged by Mrs Laverick.

Other prizewinners were: Best dressed tableaux: 1, Thornley Mothers' Club; 2, Thornley Women's Institute; 3, Thornley Road Safety.

Fancy Dress

Adult: Mrs Crisp, G Coupland. Judges were Mr and Mrs Bonar, Mr and Mrs J Williams.

Children: 5 to 7 (comic): S Wharrior, P Hoban, P Thompson, J Hubbard, S Mitchinson. 8 to 10 (comic): R Murray, B Tilley, R Saunders, K Quinn, B Musgrave. 11 to 15 (comic): A Williams, J W Cairns, L Chapman, R Mawson, J Darby and P Stanley.

Children (original): 5 to 7: J Mitchison, D Newton, P Williams, A Lofthouse, J Bowes. 8 to 10: M Slater, A Whinn, J McMenam, C Davison. 11 to 15 plus: P Cairns, V Hall, L Evans, V Lofthouse, M Clarke, J Lennox.

Arts and Crafts

C Durkin, S Dobbin, S Brownless, G Robson, G Carter, B Dobbin, J Owen, M Carter, J Iveson, K Hardy, M Dougherty, R Peacock, W Hall, A Thompson, Jean Iveson, C Frampton, J Jobes, M Wood, L Parker, E Bell, S Richardson, J Wood, M Johnson, S Bell, M Quinn, R Peacock, D Barker, A Dinsley.

Painting (11 to 15): M Crisp, K Turner, G Athey, G Iveson. Special Ann Hardy.

Handicapped children (Boys): J Johnson, W Murray, (girls): 1, M Bell; 2, A Hardy; 3, C Coldwell; joint 3rd, E Neilson.

Judges for arts and crafts were Mr Harris, Mr Howell, Miss Taylor, Mrs Lang, Mr Alderson and Mr Lamb.

Pit Ponies

Cleanest pit pony B Group No 3 Area; 1, "Pompey" Shotton Colliery, (R Young, 2, "Royal" Wheatley Hill, (L Bell), 3, "Duke" Deaf Hill, (R Bell).

Champion of Durham Division: 10 hands and under: 1, "Tiny" Thornley Colliery (R Ord), 10 to 11 hands: 1, "Pompey" Shotton Colliery (R Young), 11 hands and over: 1, "Boxer", of Easington Colliery (E Robinson).

Champion pit pony and cup, "Boxer", of Easington Colliery. Judge was Mr E Gilson, Low Pittington.

Jazz Bands

Jazz Bands Drum Major, cup and medal, Horden Blue Stars; 2 and medal, Pennywell Toreadors; 3 and medal, Peterlee Gold Stars.

Jazz Bands Band Major: 1, cup and medal, Horden Blue Stars: 2, and medal, Guidepost and Stakeford Highflyers: 3, and medal, Hedworth.

Jazz Bands Base Drummer: 1, cup and medal, Horden Blue Stars, 2, and medal, Guidepost and Stakeford Highflyers; 3, and medal, Boldon Jazz Band.

Judges for the fancy dress were Mr and Mrs Hutton, Mr and Mrs A Woodward, Mr and Mrs W Stokoe, The Reverend and Mrs Mold, Mr and Mrs Maddison, Mr and Mrs Ward and for the tableaux, Mr Bovill, W Hetherington and G Hutchings.

Field Events

Boys: 5 to 6: 1, P Lennox; 2, G Williamson; 3, K Quinn. 6 to 7: 1, S Chaytor; 2, P Watson; 3, G Pattison. 7 to 8: 1, J Purvis; 2, D Grieves; 3, R Parker. 8 to 9: 1, I Lang; 2, K Brownless; 3, J Adams. 9 to 10: 1, D Pattison; 2, J Youll; 3, D Atkin. 10 to 11: 1, R Hubbard; 2, T Wilson; 3, R Marshall. 11 to 12: 1, D Spence; 2, P Pattison; 3, Gaskell. 12 to 13: 1, J Walls; 2, A Dower; 3, W Adams. 13 to 14: 1, D Frost; 2, B Parker, 3, A Winter.

Girls: 5 to 6: 1, J Gaskell; 2, V Errington; 3, S Gradon. 6 to 7: 1, L Richardson; 2, G Day; 3, J Murray. 7 to 8: 1, S Armstrong; 2, S Armstrong, 3, A Dower. 8 to 9: 1, M Wood; 2, L Parker; 3, M McDonnell. 9 to 10: 1, J Day; 2, M Walker; 3, M Bonar. 10 to11: 1, J Wood; 2, J Foster; 3, J Sunley. 11 to 12: 1, S Green; 2, D Errington; 3, N Armstrong. 12 to 13: 1, L Walker; 2, E Dixon; 3, A Rutherford. 13 to 14: 1, A Vasey; 2, P Sunley; 3, C Winters. 14 to 15: 1, K Leck; 2, J Taylor; 3, E Worthington.

Winner of the go-as-you-please race, and the winner of the Baldasera Challenge Cup was J W Cairns. Trophies were presented by Mr F Baldasera.

Prizes for the field events were presented by Mr and Mrs Wood.

"GOLDEN DAY" FOR WHEATLEY HILL COUPLE

On July 11 1914, Mr George Lindsay Aitken was married to Miss Mary Hannah Brown in Shadforth Parish Church. Today, the couple, who reside at 14 Shinwell Terrace, Wheatley Hill, celebrate their golden wedding, with a family party in their home. Attending the festivities will be the couple's two daughters and a son, who is secretary of Wheatley Hill Workmen's Club, and two grandchildren. An honoured guest will be Mrs Aitken's sister, Mrs Jane Armstrong, of Sherburn, who was a bridesmaid 50 years ago.

Mrs Aitken said; "At the time of our wedding George came down from Scotland to Ludworth, where I was staying. He only came for the New Year holiday - at least that was his intention. However, he stayed and we were married in the July. We hadn't time to settle down to married life for in three weeks the 1914-18 War was declared and it meant parting. My husband enlisted with the Argyle and Sutherland Highlanders and later transferred to the Royal Engineers. He spent ten months in a prisoner of war camp in Germany.

From Scotland

Mr Aitken was born 72 years ago in Hamilton in Scotland and started work at the local colliery. In 1913 he moved to Wheatley Hill Colliery and spent 46 years there until he retired at the age of 66.

In the 1939-45 War he served as an ARP warden in Wheatley Hill. As a young man he was interested in football and gave many years as trainer of Ludworth Club. He has been a member of the Village Workmen's Club for many years and has served on the Management Committee.

Mrs Aitken is 68 and apart from a lame leg is in good health. She has the Scottish Army tradition in her blood. Her father was a regular soldier and she was born and brought up in Hamilton Barracks. Before her marriage she was in domestic service.

Praise for Young People

Mrs Aiken had some comments to make on today's young people. "Young people are run down by many folk. A few extremists in riots are all some folk can see. They fail to see the bulk of the youngsters who are decent and behave properly. Our young people are all right. I don't ever remember a time when the youngsters were so willing to help the old folks in every was they can".

Commenting on housework, Mrs Aiken said, "Things are a lot easier today. Labour saving devices have helped working people to have more leisure. Take washing days, I remember we had to get up early on washing day to light the fire for boiling water. Out came the big iron pan which was filled and boiled time and again. The poss stick, or 'dolly' meant hours of manual labour. After a day's washing in those conditions it meant tired arms and shoulders. Washers and spin dryers have taken the work out of washing days".

Mrs Aitken is a communicant member of Wheatley Hill All Saints' Church and is a former member of the Mothers' Union.

Both Mr and Mrs Aitken are regular members of the local Over 60 Club. Among early well wishers at their home tomorrow will be the secretary of the Over 60 Club, Mrs M E Richardson, who will present the couple with a bouquet of carnations on behalf of members.

COAL BOARD BOWLS FINALS ATTRACTED
LARGE CROWD AT WHEATLEY HILL

Under the auspices of the Coal Industry Social Welfare Organisation, the finals of the No 3 Area National Coal Board Bowls Tournament was held at Wheatley Hill Welfare Recreation Ground on Saturday.

Mr J Coates, Regional Welfare Officer stated that the competition attracted 400 entrants. Mr A Hafekost (Horden) acted as area secretary. The event attracted a large crowd of spectators.

Mr John W Burrell (Wheatley Hill), secretary of the local Welfare Club, followed up his recent success in winning the Open Singles trophy in the No 4 Area championships, by winning the Men's Doubles with Mr T Steel. Since commencing to play bowls in 1953, Mr Burrell has won ten trophies.

Results Women

Singles: 1, Mrs Robinson (Blackhall); runner-up, Mrs E Hall (Wheatley Hill). Pairs: 1, Mrs Dobson and Mrs Parker (Blackhall); runners-up, Mrs M Skellet and Mrs J Bell (Horden).

Rinks: 1, Mesdames Robinson, Allan, Scott, Barrass (Blackhall); runners-up, Mesdames Rigby, Harrison, Murray, Luxmore (Wingate).

Men - Singles: 1, Mr J English (Easington); runner-up, Mr J W Burrell (Wheatley Hill).

Pairs: 1, Mr J Steel and Mr J W Burrell (Wheatley Hill); runners-up, Mr G Iveson and Mr E Pullan (Blackhall).

Rinks: 1, Messrs J Telford, J Eggleston, J M Eggleston, J English (Easington); runners-up, Messrs R Jackson, L Parsley, J Steel, J W Burrell (Wheatley Hill).

Veteran rinks: 1, Messrs J Waister, M Robinson, A Hafekost, J Kirkbride (Horden); runners-up, Messrs R Lonsdale, J Bell, F Bissett, J Taylor (Blackhall).

10 July 1964

WORKMAN'S FALL FROM ROOF
COUNCIL'S FAULT - COURT

While using a roof ladder on the top of a council house at Wheatley Hill, the magistrates heard at Peterlee on Monday, a bricklayer employed by Easington Rural Council fell onto the concrete path at the back of the house when the ladder collapsed.

Fortunately, said Mr N Turns, HM Inspector of Factories, the bricklayer sustained only a fractured ankle.

Council Summoned

Mr Turns was the prosecutor when Easington Rural Council was summoned for failing to comply with the regulations of the 1961 Factories Act by using a roof ladder which was not of good construction. The Council pleaded "Guilty" and was fined £10.

The Bricklayer, Mr Lloyd Saunders, of Thornley, had been told to renew a chimney pot on top of the house, 32 Burns Street, Wheatley Hill, on March 31, said Mr Turns. The house was 15¾ feet high and the gable above was another 7½ feet.

Ladder Collapsed

Mr Saunders, continued Mr Turns, took a roof ladder and after climbing onto the roof went up the roof ladder to secure a rope at the top. Before he could fasten the rope, however, the ladder collapsed and fell off the roof. Mr Saunders went with it and landed on the concrete path below. It was "quite a worn ladder", said Mr Turns. Nails had been used to fasten the top of it but something "more substantial" than these was needed.

In January last year, said Mr Turns, it came to the Ministry's notice that the Council was using ladders of this construction and they were advised to replace them with ladders of a more suitable construction.

"Although this is a serious matter", added Mr Turns, "The Council, as an employer of building labour, is extremely safety conscious and they have appointed a Safety Officer".

Safety Officer Away

Mr R R Crute, defending, said that at the time the Safety Officer had been off work ill. When the recommendation came from the Factory Inspector about more suitable ladders, the Council complied with it and at once ordered them.

The old roof ladder which had been used must have been lying about and been picked up by one of the workmen and put into use without being properly looked at. There were better ladders available.

Mr Crute added, "The Council officials are rather upset about this accident because they have never been prosecuted for anything in connection with the carrying out of their work".

YOUNG SOLDIER'S FUNERAL - Many relatives and friends attended the service at Thornley of Sapper Raymond Monk (19), who died last week in Germany. His home was 6 St Cuthbert's Road, Thornley. He is survived by his parents, Mr and Mrs G H Monk, two brothers and four sisters. Services in St Stephen's Methodist Church and at Thornley Cemetery were conducted by the Reverend G Johnson.

24 July 1964

YOUTH ON PARADE AT WHEATLEY HILL

One of the most go-ahead organisations in the district, Wheatley Hill Youth Club, held an open air parade and rally of youth activities in the Girls' Modern School playing field on Saturday. It was organised by the Youth Club leaders and the committee. Club leaders were Mrs R Sinclair (Junior Club), Mr E Curry (Intermediate Club) and Mr C Gregg (Senior Club).

Mr J Andrew (Club chairman) said that it was hoped to make the rally an annual function. It was intended to show the people of Wheatley Hill what their Youth Club stood for, the type of activity it catered for and the spirit that animated their young people

The parade marched through the village, headed by Wheatley Hill Colliery silver band, in front of the three sections of the club marched the leaders and the officials of the club, Mr J Andrew (chairman) and Mr F Dunn (secretary). Wheatley Hill Miners'

Lodge was represented by Mr A Wharrier (secretary), Mr G Burnside (chairman) and Mr J Andrew (delegate). Also in the parade were the Wheatley Hill Boy Scouts and Cubs in charge of Councillor R Watson and Scoutmaster Les Barker.

Mechanised units of the DLI and the KSLI, and a detachment of the Somerset and Cornwall Light Infantry under Captain O Reynolds, who are touring Britain after service in Berlin, caused a lot of interest. The Army was commanded by Major E Burrini.

Its Own Premises

On the playing field members of the junior club gave a display of dancing and folk dancing. Personnel of the intermediate club entertained with an excellent gymnastic display. Members of the senior club showed goods they had made to be sold for the National Association of Youth Clubs' Jamaica Project, the money raised to go to the fund for starting youth clubs in Jamaica.

Christmas cards and other novelties were sold for the club's own building fund. Mrs Sinclair pointed out that the club hopes to build its own premises as soon as is practicable.

The large crowd present were keenly interested in the Army's display of the latest weapons. On show was a light armoured car, a minefield, an aerial rope way, an air rifle range and two champs (vehicles). The soldiers gave a highly efficient display of physical training.

Scouts and Cubs were in charge of side-shows and members of the Adult Management Committee did a grand job in the refreshments department.

Members of the senior club made their own banner, which was on display for the first time on Saturday, and will be paraded on all future formal occasions.

A unique feature of Saturday's parade was the appearance of Wheatley Hill Colliery Miners' banner. Under the supervision of Mr George Burnside, it was carried by five teenage girls: Eileen Barker (14), Jennifer Forster (13), Greta Beddell (16), Madeline Holmes (14) and D Cook.

WORKMEN'S, THORNLEY

Rhythm groups are appealing to the young members, the Saturday, Sunday and Monday night sessions being well patronised. It has been decided to organise rhythm for Friday nights, and the local group The Raging Storms, were given the opportunity to open the new session. They were very successful.

The half yearly ballot for the management committee resulted in the election of Ned Luke, George Hopps, John Templeton, and Percy Hird. Runners-up were George Oswald and Alf Jones. Scrutineers were Johnny French, Doug Gott and Ernie Craven.

The old thick pint glasses with clumsy handles are rarely seen in clubs nowadays, but still clinging to the old type is Jack Campbell, who enjoys his nightly pint at this regular place in the bar.

The moment old Jack hobbles in with his stick and pipe steward Stan Jackson automatically moves to lift the glass from its honoured place and fill it with Jack's favourite brew.

From opening to closing time this fine old man sits puffing away at his pipe and supping the ale, unconcerned at the continuous babble in the bar, Jack is deaf.

WHEATLEY HILL - Now enjoying his pint of beer in the bar is Alf Bramford, after a period of indisposition. A charge hand for Easington Rural Council, he fell through a bedroom floor, which had been weakened by woodworms.

"It could have been worse", commented Alf, who is still a little shaky.

The talent contest on Friday nights continue to be popular, and competition is becoming so keen that the judges are finding it quite difficult making awards. There was a packed house for the Saturday night dancing, with Keith at the organ and Tom beating out the time on the drums.

14 August 1964

WORKMEN'S CLUB TRIP - THORNLEY

The village was much quieter on Saturday, the reason being that 14 bus loads of children with their parents, went to South Shields - the annual outing for members' children.

The day was well organised thanks to Doug Gott (outing secretary).

The only odd man out was Sam Blakemore, a member of the outing committee, who had put in 12 months of hard graft paving the way for this popular event.

He took ill and was taken to Sedgefield General Hospital. Secretary Tucker Brown, visiting him the other day, tells me he is bearing up well. Members and friends wish him a speedy recovery and a quick return to the bar. "I am taking him the Club News on Friday", yelled a member from the other side of the bar. "It will be a great tonic for him".

Pybus Christopher vanished into thin air when he landed at South Shields with the children. His pals, all ready to try a pint of Tyneside brew, wondered what had happened to him.

A search was organised and Pybus was found entangled with the ropes of a beach tent he had hired for his wife and children. Pybus, unfortunately, was well up the pole, baffled as to how to erect the tent. His cronies, however, came to the rescue with the result that he was soon trying out the seaside ale.

Misfortune also dogged Jack Dawson and his father, "Ginger", minehost of the Railway Tavern. Smartly dressed, they boarded the bus for Redcar, but on reaching Wingate they discovered they had left behind their free tickets for the Silver Ring at Redcar racecourse.

They got off the bus and returned to Thornley cursing their bad luck, but a local butcher put them in better mood by volunteering to give them a lift to Redcar.

They arrived at the Silver Ring just at the start, but on the whole it was neither a golden nor a silver day for this sporting pair, they backed no winners.

SOLDIERS AND SAILORS, WHEATLEY HILL - Steward and stewardess are now back at the pumps, fit and bronzed after a holiday at Blackpool, Austin Cain acted as relief steward. Pleased to renew acquaintance with many of the members was Charlie Curry, on holiday from the Midlands. He enjoyed the fresh tang of the North East beer, "the best in the world", he says.

The domino team, Ken Hedley, Bob Hedley, John Halliwell, trounced Fishburn in the tournament.

21 August 1964

THORNLEY'S EFFORTS TO
FIND WINNING TEAM

Thornley CW are leaving no stone unturned in an effort to improve on their displays of last season, and to strengthen the positions which caused the committee some concern last term.

New faces have already appeared on the local Welfare Ground in practice matches in the last few days. Most of last season's players have put in an appearance.

Terry McGregor, outstanding last season and a former 'Pools player, and Geoff Wyhatt, who reluctantly switched to centre half last season and soon had the "scouts" interested with his displays, have left.

The biggest surprise was the loss of goalkeeper Bill Hedley to Murton CW, the Wheatley Hill youth who turned down offers from Spurs and Wolves to continue his scholastic duties.

Thornley have always been noted for having brilliant custodians. This season is no exception for they have secured the services of Harry Metcalfe, who was on 'Pools' books last season.

As in last season's team there has been a big influx on Hartlepool players to the colliery area.

With the Veart twins back in the side, Bob Spavin, Ken Peart, Billy Sutherland, Frank Boylan, newcomers Herring and Eric Clark (all from the 'Pools) it will be hard to discern which is rally the Hartlepools XI on Wednesday when Thornley play 'Pools' Reserves in a friendly game.

The two odd men out in this probable Thornley team are the two full backs, local boy John Wilkinson and Shotton junior Arnold Church.

Mich Spaving, who has been waiting patiently for a full time position in the rearguard position, played for 'Pools against Leeds and had quite an impressive debut. He played some strong games for Thornley last season but the more cultured and cool displays of ex-Durham County Captain, John Wilkinson, always kept him on the lines.

28 August 1964

WHEATLEY HILL CHURCH CLOSES

After serving the community for about 100 years, Wheatley Hill Church Street Methodist Church has closed. The society is amalgamating with Patton Street Church.

On Saturday a social function was held in Wheatley Hill Welfare Hall, the Reverend G L Nelson presiding. It was organised by Mr P H Galley and Miss S Venables. Supper was served by the ladies.

The long service of two Sunday school and church officials was recognised. Mr J O Hughes received a bowls bag and Mr G Poulson a fountain pen.

At the closing service on Sunday night the Church was filled, when the members of Patton Street Church joined their Church Street friends. The preacher was Mr Nelson, with Master Alan Howarth as organist. Lessons were read by Mrs R Chisholm (Patton Street) and Mrs A Kirk (Church Street).

An anthem was sung by the choir, with Mr L Williams as conductor and Mrs J Shutt as organist. Soloists were Mrs G L Nelson, Miss B Galley, Mr A Straughan and Mr W Warnes.

25 September 1964

THORNLEY UNCLE AND NEPHEW WERE TOP IN BIG LEEK SHOW

The 36th News of the World leek, flower and vegetable show, a magnificent display of produce from the best of the county's gardeners, was opened in the Town Hall last week by the Mayor of Durham, Councillor N W Sarsfield.

Of the 350 stands, judged by Messrs T Robinson, H Jackson, R Alexander, J Quaile, R Neale and H Shiel, well over 150 were blooms - of which the chrysanthemums, particularly, were of an exceptionally high standard.

Thornley men win 36th News of the World Leek, Flower & Veg Show at Durham City

The premier award, the first in the pot leeks section, was won by a Thornley uncle and nephew, Mr Alan Hutchinson and Mr Norman Hutchinson, whose stand measured 187 cubic inches.

"Bodies in State"

Mr A Bewick, who first organised the Durham show on behalf of the News of the World in 1927, recalled that the sponsors referred to the 25 leek stands in those days as "dead bodies lying in state". Moves were made to "brighten up" the show and he was glad to see that today the exhibits made a magnificent spectacle of which Durham could be proud.

407

The show, said Alderman Mrs H H Rushford, could not fail to uplift those who saw it. It also gave visitors an opportunity to help local charities as collections were taken during the show to benefit deserving causes.

Mr R Bachus, publicity manager of the News of the World, thanked the corporation for their help in staging the show. The speakers were introduced by Mr T Scott the Show organiser.

Results

Pot leeks: 1, A and N Hutchinson, Thornley, 187 cu in; 2, S Peacock, Witton-le-Wear; 3, J Bell, Trimdon.

Blanch leeks: 1, 2 and 3 J Defty, Trimdon.

Collection of vegetables: H A and N Hutchinson, Thornley. Collection of vegetables: 1, J Storey, Sedgefield.

Incurved chrysanthemums: 1, N Hughes, Easington. Incurving chrysanthemums: 1, N Hughes, Easington. Reflex chrysanthemums: 1, G Stonehouse, Jarrow. Vase of 12 chrysanthemums: 1, A Jackson, Easton Bolton. Artistic arrangement: 1, Mrs Armstrong, Staindrop.

Vase of gladioli: 1, C A Holmes, Tantobie. Dahlia medium decs: 1, G Fisher, Coxhoe. Dahlia medium cactus: 1, W Robinson, Bishop Auckland. Dahlia small decs: 1, G Stonehouse, Jarrow. Dahlia small cactus: 1, R Maddison, Coxhoe. Dahlia pom pom: 1, W Hope, Hetton-le-Hole. Bowl of dahlias: 1, Mrs N McKay, Sedgefield.

Bowl border flowers: 1, J A Clark, Consett.

2 October 1964

PHOTOGRAPHIC SOCIETY - Wheatley Hill and District Photographic Society serves the area twixt Durham and West Hartlepool and have acquired new premises recently decorated by club members at 24 Granville Terrace, Wheatley Hill. There are studio and dark room facilities available and a varied programme is already underway. Meetings are held every Wednesday at 7.30 pm and new members are particularly welcome whether expert or beginner. Anyone interested is asked to contact the club secretary, Mr D Griffiths, 22 Bevan Crescent, Wheatley Hill, who will be pleased to answer any queries.

9 October 1964

MANY ROAD SAFETY AWARDS
AT THORNLEY

Some 100 children with their parents and special guests attended a presentation dinner in the Thornley Miners' Welfare Hall, organised by the Thornley Road Safety Committee.

Councillor J Bosomworth welcomed the children and special guests, who included Inspector N Knowles, Accident Prevention Officer of the Durham County Police, County Councillor Edward Carter, and Councillor J Nicholson of the Easington Rural District Council.

PC Pearson, Accident Prevention Officer of the Castle Eden Division, told the children always to be road safety conscious in their school days for as they matured they would be hoping to have a motor cycle or a car.

Councillor Nicholson paid tribute to the Tutor, Mr C Woodward, the ladies of the committee for their services both in Road Safety and also for their serving of tea.

The following received cycle proficiency awards: I Brown, 100 per cent Safety Challenge Cup; Maisie Spence, 99 per cent; G Athey, 99 per cent; W Nicholson, 99 per cent. These four also received extra awards for representing Thornley at Crimdon in the ERDC road safety contests. Other children to pass were D Atkinson, D Butler, P Joyce, A Dower, K English, J Thomys, P Wilson, D Jackson, D Jones, Norma Armstrong, Marjorie Dower, K Mitchell, S Tilley, J Peachey, Christine Proud, N Stokoe, A Slater, J Spence, J Day, Susan Green, M Davidson, R Lee, D Hammond, A Ord, D Cockburn, C Frampton, B Gallant, T Kent, R Thomys, Anne Morton, K Brownless, B Tilley, J Milton, K Youll, J Lonsdale, P Cairns, R Browning, J McDonnell, Rosaleen Bowes, D White, J Bell, Elaine Parker.

Cycle rally winners were: W Nicholson and Peter Cairns Joint winners with 115 points out of 128. Third, John Tilley and John Spence.

Posters competition, Class B: K Taylorson, J Regan. Class C: Georgina Walls, Sheila Richardson, Cheryl Allison, Doreen Bell, Lorna Murray. Class D: Isobel Bowes, Valerie Lofthouse, Stephen Tilley, Elaine Parker, Arnold Slater, Raymond Fisher.

Thornley Road Safety Quiz: Seniors: Anne West, Eileen Bartley, John Hunt, John Regan. Juniors: Alan Day, Anne Williams, Shirley Bell, Stephen Tilley.

Thornley carnival float winners: Gillian Day, Ann Dinning, Doris Grieves, L Ellwood, John Bradley.

LEGION WOMEN - Mrs J Clark presided over Thornley British Legion Women. The harvest festival realised £2 2s. Mrs G Bromilow, secretary, said that the branch had contributed £17 to various Legion funds. Prize-winners were Mesdames M Barrass, M Dinning, M Dobson, S Redshaw, B Atkin and G Bromilow.

LODGE OFFICIALS - At the voting of Thornley Colliery Lodge of Mineworkers, five of the officials were elected unopposed: Secretary, Mr R Hughes; treasurer, Mr S Greener; financial secretary, Mr W Anderson; compensation secretary, Mr R Briggs and delegate, Mr D Gott. There were three nominations for chairman and after only 12 months in office, R Robson was defeated by F Walker. There were 14 nominations for the ten vacant seats on the Lodge committee. Successful were: Messrs J Templeton, E Luke, J R Barron, J Willins, B Jones, W Curry, J Sandywell, J Nicholson, J Craven, H Brierley, M O'Brien. The following were elected as representatives onto the Federation, J R Barron, J Sandywell, J Willins and W Curry.

MINERS' SAFETY DRAW - The principal prize of a £30 voucher in the quarterly draw among accident free workmen at Wheatley Hill Colliery, held in conjunction with the Divisional Coal Board Safety Campaign, was won by a coal hewer, Mr W

Banks of Wheatley Hill. Mr Banks also won a £1 Premium Bond. Other bond wnners were Messrs E Jones, C Hardy, R Holden, J Hart and L Barker.

16 October 1964

WHEATLEY HILL MAN'S SUCCESS AT BOWLS

Anyone entering the council house living room of Mr John William Burrell, 87 Wordsworth Avenue, Wheatley Hill, might well think they had entered a silversmith's establishment or a high class department store.

On one wall is a china cabinet displaying 12 silver cups, which are Mr Burrell's personal possessions. On the sideboard are two clocks. On view there is a table set and half a dozen champagne glasses.

These are some of the seven awards Mr Burrell has won as a member of Wheatley Hill Welfare Bowls Club.

He said: "Bowls is my hobby. I have played for a number of years now and enjoy every moment of it. I have had previous successes, but this 1964 season has been one of my best".

This Season's Awards

Awards which Mr Burrell has won this season, either on his own or with partners, are as follows: No 4 Area Challenge Cup in the two-wood competition at Mainsforth; Wheatley Hill Welfare Club Challenge Cup; Wheatley Hill Club Moore Cup; No 3 Area Pairs Cup, and the Durham Divisional Pairs Championship. His partner in these events was Mr J Steele.

Mr Burrell was runner-up in the No 3 Area singles final. His team was runner-up in the No 3 are rink final. His rink-mates were Messrs R Jackson, E Bushby and J Steele.

To make way for this season's trophies, Mr Burrell has given two cups away to his brother-in-law, Mr Tom Smith of London. He has also given one to his grand-daughter, Jean Warnes.

During his bowls career Mr Burrell has won 12 cups outright.

6 November 1964

PARTY - At the 34th birthday party of Wheatley Hill Women's Institute in the Welfare Hall on Tuesday, Mrs J Moorin presided and welcomed 131 members. Supper was served and during an interval Mrs Moorin cut the birthday cake, and it was distributed among the members. The cake was made by Mrs W Hodgson and iced by Mrs Moorin. A barn dance followed, with Mrs Simpson as caller and Mrs Cook pianist. A Christmas cake given by Mrs R Jordan was the prize for a special competition, was won by Mrs Sheehan.

REMEMBRANCE DAY - Members of all denominations and village organisations attended the service in All Saints' Church, Wheatley Hill. Procession was headed by Wheatley Hill Colliery Band. The church was filled to capacity for the service, which was conducted by the Reverend G L Nelson (Methodist minister) and the sermon was preached by the Vicar (the Reverend G G Graham). After the service in the church the procession marched to the Cenotaph in the Welfare Park. In the Front Street the parade halted for prayers opposite the memorial clock on the walls of the Boys' Modern School, which commemorates the fallen of the second world war.

Wreaths were laid at the Cenotaph by the following organisations: Wheatley Hill women's section of the British Legion, Women's Institute, Wheatley Hill 1st Company Boy Scouts, Mothers Club, Sherburn Hill Co-operative Society, Workmen's Club, Constitutional Club, Police, Discharged Soldiers' and Sailors' Club, RAOB.

13 November 1964

MINERS TO DISCUSS
COAL IN BAG OFFER

Delegates representing the 70,000 Durham miners will meet at a special united council meeting on Saturday to discuss the NCB offer to supply their concessionary coal washed and bagged.

After August 3rd next year the typical Durham village street scene of heaped coal on pavements will vanish - or the free coal will become very expensive.

No Coal on Highways

For Section 24 of the Durham County Council Act comes into force on that day.

It forbids anyone to leave coal, coke or wood on highways maintained by local authorities - penalty for disobedience, £5 or 40 shillings for each day the stuff is left.

The NCB at Low Fell said this week the Coal Board had made an offer to supply the miners with good quality washed coal in bags.

"The value of the tonnage offered in the proposal amounts to the same as at present", a spokesman said.

But now the miners will get less of the washed coal than they get of the unwashed coal - which may contain stones.

Neither Mr Alf Hesler, secretary of the Durham area NUM, nor the NCB would say what the offer was.

Miners have got the free coal since the beginning of the century. Now in theory they get on average between 12 and 15 concessionary tons a year.

But this is reduced by various considerations like the amount they agree to give to the retired miners and pensioners, who get an average of about four and a half tons a year.

PRESENTATIONS TO
WHEATLEY HILL BOWLERS

Cups and prizes won by members of the men's and women's sections of Wheatley Hill Welfare Bowls Club during the past season were presented at a joint supper and social evening in the Welfare Hall.

Mrs E Jones presided at the presentations of the women's prizes made by Mrs Liddle, president of the North Eastern Women's Bowling League, and Mr E Parsley at the men's prize giving. The prizes to the successful men bowlers were presented by Mr E Winter, secretary of the No 4 Area of the league in which Wheatley Hill competes.

Awards were as follows:-

Men - Championship Cup: J W Burrell; runner-up, B R Jackson. Moore Cup: J W Burrell; runner-up, K Saddler. T Todd Trophy (for veterans): J Steel; runner-up, J Horrocks.

Women - Championship Cup: Mrs E Atkinson; runner-up, Mrs E Jones. William Jones Cup: Mrs Edna Hall; runner-up, Mrs R Ord. Festival Bowl: Mrs E Hall; runner-up Mrs E Jones.

Supper was served, followed by a programme of whist, dominoes and dancing. Mrs Hall was MC for whist and Mr E Kendall for dominoes, and prize winners were - Whist: Mrs Simons, Mrs S Armstrong, Mrs A Bowes and Messrs J C Kirk, V Herron and W Shutt. Dominoes: Messrs J Hind, J Horrocks and T Tunstall. Mr J Jones was MC for the dance.

TWO CARRIED OFF AT THORNLEY

Thornley Workmen's Club entertained neighbours Wheatley Hill Workmen's Club, in a Durham Club Union League game.

This "derby" had everything - goals, thrills, excitement, and though two men were carried off the field, Billy Gaskell the Thornley goalkeeper, and Colin Smith, the Wheatley Hill forward, the game, ironically, was played in a very friendly spirit.

Thornley looked set for their first victory of the season when they were three goals up in the first ten minutes through a brace of goals from Humes and one from Hinds.

Wheatley Hill came back into the game and by the interval were in the lead through goals from Halliwell, Smith, Neil and an own goal by Ernie Peachey.

Missed - Just after the interval Robert Holden shot miserably wide from the penalty spot. In a late burst of sustained pressure Smith and Halliwell scored for Wheatley Hill and an own goal from Ray Wood made the final score 6-4 in their favour.

Outstanding for Thornley were Ray Humes, Bill Williamson and Cassius Cook, star men for the visitors were Wood, Halliwell and Newby.

4 December 1964

FRENCH NOW TAUGHT AT LUDWORTH SCHOOL:
PRIZEDAY AWARDS

There was a packed school hall on Wednesday evening when the fifth annual school concert and prize giving took place at Ludworth County Junior Mixed and Infants' School. The chairman was Councillor F Kidd, chairman of the Central Divisional Executive Committee, and he was supported by school managers, Messrs J T Hedley (chairman), G W Pritchard, G W Smith, D Thornton and J T White, with Mr R Simpson, headmaster, and staff, Mrs F Wilson, Mrs E L Walton and Miss V J Wright. The prizes were presented by the Rector of Shadforth, the Reverend A R L Prentice.

In his report, Mr Simpson spoke of additions to the curriculum which included the teaching of French in the junior classes, while in the upper junior class, in music, more attention was given to the practical work in rhythm and pitch as well as the encouragement of simple musical composition. In the infants' classes more scope was now being given to music and movement and the improvement in poise and rhythmic development is already evident.

Transfer

Last year reference was made to changes which were to come into effect concerning the transfer of pupils to secondary education at 11-plus. Speaking from the point of view of this school the new system worked well and Mr Simpson was fully confident that the allocation would have been the same if the old examination system had been in operation. Out of the 12 children transferred to secondary education in September 1964, three proceeded to a GCE course and nine to non-GCE courses.

It was always of vital importance to keep in mind that the prime factor in transfer to secondary education is to allocate the children to the type of course in which they are most likely to derive the greatest benefit, and in which they are most likely to achieve success.

Improvements

He referred to the exterior and interior redecoration of the school and other improvements in the playgrounds and surroundings, and the aerial photograph of the school and surroundings which was taken earlier in the year.

This produced a good picture in colour which drew the comment "What a lovely place", and the headmaster commented upon the effects at ground level.

He said that there were many, who through the years had showed great concern either as individuals or as members of a group to improve the appearance and amenities of the village. At the same time however, there are those who have shown a total disregard of such concern and effort and who have done wanton and irresponsible damage which shows a lack of pride in the village that is their home.

Prize List

The Rector presented prizes as follows: For progress: Fourth year juniors: Robert Milburn, Susan Wilson, David Embleton. Third year juniors: Linda Raine, Janice Niles. Second year juniors: Ian Dunbar, Ann Gascoigne. First year juniors: Susan Gradon, Ann Hooler. Second year infants: Barbara Whittle, Marion Marley, Denise Stephenson. First year infants: Jacqueline Murray, Catherine Whittle, Brian Agar. Prizes for unbroken attendance: Three years: William Youll. Two years: Glyn Hutchinson, Pauline Smith. One year: Robert Milburn, Keith Parsons, Ian Dunbar, Christine Davies, Ann Gascoigne, Howard Carr, Susan Gradon, Paul Whittle, Sandra Gradon. Drama: Margaret Whittle. Reading: Valerie Prout. Courtesy: Janet Lee. Helpfulness: Shirley Morgan.

TEACHER BIDS AUSTRALIAN FAREWELL

When Wheatley Hill county junior mixed school closes for the Christmas holidays, Mr Ian Hill, Australian teacher, will say goodbye to his scholars. He came to this country for one year under the Teacher Exchange Scheme.

Headmaster of the school Mr Alec Wright (Ferryhill) and his staff, threw a farewell party for Mr Hill at the County Hotel, Durham. The party was attended by the wives and friends of the staff. Mr Wright expressed the good wishes of the school to Mr Hill, who will spend a fortnight with friends in London and then sail for Sydney on January 6.

Helpful and Co-operative

Mr Hill said to our correspondent, "I have enjoyed my year's teaching in England. I have found the headmaster and the staff most helpful and co-operative. This has been helpful to me as I have lost some time through sickness. In a strange country this could have been an unpleasant experience but everyone has been most kind and considerate".

Mr Hill commented, "In some respects the educational system here and Australia are very similar."

"Teaching children is the same the world over, for children everywhere are the same. The administration and government is similar in both countries. Your schools are better equipped, particularly in the matter of school libraries. The teacher in Australia is better paid. At home a teacher on maximum would have £1,920 per annum, after 12 years' service".

Mr Hill has used the holidays to see the country. He has visited the Continent twice. Has motored all over Ireland, Scotland and Wales. "I liked Ireland best of all because it wasn't too crowded. There was room to get around. Scottish scenery impressed us, as did that in parts of Northumberland and the West of Durham Dales country. There will be no trek from the North to the South for scenery at any rate. Your scenery up here is superior to the South of England."

18 December 1964

1965

MR J J HUTTON manager at Thornley Colliery, presided at a social function held by the Thornley Colliery Officials' Lodge in Thornley Officials' Club, to recognise the services of three of their members. He presented Mr T Wood, under-manager for the last five years with a photographic enlarger. Mr Wood is leaving the colliery to become manager of Easington Colliery. Mr J Clark an underground official for the last 50 years and Mr M Fleming, engineers' clerk, were presented with inscribed wristwatches. Mr Hutton was also compere at the entertainment and also gave items. Mr L Mordue, manager of Deaf Hill Colliery, was also present.
1 January 1965

WORKMEN'S WHEATLEY HILL

Members have appointed a new organist. Teddy Kitto, a local man who is also a member of Thornley Colliery Brass Band. He succeeds Billy Tucker, who has held the post for six months. Teddy was organist at Thornley Club and Dawdon Workman's.

Many members were concerned about the absence of secretary Ben Aitken from the bar on Sunday. He was at Dryburn Hospital visiting club member Billy Wood. The football team were beaten 4-1 by Pallion (Sunderland) in a CIU League game, after leading 1-0 at half time Wilf Halliwell scored the consolation goal. Bill Cowie, Eddie Newby and Leslie Jones gave good performances.

The darts team won a double, the players being "Nipper" Stevenson, Tom Hoban, Dave Young and Alan Cowan. The dominoes side won 3-1, thanks to Keith Jackson, Alf Purvis, Jim Cowan and Dave Young. Tomorrow night Teddy Kitto and Tom Hargreaves (drums) will accompany the dancing. Rhythm groups, the Keystones and the Astronauts, are engaged for Sunday night and Wednesday night, respectively.

WORKMEN'S THORNLEY

Football team made a poor start to the New Year, being trounced 12-1 by Easington Lane in a CIU League game. The opponents congratulated the team on putting up a spirited fight. Ray Humes gained the lone goal. Dave Gaskell (Goalkeeper) has let in 129 goals so far, but this is no reflection on him. He is rated as one of the best 'keepers in the league.

The darts team consolidated their position at the top of the league with a win, the line-up being Alf Steel, Bobby Applegarth, Bill Race and John Morton. The dominoes side, second in the league table, suffered a setback, the losers being Alf Jones, John Morton, Dick McGarrol and Walter Mangles.
8 January 1965

CLUB BALLOT –As a result of a ballot at Wheatley Hill Workmen's Club, Mr R Armstrong was elected chairman. Mr B A Aitken and Mr J Maddison were re-elected secretary and treasurer respectively, and Mr T Wilson was elected doorman. Messrs H Marratty, senr, R O'Connor, R Bradley, J Jackson, W Gibson and G Rowlands were elected to the committee.

SCOUTS' EFFORT -The Wheatley Hill Scouts' Association raised a record sum of £34.15s by their carol singing efforts in the village over the Christmas period, the secretary, Coun R Watson, reports. The money is to be used, as in the past years, to provide gifts for the children's ward of Durham County Hospital, which the Scouts "adopted" some years ago. Arrangements are to be made to visit the ward with gifts in the near future and to discuss with the Matron the provision of a special gift for the benefit of the whole ward.

CATHOLIC'S 86 YEARS AT THORNLEY

Requiem Mass was said on Thursday in Thornley RC Church of the English Martyrs by Dr H McNeil for Mr James Galligan, who died at his home, 6 Park Street, Thornley. Burial followed in Thornley Cemetery. Since the death of his wife Margaret, two years ago, he had live with his son, John.

Mr Galligan was born in Thornley 86 years ago and for 47 years lived in one house, 11 Queen Street. He saw all the major changes come over what used to be an agricultural village.

As a boy, he attended the old RC School in Thornley Hartlepool Street (now pulled down). He was present when the Riot Act was read when there was trouble at Thornley Colliery.

Mr Galligan worked at Thornley Colliery for 45 years and retired at the age of 72. In his early mining days he worked at Deaf Hill, and all told gave the mining industry 61 years' service. He tried to enlist during the First World War but was sent back to Thornley on the representations of the colliery manager.

Mr Galligan won a reputation as a first class breeder of racing "miler" pigeons and his bird "Mecca" was well known throughout of the country because of its racing successes.

Mr Galligan was also a noted dog breeder and a member of Thornley Workmen's Club for 50 years.

He was a regular worshipper at the Church of English Martyrs, Thornley.
15 January 1965

THORNLEY GREETS A FAMOUS SPORTING SON

Representatives from all organisations in the village met in the Thornley Catholic Club to pay tribute to the Thornley youth Ernie Pomfret, who reached the finals of the 3,000 metre steeplechase in the Olympic Games at Tokyo last year.

Coun F A Walker, chairman, said that two Thornley youths represented Britain in the Olympic Games in the last few years. At Melbourne they had Charmaine

Welsh and the residents of Thornley paid tribute to her feats eight years ago. That night they praised Ernie Pomfret.

He added, "In the past we have had our world champions in the sporting field, internationals on the soccer field, men who died bravely on the battle fields and received V Cs and M Ms. We also have our own boys who have made their name in the political field, Mr Fred Peart, Minister of Agriculture, who was asked to make the presentation to Ernie Pomfret, but owing to commitments, he could not attend.

Coun Miss Griffiths, Chairman of Thornley Parish Council, presented the athlete with a furniture voucher and a trophy. The trophy he in turn passed on to Mr Lauderdale, secretary of Houghton Harriers, for annual competition.

County Coun E Carter proposed a vote of thanks. It was interesting to note that the Thornley Miner's Lodge was the first Lodge to be formed. Coun J Nicholson seconded the vote of thanks.

Also there were Coun Slater, Grieves, Bowerbanks, Bennett, Bosomworth, Bullock and Ellwood. Thornley Parish Coun Dr J Gray, C Lamb, Headmaster Thornley-School, Mr J Williams, PC Carr, Mrs E Clark, British Legion. S Wilson, W Slater, J Taylor, Clerk of Thornley Parish Council, and other village organisation representatives.

Mrs Pomfret, an ex-athlete herself, with members of both families, was also there.

Refreshments were supplied by members of the Catholic Women's League. Entertainment was by Coun Walker, J Nicholson, R Armstrong, R Foster, W Hubbard and Mrs Tilly. Pianist was Jackie Toye and the MC John Regan.

WORKMEN'S WHEATLEY HILL

Football team were beaten 7-3 in a CIU League game by Seaham Knack. They did well to hold the visitors to a 3-3 score at half-time, but in the second half the side as a whole wilted considerably. Scorers were Alf Purvis, Jack Nichols and Ben Harvey.

The dominoes team won 15-9, thanks to Jack Jackson, Alf Purvis, "Mopsie" Harper and Ted Jones. The darts line-up also did well winning by 276. Team: "Nipper" Stevenson, Dave Young, Dave Young sen , Tom Hoban.

After the football match the "ref" congratulated Archie Jobes (groundsman) on the excellent marking out of the ground.

The Club Union whist game with Easington Village Workmen's resulted in a win by 35-33. The team was Jack Durrant. Harry Maratty, Dick Holden and Stan Metcalfe.

The dominoes won 15-14, - Joe Dodds, Frank Jackson, Jim Jackson and George Jackson.

Both the whist and the dominoes sides are in the running for runners-up honours.

A keen supporter of the teams is 85-years old Ben Bowes. Ben Aitken (secretary) reports that they have shown a surplus of £442.19s.8d on the years working.

The talent contest was won by Ken Bell (Blackhall). Second Mrs Jones and third Jack Walker. Accompanist was Ted Kitto (organist).

Entertainment for this weekend: Tonight- talent contest; Saturday- dancing to Kitto and Tom Hargreaves (drums); Sunday morning-afternoon – Take Your Pick; Sunday night – a concert party, The Cordettes, from Byker; Wednesday – The Jinx (rhythm group).

22 January 1965

SCOUTS' REUNION - Among the guests when the 2nd Wheatley Hill Group of Scouts held their 30th annual reunion supper and party in the Welfare Hall, Wheatley Hill, were two of the original trustees of the Group Headquarters, Dr A P Gray and Mr Fred Simpson (Wingate). The Group Scoutmaster, Mr Leslie Barker, presided and welcomed the guests, who also included Mrs Gray, Miss E Simpson, Sister Sutton (children's ward, Durham County Hospital). Mr F Richardson (manager of Wheatley Hill Colliery) and Mrs Richardson, and Mr and Mrs F Walker. During supper, provided by the women members of the Scouts' committee, a birthday cake made by Mrs S Watson and iced by Mrs Lindsay, was cut by the assistant matron of Durham County hospital, Miss Hodgson-Laws. The continued success of the Scout movement in the village was toasted by Dr Gray. Group Scoutmaster Barker, Scoutmaster Colin Thackeray and Cubmaster Walter Saxby organised games and competitions for the 30 Cubs and 25 Scouts present, and the guests were entertained by the Scouts with a camp-fire sing-song. Before leaving for home the Scouts received a packet of sweets each. The group secretary, Coun Ralph Watson, was responsible for the arrangements.

29 January 1965

VANDALISM AGAIN AT LUDWORTH

Vandalism was once again discussed at Shadforth Parish Council meeting at Ludworth, presided over by Coun A Turnbull.

The Council passed for payment an account of £49. 10s. for repairs to the Ludworth War Memorial. The repairs had been necessary to replace the damaged surrounds and metal posts, damaged by vandalism.

Mr W N Reay told the Council that repairs to this memorial was the result of irresponsible behaviour, and had cost the Parish Council over £100. A member said that the Council should not pay any more money out over this War Memorial.

Coun J T Hedley replied that the Parish Council had accepted the responsibility of caring for the memorial and a defeatist attitude should not be adopted. An appeal was made for the public to co-operate with the Parish Council to help stop these wicked acts of vandalism.

5 February 1965

FEDERATION BREWERY PREFERRED
AT THORNLEY WORKMEN'S

Special meeting for the purpose of discussing whether it would be advantageous to remain with the Northern Federation Brewery or revert to Vaux's Brewery decided unanimously to remain with the Federation. Spokesmen in favour of the resolution to continue with the "Fed" was Coun Frank Walker, who put up a formidable case.

The football team were beaten by Newbottle Workmen's in a CIU League game. Had the score, 3-1, been reversed no one could have grumbled. There was a big improvement and with a little luck they would have probably recorded their first win of the season. "Cassius" Cook gained the consolation goal, Brian Cook and Dave Walker were outstanding performers.

The dominoes side were beaten 20-7, the losers being Walter Mangles, Dave Gaskell, John Morton, "Lol" Morton. The darts team, current league leaders, won by 366, thanks to Bob Appleby, Alf Steel, John Morton and Bill Race. They have lost only one game, and on this occasion they were minus three of their best men.

The Phonetics (beat group) are engaged for tonight. Saturday will be dancing to Rich Clark (organist) and Joe Boyle (drums). Group Unlimited from Newcastle entertain on Sunday. Monday night- Caron and the Crossfires (beat group) from Chester-le-Street.

5 March 1965

HOMESICK WHEATLEY HILL WOMAN TO "RE-EMIGRATE"
After just over two years in Australia, 45-year-old Mrs Jenny Bartram, who emigrated there with her husband and family of five from Wheatley Hill, has come back home on a "one-way ticket." With her are her youngest son Stephen, who will be five in May, and her only daughter, Doreen, who will celebrate her seventh birthday next week.

"I just could not settle there although everyone, including my husband and sons did everything possible to make me happy," Mrs Bartram, who is staying with her 72-year-old widowed mother, Mrs Hannah Coldwell, at 21 Burns Street, Wheatley Hill, told our reporter this week.

Mrs Bartram went on, "I was dreadfully homesick - in no time I lost two stone in weight with worry. But my husband and sons kept pressing me to stay two years to see how things worked out. I managed that but as soon as the two years were up I came back."

When she set sail from "Down Under," leaving her husband and three grown up sons, Fred (25), Billy (22) and David (17) behind, she thought it was "really for good" and that Australia would see her no more.

Prepared to go Back Again Now
"But," said Mrs Bartram, "after only a couple of weeks back at Wheatley Hill I had got over my homesickness and now am quite prepared to go back again and make a real go of it in Australia."

Her sun-tanned face broke into a smile as she said, " I have had to come back home to make up my mind to stay in Australia."

"Making up her mind" will have cost her nearly £700. Her passage to England cost £337 - her husband and three eldest sons, who are all happily settled in well-paid employment in Australia, saved up this money inside a year for her.

And now Mrs Bartram has written to her family telling them to hurry up and save the money again to pay her passage back. "They are looking after themselves and are managing quite nicely, they tell me "said Mrs Bartram, "but they are anxious to see me back again".

The family live in a new home at Acacia Ridge, Brisbane, Queensland. It was an easily-run labour saving house, said Mrs Bartram, and despite her big family she found she could get through her work much more easily than when she lived in England.

"The emigration authorities did all they possibly could to make me happy when they knew I was so unsettled," said Mrs Bartram. "And I made lots of good friends among the Australians, they are all nice folk, but I got the longing for my old home and to see my mother again and I just could not shake it off."

Mrs Bartram is now trying to persuade her mother to go back with her. But Mrs Coldwell feels her roots are too firmly set in Wheatley Hill. "I think I am too old now to go out there," said Mrs Coldwell. "Besides, I have two other daughters here at Wheatley Hill and Thornley.

Completely Recovered
"But whether my mother decides to go back with me or not I certainly have no doubts now about settling in Australia- I have got completely over my homesick-ness," said Mrs Bartram.

Mrs Bartram has been here five weeks and thinks she will be on her way back again to Australia by mid-summer. She had only been here a fortnight when she obtained employment at Nimmo's Brewery, Castle Eden. "I had to find work to keep myself and two young children while living with my mother," she said.

There was no denying there were wonderful opportunities in Australia for those who went with the will to work, said Mrs Bartram. Her husband Fred, who formerly worked at Wheatley Hill colliery, is a boiler-maker earning good money, and her sons all have excellent jobs.

"They love the life out there," said Mrs Bartram. "My sons go shooting in the bush at week-ends and my husband enjoys working in our big garden."

High Rent
The family arrived in Australia just before Christmas two years ago. "It was pretty tough going at first, with its being Christmas-time and the holidays, jobs were bad to get, but eventually my husband and sons found employment at Melbourne," said Mrs Bartram.

They lived in Melbourne about seven months and then moved to their present home, where they have lived since. "The rent is high, £4.16s. a week, but there is plenty of money to be made to meet rents like these and we don't feel it," said Mrs Bartram.

Apart from rents the cost of living was "much about the same as in England. Some commodities, including tea and sugar, are cheaper", added Mrs Bartram.

The Bartrams live only a ten-minute walk from Mr Bartram's brother Richard and his wife Margaret, who emigrated there from South Shields only about a year before the Bartrams went. "They are very happily settled there with their eight-year-old daughter," said Mrs Bartram.

Another relative of the Bartrams is likely to join the growing list of emigrants soon. She is Mrs Bartram's neice, Audrey Christopher, who, with her husband and baby son, hope to emigrate there shortly from Wheatley Hill.

WORKMEN'S WHEATLEY HILL Football team trounced their neighbours, Thornley Workmen's, in a CIU League game, the score being 10-2. Colin Smith completed a hat-trick, and the other scorers were John Lowther (two), Wilf Halliwell(two), "Chick" Nichols (two) and Ray Wood (one).

Eight of the goals came in the last 15 minutes. The biggest crowd of the season were disappointed, as everyone expected a tough fight for supremacy in the local "derby."

Secretary Tom Cowie was very pleased with his team's performance, and is convinced that they will beat the league leaders, Pallion (Sunderland), in the league cup.

His latest signing, John Lowther (out-side left), has strengthened the forward line considerably.

The dominoes side were beaten 16-13, the players being Alf Purvis, Dave Young, Ken Hedley and Brian Maddison. The darts side lost by 172 points, the losers being "Nipper" Stephenson, Tom Hoban, Alan Cowan and Dave Young.

Birthday greetings were extended to Ben Bowes, one of the founders of the club, who was 85. He celebrated the occasion with a family reunion. The club has lost a member by the death of "Tot" Robson. He was only 55, and was well known as a competition leek grower.

19 March 1965

CONCESSIONARY COAL:
HOW THE BAGGED SCHEME WILL WORK

With the coming into operation in August of the Durham County Council Act it will be illegal for any person to put coal on highways within the Council's administrative area. The present system of delivering miners' concessionary coal will be suspended and new arrangements have to be made to ensure the continuation of concessionary coal without contravening the law.

The easiest way of overcoming the difficulties appears to be the delivery of coal in bags direct into the miner's coalhouse.

Washed coal is specified, since obviously the men concerned would be unable to leave stones in the street, and would not normally be permitted to put them in household refuse bins. The washed and graded coal to be supplied will be of a much better quality than that generally delivered in the county, and will be transported free, present leading charges being abolished.

The Solution

The Divisional Coal Board insists that the extra costs which they will incur in the washing and bagging of the coal and its delivery into coalhouses must be met by the recipients since they are not permitted by the National Coal Board to make any increases in the present cost of supplying concessionary coal. This can most easily be achieved by the surrender by the workmen of any amount of coal equivalent in value to the extra costs involved in the new arrangements.

The gross annual entitlement per serving worker will be 8 tons 2cwt of washed bagged coal delivered into the coalhouse. From this amount each man will surrender 15cwt to provide a pool of coal for allowances to retired miners and for a six months supply of coal to widows of deceased workmen. The amount of coal actually supplied to each such recipient will be reduced in much the same proportion as the workmen's firecoal is reduced by these proposals. Here again the value of the coal supplied will be equal to the value of the existing allowance since it will be a better quality of coal and will be put directly into the coalhouse.

Meeting An Objection

Durham NUM members who live in boroughs where the Durham County Council Act does not apply, have pointed out that they can continue to receive coal tipped outside their homes, so that by surrendering the full stipulated amount of firecoal required to reimburse the Board for washed coal delivered into the coalhouse they will be paying for a service which they do not require,

To meet this objection the board have proposed the restoration throughout the county of that part of the allowance which represents the bagging and delivery charge and the payment in cash of this charge. The effect of this would be that there would be a reduction in the present coal entitlement to cover the cost of washing, the cost of bagging and delivery being met by a cash payment. The cash payment would not have to be made by those members living in the boroughs who chose to have their coal left in the street.

The new proposals represent a considerable reduction in the amount of coal supplied to miners: on the other hand, the coal, being of a better quality, will contain no waste and the men and their families will be relieved of the chore of getting the coal into their homes from the roadside.

SURPRISE FOR WHEATLEY HILL 'GOLDEN' COUPLE

Pleasant surprise for Mr and Mrs Alfred Richardson, of 18 Aged Miners' Homes, Wheatley Hill, on Saturday, when they celebrated their golden wedding, was a family party at their niece's home in Spennymoor. The party, "completely out of the blue," was arranged for the couple by their daughter-in-law, Mrs Fred Hutchinson, and niece Mrs Francis.

"What a wonderful surprise it was, I never knew there was going to be something special 'laid on' for our celebration." 77-year-old Mr Richardson told our reporter later.

The couple, who have spent all their married life in Wheatley Hill were married at St Mary's Church, West Rainton, on April 3 1915, by the Rector, Canon S Parkinson.

Forman Bricklayer

Born at Castle Eden, Mr Richardson spent most of his working career as a bricklayer at Wheatley Hill colliery and for the last 24 years, until his retirement 14 years ago, he was a foreman bricklayer.

When he left school at 14 however, his first job had nothing to do with mining. He started work in the drapery department at Sunderland Co-operative Society earning 4s.6d a week. "My mother thought this was quite a good wage, it was a 'bonny good help," said Mr Richardson.

After only six months there he started work "on the belts" at Wheatley Hill colliery, he was paid 1s.3d a shift. "And I worked from six in the morning until five at night," Mr Richardson recalled.

Soon he became an apprentice bricklayer but when he was 18 he left the colliery to "gain more experience" with several private contractors. After four years however, he returned to the colliery, where he remained until his retirement.

Pretty Good Health

Mr Richardson's wife Elizabeth Jane, was born at Pittington. She is 73, and both she and her husband enjoy pretty good health. Mrs Richardson is quite active and does all her own housework. In their younger days she and her husband both sang in the choir at All Saints' Church.

Mr and Mrs Richardson, who received many greeting cards as well as flowers and gifts from their many friends and relatives, have an only son, Frederick who with his wife and two children live near Whitehaven, Cumberland.

9 April 1965

"THE PRIDE OF SHOTTON"
GREAT WELCOME HOME FOR CHAMPION CULLEN
DRIVEN AROUND STREETS TO CHEERS OF BIG CROWD

After winning the British lightweight title in a gruelling 15 round fight with Dave Coventry at Liverpool two nights before, Maurice Cullen ("the pride of Shotton") had another hard fight on his hands on Saturday afternoon, to battle his way through the cheering crowds, up the garden path of his council house home in Ashbrooke Estate at the end of a triumphal procession through the packed streets of the village.

Maurice, who had been driven around the streets in a small car, followed by Shotton Colliery Band and a coach load of supporters, was loudly cheered and warmly congratulated on all sides. He was the hero of the day, especially for the youngsters who, after he had fought his way into his home, kept chanting, "We want Maurice- we want Maurice.

Time and time again Maurice, wearing dark glasses to cover his bruised eyes and a bandage on his right wrist, walked to the front door and, waving the dark red boxing gloves which (with his fists inside them) brought the title to the North-East for the first time in 13 years, acknowledged the prolonged cheers of the crowds.

"This was a far worse ordeal than stepping into the ring with Coventry," Maurice told our reporter after, at last, the crowds had dispersed and he was left alone with his family.

Maurice certainly deserved the fine ovation he received, for his success in winning the Lonsdale belt was the culmination of years of endeavour, which have not been without their frustration and disappointments. It is only a few months ago that Maurice, who had shown up exceptionally well in the ring in his recent fights before the championship contest, was despairing of ever getting a tilt at the title.

He was full of confidence before his fight with Coventry, and he is just as confident that he can successfully defend his title twice within the next 11 months to retain the Lonsdale belt in record time.

"But first," said Maurice, "I want a complete rest for a week or two. The championship fight was the one of my toughest, it is only the second time I have fought 15 rounds, and I need time to get rid of the stiffness and my aches and bruises."

Crimdon Lifeguards

Otherwise, Maurice says he is physically fit and after his rest he will get straight down to training again. He is hoping for a spell of duty again at Crimdon as a lifeguard, he spent all last summer there.

In the meantime Maurice's manager, his brother Terry, has called off the fight which had been arranged between the new champion and the Nigerian, Ray Adigun, at Brighton on April 17.

"This is too soon after the championship fight but we still hope to fulfil this engagement at a later date," said Terry.

After his fight on the Thursday night Maurice drove straight back home with his father and brother, arriving there in the early hours, His mother and sister Eileen listened to the fight on the radio". He put up a grand show," said his mother.

Congratulatory telegrams arrived by the dozen at his home, they include one from Easington Rural Council and another from the lads with whom he had worked at Crimdon during the holiday season.

16 April 1965

CHEAP BEER - As a holiday concession 7d a pint was slashed off the price of beer at Wheatley Hill Workmen's Club during Easter weekend. Ordinary beer was 9d a pint and best 1s. "We were packed out all the holidays," the club steward, Mr J Craggs, told our reporter on Wednesday. The beer, he said, disappeared at the rate of 430 pints an hour from Good Friday to Easter Monday, the period during which the concession lasted.

REWARD FOR SAFETY - When the quarterly draw among accident free miners at Wheatley Hill colliery was held during a social evening in Wheatley Hill Workmen's Club in connection with the Divisional Coal Board Safety Campaign, the first prize of a washing machine valued £50 was won by a surface datal worker, Mr G Hodgson, of 10 Durham Street, Wheatley Hill. The second prize of a £25 cocktail cabinet was won by Mr T Hall and the third prize of a transistor radio valued at £10 was won by

Mr T Gordon. Mr F Richardson, manager of the colliery, presided at the draw, into which went the names of those workmen who had been free of compensionable accidents during the past three months.

23 April 1965

SEAHAM 'NACK' WIN CIU CUP MARATHON

After five-and-a-half hours of football New Seaham 'Nack' Workmen's Club retained the Club Institute Union League Cup when at Eppleton they defeated Wheatley Hill by three goals to two in a thrilling final.

Two games at Murton, which ran into extra time, failed to produce a goal from either side and a third match at Hetton proved equally as close as the others.

With the score at 2-2, Lee and Dormand scoring for Seaham, and Smith and an 'own goal' for the Hill,' worried officials were mentally thinking out another venue for a further replay. Then Leslie fastened on a shot which beat the 'Hill' 'keeper after he had twice parried drives from forwards.

Determination

But the result was by no means certain for Wheatley Hill fought with determination for the equaliser which almost came in the last minute.

The ball was charged down from a corner and scrambled away to safety as Mr A Bailey sounded the final whistle.

Seaham, who narrowly missed league honours, carry off the runners up awards for the second year running, thus repeating last year's success.

The annual presentation is to be held in the South Hetton Workmen's Club on June 26.

7 May 1965

MAURICE COLLECTS HIS BELT

This week Maurice Cullen, "The Pride of Shotton," who won the British lightweight title last month when he defeated Dave Coventry over 15 rounds at Liverpool, made a special train trip to London for his prize, the coveted Lonsdale Belt.

"With this in my possession and my name inscribed on it, I now really feel like the champion, I could scarcely realise it before," Maurice told our reporter at Crimdon Lido on Tuesday when he paused from unloading scores of cartons of soft drinks from a lorry.

Maurice is again working fulltime at the Lido, "It's great there and I can get plenty of exercise," he says, and until the season gets well under way he is ready to do any task given to him by the manager, Mr Roy Isherwood. Later he will work with a team of lifeguards on the beach.

At The Lido

Maurice, in the pink of condition again after his gruelling fight with Coventry, is keeping himself fit with an hour's sprint along the beach every morning and some light work in the gymnasium at night. Next month he is hoping to fight in Brighton, his opponent is likely to be a Frenchman. "But I don't know yet who it will be, my brother Terry is making the arrangements," said Maurice.

When he was in London, Maurice was met by Mr Jack Solomons, the promoter, who escorted him the offices of the British Boxing Board of Control. "He told me he was over the moon with my performance in winning the title," said Maurice, "and said my chances look rosy for meeting Bunny Grant for the British Empire title."

On Wednesday night at a gathering of officials of the Northern Area of the Boxing Board in the Grand Hotel, West Hartlepool, Maurice was officially presented with the belt.

If he successfully defends his title twice the belt will stay in Maurice's possession "Believe me," said Maurice, "I'll be all out to keep it. Now that I have got it, I mean to stick to it."

14 May 1965

BAGGED CONCESSIONARY COAL: MINERS VOTING THIS WEEK

Durham miners must decide this week whether or not to accept the new arrangements for delivering concessionary coal, resulting from the Durham County Council Act which comes into operation in August. After that, it will be illegal to continue the present system of dumping coal on the highway.

If agreement is not reached, says Mr Alf Hesler (general secretary of the Durham National Union of Mineworkers), the NCB will be forced to suspend deliveries and the miners will have to collect the coal themselves from depots.

On Saturday delegates from collieries throughout the area attended a special meeting of the Durham Miners Council to discuss the matter and the 100 miners' lodges in the county are now voting the issue.

When the votes had been counted, a meeting of the Federation Board (comprising all the unions in the mining industry in Durham County) will be called and the Divisional Coal Board will be notified of their collective decision.

A special meeting of the Miners' Council some months ago rejected the new arrangements, but various points raised at that time have now been clarified and these were explained to delegates at Saturday's meeting. Now the matter is left entirely for the men to decide, without any recommendation to accept or reject from the Area Union.

Better Quality

The suggested means of overcoming the difficulties created by the County Council Act in prohibiting the dumping of coal on highways is to have it delivered in bags direct into the miners' coalhouses. This coal must be washed, as the men would not be able to leave stones in the street or put them in refuse bins.

The washed and graded coal will be a better quality than that generally delivered in the county and will be transported free (existing leading charges being abolished), but the Divisional Board insist that the extra cost incurred in washing and bagging the coal and delivering it into coalhouses must be met by the miners taking delivery. This could best be achieved by the surrender of an amount of coal equivalent in value to the extra costs. A major point at issue is that miners living in areas where the County Council Act does not apply can continue to have coal tipped outside their homes; consequently surrendering part of it means they will be paying for a service they do not require.

To overcome this objection, the Board proposes restoring that part of the allowance representing the bagging and delivery charge and making a cash charge instead for those areas covered by the County Council Act. This cash payment would not be demanded from miners who continue to have their coal dumped in the street.

The new proposals represent a considerable reduction in the amount of concessionary coal supplied, but it is pointed out that the coal, being better quality, will contain no waste and it will no longer be necessary to carry it into the coalhouse from the road side.

The result of the voting on the situation, following the special meeting of miners' lodges throughout the county, is expected to be known next week.

21 May 1965

4,000 ATTEND WHEATLEY HILL SPORTS

The annual sports day organised by the Wheatley Hill Colliery Federation Board was attended by a crowd of 4,000. The organising secretary was Mr W N Gibson, assisted by the Lodge officials, Mr A Wharrier (chairman) and Mr J Hedley (treasurer).

The 1,300 children of the village received a gift bag of chocolate and sweets to the value of 4s. A weekly levy on workmen at the colliery met the day's expenses, approximately £4.

The parade through the village was a colourful affair, headed by the Wheatley Hill Colliery Silver Band.

Jazz bands from Sunderland and decorated floats of local organisations created the gala spirit.

Mr B Aitken, secretary of the Workmen's Club, acted as "Mr Sports Day". He was successfully challenged by Master M Harper.

Judges of the fancy dress and field events were Rev and Mrs G L Nelson, Rev and Mrs G G Graham, Police sergeant and Mrs Pickering, the colliery undermanager, Mr H Atkinson and Mrs Atkinson, Mr and Mrs J Robson and Dr Parrikh.

The four-mile race proved an exciting and close event. It was won by John Bradshaw, second C Bramfitt, third J Bennett and fourth W Jobes.

Results

Jazz bands; 1 Sunderland Juveniles (Silver Cup); 2 Hedworth Juveniles; 3 Hedworth Legionnaires. Medals were awarded to Sunderland Juveniles (Drum Major), Sunderland Juveniles (Band Major), Hedworth Legionaires (Bass Drummer). The bands were judged by Police Sgt M Pickering, Mr E Curry and Mr C Hardy.

Fancy Dress: 1 Peter Swallow; 2 Peter Hoban; 3 Jennifer Gibson. Original: 1 Kevin Hicks; 2 Dale and Doreen Beeston; 3 Mary Bulmer and Betty Hodgson.

Comic: 1 Irene Craggs; 2 Trevor Davis; 3 Edward Rippon and Paul Hogg.

Adults: 1 Thomas Taylorson; 2 Peter Leigh; 3 George Hedley.

Decorated Floats: 1 Wheatley Hill Mother's Club; 2 Wheatley Hill Road Safety Committee; 3 Wheatley Hill Youth Club.

THORNLEY PEOPLE'S RIOTOUS WELCOME

Following a carnival at Seaton Delaval on Saturday, the Sunbeams Jazz Band was welcomed by the people of Thornley when they returned with their first trophy. The band was formed recently and this is only the third carnival they have entered. They were cheered wildly as they paraded through the village displaying the cup they had won. Apart from the cup, which was a first, members of the band also won six medals between them. The cup was given for a marching display and the medals were won by the majorettes and the bass drummer Miss Jean Dunning, won two second places and was given a medal for each. Miss Barbara Poole, the band majorette, won a second and a third and the bass drummer, Miss Denise Bennet, won a first and second place.

18 June 1965

ACCIDENTAL DEATH VERDICT ON MR F CORRY

A verdict of accidental death was recorded at an inquest at Dryburn Hospital, Durham, on a 79-year-old retired miner, who fell and fractured his skull on the steps in his back yard last week.

Mr Fred Corry, of 10 Aged Miners' Homes, Wheatley Hill, appeared well and had just asked a young unemployed labourer to move a load of coal for him when he walked back towards the house, mounted the steps and fell, hitting his head on the concrete.

The labourer, Mr N Cook, went for help, but the fracture was so severe that nothing could be done.

Mr Corry's daughter, Mrs Eva Millington, of 49 Milbank Terrace, Shotton Colliery, told the Coroner, Mr L J Heron, that her father, who was blind in one eye, had been suffering from blackouts and dizzy spells for the past three years.

YOUTHS CONVERT OLD 'JUNK ROOM' INTO A COFFEE BAR

Although no palace Wheatley Hill and District Youth Club's new coffee bar has a feature which gives club members a feeling of intense satisfaction.

This might seem surprising when you consider the appearance of "The Cabin", a drab-looking shack tucked away on the side of the decaying welfare ground, it at first seems to have nothing which one would wish to shout about.

In fact the members have every reason to be proud. They practically made the bar themselves.

Three months ago "The Cabin," originally a tennis pavilion, was little more than an untidy junk room. Then the youngsters descended with £150 which they had raised themselves.

Proof

Mr Jack Dormand, the Easington Divisional Education Officer, said at Tuesday night's official opening: "You hear a lot of talk about young people being unable to do anything for themselves. This coffee bar just proves how wrong this can be."

One of the youngsters who helped with the work is 15-year-old John Langley, an apprentice joiner of 3 Morris Crescent, Thornley. The Beatle paintings which decorate one wall are only part of his work.

John Taylorson, a 15-year-old apprentice joiner, of 48a Liddell Terrace, Wheatley Hill. said that some of their members had drifted off to the new Peterlee youth centre but when the bar had opened they had quickly returned.

One of the girl members who helped with the conversions, 17-year-old Enid Mason, of 19 South View, Wheatley Hill, said: "When we started the work we thought of it as a bit of a laugh but we didn't realise how important it would be".

2 July 1965

THORNLEY STUDENT ON AMERICAN EXCHANGE

The opportunity for a Thornley girl to spend a year in America on an exchange visit is like a ray of hope for those who fear a future mass exodus of doctors to the States.

When 17-year-old Elizabeth Gray the daughter of a general practitioner returns to this country she hopes to study to become a doctor. But although she will know America well by then her brain will definitely not be for the 'drain'.

"I am really looking forward to my year in America but I certainly will not be going back to work there when I become a doctor," said Elizabeth at her home at 'Brimmond', Gore Lane, Thornley.

A pupil at Durham Girls Grammar School she has already taken her 'A' level examinations and depending on the outcome there will be a place waiting for her in either Newcastle or Birmingham University.

4,000 AT THORNLEY SPORTS DAY

Nearly 4,000 people packed into Thornley village for the eighth annual Sports Day. Weather conditions were not good but people seemed to enjoy themselves.

Heading a mile and a half long parade from the Half Way House was the Thornley Colliery Silver Prize Band, under its conductor, Mr E Kitto. Nine jazz bands also took part as well as many other local organisations.

Mr E Farrell, a deputy at Thornley Colliery, was Mr Sports Day, and was successfully challenged by Mr J Onion (this was the third successive year that Mr Onion had found Mr Sports Day). Mrs Sports Day was Mr Farrell's wife, Margaret, who was successfully challenged by Mrs I Watson.

Champion pit pony from Durham and Northumberland was "Boxer" from Easington Colliery (Mr Robinson). Other prizes went to "Duke" of Deaf Hill (Mr Horn) and "Billy" of Shotton. Cleanest pit pony No 3 Area was "Tiny" of Thornley (Mr P Ord). Second was "Duke" and third "Topsy" Thornley.

Jazz Bands

Of the nine jazz bands, Peterlee Emeralds was the best band on display. Drum major: 1 Peterlee; 2 Hedworth Juveniles; 3 Queenslanders and Easington Tip Toppers (tied). Bass Drummer: 1 Hedworth; 2 Washington; 3 Peterlee and Easington (tied). Drum major: 1 Peterlee and Hedworth (tied); 2 Easington and Thornley Sunbeams (tied).

Judges for the jazz band contest were E Curry and A Smith. Mr Gelson judged the pit ponies.

Children's fancy dress winners: A Smith, T Saunders, R Craggs, J Hubbard, P Williams, W Stanley, A Williams. P Ramage, V Hall.

Adult winners were: G Copeland, N Hanley, Mrs Crisp, Mrs Chapman, D Parker, M Turner, J Atkin, P Hoban, P Wilson.

Children's original: R Parker; C Davidson, M Jackson, J Parker. P Cairns, P Wigham, C Hovells, I Craggs.

Judges for the fancy dress were the Rev and Mrs Mold, Mr and Mrs J Luke, Mr and Mrs W Stoker, Mr and Mrs Maddison, Mr and Mrs Williams and Mr and Mrs F Bradley.

The Baldasera Memorial Cup, was presented by Mrs F Baldasera and the large number of trophies were presented by Ald E Cowan, of Birtley; County Coun J Hughes, County Coun E Carter, and Mr F Walker, undermanager at Thornley Colliery, and his wife.

A collection taken during the parade, for Thornley Aged Miners' Homes Fund raised £48.18s.

Winners

Winners were: B Marratty, M Taylor, G Robson, C Carr, S O'Brien, R Robinson, B Tilley, V Lofthouse, M Dougherty, P Dove, S White, M Widdowfield A Martin, A Williamson, K Brownless, L Middleton, S Lowes, S Bell, R Cotton, C Proud, S Armstrong, P Lennox, P Watson, J G Adams, D Pattison, R W Hubbard, D Parker, R Gaskell, D Still, S Jackson, S Chaytor, A Jones, T Winter, F Ord, S Tilley, P Pattison, D Appleby, D Nicholson, J Purvis, I Lang, J Youll, T Wilson, D Parker, D Spence, L Greener, M Niles, A McCoy, M Walker, J Dawson, S Green, L Walker, E Worthington, A Gaskell, J Gaskell, L Richardson, L Curry, S Bell, A Vasey.

9 July 1965

SCOUTS' FIELD DAY AT WHEATLEY HILL

Members of Wheatley Hill Old Scouts Association held their annual Field Day on the Wheatley Hill Girls' Modern school playing field on Saturday.

Coun Ralph Watson, the association secretary said: "The object of this event is primarily to encourage scouting among the boys of our village. Over the years the Movement has been popular in Wheatley Hill and we wish to carry on our scouting tradition."

The effort realised over £100 and the organising secretary was Mr G Hinds.

Competition winners were: K Gardener (weight of live calf), J Nicholson (weight of log). In the lucky draw, the first prize, a week-end for two in Blackpool went to Mr

Wilson (Hartlepool). Placings in the Scouting competition (camping and kitchen efficiency) were 1 Wheatley Hill, 2 Fleming Field, 3 Easington.

Highlights

Highlight of the entertainments provided was a display of exhibition boxing under Mr K Jones as trainer. Other taking part were: J Williams, R Brooksbank, T Westhoe and T Vasey.

A Rock and Roll session with the Rocking G Days was another popular attraction. Sideshows were run by Messrs N Waugh, L Barker, Watson, Elliot, Carr, Hargreaves, Anderson, J Carr, Woodward, Horrocks, Pace, Hildrew, Henderson, Hall, Hutchinson, Thackeray, Saxby, Armstrong, Dinsley, Gibson, Abbs, Hunter, Vincent, Warnes, Walker, Berresford, Pattison and Hind. All were in fancy and traditional dress.

Ladies of the Scouts' Committee served teas and refreshments; Mesdames Andrew, M Watson, Nicholson, Warnes, S Watson, Walker, Hodgson, Cook, and Miss Shutt.

16 July 1965

WHEATLEY HILL

MINERS' SAFETY AWARDS - In the quarterly draw among accident-free workmen at Wheatley Hill Colliery, held in connection with the Divisional Coal Board Safety Campaign, the principal prize of a gold watch was won by a coal-hewer, Mr E Stamforth, of Wheatley Hill. Mr J E Bricklebank won the second prize of a tape recorder and electric shaver, and Mr L Jones the third prize of a set of car safety belts and a travelling clock. The draw took place during a social evening in Wheatley Hill Workmen's Club with the colliery manager, Mr F Richardson, presiding.

WHEATLEY HILL COUPLE WERE MARRIED IN 1905

One of six sisters whose average age is over the 80 mark, Mrs Maria Race, of East House, East View, Thornley, and her husband William celebrated their diamond wedding on Saturday with a family party in Wheatley Hill Workmen's Club where their son-in-law and daughter, Mr and Mrs Joseph Craggs, are steward and stewardess.

The couple were married at the old Primitive Methodist Church at Wingate on 15 July 1905. "We held the party two days after the actual anniversary date so that all the family could get," Mr Race, who is 83, told our reporter.

Worked At Thornley

Both Mr Race and his wife enjoy pretty good health. "My only complaint is I could do with a fresh pair of legs- I cannot get about as well as I would like," said Mr Race, "Otherwise I keep quite well." Mrs Race, who is 82, does all her own housework and keeps quite active for her years. She is one of the olderst members of the village's Over 60 Club and rarely misses a meeting.

Mr Race was born at Thornley and has lived there nearly all his life. His schooldays were spent at Haswell and when he left at the age of 13 he began work at Thornley colliery. "At first I worked on the belts on the surface and was paid about a shilling a ten-hour shift," he recalled.

Later he went down the pit and, apart from a short spell at Ushaw Moor colliery and about three years as steward at Thornley Workmen's Club, he worked at Thornley all his life until retiring about 15 years ago.

For a number of years he was treasurer of Thornley Workmen's Club and he has also served on the committee. He is still a member of the club. "But I don't get there so much these days because of my legs," he said.

*Mr and Mrs Race of Thornley
Celebrating their Golden Wedding*

Six Sons, Four Daughters

Mr and Mrs Race have a family of six sons and four daughters, 27 grandchildren and nine great-grandchildren. They were all at the celebration party.

Only two of Mrs Race's sisters, however, were able to attend. They were Mrs Hannah Lamb (74) of Buckley, Flintshire, and Mrs Isabella Simpson (80), of Thornley. Her other sisters are Mrs Jane Luke (86), of Wheatley Hill, and Mrs Margaret Bullock (84) and Mrs Sarah Gott (77) of Thornley.

23 July 1965

WHEATLEY HILL 'GOLDEN' WIFE - SCOUTING FAN

A well-known figure in the Scouting movement at Wheatley Hill is-surprisingly-a women!

And on Saturday when the woman, 69-year-old Mrs Susannah Watson, of 52 Wheatley Terrace, Wheatley Hill, celebrated her golden wedding, among the scores of congratulations she received were those from local Scouts and their parents.

Mrs Watson and her husband William were married at Easington on July 31, 1915, and all their married life has been spent in Wheatley Hill.

Mrs Watson helped to form the Wheatley Hill Scouts 29 years ago and she has since played an active part in the group's progress, as a member of the Parents' Committee. "I have always enjoyed working for them," Mrs Watson told our reporter.

Her six sons have also taken a keen interest in the Scouts. Her eldest, Ralph, who is a member of Wingate Parish Council, has been secretary of the Wheatley Hill Group Scouts for many years, and two of his brothers, George and Alf, have served as Cubmasters, while his youngest brother, Nathan, won his Queen's Scout Award.

Born At Auckland

Mrs Watson, whose maiden name was Cook, was born at Bishop Auckland but has lived in Wheatley Hill since she was eight years old. Her husband was born at Ludworth 75 years ago but was only twelve months old when his parents moved to

432

Mr and Mrs Wastson of Wheatley Hill,
Celebrating their Golden Wedding

Wheatley Hill, where apart from three years at the neighbouring village of Shotton, he has since lived.

Mr Watson retired from work at Wheatley Hill colliery ten years ago after being employed there from leaving school at 14. He earned a shilling a ten-hour shift when he began work as a trapper-boy. He has done "virtually every kind of job" down the pit, he said. When he retired he was a training officer.

Helps With Meals

Like his wife, Mr Watson enjoys good health and often gives Mrs Watson "a helping hand" with the household chores. When our reporter called at his home he found Mr Watson scraping potatoes ready for the dinner. "He's not afraid to give a hand with the meals," said Mrs Watson, "and always looks after the coals and the fire".

Mr Watson is also fond of gardening and spends many an hour cultivating the large plot attached to his home. His wife is a member of the village's Over 60 Club.

Mr and Mrs Watson have a family of six sons and two daughters, ten grandchildren and one great-grandson. They were all at a celebration party at the couple's home on Saturday, and as well as receiving a shoal of greeting cards, the couple were the recipients of many gifts and flowers.

SHIP FIRE ALTERED THORNLEY GIRL'S PLANS

Miss Elizabeth Gray, the 17-year-old Thornley student who is going to the United States on a travel scholarship, has had to change her plans because the ship on which she was to have sailed has been put out of action by an engine room blaze. She was to have sailed, along with other British students, from Southampton on August 7, but because of the fire, a revised schedule had to be drawn up and Miss Gray sailed on August 1, a week earlier than planned. The British contingent sailed to Rotterdam to meet the rest of the students, some had come from as far afield as Thailand. They sailed for New York on Thursday.

The scheme is being organised by the American Field Service, which now runs scholarships for students from over 50 countries. Miss Gray will be staying with a Doctor and his family in Amherst, Massachusetts. She will be starting off on familiar ground as her father is a General Practitioner in Thornley. Her hosts will meet her at New York and take her back to Amherst, which will be her home for the next year.

Rotary 'Ambassador'

Miss Gray has been given a small embroidered banner by Durham Rotary Club and asked to deliver it to the Headquarters of the local Rotary Club in Amherst. Durham Rotary Club hopes to develop friendly relationships, through Miss Gray, with Rotary in America.

6 August 1965

NEW THORNLEY ESTATE HAS OCCUPANTS' NEEDS VERY MUCH IN MIND

By the second week in September, the first tenants will be moving into Easington Rural District Council's new housing estate at Gore Lane, Thornley - only 13 months after the first brick was laid.

By then ten houses will be completed, with the rest of the 106 houses on the estate expected to be completed in phases, by the beginning of next year.

Work was held up in the early stages by the national shortage of building bricks- then by the siting of the estate itself, which is built on a limestone ridge. Although the limestone will ensure extra strong foundations- a pneumatic pick had to be used to dig the trenches- keen gardeners will find this a problem, or they could try a rockery.

The estate is composed of four-bedroom, three-bedroom and two-bedroom semi-detached houses, and ten old people's bungalows. It is planned in a square formation, served by one ring-road.

An outstanding featured of the estate is the way in which the fine view, which extends as far as Consett, has been incorporated into the open planning of the houses. With many open spaces, and large lawns planned in place of individual front gardens for some houses, the view is visible from most parts of the estate.

Many Garages

The view is further enhanced by a wide range of colour in the house bricks- made incidentally at Chester-le- Street. Pastel shades in Elizabethan rose, buff, terracotta, black and white as well as Shotton rustic bricks, do much to belie the traditional uniformity of a council estate.

Another attractive feature is the large number of garages, ensuring that the maximum distance which anyone will have to walk for their car is only 250 yards. Although the estate has only one access road, a further road is to be built from the East Lee Estate to the garages.

Over half the houses on the estate have two bedrooms, and tenants taking these will find an unusual feature- one of the bedrooms has a cupboard with its own window. Ideal for your smaller relatives?

Cupboards are also of interest in the three-bedroom houses where a large bulk-head cupboard in the small bedroom will make an ideal toy cupboard for the children.

Wall Units

But cupboards downstairs are out, other than under the stairs. Instead wall units have been fitted, so all it means is that your pantry is now four feet higher than you are used to.

All the houses have a toilet inside and out, with a washhouse and coal house also outside. A feature which will be appreciated in the old people's bungalow is the sun lounge on each front door.

As yet no names have been decided for the streets-but in view of the estate's attractive surroundings that should not present much of a problem.

13 August 1965

AUTOBAGGER TEAM

Miners living in Peterlee got a surprise when an Autobagger coal lorry team drew up at their homes ready to deliver 12cwt of bagged coal into their coalhouses.

Only the previous day a report had been issued stating that deliveries of clean bagged coal would begin on August 23, after the miners' holidays. This was a last-minute arrangement by the NCB who had brought two of the special lorries to Horden Colliery to start delivering coal to miners living in Peterlee.

Two Horden drivers assisted the drivers of the vehicles in delivering the coal. Mr Thomas Legg, one of the Horden drivers, said the work of delivering the coal was much harder than he expected. General opinion from the receivers was that from their point of view it was much better but they sympathised with the delivery men.

Work will go on during the miners' holidays by contractors hastening to complete part of the new coal bunkers being erected for use in the coal-bagging scheme to enable bagged coal to be delivered non-stop in the Peterlee area. Deliveries in the Horden area will not start immediately.

20 August 1965

THORNLEY BL MARKS 40th BIRTHDAY

At the 40th birthday party of the Thornley British Legion held in the Thornley Miners' Welfare Hall, the chairman welcomed visitors and members. She also gave a warm welcome to the County Chairman, Mrs Handysides.

A birthday cake specially made to mark the occasion was cut by Mrs Clark, who stressed that all the members and herself were very sorry that Mrs Brewster, the president was unable to attend, owing to a recent illness, and conveyed wishes for a quick recovery. Mrs Clark continued by wishing all the local branches present every success in the future.

A fancy dress parade followed and the lucky winners and recipients of prizes were Mrs P Luke, Mrs H Slater, Mrs Thornton and Mrs Hardy.

Entertainment and dancing followed, and all members enjoyed the final moments of the night's entertainment.

Votes of thanks were given by Mrs Morgan, of Ludworth, Mrs Bishop, of Wheatley Hill and Mrs Stubbs, area county standard bearer. Prizewinners were Mrs Richardson, Mrs Merryfield, Mrs Stewart, Mrs Head, Mrs Barrass, Mrs Winter and Mrs Hammond.

The birthday cake was made by Mrs M Langley, and elaborately iced by Mrs F Simpson.

27 August 1965

THE HUTCHINSONS - Alan, George and Norman of Thornley are making a habit of winning the trophy for most points at Durham County CIU Show. This is the fifth year in succession, added to which is the celery trophy.

17 September 1965

IN HOSPITAL - Mr Edward Barry Dobson, 21, of 29 Luke Terrace, Wheatley Hill, was admitted to Durham County Hospital early on Tuesday morning with leg and head injuries sustained when his motor cycle was involved in a collision with a baker's van at Wheatley Hill.

POLICE PROMOTION - PC R Mahan who has been stationed at Wheatley Hill for the past 14 months, moved to West Hartlepool on promotion to the rank of sergeant. PC Mahan joined the Sunderland Borough Police at the age of 18, and earned two recommendations for his work. When war came he volunteered for the Commandoes, and served as a corporal in the renowned No 4 Commandoes, Lord Lovat's Own as a leader of a troop. He went on daring raids on enemy-occupied territory in Norway, France and Holland. He joined Durham County Police and served for 16 years in the Castle Eden Division, where he captained the life-saving team, and was in the team which won the competition seven successive times. He was also secretary of the sports section and the football team. He is the son of the late Mr James Mahan and Mrs N Mahan (nee Crow) of Shotton Colliery

24 September 1965

ROBSON HITS FOUR IN HILL'S FIRST HOME WIN

Wheatley Hill Workmen's Club recorded their first home win of the season in convincing style, winning 5-0 at the expense of Houghton Glendale in a Club and Institute Union League game,

"Hill" showed big improvement, the team as a whole being more constructive and quicker in action.

Inside-right Dave Robson enjoyed a personal triumph. He gained four of the goals and with a little luck he would have rattled in two more.

Play was even in the opening stages, but in the 25th minute Robson, from a pass from Ray Wood, opened the scoring. This goal stimulated the team to greater effort and two minutes before half-time Robson lifted the ball over the 'keeper's' head to make the half-time score 2-0

Threatening

Glendale made several threatening attacks this half, but found a defence equal to all demands.

The second half was only two minutes old when Robson completed his hat-trick. He made a fine solo effort down the middle to fire into the top corner of the net.

"Hill" were now dictating the play and it was no surprise when Ray Wood, in the

65th minute, rattled home the fourth goal.   Then Robson slipped through a gap in defence to complete the scoring from 15 yards.

"Hill" were well served by George Cook (right half), Alf Purvis (centre half), Harry Hepple (left half) and Dave Young (right back). The forward line as a whole-Wilf Halliwell, Robson, Wood, Alan Hawkes, Maurice Nichols-combined effectively and if this standard is maintained they should be a trouble to most defences.

Keith Jackson made a good debut in goal. He had not a lot to do, but he brought off three excellent saves.

The team is unchanged for the league game at Seaham Knack tomorrow. Kick-off at 10-30 am. Team: Jackson, Young, Cowan, Cook, Purvis, Hepple, Halliwell, Robson, Wood, Hawkes, Nichols.
1 October 1965

THERE IS NOBODY IN THE COUNTY to beat them and the same might apply to further afield. Alan and Norman Hutchinson of Thornley, showed six wonderful pot leeks to win first and second prizes at the News of the World show in Durham Town Hall.

Produce Amazing At Durham Show Despite Bad Season

Durham's top garden produce, with pride of place going to some magnificent pot leeks, drew praise and gasps of astonishment from visitors to Durham Town Hall for the three-day Durham leek, vegetable and flower show held by the News of the World.

Over £200 in cash prizes was offered, with the major award for £20 and the County Silver Challenge Trophy in the pot leeks section going to A and N Hutchinson, of Thornley, whose champion exhibits measured 218.3 cu. ins.

The beautiful exhibits in the flower classes, with some very high standard chrysanthemums, dahlias and gladioli, filled the Town Hall with a mass of colour to delight the eye of the hundreds of visitors throughout the three days of the show.
Results
Pot leeks: 1 and 2, A and N Hutchinson (Thornley), 3 G Evans (Blackhall Rocks), 4 E Raydon (Stanley), 5 J Defty (Trimdon), 6 J Lightburn (Langley Moor), 7 J Defty, 8 R Richardson (Trimdon), 9 J Defty, 10 J Lightburn, 11 R McAdam (Clousdale), 12 J Bell (Trimdon Colliery), 13 R Raine (Vigo), 14 J Lightburn, 15 J Middleton (Wingate), 16 R Wilson (Jarrow), 17 G B Callender (Norton), 18 G Fisher (Coxhoe), 19 T W Hodgson (Wheatley Hill), 20 A A Joseph (South Shields).
Blanch leeks: 1 and 3 J Defty, 2, 4 and 5, A and N Hutchinson, 6 J Shaw (Gilesgate).
Vegetables - Four varieties: 1,3 and 4 A and N Hutchinson, 2 J Defty.
Three varieties: 1 and 2 A and N Hutchinson, 3 R Wilson, 4 J Defty.
Chrysanthemums – incurved: 1 and 2 J Hogarth (West Hartlepool), 3 W Iceton (Horden), 4 M Johnson (Bishop Auckland), 5 C Fletcher (Lanchester), 6 A Drane (Easington Colliery).

Intermediate: 1 and 6 J Hogarth, 2 and 3 N Hughes (Easington Colliery), 4 L W Watson (Dunston), 5 M Richardson (Shotley Bridge).
Reflex: 1and2 M Johnson, 3 R Dowsey (Sunderland), 4 and 6 J Pearce (Horden),5 G Evans (Blackhall Rocks). **Twelve blooms**: 1, 3 and 4 J Howarth, 2 J Seery (Hylton Castle), 5 Clarke and Jackson (East Boldon), 6 N Hughes.
Artistic arrangements: 1 Mrs E Armstrong (Staindrop), 2 A Dobson (Medomsley), 3 A Robinson (Bishop Auckland).
Gladioli: 1and 6 C A Holmes (Tantobie), 2, 4 and5 A C Thomas (Darlington), 3 J Bond (Whitburn).
Dahlias: **Medium decorative**: 1 C Walton (Stanhope), 2 and 4 E Raydon (Stanley), 3 F N Morris (Chester-le-Street), 5 W Robinson (Bishop Auckland), 6 G Stonehouse (Jarrow).
Medium cactus: 1, 4 and 6 W Wilson (Rowlands Gill), 2 W Robinson, 3 G Stonehouse, 5 A Baldwin (Gilesgate).
Small or miniature decorative: 1 R Sygrove (Bishop Auckland), 2 W Wilson, 3 C A Holmes, 4 G Stonehouse.
Small or miniature cactus: 1 and 2 J Jones (Stanhope), 3 A Raine (Stanhope), 4 J Shield (Quarrington Hill). **Pompom**: 1, 2 and 3 H Fenwick (Bishop Auckland), 4 A Robinson.
Artistic arrangement: 1 A Robinson, 2 Mrs W McNay (Sedgefield), 3 and 4 Mrs C P Webb (Durham Moor).
Artistic arrangement of herbaceous or border flowers: 1 E C Still (Durham, 2 R Adamthwaite (Crook), 3 J Gibson (Pittington).
8 October 1965

WHEATLEY HILL ROMP HOME

Wheatley Hill Workmen's Club recorded their biggest win of the season when they beat Newbottle 11-2 in a Club and Institute League game at Wheatley Hill.

In the second minute Colin Smith gained an easy goal, and five minutes later "Chick" Nichols headed in from a centre from Jim Cowan. Shortly afterwards, Smith made a fine solo effort to increase the lead from close in. "Hill" continued to pile on the pressure and Ray Wood rattled in a good goal from 18 yards.

Then Dave Robson unleashed a powerful shot from 16 yards to beat the "keeper" all the way. "Hill", encouraged by a substantial lead, slackened their pace and in the five minutes before the interval Newbottle scored two goals.

In the early minutes of the second half Cowan added another goal-direct from a free kick, the ball entering the top corner of the net. Five minutes later Robson drove the ball home from ten yards, and shortly afterwards Smith completed his hat-trick by leaping high to head in from a corner from Alan Hawkes.

Newbottle were unable to cope with the lively Hill forward line and it was no surprise when Hawkes scored one and Robson two in the closing phases.

Not Extended

Hill defence was rarely extended, but Bill Gibson (left-back) and George Cook (left-half) made the most of the opportunity to give the forwards neat though passes. Jim Cowan (out-side-left) made several scintillating runs to pave the way for three of the goals.

Tomorrow, Wheatley Hill W C visit South Hetton in a league game. Team selected is: Jobes, Winter, Gibson, Cook, Purvis, Cowan, A N Other, Robson, Smith, Wood, Howarth. Kick off at 10.30am.

15 October 1965

A SIX HOUR BED TREK RAISES £18.

A novel fund-raising stunt gave a good send-off to the annual Club Week organised by Wheatley Hill and District Youth Club on Saturday. In comic night attire members of the club pushed a single bed on wheels around Wheatley Hill and the neighbouring villages of Thornley, Shotton, and Ludworth, and collected money en route for their funds. They took turns at pushing the bed and lying on it and at the end of a six-hour trek their takings amounted to £18. 16s.

"It was a magnificent effort and we thank all those who so generously supported our appeal," said the club leader, Mrs Ros Sinclair.

A Pantomime

The week's programme was continued on Monday and Tuesday nights this week when the club members presented a pantomime, Snow White, before packed audiences in the Welfare Hall, Wheatley Hill. They designed and made all their own scenery, costumes and "props."

The show, produced by Mrs Sinclair, went with a swing from the opening curtain, the singing, acting and dancing reaching a high standard.

Kathleen Leck charmingly filled the title role and plenty of fun came from the seven dwarfs - Joyce Hubbard, Judith Hodgson, Enid Mason, Dickie Henderson, Richard Curry, "Noddy" Waites and Ena Simons. Other leading roles were filled by Margaret Simons, as the wicked stepmother, and Val Hammond as Prince Charming. Mrs Nancy Robinson was the accompanist.

Fashion Show

Last night a teenagers fashion show was held in the Welfare Hall, followed by a sherry and cheese party. Tonight there is to be a film show and the week ends tomorrow night with a hallowe'en dance in the Welfare Hall.

Club Week last year raised £140. "We have set a target for at least that amount this year," said Mrs Sinclair.

WHEATLEY HILL COUPLE MARRIED FOR 50 YEARS

A popular figure in local carnival processions during the early part of his married life, Mr James Monaghan, of 1 Fourth Street, Wheatley Hill, celebrated his golden wedding on Saturday. He and his wife, whose maiden name was Elizabeth Ann Wallace, are well-known and esteemed in the area and at their celebration party in the Soldiers' Club on Monday they were showered with good wishes for their future happiness.

Often Mr Monaghan, who is 71, was Carnival King at Thornley, where he lived before moving to his present home 26 years ago. "And I have also dressed up as the "Queen" and the "Jester," he told our reporter this week. "In those days" he said, "Carnivals were very popular and sometimes they ran for a week at Thornley, I used to enjoy myself, but it always took a pint or two of beer or a glass of rum to get me in the carnival mood when I headed the procession!"

One year, he recalled, he turned down the offer of being Jester. "I did not want to lose a shift at the pit," he said.

But the organisers, not to be denied, went to the colliery, where he had got through half his shift, and after approaching the manager, got his "release." They had to get my "marra" to take my place at work and pay me for the time I lost," said Mr Monaghan, who added that many bets were "won and lost" among the workmen that day as to whether he had been at work or not.

"I was a banksman and as they had seen me at my job when they went down the pit," he said, "many of them could not believe I was the Jester in the carnival!"

For Ten Hours' Work - 9½d

Mr Monaghan was born at Thornley and started work on the belts at the colliery there when he was 14. "I was paid 9½d a ten-hour shift," he said. "But when I went down the pit I got twopence a shift more and after about three weeks was paid 1s.1d."

He remained at the same colliery until his retirement at 65 and for more than 30 years was a banksman.

He was formerly a successful exhibitor at local shows with his leeks, vegetables and flowers. "At Thornley Workmen's Club just before the last war," he said, "I cleared the deck for prizes-I won every class I entered."

Mrs Monaghan was born at Sunderland 69 years ago, but moved to Wheatley Hill when she was 13 and has since lived in the area. "I often 'play war' about lasses marrying young nowadays," she said, "but I suppose I should be the last to talk! I was only 19 when I was married and I have never taken any harm!"

Mr and Mrs Monaghan, who are both in good health, were married at St Godric's RC Church, Thornley, on October 23, 1915. They have a family of three sons and two daughters, who are all married with the exception of a daughter, and there are five grandchildren and one great-grandchild.

PIT SAFETY PRIZES - The first prize valued £50 in the quarterly draw among accident-free workmen at Wheatley Hill colliery, held in connection with the Divisional Coal Board Safety Campaign, was won by an underground miner, Mr R Jones. The second prize valued £25 went to Mr L Freek, a putter, and the third valued £10 to Mr T Rowlands, who is an attendant at the Medical Centre. The draw was made at a meeting of the colliery consultative committee, presided over by the manager, Mr F Richardson.
29 October 1965

SHE IS 90 YEARS OLD
At the last meeting of Ludworth British Legion (women's section), Mrs Matilda Mark was honoured on the occasion of her 90th birthday. Mrs Mark, whose maiden name was Matilda Stringer, was born at Darlington. She was baptised at St Paul's Church, and was married in the same church to Mr William H Morland. They came to Ludworth 62 years ago, when her husband started work as a miner at Thornley Colliery.

Before that, her husband served in the Army as a regular. He went out to India and South Africa (in the Boer War) and was called up to serve in World War 1. After the death of her husband, Mrs Morland was caretaker at the old CE School at Ludworth and later married again, this time to the late Alfred Mark of Darlington.

There were two children of the first marriage, Mr William Morland and Miss Lily Morland, and Mrs Mark has 9 grandchildren and 14 great-grandchildren. Miss Lily Morland married Mr Michael Morgan of Ludworth, and sometime ago, Mrs Mark went to Ludworth to make her home with her daughter and son-in-law. She is a member of the Church of England and was confirmed in middle life at Shadforth Parish Church, being prepared for confirmation by a former rector, the late Rev T Perkins.

Following the example of her first husband, Mrs Mark became a founder member of the British Legion (women), at Ludworth and she is a member of the Women's Institute.

WHEATLEY HILL MINERS ARE MEALS ON WHEELS SAMARITANS
Only a few hours after finishing his shift as a stoneman at Wheatley Hill Colliery, where he had been at work all night, Mr Marcus Shevels drove his small van to the colliery canteen on Tuesday morning to begin another "voluntary shift", delivering meals to old people in the village under the Women's Voluntary Service "Meals on Wheels" scheme.

Mr Shevels was the first of seven miner-drivers on a rota of ten people who have volunteered to deliver the meals to aged and infirm people in Wheatley Hill twice a week-on Tuesday and Thursdays.

"I think it is a fine idea, these dinners for old people who find it difficult to get about, and I hope the scheme is a big success in the village," commented Mr Shevels as he was helped by the Easington Area WVS Organiser, Mrs Hilda Kilgour, and Mr

John Andrew, one of the founders of the local scheme, to load the containers with the piping hot two-course dinners into his van.

Highly Successful

Judging by the delighted smiles of the 12 old people who had the meals taken to their homes on Tuesday, there is little doubt about the scheme being highly successful.

"This is wonderful," said Mrs Margaret Anson Pattison, a 78-year-old widow, of 25 Aged Miners' Homes, who was the first "call" for driver Mr Shevals and his helper, Mrs J Milne, secretary of Wheatley Hill Women's Institute.

Mrs Pattison has been blind for the past six years. Since her husband George's death seven weeks ago, she has lived by herself. "But there's always someone popping in," she said, "and a friend comes in every night to sleep with me."

Meals on Wheels
Front: Coun Andrews and Marcus Shevels

Very Kind

Mrs Pattison's lips quivered as she told our reporter how she had missed her husband. "He helped a lot in the house," she said, " and cooked all the meals. I did not know how I was going to manage without him but these meals brought to the door are going to be a big help- I think it is very kind of everybody to organise them."

And for the oldest woman to benefit from the service, Mrs Martha Ann Fothergill, of 1 Quetlaw Road, it looks like the end of "burned fingers."

Said Mrs Fothergill, who was 90 in September, "Most of my meals come out of tins. Every time I use the oven I seem to burn my fingers - my legs are not too good and I get about badly."

Yorkshire Pud

As the meal of Yorkshire pudding and roast beef, with potatoes and cabbage, and an apple sponge and custard "sweet" was served to Mrs Fothergill, she smiled and said, "I have been looking forward to this for a long time." Mrs Fothergill has been a widow 13 years.

The Meals on Wheels service in the Easington Rural area began at Peterlee about three years ago. Later it was extended to Horden and Blackhall, where the volunteer drivers, who at first used their own cars, now have the use of a van, which was presented to them by Easington Rotary Club. Recently the number of meals delivered in Horden and Blackhall was doubled from 12 to 24.

Cooked In Local Pit Canteen

Mrs Emily Thackeray, a past president of the local Women's Institute, is in charge of the Wheatley Hill "Meals" rota. "The rota is made up until next January," she said. They have ten drivers – eight men and two women - with "mates" to accompany them.

As they are subsidised by Easington Rural Council, the meals cost the old folk only a shilling each and by arrangement with the National Coal Board, they are cooked in the local pit canteen.

There had been a wonderful response to the initial meetings organised to make arrangements, said Mrs Kilgour. Later she said, the WVS hope to run Luncheon Clubs in the neighbouring village of Thornley and at Easington Colliery, where there is no "Meals on Wheels" service. Meals would be served at these clubs to old people who were not confined to their homes and were able "to get about."

5 November 1965

NURSING GUARD OF HONOUR AT THORNLEY FUNERAL

The funeral of Miss Margaret Tunney took place last Monday at the Roman Catholic Church of the English Martyrs, Thornley. Nursing colleagues formed a guard of honour outside the church as the coffin was borne out by Miss Tunney's four brothers: Mr H Tunney, Mr T Tunney, Mr L Tunney and Mr E Tunney.

Requiem Mass was celebrated by the Rev Father H McNeill, and interment at Thornley cemetery followed. Among the friends who attended the funeral were a party who had come from Shotton where Miss Tunney worked for many years as a health visitor. Many floral tributes were sent and among them were wreaths from many medical and welfare organisations, which Miss Tunney has helped in the past.

The mourners were: Mr and Mrs Hubert Tunney (parents), Mr Hubert Tunney, Mr Thomas Tunney, Mr Leo Tunney, Mr Eugene Tunney (brothers) and their respective families, Mrs J L Rowley and Mrs Atkins (sisters).

Miss Tunney began her studies to be a nurse at St Mary's Hospital, Armley, Leeds. One of her companions who began her studies at the same time, Miss Carr, is now Matron at Sedgefield General Hospital, where Miss Tunney died last Thursday.

After completing her studies and becoming a State Registered nurse, Miss Tunney took up duties at the Hartlepools General Hospital at Howbeck where she stayed until 1939. On the outbreak of war she joined the Queen Alexandra's Imperial Military Nursing Reserve and served as a nursing sister in North Africa, India and Palestine.

While she was serving in Palestine, Miss Tunney was attached to a hospital in Jerusalem.

While sight-seeing she found a small coin about the size of sixpence. After returning to England an expert informed her that it was a Byzantine coin and that it had been minted in the year 578 AD, Miss Tunney gave it to the British Museum.

After the armistice Miss Tunney served in Germany. When she returned to England she took up duties as a health visitor in East Durham. Later she qualified to join the Soldiers, Sailors, and Air force Families Association. Her work for SSAFFA took her to East Africa. She worked among servicemen's families in Nairobi for three years before returning to Britain.

In recent years Miss Tunney has become well known to Women's organisations throughout the North-East for her lectures on travel and nursing.

In recognition of Miss Tunney's devoted service to nursing she was elected as a Fellow of the Royal Society of Health.

2 November 1965

COLLIERY VILLAGES REMEMBER
THORNLEY

At Thornley the Thornley Colliery Band headed a large procession of local organisations. St Bartholomew's Church was well filled for the service of remembrance which was conducted by the Vicar (the Rev P G Mold). The lessons were read by Mrs Dowson (representing the Salvation Army). The address was given by the superintendent minister of Thornley Methodist Circuit (the Rev G Johnson).

The procession re-formed and marched to the village cenotaph in the market place where wreaths were placed by the following organisations- British Legion, British Legion Women's Section, Thornley Colliery Federation Board, Parish Council, Labour Party, Mothers' Club, Workmen's Club, Thornley Colliery Officials Club, Over-60 Club, Jazz Band, Thornley St Stephen's Greenwood's Girls Guild, Life Boys, Boys' Brigade, St Stephen's Youth Club. Mr Burrell, Mrs Lawrence. Mrs E Gordon acted as Thornley Women's Section Standard-bearer.

WHEATLEY HILL

Anglicans and Methodists united for the British Legion service at Wheatley Hill. Organisations taking part in the parade, which was headed by Wheatley Hill Colliery Band, were British Legion Women's Section, Fire Brigade, Police, Workmen's Club, Mothers' Club, Constitutional Club, Discharged Soldiers and Sailors Club, Women's Institute, Sherburn Hill Co-operative Society and Wheatley Hill RAOB.

All Saints' Church was filled to capacity for the service which was conducted by the Methodist minister (the Rev G L Nelson). The address was given by the Vicar (the Rev G G Graham). On their way to the cenotaph in the Welfare Park, the procession halted beside the memorial clock in Front Street on the Boys' School, to mark the memory of those killed in the Second World War. The organisations represented in the parade placed wreaths on the cenotaph. Last Post and Reveille were sounded.

19 November 1965

MAURICE CULLEN RETAINS TITLE _

In the first defence of his British lightweight title, Shotton Colliery boxer Maurice Cullen scored a points win over the Hoxton market porter, Vic Andreetti over 15 rounds at Wolverhampton on Tuesday night. He had matters far from his own way and in the end Andreetti was fighting hard to build up points, but Cullen still ended a worthy winner, delighting the band of supporters who had made the cold journey from his home village to cheer him on.

As usual, it was Cullen's lightning left-hand punches which scored points- he was "prodding into Andreetti's face like a mosquito", said the radio commentator, adding, "He is so fantastically fast!"

Cullen will remember this fight if only for the right handers he had to take in the early rounds. After attempting to establish the usual left hand pattern in the first round, the Shotton boxer was shaken by two punches on the chin in the second.

Gradually, however, Cullen's speed of hand and foot began to tell. By the tenth round he was jabbing with authority and also finding time to throw his right hand into the battle with good effect.

In a whirlwind last round Andreetti gave everything he had, but Cullen stood firm and after the gong had gone his hand was held up in victory. It was a "beautifully clean and clever contest throughout," summed up the radio commentator.

BOY KILLED - shortly after four-o'clock on Tuesday afternoon a nine-year-old Thornley boy, Stephen O'Brien, was killed in an accident with a moving set of trucks in the local colliery yard not far from his home. It is believed he was crawling through one of the truck wheels when he was trapped and died almost instantly from his injuries. Stephen was the son of Mr and Mrs Mathew O'Brien, of 77 East Lea, Thornley.
3 December 1965

MANY ATTEND THORNLEY BOY'S FUNERAL
More than 300 local people made their way to Thornley RC Church on Saturday morning to attend the funeral of nine-year-old Stephen O'Brien, son of a colliery worker, who was killed in an accident last week.

A bazaar, which had been scheduled for last Saturday at St Godric's school, was postponed in order that Stephen's school friends could attend the funeral. Over 150 children were among the congregation and, under the direction of their headmaster, they sang hymns as Requiem Mass was celebrated by the Rev Fr H McNeill. After the funeral they lined up on the church steps to form a guard of honour. The coffin was carried by Stephen's uncles, Mr Mark O'Brien and Mr Patrick O'Brien, Mr R Weller and Mr W Scott.

WHEATLEY HILL BOWLS CLUB PRESENTATIONS
Though road conditions were bad, preventing a number of league officials attending, there was a good turn-out for the joint presentation social evening in Wheatley Hill Welfare Hall organised by the men's and women's sections of the local Welfare Bowling Club.

About 150 members and friends were present and were given a warm welcome by Mrs E Jones, president of the women's section and Mr E Parsley, president of the men's section.

Lady Winners

Mrs A Ord, Chairman of the North-Eastern Women's Bowling League, who was introduced by Mrs Jones, presented trophies and prizes to the following winners of the season's tournaments organised by the women's section: Championship Cup, Mrs Edna Hall, runner-up Mrs E Atkinson. William Jones Challenge Cup Mrs E Jones, runner-up Mrs B Reed. Festival Bowl, Mrs J Grant, runner-up Mrs E Atkinson.

And The Men

Mr Winter, of the No 4 Area of the National Coal Board League, who was introduced by Mr Parsley, presented the following members of the men's section with their trophies and prizes: Club Cup, Mr J Steel, runner-up Mr J Watson. Moore Cup, Mr J Watson, runner-up Mr A Franks. Veterans' Trophy Mr J Steel.

An excellent supper was served, followed by a programme of whist, dominoes and dancing. Prizes were won by the following: Whist, Mesdames Robinson, L Bates and E Champley and Messrs E Parsley, J Blakemore and J Jones. Dominoes: Mrs Tattersall, Mr J Hughes and Mrs Wigham.

WHEATLEY HILL FUNERAL OF EX-POLICEMAN

The funeral has taken place of one of Wheatley Hill's most colourful personalities, Mr Thomas Dodd Collingwood (79), who died at the home of his son-in-law and daughter, Mr and Mrs William Walker, 1 Cemetery Road, Wheatley Hill, with whom he went to live five years ago.

Mr Collingwood was born in Bedlington, and at the age of 13 was living at Wingate. He started work at Wingate Grange Colliery, and seemed to be all set for a mining career. He was a Salvationist in his younger days, and played in the Wingate Salvation Army band.

25 Years Service

In 1914 he joined the Durham County Constabulary and gave 25 years service. He served 17 years as a constable at Wheatley Hill, and was also at Stockton, Felling and Hetton, where he retired in 1939. He volunteered for service in the 1914-18 war, and joined the Royal Engineers, and rose to the rank of sergeant major.

He was awarded the Military Medal, was mentioned twice in despatches, and was also in the King's Honours List for distinguished services.

When he resumed his police duties, Mr Collingwood was always very proud of one special task. He was one of the Durham County Force selected for duty at the Coronation of King George VI in London in 1937.

After his retirement in 1939, Mr Collingwood made a useful contribution in the 1939-45 war. He joined the first aid staff of a munitions factory and held a number of certificates of the St John Ambulance Brigade.

Bowls became one of his chief recreations, and he became an active player with the Wheatley Hill Welfare team. He was married more that 50 years, his wife dying two years ago. He is survived by two married daughters, two grandchildren and three great-grandchildren.

Funeral service was conducted at The Rest, Wheatley Hill, by the Methodist minister, the Rev G L Nelson.

Durham County Constabulary were represented by Supt English and Insp Bailes. Police Constables Carr, Fletcher, Donaldson and Magee acted as bearers.

At the wish of his grandfather, Mr Thomas Dodd Collingwood Walker (grandson) and his wife headed the procession of family mourners.

10 December 1965

WHEATLEY HILL WC HAVE 11-0 WIN

Wheatley Hill Workmen's Club improved their CIU League championship chances with an easy win over West Lea, the score being 11-0.

In the seventh minute Colin Smith opened the scoring after collecting a rebound from the bar, and four minutes later he took up a pass from Wilf Halliwell to shoot in from close in. Then Dave Robson, five minutes afterwards, gave the 'keeper' no chance from 16 yards.

West Lea remained under sustained pressure and slipped further behind, Smith completing his hat-trick by converting a penalty for "hands." In the 30th minute Robson made a fine solo effort to score from 12 yards, and just before half-time Smith, after beating two defenders, added another good goals.

The pattern of play in the second half was similar to the first, Wheatley Hill piling on the pressure. Smith proved to be an indomitable leader and in the first ten minutes of the second period he gained two more goal.

Robson (inside-right) was also in dazzling form and he completed his hat-trick in the 70th minute. Five minutes later Jack Lowther gained a goal from a penalty kick.

Towards the end Robson made a solo effort, beating two players before driving the ball home from 15 yards.

Tomorrow, Wheatley Hill WC visit Seaham York House in a league game and are expected to line- up as follows; Jobes, Craggs, Gibson, Young, Purvis, Hawkes, Halliwell, Robson, Smith, Wood and Nicholson. Kick-off at 10.30am.

YOUTH CLUB WIN

Wheatley Hill WC Youth XI did well to gain a 5-1 win over the Hartlepools and District League Division II team, Nimmo's, in a Durham Minor Cup game. They gained a three-goal lead in the first ten minutes, Million scoring two and Wesley Howarth one. Nimmo's were on the retreat for most of the game and did well to limit the opposition to only two more goals, Sid Luke and Eddie Newby being the scorers.

Tomorrow, the Youth XI entertain a formidable side in Seaton Holy Trinity (Hartlepools and District League) in a Horden Aged Miners' Cup first round game. Kick-off at 2.15pm.

Wheatley Hill WC Youth will be represented by, Curry, Newby, Cowan, Cook, Winter, Grady, Howarth, Million, Tempest, Lowther and Luke.
17 December 1965

COLLIERY MANAGER PRESENTS TROPHY

Mr W S Hutton, manager of Thornley Colliery, presented a trophy to the Sunbeams Jazz Band at a presentation tea on Saturday afternoon in the Welfare Hall Thornley. The trophy was won at Brandon Carnival six months ago when the Sunbeams tied for first place with another Durham band.
Accordingly it was agreed that the Sunbeams should hold the cup for the latter part of the year.

In presenting the trophy, Mr Hutton congratulated the people of Thornley on the band. He commented on the need for some activity to fill the "vacuum" in a child's mind and to keep him out of trouble. He added that this venture besides fulfilling that purpose gave enormous pleasure in the older residents of Thornley.

Following the presentation of medals to each individual member of the band, a bouquet was presented to Mrs Hutton by a younger member of the band, Gillian Newton. Then the drummers (numbering13 in all) gave a demonstration.

Mr S Greener, secretary of the Federation Board, congratulated the children on behalf of the miners of Thornley.
17 December 1965

PARTY - Mrs E Clark (Chairman) welcomed a large number of members and guests at the annual party of Thornley Women's Section of the British Legion. The function was held in Thornley Colliery Miners' Hall. The chief guest was Mrs L Park (Durham County Chairman), who extended the season's greetings to all members. A supper was enjoyed and each member received a Christmas gift. A fancy dress parade attracted a large entry. Prizes were awarded to; 1 Mrs C Cooper, 2 Mrs E Clark, 3 Mrs C Saunders. McNamara's Band under the leadership of Mrs E Clark proved to be hilarious fun. Vocal solos were contributed by Mrs E Middleton. A comedy sketch was presented by Mrs M Maddison, Mrs M Greener and Mrs B Atken. Dancing followed and the evening closed with the community singing of traditional Christmas carols. Organising secretary was Mrs G Bromilow.

CLUB PARTY - When they were entertained to their annual party by Wheatley Hill Workmen's Club, the retired club members and their wives, as well as widows, received Christmas gifts of £2 each. They were welcomed by the chairman of the club, Mr R Armstrong and secretary, Mr B Aitken, and during an excellent tea the oldest guest, Mr B Bowes, who is 85, cut the Christmas cake. Carols were sung and entertainment was provided by a South Shields concert party and members of Wheatley Hill District Youth Club.
31 December 1965

1966

SCOUTS

The 2nd Wheatley Hill Group of Scouts and the Old Scouts' Association raised a record sum of £45.11s by their annual carol-singing round of the village at Christmas and New Year. In thanking all those who supported the effort, the secretary, Coun Ralph Watson, says that the total was £12 more than the previous record. The money, as in the past, will be used for the benefit of the young patients in the children's ward of Durham County Hospital, which the Scouts "adopted" some years ago. The Scouts' annual "re-union" is to be held on Saturday.
22 January 1966.

WHEATLEY HILL FUNERAL

The funeral took place on Tuesday of Mr Alfred Carr, 9 York Street, Wheatley Hill. He was 64 and went to Wheatley Hill as a child. He is survived by his wife, Mrs Barbara Carr, to whom he has been married for 41 years, three sons, four daughters and 11 grandchildren. He was born at Yarm. Mr Carr gave 50 years to Wheatley Hill Colliery retiring in February last year because of ill-health.

He was a member of Wheatley Hill Discharged Solders and Sailors Club for 45 years, and served for many years on the management committee. He served as chairman for five years.

His six brothers, William, Herbert, Christopher, John, George and Norman were bearers. A service was conducted in All Saints' Church by the Rev G G Graham.

Family mourners included Mrs B Carr (widow), Mr and Mrs R Smith, Mr and Mrs J Gibson, Mr and Mrs G Hodgson, Mr and Mrs R Williams, Peterlee (sons-in-law and daughters; Mr and Mrs A Carr, and Mr and Mrs R Carr (son and daughters-in-law), Mr Norman Carr (son), Miss E Smith (granddaughter), Mr and Mrs W Carr, Mr and Mrs H Carr, Mr and Mrs C Carr, Mr and Mrs J Carr, Mr and G Carr, Mr and Mrs N Carr, (brothers and sisters-in-law), Mr and Mrs G Hutton, Shotton, Mrs H Brown, Newbiggin, Mr and Mrs J Bryson, Easington Colliery, Mrs D Hunter, Mrs M Davies, Mr and Mrs R Hutton, Nottingham (brothers-in-law and sisters-in-law).

The Wheatley Hill Discharged Soldiers and Sailors Club was represented by officials and members.
7 January 1966

POPPY DAY RESULT

Mrs G M Bromilow, organising secretary of Thornley British Legion Poppy Day sales and collections, said the effort realised £106.7s.6d. This was Mrs Bromilow's first year as organiser and the result has broken all previous records by £15. Sale of wreaths, car poppies and door to door collections were all up.

THIEVES HAUL

Detectives from the Castle Eden Police Division are investigating a break in at Thornley Welfare Hall at the week-end, when thieves made off with almost the entire stock of the canteen. After entering the building, by breaking a small window at the back, they forced the shutters of the canteen and got away with a haul of more than 8,000 cigarettes and a large quantity of chocolate and sweets to the total value of £108. All they left behind were a few boxes of matches.

14 January 1966

FOUR FOR PARKES IN THORNLEY'S CUP WIN

Thornley CW broke new ground when they travelled to Blaydon to play the Northern Combination League side in the Durham Challenge Cup, and celebrated the occasion by romping home to a comfortable 7-1 victory.

Thornley had long periods of supremacy throughout and very little was seen of the home attack. The Wearside League team assumed command from the kick-off and were a goal up in the 5th minute. Thubron collected a centre from Whyatt, and found Gofton on the left wing with an astute pass. The winger left full back Ward in his wake and put in a terrific drive which left Workman in the home goal helpless.

The ex-Pools player Barry Parkes was in his most tantalising mood, and was a constant menace to the Blaydon defence. He had a say in Thornley's second in the 11th minute when he picked up a loose ball on the left wing and found Connell in the penalty area with a pin-point centre. The centre forward headed the ball into the roof of the net.

Parkes nearly scored a third when he outwitted the home defence, and chipped a shot over the advancing goalkeeper's head, but the ball perched precariously on the crossbar before dropping behind. However, the diminutive player made amends when he unleashed a shot from 18 yards that had Workman well beat. Just before the interval he made it 4-0 when he waltzed through the home defence to score from close range.

In a lone attack by the home side Whyatt did well to dispossess Mac-Winney, but the Thornley defence in its most resolute mood, gave the Blaydon attack very little chance to shine.

Parkes was soon in action after the interval and from one of his passes MacGregor ran in to score Thornley's fifth. Blaydon did eventually get the ball past the Thornley defence in the 59th minute, when Oliver broke through to score.

However, it was the Colliery side who kept on top and Parkes scored another two goals to make his tally up to four and the final score 7-1.

WHEATLEY HILL TEAMS

Wheatley Hill Workmen's Club's away game with Newton Aycliffe Rangers last Saturday in the replayed fourth qualifying round of the Durham Minor Cup was postponed because of the snow. The match has been rearranged for tomorrow and representing the "Hill" will be: Curry. Newby, Cowan, Cook, Winter, Gibson, Howarth, Luke, Tempest, Million, Lowther. Kick-off, 1.45pm.

Wheatley Hill's other team visit Newbottle Workmen's Club tomorrow in the Durham Club Union League, the selected side being: Jackson, Craggs, Jones, Purvis, Young, Wood, Halliwell, Robson, Smith, Hawkes, Ainscough. Kick-off 10.30am.

21 January 1966

COMMUNION TABLE DEDICATED

Before a large congregation, the Rev George L Nelson dedicated a new oak communion table in Wheatley Hill Methodist Church. It was the gift of Mr and Mrs William Poulson and was in memory of Mrs Poulson's father and mother, Mr and Mrs William S Hedley. Mr Hedley was well known as a butcher in the village. Mrs J Shutt was organist. Mrs Poulson is secretary of the church sisterhood.

28 January 1966

WHEATLEY HILL BOY AWARDED QUEEN'S SCOUT BADGE

A member of the 2nd Wheatley Hill Group of Boy Scouts, William Smith, who has qualified for his Queen's Badge, was presented with this award by the District Commissioner, Mr Ashton, when the Group held its 30th annual re-union supper and social evening at their newly-decorated headquarters.

Mr Ashton, who congratulated Mr Smith on his splendid achievement, also presented swimming badges to five members of the Wolf Cub Pack – twins M and J Youll, cousins R and G Lambert and T Farrell.

Mr A Lambert presided and welcomed the guest who, in addition to the District Commissioner, included Mr Fred Simpson, Miss E Simpson, Sister Sutton, of the Children's Ward of Durham County Hospital, and Mr Waring.

Supper was served by the Group committee – Mesdames S Watson, M Watson, Cowan, Rowland, Armstrong, Hodgson, Walker, Richardson, Andrew and Nicholson, Miss Shutt and Messrs R Booth, N Waugh, A Watson and G Hird.

Best Wishes

A birthday cake, made by Mrs S Watson and decorated in the Troop colours by Mr Lindsay, was cut by the District Commissioner, who extended best wishes for the future of the Scouting movement in the area

Thirty-six Cubs with Arkela Mr W Saxby, were present, together with 24 Scouts, under Scoutmaster Colin Thackeray, six senior Scouts and a number of old Scouts.

After supper, a programme of games, competitions and sketches was organised and the Group Scoutmaster, Mr Leslie Barker, was in charge of a campfire sing-song, assisted by Mr G Watson. The old Scouts enjoyed the singing and joined in the traditional Scout songs. Before leaving for home each Scout and Cub received a packet of sweets.

During recent weeks members of the Old Scouts' Association have worked hard in their spare time altering and re-decorating the Scout building and after the re-union they held a celebration of their own. Mr G Watson was responsible for the cooking of hamburgers, assisted by Messrs A Watson and T White, and among those who entertained were Messrs W Vincent, J Carr, C Thackeray, W Saxby, R Woodward, G Watson and J Fishwick.

Arrangements for the evening were made by the secretary, Coun Ralph Watson,assisted by the ladies' committee, the Scouters and the Old Scouts' Association.

4 February 1966

RUMBLING OVER THORNLEY ALLOTMENTS
RENT RISE PROPOSALS

A LETTER from the solicitors of Professor Kirk, a former resident of Thornley, saying he proposed to increase the rent of the allotments to £40 per year, roused mixed feelings at the Thornley Parish Council meeting. Members were told that two thirds of the allotments had been lost to horticultural enthusiasts, by the implementation of a scheme by the Easington Rural District Council to build some 200 new houses under a slum clearance order.

The Council decided the increase in rent was "a little steep" and the Clerk was instructed to write to Professor Kirk asking for the possibility of a five year lease on the allotments with a much smaller figure proposed.

Back to the old roue

A letter was read from the G and B Bus Company stating that they intended to revert back to the old route through Thornley i.e. through the Villas down High Street to the Colliery Inn. Most members were disturbed by the news of this re-routing, Coun F A Walker made strong objection. He said that within the next two years there would be some 300 new council houses erected on this estate, and also that the re-routing had alleviated some of the traffic chaos prevailing in the Villas. Coun Walker continued that this company were not running a public service but a profitable one. The Council should make known their views on this issue to the Traffic Commissioners.

A setback

Coun Nicholson told members that there had been a setback to the proposed new playing fields. The NCB had stated that the 11 acres involved in the proposed scheme should be fenced. A rough estimate of the cost, said Coun Nicholson, would be nearly £2,500. It was finally resolved that the Clerk write to the Area Estates Manager, Mr Fleming, on the possibility of meeting a delegation from the Council.

The chairman, Coun F Walker, spoke indignantly of the disposal of coal dust in the main street of the village. While appreciating the productive liaision between these private lorries and the miners at the Thornley Colliery in taking away the coal to the local ICI works, steps should be taking to prevent this holocaust of coal and shale which littered every corner of Hartlepool Street. Besides being a hazard to motorists and road safety, it was spattering pedestrians with an unsavoury mixture of coal dust, red shale and slush whenever vehicles were passing. Coun Walker stated this complaint had been a hardy annual, and these wagons should be covered with tarpaulins, to prevent the deposit of coal in their wake.

18 February 1966

CHILDREN'S PLAYGROUND FOR WHEATLEY HILL?

Following a meeting between representatives of the Council – the chairman Coun Jack Horan, and the Clerk, Mr John Etherington – and Wheatley Hill Welfare Committee, prospects are brighter for a childrens play-ground the Council are seeking to provide in the Wheatley Hill Welfare grounds.

This was revealed at Wingate Parish Council on Monday night when the Clerk, reporting on the meeting, said that the Welfare Committee were agreeable to allowing the Council the use of a site near the tennis courts. "But, of course," the Clerk added, "the Parish Council will be expected to provide the cash for the maintenance of the playground."

The Welfare Committee themselves, pointed out Coun Mark Alderton, who is the committee's secretary, were in "no position to foot the bill," but they were fully in favour of giving permission for the land to be used for a play area.

No Difficulties

Since the meeting, added Coun Alderton, he had written to the area Welfare Officer of the Coal Industry Social Welfare Organisation, who had replied that no difficulties were anticipated in allocating the land to the Council. But, wrote the officer, they would like to meet the Welfare Committee and representatives of the Council to discuss the matter further.

Said Coun Alderton, "We will have to go into the pros and cons of the situation."

It was agreed that a meeting be arranged in the near future for a full discussion on the project. The sooner they had a playground the better, commented Coun Horan, for parents were very perturbed about their children playing in the streets.

25 February 1966

STACK BLAZE AT WHEATLEY HILL

Thirteen tons of unthreshed wheat in two stacks were destroyed by fire in a field bordering the Durham road, near Wheatley Hill, on Monday morning.

Wheatley Hill retained unit of the Fire Brigade found the stacks, fanned by a strong wind, burning fiercely and they were unable to save them. Valued at about £450, they were the property of a Trimdon Station farmer, Mr Thomas Edward Hopper, of West Farm.

The fire was spotted by Mrs Wilson, of Whitehouse Farm, Wheatley Hill. She told her husband, who immediately called the Brigade.

The cause of the fire is being investigated.

4 March 1966

THORNLEY COUNCIL DISCUSSES WALLS AND WAR MEMORIAL

Mr W Barnett, caretaker of the Ludworth Road Burial Ground, gave a report to Thornley Parish Council on the number of burials, and answered members on the general cleaning and maintenance of the burial ground.

Coun Miss Griffiths said that many complaints had come to her about the dilapidated condition of the War Memorial. She said that Spring was just around the corner, and the rose trees given by the manager of Thornley Colliery, Mr Hutton, needed attention and nurturing for future blooms.

The chairman Coun F A Walker told the members that this Council two years ago had passed a resolution that Mr Barnett should spend four hours a week on the preservation of the war memorial grounds, and to meet any disputes from the Trade Union, the local organiser of the Caretakers Union had been approached.

The resolution had been fully accepted. However, with the arctic conditions which had prevailed and the large number of burials in this period Mr Barnett had been fully employed at the cemetery, and it was hoped that more pleasant weather conditions would enable work to proceed on the war memorial.

Fantastic

A letter from the solicitors of Prof Kirk, who was born and bred in the village, and is now living in the Leicester area, in answer to the Parish Council's plea, that the rent required for garden allotments was a little to high stated that he would accept £32 per annum instead of his previous figure of £40. Coun Walker stated this figure was fantastic.

In previous years the figure had been £25 for the whole area. Now the horticultural enthusiasts of the village had lost two-thirds of this ground by the implementation of a scheme by the Easington Rural District Council to build over 100 houses under a slum clearance order.

With only a third of arable land at their disposal, surely this was a case of a cut in rent instead of an exhorbitant rise. Members were reluctant to make any proposal on this new development and it was finally resolved that the Thornley Allotments Secretary, Mr Smith be informed of the issue, and their views sought.

Time stands still

The Coronation clock in the Market Place, which was causing quite a lot of inconvenience to the miners working at the adjoining colliery, had been standing at the time of 1.40 for a number of weeks. The Clerk, Mr J Taylor, had said that it had been broken by local teenagers, with snowballs, and that the man responsible for maintenance was ill.

A letter from the Vicar of St Bartholomew's Church, the Rev P G Mould, requested that it was imperative that the Parish Council make the necessary repairs to the old churchyard wall.

Age, time and weather had brought the old limestone wall down onto the footpaths. This was proving a hazard to pedestrians and a danger to young children.

New Wall

The chairman told the members that they had examined the damaged wall, and with members from the Easington Rural District Council had decided that the only solution was to erect a new wall which would cost £1,669. Of this £918 would be met by the Parish Council and £750 by the Parochial Church Council. This was for a wall of three feet high, but the vicar had said that a wall of this size would be easily accessible to younger children and that a four feet structure would be more favourable. The vicar in his letter asked that the additional cost could be met by a 1d rate.

It was finally decided that the Ministry of Housing and Local Government be approached on the matter and that a deputation from the Council meet the Parochial Church Council on the site.

Playing Fields

Coun J Nicholson gave a report of his meeting (with other members) with Mr Fleming, Area Estates Manager of No 3 Area NCB on the proposed new playing fields envisaged to begin within the next few years.

He reported that he had been highly satisfied with Mr Fleming's report, and that he Council should go ahead to purchase the land. A sum of £1,750 has been received from the Easington Rural District Council. This money could only be spent on recreational amenities.

One year would have to be given to the present tenant to quit, and it would be 1970 before the playing fields would be in use.

"This village is void of recreational facilities for the children, at the present time they are using roads and back streets to play football and cricket, causing a nuisance to nearby residents and quite a hazard to road safety."

Nauseating, deplorable, pathetic, chaotic, a slimy mass of mud and coal dust, were some of the expressive terms mentioned by members, about the "Gassy Gutter" (a name derived from its contents by parishioners some 100 years ago) on the main road between Thornley and Wheatley Hill.

One member said this was a matter for the Health Authorities, yet in the latest Health Report, it was ironically intimated that rats have been destroyed, and that it has been given a clean bill of health.

While appreciating that it was linked with production at the nearby colliery, steps should be made immediately to have the whole place cleaned up

It was decided that the members of the Wheatley Hill Parish Council, ERDC members and Thornley Parish Council meet on the site of the "Gassy Gutter".

11 March 1966

PET CORGI FIGURES LARGELY AS WHEATLEY HILL SEVEN PLAN TO EMIGRATE TO AUSTRALIA SOON

When they emigrate shortly to Australia, a Wheatley Hill family of seven will be parted from their pet Corgi – a dog they took into their home just over six months ago to save it being put down. But the parting will be only for a few weeks. Under the Government assisted emigration scheme, Mr and Mrs Joe Lamb are flying to Melbourne from London, but Randy, their four year old Corgi, must go by sea.

He will receive VIP treatment on his lone five-week voyage. A special kennel has been built for him – it has to conform to exact specifications – and with him will go a store of food to last him the whole trip.

"Arranging for Randy to go has given us more running about than for ourselves – and his passage is costing more than the lot of us put together." Mr Lamb, a pit deputy, told our reporter this week. The dog had to have a special medical check and injections and a clearance certificate to leave the country. "But it has all been

455

worth while," said Mr Lamb. "We would not have dreamed of leaving him behind – the children all love him. They would never have gone without him!"

The Lamb Family from Wheatley Hill
Back: Jeff, Jennifter, Keith
Front: Beverley, Olive, Joe, Ian

Not superstitious

Mr and Mrs Lamb, who are looking forward tremendously to their new life "down under", are far from being superstitious. All their married life of 19 years has been spent in the same house in Lynn Terrace – No 13.

"But it has never brought us any bad luck," smiled Mrs Olive Lamb, who is 43 – the same age as her husband. She added, "In fact, we have lots to be thankful for and we hope this good luck will continue when we leave the house after all these years."

The couple have three sons and two daughters – Keith (18), a miner at Wheatley Hill Colliery, Jeffrey (17), a shop assistant in Duncan's grocery shop in Wingate, Jennifer (15), who works in Alexandre's clothing factory in Peterlee, and Ian (10) and Beverly (7), who are both at school.

Mr and Mrs Lamb have already taken the first steps to buying a bungalow at Elizabeth, a town about 18 miles from Adelaide, where they are to live. Mr Lamb who has worked at Blackhall Colliery for the past 14 years, has no special job awaiting him in Australia. But he said, he can turn his hand to "almost anything."

He has been a shot-firer at Blackhall Colliery and before taking up mining was a driver for the East Durham Co-operative Dairies at Wingate. He is a bricklayer by trade – this was his first job when he left school. His wife also drove for the East Durham Co-operative Dairies before her marriage. "During the war," she said, "I was the only girl driver, I left to get married."

He and his wife also have many friends in Wheatley Hill, where all the family are associated with the Methodist Church. Mr Lamb's parents are dead, but his wife's mother, Mrs Mary Stockport, lives at Wingate.

"When we get nicely settled there we are hoping my mother will follow us out," said Mrs Lamb. Mr Lamb's older brother Frank, a bachelor, who lives at Wheatley Hill, may also join the emigrants later.

18 March 1966

MAGISTRATE RETIRES

On Monday – the day before his 75th birthday – Coun Edward Cain, of 11 Burns Street, Wheatley Hill, made his last appearance on the Bench at Peterlee court before retiring after 20 years' service as a magistrate.

It had been a "tremendously interesting 20 years," he told the court before the day's business began, and tributes were paid to the fine service he had given. He had met "all sorts of people on all sorts of occasions," and he regretted that the time had now come when he must retire. He added, "I wish to thank the police and the legal profession and my colleagues especially, for the tremendous amount of help I have received."

Tributes were paid by Mr H E Bailey, on behalf of the practising solicitors; Supt J K England, head of the Castle Eden Police Division, and Mr Gerald J Cohen, clerk to the magistrates.

Mr Bailey said they had enjoyed their association with Coun Cain, particularly in this and other courts. He added, "There have been moments when we have not understood each other perfectly, but there have been many more times when we have been thoroughly impressed by the sincerity with which you have dealt with your responsibilities from the Bench, and that is perhaps one of the great attributes a magistrate can have. We are sorry you are going, and thank you for all you have done over the years, and we hope you will have a long and happy retirement."

From time to time, said Supt England, Coun Cain had commended police officers on their work. He added, "May I now thank you for your work in the past 20 years in helping the police to keep the peace and preserve law and order in this Division."

Good wishes were also extended to Coun Cain's wife, Frances, who is now making a fine recovery at home after having her leg amputated in Sedgefield General Hospital. She and Coun Cain, who was appointed a magistrate in 1946, and has been a deputy chairman for the past nine years, celebrated their golden wedding two years ago. Mrs Cain was 77 on Monday.

18 March 1966

THORNLEY GIRL LOST PURSE BUT WON PRIZE

An attractive 18-year-old Thornley girl, Joyce Hubbard of Office Villas, Thornley, was nominated by the Durham Association of Youth Clubs, to go to the finals of a competition, (An essay in Youth Leadership) from the thousands of young people competing from all over Britain. Joyce a miner's daughter, won a cheque for £10 for the first prize.

The competition was organised by Remington the razor firm, and Mr Simon Lloyd presented Joyce with the cheque in the Savoy Hotel.

The Thornley girl was a little perturbed for she thought she had lost her purse with £8, but the remuneration she received from her victory made her better off than she was when she arrived. Joyce was all smiles later for after the presentation she found her purse in her handbag.

Joyce has been an active worker for the Youth Movement for quite a number of years, she became chairman of Wheatley Hill and District Youth Club when it opened in March, 1963, and has occupied the post ever since, she became Press Offlcer of the Members Council in October 1963 and represented Durham County Association Youth Club at National Conference in Hampshire in 1964, both at Whit and in August.

In September, 1964, at London, she was chosen as secretary, and also chosen to represent the Council National Youth Clubs, the chairman being the Hon Angus Ogilvey and she also represented the National Leaders' Conference in Nottingham and the Scottish Members Conference in Edinburgh.

Daughter of Mr Henry Hubbard, she works at the NCB No 3 Area Castle Eden. Her father is a Training Officer at Thornley Colliery.

25 March 1966

PETER, 15, AGAIN CARRIES OFF PIANO HONOURS

For the last five years, Peter Galloway, of Wheatley Hill, has entered the Coal Industry Social Welfare Organisation's annual musical festival and each year 15-year-old Peter has won the piano section for his age. Again on Saturday, Peter won the under-16 and under 18 classes for piano solo, when the festival was held at Durham Technical College.

Mr W Churchill, of the CISWO, said that there had been a very good response at the festival-in particular from young people.

Results – Friday-Junior school choirs: Byron Terrace Junior Modern School. Secondary school choirs: Chester-le Street Grammar School. Youth choirs: Washington Grammar School. Saturday-Girls solo, under 12: Doreen Wheatley, Quarrington Hill. Girls' solo, under 14: Lyn Harris, Willington. Girls solo, under 16: Marilyn Mason, Sunnybrow. Boys solo, under 12: Malcolm Bunton, Sunnybrow. Boys' solo, under 14: James Laing, Easington Lane. Boys' solo, under 16, Malcolm Bunton, Sunnybrow.

Piano solo, under 12: Alan Kirkbride, Easington Colliery. Piano solo, under 14: Barry Kitto, Peterlee. Piano solo, under 16: Peter Galloway, Wheatley Hill. Piano solo, under 18: Peter Galloway. Piano duet, under 18: John and Doreen Wheatley, Quarrington Hill.

Instrumental brass solo, junior: Leslie Ramsey, Peterlee. Instrumental brass solo, juvenile: Wayne Kenneth Cessford, Consett. Instrumental brass solo, open: Wayne Kenneth Cessford. Oratorio: Winifred Tempest, Washington. Female voice choirs: Deneside WI Choir.

Operatic aria: Brian Craig, Waterhouses. Open choirs, Deerness Male Voice Choir. Rosebowl, 1, Brian Craig, 2 Winifred Tempest.
8 April 1966

GOLDEN WEDDING OF WHEATLEY HILL COUPLE

All their four daughters, who are married, were present when a party was held at the home of Mr and Mrs Thomas Freeman, of 3 Cemetery Road, Wheatley Hill, on Good Friday, to celebrate their golden wedding. The couple who were married at All Saints' Church, Wheatley Hill, on 8 April, 1916, have spent all their married life in the village.

Mr Freeman, who will be 73 in July, was serving in the Durham Light Infantry during the 1914-i8 war when he was married. "I was serving in France," he told our reporter this week, "and was married during a 48-hour leave. The wedding was on the Saturday and the next night I was off back to France again. It was some months before I saw my wife again."

A native of the South of England – he was born in Herefordshire –Mr Freeman came North as a boy and started work at East Hetton colliery. Later he continued his mining career at Wheatley Hill and Thornley collieries, but went back to East Hetton pit, where he retired when he was 65 after 51 years' service.

"I have done most jobs down the pit," said Mr Freeman. Now that he is retired he enjoys pottering about his council house garden. "I only wish the warmer weather was here so that I could get in it more," he said.

Mr Freeman is a member of the village's Over-60 Club. His wife Charlotte was formerly a member, but stopped going to the meetings about three years ago because of ill-health.

Mrs Freeman, whose maiden name was Wylie, is 72. The couple's four daughters all live in the area, and they also have five grandchildren
15 April 1966

GAMING MACHINE STOLEN

Thieves who broke into Baldasera's café in Hartlepool Street, Thornley between Sunday night and Monday morning made off with a gaming machine. Detectives from the Castle Eden Police Division, who are making enquiries, later found the machine broken in an empty house a short distance away, with most of its contents missing. The café was entered after the front door window had been smashed.

FOR THE SECOND YEAR

Six-year-old Denise Newton has won a silver cup at the Northern Counties Dancing Teachers' Association competition. This year it was the silver star cup that Denise took back to her home at 12 Collingwood Street, Thornley. Already in her two-and-a-half years of dancing, Denise has won five cups and two medals. Her teacher is Miss H Greenfield, of Peterlee. The competition is an annual event held at South Sheilds.
22 April 1966

LORRY, CAR, CRASH INTO WHEATLEY HILL SHOP

The lower walls of a corner shop at Wheatley Hill crumbled and partly caved in when a six-ton National Coal Board lorry, which had been delivering coals, crashed through the front door on Saturday afternoon. Virtually at the same time a car with four people inside plunged through the plate glass window at the side of the shop, throwing glass and debris around... but the shop-owner's wife and a customer she was serving, as well as an 18-year-old youth, all escaped injury.

The driver of the car, Mr Bernard Dawes (25), and his three passengers were rushed to Durham County Hospital, suffering from shock and injuries.

Mr Dawes who, after travelling all night from London had arrived at his mother's home in Wheatley Hill only a few hours before the crash, received a dislocated hip and facial injuries. His mother, Mrs Mary Dawes (53), of 8 Durham Street, who was in the car with him, was discharged from hospital after treatment for leg injuries, and Mrs Ruth Hildrew (28), of 13 Wheatley Terrace, Wheatley Hill, was also allowed home after treatment for minor cuts and bruises.

Mrs Hildrew's mother, Mrs Jane Henderson (54), of 13 Weardale Street, Wheatley Hill, was detained with facial injuries and later she and Mr Dawes were both said to be "improving."

At Crossroads

The driver of the auto-bagging coal delivery lorry, Mr Charles Thompson (35), 28 Dunelm Road, Thornley, and his mate Mr David Dougherty (27), 13 Bevan Crescent, Wheatley Hill, both escaped with only a shaking. The front of the vehicle was badly damaged and the car was wrecked.

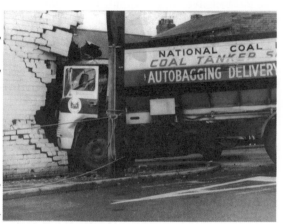

The NCB lorry which creashed into a shop in Front Street

The lorry had been travelling down Cemetery Road and the car along Front Street when the accident happened at the crossroads.

Mr Dawes was trapped for about ten minutes behind the steering-wheel of his left-hand drive car. He was freed by members of Wheatley Hill retained unit of the Durham County Fire Brigade, who were called to the scene, with the assistance of Dr Todd, of Thornley. Police were also quickly on the scene and helped to control traffic at this dangerous corner.

Mrs Marjorie Baker, wife of Mr John E Baker, owner of the hardware and general dealer's shop was serving an elderly customer when the crash occurred.

Twofold Blow

She told our reporter: "We both got the shock of our lives! I knew nothing whatever until I heard this terrific crash and the Coal Board lorry smashed its way through the shop door. Practically at the same time the car crashed through the plate glass window. The walls caved in, goods tumbled all round us from the shelves, and there was a shower of debris."

Luckily, said Mrs Baker, they were not hurt, but an 18-year-old youth, Mr Martin O' Hara, of Fairfield, Stockton, who was visiting their 18year-old son, David, had an even luckier escape.

Only seconds before the crash, said Mrs Baker, he had come into the shop and slammed the door behind him. "The lorry practically followed him in, he was barely a foot from it," she added. "We all made one dash for the back of the house out of danger."

Supports Needed

As well as extensive damage being done to the shop, where Mr and Mrs Baker moved from Trimdon only two years ago, the walls of the sitting-room upstairs were badly damaged – daylight could be seen through cracks. Workmen had to erect supports in this room and they also carried out shoring-up operations outside the shop.

"We have just spent a lot of money on alterations and decoration to the shop and house," said Mrs Baker.

Mr Dawes, who formerly lived at Wheatley Hill, has been working in a plastic factory in London for the past five years.

"But he has left his job," his mother told our reporter on her return home from hospital, "and came up here this weekend to stay with me and look for a fresh job in this area. He was going back to London with a van for his furniture, and his wife and seven-months-old baby were coming up by train, but friends have now gone to bring them in their car."

NEW MEN DID WELL IN 6-0 WHEATLEY HILLWIN

Wheatley Hill WC tried out several new players in their CIU League game at Hetton WC and performed better than was expected to win 6-0.

In the first minute newcomer John Tempest, from a pass from Russell Lowther, opened the scoring, and two minutes later Tempest rattled in another good goal from 12 yards.

Hill, inspired by the flying start, continued to press and Bill Milliner added two goals within the next ten minutes. Just before half-time Howarth made a fine solo effort to make the score 5-0.

Hill remained in command throughout the second half, outplaying the home side with fine constructive efforts, but efforts in the target area were not so fruitful, the only goal this half coming ten minutes from the end. Howarth gave the keeper no chance from ten yards.

For Hill, Tempest, Ralph Winter (centre half), Bill Gibson (full back), and George Cook (inside left) were most effective.

WHEATLEY HILL MAN, 60 YEARS WED,
HELPS WITH HOUSEHOLD CHORES

A Wheatley Hill couple, Mr and Mrs Christopher George Dobbin, of 2 Fred Peart Square, who have spent all their married life in the village, yesterday celebrated their diamond wedding, and tomorrow are holding a family party in their Council bungalow. Both are aged 83, Mr Dobbin, who enjoys excellent health, being three months older than his wife.

Mrs Dobbin has not been so well during recent months. "But I have a fine help-mate in my husband," she told our reporter this week. "He helps a lot with the housework – I don't know what I would do without him! He's a good husband – one of the best."

The couple were living at Wheatley Hill when they were married at Thornley Parish Church on 5 May, 1906. "And we were taken to church in a horse-drawn covered wagonette," Mr Dobbin recalled.

With the exception of a period two years, all Mr Dobbin's mining career of 53 years was spent at Wheatley Hill colliery. "But it was pretty hectic those two years I wasn't at the colliery," he said.

In those days, he said, miners often moved from one colliery to the other when they thought they could earn better money. "My father did this," said Mr Dobbin, "and, of course, I had to go with him. In the space of two years we worked at no fewer than six pits – Kelloe, Trimdon Colliery, East Howle, New Herrington, Monkwearmouth and Whitburn." At one colliery they stayed only three weeks.

Until His Retirement

But eventually Mr Dobbin returned to Wheatley Hill colliery and remained there until his retirement shortly before he was 67. Most of the time he was a coal- hewer and chock-drawer.

A native of Wingate, Mr Dobbin began work at Thornley Colliery when he was 14 as a trapper-boy. He was paid tenpence a ten-hour shift. "Times have certainly changed since those days!" he smiled.

His was far from an accident-free career. On one occasion he lost four months' work with broken ribs and another time was off work six months with a rupture.

In his younger days, Mr Dobbin was a keen member of Wheatley Hill Colliery Band. He played the cornet in the band for 24 years.

He and his wife have both been members of the village's Over-60 Club for many years. Mr Dobbin is a regular attender, but Mrs Dobbin, because of her health, does not get there so much these days. "But when I can get I thoroughly enjoy the meetings," she said.

Mrs Dobbin, whose maiden name was Jane Yule, was born at Spennymoor. Before her marriage, she recalled, she worked in domestic service, but the "pay was very poor."

"I have often done a heavy fortnight's washing for 1s.9d or two shillings," she said. Mr and Mrs Dobbin, who are well known and held in highest esteem in Wheatley Hill, have a family of four sons and two daughters. They are all expected at tomorrow's party, together with their 22 grandchildren and 17 great-grandchildren
.

SOUTH HETTON IN ROAD SAFETY QUIZ SEMI-FINAL

In the second round of Easington Rural District Council's Road Safety Quiz for schoolchildren held in South Hetton British Legion headquarters, South Hetton defeated Peterlee in both the Junior and Senior events.

The South Hetton Juniors had the unique distinction of gaining maximum points of 96 against 89 gained by Peterlee, while the South Hetton Seniors won by 84 to 76.

Teams were:- South Hetton Juniors: Brian Scott (capt), Brian Coman, Trevor Clark and Sandra Reed. Peterlee: Beryl Greenwood (capt), Lynn Sinclair, Carol Gordon and Lynn Bainbridge. South Hetton Seniors: Anne Clark (capt), Julie Kane, Carol Bainbridge and Susan Ridley. Peterlee: Christopher Boyd (capt), David Porter, Keith Anderson and Ruth Castle.

Questionmaster was PC R Pearson, Accident Prevention Officer for the Castle Eden Division, and adjudicators Coun J Nicholson, of Thornley, and Mr A Golightly, of Easington Colliery.

Thanking PC Pearson and the adjudicators, Mr J Mann, chairman of the South Hetton Committee, said that he was pleased to see some parents present but would like to see many more take an interest in this worthy cause. Great credit he said was due to the children and their tutors for they had shown that they had a great knowledge of the subject. He also thanked Mrs D M Crinson, the South Hetton secretary, for carrying out the arrangements. He was supported by Mr J H Moses, vice-chairman of the Peterlee Committee South Hetton will now meet Shotton in the semi-final at Shotton.

6 May 1966

MINER WHO WENT INTO BUSINESS

The funeral took place on Wednesday of Mr Thomas Henry Vincent (79), Lambourne House, Alexandra Terrace, Wheatley Hill. A service was conducted in Wheatley Hill Methodist Church by the Rev G L Nelson, followed by cremation at Durham. Mr Vincent's wife, Jane Ann, died 15 years ago. He is survived by a daughter.

Born at Coundon, Mr Vincent went to Wheatley Hill when he was 10. His first work was at Thornley Colliery. For a while he was attracted into insurance and rose to be an assistant superintendent with the Pearl Assurance Company. He returned to the pits and was for many years employed at Wheatley Hill Colliery.

Was Prisoner Of War

At the age of 50 Mr Vincent entered the family hardware business. He was active in the business until his sudden death on Saturday. Mr Vincent served in the first world war with the East Yorkshire Regiment. He took part in the Dardanelles campaign and in France. He was a German prisoner of war for seven months. Mr Vincent was a member of the Methodist Church for many years.

He was actively connected with the Thornley Bow Street and Wheatley Hill Patton Street churches and was a local preacher for 40 years. He resigned that position following a strong disagreement on the administration of the church.

Since its inception, Mr Vincent has been active in the affairs of Wheatley Hill Over- 60 Club. For some years he was chairman, a member of the executive committee and an active member of the club's concert party. The club and concert party were represented at the funeral by officers and members.

27 May 1966

THORNLEY JAZZ BAND DISPLAYS NEW UNIFORMS

Last Saturday the people of Thornley caught their first glimpse of members of the local jazz band in their new uniforms as the children marched proudly through the village.

Since the Sunbeams were founded two years ago they have won no less than two cups and 33 medals. They have already been booked for 14 more carnivals this season and they are confident of carrying off more honours than ever before. As the 58 children marched through the village a collection was taken in order to off-set the cost of the new uniforms which are costing over £600.

The street collection amounted to £26 12s.

3 June 1966

CULLEN KEEPS BELT THIS TIME

"Pride of Shotton" Maurice Cullen made the Lonsdale Belt his own property on Monday when he left no doubts about his superiority in successfully defending his British lightweight title for the second time against Terry Edwards, of Birmingham.

Maurice had the belt placed round his waist for the first time 14 months ago and he has always said he would "never let it go."

He proved himself a real champion in Monday's fight at St James's Hall, Newcastle, and, surprisingly, it was with his right hand that he did the damage in the fifth round which led to the referee stopping the contest. It landed squarely on his opponent's face to send Edwards reeling.

On his slight recovery Cullen moved in determinedly to end the fight and swung punch after punch at the luckless Edwards for fully half a minute until the challenger seemed insensible. And then the referee stepped in and stopped the fight to save Edwards further punishment.

The only disappointment of the night was the "gate." Only about 1,000 turned up to watch the fight in a hall which has a capacity of 4,000.

Before the fight Maurice was brimful of confidence about the outcome, "I'm sure I will make the Lonsdale Belt my own," he told our reporter.

464

Maurice can now look forward to an Empire title fight with Bunny Grant, whom he beat convincingly last year, and, who knows, it may not be long before he gets a crack at the world title against Carlos Ortiz.

WHEATLEY HILL SPORTS ATTRACTED BIG TURNOUT

It was estimated that over 5,000 people watched the parade and sports organised by the Wheatley Hill Colliery Federation Board, and held last Saturday. Tableaux, fancy dress entrants and jazz bands made a colourful scene as the procession, headed by the Wheatley Hill Colliery Prize Band, wound its way through the village to the Modern School playing field, where the sports took place. A sum of £600 had been raised by a weekly levy, on the miners at the colliery, to cover the expenses of the day. Every child in Wheatley Hill under 15, to the approximate number of 1,500, received a bag of sweets valued at 4s and every child taking part in the sports a half-crown savings stamp.

Trophies and prizes were presented by police Sgt Pickering, and judges for the various events were Mr and Mrs Bowman, Dr and Mrs Penrose, Mrs G G Graham, Mr W Atkinson, Mr T Smyth, Sgt Pickering and PC's J Carr and Maxwell acted as judges for the jazz bands.

The long distance race (open), provided an exciting and close finish. Result: 1, W Waistell; 2, J Bennett; 3, J Bradshaw; 4,W Jobes.

Prize for best tableaux went to the Wheatley Hill Mothers' Club. The fancy dress parade drew a large entry and revealed artistic taste and originality. Winners: Children : 1, C Dunn and I Gibson (clowns); 2, T Ord (Made in Japan); 3, C Million and D Million (Bride and Groom).

Original dress: 1, C Taylor (Mary Poppins); 2, M Hicks (Wee Willie Winkie); 3, S Hicks (Oliver Twist). Comic dress: 1, I Snowdon (Wilma Flintstone); 2, P Hoban (Shackleton); 3, E Simmons and M Ogden (Munsters).

Mr B Aitken, a well known figure in Wheatley Hill, was "Mr Sports Day." He was correctly challenged shortly before five o'clock by Margaret Craggs who was awarded the £2 prize.

Horden Melody Makers won the trophy for jazz bands, the various section points were won as follows: Parade; Band Major: 1, Horden (78); 2, Thornley (77½); 3, Hedworth,Easington, Sunderland (75). Drum Major; 1, Horden (84); 2, Sunderland (77), Thornley (76). Bass Drum; 1, Sunderland (82½); 2, Horden (82); 3, Thornley (76½).

Field Display: Drum Major; 1, Horden (84½); 2, Thornley (80½); 3, Hedworth (80).

Band Major : 1, Horden(82); 2, Hedworth (78); 3, Sunderland and Thornley (77).

Bass Drum: 1, Horden (83); 2, Hedworth (78); 3, Easington (77½).

Overall result: 1, Horden Melody Makers (762 points); 2, Sunderland (724); 3, Thornley(717).

CHILDREN'S SPORTS

BOYS EVENTS:

Sprint: five years; 1, Trevor Pace; 2, Frank Lye;3, Stephen Dobbin.

Six years: 1, Brian Connor; 2, Ronald Saiger ; 3, Michael Carr.

Seven years: 1, Lloyd Hedley; 2, Gerald Darby, Kevin Quinn (tie).

Eight years: 1, J Burnham; 2, J Gutcher; 3, G Pace.

Nine years: 1, M Smyth; 2, J Starkey; 3, K Bradley.

Ten years: 1, R Lambert; 2, M Billingham; 3, D Starkey.

11 years:1, D Pattison; 2, F Mitchell; 3, P Langlands.

12 years: 1, J Dunn; 2, J Dunn; 3, E Starkey.

13 years: 1, D Parker; 2, A Pattison; 3, B Venables.

14 years: 1, D Evans; 2, K O' Connor; 3, B Booth.

15 years:1, J Barker; 2, R Kirk; 3, J Langlands.

Potato Race:

Five years: 1, Michael Dunn; 2, Frank Lye.

Six years: 1, Ronald Saiger; 2, Brian Connor; 3, Robert Hardy.

Seven years: 1, Lloyd Hedley; 2, Gerald Bradley; 3, Steward Appleby.

Eight years: 1, T Burnham; 2, J Gutcher; 3, S Chaytor.

Nine years:1, B Harker; 2, N Smythe; 3, A Warnes.

Ten years: 1, D Hardy; 2, M Rutherford; 3, S Kell.

Hurdles:

11 years: 1, a tie; F Mitchell and B Gutcher; 2, a tie J Yuill and N Cain; 3, D Pattison.

12 years:1, a tie; E Starkey and A Dyson; 2, a tie J Dunn and J Oswald.

13 years: 1, D Parker; 2, B Venables; 3, a tie A Pattison and T Anderson.

14 years:1, D Evans; 2, R Pattison; 3, C Woodley.

15 years: 1, J Barker; 2, J Langlands; 3, N Ayre

GIRLS EVENTS:

Five years: 1, Kathleen McDonnell; 2, Christine Armstrong; 3, Christine Williams.

Six years: 1, Linda Hutchinson.

Seven years: 1, Susan Jackson; 2, Valerie Errington; 3, Lesley Hunter.

Eight years:1,C Thubron; S Dixon; 3, C Welsh.

Nine years: 1, S Quinn; 2, D Taylor; 3, J Gratton.

Ten years: 1, J Luke; 2, L Stephenson; 3, L Parker.

11 years: 1, M Bulmer; 2, A Battey; 3, S Cook.

12 years: 1, A Gilling; 2, M Luke; 3, S Luke.

13 years: 1, A Loftus; 2, K Nuttall; 3, K Fleetham.

14 years: 1, D Rushton; 2, A Peacock; 3, E Simons.

Potato Races:

Five years: 1, Linda Warnes: 2, Kathleen McDonald; 3, Christine Million.

Six years: 1, Beverly Robson; 2, Ann Dunn; 3, Carol Richardson.

Seven years: 1, a tie Marjorie Carr and Susan Dobbin; 2, a tie Patricia McDonald and Eileen Cullen.

Eight years: 1, S Cain; 2, K Thubron; 3, S Dixon.

Nine years: 1, S Howe; 2, D Stephenson; 3, P Hitch.

Ten years: 1, J Luke; 2, L Parker; 3, L Stephenson.

Hurdles: 11 years: 1, a tie M Bulmer and A Battey; 2, a tie G Carr and C Hodgson.

12 years: 1, a tie A Gilling and M Luke; 2, a tie S Luke and C Hardy.

13 years: 1, K Nuttall; 2, A Loftus; 3, K Fleetham.

14 years: 1, F Simons; 2, A Peacock; 3, A Rutherford

Members of the Wheatley Hill Old Scouts Association rendered good service at the many side-shows and competitions, while members of the village's women's organisations did a good job of work looking after teas and refreshments.

Although having to miss most of the day's events owing to his father's funeral, Mr Stephen Ragg, the organising secretary, said: "The event is proving to be more popular year by year. Fully 5,000 people would see the parade and sports. Our sports and gala day is one more piece of evidence showing the changing pattern of the miner's world. This event has won its place in the calendar of the village. On behalf of the Federated Board, I want to thank all who have contributed in any way to this year's most successful effort."

The other organising officials were Mr H Peacock, chairman; and Mr J Hedley, treasurer.

BIG IMPROVEMENT PLAN AT WHEATLEY HILL

Greyhound racing has been revitalised at the Wheatley Hill Stadium following its purchase by a Shiney Row man. Mr Norman Fannon, 36-year-old salesman, of Gainsborough Crescent, Shiney Row, an experienced greyhound owner, has great plans for improving the existing amenities at the track.

The Wheatley Hill track, established on waste ground near the colliery some 20 years ago, in the shape of a horse-shoe, was transformed into a circular track about five years ago, allowing for racing over 270 yards and 450 yards. It is equipped with a drag-type hare, electrically driven, and at the end of each race two youths pull it back to the starting position.

In the large paddock punters have the benefit of a good betting market, with five bookmakers giving win and place betting, and one a forecast on the first two dogs to finish.

600 -Yard Races

Mr Fannon told our reporter, that he plans to returf all four bends on the circuit, and hopes to extend the programme to include races over the 600 yards distance, in addition to open races, for the first time at the stadium.

The judge's box, which incorporates a photo- finish camera, is to be extended and improved, and he has plans for improvements to the bar and the addition of a canteen for light refreshments.

Another innovation is the sprint sweepstake which started last weekend and ends with the final on Saturday week, when the winning owner will receive the Nimmo's Sprint Trophy.

"Although one of the smallest of tracks in the county, Wheatley Hill is a good one, and when the plans for improvements are complete it will compare favourably with any other in the district," said Mr Fannon this week. Already there has been a decided improvement in the attendances, and under Mr Fannon's guidance it is anticipated that more enthusiasts will patronise the Wheatley Hill track each Saturday and Monday evening.

Greyhound racing has been Mr Fannon's chief hobby almost all his life, and he estimates that more than 200 dogs have passed through his hands.

He has enjoyed many successes, particularly at Houghton and Wheatley Hill, and his brindle dog, Lingering Hope, last year shattered the 290 yards lap record at Houghton.

Big Appetites!

Training a record breaker is no mean task, and "Hope," with another three stable companions, get through 40lb of meat each week, in addition to four dozen loaves of bread and 18 pints of milk.

The dogs also need plenty of exercise and Mr Fannon is astir at 7.30 every morning to give them a two mile walk. In the evening, after completing his work, he is out again with his charges, for another three miles stint.

He scorns talk of pep pills and laughs at the label he gets from racegoers who claim he has the "magic touch."

Dogs Enjoy It

"Greyhound racing is a fine sport and the dogs enjoy it, too," he says. "Racing is their whole life and they love a bit of competition and keeping themselves in tip-top condition."

If Mr Fannon's venture into the management side of greyhound racing is as successful as that as an owner, enthusiasts in the Wheatley Hill area can be assured of some tip-top racing under first-class conditions.

10 June 1966

WINGATE COUNCIL GETS SUCCESS WITH THE 'BUSES

Wingate Parish Council, who had sought the help of Easington Rural Council to secure a better bus service between the Wheatley Hill area and Crimdon lido during the summer months, were told at their monthly meeting that the Council had taken up the matter with the United Bus Company.

The Company wrote that they were arranging to operate the same service between Wheatley Hill and Crimdon as last summer. There would be a special service every Sunday; and a special bus on Mondays in August.

Coun Mrs Dodds said that the services needed a big public notice in the village. More publicity about these extra buses would help.

Further complaints were made about the untidy state of paths and streets in the parish because of the absence of a road length-man.

Coun J H Charlton said it was not sufficient for a mechanical sweeper to go around only once every three weeks.

Would Aid Tidiness

It would make a vast difference to village tidiness, Coun Ralph Watson claimed, if a man was employed to clean up the paths after every weekend.

It was agreed to write to the Rural Council asking for their comments on the matter and to see if they could help.

A letter was read from Wingate Community Association outdoor section, thanking the Council for their £500 grant.

Trimdon Station Recreation Community Scheme also wrote seeking financial help and it was agreed to make them a similar grant of £500. They wrote the plans were in hand to increase the playing facilities for children and provide equipment for the Youth Club.

The meeting was presided over by the newly-elected chairman Coun M Telford. The new vice-chairman is Coun G H Mills, of Deaf Hill.

24 June 1966

THORNLEY COLLIERY SPORTS REMEMBERED EVERYONE

Mounted Police did a magnificent job of controlling some 8,000 people that lined the 1 and a half mile route at Thornley Sports.

Local miners and residents from nearby colliery localities helped to swell the crowds.

There were no losers in the sports. Every child in the Parade received 2s.6d and also the chance to receive a better prize in the judging.

The cost came from the Miners employed at the colliery, who gave a levy each week.

For the secretary, Sam Greener and his working committee, it was quite an arduous afternoon and there was never a flaw in the organisation.

Jazz Bands – Jazz band results, were: Best Band on Display, Horden Melody Makers; Best Drum Major, Hedworth Legionnaires and Horden Melody Makers (Tied); Band Major, Burnmoor Coldstream Guards; Bass drummer, Horden Melody Makers.

Tableaux: Thornley WI, Trimdon RAFA, Thornley Youth Club.

Adult fancy dress, comic, G Hewitson, R Routledge, N Handley.

Original: J Morriss, G Copeland, J Dunnet. Judges: Mr and Mrs G Hutchinson, Mr and Mrs W Ruth, Mr and Mrs Bonar.

Childrens fancy dress, comic, D Parker, F Peacock, J Bowes, M Atkin, M Turner, B Bowes, T Cullen, K Mather, M Slater, J Hubbard, J Lennox, C Dowson, N

Hogg, B Bell. Judges: Mr and Mrs Woodward, Mr and Mrs Maddison, Mr and Mrs J Luke.

Childrens fancy dress original, M Lennox, P Lennox, L Coxon, E Cutter, S Parker, A Barker, M Jackson, P Williams, T Carr, B Tilley, D Griffiths, B Musgrave. Judges, Mr and Mrs Crosman, Mr and Mrs Stokoe, Mr and Mrs J Ward.

All handicapped children unable to participate in the sports and other competitions received £2 in saving stamps.

Champion pit pony of Northumberland and Durham was "Boxer" of Easington Colliery, under its handler E Robinson. Other prize winners, 10 hands and over, Top, Thornley, handler, J Holden. 10 to 11 hands, Lester, Blackhall, handler, P Butters.

Cleanest pit pony in C Group, 1, Toby, Thornley, handler, R Ord; 2, Duke, Deaf Hill, handler, C Horn; 3, Top, handler, J Holden. Prizes for the champion pit pony were presented by County Councillor S C Docking, chairman of the Durham County Council, and his wife Mrs Docking presented the prizes for the cleanest pit pony.

Mr and Mrs Sports Day were Mr W Wetherall, a telephonist at Thornley Colliery, and Mrs J Adams, wife of Jack Adams, Horse-keeper at Thornley Colliery.

Arts and crafts: K Woore, D Wood, C Dunkin, A Barker, G Robson, A Barker, L Gray, J Gratton, B Brownless, R Murray, H Oswald, K Brownless, W Armstrong, J Crisp, T Cullen, E Watson, F Ord, J Foster, A Williams, S Bell, J Marley, P Stanley, L Baldasera, D Griffiths, G Walker, J Barron, J Burgin.

Painting, crayoning, drawing: C Booth, T Saunders, J Watson, K Richardson, F Dye, C Swinburn, C Young, S Bowes, J Stokoe, G Robson, J Bowes, K Stokoe, S Eslick, M Marley, J Featonby, M Evans, L Maddison, S Stokoe, T Cullen, J Lowther, B Tilley, M Moody, M Davison, E Parker, A Slater, J Greener, P Wilson, M Bartley, R Bowes, K Wetherall, T Fisher.

Field event prizes were presented by County Coun.W E Reavey, Coun. J Cummings, Sedgefield Rural District Council; Mr and Mrs J Crossman, Further Education officer of Durham. A collection taken on sports day for the Thornley Aged Miners' Homes raised £61.

Field Event Results

Boys flat races: 5 to 6 years, S White; 6 to 7, P Ord; 7 to 8, C Williamson; 8 to 9, D Nicholson; 9 to10, J Purvis; 10 to 11, T Leathers; 11 to 12, D Pattison; 12 to 13, T Wilson; 13 to 14, D Parker; 14 to 15 plus, I Barber.

Girls Egg and Spoon: 5 to 6, C Williamson; 6 to 7, A Gaskell; 7 to 8, V Errington; 8 to 9, F Lonsdale; 10 to 11, L Parker, 11 to 12, L Curry; 12 to 13, M Peachey; 13 to 14, P Nicholson; 14 to 15, plus, A Vasey.

Girls flat races: 5 to 6, L Greener; 6 to 7, A Gaskell; 7 to 8, J Gaskell; 8 to 9, G Day; 9 to 10, A McCoy; 10 to 11, H Davies; 11 to 12, J Day; 12 to 13, J Sunley; 13 to 14, S Green; 14 to 15 plus, L Walker.

Boys sack race: 4 to 6, A Wood; 6 to 7, S Jackson; 7 to 8, S Brownless; 8 to 9, S Chaytor; 11 to 12, D Pattison; 12 to 13, T Wilson; 13 to 14, D Parker;14 to 15, R Gaskell.

470

Go as you please - R Peachey.

8 July 1966

SON OF NOTABLE SOCIALIST MOTHER, MR BOSOMWORTH IS NEW COUNCIL CHAIRMAN AT THORNLEY

One of Thornley's most prominent personalities, Mr Jonathan Bosomworth, has been elected chairman of Thornley Parish Council. Since he was a teenager this 44-year-old, better known as "Jonty," has played a major part in the political and social life of his village, and soon after starting work as an apprentice plumber for Easington Rural Council he became an active member of his trade union.

His mother, the late Mrs Bessie Bosomworth, was an active member of the Labour Party from being a girl and was Thornley's first woman Councillor (writes HH).

"Sidney Webb, Ramsay MacDonald, Jennie Lee, Emanuel Shinwell, Phillip Snowden and other Socialist campaigners were friends of my mother, and all of them had, at different times, lunched in our home, and the conversation was inevitably political," said Mr Bosomworth.

"Shortly after Mr MacDonald became Prime Minister my mother was invited to have tea with the MacDonald family at 10 Downing Street.

First Visit

"It was my mother's first visit to the Capital and due to misinterpretation of procedure she called at the headquarters of Scotland Yard."

Mrs Bosomworth was looked upon as a suspect. "She waited some considerable time before they got official confirmation that the Prime Minister was waiting for the arrival of his friend," said Mr Bosomworth. From then onwards Mrs Bosomworth was given VIP treatment.

"My sister Eleanor slept at 10 Downing Street when she was a teenager," said Mr Bosomworth. Mr Bosomworth recalled another incident involving his mother at 10 Downing Street.

Mr Bosomworth has inherited his mother's flair for public life. He has served on the Parish Council for some years, and on the Executive of the National Playing Fields Association and is still delegate to this Association. He has been a Governor of Wellfield Grammar School and a member of the Management Committee of Wheatley Hill Boys Modern School.

Road Safety

He is chairman of Thornley Road Safety Committee, and represents the committee on the Easington Rural Council Area Road Safety Committee.

For many years he has served on Thornley Ward Labour Party Committee, was treasurer for two years, and is now auditor.

Until a few weeks ago he was employed as a plumber for Easington Rural Council, starting as an apprentice when he was 14.

He was a chargehand when he left the RDC on being appointed a foreman plumber for a Tyneside firm.

Mr Bosomworth was an active member of Easington branch of the Plumbers' Union for many years, serving first as treasurer and then secretary from 1948 to 1965.

War Service

Mr Bosomworth served in the Royal Air Force during the 1939-45 war, becoming a corporal and for some time a temporary sergeant.

He served in Italy and helped in the evacuation of the civil population when Vesuvius erupted. He also served in Cape Town and Rhodesia, and with the Desert Air Force based in Cairo.

In Tripoli he formed a "Geordies Club" and raised funds to buy Christmas gifts for the elderly people in Durham County.

He received a letter from the Dean of Durham expressing appreciation of gifts for the old people.

Mr Bosomworth has also played a major part in organising competitive football in Thornley. He helped to form the football team in the 1945-46 season, and served on the committee. "There were two teams, the Rovers and the Sports Club. They amalgamated and the club adopted the name of Thornley CW FC," said Mr Bosomworth.

Keen Footballer

The club became members of the Wearside League and Mr Bosomworth is now secretary.

In his earlier days, playing at right half for Deaf Hill Junior FC, he turned down invitations to undertake a trial with Tottenham Hotspur and Bolton Wanderers.

GAMING MACHINES STOLEN

Detectives from Castle Eden Divisional Police headquarters are investigating a break-in at the coffee bar belonging to Mr A Baldasera in Hartlepool Street, Thornley. The intruders got into the building after smashing a back window and, after forcing open two inner doors leading to the coffee bar, they made off with two gaming machines valued £654. Each machine contained about £12 in sixpences. Two hundred cigarettes were also taken.

WHEATLEY HILL FIELD DAY RAISED £70

Wheatley Hill Old Scouts Association held a successful 8th field day in the Wheatley Hill Peter Lee Girls' Modern School playing field. The effort realised some £70 and was organised by Mr L Barker (chairman), Coun R Watson (secretary), and Mr C Snowdon (treasurer), backed by a strong committee.

The Five Shades Rhythm Group, were popular while a display of fire-fighting, by the Auxiliary Fire Service, thrilled the crowd.

A tug-of-war competition resulted in a win for Wheatley Hill Auxiliary Fire Service with Wheatley Hill Workmen's Club second. Other competition winners were: Log sawing; Messrs W Mercer and S Hall. Guessing the cubic inches in the log; 1 R Cooper, 2 A Maddison 3 A Burnip.

Competitions were in charge of Messrs T Carr and J Douglas.

A feature was an exhibition of paintings by a local artist, Mr W Hollins.

Scouts and members of the Association were in charge of sideshows: Penny on the plate: R Hargreaves and A Carr; Darts: J Metcalfe, B Aitken and R Hunter; Shooting tins: A Watson, W Hall assisted by Cubs; Coconuts: N Waugh, J Fishwick, B Lindsay, W Saxby; Football: T Walker, M Dunn; Bowls: C Thackeray, S Saxby, Y Richards; Soft drinks: W Vincent, C Harris, E Hutchinson; Lucky dip: W Smart, A Hildrew; Ball in the bucket: G Henderson, J Drysdale; Dart board: L Barker, R Elliott;

Prizes await lucky ticket holders in the grand draw, conducted by Mr A Lambert, assisted by J Pyle, T Meechin, F Alderson and J Carter.

Ladies of the parents committee served teas and refreshments, Mesdames Rowlands, Carr, M Watson, S Watson, Armstrong, Andrews, Nicholson, Walker, with the assistance of Mr R Booth.

Messrs G Hind, G Pattison and T Cowie assisted as announcers and MCs for the various events.

Coun R Wastson thanked the villagers for their support.

15 July 1966

FAMILY GAVE WHEATLEY HILL PAIR A HOLIDAY
AS "GOLDEN GIFT"

Mr and Mrs Joseph Dodds, of 50 Luke Terrace, Wheatley Hill, received more than 60 cards and many gifts and flowers when they celebrated their golden wedding with a family party at their home on Saturday. . .but the loveliest surprise of all was a fortnight previous when their family combined to pay all their expenses for a week's holiday at Blackpool.

"It was a wonderful surprise and we enjoyed every minute of the holiday, which did not cost us a penny," Mrs Dodds, who is 70, told our reporter.

The couple, who both enjoy good health, were married at All Saints' Church, Wheatley Hill. They have spent all their married life in the village. They have been in the village's Over-60 Club since its inception.

Mr Dodds, who is 73, was born at Thornley. A miner all his life, he spent the whole of his 51 years down the pit at Thornley Colliery, retiring when he was 65. He did all kinds of work underground, but was principally on piecework.

In his younger days Mr Dodds played an active part in local cricket and football administration, and was particularly interested in coaching young players. For many years he was secretary of Wheatley Hill Juniors FC.

"And while I was secretary the club set up a record which has never been beaten," said Mr Dodds. They reached the final of the Durham Junior Cup one year, he explained, and played no fewer than six draws with their opponents, Coxhoe Juniors, before the match was decided with a goal scored in extra time by Wheatley Hill.

473

Mr Dodds was also a referee for school soccer matches, and some years was on the committee of Wheatley Hill Cricket Club.

Mrs Dodds, whose maiden name was Jane Walker, was born at Chester Moor. As well as three daughters and two sons, the couple have three grandchildren.
22 July 1966

HEAD TEACHER RETIRES AT THORNLEY

When school closed last week it marked the end of the school year and the end of term. For Mrs Catherine Wilson, of Rosneath, Dunelm Road, Thornley, it marked the close of a devoted career as a teacher. Except for one month at Bishop Auckland she has been a teacher on the staff of Thornley St. Godric's Infant School for 40 years. She took up work in this school, where she had been a scholar, in September 1926.

Mrs Wilson served on the staff under Miss O'Hara and Miss B Kevany. When Miss Kevany retired eight years ago Mrs Wilson was appointed headteacher. Mrs Wilson said: "It will be a change not to have two jobs; school and home. But it has been very exciting and challenging being at school."

Changes

Mrs Wilson's retirement has brought changes to the Roman Catholic schools. During Mrs Wilson's headship the number on the roll have doubled. For many years there have been two departments, Mixed and Infants. In September the departments will be merged into a Junior Mixed and Infants school with Mr E Smith as headmaster.

Mrs Wilson was guest at a school concert in the Junior Department when a programme of songs, music and mime was given.

Pianist was Miss E McKiernan. Tributes were paid to the work of Mrs Wilson by Mr E Smith and on behalf of the staff and scholars. Mrs Wilson was trained at Sedgeley Park Training College, Manchester.
29 July 1966

"COUNTY" SUCCESS – DURHAM COUNTY SHOW

Scottish farriers carried off the second and fourth prizes in the Open Hunter Shoeing competition at the County Show on Saturday.

Entries were up on last year and the judges Mr J Hauxwell, of Durham, former National President of the Worshipful Company of Farriers, and Mr H W Wrightson, of Loftus, had a difficult task and remarked on the high standard of shoeing.

Throughout the day many interested spectators watched the blacksmiths fashioning the shoes on the open air forges which had been set up.

Prizes were donated by Messrs Vaux Breweries Ltd, horses were loaned by Mr S N Hannah, of Sunder-

474

land, and the shoeing iron and nails was given by Messrs Monkhouse and Brown Ltd, of Blaydon.

Results

First prize : Pewter tankard, cash and silver medal presented by The Worshipful Company of Farriers, E K Readman, Cloughton, Scarborough; 2, Cash and bronze medal, A Duff, St Boswald's, Roxburghshire; 3, Cash and bronze medal, F L Baty, Hexham; 4,T Wilson, St Boswald's, Roxburghshire; 5, C Cooper, Barnsley; 6, A Hood, Thornley. Special and silver medal for best competitor under 26 years of age, A Hood, Thornley; best hind shoe, E K Readman; best dressed foot, C Cooper, Barnsley.

A VISIT FROM OVERSEAS SON
WOULD HAVE MADE THEIR GOLDEN

Both in excellent health, Mr and Mrs Mark Waters Brain, of 31 Henderson Avenue, Wheatley Hill, are celebrating their golden wedding today (Friday) and on Sunday are holding a family party at their home.

All their three daughters, who are married and live in the village, will be there, but missing will be the couple's only son Mark, who emigrated to Victoria, Canada, 18 years ago.

"We have never seen him since he went there – it would have made the party complete if he had been able to come, but we hope we will see him again one day", said Mrs Brain. When he first emigrated Mark was in the building trade, but now he has a responsible job in a naval dock-yard.

Mr and Mrs Brain, who were married in All Saints' Church, Wheatley Hill, have spent all their married life in the village, where they are well-known and respected. They have nine grandchildren.

Mrs Brain, who was born at Croxdale, was one of the founders of Wheatley Hill women's section of the British Legion early in 1930 and has been actively associated with it ever since

Present Chairman

She is the section's present chairman – a position she formerly filled for 27 years – and she has also served as vice-chairman, delegate, standard bearer and assistant standard-bearer. For many years she has also been chairman of the Benevolent Fund.

Mrs Brain has also been Poppy Day Organiser and on a number of occasions has organised flag days in the area for the blind and the Soldiers' Sailors' and Airmen's Fund.

Mrs Brain, who will be 69 in October, was 18 when she was married. "And I don't think this is too young to get married if you feel you have the right partner", she said . " I certainly got the right partner – he's been a good husband and a good father throughout the years."

Mr Brain retired from work at Thornley Colliery five years ago after a min-ing career of 53 years. He was born at Coxhoe 70 years ago.

Virtually all his mining career was spent at the same colliery and he often served on the committee of Thornley miners' lodge and for some years was lodge secretary.

He is fond of walking and has a good appetite.

5 August 1966

WHEATLEY HILL "GOLDEN" PARTY WAS A SURPRISE

A surprise party at the home of their eldest son was organised for Mr and Mrs John Chapman, of 11 Fourteenth Street, Wheatley Hill, when they celebrated their golden wedding on Saturday.

"We knew nothing about it until a few days before our wedding anniversary." Mrs Chapman (whose maiden name was Rebecca Calvert) told our reporter.

She added: "I was sitting sewing at home when my daughter-in-law came in and said we had to be ready to go to her house for the party. It was the surprise of my life for there had never been any mention of a party and we were just going to celebrate our golden wedding quietly."

The party was held at the home of Mr Jack Chapman and his wife Martha, at 28 St. Aidan's Crescent, Thornley. Altogether Mr and Mrs Chapman have three sons and four grandchildren. Mrs Maureen Malt, of Horden - a daughter of the eldest son – made and decorated the cake for the party.

"Bit of a Struggle"

Mr and Mrs Chapman, who both enjoy good health, were married at Easington. All their married life has been spent in Wheatley Hill.

Mrs Chapman was only two months off her 19th birthday when she was married. Her husband worked at the local colliery. "And in the early days of our married life I had to manage on 25s a week," she recalled. "It was a bit of a struggle until my family grew up, but none of us ever took any harm."

At one time, she said, she had "four workers" coming in from the pit – her husband and three sons. "Many a time," she smiled, "there have been two bath tubs on the hearth for them when they returned from the pit."

Mr Chapman, who will be 72 in September, was born at Wheatley Hill and has lived there all his life. He started work at the colliery when he left school and remained there throughout his working career of more than 51 years until his retirement at 65. He has done most jobs down the pit.

A keen gardener, Mr Chapman has his own big allotment. Many of his leisure hours are spent there, and helping him to cultivate it is his second eldest son Harry, who is unmarried and lives with the couple.

Mr Chapman is a member of both the Soldiers' and Sailors' Club at Wheatley Hill and the Workmen's Club at Thornley. ,His wife was born at Thornley, but has lived in Wheatley Hill since she was a girl of nine.

SUDDEN DEATH OF WHEATLEY HILL SUB-POSTMASTER

Following a service in St. Mary Magdalene Church, Prudhoe, on Monday, the funeral took place at Prudhoe cemetery, of a well-known business man at Wingate Lane, Wheatley Hill, Mr Henry Ruddick Shield, who died suddenly in Sedgefield General Hospital at the age of 61. He had been in hospital only three days.

Mr Shield, who was held in the highest esteem in the area, moved to Wheatley Hill from Prudhoe 17 years ago on taking over a general dealer's business. Two years ago a sub Posit Office was opened at Wingate Lane attached to his business and he became the first sub-postmaster there.

Before going to Wheatley Hill Mr Sheild was employed by Blaydon Co-operative Society from leaving school at the age of 14. He was an apprentice in the drapery department at Barmoor, Ryton, and later was foreman at the central premises at Blaydon before his promotion to drapery manager of the Chopwell branch. He was manager for about seven years before he left to go to Wheatley Hill.

Mr Shield is survived by his widow and an only married daughter, Mrs Eileen Archer, of Thornley.

The funeral service was conducted by the Vicar of Prudhoe (the Rev F Lomax).

CIGARETTE HAUL AT WHEATLEY HILL

Breaking into Wheatley Hill branch of Co-operative Society at the weekend after scaling a high wall at the rear, thieves made off with a haul of 83,000 cigarettes worth £1,000.

The Regional Crime Squad have been called in to help the detective force in Castle Eden Police Division with their enquiries, a senior police detective told our reporter on Tuesday. A vehicle was used to take away the stolen property, the spokesman added.

The intruders forced a rear door which gave access to the warehouse, and then forced an inner door leading to the grocery department, where the cigarettes were stored.

Castle Eden detectives are also investigating two weekend thefts from parked cars in Peterlee.

A roof rack was stolen from a Ford Classic saloon parked in Skerne Close, and a new spare wheel, bright yellow in colour, from a Morris 1,000 parked in Dunn Road. The wheel measured 520x14. Anyone with any information about these thefts is asked to contact the nearest police officer.

12 August 1966

THORNLEY TALE OF PROGRESS BY LEGION WOMEN

Thornley Women's Section of the British Legion celebrated their 41st birthday with a party in the Welfare Hall. Mrs E Clark (chairman) welcomed 90 members and the guest of honour, the County Chairman, Mrs L Parks (Blackhall). She expressed sympathy with Mrs R Brewster (President) who was unable to attend owing to illness.

Looking back Mrs Clark said, "Our branch was formed in August, 1925. We owe a lot to our founders: Mrs M Bovill, the first chairman, Mrs A Wallis (secretary), and Mrs E Fort (treasurer), Mrs O Burlison was our first standard bearer. We started in the old reading room in the Front Street with a membership of 12 and paid a penny a week.

Dwindled

We have had our ups and downs. The membership rose from 12 to 20 and at one point dwindled to six. With hard work, a recovery was staged, rallying our present membership to 105. We always worked well with the Men's Section and provided them with their first standard."

Mrs Clark said that the section had always been active.

Twice headquarters have been moved. First to the Thornley Workmen's Club and then to their present meeting place, the local Welfare Hall.

Mrs Clark continued: "In the Second World War we held our meetings in the afternoon. We manned a mobile canteen for the troops stationed in the area at gun emplacements and searchlight sites. We also formed knitting parties which provided woollens for the Forces." Mrs Clark herself has been associated with the branch since shortly after its formation. She has been chairman for 25 years and vice chairman for eight years. She has served as chairman of the Benevolent Fund for many years and is County representative.

Others who have given excellent service over the years are Mrs R Brewster (president for 12 years), Mrs G Bromilow (secretary), Mrs H Langlands (treasurer): Standard Bearer, Mrs E Gordon and Mrs B Crane (Assistant standard bearer). As Poppy Day Organiser, Mrs G Bromilow achieved a record success last year with a collection of £105.

Supper was served by the Committee and the birthday cake was cut by Mrs Clark. The toast was proposed by Mrs L Parks who complimented the branch on their fine work and increased membership.

"This," she said, will encourage you to reach your former high level of membership." Highlight of the party was a fancy dress parade. Winners were: 1, Mrs I Osbaldestin (Batman); 2, Mrs G M Bromilow (Hunchback); 3, Mrs M Harrison (Gypsy).

Entrants were judged by Mrs L Parks. Other competition winners were Mesdames M Barker, D Laverick, E Gordon, P Dunning, J Brookes and M Clough.

Games and singing were organised by Mrs S Redshaw and Mrs M Harrison. Dancing was enjoyed to the music of Mr R Smalley and his band. "Spot" prizes were awarded to Mesdames C Cooper, J Hillmam, J Burnham and S Crane.

Sick members had teas sent out to them. Mrs G M Bromilow was organising secretary.

2 September 1966

FIRST AWAY WIN FOR WHEATLEY HILL WC

Wheatley Hill WC gained their first away points in the CIU League by beating Seaham York House 3-1.

With the wind behind them, "Hill" exploited the elements and in the 10th minute went ahead through Colin Smith (inside left), who headed in from a centre from Wilf Halliwell.

The home side were mainly on the defensive and it was more or less expected when Jack Lowther (outside left),from a pass from "Noddy" Hammond, increased the lead. Then Jack Lowther hit the upright.

Seaham tried hard to level matters before the interval, but were kept at bay. Hill, facing the wind in the second half, were hard pressed for long spells and did well to contain the fast-moving Seaham forwards. The home team managed to score 15 minutes before the end.

It was a ding-dong struggle for supremacy in the latter phases, and Dave Robson (centre forward), settled the issue from a cross from Hammond.

Ralph Winter (centre half), was Hill's powerman in defence. Jobes made some fine saves, and Colin Smith impressed in his new position, (inside left). Sid Craggs and Jimmy Cowan (full backs) worked well together.

Wheatley Hill WC, for their league game at Easington Central, are to rely on the same team: Jobes; Craggs; Cowan; Cook; Winter; Gibson; Hammond; Halliwell; Robson; Smith; Lowther. Kick off at 10.30 am. Bus leaves club at 9.30am.

16 September 1966

LEEK AND PRODUCE SHOW – THORNLEY WORKMEN'S CLUB

Thornley Workmen's Club – Judge, Mr Mather. Leeks: J R Greener (98.5); 2, R Youll; 3, A Miller; 4, W Smith; 5, W Hammond; 6, R Kell. Intermediate leek: 1 and 2, J R Greener; 3, J Bellwood. Onions:1, J Bellwood; 2 and 3, J Greener. Long carrots: 1 and 2, J Bellwood; 3, G Still. Short carrots: 1, A Miller; 2 and 3, S Hargreaves, Parsnips: 1, D Maitland; 2, G Still; 3, J Bellwood. Cauliflower: 1, 2 and 3, J Bellwood. Celery (white): 1 and 3, R Youll; 2, J Bellwood. Celery (pink): 1 and 2, R Youll; 3, J Bellwood. Potatoes: 1, R Youll, 2, S Hargreaves; 3, J Bellwood; Beet: 1, 2 and 3, J Bellwood. Beet (long): 1, S Hargreaves; 2, R Errington;3, J Bellwood. Tomatoes: 1, D Betts; 2 and 3, J Bellwood. Shallots: 1 and 2, J Bellwood; 3, J Greener.

Vase of flowers: 1, J Bellwood; 2, J Greener. Dahlias (cactus): 1 and 2, J Bellwood; 3, A Miller. (Decorative): 1, A Worthington; 2, D Betts; 3, A Miller. (Poms): 1 and 2, A Miller; 3, J Bellwood. Display: T Robson, R Errington.

DEATH OF WHEATLEY HILL MILITARY MEDALLIST

All Saints' Church, Wheatley Hill, was filled to capacity for the funeral of one of the village's best known and respected residents. He was Mr Cuthbert Raffell, of Ryan Terrace, Wheatley Hill. The service was conducted by Rev G G Graham and creamation followed at Durham.

Mr Raffell's wife died 13 years ago and he is survived by two sons and a daughter.

Born at Spennymoor, he went to Wheatley Hill when he was 17. He started work at Tudhoe Colliery but spent most of his working life at Wheatley Hill. Passing through various grades of mining he was promoted to deputy. Retiring at 65, he had given the coal industry 52 years' service.

He fought in the First World War with the 5th Durham Light Infantry Regiment in France and for bravery "in the battle of the Somme" he was awarded the Military Medal.

Mr Raffell was a keen sportsman. He was interested in bowls and was a member of the Wheatley Hill Welfare team for many years. He was a keen supporter of Sunderland Football Club. He played his part in the life of the village and was a regular worshipper at All Saints. He was a member of the Wheatley Hill Workmen's Club.

Always interested in the welfare of the aged, he took a prominent part in the founding of the village Over-60 Club. He served as chairman for some years and was a regular visitor to the club until his last illness. The club was represented at the service by officials and members.

WHEATLEY HILL MINER KILLED

A 24-year-old miner at Wheatley Hill Colliery, Thomas Mercer, of 6 Shop Street, Wheatley Hill, was fatally injured in a shot firing accident on Wednesday morning. Mr Mercer, who was employed as a power-loader, was working in the Main Coal Seam when the accident occurred mid-way through his shift. He was extensively injured and was dead on arrival at the surface.

Mr Mercer, who was the twin son of Mr and Mrs T Mercer, of Stanhope Street, Wheatley Hill, leaves a widow and two young daughters.

23 September 1966

WHEATLEY HILL CHALLENGING IN CIU LEAGUE

Wheatley Hill WC, having gained ten points from a possible 12, are now second in the CIU League table.

Their latest two points were gained at the expense of Seaham Knack, whom they beat 2-1. This was the first time that they have beaten this side.

"Hill" took the lead in the ninth minute when John Tempest (centre forward) receiving from a free kick by Jimmy Cowan, headed in from five yards.

Both teams produced a good standard of play and attacked in turn, only to find that the defences were equal to all demands. Towards half-time Knack equalised.

It was a tough struggle for supremacy in the second half, but neither side managed to gain a great degree of command. Fortunes fluctuated, and a draw seemed certain, but Tempest gained the decisive goal four minutes from the end. A shot from

Wilf Halliwell (inside right) rebounded from the 'keeper and Tempest showed fine opportunism by running in to tap it home.

On the whole, however, Hill deserved the points, but Seaham emerged with a fair share of credit for contributing much to making it a very good game.

Ralph Winter (centre half) was again the strong man in "Hill" defence. His brother, "Bob," having his first game, impressed at left half. Jimmy Cowan and Sid Craggs were sound full backs. Dave Hammond and Colin Smith were the most forceful in a smart forward line.

Wheatley Hill WC, for their league game at Murton British Legion tomorrow, have chosen: Jobes; Cowan; Craggs; Winter; R Winter; Lowther; Gibson; Hammond; Halliwell; Robson; Smith. Kick-off at 10.30am. Bus leaves Club at 9.30am.

FINE LEEKS AT DURHAM SHOW

A Judge at the News of the World (Durham Area), leek, vegetable and flower show in Durham Town Hall yesterday said that the three pot leeks, measuring 201.65cc, which won for Mr E Raydon, of Oxhill, the County Silver Challenge Trophy were the best leeks he had handled this year.

Over 300 stands of leeks were entered and the general quality was higher than it has been for some years.

Top six awards for pot leeks were: 1, E Raydon; 2, W Crummie (Tow Law); 3, A and N Hutchinson (Thornley); 4, F Marley (Shotley Bridge); 5, G Marwood (Seaham); 6, J R Greener (Ludworth).

In the class for blanch leeks the two winning exhibits measured 153.8 cc awards in this class were: 1, A and N Hutchinson; 2, B Howe (Darlington); 3, J Defty (Trimdon).

The show, which offers over £200 in cash prizes, will be officially opened this afternoon at three o' clock and will be open to the public throughout tomorrow (10am to 9 pm), and Sunday (11am to 8pm).

30 September 1966

WHEATLEY HILL WC MAINTAIN THEIR CHALLENGE

Wheatley Hill WC made headway in the CIU League at the expense of Easington Colliery WC, winning 4-1 at Wheatley Hill. They are now second in the league table and are only one point behind the current leaders, Houghton Social Club.

In the fifth minute Dave Robson (centre-forward) put through by Jack Lowther (outside-left) scored from close in, and ten minutes later he made a fine solo effort to increase the lead.

The home team were limited to spasmodic raids, but were kept in check by a sound defence in which the full-backs, Sid Craggs and Jimmy Cowan, were most prominent. The few shots that hit the target were smartly dealt with by Sid Jobes.

"Hill" were on the retreat in the opening stages of the second half with the result that centre-half Ralph Winter was given plenty of scope to show his paces and he managed quite nicely.

Then "Hill" improved and in the 70th minute Robson completed his hat-trick. The home team were now held in a defensive role, but in a breakaway they gained a consolation goal.

Three minutes from the end Robson, from a pass from Halliwell, added another goal to gain the distinction of the highest individual score this term so far. He is now leading scorer with 17 goals to his credit.

Robson was well supported by inside-right Bobby Winter, and the forward line as a whole made good use of the generous support from the half-backs, Cook, Winter and Billy Gibson.

Tomorrow, Wheatley Hill WC visit Seaham West Lea Club in a league game, for which there is no change in the team: Jobes; Craggs; Cowan; Cook; Winter; Gibson; Halliwell; Bob Winter; Robson; Smith; Lowther. Bus leaves Club at 9.30am. Kick-off at 10.30am.

28 October 1966

WHEATLEY HILL MINER DIES IN 1,000 TO ONE CHANCE - INQUEST TOLD

A young miner at Wheatley Hill colliery was killed, it seemed, by more than a 1,000 to one chance, commented the Coroner, Mr LG Appleby, in his summing-up at the inquest at Peterlee on Monday night. "It was very unfortunate," he added.

The inquest was on Thomas Mercer (24), a married man with two children, of 6, Shop Street, Wheatley Hill, who was fatally injured in a shot-firing incident on Wednesday, 21 September.

"Scuttling" out of the way from where he was working when it was noticed that the roof was unsafe and beginning to move, said the Coroner, Mercer had headed straight into the danger zone where a shot was being fired. The Coroner added: "He ran slap into the danger area at the precise moment the shot was fired, and took the full blast. It was the explosion which caused his death."

Dr. Bernard H Knight, pathologist, said that death was caused by a haemorrhage due to blast injuries to the chest.

Verdict

After a brief retirement the jury returned a verdict of "Accidental death."

A deputy, Mr Benjamin B Aitken, of 42 Johnson Estate, Wheatley Hill, said he went down the pit at 3am to start his shift and directed Mercer and another man to work on the face and clear the coal left at the tail gate end. He then went to the face as far the flighter – the machine which threw coal on to the belt – and after a few minutes heard a call for timber up the face. He went back to the main gate to supervise the passing of timber and then Robert Clarkson said he was going to fire a shot in the main gate stall.

"I went to a safe place in the main gate, taking two men with me," added witness, "and acted as a sentry to stop anyone coming into the danger zone. I heard a shot fired and then Mr Clarkson came running towards me and said someone had been hurt."

Lying Injured

Witness said he then saw Mr Mercer lying injured and being attended to by workmates.

Harold Syson (21), a power-loader, of 8 Sunderland Street, said he was working on the flighter when he was told shot-firing was to take place. Men were coming up the face and they all stopped where he was, except Mercer, who "went rapidly over the machine and climbed over the belt."

Witness added: "I shouted to him that shots were being fired. He seemed to take no notice and disappeared down the face towards the shot-firing area."

Replying to Mr D C Kinnair, HM Inspector of Mines, witness said it was impossible to stop Mercer running down towards the main gate – another miner, Brian Miller, made a grab to try and stop him, but failed.

Brian Miller (23), another power-loader, of 1 Fourteenth Street, Wheatley Hill, said he and Stephen Raffell were sent up the face to act as sentries before the shot was fired and were three yards from the flighter. He added, "I heard someone say the tail and the face was on the move and then I saw the lights from workmen's helmets coming towards me. Then Mercer scuttled past me on the goaf side of the conveyor. Harry Syson and I shouted to him that shot firing was in progress, "but it was all over in seconds."

Roof Began To Move

Normally, said witness, replying to Mr Kinnair, he would not have expected a workman to go down the face on the goaf side.

Evidence that the roof began to move and "fall heavily into the face" where he and Mercer were working, was given by George M Johnson, of 8 Morris Crescent, Thornley. He added, "We all ran back towards the main gate end of the face – the sentries there would see our lights. We ran back, scrambling over the flighting machine. I did not see where Mercer was as I ran down, but I heard the shot fired and later helped to get Mercer on the stretcher."

Mercer, he added, would be fully aware that shots were being fired.

Coroner: "Why do you think he crossed the conveyor and dropped down the goaf side? – I haven't the slightest idea.

The shot-firer, Robert W Clarkson, of 35 Luke Terrace, Wheatley Hill, told the Coroner that about three minutes elapsed between placing the sentries and firing the shot. He added, "I heard nothing to indicate anything was wrong – everything was straightforward as far as I knew."

Unfortunate

It was perfectly obvious from the evidence what had happened, said the Coroner. He added, "The roof began to move at one end where the men were working and shortly afterwards a shot was fired at the other end. If the roof had not moved there would have been no necessity to get away from there and if the shot had not been fired there would have been no danger running there. The two things happened more or less at the same time – it was extremely unfortunate."

The sentries, the Coroner added, had carried out their duties correctly as far as he could see. There was nothing they could do once Mercer had gone over the belt on the goaf side and ran into the danger area. He must have panicked and, said the Coroner, in the circumstances there was no disgrace in being frightened .

Sympathy with the relatives of the deceased were expressed by the Coroner, HM Inspector of Mines, the colliery manager (Mr Frank Richardson) and the secretary, Mr J P Cain.

4 November 1966

REMEMBRANCE DAY

All denominations in Wheatley Hill supported the service in All Saints' Church, Wheatley Hill. The parade, organised by the British Legion, was headed by the Colliery Band. Legion Women's Section, Fire Service, Police and uniformed youth organisations were represented. Wingate Parish and Easington Rural Councils were represented at the service for there was a packed church.

Devotions and lessons were read by the Vicar (the Rev G G Graham). The address was given by the Rev M Henderson, Methodist minister.

After the service the procession marched to the Cenotaph in the Welfare Park. A halt was made in the Front Street, where a clock hung on the wall of the Boys' Modern School is the memorial to the dead of the second world war. Prayers were said. At the cenotaph, the Last Post and Reveille were sounded. Wreaths were laid by local clubs, churches and the public services.

There was a big turn out at Thornley where the Colliery band under Mr E Kitto, headed the parade. British Legion's standard was borne by Mrs S Crane. Among the many organisations in the parade was the Sunbeams Jazz Band.

St Bartholomew's Church was filled for the service which was shared by the Rev G Johnson (superintendent minister of Thornley Methodist Circuit), Mrs Dowson (Salvation Army) and the Vicar of Thornley (the Rev P G Mold), who gave the address.

The procession re-formed and marched to the War Memorial in the Market Place, were wreaths were laid by the following organisations: Thornley Women's Section of the British Legion, Thornley Colliery Federation Board, Parish Council, Labour Party, Mothers' Club, Over-60 Club, Workmen's Club, Officials Club, Thornley St Stephen's Methodist Boys Brigade, Girls' Guildry and Jazz Band.

18 November 1966

A BLACK WEEK FOR WHEATLEY HILL FOLK

Six hours after being severely injured when struck by a car on the A19 Stockton to Sunderland road late on Saturday night, a 21-year-old schoolteacher, Mr David Peaceful, of 2 Percy Street, Wheatley Hill, died in Sunderland Royal Infirmary on Sunday morning.

The accident happened about half a mile north of Old Shotton as Mr Peaceful was walking towards the bus stop at Shotton Colliery road ends to catch a bus home. The only son of Mr and Mrs Fred Peaceful, Mr Peaceful taught at a school in Sunderland. He was unmarried.

The car involved in the accident was driven by Mr John George Middleton (21), of 25a Sandringham Road, West Hartlepool.

Another Wheatley Hill man, Mr Thomas Archibald Dixon (32), son of Mr and Mrs Dixon, of 9 Sunderland Street, who received extensive injuries the previous Saturday night when he was struck by a bus on the road between Wheatley Hill and Thornley railway crossing, also died in hospital on Saturday. He had lain critically ill in Durham County Hospital since the accident.

Mr Dixon was cremated at Durham yesterday, Thursday, following a service in All Saints' Church, Wheatley Hill.

Pit Fatality

Last Thursday, six days after being severely injured in an underground accident at Wheatley Hill colliery, a 43-year-old miner, Mr Eric Snowdon, of Briarholme, Cemetery Road, Wheatley Hill, died in Durham County Hospital. Married, with a son and daughter, he and his wife had a general dealer's business in Cemetery Road. He was cremated at Durham on Tuesday, following a service in All Saints' Church, conducted by the vicar, the Rev G G Graham.

Another 43-year-old Wheatley Hill miner, Mr Joseph David Lowther, of 77 Johnson Estate, was killed by a fall of stone at Thornley colliery at the beginning of last week, and last Wednesday one of the village's post women, Mrs Elizabeth Fulcher (49), of 8 Alexandra Terrace, collapsed and died while delivering letters in a confectioner's shop in the street where she lived.

To crown this fateful week for the pit village, local people were shocked at the tragic death of the two young sons of a former Wheatley Hill miner, Mr William Bennett.

Found In Canal

The children, Colin (4) and Barry (3), disappeared from their home at Hamstead, West Bromwich, last Friday and the following day were found dead in a canal near their Staffordshire home. The discovery ended a search by almost 400 people, including off-duty firemen, neighbours, police with dogs and frogmen.

Their 25-year-old father transferred from Wheatley Hill colliery three years ago to Baggeridge Colliery, Staffordshire. He and his wife Audrey have one other child, Derek, aged two. His widowed mother, Mrs Gladys Bennett, who lives in Stephen's Terrace, Wheatley Hill, is a school crossing patrol warden in the village.

WHEATLEY HILLMAN BROKE HIS NECK

A verdict of accidental death was recorded at the inquest on a 43-year-old fitter at Wheatley Hill Colliery, who died a week after being injured in an accident at the coal face.

The Coroner, Mr L J Heron, was told how a 15ft pipe weighing 21cwt had fallen on the man, Mr Eric Walker Snowdon, of Briarholme, Cemetery Road, Wheatley Hill. He died in Durham County Hospital with a broken neck. Mr Mark Jasper, a fitter at the colliery, said he was helping Mr Snowdon erect a tube across the main trunk conveyor belt line. The accident happened as they were carrying the pipe with chocks and bars. "We began to remove the chocks. I saw the tube move slightly. I heard a shout and I jumped clear." The tube had dropped about a foot and been stopped from falling further by a wall.

Mr Heron said there was no real evidence to say that the pipe actually struck Mr Snowdon. There was only circumstantial evidence from the men working with him who did not actually see the pipe hit him

2 December 1966

WHEATLEY HILL BOXERS' FRIEND MARKS "GOLDEN"

A 75-year-old retired miner, Mr William Curry, of 5 Liddell Terrace, Wheatley Hill, who played a big part in the training of young boxers, including four of his sons, in his younger days, celebrated his golden wedding on Friday. He and his wife Florence, who is 71, have spent all their married life in the village. They were married at Easington on 2 December 1916.

"I have always been interested in boxing," Mr Curry told our reporter, "and I did everything I could to encourage young lads to take up the sport."

Four of his five sons – Charlie, Johnnie, Billy and Ernest emulated his enthusiasm for the sport and they all went on to win quite a number of contests in the North-East. The trophies they won, including shields, cups and statuettes, fill the entire length of the sitting-room windowsill at their parents' home, as well as the sideboard.

NCB Champion

With the exception of Ernest, the brothers all became professionals and put their family name well and truly on the local boxing map. Keeping his amateur status, Ernest, now the only brother not married, won the National Coal Board Divisional Novices' Championship as a lightweight in 1951. Mr Curry used to run two gymnasiums in Wheatley Hill. "They attracted a lot of youngsters and they were all tremendously keen," he said. The members paid a weekly subscription and this covered the use of the gymnasium and the cost of the boxing "gear."

"Unfortunately", Mr Curry recalled; "one of the gymnasiums was burned down when an incendiary bomb fell on it during the Battle of Britain."

Mr Curry was also formerly interested in whippet and greyhound racing and for eleven years was a handicapper at Wheatley Hill. He has been a keen gardener all his life, leek-growing being his speciality, and continues as a successful exhibitor at the local shows.

"Flatting"

Born at Byers Green, Mr Curry began work at the colliery there when he was 13. "Flatting" was his job. "I used to couple on the tubs down the pit ," he said, "and worked five 10-hour shifts and a six-hour shift every week."

For his first fortnight's work of 112 hours – 56 hours each week - he was paid eleven shillings after offtakes. "And I got a bob back for my pocket money," Mr Curry smiled.

When he was 18 he moved to Wheatley Hill and started work at the neighbouring colliery at Thornley, where he remained, doing virtually every kind of job down the pit, until his retirement at 65. He was on stone-work when he retired.

Mrs Curry, whose maiden name was Bainbridge, was born at West Cornforth 71 years ago. Both she and her husband are in good health. She said: "We do not go far these days – we are very happy and content by our own fireside."

The couple have a family of five sons and one daughter and 17 grandchildren. They have taken the Durham Cronicle practically all their married life. We extend to them best wishes for many years of happiness and good health together

9 December 1966

WHEATLEY HILL MINER DIED
IN ONE OF THE PERILS OF COAL MINING

Referring to the accident as "one of the perils of coal mining," the Coroner, Mr L G Appleby, at an inquest at Peterlee on Friday on a 43-year-old miner killed by a roof fall at Thornley colliery on 21 November, said it was clearly an accident which could not have been foreseen. No blame, he added, was attached to anyone.

The inquest was on Joseph David Lowther, a married man with two children, of 77 Johnson Estate, Wheatley Hill, who was described by his deputy overman as a "very good, conscientious workman."

Returning a verdict of "Accidental death", the jury recommended that wooden pads should always be used to give added strength to hydraulic props when supporting the pit roof. The recommendation, they were told by the Coroner, would be forwarded to the appropriate authority.

A stoneman, Raymond Atherton, of 7 South View, Sherburn Hill, said he went down the pit with the deceased at 3am. Conditions appeared to be quite normal when they started cleaning the coal from the face side of the conveyor.

Roof Collapsed

They then made preparations to move forward one of the two 15-ft girders. They had moved three of the four hydraulic props and Lowther was "easing" the last one when suddenly the girder "flew" – it was knocked aside, witness explained, and the roof collapsed, burying Lowther.

There had been "no warning whatever" of roof movement, said Mr Atherton. He was quite satisfied, he added, in reply to a question from the colliery manager, Mr W Hutton, that the roof was timbered in accordance with the regulations.

The deputy overman, Mr Walter Dixon, of 4 Shinwell Crescent, Thornley said he went down the pit at 11pm. and made a pre-shift inspection of the face. He was quite satisfied that conditions were safe for working. About 3 40am. he sent Lowther and Atherton to their working places.

When he was told about the fall he immediately organised rescue operations but it was about two hours before Lowther was released. Witness added, "We worked our way into the coal side to release him, but the stone was heavy and hanging down and we had to work our way very carefully."

Pads Not Used

Replying to the local inspector of mines, Mr Dixon said that sometimes wooden pads were used below the hydraulic props to prevent them sinking into wet ground. On this occasion, however, pads were not used.

Addressing the jury, the Coroner said that obviously there had been no indication of roof movement at all when the props were released. Without any warning the roof had collapsed.

He added, "You may feel, however, that a suggestion could be made that when these hydraulic props are used on a damp or wet surface they should have wooden pads underneath to minimise as much as possible the sinking of the prop into the ground."

Mr and Mrs Joe Lowther

Sympathy with the dead man's widow and family was expressed by the Coroner, the colliery manager and Mr P Blunt, H M Inspector of Mines.

16 December 1966

FLEW FROM CANADA TO WHEATLEY HILL FOR FUNERAL

When she received news of the death of her 85-year-old mother at Wheatley Hill, a former Wheatley Hill woman who emigrated to Canada 16 years ago, Mrs Elizabeth Davison, quickly booked a flight to England and reached Wheatley Hill two days before the funeral last Thursday.

Mrs Davison and her husband Robert, who formerly lived at Shotton Colliery, live in Toronto. Mrs Davison was last here on holiday two years ago.

Her mother, Mrs Martha Prince, of 58 Peterlee Cottages, Wheatley Hill, died in St Margaret's Hospital, Durham. She had been in hospital about a year.

Mrs Prince, who was well known and esteemed in the area, had spent most of her life in Wheatley Hill. Her husband died in 1927 and she is survived by three sons and two daughters. Her younger daughter, Mrs Hilda Davidson, lives in Aberdeenshire, and her sons all live in the area.

The funeral service, which preceded interment at Wheatley Hill Cemetery, was conducted in Wheatley Hill Methodist Church by the Rev Maurice Henderson.

LABOUR PARTY NOMINATIONS

Wheatley Hill Labour Party have nominated Messrs A D Wharrier, R Hughes and J Harper snr, as their candidates to contest the forthcoming Easington Rural Council elections in the Wheatley Hill ward. Messrs Wharrier and Hughes are at present serving on the Council. Nominations for Wheatley Hill ward of Wingate Parish Council for the triennial elections are Mr Mark Alderton, Mrs Dodds and Mr E Goyns (present members), Mrs Golightly, Mr George Harper and Mr W Newby.

SAILOR MARRIES

The wedding took place of Mr William Burrell, youngest son of Mr and Mrs William Burrell, Jack Lawson Terrace, Wheatley Hill, and Miss Myra Hunter, only daughter of Mr and Mrs Alfred Hunter, 81 Luke Terrace, Wheatley Hill. The ceremony took place in All Saints' Church, Wheatley Hill, Rev G G Graham officiating. The bridegroom is serving with the Royal Navy. Given in marriage by her father, the bride wore a full-length gown of white flocked nylon with train and bouffant veil and coronet of pearls and diamante. She carried a bouquet of pink chrysanthemums. Bridesmaids were the Misses Anne Taylorson and the bridegroom's sister, Eva Burrell. The former wore a dress of blue flocked nylon and the latter a dress of apricot flocked nylon. Both wore head-dresses to match and carried bouquets of white chrysanthemums. Attendants in dresses of white nylon

Wedding of
Mr William Burrell & Miss Myra Hunter

were Lesley Hunter (bride's niece), Anne Burrell (bridegroom's sister) and Lesley Featonby, Mr Brian Kears was best man and groomsman Mr Donald Poole.
23 December 1966

SNOW CANCELLED THEIR HONEYMOON, BUT FIFTY HAPPY YEARS FOLLOWED

Mr William Williams married Miss May Stones in Thornley St Bartholomew's Anglican Church on 23 December, 1916, the Rev William Hodgson officiating. On Friday they celebrated 50 years of married life together. The day was spent quietly at their home, 6 Handel Terrace, Wheatley Hill. The couple have two daughters, Mrs Doreen Mitchell (Wheatley Hill) and Mrs May Winter (Cheltenham).

Mr Williams who is 75 was born at South Hetton. He moved to Thornley as a child and started at bank at Wheatley Hill colliery at 14. He remained there till he was 18 and then went down the pit at Wheatley Hill. In1931 an accident ended his mining career. For some years he was employed as an agent-collector and retired at 65.

Mr Williams has always been interested in sports of all kinds. Cricket and hand-ball were his favourite games. He met most of the prominent hand-ball players in the county.

Music has always been his greatest interest. With a fine tenor voice, he was always in demand as a singer. At Thornley Bow Street Methodist Church he was choir secretary for eight years.

Under Three Conductors

On going to Wheatley Hill, he joined the Patton Street Methodist Church choir. He also found time to sing with the Wheatley Hill Male Voice Choir and sang under three conductors: Mr William Howarth, Mr Jack Hamilton and Mr Norman Strong. He has also sung in the Hetton Lyons Male Voice Choir under Mr Tennyson Kay. Mr Williams has also sung the leading roles of various operas with the Wheatley Hill Operatic Society, when it was in its heyday.

He was one of the 25 founder members of Wheatley Hill Over-60 Club. He founded the Club's first concert party, with Mrs Smith as producer. He sang regularly with the party and with his wife, May, who is no mean performer, often brought the house down with the duet, My Old Dutch. It was a blow to Mr Williams when a thrombosis attack caused him to have to give up his singing activities.

Married In A Snow Storm

Mrs Williams is 73 and was born in Thornley. When she left school she went straight into domestic service. She commented: "Domestic service was different in those days. Wages were small and hours long. I received half-a-crown a week for a seven-day stint. My only time off, after the washing up at Sunday lunch time."

Recalling her wedding day, Mrs Williams said: "It was awful weather when Bill and I got married. It was snowing heavily and was bitterly cold.

The horse drawing our cab could hardly pull it through the thick snow and you couldn't see more than a yard or two ahead. The blizzard got so bad roads between Thornley and the station were soon blocked by huge drifts. So we had to cancel our honeymoon. The snow affected the colliery wagons so much that Bill could only work one shift the first fortnight of our married life."

As a young women Mrs Williams worshipped in Thornley Bow Street Methodist Church and was a member of the choir. At Wheatley Hill Patton Street Church she was active in the Women's Own and was its secretary for three years. She was also a member of Wheatley Hill Over- 60 Club and a member of its concert party.

The couple who are well known in Thornley and Wheatley Hill, were the recipients of many messages of greeting and goodwill.

30 December 1966

1967

WHEATLEY HILL SCOUTS' "GOOD TURN"

Once again the young patients in the children's ward at Durham County Hospital can expect "something new" in their ward for their entertainment and recreation as a result of the carol-singing efforts of the 2nd Wheatley Hill Group of Boy Scouts.

Every Christmas since they "adopted" the ward about twelve years ago, members of the Group old Scouts, Boy Scouts and Wolf Cubs have toured Wheatley Hill singing carols to raise money to provide "extras" for the children's ward. This Christmas they raised a record sum of £53.

In thanking all those in the village who supported the effort, the Group Secretary, Coun Ralph Watson, who is an official at Wheatley Hill colliery, says that early in the New Year the Scouts will be visiting the young patients. "And after discussing the matter with the Matron and Sister – we always like to have their suggestions – we will be spending the money on some suitable equipment", he adds.

6 January 1967

WHEATLEY HILL SCOUT'S NET QUEENS AWARDS JAMBOREE JOURNEYS

The announcement that two more members of the 2nd Wheatley Hill Troop of Boy Scouts, Edward Waistell and Benny Aitken, have qualified for their Queen's Scout Badge and Certificate brings the total number of Queen's Scouts in the group to six.

The others are Billy Waistell – a brother of Edward – Billy Smith, Billy Hedley and Tom Brownless.

Edward Waistell (18), the second son of Mr and Mrs W Waistell of 32 Quetlaw Road, Wheatley Hill, is employed as a motor mechanic at a sausage factory at Gilesgate, Durham. He has been actively associated with the Scouting movement for eight years. His brother Billy, who is a year older, was made a Queen's Scout two years ago and at present is acting assistant Cub master in the Group.

Benny Aitken, also 18, is the elder son of Mr and Mrs B Aitken, of 42 Johnson Estate, Wheatley Hill. He has been a Scout for six

Caps off and three rousing cheers for Eddie Waistell and Benny Aitken of the Wheatley Hill Boy Scouts who received Queen's Scout awards at a re-union party on Saturday. Mr A. Otterton, Assistant County Commissioner, made the presentations. Bill Smith also received the Silver Duke of...

years and before that spent four years in the Cubs. His father is secretary of Wheatley Hill Workmen's Club.

Benny is a student at St Aidan's Grammar School, Sunderland. His 14-year-old brother, Ian is also a member of the local Scouts.

Benny and another Queen's Scout, Billy Smith, who is 18, have also qualified for their Duke of Edinburgh Silver Award.

For World Jamboree

Another member of the Wheatley Hill Troop, 15-year-old David Hedley, second son of Mr and Mrs W S Hedley, of Front Street, Wheatley Hill, has been shosen, together with a Shotton Scout, Paul Pattison, to attend the World Scout Jamboree at Idhowa, USA, this summer.

David, whose father is a well-known butcher in the village, will be following in the footsteps of his older brother Billy, a Queen's Scout, who attended the Jamboree when it was held at Sutton Coldfield nine years ago. Billy was 16 at the time.

"It's a great thrill having been chosen to go – I am looking forward to it very much, especially as I have never been abroad before", David, a pupil at Shotton Colliery Secondary Modern School, told our reporter this week.

David is at present working hard for his Queen's Scout Award. He and Paul Pattison will represent the Castle Eden and Easington District of the Boy Scout movement at the Jamboree. Paul of 8 Fleming Field, Shotton, is a member of the Fleming Field Troop of Scouts.

13 January 1967

"DIAMOND" CELEBRATION AT WHEATLEY HILL

A well-known Wheatley Hill couple, Mr and Mrs Thomas William Trisnan, who are regular worshippers at the village's Roman Catholic Church, celebrated their diamond wedding quietly at their home last week.

The couple, who live at 4 Aged Miners' Homes, were married at Hutton Henry Roman Catholic Church on 10 January, 1907. They are life-long Roman Catholics. "We rarely miss going to church", Mrs Trisnan, who is 82, but looks years younger, told our reporter.

Like her husband, Mrs Trisnan enjoys fairly good health. She does practically all her own housework "but I give her a hand with the washing-up and don't mind doing other odd jobs about the house", said Mr Trisnan.

Mr Trisnan was born at Wellfield, near Wingate, 87 years ago. He was just turned 13 when he began work as a gardener for the Castle Eden Brewery of J Nimmo and Son, Ltd.

"But later", he recalled, "I worked in the Brewery itself". Eventually he left the Brewery and began work at Wheatley Hill colliery, where he remained until his retirement 20 years ago. Most of his career was spent in the colliery weigh office – he was an official for more than 30 years.

For a number of years Mr Trisnan worked alongside the well-known miners' leader and social reformer, Mr Peter Lee, who was employed at the colliery as a miners' checkweighman.

Mr Trisnan and his wife, Mary, have lived in Wheatley Hill since 1914. They moved there from Wellfield. Mrs Trisnan is a native of Hartlepool and later lived for a time at Hart Village.

The couple have a family of two sons and a daughter, nine grand-children and three great-grandchildren. Their eldest son, Thomas, was killed in the Easington pit disaster 16 years ago.

20 January 1967

GOLDEN YEARS FOR WHEATLEY HILL PAIR

Well-known figures in Wheatley Hill, where they have spent most of their married life, Mr and Mrs James Wylie, of 4 Peter Lee Cottages, have just celebrated their golden wedding.

They held a family party at their home for the occasion and visiting them was their only son James, who had travelled up from Catterick Camp with his wife and son. Their son is a hairdresser at the camp.

Mr and Mrs Wylie, who are both in fairly good health, were married at Kelloe Parish Church. The first two years of their married life were spent at Wheatley Hill and then they moved to Trimdon Grange, where they lived for about ten years before returning to Wheatley Hill.

In his younger days Mr Wylie, who will be 71 next month, was keenly interested in local football and cricket. He was one of the founders of the National Orphanage Cup soccer competition, serving on the first committee, and served on the committee of a number of local football clubs in the area. For many years also he was on the committee of Wheatley Hill Cricket Club.

Retired at 65

When he was 14, Mr Wylie began work as a trapper boy at Wheatley Hill Colliery for eighteen pence (12½p) an eight-hour shift. After seven years there he switched to Trimdon Grange Colliery and later worked at Thornley Colliery where he retired at 65 after a 51-year mining career.

Mr Wylie formerly served on the committee of Wheatley Hill Constitutional Club, where he is still a member. "I like to pop down and have a 'bit crack' with the men", he told our reporter.

Mrs Wylie, whose maiden name was Isabella Welch, is a member of Thornley Over-60 Club. She will be 70 in March and does all her own work in her spic and span, brightly decorated home. Shortly after celebrating her golden wedding she accompanied her niece on a week's holiday in London.

Mr and Mrs Wylie were the recipients of many beautiful greetings cards, bouquets and gifts on their golden wedding day and best wishes were extended to them for many more happy years together.

THORNLEY METHODISTS ARE PROUD OF THEIR
GOLD MEDAL AWARD WINNERS

Members of Thornley St Stephen's Methodist Church attending the annual Society meeting found the occasion combined business with pleasure.

The Rev Gordon Johnson (superintendent minister) presided. Musical items were given by the Thornley St Stephen's Youth Group. The Witnesses, soloists, Mr R Hedley, Mrs B Wilson and Mrs J Bullock; Male Voice Quartet, Messrs J Bulmer, R Hedley, P Wood and T Robinson.

Reports by the church organisations showed that progress was being made. The report on the society was given by the senior Society Steward, Mr J H Pattison. He said the membership was 148 and that the impact of the church on the life of the village did not wane.

Mr K Hetherington reported on the Boys' Brigade and the new church building project. The Brigade is a popular part of church life and two of its members, Colin Davies and Joe Bennett have received the Gold Award in the Duke of Edinburgh's scheme. They go to London to receive their awards in February.

Honour to the Community

Mr Hetherington commented; "These two young men have brought honour not only to our church and Brigade but to the village in these days when youth is being criticised for so much delinquency and lack of purpose, it is pleasing to note that there are young people, who by their own efforts and consistency reach a worthwhile goal".

Referring to the new church building project, Mr Hetherington said the scheme had received the blessing of the District and Connexional Chapel Committees.

With the help of grants, the scheme would be carried out and a new building would take the place of the present premises in Waterloo Street.

The proposed building will be in the centre of population. Thornley people to date have raised £1380. Mr A L Miller dealt with Trust affairs and the Church Fellowship. The annual autumn fayre had raised £140.

Mr P Wood (choirmaster) said that choir and Sunday School were doing well. The great need was workers. He appealed for more choristers and said the Sunday School could be more effectively carried out if there were more teachers.

The Cradle Roll, according to Coun Miss A Griffiths, is in a healthy state. Every child baptised is placed on that roll and on its birthday Miss Griffiths sends it a birthday card.

At Early Age

So a link between the home and church is forged at an early age. Mrs J Hedley reported on a successful year for the Sisterhood, with a sound financial position and a good attendance at the weekly meetings.

Society representatives to the Leaders' and Quarterly meetings were appointed: Mesdames J Bott, G Wigham, G Thornton, J Bullock and Wilson; Messrs R Hedley and T Lincoln.

Supper was served by Mesdames J Bott, J Thornton, O Lincoln, D Galloway, J Hedley and J Mather.
27 January 1967

YOUNG DANCER ON TV – Monday was a big day for seven-year-old dancer, Denise Newton, daughter of Mr and Mrs G R Newton, of Thornley. In Tyne-Tees Children's Hour she appeared in the programme Fanfare. Denise is a pupil at Thornley County Junior Mixed School. Success has not spoiled her. She has won seven trophies for dancing and 11 medals. For two years in succession she won the Northern Counties Championship and in some events has carried off the overall winners cup, competing with those up to 14. She took part in shows for the Aberfan Disaster Fund and often entertains old folk at the Over-60 Clubs of Thornley, Shotton, Easington, Horden and Peterlee.
3 February 1967

ACCIDENTAL DEATH VERDICT ON WHEATLEY HILL TEACHER
A young Wheatley Hill teacher, who took the precaution of facing oncoming traffic when walking along the A19 near Old Shotton late on 26 November last year, forgot about the danger of cars overtaking when coming from behind him, a jury heard at an adjourned inquest at Sunderland.

The inquest was on David Peaceful (21), of Percy Street, Wheatley Hill. "He was very wise to walk facing approaching traffic", commented the Coroner, Mr Cuthbert Morton, "but unfortunately the unexpected happened".

The jury heard than an estate car travelling in the same direction as Mr Peaceful was walking, swung out to overtake a slower car and struck Mr Peaceful who, the driver, Mr John G Middleton (21), of Sandringham Road, West Hartlepool, told the police, "was walking in the middle of the road".

"I did not see him", Mr Middleton told he police, "until I put on full beam to overtake the other car. He was wearing dark clothing. I braked but could not avoid him".

Mr Peaceful was thrown onto the grass verge. He never regained consciousness and died early next day in hospital from brain damage.

Mr Geoffrey Reed (42), of Stafford Grove, Ryhope, driver of the car which was overtaken, said Mr Middleton's vehicle was not speeding and "overtook in a normal manner".

He added, "Just as it passed I heard a thud and the sound of breaking glass. The other driver stopped on his right side of the road. He told me, thought he had hit something".

A verdict of "Accidental Death" was returned.

"It is tragic", commented the Coroner, "that a young man just starting out in his teaching career should die in this way".

THORNLEY BRITISH LEGION REVIVED

Six years ago, after a long and honourable existence, Thornley Men's section of the British Legion was compelled to disband, owing to lack of support. Founder members were dying or moved away from the village and these losses were not being replaced.

The spirit of the Legion was not dead, however, and it has always been the hope that the section might one day be re-formed with new and young blood to give it vigour. Their friends in the Thornley Women's section kept going and last year under the impetus of the new recruiting campaign, they not only increased their own strength but their chairman, Mrs E Clark, canvassed the men of the village. She found over 30 men who were willing to re-start the Thornley Men's section of the British Legion.

Dream became fact when the first meeting was held in Thornley St Stephen's Methodist church schoolroom. There was an attendance of 26 and a lot more promised support.

The meeting was visited by Mr Norman Dodds (County Chairman) who presided and Mr J Bell (County secretary).

A Blend

In his opening address, Mr Dodds said: "I am delighted at the support that the re-formation of Thornley Men's section has received and to see the blend of those who fought in the First and Second World Wars represented at this inaugural meeting.

"I am glad that all of you, whether belonging to the original section or not, are eager for Thornley to regain its honourable place in the No 10 Group. I know that the re-formation of the section owes a lot to the ladies and particularly, Mrs Clark, who canvassed the village for our cause. I shall be pleased to report to the County Committee, the splendid work she has done in an all out effort to win recruits".

Mr Dodds outlined the work of the Legion to show that it is worthy of support. Its funds are not wasted but are used for benevolence, pensions, allowances and rest homes for those broken in health and need a recuperative break. These are the benefits which are provided by the generosity of the British Legion.

The following officers were chosen: Chairman, Mr R Smith; secretary, Mr J Bosomworth; treasurer, Mr D Gott.

Executive committee: the officials together with Messrs J Ollett, R Bullock, W Brereton, J Harrison and S Davies. Mr Smith, the new chairman, appeals to men of Thornley to rally round the Legion Standard. He announced that the area secretary, Mr Ward, would be the speaker at the next meeting.

17 February 1967

DAY OF PRAYER SERVICE – The annual World Women's Day of Prayer service was well attended, Thornley St Bartholomew's Church being filled. The service was attended by members of Thornley, Wheatley Hill, Haswell and Cassop women's organisations, including Mothers' Unions, Methodist Sisterhoods, missionary organisations, Salvation Army Home Leagues and Catholic Women's Guild. The service took the form of an order of service compiled by the late Queen Zalote of Tonga. It was conducted by Mrs Mold and Mrs Johnson. Scripture readings were taken by Mrs R E Gratton and Mrs V Dowson. The address was given by Mrs Davison and Mrs Armstrong was organist.

LEGION WOMEN MEET - An attendance of 80 at the meeting of Thornley Women's Section of the British Legion is indicative of rising interest in the village. Mrs Clark presided and Mrs Bromilow undertook secretarial duties. Talk was given by Mrs Clark, who welcomed two new members. Nightwear was the subject of the competition. Mrs Bromilow and Mrs Saiger judged the pyjamas and Mrs Dunlavey was awarded the prize. They awarded first place for the nightdress to Mrs Luke. Mrs Woodward and Mrs Middleton judged the sandwich cakes and Mrs Langley was declared the winner. Mrs Coxon was MC for games and dancing. Tea hostesses were Mrs Osbaldestin and Mrs Nicholson.
24 February 1967

LEGION CONFERENCE - Mrs G M Bromilow and Mrs S Crane were elected by members of the Thornley Women's Section of the British Legion to represent them as delegates at the annual British Legion conference in London. When Mrs Bromilow read the correspondence one item from headquarters concerning the hire of the Albert Hall for the conference caused grave concern. Mrs E Clark, who presided, said that the cost of using the Albert Hall was becoming prohibitive. The cost for a day and a half conference was £750. Now they had been informed that the hire was going up to £1500 for the same period. The delegates were instructed to vote for a one-day conference. Silent tribute was paid to the memory of Mrs E Bosomworth, who had served the Thornley Women's Section as treasurer from many years. The social half-hour provided some enjoyable humour with members having to "Sing Say or Pay". Mrs M Dobson was in charge of entertainments and competitions. Prize-winners were Mesdames E Willey, L Newton and M Myers. Tea hostesses were Mesdames S Crane, I Ross and S Richardson.
3 March 1967

PRIVATE DAVID SMITH from Thornley, fires his rifle on skis during a winter warfare exercise by "C" Company, 1st Battalion The Somerset and Cornwall Light Infantry, in Norway. David is the son of Mr and Mrs A Smith, of 6 St Aidan's Crescent, Thornley. While he was in Norway, his brother, Pte Tucker Smith, was on a similar exercise in Canada

with "B" Company of the battalion. David went to Wheatley Hill Secondary Modern School and enlisted in 1964 in the Infantry Junior Leaders' Battalion at Oswestry
.10 March 1967

ACCIDENTAL DEATH VERDICT ON MINER
After hearing evidence given by miners from Thornley pit, a Durham inquest jury returned a verdict of Accidental death on Norman Greener (17), who died after an accident at the pit on 21 February.

Dr G S Graham, a pathologist at Dryburn Hospital, said that Mr Greener had died of crush injuries to his face.

Mr Greener, of Shinwell Crescent, Thornley, had been working with a Mr George Iddon clearing up spillage and keeping the tubs in running order underneath a conveyor belt in the County Busty Loader Shaft.

There had been some difficulty with one of the tubs and Mr Greener had gone to the back of the line of tubs. "After I released the tub I called out to Norman but he didn't answer. I called again and there was still no reply", said Mr Iddon.

It was at this point that he had gone to the rear and found Mr Greener lying between two empty tubs.

After seeking help, Greener was taken out on a stretcher and died at Durham County Hospital. A Safety Officer inspected the scene of the accident and found traces of blood on the top of the tub and the base of the conveyor belt with a four inch space in between.

Coroner Mr L J Heron said that trucks stuck and sometimes miners had to stoop over to couple or uncouple them. "There is, however, no evidence as to why or how, or in what circumstances he had stooped between the belt and the tub. As he was found between two tubs, which had not been moved, he must have fallen on to the buffers, after being caught.
17 March 1967

FROM WHEATLEY HILL AT 74,
SHE JOINS FAMILY DOWN UNDER
Four years after her second daughter had emigrated to Australia with her husband and family of five, a 74-year-old Wheatley Hill widow, Mrs Hannah Coldwell, of 21 Burns Street, flew there at the weekend to rejoin them.

And accompanying Mrs Coldwell, whose husband William died six years ago, were her youngest daughter, Mrs Doris Walker, her husband William and their 17-year-old son Gordon.

Mrs Coldwell told our reporter before setting out on her flight from London airport, "I am looking forward to seeing them all again. It will be a 'bit of a pull' leaving Wheatley Hill, where I have spent most of my life, but they speak well of their new life in Australia and I am sure I will be all right there".

It was the first time she had ever been on an air trip. "But I have no qualms whatever", Mrs Coldwell, who enjoys quite good health, said with a smile.

Brighter Opportunities

Mr Walker, formerly an overman at Wheatley Hill colliery, said he had decided to emigrate with his mother-in-law because he thought opportunities were much brighter in Australia. "My brother-in-law and his family have certainly never regretted going and in letters back home speak highly of the prospects out there", he said.

It is only about 14 months ago that Mr Walker, who is 43, left the pit at Wheatley Hill to start work at a textile factory in Darlington, where for most of the time he has been a foreman.

He said, "I don't know what I will be doing when we get to Australia ... one thing is certain, it won't be mining. But I am prepared to do anything else and am sure we can made a 'go' of it".

His son, too, who has been employed by Durham County Council, was full of enthusiasm for his new life as an emigrant.

Take the Plunge

Said Mr Walker, "You have to take the plunge sometime if you want to get on and we feel that now is the time".

It was four years past November that Mrs Coldwell's second daughter, Mrs Jennie Bartram, emigrated to Brisbane from Wheatley Hill with her husband and family of five.

Two years later, Mrs Bartram was back at Wheatley Hill with two of her children for a holiday at her mother's home. At first, she said then, she had found it difficult to settle in Australia. "But now that I have been back for a holiday I am ready to settle for good there", she said before returning 'down under'.

"They have a nice home and they are all doing fine", said Mrs Coldwell, who has lived in Wheatley Hill for the past 31 years. Before that she lived in the neighbouring village of Thornley from childhood.

Leaving a Friend

One regret Mr and Mrs Walker, who lived at 7 Bevan Crescent, Wheatley Hill, had about emigrating, they said, was leaving behind their three-and-a-half-year-old miniature Shetland sheepdog, Sheltie. "We have got a good home for her and we are sure she will be all right, but we will certainly miss her", said Mrs Walker.

They had been unable to get permission to take the dog with them. "But even if we could have taken her", said Mrs Walker, "I don't think she would have settled – she's a very fretty animal".

Mrs Coldwell spent her last few days in this country with her eldest daughter, Mrs Hilda Potts, a widow of St Bede's Crescent, Thornley – the only member of her family left in England. "But we hope we will all see her again some day", said Mrs Coldwell. Mrs Potts has three daughters and a son.

Mr Walker is the third eldest of the family of five sons and three daughters of Mr and Mrs George William Walker, of 7 Durham Street, Wheatley Hill.

24 March 1967

499

WHEATLEY HILL
FIRST-AID SUCCESSES
The following members of Wheatley Hill First-aid Class were successful in a recent examination: Messrs R Mallory, E Warnes, T Carr, B Aitken, P Hollis, E Robson, J Iveson, A Devine, T Ramage, L Taylorson, R Maughan, H Lonsdale, W Waistell, E Waistell, T H Ashford, H Wilson, E Edwards, J Tully, W Higham, M Conway, W Vincent, N Osbaldestin, W Smith, J Cook and R W Foster.

The class lecturer was Dr J Gray and Mr J Cook was local instructor. The examiner was Dr A Todd, of Thornley, and Mr R W Storey was class secretary.

31 March 1967

WHEATLEY HILL COUPLE FIFTY YEARS WED
The early days of his mining career when he received 13s *(£1.15)* a fortnight for twelve shifts down the pit, are recalled by Mr Richard Frampton, of 42 Peter Lee Cottages, Wheatley Hill, who recently celebrated his golden wedding. He and his wife Catherine, whose maiden name was McCoy, have spent the last 40 years of their married life in Wheatley Hill. They were married at Thornley Roman Catholic Church on 28 March, 1917.

For two years before leaving school at the age of 14, Mr Frampton, who was born at Hartlepool, was a butcher's errand boy at weekends. "I used to carry baskets of meat from Hartlepool to the ships every Friday and Saturday", he told our reporter, "and for this I was paid eighteenpence". *(this is 12½p in today's money)*

Thornley Miner
All the money was tipped up to his parents. "And I rarely got any back", he said. Even when he started work at Thornley Colliery he was only given threepence pocket-money out of his fortnightly pay. "Times have certainly changed", smiled Mr Frampton. All Mr Frampton's mining career of 51 years was spent at Thornley Colliery and he used to walk there every day from his home at Wheatley Hill. He retired when he was 65.

Mr Frampton will celebrate his 73rd birthday later this month. His wife, the last surviving member of a family of 15, is 71. The couple have only been in moderate health during the past few years. "We cannot get far these days", said Mrs Frampton.

They were both formerly members of the village's Over-60 Club. "I have gone there since its inception", said Mrs Frampton, "and I am only sorry I cannot get nowadays because of poor health".

The couple have two sons, both married. They are Thomas, who lives at Fishburn, and Joseph, who lives with them. They also have nine grandchildren and one great-grandson. Their only daughter, Mrs Dinah Poulson, died eighteen months ago.

Mr and Mrs Frampton celebrated their "golden" with a family party at their home, when they were the recipients of many good wishes for the future.

7 April 1967

WORK SOON ON A181 AT THORNLEY HALL

Work will start soon on a scheme to improve about 2/3 mile of A181 at Thornley Hall.

Mrs Barbara Castle, Minister of Transport, has made a grant of £29,850 towards the £39,800 estimated cost of the work.

The scheme will provide a 24ft wide carriageway on a straighter and flatter alignment than the existing road. It will start 60 yards east of the junction with B1279 and run eastwards for about 1200 yards. One 4.5 feet wide footpath will be constructed on the north side of the road and there will be verges varying in width between 10ft and 25ft.

The stretch of road involved will form part of an improved link between Teesside and Durham City.

The scheme will be carried out by Durham County Council's Direct Labour Organisation and is expected to take about 15 months to complete. It was designed by the Durham County Surveyor, Mr W H B Cotton, who will also supervise the work.
21 April 1967

WHEATLEY HILL FIREMEN'S SUCCESS

A team from the Wheatley Hill retained unit of the Durham County Fire Brigade have again excelled themselves in the biennial national technical "Quiz" organised among firemen from retained stations from all over the British Isles.

In the final, staged at the Fire Services' College at Dorking, Surrey, they finished as runners-up, only two points separating them

The Wheatley Hill Fire Brigade quiz team, who were runners-up in the National Quiz Competition. Left to right: Leading Fireman P. E. Whinn, Fireman M. Dunn, Fireman J. Starkie; Fireman R. Widdowfield and Leading Fireman L. Barker.—[D.A.]

from the winners, a team from Worksop, Notts.

This was the second time running Wheatley Hill have been runners-up. They won this distinction when the competition was last held in 1965 and on three earlier occasions – in 1956, 1961 and 1963 – they finished as champions.

Members of the Wheatley Hill team, who were awarded 29½ points, were Leading Firemen P E Whinn and L Barker and Firemen M Dunn, J Starkey and R Widdowfield. The three last-named firemen were making their first appearance in the final, but the two others were "old hands".

501

A team from Pembroke, Wales, were third with 19½ points, and Whitchurch (Shropshire) were fourth with 11½.

The Wheatley Hill team were accompanied by their Station Officer, Mr Frank Horner, and the trip South was also made by the Durham County Fire Officer, Mr J Smith.

WEAKENED THORNLEY CW PUT UP GOOD FIGHT

Thornley CW fielded a greatly weakened side for their Wearside League game against Roker FC at Dawdon on Saturday, and faced an uphill task. With centre forward Best, playing in goal and the trainer, Johnson, at outside right, the forward line had been reshuffled. Under the circumstances, Thornley performed well and were at one stage leading 2-1, so their 4-3 defeat by the Roker side, was no shame. Thornley's effort, particularly in the second half, and a flurry of goals in the last five minutes, were the only things that lifted an otherwise moderate display.

Roker were first to score after seven minutes, when outside left Taylor, after getting through alone, headed in out of the reach of Best, in the Thornley goal. The only other real scoring chance in the first half went to Roker, when inside right Hall crossed and Wilson got in a fine header which Best only just managed to push over the bar for a corner.

In the second half, Thornley looked much more dangerous, and soon proved it in the 53rd when they equalised through inside right Denham who pounded home a rebound after Jones, in the Roker goal, had pushed away a shot from centre forward Parks. After 60 minutes, Thornley took the lead when centre half Connell broke through on his own and from just outside the penalty box shot in.

Taylor scored a second goal for Roker after 78 minutes. In the 85th minute Roker pulled ahead when Taylor made the score 4-2, two minutes later, he completed his hat-trick and then a minute later Thornley pulled back a goal when Taylor crossed from the right corner flag for Wilson to shoot home.

FOUR CANDIDATES FOR NUM BALLOT

Mr Ronald Hughes, of Thornley Colliery, is one of the strongly favoured candidates for the post of Agent for the Durham Area of the National Union of Mineworkers, a post vacant with the retirement of Mr C Pick.

Other candidates are Messrs T Finnegan (Washington Glebe), W Malt (Horden) and T Callan (Seaham Vane Tempest).

Mr Hughes, aged 44, is a coalface worker, and Services secretary of Thornley Miners; Lodge, a position he has held since May, 1958. He is in his second term of office as a member of the Durham Area Executive Committee.

During the War he served over four years with the Royal Scots Fusiliers in France, Holland and Germany.

Mr Hughes obtained a NUM Scholarship to Ruskin College, Oxford, in 1954, and he graduated two years later with an Oxford University diploma in Economics and

Political Science. During vacation periods from the college he continued his work at the coal face of the local colliery.

Mr Hughes is a district councillor on Easington Rural Council, and has been nominated by the local Labour Party for a third term of office. The result of the ballot will be announced some time in May.

28 April 1967

MEALS ON WHEELS FOR THORNLEY SOON

Their efforts to launch Luncheon Clubs for elderly people at Thornley and Easington Colliery have made considerable progress, Mrs Hilda Kilgour of Easington Colliery, the area Centre Organiser for the Women's Royal Voluntary Service, told our reporter this week.

"In fact", she said, "we are hoping to open the club at Thornley very soon with meals provided twice a week – on Tuesdays and Thursdays".

The Miners' Welfare Committee there have granted the use of the Welfare Hall for the club to meet and, said Mrs Kilgour, it was planned to provide 25 meals each day.

She added, "There has been a very good response for helpers to run the club. Drivers are still a bit of a problem – we need voluntary drivers to bring the meals in from the colliery canteen – but we expect we will have sufficient when the club is opened".

At Easington Colliery, Mrs Kilgour revealed the Women's Voluntary Service have been successful in obtaining the use of a room in the Workmen's Club for a Luncheon Club.

"We are still busy with our arrangements here", Mrs Kilgour went on, "but we are hoping to establish a club in the near future. A meeting is being called of the various organisations in the village to see how many helpers we can enrol to help with the meals".

As at Thornley, they were hoping to obtain cooked meals from the local colliery canteen.

The WRVS already run a "Meals on Wheels" service at four places in the Easington Rural Area – Peterlee, Horden, Blackhall and Wheatley Hill – but the Luncheon Clubs at Thornley and Easington will be the first to be set up.

"From our enquiries there seems to be quite a demand for them", said Mrs Kilgour.

5 May 1967

COAL OUTPUT

While the total production from the 31 pits in the South Durham area last week of 298,352 tons was a decrease of 1443 tons, two of the largest pits had all time production records.

Dawdon, with a production of 41,150 tons, had a new record output, as had Horden with 35,699 tons.

Other individual returns were: Seaham 16,156, Vane Tempest 20,008, Blackhall 18,166, Easington 28,258, Elemore 5,442, Eppleton 16,268, Murton 17,311, South

Hetton 5,162, Shotton 8,861, Wheatley Hill 3,975, Bearpark 3,817, Brancepeth 3,134, Brandon Pit House 7,786, Esh 1,281, Kimblesworth 1,002, Langley Park 4,164, Stanley Cottage 856, Thornley 10,560, Tudhoe Park 1,355, Whitworth Park 2,117, Brusselton 2,891, Bowburn 2,635, East Hetton 10,230, Metal Bridge 1,726, Staindrop 535, Trimdon Grange 4,420, West Auckland 2,209.

FORMER MINER DIES AT LUDWORTH

The death occurred suddenly at his home, 78 Barnard Avenue, Ludworth of Mr Thomas Gradon (66). He worked as a miner at Wheatley Hill until his retirement. A keen pigeon fancier, he was for several years a member of Ludworth Homing Society, and as recetly as last week he took part in the Retford race. For a time he and his wife (nee Atherton) lived at Shadforth, afterwards at Wheatley Hill and Ludworth.

The funeral took place on Monday at Shadforth Cemetery, preceded by a service in St Cuthbert's Parish Church, the Rector (the Rev C E Woolstenholmes) officiating. *(A list of mourners is included in the original article)*
12 May 1967

FORMER WHEATLEY HILL RESIDENT RETURNS
AFTER 43 YEARS

Forty-three years after emigrating to Canada when she was only 21, a former Wheatley Hill girl has been back to her native village for a whirlwind three-week holiday ... with all expenses for the trip paid by her employer.

"It has taken me a long time to get back to the old country for a holiday but it has certainly wetted my appetite for more", Mrs Martha Hemsley, a 64-year-old widow, told our reporter before leaving for Prestwick at the weekend for her return flight to Ottowa.

Mrs Hemsley, who was widowed six years ago, added, "I have had a wonderful time and, believe me, I will be back again as soon as I can possibly make it".

She has been staying with her widowed sister, Mrs Ada Raffell, of 8 Shinwell Terrace, Wheatley Hill, and has also crammed in visits to her two other sisters, Mrs Alice Adam and Mrs Margaret Robinson, who both live in Whitby, and her brothers, 82-year-old Mr Jack Brown, who lives in Wheatley Hill and Mr James Brown of Middlesbrough.

And for the first time she has seen all her nieces and nephews, "And even great-nieces and nephews", smiled Mrs Hemsley.

When her plane touched down at Prestwick Airport on her arrival here her three sisters were all waiting to welcome her. "We recognised each other immediately, although it was all those years since I left England", said Mrs Hemsley.

A daughter of the late Mr and Mrs W Brown, Mrs Hemsley was born at Cassop, but a few years later the family moved to Wheatley Hill and she went into domestic service when she left school. "And I've been in service ever since, mainly as a cook", she said.

On Governor General's Staff

It was as a member of the domestic staff that she first went to Canada with Lord and Lady Willingdon on Lord Willingdon's appointment as Governor-General there.

"I was only 21", Mrs Hemsley said. "It was the spirit of adventure which took me there – at first I never thought I would be there so long before coming back to England, but when I was 24 I married an Englishman from Brighton who had been in Canada about the same time as me and after that I was quite settled there". During her three years at Government House in her early days in Canada, Mrs Hemsley came in contact with many members of royalty and the aristocracy from a number of countries.

"A lot of entertaining was done at Government House", she said, "and visitors of high rank staying there always shook hands with the domestic staff before they left".

Among those she remembers being introduced to were the Duke of Windsor – he was Prince Edward at the time – and the late Duke of Kent.

Mrs Hemsley's husband, Edward, who was a gardener, died after they had been married only five years. They had only one son, Nelson – he now holds a good post as an engineer with the Canadian Government and is unmarried.

Wheatley Hill "Scarcely Recognisable"

Mrs Hemsley continued in domestic service after her husband's death and spent 28 years in the job – as cook for the first lady of Canada. When she died Mrs Hemsley took up employment as cook-housekeeper to Mrs Hyacinth Willis O'Connor. "Though I have been with this lady only three years", said Mrs Hemsley, "it was she who made it possible for me to have this trip back home – she paid every dollar of the fare. It was extremely kind and generous of her".

By a coincidence, Mrs O'Connor's late husband was an aide-de-camp at Government House when Mrs Hemsley first worked there.

Mrs Hemsley said she could "scarcely recognise" Wheatley Hill when she came. "About the only place I could remember from my girlhood days was the Front Street and the Co-operative Store ", she said.

She had been greatly impressed by the high standard of living conditions in this country.

Holiday "Just Like a Dream"

She added, "It was much more prosperous than I had expected – all the children look well cared for – and I think your National Health Scheme is absolutely marvellous. It would be a great boon if the same sort of scheme could be extended throughout the world.

Medical treatment was expensive in Canada, she said, although there had been some improvement, with their "hospitalisation" scheme. Under this you pay about £1 a month and this "covered you for bed and accommodation if you had to go into hospital. "But", said Mrs Hemsley, "you still have to pay for medical attention, drugs and medicine while you are there".

Mrs Hemsley thought the cost of living here was about the same as in Canada. "I think the clothes here are very smart and of excellent quality", she added.

Her holiday, Mrs Hemsley summed up, had been "just like a dream". Everybody has been kind to me wherever I have gone", she said, "and I am going back loaded with presents. It has been a big thrill coming back and I certainly hope it won't be long before I can come again!"

JAZZ BAND DISPLAY AT LUDWORTH

Continuous rain did not daunt the spirits of six jazz bands with their attendant members numbering over 300 children on Saturday, the opening rally of the season of the Durham County Jazz Band Association (Northern Area) which took place at Ludworth.

The six bands competing were Trimdon Village Happy Wanderers, Easington Lane Fusiliers, South Hetton Royal Scots, Ford and Hylton Lane, Seaham Grenadiers and Ludworth Rising Star.

Weekly rallies will be held during the summer and for this first meeting there were three cups and 23 medals to be competed for.

Association officers were: Mr E Bennett of Easington Lane (Secretary); Mr R Richards of Trimdon (Chairman) and Mr W Hassell of South Hetton (Treasurer).

After the opening parade through the streets of Ludworth watched by hundreds of onlookers the bands gave displays of marching and counter-marching.

Scoring was very close, in fact, there was a number of ties for the trophies. The judges were Mr T Rutherford, Mr J Nugent and Mr W Johnson.

The prizes were presented by Mr R Simpson, Headmaster of Ludworth Junior County School. Ludworth ladies served teas in the adjoining British Legion Memorial Hall.
19 May 1967

DINNER LADY LOSES JOB, BUT DOES NOT KNOW WHY

After working for a year as a 'dinner lady' in Thornley infants' school, a woman was dismissed and her job readvertised.

Mrs Violet Dowson, of 9 Hillsyde Crescent, Thornley, senior dinner lady at the school said, "I haven't the faintest idea why it happened".

Her colleague, Mrs Molly Liddle, of South Street, Thornley, had been dismissed after a year working on a temporary basis. Three dinner ladies are allotted to the school if the numbers staying to dinner remain steadily over 100.

Mrs Dowson said that Mrs Liddle was employed temporarily until the numbers had been over 100 for a certain length of time. The job was then due to be made permanent.

It is stated that she was told that she was dismissed, but was asked to continue until there was a replacement, but she could not be considered for interview. "We were put out to think she was going to be permanent and then was finished", Mrs Dowson said.

Coun James Nicholson, of Easington Urban Council, said it was correct that another dinner lady was to be taken on, but it was in the rules that whenever a temporary post was made permanent, it was to be re-advertised.

There had been 30 applicants for the job and in his opinion, widows and women with no children would be more suitable. When a mother with school age children had a sick child she stayed off work. At one time it was difficult to find dinner ladies but now, there were enough applicants.

TELEPHONED DOCTOR THEN COLLAPSED AND DIED

Feeling unwell while on his business rounds a 45-year-old Wheatley Hill commercial traveller, Mr Joseph Warnes, of 85 Johnson Estate, returned home and then telephoned his doctor ... but shortly afterwards he collapsed and died.

Well-known and esteemed in the village, where he had spent all his life, Mr Warnes had appeared to be in his usual good health when he left home on his rounds. His death cast a deep gloom over the village.

Mr Warnes, formerly worked as a miner at Wheatley Hill and Blackhall collieries, but gave up pit-work to take up a new job as a traveller for the Sunderland house furnishing firm of F Clark Limited.

Lifelong Methodist

A life-long Methodist, he formerly sang in the choir of the old Patton Street Methodist Church at Wheatley Hill, and he was formerly secretary of the Welfare Tennis Club when it was in existence. He was keenly interested in amateur photography.

Some years ago Mr Warnes and his brother Wilfred ran a part-time printing business in Wheatley Hill. It was only in January that his sister-in-law, Mrs Mary Ann Warnes, died at the age of 45 at Wheatley Hill.

Mr Warnes is survived by his widow and an 18-year-old daughter, Jean, who is employed at the same firm where he worked.

Following a service in Wheatley Hill Methodist Church on Saturday, conducted by the Rev M Henderson, Mr Warnes was buried at Wheatley Hill Cemetery.
26 May 1967

THE SUCCESSFUL CANDIDATE in the election for a new agent for the Durham Area of the National Union of Mineworkers is Mr W Malt, of Horden, Mr T Finnigan, of Washington Glebe was second, Mr T Callan, of Vane Tempest, third and Mr R Hughes, of Thornley, fourth.
2 June 1967

CLOTHES THEFT – Detectives from the Castle Eden Police Division were this week making extensive enquiries into a break-in at a draper's shop in Hartlepool Street, Thornley, at the week-end, when a quantity of ladies coats and dresses were stolen. The thieves entered the lock-up shop, belonging to Latest Fashions, of Nunn Street, Newcastle, after smashing a plate-glass window near the entrance door.
9 June 1967

LUDWORTH'S BOON TO BOWES

One of the features of the little village of Ludworth was the natural history museum owned by Mr Bob Lofthouse and housed in his small council house in Barnard Avenue. At the age of 86 years, Mr Lofthouse finds the duties of maintaining and attending to his hundreds of exhibits a bit too much. It is pleasing to note however that this unique collection of wild life will not be lost to the county: it has been taken by the Bowes Museum and will be available for educational purposes in a wider sphere.

On entering the bedroom of Bob Lofthouse, one was immediately struck with the sight of a full grown fox (stuffed of course), and from there could be seen specimens of the taxidermist's art in the way of stuffed birds, both large and small, from sparrows up to owls, all in perfect condition. In addition to his cases of birds and small animals, there could be inspected several cabinets housing hundreds of specimens of Lepidoptera, all superbly mounted and docketed for reference. This was not the only talent possessed by Mr Lofthouse; he was a first class artist with pen and ink, and the walls of his home are covered with delicate sketches of birds, cats etc as well as countryside scenes. And his intimate friends were proud possessors of gifts drawn by Bob Lofthouse. At Christmastide, he drew his Christmas cards. One recipient, the late Mr T H Holder never failed to acknowledge in print his gratitude for a greeting on a card bearing a lovely pen and ink drawing.

Mr Lofthouse, an old standard of Ludworth, educated at the old church school of Ludworth by Mr R M White, was a miner at Ludworth and Thornley Collieries. He served in the First World War. He has never taken part in sport, and was content to pursue his studies and activities in the field of natural history. Another considerable part of the life of Mr Lofthouse is his devotion to his church; this being the little mission church of St Andrew, Ludworth, where he attends with his sisters so long as his health permits. He is a confirmed bachelor. The collection has been inspected by hundreds of visitors and a recent one was Bishop G E West, who learned about Mr Lofthouse while conducting a service at Ludworth, and insisted on being taken to visit Mr Lofthouse and his specimens.

Mr Lofthouse has viewed the departure of his collection with sorrow, but expressed his intention of visiting Bowes Museum from time to time to see the birds, eggs, butterflies etc which he knew each and every one.

16 June 1967

NEW DETECTIVE SUPERINTENDENT IS WHEATLEY HILL MAN: MANY LOCAL LINKS

Detective Chief Inspector George Clarkson, of the Metropolitan Police, who comes from Wheatley Hill, has been promoted Detective Superintendent and has taken charge of

Mr G Clarkson (right)

the CID offices on 'A' (Whitehall and Westminster) Division. His headquarters are at Cannon Row Police Station.

Sup Clarkson, who is 49, is a son of the late Mr William Clarkson, formerly a mining engineer at Wheatley Hill. Educated at Wheatley Hill School and later Wellfield Grammar School, Supt Clarkson first worked as a clerk in the Architect's Department of Easington Rural District Council, but, after three years, he went to London and joined the Metropolitan Police.

First Posting

His first posting was to City Road Police Station in north-east London. After two years on the beat, he was attached to the CID. A volunteer for flying duties with the RAF on the outbreak of the War, he was released from the Police in 1943 and became a pilot with Coastal Command serving mainly in the Middle East. Later he was a Flying Officer with Fighter Command in Europe.

On demobilization, he returned to City Road where he was appointed as detective. He became a Sergeant in 1952, and Inspector in 1960, serving at various stations in north London and also with the Flying Squad. For two years he was an instructor at the Metropolitan Police Detective Training School.

Since his promotion to Detective Chief Inspector in 1963, he has been a member of the Research and Planning Branch at New Scotland Yard, later senior liaison officer at the Metropolitan Police Forensic Science Laboratory and, for the past two years, first on 'G' Division in north London. During the past 12 months he has investigated four separate murders in London.

Sportsman

A keen sportsman, Supt Clarkson represented his school at rugby football and cricket, later played for three seasons with West Hartlepool RFC and, during the same period, played soccer with the Wheatley Hill Juniors.

He is a former rugby trialist with Durham County Juniors. During his earlier service in the Force he kept up his interest in rugby, and was also a tennis enthusiast. At present he keeps fit, when duties permit, by the occasional game of squash rackets or golf.

Although he left Durham many years ago, Supt Clarkson still keeps in touch with the district. Each year he and his wife, Irene, visit Durham City where her father, Mr Thomas Robinson, a well-known former City Rugby player now lives.

Supt and Mrs Clarkson have their own home at Wood Green in North London; with their 13-year-old son, Peter. Their daughter, Pamela, who is 20, is at College in Bognor Regis.

It is said that behind every successful man there is a woman and this is so in Supt Clarkson's case. In her own way his wife, Irene, is perhaps equally committed to public service. About a year ago she gave up an office job to take up nursing and is at present an auxiliary at the north Middlesex Hospital. She is also an active member of both St Michael's and the Good Shepherd Churches, Wood Green, and is in charge of the cub scout pack.

WHO CAN BLAME THIS CLASSIC BOXER?

Maurice Cullen's weekend announcement that he is 'hanging up his gloves' came as a shock not only to the village where he lives, but to the wide following he has throughout the North-East.

The boxing scene will not be the same without him, but who will blame him for his decision?

Often he has hit the sporting headlines with his successes as a lightweight, with two Lonsdale belts in his possession ... but still the 'big money' in the game eludes him.

As a professional and a champion he should have commanded much bigger purses for his fights especially after tucking the British title under his belt.

There were plenty of promises for a tilt at the world title, but little action.

This has left Maurice a sad going," he says wryly, "I am like world title".

Maurice – the "pride of Shotton" – has suffered much frustration in the boxing game. He has had more than his share of disappointments.

But after winning the British title he expected the fights, with accompanying good offers, to come flooding in. But they didn't and the few that did come were a mockery, as far as finance was concerned, for a champion of his calibre.

Maurice has always been a stylish boxer, a purist. Often he has been dubbed "the man with the most punishing left hand in the business".

When people saw him fight there was no "blood and thunder" just a classic display of superb boxing by a man who was seldom out of training.

Whether this has not pleased some of the fans, or whether it is because he is not a Cockney, that the big money has by-passed him is anybody's guess.

Certain it is, however, that Maurice, a likeable lad and undeniably an expert in the ring, has not received the full recognition he so richly deserves.

510

His shock announcement may make the big promoters sit up and take notice and out of the blue may come a lucrative offer to fight for the world championship.

Would this make Maurice change his mind?

Here again no one can prophesy. But his many fans would certainly like nothing better than to see him wearing the world crown ... it would be a fitting reward to an unblemished career

5000 AT WHEATLEY HILL SPORTS DAY

Under blue skies and flaming June sunshine there was a record attendance at the Wheatley Hill Colliery Federation Board's annual Sports Day, held in the Wheatley Hill Peter Lee Girls' Modern School playing field. A crowd of 5000 watched the parade through the streets of the village and events at the school.

Officiating handling arrangements were Coun W Newby (chairman); Coun M Alderton (organising secretary); Mr J Hedley (treasurer).

The miners of Wheatley Hill were generous to their children. Every child taking part in the fancy dress parade, who walked in the procession, received a 2s savings stamp. Some 1800 children up to school leaving age received a bag of sweets and chocolate valued at 3s.6d. By levy and special efforts the miners raised £500 to meet the costs of the day.

Five jazz bands from Thornley, Peterlee, Felling, Horden and Burnmoor took part in the procession headed by the Wheatley Hill Colliery Prize Band.

The fancy dress parade attracted a large entry. Judges were Mr F Richardson (colliery manager) and Mrs Richardson, Mr W Bowman (under-manager) and Mrs Bowman, The Rev and Mrs M Henderson (Methodist Minister) and Mrs G G Graham (wife of the vicar of Wheatley Hill).

Wheatley Hill Scouts helped to look after side-shows and erecting tents and Women's Organisations in the villages manned the teas and refreshments tents.

Wheatley Hill Workmen's Club and the Soldiers and Sailors Club provided prizes for a lucky draw.

A well known personality in the village, Mr Tom Kelly, acted as Mr Sports Day and was correctly challenged before 'closing time'.

A popular feature of the programme which attracted many visitors was the road safety exhibition in charge of Sergeant Gee, of Aycliffe.

The jazz bands in their colourful uniforms added rhythm and gaiety to the occasion. Judges were Sgt C Pickering, Special Sgt J Local and PC R Maxwell.

Jazz band results: Parade Efficiency and Performance on field: Overall winners Baldasera Cup; Felling Royals. Parade Medals: Drum Major; 1 Felling Royals; 2 Burnmoor; 3 Thornley.

Field Events

Field events provided some close finishes in children's races. **Boys flat races**: **5 years:** 1 John Walker; 2 Graham Maxwell; 3 Gary Mason. **6 years:** 1 Alan Wood; 2 Trevor Pace; 3 Paul Raffell. **7 years:** 1 Michael Carr; 2 Ronald Saigar; 3 Tony Dixon. **8 years:** 1 Terry Purvis; 2 Stewart Robinson; 3 Kevin Quinn. **9 years:** 1 Ian

Burnham; 2 John Gutcher; 3 George Pace. **10 years**: 1 Harry Banks; 2 Stewart Atkin; 3 Brian Harker. **11 years:** 1 Raymond Lambert; 2 Stephen Kell, 3 Donald Million. **12 years:** 1 David Patterson; 2 Frederick Mitchell; 3 John Youll. **13 years:** 1 Tie – Ian Oswald and Jeffrey Dunn; 2 Alan Patterson; 3 Bruce Laverick. **14 years:** Brian Venables; 2 Colin Bradley; 3 Alan Pattison. **Potato races: 5 years:** 1 Tie – Paul Lye and Thomas Lowther; 2 Tie – Leslie Thompson and Kevin Connor; 3 Dennis Spencer. **6 years:** 1 Alan Harker; 2 William Hodge; 3 Paul Raffell. **7 years:** 1 Tie – Colin Foster and Michael Carr; 2 Ronald Saigar; 3 Tie – Gary Coxon and Brian Richardson. **8 years** – 1 Kevin Quinn; 2 Stewart Appleby; 3 Christopher Durkin. **9 years**: 1 Gordon Pattison; 2 John Gutcher; 3 Ian Burnham. **10 years:** 1 Brian Harker; 2 Stewart Atkin; 3 Michael Smyth. **Hurdles: 11 years:** 1 Raymond Lambert; 2 Donald Million; 3 Stephen Kell. **12 years**: 1 Frederick Mitchell; 2 David Patterson; 3 John Youll. **13 years:** 1 Jeffrey Dunn; 2 Alan Patterson; 3 Alan Dyson. **14 years:** 1 Brian Venables; 2 Colin Bradley; 3 Alan Pattison.

Girls' Flat Race

5 years: 1 Tie – Elizabeth Bulmer and Lynn Holdcroft; 2 Tie – Gloria Ragg, Trudy Ord, Christine Carr; 3 Tie – Janice Law and Elizabeth Parnham. **6 years**; 1 Christine Million; 2 Deborah Errington; 3 Susan Davies. **7 years:** Anne Amies; 2 Beverley Robson; 3 Linda Hutchinson. **8 years:** 1 Lesley Robson; 2 Patricia McDonald; 3 Christine Lambert. **9 years:** Fredeen Lonsdale; 2 Linda Patterson; 3 Pamela Atwood. **10 years:** 1 Glenis Dunn; 2 Shirley Quinn; 3 Dawn Taylor. **11 years:** 1 Margaret McDonald; 2 Linda Parker; 3 Olive Telford. **12 years:** 1 Jean Carr; 2 Anne Battye; 3 Karen Million. **13 years:** 1 June Forster. **Potato Races: 5 years:** 1 Karen Taylor; 2 Janice Law; 3 Trudy Ord. **6 years:** 1 Kathleen Atkinson; 2 Christine Million; 3 Diane Patterson. **7 years:** 1 Beverley Robson; 2 Christine Smyth; 3 Monica Barley. **8 years:** 1 Lesley Robson; 2 Lesley Hunter; 3 Susan Clish. **9 years:** 1 Fredeen Lonsdale; 2 Susan Jackson; 3 Linda Patterson. **10 years:** 1 Glenis Dunn; 2 Shirley Quinn; 3 Tie – Anne Ayre and Dawn Stephenson. **Hurdles: 11 years:** 1 Linda Parker; 2 Linda Stephenson; 3 Olive Telford. **12 years:** 1 Mary Bulmer; 2 Ann Battye; 3 Marie Spencer.

Fancy Dress Parade: Original: 1 J Thompson; 2 Shirley Parkin; 3 John Hind and John Foster. **Fancy dress:** 1 Peter Hoban; 2 Susan Carr; 3 Julie Maxwell. **Comic:** 1 Gary Warnes; 2 Gillian Burnett; 3 Linda Warnes.

In the adults fancy dress, winner was Jimmy Morris and partner. Russell Kirk correctly challenged "Mr Sports Day" and won the prize.

The 4-mile race was won for the second year in succession by William Waistell; 2 Jack Jordan; 3 Russell Kirk and 4 Renee Carter.

Coun Alderson said, "The effort has been well worth while and we would express our appreciation to all private individuals and village organisations who have helped to make the event so successful. Certainly the weather helped us but the over-riding element in our success is the willingness of the miner to give pleasure and generosity to the old and the children in this community".

23 June 1967

LUDWORTH MAN'S ROAD SAFETY RALLY SUCCESS

Mr D Ingleby of 6 Barnard Avenue, Ludworth, drove very well indeed to drop only two penalty points out of a possible 80 when he won the sixth eliminating safe driving rally held at Hartlepool last Sunday.

Ten of the 28 entrants in Sunday's rally go forward into the final rally to be held at the County Hall in Durham on Sunday 9 July. Both the second and third drivers drove well. Mr E Johnson of Peterlee dropping only five points and Mr R T Collings of Hartlepool seven.

The rally is an annual event organised by the Durham County Police in conjunction with the County Committee of Road Safety with the hope of promoting better and safer driving in the county.

30 June 1967

THORNLEY COLLIERY SPORTS DAY HAD GAIETY AND FUN

Cloudy skies did not abate the enthusiasm that one usually connects with the annual sports day at Thornley, and once again some 6000 people from Thornley and nearby Colliery communities lined the streets and joined in the gaiety and fun as the 1½ mile procession wended through the main street, headed by the Thornley Colliery Silver Prize Band, for the Welfare Grounds.

Mr Sam Greener was organising secretary and was well backed by an enthusiastic committee.

The money for this special children's day was raised by a voluntary levy each week from the miners employed at Thornley Colliery, a gesture warmly appreciated by the mothers and children of this mining community.

Some years ago the Miners' Federation Board adopted a procedure that each child who entered in the Fancy Dress Parade receive 2s.6d, so there were no 'also rans', no losers in this event.

As an added titbit for 1700 children in the village, and employees' children living in nearby areas Wheatley Hill, Wingate, Ludworth, Haswell and other places, there was a bag of assorted sweets. Surplus stocks often left are sent to Earls House Hospital.

Mr Sports Day was Mr Dick Bell, successfully challenged by Mr Stan Lowther and Mrs Sports Day, Mrs Douglas Gott, successfully challenged by Mrs Hodgson. Both received a £5 prize.

Besides painting, crayoning, drawing, knitting, needlework crafts and model making competition in the Welfare Hall, there was Kiss of Life demonstration using the Blonde Model, Resusci Anne, demonstrated by Mr J Ellis and Mr H Hubbard.

Judges: Tableaux, Mr and Mrs W Fawcett (Manager Thornley Colliery) and Mr and Mrs F Walker (Colliery Undermanager), Mr and Mrs J Crossman (Education Officer, County Hall).

Results

Painting and crayoning: 12 to 13 years: 1 T Winter; 2 J Foster; 3 M Hagan. **13 to 14 years:** 1 B Tilley; 2 C Fort; 3 B Tilley. **14 to 15 years plus:** 1 H Tunney; 2 H Tunney; 3 L Thomas. **5 to 6 years:** 1 J Atkin; 2 P Darby; 3 A Hall. **6 to 7 years:** 1

D Pattison; 2 J Aspinall; 3 D Million. **7 to 8 years:** 1 J Purvis; 2 S Eilbeck; 3 J D Lee. **8 to 9 years:** 1 M Carr; 2 N Hummerston; 3 R Frampton. **9 to 10 years:** 1 G Youll; 2 W Curry; 3 P Lennox. **10 to 11 years:** 1 P Carr; 2 K Tunney; 3 M Graney. **11 to 12 years:** 1 M Hoban; 2 C Cowan; 3 A McCoy.

Children's Fancy Dress

Original 7 years and under: 1 P Hoban; 2 C Dowson; 3 T McCarroll; 4 D & S Parker. **Original: 8 to 10 years:** 1 Y Atkinson; 2 R Craggs; 3 S Parkin; 4 S Walker. **Original 11 to 15 years plus:** 1 C Dowson; 2 A Batty; 3 N & M Walker; 4 S Walker. **Arts and Crafts 12 to 13 years:** 1 M Hewitson; 2 M Fawcett; 3 W Armstrong. **13 to 14 years:** 1 C Fort; 2 B Tilley; 3 D Summerson. **14 to 15 years plus:** 1 S Marley; 2 M Lincoln; 3 J Inchcliffe. **6 to 7 years:** 1 G Booth; 2 L Robinson; 3 J Bell. **7 to 8 years:** 1 K Hammond; 2 S Shutt; 3 K Lowther. **8 to 9 years:** 1 P Whittle; 2 P McDonnell; 3 S Brownless. **9 to 10 years:** 1 A Barker; 2 M Robson and R Pickles; 3 C Barker and S Allan. **10 to 11 years:** 1 R Vasey; 2 A Lofthouse; 3 L Richardson. **11 to 12 years:** 1 K Brownless; 2 J Lennox; 3 P Harriman.

Tableaux

1 Thornley WI; 2 Thornley Youth Club.

Adult Fancy Dress - Comic: 1 R Craggs; 2 N Hanley; 3 R Routledge. **Original:** 1 G Copeland; 2 J Morriss; 3 Mrs Crisp.

Children's Fancy Dress – Comic: 8 to 10 years: 1 Y Atkin; 2 J Hubbard; 3 K Mather; 4 D Simpson. **Comic 11 to 15 years plus:** 1 D Mather; 2 J Darby; 3 R Saunders; 4 M Jackson.

Jazz Bands – Display

Best Band: Horden Blue Stars, 324 points; Felling Royals, 306 points; Thornley Sunbeams, 302.

Field Events

Boys Field Events – Flat Race 5 to 6 years: 1 G Thompson; 2 K Lonsdale; 3 P Nicholson. **6 to 7 years:** 1 S White; 2 A Wood; 3 J Barron. **7 to 8 years:** 1 T George; 2 P Ord; 3 K Lowther. **8 to 9 years:** 1 G Williamson; 2 K Raine; 3 P Lennox. **9 to 10 years:** 1 G Pattison; 2 P Watson; 3 D Nicholson. **10 to 11 years:** 1 C Ramage; 2 A Hood; 3 J Purvis. **11 to 12 years:** 1 T Leather; 2 K Brownless; 3 J Watson. **12 to 13 years:** 1 D Pattison; 2 J Youll; M Youll. **13 to 14 years:** 1 T Wilson; 2 R Marshall; 3 F Ord. **14 to 15 years:** 1 D Parker; 2 J Peachey; 3 D Ord.

Sack Race 5 to 6 years: 1 B Crisp; 2 P Langlands; 3 T Lowther. **6 to 7 years:** 1 S White; 2 P George; 3 A Wood. **7 to 8 years:** 1 T George; 2 P Ord; 3 D Appleby. **8 to 9 years:** 1 G Williamson; 2 S Brownless; 3 R Saiger. **9 to 10 years:** 1 S Chayter; 2 A Barker; 3 R Marshall. **10 to 11 years:** 1 J Orton; 2 A Hood; 3 P Swallow. **11 to 12 years:** 1 K Brownless; 2 W Bowes; 3 J Adams. **12 to 13 years:** 1 T Winter; 2 D Pattison; 3 M Youll. **13 to 14 years:** 1 T Wilson; R Hubbard; 3 R Marshall. **14 to 15 years plus:** 1 J Peachey; 2 D Parker; 3 D Ord.

Baldasera Memorial Cup: 1 D Spence; 2 J Million; 3 D Ord.

Girls Field Events. Flat Race 5 to 6 years: 1 T O'Brien; 2 S Armstrong; 3 E Connelly. **6 to 7 years:** 1 L Greener; 2 K McDonnell; 3 N Appleby. **7 to 8 years:** 1

A Gaskell; 2 C Williamson; 3 K Robson. **8 to 9 years:** 1 J Gaskell; 2 J Bowes; 3 C Robson. **10 to 11 years** 1 S Armstrong; 2 A Dower; 3 A McCoy. **11 to 12 years:** 1 M McDonnell; 2 L Parker. **12 to 13 years:** 1 J Day; 2 A Batty; 3 M Walker. **13 to 14 years:** 1 J Sunley; 2 M Peachey; 3 J Marley. **14 to 15 years plus:** 1 L Walker; 2 P Smith; 3 S Green.

Egg and Spoon Race 5 to 6 years: 1 E Connelly; 2 S Armstrong. **6 to 7 years;** 1 K McDonnell; 2 C Williamson; 3 B Filon. **7 to 8 years:** 1 K Robson; 2 A Gaskell; 3 M Lennox. **8 to 9 years:** 1 J Bowes; 2 L Williamson; 3 J Gaskell. **10 to 11 years:** 1 A McCoy; 2 F Walker; 3 E Hutchinson. **11 to 12 years:** 1 L Parker; 2 M Gaskell; 3 M McDonnell. **12 to 13 years:** 1 J Day; 2 L Curry; 3 A Batty. **13 to 14 years:** 1 J Sunley; 2 E Rutherford; 3 J Foster. **14 to 15 years plus:** 1 E Parker; 2 P Smith; 3 S Marley.

SURPRISE PARTY FOR WHEATLEY HILL PAIR

On 30 June, 1917, Mr James Gair was married in All Saints' Church, Wheatley Hill to Miss Winifred May Barnett. A well remembered vicar officiated at the wedding, the Rev P T Casey. The couple's family arranged a pleasant surprise on Saturday when Mr and Mrs James Gair, of Wheatley Hill, celebrated their Golden Wedding.

The couple have three sons, seven grandsons and a grand-daughter and two great-grandchildren. Their sons and daughters-in-law, Mr and Mrs James Gair and Mr and Mrs Eric Gair arranged the party at which some 60 guests assembled in Wheatley Hill Methodist Sunday School Hall and among them were friends and relatives whom the couple had not seen for between 30 and 40 years. Although some travelled long distances and had to be put up overnight, Mr and Mrs Gair did not know of their arrival till they met at the Golden Day party.

Among these guests were Mr and Mrs H Reed (Leicester), Mr W E Brookes (brother) and Mrs Brookes, from Oxford; Mrs Fisher, formerly Lieut Codling, an officer in charge of the Thornley Salvation Army Corps 40 years ago; Miss M Campbell and Miss M Reed, who went from the Thornley SA Corps to become SA officers (they are now retired and live in Hartlepool).

Absent Through Blindness

The family tried to bring up from Staines the bridesmaid of 50 years ago, Mrs Sarah Bowman. Blindness, however, prevents Mrs Bowman travelling far.

The only granddaughter, Lesley Gair, presented her grandparents with a bouquet. Among the many congratulatory messages were cables from grandchildren Mr and Mrs James Arthur Gair who emigrated to South Africa and Cpl Laurence Gair serving with the Army in Germany.

Mr and Mrs Gair had a family party in their own home on Sunday. "So ended for us", said Mr Gair, "a wonderful weekend". Mr Gair, who is 69, came to Wheatley Hill in 1912 and worked at the local colliery till he was 63, after giving 49 years to the mining industry.

He spent many years as a deputy. Arthritis keeps him mostly in the house but as he says, "Otherwise I am OK". He served in the First World War and was with the Royal Artillery in France.

Band Music His First Interest

He played in junior football for a while but band music was his main interest. As an active Salvationist, Mr Gair played in the Thornley and Spennymoor SA Bands. He was an expert on the euphonium and the double bass. Mr Gair conducted the Wheatley Hill Methodist Church choir for 11 years.

Speaking of mining, Mr Gair had a lot to say about the industry. He commented, "I have seen ups and downs in the mining industry. Strikes hit us hard. I remember in the 1926 strike we spent all our savings. It had been our hope to see it through without help, but towards the end our store book was empty and we had to apply for assistance. "I believe nationalisation of the mines was the best thing that ever came to the miner. Conditions, holidays and wages have all been transformed. When I was a deputy I earned 8s.2d a shift. Compare that with wages today".

Mr Gair was a keen amateur gardener and grew flowers and vegetables for shows, until he was told by the SA Officer that that was not quite was expected of a good Salvationist.

Rules to be Kept

He said, "Rules and regulations are there to be kept. If you are a member of any organisation you must keep the rules. The Army has changed a good deal in recent years. So it must, if it is to appeal to our young people. "Look how it adapted itself to the pop group craze. We have the Joy Strings and other Army groups using this medium to reach the crowds. In my younger days at the Army in Thornley, Sunday was a busy day. Prayer meetings first, at least two open-air services, Sunday School testimony meeting in the morning and service at night".

Many Grapes

Of his gardening days, Mr Gair recalled that he had two greenhouses and grew 100 or more bunches of grapes in a season, and gave most of them away.

Mrs Gair is 67 and was born in Tavistock in Devon. Her father was a tin miner, and came to Wheatley Hill when she was 8. She recalled the days when a miner paid a shilling a week to his local doctor. For some years Mrs Gair collected the miners' subscriptions to a well-loved Wheatley Hill doctor, Dr Ryan.

Mrs Gair too, was active in the Thornley SA Corps before its closure. She was an active member of the Home League and was a teacher in the Sunday School.

Mrs Gair's smiling last comment, "The next big event will be our diamond wedding. Come back and report that".

7 July 1967

GOLDEN DAY FOR THORNLEY COUPLE

The Rev P T Casey married Mr and Mrs Charles Edward Lowe, 31 Aged Miners Homes, Thornley, on 7 July 1917, in All Saints Church, Wheatley Hill. The couple had ten children, of whom seven survive, five sons and two daughters.

Recalling her wedding day Mrs Lowes said, "We walked to church and had no honeymoon. When we were married the pits were only working one, two or three days a week. Money was scarce".

Mr Lowes was born at Plawsworth Station and moved to Durham when he was a year old and lived there till he was 20. His mother got him a job in a barber's shop and he later became a miner.

He had spells of work at Framwellgate Moor colliery and Durham Main before moving to Thornley pit in 1908. He worked underground till he was 68 and gave 55 years to mining.

Mr Lowes commented, "The Durham Miners' Big Meeting always attracted a big crowd and until three years ago I never missed a meeting. The number of people attending may appear to be the same but the number of bands and banners going into the gala are diminishing. They will get less as more and more collieries close down. That to me is a very sad thing".

Mr Lowes, who is 79, is an old boy of the Blue Coat School. In his younger days he played full back for the Blue School Old Boys' FC and later for Wheatley Hill.

Hard Days

Mrs Lowes was born 70 years ago in Coolgardie, Western Australia. She came to England in 1902 and for a while lived at Haswell Plough. At the time of her marriage she was living at Shotton.

Recalling hard times Mrs Lowes said, "The long strikes played havoc with our savings. We would have been far worse off if the tradesmen of Thornley hadn't allowed us credit through the strikes. They were repaid by an arrangement that the miners agreed to have a weekly amount deducted from the pay notes to be handed over to those tradesmen who had helped us"

Mrs Lowes attends the Mothers' Union and the Over 20 Club at St Barthlolomew's Church, Thornley. None of the couple's five sons has entered mining but have entered the professions.

Both are active members of the Thornley Over 60 Club and are useful members of the Club's concert party. "We have travelled hundreds of miles all over Durham County entertaining the old people", commented Mr Lowes.

Mrs Lowes had the last word, "I think the over 60 Club movement is the finest thing that has ever happened to old people".

14 July 1967

CLUB COMMITTEE - As a result of a ballot the following have been elected to serve on the committee of Wheatley Hill Workmen's Club for the ensuing year: Messrs J Topham, G Henderson, Jnr, B Harvey, Jnr, B Maddison, A Cooper and W Newby. There were 27 nominations. Messrs S Raffell, A O'Connor and E Bulmer were elected scrutineers.

NEW MINERS' CHAIRMAN - In the annual ballot at Wheatley Hill miners' lodge, Mr W Newby, chairman of the past three years, was defeated by Mr Brian Miller, who was elected to fill the position for the ensuing year. Principal officials returned unopposed were: Correspondence secretary, Coun A D Wharrier; Treasurer, Mr S Ragg; Financial Secretary, Mr J Hedley; Compensation Secretary, Mr J Cain;

Delegate, Mr J Andrew; Auditors, Messrs T Buxton and J Poole; Local Pit Inspector, Mr J Topham.

RETIRED MINERS' TRIP – Eight coaches took 280 retired miners at Wheatley Hill colliery and their wives and widows over 55, on their annual outing to Redcar organised and financed by the local Aged Miners' Committee. Each tripper received 10s pocket money and at Redcar they were entertained to a concert in the Pavilion, where tea and biscuits were also provided. In charge of the arrangements were the secretary and treasurer of the fund, Mr R Cook and Mr J Hedley, assisted by members of the committee.

21 July 1967

WHEATLEY HILL SOLDIERS' CLUB
TO GET LUXURIOUS NEW HEADQUARTERS

In about three months time Wheatley Hill Discharged and Demobilised Soldiers' and Sailors' Club – known locally for short as the Soldiers' Club – is to move into more spacious, luxuriously-furnished premises in Front Street, Wheatley Hill, after having occupied its present site near the Greyhound Stadium for nearly half a century.

"We aim to make this new building one of the show places in the county", the secretary, Mr J L Peacock, told our reporter this week.

The club has bought a former drapery and outfitter's shop and this is being converted at a cost of £23,000 into an up-to-date two-storeyed club.

Upstairs there will be a brightly lit, tastefully-furnished concert room, while downstairs will be the bar and comfortable lounges.

With the Times

"We have to move with the times", said Mr Peacock. He explained, "Our present building is in too isolated a spot, well away from the main part of the village, but our new club will be in the centre of the main thoroughfare and should prove an added attraction to club life in the village. When we eventually move in – and I expect it will be ready by October – we hope to double or treble our takings".

The present club was opened shortly after the end of the 1914-18 war. Originally it was a wooden hut, but later it was replaced by a brick building and in more recent years, with growing membership, an extension was built. The building, with a house attached, is now up for sale, although it

Committee of Wheatley Hill Soldiers & Sailors Club

will continue to be used until the transfer is made to the new club.

New House

Work has been proceeding for some weeks now on the new premises, which also include a new house for the club steward, Mr William Hackworth – Mr Hackworth has been steward for the past two years.

Membership of the club is around the 300 mark. "We also expect this to increase once we get into our new building and we are quite confident that the big step we have taken in launching out into modern premises will be fully justified", said Mr Peacock.

The new club will be heated electrically and will incorporate every modern amenity for the comfort and enjoyment of its members.

4 August 1967

DOCTORS OBJECT TO "NO WAITING" ORDER
AT THORNLEY

Because of the inconvenience to patients two Thornley doctors are objecting to the proposed "No Waiting" order for The Villas, Thornley, where they have their surgeries, members of Easington Central Road Safety Committee were told at their meeting.

At the District Road Safety Committee meeting, a letter was read from Durham County Council, enclosing copies of two objections to the "No Waiting" order received from Dr J Gray and Dr A Todd, and they asked for the Committee's observations.

Dr Todd's grounds for objections were that the order would affect the road in front of his house, and part of these premises had been used as a surgery since 1929.

Patients were frequently brought by car and especially on Sundays, children and other victims of accidents or sudden illness, had to be seen, whilst a car was waiting to take them either back home or to hospital.

In addition, said Dr Todd, he frequently had to interrupt his round and return to the surgery to telephone to get urgent cases into hospital or pick up late messages, and any delay could be serious.

Difficulty and Hardship

Dr Gray's grounds for objection were that the restrictions would cause difficulty and hardship to the more seriously handicapped and the emergency accident patients attending the surgery.

There would also be difficulties imposed upon the doctors attending surgery in not having easy access to their cars, particularly when required to leave the surgery to attend to urgent cases. Any resultant delay could be serious.

The local Road Safety Committee members said that in both cases car parking facilities could be obtained for the doctors at places in the vicinity of the surgery, and that the complaints were unfounded. They agreed to forward these observations to the County Surveyor.

18 August 1967

THORNLEY LEGION WOMAN RECEIVES TOLD BADGE

Over 100 members and friends gathered in Thornley Welfare Hall last week for the 42nd birthday party of Thornley Women's Section of the British Legion. Mrs E Clark (chairman) welcomed the guests.

The party had a special significance for Mrs Clark, who was presented with the Legion's Gold Badge for meritorious service. The presentation was made by Mrs L Park, Blackhall County Chairman. Other County representatives present were Mrs A Hamilton, Darlington (County secretary), Mrs E Johnson, South Hetton (County treasurer), Mrs M Ford (Hetton Downs) and Mrs E Forster (Darlington).

Mrs Elizabeth Clark has served the British Legion for 42 years. She said, "I joined the Thornley Women's section three weeks after its formation. At the time the membership was 19 and we paid a weekly subscription of one penny and we got a cup of tea thrown in. The movement soon became popular and our peak membership was 205 and we had moved from the old reading room into the Workmen's Club".

During the Second World War Thornley section knew hard times. Through war work many ladies left the area or went into full time work and the membership shrunk to 12.

Loyal Core

Mrs Clark commented: "But we had a loyal core who decided, come what may, we would keep the flag flying – and we did. We built on that small foundation and today our membership has risen to 112. Mrs Clark herself has played more than a major part in the activities of the Thornley section. For ten years she served as a committee member, organising whist drives to raise finance when it was sorely needed, arranging field days for the children and in the war years she served with the WVS, looking after a canteen for soldiers who manned the searchlight batteries and gun emplacements between Thornley and Durham.

Mrs Clark has taken part in various recruiting campaigns for membership. Last year she helped her section to win the County Cup for the highest increase and she was awarded a trophy for the highest individual effort.

Personal Canvas

Perhaps Mrs Clark's most valuable service for the Legion was her work in re-forming the Men's section six months ago. Thornley Men's Section had to disband through lack of support. Mrs Clark commented; "The County Executive were worried at the failure of some of the Men's section and urged that efforts be made to reform branches that had closed down. We women came to the conclusion that something must be done at Thornley. I made a personal canvas of the village and was promised enough support to appoint the necessary officers and personnel for a reasonably strong section". Mrs Clark's work was not in vain. "The men are back on the job".

Mrs Clark served eight years as vice-chairman of the Thornley Women's Section and 23 years as chairman. She had a break of two years, owing to ill-health. For many years she has been No 10 Group representative. Tea was served and the birthday cake was cut by the President, Mrs Hannah Brewster.

Entertainment took the form of a play, Wedding Fever, which was presented by members: Mesdames E Atkin, B Coxon, M Dobson, J Harvey, S Crane, S Richardson, K Dunleavy, M Thompson, I Ross, B Vasey, G M Bromilow, J Brooks and L Osbaldestin. Dancing was enjoyed to the music of Gordon Cutty's band from Kelloe. Organising secretary was Mrs G M Bromilow.

The cake was cut by Mrs E Clark in the absence of president, Mrs Brewster, through illness. The cake was made by Mrs M Langley, iced by Mrs Osbaldestin.

Prizewinners: Mesdames F Peacock, M Morgan, B Atkin, M Soppit, M Greener, F Smithson, G Bromilow, S Gray, E Cowan, J Burnham.

25 August 1967

WHEATLEY HILL WPC IS AGAIN PRAISED

Irene Elizabeth Alderton (22), daughter of Mr and Mrs Mark Alderton, of 63 Wordsworth Avenue, Wheatley Hill, has again been commended by her Chief Constable, Sir George Scott.

When WPC Alderton, on plain clothes duty with an 18-year-old girl cadet, Pamela Jane Rymer, daughter of Mr and Mrs G H Rymer, of 9 Topcliffe Road, Thirsk, saw a man committing an offence in Harrogate earlier this month, they promptly told him who they were and, each taking hold of an arm, told him they were arresting him.

As the man began to struggle violently, Cadet Rymer and WPC Alderton were both dragged some 25 yards and covered with mud. Both officers were bruised on their legs and ankles but their injuries were not serious.

Now Sir George has officially commended WPC Alderton and Cadet Rymer "For physical courage and determination when effecting an arrest in a case of indecent exposure".

On 14 June this year, WPC Alderton was commended by the Chief Constable in respect of a similar arrest.

Miss Alderton, who joined the West Riding Constabulary in July 1965, has three cousins in the Durham County Police Force and another in the Coventry City Force.

8 September 1967

WELCOME TO THORNLEY MINISTER

The Rev S Thompson, who succeeds the Rev Gordon Johnson as superintendent minister of Thornley Methodist circuit was officially welcomed at circuit services held in the Thornley St Stephen's Methodist Church on Saturday.

Mr Thompson is a native of Castle Howard in Yorkshire and was educated at the Scarborough Boys' High School. Being the son of a farmer, his first occupation was on the land. He became a local preacher and entered the ministry from the Malton circuit.

Mr Thompson received his theological training in Headingley College, Leeds. The whole of his ministry has been spent in North-Yorkshire, Lancashire and Durham. His circuits include Reeth, Oldham, Manchester, Houghton-le-Spring, Doncaster and Durham. Thornley is his first superintendency.

The service on Saturday afternoon was well attended. The service was conducted by the Rev Robert J Figures (Coxhoe) and the sermon was preached by the newly appointed superintendent minister. Mrs V Wilson was organist.

Tea was provided and served by the ladies of Thornley St Stephens Sisterhood.

Mr Ambrose Johnson (Trimdon Station) presided over the official service of welcome in the evening, when there was a full church.

Devotions were conducted by the Rev Robert J Figures.

The good wishes of the Anglican community were expressed by the Vicar of St Barholomew's, Thornley, and Captain Pye of the Wingate Salvation Army Corps welcomed Mr Thompson on behalf of Salvationists in the area.

The circuit welcome was extended by Mr Jesse Craig, Trimdon Grange (senior circuit steward). The Rev W Anthony Stones (Wingate) pledged the loyalty of the staff to their new superintendent. Mr Thompson replied.

Mr Thompson comes to Thornley with his wife, a son and daughter. Mrs Thompson is a native of County Durham, being born at Stanley and living for some years at Ferryhill.

Mr J Gillmore (Coxhoe) was organising secretary.

15 September 1967

WHEATLEY HILL

At the annual leek show in Wheatley Hill Workmen's Club at the weekend, there were 29 stands of leeks and prize-money totalled £750. The first prize went to Mr R Greener, with a pair of leeks 101 cubic inches capacity, and second to Mr J Nattrass (94.9 cubic inches), who also had the distinction of exhibiting the best single leek in the show.

Mr W Myers of Sedgefield, was the judge, and the arrangements were made by Mr T W Hodgson (chairman and secretary) and Mr R Carr (treasurer).

Prize winners were:

Pot leeks (in order of merit): R Greener, J Nattrass, R Cook, T Kelly, R Carr, S Jobes, W Middleton, W Walker, W Hogan, T W Hodgson, T H Appleby, W Pearock, P Nuttall, J Wilson, G Bowes, E Lowther, S Hughes, F Wilson, W Oswald, W Curry.

Other Vegetables: Intermediate Leeks – 1 J Nattrass; 2 T W Hodgson; 3 T Kelly. **Kidney Potatoes:** 1 W Curry, 2 and 3 R Cook. **Round Potatoes:** 1 W Curry; 2 W Walker; 2 S Hughes. **Tomatoes:** 1 J Nattrass; 2 and 3 W Walker. **Onions:** 1 and 2 T W Hodgson; 3 J Nattrass. **Long Beet:** 1, 2 and 3 W Walker. **Short Carrots:** 1 W Curry; 2 and 3 W Middleton. **Long Carrots:** 1 E Lowther; 2 S Jobes; 3 W Hogan. **Round Beet:** 1 S Jobes; 2 J Nattrass; 3 S Hughes. **Cauliflowers:** 1 T W Hodgson; 2 and 3 R Waites. **White Celery:** 1 W Curry; 2 S Owens; 3 J Greener. **Pink Celery** 1 W Curry; 2 and 3 J Nattrass. **Bunch of Flowers:** 1 T W Hodgson; 2 J Nattrass; 3 R Carr.

WHEATLEY HILL CONSTITUTIONAL CLUB

With a pair of leeks measuring 101.8 cubic inches, Mr J Scott won first prize at the annual leek show in Wheatley Hill Constitutional Club. Mr C Rose was second and his son, Mr J Rose, third. Fourth prize went to Mr R Foster and fifth to Mr W Worthington.

The show, which attracted 31 stands, was judged by Mr W Myers, of Sedgefield.

WHEATLEY HILL COLLIERY MANAGER RETIRES
After full, active Career

Manager of Wheatley Hill Colliery for the past 12 years, Mr Frank Richardson, who began his mining career as a trapper-boy at the age of 14 but, through zealous studies at evening classes, eventually qualified for his mine manager's certificate, is retiring next month.

Retirement of Mr F Richardson (3rd left)
L-R: Dick Storey, Tommy Smythe, ? ?, Benny Aitken

And on Saturday evening, when he was the guest of honour at the annual dinner-dance of the Wheatley Hill Colliery Officials and Deputies, many tributes to his sterling work were paid when he was presented with a wallet of notes to mark his retirement.

"I suppose it was only natural that I would make mining a career, for both my father and grandfather worked in the mines", Mr Richardson, who lives at Weardale House, Church Street, Wheatley Hill, told our reporter this week.

"It has been a well worthwhile career", he added. "There has been plenty of hard work – and not a little worry – but I have enjoyed it and am now looking forward to a happy retirement."

Mr Richardson's father, Mr Benjamin Richardson, was the first workmen's mines inspector to be appointed in Northumberland – no fewer than 27 collieries were in the area he covered.

Began at Mainsforth

Born at Ferryhill, Mr Richardson, who is 60, began work at Mainsforth Colliery and went through all the grades of mining underground, including driving, putting, hewing and stone-work.

In his spare time he studied at evening classes and other special classes held on a Saturday and when he was only 23 – he was employed at Hazlerigg Colliery at the time, in Northumberland – was successful in passing his examination for his under-manager's certificate. Twelve years later, while at Seaton Burn Colliery, he qualified for his manager's certificate.

Mr Richardson worked at Mainsforth Colliery until he was turned 20 and then moved to Northumberland and became a deputy at Hazlerigg Colliery. Later he spent three years as fore-overman at Mickley Colliery.

First Post

In 1939 he took up his first appointment as an under-manager at Wingate Colliery and remained there until 1954 when he was appointed a 'spare' manager for the collieries in No 3 Area of the Divisional Coal Board. A year later he went as manager to Wheatley Hill and has remained there since.

While living in Wheatley Hill Mr Richardson has been a generous supporter of many local organisations and won the respect of a wide circle of friends. Throughout the time he has been manager he has been chairman of the local Miners' Welfare Committee and he has also taken a keen interest in the local Boy Scout movement.

Mr Richardson and his wife – they have no family – are to live in Whitley Bay during their retirement. He said, "My wife is a native of Newcastle and so we are looking forward to going back to that area".

Mr T Smyth, Safety Assistant at the colliery, presided at the presentation on Saturday night which was made by Mr R Bowman, undermanager. Arrangements for the function were made by Messrs R Storey and B Aitken.

22 September 1967

THORNLEY "GOLDEN PARTNER"
ONCE BATMAN TO GENERAL SMUTS

On 6 October 1917, Mr Joseph Henry Pattison married Miss Catherine Bulmer in Thornley Waterloo Street Methodist Church. The Rev Harold W Stephenson officiated. On Saturday Mr and Mrs Pattison, 88 Dunelm Road, Thornley, celebrated their golden wedding in a way that had a distinct Methodist flavour.

With members of their family and friends they went to Thornley St Stephen's Methodist Church (the old Waterloo Street Church) and attended a service of thanksgiving. This was conducted by the Rev Gordon Johnson, a former superintendent minister of the Thornley circuit. He was assisted by the present superintendent, the Rev Robert S Thompson. Mrs V Wilson was organist.

A family party followed in the Sunday School and the guests were entertained by the Thornley Over-60 Club concert party, who gave a musical version of the Golden Wedding, which formed part of the party's latest variety show, which has been given in many parts of the county. Those taking part were Mesdames C Lowes, G Hodgson, S Blakemore, J Greenwell, R Hall, J Harrison, B Wilson, J Bullock; Messrs C Lowes, J Oswald, J Harrison, B Pattison, S Davies, J Broomfield.

Born at Wingate

Mr Joe Pattison was born at Wingate and then moved to West Hartlepool where his school days began. On moving to Thornley he came under schoolmaster Mr Daniel Hagan. Leaving school at 12 Mr Pattison's first job was at the belts at Wheatley Hill colliery. He commented "For working 10 hours a day I received 9s.2d *(About 47p in todays money)* for an 11 shift fortnight and took 8s home *(40p)*. I then trained to be a winding engineman. The First War interrupted my training, which I never completed". After the War he was then transferred to Thornley Colliery where he became a wagonway man.

Mr Pattison retired as head wagonway man when he was 65, giving 53 years service to the industry. He is now a sprightly 74.

Mr Pattison, although reserved, volunteered for service in the First World War and served with a Northumbrian Divison in the RAMC in France and Belgium. He trained under Dr Clay at the Royal Victoria Infirmary, Newcastle. His Army service brought him a memorable experience. He met General Smutts, the great South African soldier and statesman, and was for a time the General's batman. In his younger days, Mr Pattison played goalkeeper for Thornley Wednesday's (tradesmen's) team.

A prominent and life-long Methodist, Mr Pattison has given yeoman service to the Thornley Church. He has been a Sunday School worker as teacher and superintendent. For many years he has been a trustee of the church, church secretary and Society steward. At district level, he served on the Overseas Missions Committee in the Sunderland and Durham and Darlington Districts. Prior to 1948, Mr Pattison was a governor on the General Board of Durham County Hospital and a member of the House Committee.

Mr Pattison is keenly interested in the Over-60 Club movement. He commented, "I am not a founder member of the Thornley Club but joined soon after its foundation. The Club had a good friend in the late Mr J H C Scott, a Thornley tradesman and Methodist. I believe this movement to be the best thing that has ever been introduced for old people. For many it is the only contact with the outside world and stands between them and utter loneliness. The club serves as a meeting ground and brings people together who would otherwise ignore one another's existence", he says.

Society Stewards

Methodist ministers coming to Thornley have cause to be thankful for the help of Mr Pattison. As society steward he has taken the minister round and introduced his members to him. This is a service that has gone on for many years.

Mrs Pattison is 72 and like her husband is a life-long Methodist. She was born in Thornley and before the marriage was in domestic service, first for Mrs J T Scott in Thornley and then for a Stockton tradesman, Mr Adam Tate.

Mrs Pattison has been a keen worker in the Sisterhood and was its first organist at Waterloo Street. She has been hostess to many ministers and local preachers who visited the church over the years. For many years she organised the tea for the quarterly meeting which was usually held in Thornley in March.

Both Mr and Mrs Pattison were choir members. Mrs Pattison recalled that they had served under two choirmasters, Simon Henderson and Wilf Potts.

The couple have a married son Mr J Pattison, who lives in Cheshire, and is a local preacher; and a married daughter, Mrs Elsie Fidler, of Caterham in Surrey.

DEATH OF MRS SCOTT, THORNLEY

The death of Mrs Jeanie Miller Scott took place in a Durham nursing home. She formerly resided at Glenside, Thornley. Mrs Scott, born in Yorkshire, had spent about 50 years in Thornley. She came to the village on her marriage to Mr James Hamilton Scott, a Thornley businessman, who died some years ago.

Mrs Scott was very active in the Women's Institute movement, and was the leading figure in the formation of a joint Thornley and Wheatley Hill branch. A branch was later formed at Wheatley Hill.

Mrs Scott was president of Thornley WI for many years, and was also interested in the Scouting movement. Area meetings were frequently held in her home.

She was a staunch Methodist and held membership with the Thornley Waterloo Street Church for 50 years. She acted as hostess to Sunderland and Durham District when she and her husband entertained the Synod to luncheon on the occasion of their silver wedding. Until recently she was a trustee of the church.

Funeral service was held at Thornley St Stephen's Methodist Church on Monday, conducted by the superintendent minister, the Rev Robert S Thompson. Cremation followed at Stranton Grange, Hartlepool.

13 October 1967

THORNLEY BRITISH LEGION – reformed about six months ago, devoted their last meeting to appointments for the benevolence side of their work. Mr R Smith presided. Following officers were appointed: President, Dr J Gray; vice-president, Mr C Lamb; chairman, Mr R Smith; vice-chairman, Mr R Brookes; secretary, Mr R High; treasurer, Mr W Brereton; employment officer, Mr R Brookes; pensions officer, Mr W Brereton; representatives from the Women's Section: Mesdames E Clark, G. M Bromilow, J Brookes and E Middleton.

27 October 1967

WHEATLEY HILL HOMING PAY-OUT

When cups and prizes won by members of Wheatley Hill Homing Society during the past season were presented at a supper and social evening in Wheatley Hill Workmen's Club, the secretary, Mr F Parkin, disclosed that more than £800 had been paid out this year in pools and points money. They had, he said, enjoyed "a very good racing season".

Top honours went to the "B" team of Frost Bros. As well as collecting most points (21½) they won four trophies, the Old Bird Averages Cup, the Inland Averages

Cup, The Yong Birds Averages Cup and the Combined Averages Cup. They were also awarded three specials.

Marley and Davies collected the next highest points, 15, and also won the Young Bird Hatfield Cup.

Other principal winners were: Heal Bros, Watson and Etherington, 12½ pts; Mr and Mrs Maughan and Son "A" team, 12 pts (also winners of Channel Averages Cup and Nomination Lady's Special); Lowther Bros, and Dinsdale "B" team, 10 pts; Law and Humes, 8½ pts; Frost Bros "A" team, 7 pts (also winners of knock-out competition).

Lonsdale and Sons, 6 pts. Winners of Vaux Long Distance Cup, Constitutional Club Cup and Mr T Scorer's Cup; Carr and Hodgson, 6 pts; Mr and Mrs Maughan and Son "B" team, 5½ pts; Million and Son, 5 pts; Wake and Son and Parkin, 4½ pts; Morgan Bros and Robson, 4½ pts; Burnside Bros 3½ pts; W Broomfield, 3½ pts.

M O'Connor, 3 pts (also A Baldasera's Ashford Cup); R Harrison, 3 pts; Routledge and Son and Gardner, 3 pts (also Workmen's Club Cup and Special); F Lye, 3 pts; Hammond Bros 2½ pts; Morrow and Briggs, G Routledge and Crisp, Parsley and Williams, one point each; Lowther Bros and Dinsdale "A" team, half a point.

3 November 1967

REMEMBRANCE DAY – At Thornley there was a massive turnout of organisations. Mr R Smith was parade marshal. Parade was headed by Thornley Colliery Silver Band under the direction of Mr E Kitto. Taking part in the parade were Thornley British Legion (Standard carried by Mr R High), Thornley Women's Section (standard bearer, Mrs B Atkin), 1st Thornley Boys' Brigade (under Capt R Speckman), Girls' Brigade (under Miss A Griffiths and Mrs E Speckman), Church Lads' Brigade, Sunbeams Jazz Bands, Over-60 Club, WI and Mothers' Club. The processions marched to the Parish Church of St Bartholomew, filled to capacity. Service was conducted by the Vicar (the Rev P G Mold) and lesson was read by Captain Fye of Wingate Salvation Army. The address was given by the Rev R S Thompson, superintendent minister of Thornley Methodist Circuit, and Mrs M Mitchell was organist. Following the service, the parade proceeded to the Cenotaph, where many wreaths were laid.

WHEATLEY HILL REMEMBRANCE DAY - Arrangements were made by the Women's Section of the British Legion. The procession was headed by Wheatley Hill Colliery Silver Prize Band. All Saints' Church was filled to capacity. The Methodist minister (The Rev M Henderson) conducted the service and read L Binyon's Ode to the Fallen. The Vicar (the Rev G G Graham) gave the address. After re-forming, the parade moved to the Memorial Clock in Front Street, where Mr Graham offered prayers. At the Cenotaph in the Miners' Welfare Park, wreaths were placed by the Women's Section of the Legion, Girls' Brigade, 1st Wheatley Hill Scouts, Women's

Institute, Mothers' Union, Over-60 Club, Mothers' Club, Soldiers' and Sailors' Club and Workmen's Club.

CULLEN MUST FIGHT BUCHANAN

Maurice Cullen (Shotton), the British lightweight champion, and Johnny Cooke (Bootle), the British welterweight champion, have been ordered to defend their titles by the British Boxing Board of Control.

Cullen's defence will be against Ken Buchanan, the brilliant 22-year-old unbeaten Edinburgh boxer. West Ham's Ralph Charles is given a title chance against Cooke.

Both contests are to take place before 29 February 1968.

17 November 1967

POST AS WHEATLEY HILL MANAGER IS A SUCCESS STORY

A former pit-lad at Shotton Colliery who went through all the grades of mining and since the war has been a mine manager in India and has also spent nine months in Germany as a technical representative of a mining machinery engineering firm, has been appointed manager of Wheatley Hill Colliery.

He is Mr Wilfred Hall, of Hazelhurst, Durham Road, Wheatley Hill, who took up his new duties last week. He has succeeded Mr Frank Richardson, who retired recently after being colliery manager for 12 years.

Mr Hall was born at Shotton Colliery 55 years ago and after starting work at the local pit when he was 14 remained there until the outbreak of war in 1939. He was on deputy work when he left to join the staff of the Houghton-le-Spring Underground Fire and Rescue Brigade.

Two years later he resumed his mining career at Wheatley Hill Colliery as a master shifter and later became assistant to the under-manager.

He filled this position for about six months until November 1945, when he left this country to take up a new appointment as assistant manager for the New Beerbhoom Coal Company in West Bengal, India.

"I went as assistant manager", Mr Hall told our reporter this week, "but actually when I arrived there I was made manager and filled this post throughout the four years I was there, being in charge of 2500 men".

When Mr Hall returned to England in 1949 he was appointed under-manager at Thrislington colliery, near Ferryhill, but two years later left the Coal Board to become a technical representative with the mining machinery firm of Campbell Ritchie.

In this capacity I visited collieries all over the British Isles as well as spending nine months in Germany", said Mr Hall.

After five years with the firm Mr Hall returned to the Coal Board, becoming under-manager at Horden Colliery, where he remained for seven years until his appointment as manager of Sherburn Hill Colliery in 1963. "But when this pit closed down in July 1965", said Mr Hall, "I became a 'spare' colliery manager until taking over as manager of Bowburn and Metal Bridge collieries at the beginning of this year".

Mr Hall, who has packed a lot of variety in his mining career of 41 years, is married with an only daughter.

THIEVES' HAUL AT WHEATLEY HILL

Thieves who broke into Wheatley Hill branch of the Sherburn Hill Co-operative Society in Quilstile Road between Thursday night and Friday morning last week made off with a huge amount of property, mostly electrical goods. Detectives from the Castle Eden Police Division are investigating.

The intruders forced their way into the hardware department after climbing onto the roof and opening a hatch.

The stolen property, including transistor radios, electric food mixers, electric irons, electric razors, watches, jewellery and cutlery, was valued at £839.

It is believed that a waiting vehicle was used to take away the 'loot'.

24 November 1967

PLUCKY WHEATLEY HILL MAN, DESPITE PARALYSIS, CRUISES ALL OVER THE WORLD

44-year-old Albert Burnside, of Wheatley Hill, who has been crippled with paralysis down the whole of his left side since he was a baby, uses a mechanised invalid carriage not only to travel to his work as a clerk at Easington... but also as a cruising ship to see the world. Cheerfully Albert told me at his paraplegic bungalow home, 5 Fred Peart Square, this week (writes Norman Passfield), "I have never been able to walk properly since I was a baby but I have never let it get me down ... and it has certainly never stopped me getting around!"

And 'getting around' for Albert does not mean an odd trip in this country, but sailing the high seas for two or three weeks at a time.

He has just returned from his tenth cruise – a three-week Caribbean trip which took him to 90 degrees of sunshine at Las Palmas, Barbados, St Vincent, St Lucia, Grenada, Trinidad and Madeira.

"And I have enjoyed every minute of it – but then I always do", said a sun-tanned Albert, who caught the 'cruising bug' in 1951 when he made his first holiday trip through the Mediterranean.

"Since then", he said, "I have only missed an odd year when I have not gone cruising but even then I have gone abroad, having been on trips to Paris, Barcelona and Switzerland".

How does he manage going off on his cruises?

"No Bother at all"

"No bother at all", smiled Albert. Naturally I have to depend on porters to carry my luggage but once I am on board it is all plain sailing. They always fix me up with a cabin near the ships lift so it is not too difficult for me to get about and then I just sit basking on deck in the sunshine ... lapping it up".

Albert, who wears a heavy boot and calliper on his left foot, is limited when it comes to taking part in the packed daily programme of entertainment on board a cruiser. "I cannot dance, of course", he said, "but I enjoy watching others and there's lots of other good fun to occupy your time ... in fact there's never a dull moment!"

Generally when he returns from one cruise Albert quickly books up for another next year.

Albert, who lives with his widowed mother, Mrs Isabella Burnside, said that despite his infirmity he believed in "enjoying life to the full".

He philosophised, "If I kept thinking about the way I am physically I would probably take it badly. But I never do. I forget all about it and I like to see as much of the world as possible".

Much Travelled

Having enjoyed so many cruises, Albert knows the Mediterranean "like the back of his hand". He has landed at most ports there.

"It's the sun I like", he said. "I am a real sun worshipper. Even when I am at home I snap up every opportunity to sit in the garden when the sun is shining".

Among the places Albert has visited during his ten cruises are North Africa, France, Portugal, Italy, Malta, Gibraltar, Yugoslavia, Greece, Turkey, Sicily and the Isle of Capri. "They were all wonderful", he says.

Lots of Friends

Cruising has brought Albert lots of friends. He said, "You quickly make friends on board and I still correspond with people I met years ago. There's always a wonderful friendly, carefree atmosphere!"

Saves All Year Round

Albert, who said he "saved all the year round" for his holiday cruises, has worked as a clerk at Easington Rural Council offices since 1942. Before that he was employed in the local colliery offices at Wheatley Hill.

He was a normal healthy baby until he was nearly three years of age, "and then one night he went to bed as right as rain, but next morning we found him lying unconscious", his mother told me. "He remained like this a day or two and when he came round he could not walk ... and he was nearly twelve before he could walk again".

He must have inherited a love of the sea from his father said Albert, his father, Mr John Burnside, who died five years ago, served in the Royal Navy during both World Wars, and his brother John, who was 26, was lost at sea while serving on a French destroyer shortly after Dunkirk in the last war.

Albert has not yet fixed up his holiday for next year, but already he is browsing through the cruise brochures. "I must have been vaccinated with sea water!" he quipped as I left him.

8 December 1967

WHEATLEY HILL LEGION PARTY

When Wheatley Hill women's section of the British Legion held their 37th Christmas party in the Workmen's Club, a special letter of good wishes for her recovery was sent to a past president, Mrs Freeman, who was unable to attend through illness.

About 100 members attended and during an excellent supper a special toast in her absence was proposed to a member from Wingate, Mrs M Glasby, at present enjoying holiday overseas. Mrs Glasby is returning home in the New Year.

Seasonable wishes were extended to the members by the chairman, Mrs M Brain, and Mesdames Cowan, Saxby, Walls and Robinson.

After supper members joined in a programme of games, competitions and dancing. Winners of a fancy dress parade were Mrs Farrer and Mrs G Smith (hippies); Mrs Hanley and Mrs Gaines (bride and 'groom); Mrs B Robinson (black and white minstrel) and Mrs O Rowbotham (beggar). The judges were Mrs Johnson and Mrs Watson.

A Christmas cake given by Mrs L Saxby was won by Mrs Phillips, and Mrs Waddell won a basket of fruit. Door prizes were won by Mrs Foster and Mrs Lister, and numerous prizes were also awarded for spot dances.

CULLEN CONFIDENT FOR NEW YORK FIGHT

Before leaving his home at Shotton Colliery at midday on Monday on the first stage of his trip to New York, where he is to fight the world's No 2 lightweight, Mike Cruz, today, Maurice Cullen, the British lightweight champion, had a final training session in the gymnasium at Horden, where he does most of his sparring.

It will be Maurice's first visit to the States and he is looking forward tremendously to the fight, brimful, as usual, of confidence. "I know Mike is a hard puncher and an aggressive fighter," said Maurice, "but I am confident I can clinch the verdict".

Maurice left for London on Monday and flew to the States the following day. His parents set him off from the station. "His father would love to have gone to America with him but the fare was just a bit too steep", Mrs Cullen told our reporter.

Although he faces tough opposition, Maurice's chances must be rated quite high for only last month in Helsinki's Ice Palace he left-jabbed the top Swede boxer, Olli Maeki, into a points defeat.

Big Incentive

Victory over Cruz today could well strengthen his claim for a European title fight and put Maurice in line for a world championship fight with Carlos Ortiz – a fight for which he has been itching since he was last narrowly beaten for the title when the two boxers met in 1963.

Maurice has improved tremendously since then – he is the proud possessor of a Lonsdale belt – and his many fans in the North-East will certainly be "rooting" for him when he steps into the ring with Cruz today even though they won't be there to see him.

Accompanying Maurice to the States is his manager, Arthur Boggis. The fight will take place over ten rounds at Madison Square Gardens.

15 December 1967

WHEATLEY HILL CLUB GIFTS

When Wheatley Hill Workmen's Club entertained their retired members and their wives and widows over 60 to a Christmas party in the club's concert hall last Thursday night, they presented each with a Christmas gift of £2. About 250 old folk were entertained and the gifts were distributed by the secretary, Mr Ben Aitken, and members of the committee.

531

The guests were welcomed by the chairman of the club, Mr S Hughes, supported by Mr Aitken, and during an excellent knife-and-fork meal a Christmas cake was cut by the oldest pensioner, Mr Ben Bowes, who will be 88 next March. Seasonable greetings were extended to all the guests.

Mr Alf Hunter played selections on the electric organ and an enjoyable entertainment, consisting of vocal, musical and comedy items, was given by Messrs G Ebden, E Peachey, W Foster and G Luke.

MAURICE CULLEN READY TO FIGHT IN STATES AGAIN

Shotton Colliery's popular boxing champion, Maurice Cullen, delighted his many fans on Saturday when news came through of his victory over Mike Cruz in the famous Madison Square Garden, New York. The contest was over ten rounds and the sportswriters were unanimous in giving full credit to the Shotton lad for his comfortable points win.

Maurice, now the only reigning British champion to have boxed in America, arrived back home on Sunday morning, but had to go straight to bed with a heavy cold. "Apart from that he is all right, but he is stopping in bed until he recovers", his mother told our reporter on Monday.

After four fairly close rounds against Cruz, Maurice built up a big points lead and finished his first fight in the States looking almost as fresh as when he stepped into the ring.

Cruz, bewildered by Cullen's punishing left jabs, was back-pedalling from the fifth round onwards and the referee and two judges were unanimous in giving the verdict to the British lightweight champion.

Maurice was quite pleased with his first fight in the States. He said, "I am ready to go back any time they care to put up a rated opponent".

22 December 1967

WHEATLEY HILL DERELICT LAND
MAY SOME DAY BECOME A GOLF COURSE

Land at Wheatley Hill which is lying derelict and which is to be reclaimed may one day become a golf course. Easington Rural Council decided that the surveyor, when briefing consultants for the land reclamation scheme at Wheatley Hill, is to ascertain the feasibility of including in this scheme a golf course.

The decision arose out of consideration of a letter from the secretary of the North Regional Planning Committee stating that a study of golf facilities in the northern region had just been completed by the committee and the Northern Advisory Council for Sport and Recreation.

The letter said the increasing pressure on golf courses and the relatively large areas of land required for new courses made the subject of existing and future possible provision one of some importance, particularly in view of the need to increase the attractions of the region.

In order that the Committee could have an overall picture they asked the council if they would consider the extent to which they felt that the improvement of existing golf courses or the creation of new courses would be carried out either by them directly or by private courses within the next 15 years or so.

The council in agreeing that the feasibility of the Wheatley Hill land be considered is advising the Regional Planning Committee that Castle Eden Golf Club intended increasing the number of holes on their course.

29 December 1967

1968

WHEATLEY HILL SCOUTS' EFFORT

As in the past years members of the Wheatley Hill Old Scouts' Association went carol singing in the village during the festive season and the secretary, Mr Ralph Watson, reports that they collected a record sum of £60 as a result of their "rounds."

The money is to be spent on "something useful" for the children's ward of Durham County Hospital.

Years ago the Association "adopted" this ward and since then they have kept in regular touch with it, especially at yuletide when they have always bought a special gift for the general use of the young patients.

"We will be visiting the hospital shortly to extend our greetings to the youngsters and sing carols" says Mr Watson, "and we will leave it to the Matron and Sisters to decide what they would like to buy from the money we have raised."

5 January 1968

FOUR HURT IN CRASH

Four people, including the two drivers, were rushed to St Hilda's Hospital, Hartlepool, on Friday morning, but only one of the drivers was detained, following a collision between a National Coal Board van and a car on the road between Blackhall and Hesleden. The accident happened at a bend close to Blackhall Modern School.

The driver of the car, Leslie Davison (41), of Eastleigh, Thornley, was detained in hospital with chest injuries and later his condition was reported to be "fairly good."

Two of his passengers, Mrs Sandra Thompson (41) and Mr Colin Thompson (20), both of Emmerson Square, Thornley, were allowed home after treatment for minor injuries, and the driver of the van, Leslie Middleton (45), of Whitroute Road, Hartlepool, was also allowed to return home after being treated for facial cuts and a broken wrist.

After the crash Peterlee Fire Brigade were called to put out a fire, which broke out in the engine of one of the vehicles.

19 January 1968

FUNERAL OF MRS PEART (FORMERLY OF THORNLEY)

Funeral took place at Carlisle crematorium of Mrs F M Peart of Borrowdale, who died in Carlisle Hospital after a short illness. Before moving to the Lake District, on her retirement some years ago, Mrs Peart resided at Thornley for some 30 years. Mrs Peart with her husband, sons Fred and Harry came to Thornley in 1929 when Mr Peart took over the headmastership of the Thornley Junior School. Mrs Peart, herself a school teacher, mainly did her teaching in the Trimdon area.

It was not long before their presence was felt in local politics, and both Mr and Mrs Peart became Rural District Councillors in the Easington area as well as holding a number of positions in area politics.

In 1937 Mr Peart became a County Councillor and Mrs Peart once again sought nomination for the Easington Rural District Council and alongside her came her son Fred, who since those days as a party member of the Thornley Labour Party has now reached the pinnacle of politics, and is now present Minister of Agriculture.

On the way to the funeral Mr Peart and his wife Elizabeth and son Emmerson, were involved in a car crash at Keswick, but after hospital treatment they continued to the service suffering from shock and bruises.

Representing Thornley villagers at the service was Coun Nicholson and Coun J R Bosomworth.

SISTERHOOD – Mrs Gratton was speaker at Wheatley Hill Methodist Sisterhood. She was thanked by Mrs Galley, who presided. The lesson was read by Miss H King and a solo was sung by Mrs Herd. Accompanist was Mrs Ord. Minutes and correspondence were read by the secretary, Mrs Lister.

WHEATLEY HILL WORKMEN'S CLUB - Annual ballot for officers and committee resulted in a defeat, by a narrow margin, of Mr B Aitken, the long-serving secretary, by Mr L Jones, a 22-year-old local government official. Others elected were, Messrs S Hughes (chairman) and J Maddison (treasurer) and R O'Conner (doorman). There were 32 candidates for the committee, and the six elected were Messrs J Bradley, J Tempest, R Bradley, M Bailes, R Carr and G Rowlands.
26 January 1968

'MINE HOSTS'

After two years as 'Mine Hosts' at the Jolly Potter in Newbottle, Mr Bobby Raine and his wife Mary, left to take charge of the new Tavern at Wheatley Hill.

Although Mary's name has been painted above the door at the 'Potters,' which naturally derives its existence from the pottery which functioned nearby, Bobby has assisted her after completing his work as a locomotive fireman at the NCB Engine works at Philadelphia.

At Wheatley Hill the licence is in his name, for he has given up pulling trucks of coal in favour of pulling pints.
2 February 1968

GOLDEN WEDDING

Still wielding his baton as conductor of Thornley Colliery band, although only a month off his 76th birthday, Mr Edward G T Kitto, one of Durham County's best-known and well-loved bandsmen, celebrates his golden wedding today. He and his wife Ethel, whose maiden name was Brereton, were married in Bow Street Methodist Church, Thornley, on February 23 1918, by the Rev Amos Ryder. They live at 37 Greenwood Cottages, Thornley.

In 1921 Mr Kitto took over as bandmaster at Thornley, and with the exception of a short break he has since filled this important position- a record of service with one band that surely must be unparalleled in the county.

During his conductorship the band has won more than 200 prizes as a combination, while individual bandsmen in solo contests have won 150 more.

"Music has brought me great joy throughout my life," Mr Kitto, who enjoys excellent health, told our reporter this week. He added, "I have had my discouragements but I have always been one to look on the bright side, and looking back I feel I have a lot to be proud of."

Top honour

One of the band's outstanding successes was winning in 1929 a contest in the City Hall, Newcastle, sponsored by the BBC- stiff opposition came from 27 other bands. Three times also they won prizes at the Crystal Palace contest - on one of these occasions, Mr Kitto was presented with a silver-mounted ebony baton, which he still treasures – and they also won the Durham County Brass Band Championship which carried with it "The Northern Echo" One Hundred Guinea Challenge Trophy.

As well as still regularly attending two band practices every week, Mr Kitto is "booked up" virtually every other night of the week teaching other members of the band in twos and threes either at his home or the band headquarters. He said "I can safely say I have never had less than 80 per cent of my own pupils in the band,"

Mr Kitto's conductorship is not confined to the Thornley Band - he has been guest conductor for many other bands in the area – and he remembers in his younger days taking no fewer than three bands on a Sunday.

Busy life

He recalled: "I used to conduct Shotton Colliery Band in the morning, return home for dinner and then go off to Trimdon to conduct the Temperance Band there. And then at night I had weekly band practice with my band at Thornley. It was a busy life, but I loved it and my wife gave me every encouragement."

Another proud moment for Mr Kitto was when Thornley Band was invited to take part in the Durham Cathedral service on Durham miners' gala day.

Mr Kitto's career as a bandsman began when he was only 15 as a solo cornetist in Spennymoor Salvation Army Band. Soon he was made deputy bandmaster and after four years in this position, conducted Thornley SA band for six years before taking over the baton of the Colliery band.

Composed too

Apart from his work with the band Mr Kitto is an accomplished organist and pianist and he has also found time to compose marches and hymns and arrange music for various combinations of instruments.

Mr Kitto played in the orchestra, which was formed to accompany the augmented choir of the former Patton St. Methodist Church at Wheatley Hill when they presented their annual Good Friday oratorio and he was also choirmaster at this church for two years. At one time also he was conductor of the now defunct Thornley Orchestral Society.

Mr Kitto's love of music is shared by his only two sons, Edward of Thornley and Gordon of Peterlee, who have both played in Thornley band, and his six grandchildren, who either play the piano or a brass instrument.

A native of Spennymoor, Mr Kitto began work at Page Bank colliery when he left school at 14, he left home at 3.40 every morning to start his shift and did not get back until six at night. "I had two miles to walk to get the carriage which took me to work," he said. And his early wages, he recalled, were 15s 7d a fortnight.

Apprenticeship

Mt Kitto worked there only a short time and then began serving his time at Spennymoor as a monument mason. But after three years his parents moved to Thornley and he went back down the pit, working there for 48 years until his retirement t en years ago. Mrs Kitto, who was 71 last week, is a native of Staffordshire. Like her husband, she enjoys good health. The couple met at Wheatley Hill and most of their married life was spent there until they moved to an aged miner's home three years ago.

Mr and Mrs Kitto are both members of Wheatley Hill Over 60 Club, and Mrs Kitto, who still has a good voice, is a member of the concert party. They are also members of Wheatley Hill Methodist Church.

Tomorrow the couple are holding a celebration party in Thornley Welfare Hall.

WHEATLEY HILL PIT TO CLOSE

The early closure of another Durham pit – the 100-year-old Wheatley Hill Colliery-was announced by the National Coal Board on Tuesday. They say it has now reached the end of its economically workable reserves.

There are 500 men employed at the colliery and when it closes on 3 May only about 40 of them will remain on salvage work. The Board will be able to find jobs for the younger men at other collieries within daily travelling distance, but it is expected that the older miners will become redundant.

The closure was announced by Mr Sam W Potts, the NCB's South Durham Area Director, at a special meeting of the Colliery Consultative Committee. He explained that for a long time the colliery had been working at a loss in extracting the remaining reserves.

Further Discussions

This had been made worse in the last few months because of deterioration in the quality of the coal at a time when the Board was faced with a declining market.

Mr John Rooney, general treasurer of the Durham Area NUM, said that while the workmen's representatives accepted the problems facing the Board they were concerned about the social consequences of possible redundancies.

The meeting was also attended by Mr John Varley, Regional Officer of COSA, and Mr Rees Irvin, general secretary of Durham Area NACODS.

Further discussions will take place between representatives of the unions and the Board about the details of alterative jobs for the Wheatley Hill men.

23 February 1968

JOBS AT OTHER COLLIERIES

As Wheatley Hill miners streamed out of a packed meeting at the Welfare Hall on Sunday, which had been called by their lodge officials to give them details of the closure of their 99-year-old pit, they faced a warm February sun…. but their future prospects in the mining industry were anything but sunny. In fact (writes Norman Passfield) for many of the 605 men employed at the colliery, whose closure on 3 May was officially announced last week, redundancy stares them blankly in the face, with bleak prospects of alternative employment.

So far, the meeting was told by miners' lodge secretary, Coun Anthony Wharrier, who has six years to go before reaching retirement age, the Coal Board has made plans for the transfer of 75 miners to other collieries, about an eighth of the number at present employed at the colliery. Fifty will be transferred to Easington Colliery, 15 to South Hetton and ten to Shotton.

These figures, Coun Wharrier told me after the meeting, did not include mechanics or enginemen. Forty men will be retained at the colliery on salvage work after it closes down. "But at the moment," said Coun Wharrier, "we do not know what will happen to the rest of the workmen."

Between now and the closure there will be quite a number of meetings with the Coal Board and Durham Area NUM. to discuss the men's future. "And," said Coun Wharrier, "we will be pressing our utmost for more jobs to be found for the men at nearby collieries."

The lodge officials are also to try and obtain "concrete information" from the Coal Board about the future of the pits to which the men from Wheatley Hill are being transferred.

"While we had quite a good meeting, with the men promising to give the Coal Board their fullest co-operation," said Coun Wharrier, "much concern was expressed about the working prospects at these other pits. With the industry in such a precarious state they do not relish being transferred to another pit and then finding it closing down after they have been there perhaps only a few months – they do not want to be like yo-yos, moving from one pit to another."

Another complaint

They were also against being transferred to South Hetton colliery, for they thought it was much too far to travel from their home in Wheatley Hill. "We are to point this out to the Coal Board and see what can be done in the matter," said Coun Wharrier.

Another complaint of the miners, said the lodge secretary, was that although the Coal Board must have known for years that pits would have to be closed in the area there had been no attempt to bring alternative employment. Coun Wharrier added, "They are very dissatisfied about the lack of industry here."

Presiding over the lodge meeting was Mr Brian Miller who, at the age of 24, is believed to be the youngest miners' lodge chairman in the country. He was elected to office a year ago.

Married, with an eighteen-month-old son, Mr Miller is a power-loader at the colliery. Like his colleagues he has no idea yet what will happen to him when the pit-cage wheels turn for the last time. "These pit closures hit young married men particularly hard," he said.

Miners with young families, who know nothing else but pit work, have anything but a happy outlook – especially those who have been earning good money at the coal-face.

Father of five

Typical of these is 31-year-old Mr Harry Maratty, father of five young children between the ages of three and eight, who lives with his wife Norma at 6 Wheatley Terrace, Wheatley Hill. As a power-loader he brings home about £21 a week.

He told me, "We felt at the colliery there was something 'in the wind' during the past six months because there has been little development, but we did not expect the pit to close so soon."

Mr Maratty, who also has an 18-year old stepdaughter, has worked at the colliery since he left school at 15 but now, he said, he was seriously thinking of leaving the pits for good. He added, "The way things are going all around here there does not seem much future – and what is the good of being transferred to another pit only to find it closing as well, just as you are nicely settled in."

It would mean a "big drop in their income" if her husband did not get another job, said Mrs Maratty – as well as themselves their children would have to "go short" of a lot of things.

"Not fair play"

She added, "I don't think they have played fair with the miners – steps should have been taken long before now to bring other employment. There is just nothing for them."

Another miner, 34-year-old, Mr Jim Rowbotham, of 8 York Street, Wheatley Hill, accepts the pit closures philosophically. He said "We cannot make any better of it. There is, apparently, no life in the pit and so the Coal Board have no other option but close it."

Though married with a young daughter, Mr Rowbotham said he was not particularly worried. He had been working "at bank" for the past eight years and was used to "small money."

He added," If I'm transferred all well and good, if not, I will have to start looking for another job and it cannot mean less money than I am making now."

Mr Robert Cowie (46), a bachelor, of 4 Weardale Street, Wheatley Hill, said he thought the pit "would have lasted at least another year." Employed as a hauler-man at the colliery for the past 15 years, Mr Cowie said he would not mind going to Easington Colliery – but the collieries at South Hetton and Shotton did not look so good where the future was concerned.

Too many

Mr Cowie maintained there had been "too many closures" in too short a time. "They should have been spaced out better to give the men better chances of employment. First Wingate, then came Deaf Hill and Trimdon Grange and now Wheatley Hill."

And what did a former miners' leader at Wheatley Hill have to say about the closure?

Mr Edward Cain, a retired rural councillor and magistrate, who will be 77 in a fortnight's time, was a lodge official for 35 years until his retirement 11 years ago, for most of this time he was secretary. He said, "The closure is inevitable. It is part of the great industrial revolution which has been going on since man began to think, and it will go on."

He was sorry for the men that the colliery was closing, throwing so many of them out of work, but at the same time he would not call it a "tragedy", in fact it could be a "Godsend." "The sooner men can get away from the dangers, hazards and dirt of mining, the better," declared Mr Cain. "If a man can get a job out of the pit he wants to take it, and I know what I am talking about for I first started work down the Dolly Pit at Herrington in 1905."

Historical Note

Wheatley Hill colliery was sunk in 1869.

Only two years later, on 19 January 1871, disaster struck the pit. Five miners lost their lives during an inrush of water and many others had narrow escapes.

1 March 1968

WHAT, ANOTHER TIP?

Household refuse has to be tipped somewhere, but Wingate Parish council feel that their area is getting more than its fair share of rubbish dumps.

Despite strong protest from the council, Hartlepool Corporation were recently given permission to tip on a site at Tilery Farm, Wingate, and there have been many complaints from local residents about the tip Easington Rural Council are using near Durham Road, Wheatley Hill.

At their meeting this week the parish council heard that yet another tip is proposed for the area, at an old quarry near Wheatley Hill.

When Hartlepool Corporation applied for planning permission to tip at Wingate the parish council were too late with their objection, but this time they have been quick off the mark and an objection to the quarry tipping has gone to Durham County Council.

Whether this will have any effect remains to be seen. But Coun Mrs Doreen Dodds warned at this week's meeting that they should be "careful" about their objections. She felt it could serve a useful purpose to fill in the quarry and it should not give rise to the same complaints as the other tips.

Rubbish, of course, has to be tipped somewhere and as long as it is not causing a nuisance to householders, with debris flying about their doors and windows, there should be no objections.

One suggestion at the parish council was that the rural authority should investigate the possibility of incinerators to dispose of the refuse.

This would probably be a costly affair, but it might be one solution to the whole vexed question, and end the complaints of those who have to "live with the tips."

LUDWORTH COUPLE'S GOLDEN

On 9 March 1918, at the Parish Church of Wheatley Hill, Mr Thomas Alfred Bell, of Wingate, was married to Miss Annie Dobbin, of Wheatley Hill.

The father of Mr Bell belonged to the North-East, and when he left the sea he became a colliery sinker and worked down the coast at various pits including Easington and Horden. He settled at Station Town, Wingate, and worked at Wingate Grange Colliery. He was in the mine at Wingate when the explosion occurred in 1906 causing loss of life of 24 workmen. He was more fortunate than many of his fellows and sheltered in an air lock. He was in the pit from 12 o'clock on Saturday night and got out at 3 pm on Tuesday.

Mr Thomas Alfred Bell began work at Wingate pit, but later went to Deaf Hill. He was a pony putter at 15 years of age, a hand putter at 17 years and started hewing at 18½ years. He worked at Thornley, Wheatley Hill, Shotton, Kelloe, Deaf Hill and finally Sherburn Hill, retiring at 65 after 50 years in mining.

Mr and Mrs Bell set up housekeeping at Wheatley Hill, afterwards getting a colliery house at Ludworth. A likeable couple, modest and unaffected, they are highly respected in the village. Mr Bell has one interest, greyhounds and he rears dogs for racing, at various local courses.

Mrs Bell is a Methodist and devoted to her church. She was for some years a member of Wheatley Hill Methodist Choir. Her eldest son John was the first boy to be presented with a Bible from the Women's Bright Hour.

The family of Mr and Mrs Bell consists of three sons, John, Desmond and Clive, and two daughters, Violet and Nancy. They are all married and there are nine grandchildren.

A surprise celebration for their parents was arranged by the youngest daughter and her husband, Mr and Mrs Williamson, 28 St Bede's Crescent, Thornley. This took place on Saturday at the British Legion Hall at Ludworth

COLLIERY ACCIDENT

One miner was killed and another injured in an accident at the Tilley Seam of Thornley Colliery early on Wednesday morning. The dead man was Mr Russell Eric Fulcher (42), 6 Eighth Street, Wheatley Hill.His workmate was Mr Joseph Hartley (43), Barnard Avenue, Ludworth, who was taken to Durham County Hospital with head and facial injuries. Later he was transferred to Sunderland General Hospital, where his condition was said to be "poorly."

It is believed that the men were struck by a flying girder when there was a fall of stone.

Mr Fulcher, who has worked at the pit since leaving school, leaves a widow and a family of three sons and one daughter ranging in age from two to 17.
29 March 1968

GOLDEN AT THORNLEY

On April 13, 1918, Mr Thomas Lambert and his bride Miss Hannah Ward drove in a horse-drawn hansom cab to St Saviour's Church Shotton to be married. The Rev E Fenton officiated at the ceremony. On Saturday they celebrated their Golden Wedding.

The couple have two sons, George and Allan. They and their wives arranged a quiet family party at the eldest son's home in Wheatley Hill. It was attended by their four grandchildren. On Monday, Mr and Mrs Lambert were at their own home to celebrate with their friends and neighbours.

Mr Lambert was born in Thornley and spent about 12 years at Thornley Colliery. He always felt the lure of an open air life and found employment with Sedgefield Rural Council housing department. He was employed as a labourer on drains and road making. Then after five years he transferred to Durham County Council laying curbs and flags. He served the County for 34 years until he retired at 65.

An accident to his back prevented his acceptance for war service in the First World War.

Always interested in the land and farming he helped out at local farms.
Was Keen Pig Breeder
At haytime and harvest he worked long hours. He was a keen pig breeder on his own account. When the old steam threshers went round the farms, he was a regular hand.

Mr Lambert, who is 74 is a life long Methodist. For 45 years he sat in the family pew in Thornley Waterloo Street, Wesleyan church, where he was christened. He commented, "I remember when the churches were full for ordinary services. At Waterloo Street on Sunday School anniversary days I have seen 500 in the church. Things are different today. Lack of example on the part of the parents and lack of discipline among the children and young people are contributory factors in the decline of church attendance. People would rather go to bingo than go to church."

542

With his wife, who is 72, Mr Lambert is a member of Thornley Over 60 Club. Mrs Lambert has been very active in the movement and for six years was assistant secretary,

Mrs Lambert was born at Shotton. She was a regular worshipper at St Saviour's Anglican Church. She also Worshipped at St Luke's Ferryhill, where she spent some years in the service of Canon Lomax. Her chief interest has been helping old people. Wherever there was need or illness Mrs Lambert was there to help.

She would wash and clean for those who could not help themselves. The couple enjoy reasonably good health and with the help of their daughter-in-law, get along fine.

Mr Lambert's last comment "Fifty years is a long time, but Hannah has been a good wife in fact one of the best."

LONG ODDS ACCIDENT KILLED MINER AT THORNLEY

A verdict of accidental death was returned by the jury at a Peterlee inquest, last week, on Mr Russell Eric Fulcher (42), of Eighth Street, Wheatley Hill, who died in an accident at Thornley Colliery on March 27.

Mr Frank Purvis, a stoneman, of Hillsyde Crescent, Thornley, said that he was working underground at the colliery removing stone with a group of other men in the early hours of March27.

Mr Purvis was working with some other men and they wanted a girder to support the roof.

Mr Purvis added "We had this 14 foot long girder for them and it was lowered on to the caunch table which is a metal table placed over the conveyor belt to protect the conveyor from damage." The girder was brought to its point of balance and then slid forward towards the place it was required until only 18ins to two feet were left on the table and the remainder was on the ground.

The front end of the girder had become lodged in some coal and Mr Fulcher and another man were bending over it trying to free it so that it could be moved back a few inches then moved to the place it was needed.

Massive Stone

Mr Purvis continued, "At that moment a massive stone broke away and caught the end of the girder on the table lifting the other end up. They must have just got it loose when this happened because it came up at a terrific rate."

He could not see what had happened to Mr Fulcher as the stone blocked his view,

Mr William Smith, an overman, of Emmerson Square, Thornley, said he believed that when the girder came up it had pressed Mr Fulcher by the head against the roof. He was severely injured and although first aid was administered there was little they could do.

Mr Smith said he had never known a similar sort of thing happen before. The practice of passing girders over the caunch table had now been stopped.

The Coroner, Mr P Ord, said that when the inquest was opened Dr J Grey had said that Mr Fulcher had severe head and neck injuries and had died from asphyxia.

The doctor had also paid tribute to the first aid carried out by Mr Smith and other men at the time of the accident.

Mr Ord commented, "It must be long odds against a stone falling down and hitting one end of the girder and lifting the other up so that it struck Mr Fulcher."

19 April 1968

REDUNDANT MINERS LESS THAN FIRST FEARED
AT WHEATLEY HILL

When Wheatley Hill Colliery closes next Friday the number of redundant miners will be much less than was first feared, the miners' lodge secretary, Coun Anthony D Wharrier, disclosed this week.

"In fact," he told our reporter, "I think I can go so far as to say we are quite pleased with the large number of men who have been found jobs at other collieries. In these depressing days in the industry, when you can switch between 60 and 70 per cent to neighbouring collieries when a pit is closed down there is not much to grumble at."

When the closure of the colliery, because it had reached "the end of its economically workable reserves", was first announced by the Coal Board in February, the miners' lodge at a meeting a few days later heard that only about 75 of the 500 men would be transferred to other collieries.

But now, said Coun Wharrier that figure has shot up to 320. Of the remaining180, 42 will be retained on salvage work at the colliery for some time. The rest who will become redundant are mostly over 60 years of age.

Gloom Dispelled

On the whole, said Coun Wharrier, this was quite a satisfactory position, much better than the gloomy outlook prevailing when it was first announced that the 100- year-old was to close.

No fewer than 108 men are being transferred to Easington Colliery, in the initial stages only 50 were going there, and this week 52 miners began new jobs at Blackhall Colliery, 42 of them piece workers and the other ten datal workers.

"Mostly", said Coun Wharrier, "the datal workers are going to the collieries of their choice but we had to put 'cavils' in for the piece workers". Twelve miners are being transferred to Shotton colliery and others are going to Horden, East Hetton (Kelloe) and Thornley collieries.

Well Satisfied

"Quite a number of meetings had been held with Coal Board officials", said Coun Wharrier, "and there had been long negotiations. But," he said, "there had been "splendid" co-operation all round" with the management and miners' lodges at the neighbouring collieries. He added, "We are well satisfied with the progress that has been made."

When Wheatley Hill colliery eventually closes, said Coun Wharrier, more men, about 40 to 50, are expected to be added to the Blackhall colliery where, over 60 were interviewed and given the chance to become redundant and make way for younger men.

BANNER TO LEAD MAY DAY PARADE

Though the colliery works its last shift next Friday, the miners' lodge banner will not be in "cold storage" for long, the following day, accompanied by the colliery band, it will be flying aloft at the head of the Easington Division Labour Party May Day annual parade at Wheatley Hill.

"By a coincidence," said Coun Wharrier, "it is Wheatley Hill's turn as hosts for the May Day parade and so, the day after our pit closes, we will be out in full force to take part in the May Day celebrations in the village." Bands and banners will also be on parade from all the other mining villages in the Easington Area.

The Wheatley Hill Band has also been invited to take part in the Durham Cathedral service at this year's Miners' Gala Day. "We were delighted to accept this invitation and so our band and banner will be on view again that day." Said Coun Wharrier.

WHEATLEY HILL CLOUD HAS SILVER LINING

The outlook for the 500 miners employed at Wheatley Hill Colliery, which is to close next Friday, is not so gloomy after all.

It was welcome news this week to hear from the miners' lodge Secretary, Coun Anthony Wharrier, that jobs have been found at other collieries, all within reasonable travelling distance, for no fewer than 320 men. Some of the remainder will be kept on at Wheatley Hill for salvage work.

A number are going to the coastal collieries at Easington and Blackhall, where over-60's were interviewed and given the chance to become redundant to make way for younger men from Wheatley Hill.

The response was quite good, and in keeping with the neighbourly spirit to be found in mining communities.

On Monday, 52 miners from Wheatley Hill already took up new jobs at Blackhall. And there are prospects of this number being increased.

Generally speaking, it is a shattering blow to a mining village these days, when the Coal Board announced that the axe is to fall on their colliery. But it is heartening, as in the case of Wheatley Hill, to find that things do not turn out quite so badly as originally feared, that it is not "the end of the world" after all.

At Wheatley Hill, says the lodge secretary, there has been fine co-operation between the Coal Board officials and men. This has undoubtedly helped considerably in the protracted negotiations to find the men employed elsewhere.

It is to be hoped that such co-operation continues at other collieries in the county when it comes to their turn for closure.

26 April 1968

WHEATLEY HILL CLOSES
But Other Pit Jobs Elsewhere If They Are Needed

Though the depressing weather, it was dull, wet and misty, matched the thoughts of the men at Wheatley Hill Colliery as they worked their last shift at the 100-year-old pit last Friday (writes Norman Passfield), the outlook as far as their future jobs were concerned was quite bright.

A total of 505 workers at the colliery, which was closed because it had reached the end of its economically workable reserves and Mr Wilfred Hall, the 56-year-old manager, told me the good news that "every man who wanted another job in the pits has got one."

There were, he said, only 103 redundant, and these were mostly men who were turned 60, were in ill-health, or, because of home circumstances, had decided to finish work a year or two before they were 65. More than 100 miners were transferred to both Blackhall and Easington collieries, 16 to Shotton, while fitters, deputies and officials had gone to Horden and other collieries in the area where they were required.

Forty-five men are being retained at the colliery on salvage work and this is expected to last about 22 weeks. One of these, Mr Reg Presho (58), of Kings Road, Wingate, who has been training officer at the colliery for the past two and a half years will act as salvage foreman.

The Second

"But when this work is completed, I will be quite satisfied to pack up work altogether," he told me. It is the second pit he has worked at which has been closed down. The other was Wingate, where he was an official for many years. When this pit closed in 1962 he was transferred to Horden colliery and remained there until his appointment as training officer at Wheatley Hill.

Friday marked the end of 44 years unbroken service at the colliery for Mr Jack Booth, also 58, of 34 Johnson Estate, Wheatley Hill. "It's rather a sad day, the colliery has many memories, both happy and sad, for me and it seems rather strange coming out of the pit, knowing it is for the very last time," said Mr Booth, when I spoke to him in the colliery lamp cabin at the end of his last shift.

Decided To Retire

About a year ago Mr Booth, who is married with a son and daughter, was in hospital and is still not in the best of health. "And so," he said, "although I had the chance of going to another colliery, I decided to retire. I didn't fancy going to another pit at my time of life, after spending so many years at Wheatley Hill."

Mr Booth has worked at the colliery from leaving school at the age of 14 and for the past 19 years has been a deputy.

Mr William Higham (53), of 97 Wordsworth Avenue, Wheatley Hill, who has also worked at the colliery the whole time since leaving school, said he was "quite worried" when it was first announced the pit was to close, especially at my age," he added.

But, he said things had turned out much better than anyone had expected. He was among those transferring to Blackhall colliery. He added, "It is a different type of mining there, more mechanised, but I expect I will get used to it. I am only too happy not to be out of work."

For Peterlee Flat

A widower, with a married daughter, Mr Higham hopes soon to move to a new flat in Peterlee to be nearer his new job.

One of the younger men, 26-year-old Mr Robert Burns, who has worked as a mechanic at the colliery for the past ten years, will find his new job much nearer home. He lives at 54 Alnwick Street, Horden, and he is being transferred "either to Horden or Blackhall."

He said, "Although I will not have so far to travel to work I will miss Wheatley Hill, it has been a homely colliery and I have lots of good pals among my workmates."

Only six miners will be leaving the industry altogether. "I had the chance of going to Blackhall," one of these, 40-year-old Mr Joseph Ronald Craggs, a deputy and shotfirer, of 4 Durham Street, Wheatley Hill, said, "but I thought now was the time to get out of the pits and try my hand at something else, better now than waiting another few years."

Mr Craggs, married with three children, took up new employment this week with the Peterlee Cabinet Company. He said, "It is all right being transferred to these other collieries, but how long will they last? No one can say and I don't fancy being shifted from one colliery to another all the time."

Stuck Together

His friend, Mr John Findley (39) also a shot firer, of 12 Gowland Terrace, Wheatley Hill said, "we have always stuck together at work and in social life. "Mr Findley, has also quit mining, though he has worked at Wheatley Hill since leaving school.

At the moment, he said, he had no job, but he was having an interview for the Government Training Scheme, and he was not particularly worried. "Anything is better than the pit," he declared. "We don't want to be left on the shelf when we are about 50."

Friday was "rather a sad day, too," for the manageress of the pit canteen at Wheatley Hill, Mrs Annie Coates (64), of 47 Thornlaw North, Thornley. As she stood over the cooking range frying the last dinners to be served in the canteen, traditionally enough for a Friday, fish and chips, she told me, "It is with real regret that I am leaving here today. I have enjoyed my work among the miners, they are a jolly lot and I have made hundreds of friends.

Disabled

Mrs Coates, whose husband Edward has been a disabled miner for 30 years, he was injured in an accident at East Hetton colliery, will not be seeking a new job. She said "I have had to work to eke out the family income all these years, now, like some of the men, I am going to retire."

Mrs Coates has worked at the canteen for the past 15 years and has been manageress for five. Her daughter Mrs Rita Maughan has been one of her assistants for the past two years, and the other member of staff, Mrs Vera Templeton, has been there four years.

Mrs Coates said it had been her "particular pleasure" to cook the meals twice a week for the local "Meals on Wheels" service for the old people in the area.

Final tribute

A final tribute to his workmen came from the colliery manager in a letter posted at various points on the surface during the pit's last few working days.

It read, "May I thank you for the splendid effort you have made to keep the colliery going on an even keel to the end? I feel sure you can be really proud of the example of conscientiousness and commonsense which has prevailed during a difficult period. May I also take this opportunity of wishing you all good luck at your new colliery, I feel sure you will give them the same cooperation which you have given me."

By a coincidence Wheatley Hill colliery is the third to close while Mr Hall has been manager in the last three years. The first was Sherburn Hill in 1965, the next Bowburn last July, and now Wheatley Hill, where Mr Hall has been manager since November.

At the moment Mr Hall does not know where he is going next. "I am off on a week's course and then I have a fortnight's holiday, but after that, well I just don't know," he said.

PROUD LODGE BANNER IN WISTFUL MAY DAY EVENT

In contrast to the dull weather, which marked the closure of Wheatley Hill colliery the previous day, bright sunshine greeted Easington Divisional Labour Party's annual May Day parade in the village on Saturday afternoon, and crowds lined the main street to catch a final glimps of their local miners' lodge banner.

When the pit closed, the banner will no longer be seen at a May Day parade, but, with the colliery band having been invited to play in Durham Cathedral, it will make "positively its last appearance" on Durham Miners' Gala Day.

It was "deplorable" said Mr Emanuel Shinwell, MP for Easington, who marched proudly, and buoyantly for his 82 years, at the head of the parade, that they should be celebrating May Day immediately after the Coal Board had closed the local colliery. He added, "It is more like a funeral ceremony than a May Day celebration. May Day was for many years associated with that great miners' leader Peter Lee. What has happened now is enough to make him turn in his grave."

Sprightly

Marching alongside Mr Shinwell and the banner and band of Wheatley Hill miners' lodge was sprightly Mr Edward Cain, who was a lodge official for well over 40 years before his retirement in 1956. Mr Cain, now 77, was also a magistrate on the Castle Eden Bench for many years until he retired two years ago.

It was at the special invitation of the lodge that Mr Cain took part in this "last march," "it was a pleasure for us to invite him and a delight when he accepted," said the lodge secretary, Mr "Anty" Wharrier who, with the lodge's 24 year-old chairman, Mr Brian Miller, treasurer Mr Stephen Wragg, and committee members, also marched beneath the silken banner.

Honoured to be banner-carriers on this rather sad but memorable day were Messrs J Dunn. E Stanforth, T Broughton, R Starke, E Redshaw, W Howarth, C Robinson and R Teasdale.

Other Lodges

Six other miners' lodges from the Easington area, Murton, Thornley, Blackhall, Horden, Easington and Shotton, with their banners and bands also joined the parade, together with several women's sections of the Labour Party carrying their green and white standards.

Mr Derek Scollard conducted the Wheatley Hill Band, and the secretary Mr Edward Newby said

Wheatley Hill Colliery Band and Banner

that although they would lose financial help from the Welfare sources, now that the colliery was closed, they were thinking of approaching the local council and the public for support to keep it from disbanding.

The parade went to the Workmen's Club Hall where the Divisional chairman, Mrs Ivy Spry, introduced the speakers, Mr Shinwell and Mrs Buchan, wife of Mr Norman Buchan, MP for Renfrew West.

Speaking on the national situation, Mr Shinwell said nothing would please him more than that devaluation should meet with success, that the standard of living should improve and that a clash with the trade unions could be avoided.

He went on "Confidence in Government policy might then prove to be a winner at the next election. But if it should fail, not only would the Government suffer defeat, but Labour could lose trade union support. That would spell disaster for the Labour Party. The Government should take note that the days when MPs could be herded into the Division lobbies, despite their doubts about Government policy, are coming to an end." Mr Shinwell said that unless some defects in the Prices and Incomes policy were removed loyalty of many Labour MPs could be "severely strained."

He added, "far too many decisions are left to the Prices and Incomes Board, where the dice seems to be heavily loaded against the workers. Demands for wage increases are regarded as a crime against Society, yet profits which are on the increase are considered to be a sign of prosperity and economic recovery. That is not the kind of policy to celebrate on May Day."

10 May 1968

THORNLEY – Mr R Smith presided over a meeting of the Thornley British Legion in the Officials' Club. Business details were dealt with by the sectetary, Mr J High, Mr R Brookes presented a satisfactory financial statement. Mr A Johnson, delegate to the No 10 Mixed Group meeting at Ferryhill Station, reported on decisions taken. He was elected delegate to the national conference at Hastings in June.

DANCE – The newly-formed Thornley Men's Section of the British Legion continue to make an impact on the life of the village and on Saturday evening held its first annual dance in the Welfare Hall. The chairman, Mr R Smith, introduced the president, Dr John Gray, who welcomed 250 members and guests. Dr Gray gave a short address on the work done by the Legion. Dancing was enjoyed to the music of Billy Pratt's Band. Mr C Laidler was MC. The lucky door prize number, a hamper of food, was won by Mr H Cockerham. The event was organised by Mr R Smith (chairman), Mr J High (secretary), Mr R Brookes (treasurer) and the entertainments committee.

17 May 1968

LEAVING LUDWORTH – Mr Clifford Collingwood, an advertising representative with the Durham Advertiser Series of newspapers for the past five years, left this week to take up a post as general manager of a Dartmouth newspaper. Mr Collingwood has been living at Ludworth with his wife Linda and two-year-old daughter Ashley. Mrs Collingwood is daughter of Mr and Mrs L Stogdale, licensees of the Queen's Head Inn there

24 May 1968

VILLAGE SPORTS ARE ON DESPITE WHEATLY HILL PIT CLOSURE

Though the recent closure of Wheatley Hill colliery has meant the end of the miners' threepence-a-week levy which went towards the cost of the children's annual sports day, this year's sports day will still be held, on Saturday 22 June.

"We have built up quite a large balance over the years the pit has been working and there should eventually be sufficient to cover the cost of the day," the treasurer of the organising committee of the Wheatley Hill Colliery Federation Board, Mr Jack Hedley, told our reporter. He added, "if it is a sunny day we should end on the right side financially for it will mean a good turn-out of people, with support for side-shows, refreshments, etc."

And once again it will be a case of " all prizes and no blanks" for the children. Every child taking part in the sports will receive a two-shilling savings stamp, whether or not among the winners. In addition, there will be a mass distribution of bags of chocolate valued 3s 6d each to all the 1,800 children eligible.

Eligible for the gifts are all the village children of school age and children of miners who travelled to work at Wheatley Hill Colliery from neighbouring villages. "There fathers paid the levy even though they did not live in Wheatley Hill and so the children are entitled to the gifts," Mr Hedley explained

Fancy Dress Parade

The day's programme starts with a fancy dress parade through the main streets of the village, headed by Wheatley Hill Colliery band. Jazz bands will also be in attendance and village tableaux, and the sports will be run off on the Girls' Modern school field.

There will be eight age groups for the sports, from five to 13 years. An arts and crafts exhibition is being held for children from 13 to 15, "usually children in this age group do not enter the races and so we thought it would be a good idea this year to invite them to send entries for arts and crafts, we hope there will be a good response," said Mr Hedley.

Once again a "mystery lady" will mingle among the crowds and the first person to challenge her correctly will receive a prize of £2. She is described on the official programme as "a well-known lady of Wheatley Hill aged between 40and 65." Resignation – Coun A D Wharrier has taken over as organising secretary in succession to Coun Mark Alderton, who has resigned for health reasons. Coun W Newby is chairman of the committee.

The officials hope that although the local pit has closed this will not be the last sports day in the village.

Said Mr Hedley, "We will, of course, no longer have any income from a miners' levy. But after these we are hoping to call a public meeting to consider ways and means of raising money to keep this sports day, a big day in the life of the village, going year after year. The future will depend on the response we get from the villagers themselves.

7 June 1968

MINERS TO PAY FOR VETERANS

Durham miners will be paying 1s.6d a week until September, to make sure the county's retired pitmen continue to get their free coal.

This payment is on top of their yearly 15cwt of concessionary coal to the free coal pool, which has been completely drained due to the reduced manpower in Durham.

Pitmen have agreed to pay the extra to help clear half a £184,000 debt, the Coal Board will pay the rest.

Mr George Atkinson, area industrial relations officer, said an alternative would have been to sacrifice more coal, to get the pool re-stocked.

In 1963 there were 66,500 pitmen contributing to the pool, and 17,000 receiving. Now there are about 20,000 receiving, but only 41,500 contributing.

Retired miners get two tons of free coal a year from the pool.

BEM FOR WHEATLEY HILL FIRE OFFICER

A Colliery fitter, Mr Harold Frank Horner, of Wordsworth Avenue, Wheatley Hill, who joined the Wheatley Hill retained unit of the Durham County Fire Brigade in his late teens and has now completed more than 26 years' service with the unit, was awarded the British Empire Medal in the Queens' Birthday Honours List published at the weekend.

Mr Horner who is 45 and married with three sons, joined the unit during the last war as an auxiliary fireman and remained with it when in 1947 it became a retained station of the local authority/

Four years ago Mr Horner was promoted Station Officer in charge of the unit and now has a force of 20 volunteers under him who deal with an average of 120 fires a year. Since April this year the unit has attended no fewer than 30 fires.

Honour For Station

Mr Horner already holds the Queen's Long Service Medal for 20 years service as a fireman and also has the Civil Service Medal.

Born at Tudhoe, Mr Horner moved to Wheatley Hill when he was 13 and a year later began work at the local colliery, he remained there until the pit closed down early last month and he was transferred as a fitter to Easington Colliery.

On receiving news of his award Mr Horner said he was quite proud of it but regarded it "as an honour for the station as well as himself.

14 June 1968

WHEATLEY HILL CA WILL CALL ITS OWN TUNE

Though his committee were prepared to pay up to 75 per cent of the cost of running the Association, the Association would virtually be left to make its own decisions, Mr Jack Dormand, Education Officer to the Easington Excepted District, assured a well-attended public meeting in Wheatley Hill Welfare Hall last week, when it was decided to form a Community Association in the village.

The Association will take over the responsibility of running the former Miners' Welfare Scheme in the village, a scheme which will become defunct through the recent closure of Wheatley Hill colliery and the end of the miners' levy which was its chief source of income.

The new Association said Mr Dormand, would have little interference from the Education committee. "in fact," he added, "I promise you this, that the Education Committee's hand on your shoulder will be as light as a feather, the Committee is really there to pay the piper without calling the tune, largely, decisions will be your own."

Leaflet "Raid"

Five thousand leaflets inviting the people of Wheatley Hill to the meeting had been distributed during the previous fortnight and although little more than 100 attended the meeting they were representative of virtually every local organisation and Mr Dormand and his fellow officials said they were delighted at such a splendid response.

Mr Dormand, who was introduced by Coun Jim Nichloson, chairman of the Education Committee, outlined in clear detail the aims and function of a Community Association.

The situation which faced Wheatley Hill people, he said, was one "of great challenge." He explained, "It was the first village in the Rural District where this situation has occurred after a colliery has been closed. The colliery was closed at Wingate a few years ago and there was a Welfare Scheme there but the position was slightly different. They had no Welfare Hall like you have here and, secondly, a Community Association was already in existence and they eventually took over the outdoor scheme with great success."

With the closure of the colliery at Wheatley Hill, said Mr Dormand, it was urgent that steps should be taken immediately to consider the future of the Welfare Scheme, which not only had a large Welfare Hall but also extensive playing areas, with bowling greens, tennis courts, etc.

To Give A Lead

The Education Committee had stepped in to give a lead because under the Education Act, they were not only concerned with schools but it was their legal liability to provide the kind of communal activities which the Welfare Scheme has been running, Mr Dormand added, "it is the genuine desire of the committee that this communal life continues, we want to see the conversion of the scheme into a Community Association."

The committee regarded a Community Centre as "the focal point of all community activity in a village", but he emphasised it was not their intention to "break up or fragment" existing village organisations. Rather, they wanted to co-ordinate them and help each section, with the principal aim of raising standards throughout the village and enriching its life.

No Limits

Mr Dormand continued, "There are no limits to the kind of activities which can be stimulated within the confines of a Community Association. We would like to see every organisation in the village become affiliated to the Association and be linked up as part of the fabric of the whole village."

Regarding maintenance of the premises and grounds, equipment and repairs, the Education Committee, said Mr Dormand, was empowered to grant financial aid up to 75 pre cent, the rest of the money, of course, would have to be raised by the Association itself.

The local parish council was also in order in making a financial contribution towards the upkeep of the Association and indeed, Wingate Parish Council had already assisted the local Miners' Welfare Scheme, said Mr Dormand.

Immediate Start Is Vital

Coun Nicholson, wishing the new Association every success, said it was imperative that they "got down to work" immediately. The Welfare Scheme funds were low, there was a balance at the moment of £133 and this would likely meet expenses for only about a month. Mr A Byass, representing CIS-WO, trustees for the Welfare property, said nothing would please his organisation more than to see the Community Association take over the Welfare Hall and grounds, and use them for the good of the village.

The following "holding" committee was elected to serve the new Association: Mrs E Powell (representing the Mothers' Club), Mr A Parsley (men's Bowling Club), Mrs Edna Hall (Ladies Bowling Club), Mrs J Mooring (Women's Institute), Mr R Hunter (Youth Club), Mr S Ragg (Welfare Committee), Coun W Newby (Parish Council), the Rev Maurice Henderson (Methodist minister), Father D Meagher (local Roman Catholic priest), Mr Les Barker (Scouts), Mr C Oswald (Photographic Society) and Mr Jack Andrew (Youth Club.

Rain hits Wheatley Hill sports day

In spite of the heavy rain, which fell in Wheatley Hill on Saturday morning and early afternoon, the local Miners' Federation Sports Day and Gala was not a complete washout. The jazz bands made a splash of colour in the grey streets of the village as they participated in a procession.

The heavy rain made the Wheatley Hill Peter Lee Girls' Modern School playing fields quite unfit for the children's sports. These were postponed until this week. The display of jazz bands took place in the Girl's school-yard. This was watched by a crowd of between 200 and 300.

Awards

Tableaux. 1 Wheatley Hill Mother's Club, 2 Wheatley Hill Women's section of the British Legion.

Jazz Bands parade, Band 1 Thornley, 2 Hedworth, 3 Pelton. **Drum Major** 1 Thornley, 2 Pelton, 3 Hedworth. **Bass drummer**, 1 Thornley, 2 Hedworth, 3 Pelton.

Display Band, 1 Thornley, 2 Hedworth, 3 Pelton. **Drum Major,** 1 Pelton, 2 Thornley, 3 Hedwrorth. **Band Major**, 1 a tie- Thornley, Hedworth and Pelton.

Bass drummer, 1 Thornley, 2 Hedworth, 3 Pelton. **Overall champions,** Thornley.

Fancy Dress, Children, 1 P and M Carr, 2 G Maxwell, 3 B Martin. **Original,** 1 C Thubron and C Wilson, 2 D Carr, 3 C Warnes. **Comic,** 1 S Charlton, 2 L Warnes, 3 P Hoban. **Adult Fancy Dress,** 1 J Morris, 2 G Dunnett.

Arts and Crafts, Girls 11-14, 1 K Bennett, 2 Marina Million, 3 L Armstrong. **Boys 13-14,** 1 C Davison, 2 J Youll, 3 J Darby. **Girls 15,** 1 J Smith.

Art, Girls 13-14, 1 Lynne Curry, 2 Jean Lowther, 3 Freda Haswell. **Boys 13-14,** 1 William Stanley, 2 Maurice Youll, 3 Fredrick Carr.

Mr J Hedley, Miners' Lodge treasurer, said that these sports would be the last under the auspices of the Wheatley Hill Miners' Federation Board. He expressed the hope that the community would take them over and the costs be raised by public subscriptions and contributions. The cost of this year's events, had been raised by the miners prior to the colliery closing, and amounted to £400.

About 1,600 children in the village received a bag of sweets and chocolate valued at 3/6.

Arrangements were in the hands of a committee headed by Mr W Newby (chairman), Mr A Wharrier (organising secretary), Mr J Hedley (treasurer). In spite of the adverse weather conditions, Mr Hedley said that all expenses had been cleared.
28 June 1968

COMMUNITY ASSOCIATION AT WHEATLEY HILL

The responsibility for Wheatley Hill Miners' Welfare Hall and the surrounding grounds has been taken over by the recently formed Wheatley Hill and District Community Association.

Previous responsibility for the hall lay with the Miners' Welfare Association, but at the first meeting of the association's management committee it was suggested that the property be invested in the name of Easington Rural District Council, and that a modest constitution be adopted.

Until the committee's next meeting at least, it was decided to continue lettings and charges for the hall as they were under the Miners' Welfare Association.

Formed only three weeks ago this was the first meeting of the association's management committee. The committee is now inviting members of the village to become members of the Association. Membership is available under the following categories, Individual, junior, family and associate and in addition the committee are giving organisations the opportunity to become affiliated.

Officers elected to the management committee, Coun A D Wharrier (chairman), Mr J Andrews (vice-chairman), the Rev M Henderson (hon secretary) and Mr C Oswald (hon treasurer).
5 July 1968

COLOUR, COMEDY, MUSIC IN THORNLEY COLLIERY SPORTS

After a week of rain, hail, gales, thunder and lightning, and even "black outs" the sun came out for Thornley Colliery sports day. The procession, headed by Thornley Colliery Silver Prize Band under Mr E Kitto, was flanked by mounted police who, with the local constabulary helped to keep the traffic moving through this 1½ mile parade. Enthusiastic spectators had come from adjoining colliery areas to help swell the ranks of the home crowd.

The crowd applauded the smartness of the eight jazz bands that were on parade.

There were no losers in the fancy dress procession for all the children who entered received 2s 6d with the chance of a larger prize.

A hardy annual at these functions is George Copeland from Shotton who dresses as a Zulu, and causes immense amusement as he runs berserk among the crowd. George always a good bet for a prize, turns his prize money over to charity.

Also taking part in the parade were members of the Thornley Boys Brigade and the Girls Guildry. There was also a Mr and Mrs Sports Day successfully challenged by Mrs F Spence and Mr Thompson. The two individuals who kept their cloak of secrecy until mid afternoon were Mr E Peachey and Mrs M Day.

Each child up to the age of five living in Thornley and the families of men working at Thornley Colliery received a bag of sweets. Committee men had a busy time giving out these 1,700 bags. Bags left went to the Earls House Children's Hospital at Durham.

Arts and Crafts

In the Welfare Hall were arts and crafts, needlework, painting, crayoning and drawing. There were over 600 entries. There was also a "Kiss of Life" demonstration by Mr J Eliss and Mr H Hubbard using the blonde model "Ressusci Annie."

The judges were, Mr and Mrs W Bradford, Mr and Mrs S D Fawcett, Mr and Mrs B Carse, Mr and Mrs Stewart, Mr and Mrs J Williams, The Rev and Mrs Mold, Mr and Mrs Bonar, Mr and Mrs Ruth, Mr and Mrs G Mills, Mr and Mrs W Maddison, Mr and Mrs D Cairns.

There were also many County Councillors who helped in presentations. They were Coun W Reavely of the New Teesside Borough, County Coun M Johnson of Lanchester, County Councillors J Clarke, J Wears, L Hawkshaw and E Carter of Thornley.

Also participating in the presentations were Dr and Mrs Wingfield, Mr and Mrs L B Bates, Mr and Mrs Whiteman.

Jazz Bands

After the sports on the Welfare Field, a display by the North-East Jazz Band Association followed. The final results were, **Best band on parade**: Burnmoor Coldstreamers, **Best band on display:** Sunderland Juveniles, **Best band major**: Burnmoor Coldstreamers, **Best drum major**: Burnmoor Coldstreamers, **Best bass drummer:** Sunderland Juveniles and Felling Royals (tied). Other bands taking part were Thornley Sunbeams, Birtley Grenadiers, Pelton Happy Wanderers, Winlaton Vulcaneers.

Best dressed tableaux: 1 Thornley Women's Institute, 2 Cassop Ladies Club, 3 Thornley Mother's Club.

Adult fancy dress, Comic: Mr Brooks, Mr G Hewitson, J hewitson. **Adult fancy dress, original:** Mrs Crisp (The Cavalier), G Copeland (Zulu), B Hinds (Rifleman and Son).

Comic children's fancy dress: T Saunders, N Iddon, d Mather, G Mather, K Thubron, S Carr, J Hall, S Walls, K Mather, A Batty, N Taaylorson, D Stephenson, E Peacock, J Hubbard, J Darby.

Children's fancy dress original: S Marr, C Abbs, R Stones, J Jobes, I Pratt, G Maxwell, S Parkin, P Williams, L M Gray, S Hammond, W Hogg, L Stephenson, M Walker.

The long-distance race for the Baldasera Memorial Cup was won by G Million, 2 J McDonnell, 3 H Tunney. The cup was presented after the race to the winner by Mr T Baldasera.

The money for these sports was as usual given by the workmen of Thornley Colliery, coming from a weekly levy. The organising committee was the Thornley Miners' Federation Board with the new organising secretary, Mr Ray Briggs.

Other Results

Results – Arts and Crafts and Needlework, 5-6 years 1 Bernadette Lennox, 2 Neville Worthington (Thornley R C), **6-7 years**, 1 S Lenehan, 2 Columba Smith, 3 Anglea Hepple (Thornley RC), **7-8 years**, 1 Shiela Coles, 2 Susan Wright and Teresa O'Brian (Thornley RC), 3 Karen Ingleby (Ludworth). **8-9 years**, 1 S Ragg and K Straughan, 2 J Milne (Wheatley Hill JM), 3 S Pugh (Thornley JM). **9-10 years**, S Brownless (Thornley JM), 2 Alison O'Conner, 3 Lesley Robson (Wheatley Hill JM). **10-11 years**, 1 A Martin (Wheatley Hill JM), 2 Lynne Fort, 3 Anne Barker (Thornley JM).

11-12 years, 1 Dawn Taylor, 2 Jeannette Parkin (Wheatley Hill JM), 3 L M Gray (Thornley JM). **12-13 years**, P Harriman (Wheatley Hill Boys), 2 B Martin (Shotton Seconary Modern), 3 Alison Inchcliffe (Spennymoor). **13-14 years**, 1 Sandra Barker (Bowburn Secondary Modern), 2 Marina Million (Wheatley Hill Girls), 3 C Davison (Wheatley Hill Boys). **14-15 years**, 1 Ann Hardy (Wheatley Hill Girls), 2 Shirley Bell (Shotton Secondary Modern), 3 Brian Tilley (Wheatley Hill Boys) and David Ord (Horden RC).

Painting, crayoning or drawing 5-6years 1 Claire Hudson (Wingate Nursery), 2 Wendy Ruth (Thornley RC), 3 Sharron Charlton (Wheatley Hill Infants). **6-7 years**, 1 G Maxwell, 2 T Bean, 3 G Carr (Wheatley Hill Infants). **7-8 years**, 1 B Dinsley (Wheatley Hill I), 2 Janet Duffy (Thornley RC), 3 Deborah Million (Wheatley Hill I). **8-9 years**, 1 Susan Williamson, 2 Marie Gilling (Thornley RC), 3 Susan Eelbeck (Wheatley Hill I) **9-10 years**, 1 C Swinburn (Wheatley Hill Boys), 2 Karen Liddle (Thornley JM), 3 Ann Dunn (Thornley RC). **10-11 years**, 1 K Mather (Thornley JM), 2 Gloria Robson (Wheatley Hill JM), 3 Allan Hewitson (Cassop JM). **11-12 years**, 1 A Lofthouse, 2 P Watson, 3 A Bartram (Thornley JM). **12-13 years**, 1 T Nuttall, 2 J Purvis, 3 D A Langley (Wheatley Hill Boys). **13-14 years**, 1 Lynne Curry, 2 Janice Lowther (Wheatley Hill Girls), 3 Maurice Youll (Wheatley Hill Boys). **14-15 years**, 1 H Tunney (Thornley RC), 2 B Tulley (Wheatley Hill Boys), 3 Valerie Lofthouse (A J Dawson Grammer).

Sports

Boys' flat race 5-6years: 1 P Nicholson, 2 P Langlands, 3 B Telford. **6-7 years:** 1 G Thompson, 2 K Lonsdale, 3 G Marley. **7-8 years**: 1 A Wood, 2 J M Barron, 3 P George. **8-9 years:** 1 K Lowther, 2 D Appleby, 3 M Nicholson. **9-10 years:** G Williamson, 2 K Raine, 3 K Quinn. **10-11 years:** 1 D Pattisom, 2 D Nicholson, 3 Chaytor. **11-12 years:** 1C Rammage, 2 A Hood, 3 J Purvis. **12-13 years:** 1 K Brownless, 2 S Ryan, 3 J Watson. **13-14 years:** 1 D Pattison, 2 J Youll, 3 T Winter. **14-15 years**: 1 D W Parker, 2 J Peachey, 3 G Cook. Baldasera Cup, 1 J Million, 2 J McDonnell, 3 H Tunney.

Boys' sack race 5-6 years: 1 B Telford, 2 P Langlands, 3 T Orton. 6-7 years: G Thompson, 2 G Marley, 3 B Crisp. 7-8 years: 1 A Wood, 2 S Lee, 3 P George. 8-9 years: 1 B Richardson, 2 P Ord, 3 D Cotsgrave. 9-10 years: 1 S Brownless, 2 I Carter, 3 D Crisp. 10-11 years: 1 A Parker, 2 B Dobbin, 3 P Watson, 11-12 years: 1 J Orton, 2 J Rammage, 3 T Raine. 12-13 years: 1 K Brownless , 2 R Murray, 3 W Bowes. 13-14 years: 1 T Winter, 2 J Youll, 3 M Youll. 14-15 years: 1 J Peachey, 2 D Ord, 3 R Marshall.

Girls' flat race 5-6 years: 1 K Greener, 2 R Scott. 6-7 years: 1 E M Connelly, 2 T O'Brien, 3 S Armstrong. 7-8 years: 1 L Greener, 2 R McCoy, 3 K McDonnell. 8-9 years: 1 A Gaskell, 2 K Robson, 3 C Williamson. 9-10 years: 1 J Gaskell, 2 D Worthington, 3 L Robson. 10-11 years): 1 D Winter, 2 G Day, 3 F Lonsdale. 11-12 years: 1 S Armstrong, 2 A McCoy, 3 H Lowther. 12-13 years: 1 L Parker, 2 M Gaskell, 3 O Telford. 13-14 years: 1 J Day, 2 A Battey, 3 L Curry. (14-15 years: 1 P Smith, 2 M Peachey, 3 E Rutherford.

Girls' egg and spoon race 5-6 years: 1 G Hunt, 2 R Scott, 3 J Vasey. 6-7 years: 1 J Bowes, 2 E M Connelly, 3 S Gradon. 7-8 years: 1 M Murray, 2 C Williamson, 3 R McCoy. 8-9 years: 1 S Dobbin, 2 K Robson, 3 A Gaskell. 9-10 years: 1 J Gaskell, 2 L Hood, 3 S Gradon. 10-11 years: 1 V Brown, 2 M Gaskell, 3 D Winter. 11-12 years: 1 S Armstrong, 2 A McCoy, 3 H Lowther. 12-13 years: 1 O Telford, 2 S Gradon, 3 L Parker. 13-14 years: 1 L Curry, 2 J Day, 3 A Battey. 14-15 years: 1E Rutherford, 2 M Peachey, 3 P Smith.

WHEATLEY HILL SPORTS FOR CHILDREN

About 300 people watched the children's sports connected with the Wheatley Hill Colliery Miners' federation Sports and Gala.

Mr W Ward acted as starter and judges of the various events were Mr W Neby and Mr S Ragg. Messrs A Wharrier, J Dunn, G Burnside and J Harper acted as marshals. Flat Races, girls, 5 years: 1 A Coulton, 2 J Billingham, 3 R Scott. 6 years: 1 T Ord, 2 E Parnham, 3 J Durkin. 7 years, 1 V Adams, 2 C Armstrong, 3 C McDonald. 8 years, 1 D Errington, 2 Smyth, 3 C Meekin. 9 years, 1 J Simms, 2 M Peacock, 3 P McDonald. 10 years, S Cain, 2 F Lonsdale, 3 S Jackson. 11 years, 1 D Taylor, 2 D Stephenson, 3 S Howe. 12 years, 1L Parker, 2 L Stephenson, 3 M McDonald. 13 years, 1 A Battye, 2 M Bulmer, 3 C Million.

Boys, 5 years, 1 F Peacock, 2 D Langlands, 3 G Hewitson. 6 years, 1 J Walker, 2 G Westgarth, 3 K Lonsdale. 7 years. 1 J Purvis, 2 T Pace, 3 tie A Wood and D Durkin. 8 years, 1 A Turnbull, 2 G Coxon, 3 J Hall. 9 years, 1 G Bradley, 2 S Metcalfe, 3 T Purvis. 10 years, 1 M Graney, 2 G Patterson, 3 T Hagan. 11 years, 1 H Banks, 2 S Atkin, 3 B Harker. 12 years, 1 M Billingham, 2 D Million, 3 D Welsh. 13 years, 1 F Mitchell, 2 D Patterson, 3 M Youll.

Potato Races, Girls 5 years, 1 A Coulton, 2 M Stephenson, 3 J Aincough. 6 years, 1 T Ord, 2 L Morris, 3 D Peacock. 7 years, 1 C Million, 2 S Wilkinson, 3 C McDonald. 8 years, 1 C Smyth, 2 C Meekin, 3 M Bartley. 9 years, 1 L Robsom. 2 P McDonald, 3 M Peacock. 10 years, 1 P Atwood, 2 L Patterson, 3 S Cain. 11 years,

1 S Rowe, 2 D Taylor, 3 D Stephenson. **12 years,** 1 L Parker, 2 L Stephenson, 3 M McDonald. **13 years,** 1 A Curry, 2 M Bulmer, 3 D Curry.

Boys, 5 years, 1 D Langlands, 2 W Martin, 3 N Pearn. **6 years,** 1 J Walker, 2 P Lye, 3 G Westgarth. **7 years,** 1 J Purvis, 2 D Durkin, 3 A Wood. **8 years,** 1 A Turnbull, 2 J Hall, 3 B Mitcheson. **9 years,** 1 S Metcalfe, 2 S Appleby, 3 P Stephenson. **10 years,** 1 G Patterson, 2 J Gutcher, 3 A Parker. **11a years,** 1 S Atkin, 2 G Rowbotham, 3 R Craggs. **11b years,** 1 S Harker, 2 J Carr, 3 S Hicks.

Hurdles, 12 years, 1 M Billingham, 2 D Million, 3 S Carr. **13 years,** 1 F Mitchell, 2 J Youll, 3 D Patterson.

There were 230 entries for these events and prizes took the form of Saving Stamps.

Mr W Newby (chairman), Mr Wharrier (organising secretary), and Mr J Hedley (treasurer), thanked the police and other helpers who nobly assisted in "this second edition of Sports day.
12 July 1968

PROGRESS IN FLIGHT DISPLAY AT WHEATLEY HILL SCHOOL KINDLES MOOD OF ENTHUSIASIM

The history of flight, from the earliest legendary efforts of Daedalus and Icarus to fly with handmade wings, to the modern jet age, was vividly portrayed in an exhibition, "Man's Progress in Flight," arranged in Wheatley Hill Boys Modern School this week by a member of the teaching staff, Mr John E Etherington.

Pupils of the first and second forms in the 11-13 age group provided most of the exhibits, cuttings, models and souvenirs, but valuable support also came from other members of the staff and a number of parents of the pupils.

"The idea of staging an exhibition to coincide with the 50th anniversary of the Royal Air Force soon caught on among the pupils, and their keenness and enthusiasm grew as the weeks passed by," Mr Etherington told me on Monday as he escorted me around the exhibition neatly arranged in one of the classrooms (writes Norman Passfield).

Exhibits Poured In
The exhibits started "pouring in" and no

Progress of Flight at Wheatley Hill School with teacher. Mr J Etherington

559

fewer than 100 models of aircraft, from the oldest type to the modern jets and even the "Concord," were provided by the boys. Essays, and even poems, were written describing man's earliest flying attempts and pictures and newspaper and magazine cuttings illustrated the progress of the Royal Flying Corps during World War 1 and the Royal Air Force during the last war.

Mr Etherington said, "It was a really popular school project and it has provided much enjoyment for all those who have seen it."

Mr Etherington himself, who served six-and-a-half years in the RAF during the last war, and has two of his three sons serving in the same Force, in Singapore and Cyprus, provided some of the photographs and souvenirs for the exhibition.

Personal Touch

Of special interest among these are some of Group Captain Douglas Bader, the legless pilot, who was on the same station at Tangmere, in Sussex, where Mr Etherington was serving. Two other members of the school staff, Mr Arthur E Jones and Mr Athur Stabler, who were pilots in the RAF, the former was a Flight Lieut and the latter a Warant Officer, also brought along photographs and these lent a personal touch to the attractively arranged historic display.

The exhibition also includes RAF uniforms and medals, a pair of flying boots worn on "ops" during the last war, a letter from a prisoner of war and scores of coloured pictures of every type of aircraft in use during the last 50 years.

Phases Of The War

Charts were provided by the art master, Mr Dennis Fox, to illustrate various phases of the last war, including the Battle of Britain.

And one pupil, David Langley, was so anxious "to do his bit" for the exhibition that he modelled a foot-long aircraft, a biplane, entirely from match sticks.

Said David, "It took me all my spare time for a month to make it but it was a pleasure to do it."

When I asked him how many matches he had used, David said, "I have no idea, but there were hundreds, I got my mother and all the neighbours to save them for me and then got to work on my own design with a pot of glue.

WHEATLEY HILL HEAD RETIRES

Miss G Alderslade, who has lived in Thornley and Wheatley Hill for many years, bids farewell to a teaching career which has spread 43 years, when the clock strikes four today (Friday).

She was educated at Henry Smith Grammar School, Hartlepool, and Durham University (King College, Newcastle).

Miss Alderslade has given her 43 years as a teacher to Wheatley Hill Girl Modern School. Until 1938 she taught the girls in the school building in the Front Street, which also housed the boys department, but when the present girls' school was built in 1938 and under reorganisation, she moved into the present spacious premises.

In 1947 Miss Alderslade became headmistress, succeeding Mrs McCleod. During her headship Miss Alderslade has widened the scope of education. At one Speech Day she intimated that education was more than driving in of the three R's. It included moral training and the inculcating of principles that would make girls worthy citizens.

In 1955 a Commercial Course was introduced.

On behalf of past and present staff members, the deputy head, Miss M Griffiths, presented her with a chiming clock and leather handbag. On behalf of pupils of the school, the head girls Norma Armstrong and Lillian Thomas presented her with a set of electric door chimes and cutlery.

This week she has left Thornley to reside in Blackhall.

Reorganisation

Miss Alderslade's retirement coincides with another scheme of re-organisation. When school reassembles in September, the system will become co-educational, and both boys and girls will be accommodated in the present Wheatley Hill Peterlee Girls School. The present boys school will be retained in use as a craft centre. The school takes in approximately 400 pupils under a headmaster, Mr Arthur Harris (Sunderland). Mr Harris has been a popular head of the present boys school for some years, succeeding the late Mr J Andrews.

The boys' school has been built since 1877. Among its well-known headmasters were Messrs Bowhill, T Arnold, Rees and J Andrews who moved from Wheatley Hill to County Hall to take charge of School Meals Organisation.

Mr Ned Ward will be deputy head of the new combined school with Mrs Pamela Baxter as headmistress.

The school is to be channelled into a structure that will take in Northern Counties examinations CSE and Commercial Courses.

19 July 1968

DURHAM MINERS' GALA, THE FIRST THERE

As Mainsforth Lodge was played on to the Racecourse at 9.15 to start the 85th Miners' Gala, Old Elvet had quite a deserted look, a strange sight on Durham's traditionally "Big Day."

A close second to Mainsforth was Eden Lodge, and Hylton Lodge, who were last year the last lodge to reach the Racecourse, this year managed third place.

Several people lined the road outside the Royal County Hotel but the heavy drizzle may have stopped many people coming to the Gala. Outside the prison only policemen patrolled the footpath.

Miss Rita Browning, Durham County Constabulary's first mounted policewoman, and indeed the country's first mounted policewoman, was on duty at Saturday's Gala.

WHEATLEY HILL GOLDEN PAIR RECALL EVENTFUL YEARS

A Wheatley Hill couple, who started their married life on a weekly wage of 30 shillings, out of which they paid 4s.2d rent, celebrate their golden wedding tomorrow.

The couple, Mr and Mrs Thomas Foster, of 54 Jack Lawson Terrace, spent the early years of their married life at Station Town. Later they lived in the adjoining village of Wingate before moving to Wheatley Hill some 30 years ago.

"We have certainly had our hard times and often it has been a struggle to make ends meet," Mrs Emily Foster, whose maiden name was Lang, told our reporter this week. "We have gone through quite a number of strikes and lock-outs. For weeks on end we got no pay and had to make do with vouchers which we could exchange for the bare necessities of life."

Often, when her family was young, said Mrs Foster, she was able to make "a real good dinner with sixpennyworth of steak and a pennyworth of suet," She smiled, "It smelled good and tasted good."

Mr and Mrs Foster were married at St Mary's Church Horden, on August 3, 1918.

Paid In Gold

Mr Foster, who is 75, was born at Wingate and started work down the pit there when he was 13 years of age. "I was trapping and driving," he said, "and for quite a time my wages were only ten shillings a fortnight. We were paid in gold those days and it was a great thrill to be able to take home a half sovereign."

Later he was employed at Wheatley Hill colliery, where he retired at 65. Mr Foster was a keen brass bandsman in his younger days and played the trombone in Wingate and Wheatley Hill Colliery Bands for about 30 years.

Before her marriage Mrs Foster, who was born at Old Trimdon 70 years ago, worked in domestic service on a farm at West Hartlepool. She recalled, "I was 14 on the Friday and I started work the next day."

Never A Penny

She was paid three shillings and sixpence a week, "We were living at Horden at the time," she said, "and my mother used to come to the farm every fortnight to collect my pay. I never got a penny for myself, but I did not really need any money for the farm was well out of town and you could never get out."

She helped to look after a family of ten for her employers, "And later," she said, "I helped in the fields, feeding the cattle and hay making. I sometimes got extra money for this and so was able to save a little for my wedding clothes."

Fairly Good Health

Mr and Mrs Foster, who are both in fairly good health, have two sons and a daughter. Their sons John William and Mark, live at Wheatley Hill and Thornley respectively, and their daughter Mrs Joyce Lonsdale, at Wheatley Hill. They also have eleven grand- children and four great- grand- children.

Shortly the couple are moving into an aged miners' bungalow in the village but tomorrow they are holding a family party in their present home. "The family have provided the cake and wine and we are looking forward to a happy time together," said Mrs Foster.

2 August 1968

"IS THORNLEY BECOMING A HAWKERS PARADISE?"
ASK SOME COUNCIL MEMBERS

Claims that Thornley was becoming a hawkers' paradise were made at Thornley Parish Council meeting by one member and repudiated by another.

A long discussion took place on the "lethargic attitude adopted by the Easington Rural District Council Health Committee," on a recent deputation to Thornley, at the request of the Parish Council.

Coun Mrs Grieves alleged that a number of unsavoury characters had moved into Thornley over the last few months and had "set up shop."

Thornley had now become a "Hawkers Paradise."

One Councillor was quick to repudiate the statement when he said that many hawkers in the area were sincere and had a sense of value.

He would be more apt to term the present situation in Thornley as being a "Scroungers Paradise."

Various premises had all come into prominence in the last few weeks, all being erected without Council planning permission.

Deplorable

They had brought their own living accommodation, with a primitive brand of toilet necessities, which was far from hygienic and proving a constant menace to children living in nearby residential areas.

Coun Mrs Grieves continued that the East End of Hartlepool Street was in a deplorable condition, and that steps should be taken immediately to have the whole area cleaned up and the instant removal of these caravans and junk- yards removed.

Mr Scanlon from the Health Department had toured the area with a special sub-committee, but nothing whatsoever had been achieved. Coun J Wright said that the night had been a complete waste of time. It was finally decided that a strong letter of protest be sent to the Clerk of the Easington Rural District Council at the "apathy and lack of interest shown by the Council" on this important issue.

WHEATLEY HILL BEAUTY SUCCESSES

Two young married sisters at Wheatley Hill carried off the major prizes at a beauty contest at a dance in the Welfare Hall, Wheatley Hill, on Friday night, organised in connection with Crimdon Lido's annual beauty queen contest.

Mrs Barbara Taylor, of Granville Terrace, won the "Miss Wheatley Hill" title and a prize of £10, and her sister, 17-year-old Mrs Jennifer Walker, of Luke Terrace, was presented with £5 as runner-up for the title.

Mrs Taylor who is 21, is the mother of a 2 year-old son and works as a clerk in a local betting shop. She will now compete against other village "Queens" from the Easington Rural Area at the lido on September 2 for the title of "Miss Crimdon 1968" and a prize of £20.

The contest was judged by Mr Alf Hesler, secretary Durham Area NUM, and his wife, and Mrs Jane Reynolds wife of Crimdon's resort manager. The resort manager, Mr Tom Reynolds, compered the programme and the prizes were presented by Mrs Wharrier, wife of Coun A D Wharrier, a local member of Easington Rural Council.

9 August 1968

WHEATLEY HILL MINERS' LODGE

Though the local colliery was closed in May, with most of the miners transferred to neighbouring collieries, Wheatley Hill miners' lodge is still functioning and at the recent meeting officers elected were, Chairman, Mr John Andrew, correspondence secretary, Coun A D Wharrier, financial secretary, Mr Jack Hedley, treasurer, Mr R Cook. A committee of five was also elected.

With the exception of Mr Hedley, who became redundant when the pit closed, all the officials are still employed at the colliery on salvage work.

"We expect the salvage work being completed by November," Coun Wharrier told our reporter this week, "But we will keep together as a lodge to look after any local problems that may crop up."

They would also, he said, continue to receive contributions from local retired miners who have been paying into the lodge's Death Fund. Coun Wharrier said, "We would not like to see this fund fall through."

23 August 1968

PRESENTATIONS AT COUNTY HALL

A part time fireman at Wheatley Hill, yesterday received the British Empire Medal from the Lord Lieut of County Durham, Sir James Duff. Station Officer Frank Horner aged 56 of Wordsworth Avenue received the medal in recognition of 26 years service, all at Wheatley Hill.

Station Officer Horner, who is also station officer at the ICI industrial Fire Brigade at Billingham, joined the National Fire Service as a part-time fireman in 1941. He became a leading fireman in 1946 and two years later joined the Durham County Fire Brigade as a part-time leading fireman. In 1958 he was promoted to sub-officer and for the past four years has held his present post.

6 September 1968

BIRTHDAY PARTY FOR THORNLEY LEGION WOMEN

Members of Thornley Women's Section of the British legion celebrated the 43rd birthday with a party in the Thornley Welfare Hall. Arrangements were in the hands of the secretary, Mrs G M Bromilow.

Mrs E Clark (chairman) welcomed 100 members and visitors, who included Mrs L Parks (county chairman) and Mrs Johnson (county treasurer). She expressed the branch's regret that the president, Mrs H Brewster, was unable to be present owing to illness.

Proposing the toast, Mrs Clark urged members to work hard in order to bring success in the coming year. She encouraged other branches to be always on the alert for new members. She cut the birthday cake, which had been made by Mrs M Langley and decorated by Mrs J Inchcliffe. Mrs Parks and Mrs Johnson responded to the toast. Congratulations to the branch were given by visiting branch presidents, Mrs M Morgan (Ludworth), Mrs Hardy (Shotton) and Mrs M Coats (Cassop).

13 September 1968

DEATH OF MR R H LOFTHOUSE, OF LUDWORTH

The death occurred suddenly in hospital of Mr Robert Henry Lofthouse (87), a bachelor, who lived with his sister at 41 Barnard Avenue, Ludworth. He was a native of Ludworth and spent all his life in the village. A retired miner, he worked for many years at Thornley Colliery, where he was a banksman.

Mr Lofthouse was a staunch member of the Church of England, and was always to be found in the same seat at the little Mission Church of St Andrew's, Ludworth. With his sisters and other church members he helped in many ways towards the building of the Mission Church in 1902.

Naturalist

He was a naturalist and country lover and his fame was more than local. He possessed a unique collection of stuffed animals and birds and butterflies and moths.

Several months ago Mr Lofthouse found that advancing age handicapped him so that he could not look after his "museum" as he would have liked. He offered his collection to Bowes Museum and County Council of Durham gratefully accepted the gift.

Mr Lofthouse was an expert pen and ink artist and scores of his sketches are found in many of the cottages of Ludworth and homes of his friends elsewhere. The subjects were almost all nature studies. He invariably produced his own greeting cards for close friends.

The funeral service took place on Tuesday morning at St Cuthbert's Church, Shadforth, conducted by the Rector, (the Rev C E Woolstenholmes). Mr C Woolstenholmes jun was organist. Cremation followed privately at Durham.

AFTER RDC ASSURANCES WINGATE REVERSES
"NO REFUSE TIPPING" VETO

It was agreed at a meeting of Wingate Parish Council, to withdraw the council's objections to a proposal to allow Easington Rural District Council to tip household refuse in the disused Wingate Quarry at Wheatley Hill.

The Council had objected to the proposal on the grounds that the tipping could cause a nuisance to residents of the houses in the vicinity by paper being blown about and the smoke and fumes from burning refuse.

Following the objection Durham County Council had invited the Parish Council to send a delegation to a site meeting with the other interested parties.

And at their meeting members of Wingate Parish Council delegation said that they had been given assurances that tipping would be strictly controlled.

Assurance

Coun W Newby said, "They listened to our objections and assured us that steps would taken to ensure our conditions were met and all the members of the delegation felt that if this was done the council would not need to persist in its objections."

Another member of the delegation, Coun D Dodds, said, "I am quite satisfied that tipping on the site will be strictly controlled. The County Council have told us that they will keep an eye on the position."

The chairman, Coun J H Charlton, commented," It was agreed by the Council that this matter should be left in the hands of the representatives of the Wheatley Hill Ward who attended this meeting.

"It is apparent that we have done some good in objecting and that they have agreed to the conditions we asked for to control this nuisance."

Must Be Watched

But Coun Charlton warned that the position would have to be watched as there was still a nuisance being caused by the burning of refuse on another tip in the parish.

The Council agreed to accept the delegation's report and withdraw its objections to the tipping of refuse in the disused quarry by Easington RDC.

THORNLEY MAN SPENDS EVERY DAY IN GARDEN

Behind the success of the Thornley Working Men's Club at the 49th annual Horticultural and Floral Show organised by the Durham County Branch of the Working Men's Club and Institute Union stands one man.

Mr Alan Hutchinson, a member of the club at Thornley, shows for the club at this annual event but all the produce entered for the show is grown by himself.

On Saturday, Thornley were presented with the Premier Club Award, for gaining the most points in the show, for the seventh consecutive year out of eight. And the Tom Nelson White Celery Trophy was also won by Thornley for the seventh time.

Mr Hutchinson, a 46-year-old miner at Thornley Colliery, is married with two children, one of whom is married. He lives at 2 Albert Street, Thornley.

After his successes on Saturday he said, "All the lads at Thornley Club will be pleased when they hear about this."

He spends every day in his garden and said that he has no secrets about growing stuff for the shows, "Its just all hard work."

20 September 1968

566

"GOLDEN DAY" AT WHEATLEY HILL

On September 28, 1918, Mr James Gibson was married to Miss Margaret Stark in All Saints Church, Wheatley Hill. The Rev E T Casey officiated.

Last Saturday the couple, who reside at 17 Peter Lee Cottages, Wheatley Hill, celebrated their golden wedding with a family party at the home of their daughter, Mrs J Jordan. Among the 20 guests were their two sons, two daughters and seven grandchildren.

Mrs Gibson, who like her husband is 70, said, "I know we have reached an event many do not see. We are profoundly thankful. That is perhaps the main feature of our emotions at the moment."

Mr Gibson has lived in Wheatley Hill all his life. As member of the mining community he was a one colliery man. He worked at Wheatley Hill Colliery for 51 years. Most of that time was spent as an engine driver. In the early days of reaching that goal, he received 6s 7d a shift.

Difficult Days

Mrs Gibson said, "The thirties and 1920's were difficult days for miners. My husband was never on the dole. There were two engines at the colliery and in slack times they were run on alternate days. That meant, although only working half-time, the drivers could not claim dole."

In his younger days Mr Gibson played football for his church team.

Worshipers At Parish

Mrs Gibson was born at Shadforth and came to Wheatley Hill when she was 13. On leaving school, she became well known as an assistant in the boot and shoe department of Shotton Co-operative Society. She served the store for 4½ years.

The couple are regular worshipers at Wheatley Hill Parish Church. Both are former members of the Parochial Church Council and both served for many years as choristers. Mrs Gibson commented "I'm still going strong at 70."

Both are members of the church's Over 20 Club. Mrs Gibson has been a member of the Mothers' Union at All Saints for 57 years. She is a former member of the Wheatley Hill Women's Institute.

NEW £17,500 METHODIST CHURCH OPENED
AT THORNLEY- 300 THERE

Vision and foresight, which had its birth in 1946, came to fruition on Saturday when the new £17,500 Methodist Church was opened at Thornley in the presence of 300 members and friends. A £10,000 grant from the Joseph Rank Trust, £1,000 from the Methodist General Chapel Committee, weekly giving by local people and special efforts by the New Building Fund committee has turned vision into reality.

This new church takes the place of two older buildings, Waterloo Street and Bow Street. The first sod was cut on October 28 by Mr Joe Gatenby (Quarrington Hill) and the Foundation Stone was laid on May 11 this year by Mr Wesley Weightman (Silksworth). At that ceremony £1,000 was raised.

Mr A L Miller, a member and Trust Official of many years, opened the door of the new church. It was dedicated by the new Chairman of the Darlington District, the Rev E Lincoln Minshull. The opening service was conducted by the superintendent minister, the Rev Robert S Thompson and the sermon was preached by the Rev Gordon Johnson (Bedale), a former superintendent of the Thornley Circuit.

The lessons were read by Mrs M Harris, Mr R Potts and Miss M Dent. The Witnesses Youth group gave a musical item.

REPRESENTATIVES

Representatives, Thornley St Bartholomew's Church, the vicar Rev P G Mould, Thornley R C Church of the English martyrs, the Rev Dr H McNeill, Easington RDC and Thornley Colliery Federation Board, Coun J Nicholson (Chairman of the Easington Education Executive), Thornley Parish Council, Couns Miss A Griffiths and R Day, Thornley Methodist Circuit, Mr J Craig, Mr J Gilmore (circuit secretary) and Mrs Gilmore, Mr T A Walker (Preachers' secretary) and Mrs Walker, Mr and Mrs Brown, Mr and Mrs W Dunmore (Building Contractors). Tea was provided for 360 by Thornley members in the Bow Street Youth Centre.

Greetings and good wishes for the new church were given by the Rev E Lincoln Minshull, the Rev P G Mold, Coun J Nicholson and Mr J Craig.

Mr Ken Hetherington (treasurer) said that the opening ceremony had raised £540. A vote of thanks to all was proposed by Mr J H Pattison) Chirman of the New Builing Fund). This Fund Committee has had Mrs J Mather as an active secretary.

The first Sunday services in the new church were conducted by the minister, the Rev Robert S Thompson. At the morning service Alan Fox was baptised. To mark the first christening Coun Miss A Griffiths (Cradle Roll secretary) presented him with a Bible.

4 October 1968

FATAL HUSTLE TO CATCH A BUS

While crossing the road at Wingate Lane, Wheatley Hill, shortly after seven o'clock on Tuesday morning, three factory girls, living only a short distance away, were involved in an accident with a workmen's bus they were hurrying to catch, one of them was killed, and another seriously injured, but the third had a lucky escape.

The dead girl was Miss Sheila Cowan (21), youngest of 12, of 12 Dalton Terrace, Wheatley Hill. Taken seriously injured to Durham County Hospital was Mrs Enid Nuttall (23), of 2 Dalton Terrace, who only the day before had celebrated her first wedding anniversary. Later she was transferred to Newcastle General Hospital, with multiple injuries.

The girl who escaped was 18 year-old Miss Marjorie Ord, a cousin of the dead girl, of 22 Liddell Terrace, Wheatley Hill. Her mother, Mrs Jennie Ord, who was bereaved by the sudden death of her husband only a month ago, told our reporter, "She was very lucky. She was crossing the road with two other girls when the accident happened. Her shoe was torn off but apart from a bad shaking she was unhurt. She is very upset for they always went off to the factory together."

Miss Cowan and Mrs Nuttall worked at the same factory at Spennymoor, Smart and Brown's, but Miss Ord recently left there for another factory on the trading estate.

On her 21st birthday in August Miss Cowan, whose mother Mrs Elizabeth Cowan is a widow, became engaged to a South Hetton man, Mr Phillip Howes. "She was a very happy girl and only the night before her death was talking about her future" said Mrs Ord. Miss Cowan's father died about 12 years ago.

The bus was travelling down the bank, belonged to Gillet Bros, of Quarrington Hill. It was driven by Mr Michael Norman Wood (22), of 22, Dene View, Cassop.

THE REV ROBERT S THOMPSON, SUPERINTENDENT MINISTER

Conducted the first wedding service in the new Thornley St Stephen's Methodist Church when Mr Colin Bullock, younger son of Mr and Mrs Robert Bullock, 57 St Aidan's Crescent, Thornley, was married to Miss Maureen Mathews, youngest daughter of Mr and Mrs Robert Mathews, 19 East Lea, Thornley.

To mark the occasion, Mr Thompson presented the couple with an inscribed Bible.

The new church has only been opened a week. The couple have been Sunday School teachers at St Stephen's for some years.

Given away by her father, the bride wore a crinoline style gown of white lace and satin with full-length veil. She wore a headdress of roses and drop pearls. Her bouquet was of pink roses with an orchid in the centre.

Bridesmaid was Miss Anne Walls, the bride's cousin. She wore a full-length dress of lemon satin and nylon with matching headdress. She carried pink roses. Best man was Mr Richard Edwards.

The bride received lucky horseshoes from Allison and Carol Bullock and David Ward (Peterlee).

11 October 1968

HERE'S TO GEORGE AND RICHARD

Members of Wheatley Hill Homing Society drink a toast to George Morgan and Richard Robson who have won the Up North Combine race from Lille trophy. It is 33 years since the award was won by a man in the village.

25 October 1968

REMEMBRANCE SERVICE

As well as the Thornley Women's section in the parade, there was the newly reformed men's section. Standard bearers were Mr R Brookes (Men's section), Mrs J Harvey (Women's section). The service was conducted by the superintendent minister of the Thornley Methodist Circuit. The sermon was preached by the vicar, the Rev P G

Mould. Prayers were said at the village War Memorial where many wreaths were placed. Men's section Dr John Gray (President), Women's Section, Mrs E Clark (chairman), Thornley Over 60 Club, Mr William Brereton (Chairman), Women's Institute, Workmen's Club, Mother's Club and many others.

AT WHEATLEY HILL the Remembrance Day parade was led by the Wheatley Hill Colliery Prize Band. The event was organised by the Wheatley Hill Women's Section of the British Legion. Ex-members of the Forces, Boy Scouts, Church Lads and Girl's Brigade, the Fir4 Services and Police took part. At the service in All Saints the vicar the Rev G G Graham (vicar) and Father Meagher (RC Church of our Lady the Queen) read the lessons and prayers, and the Rev Maurice Henderson (Methodist) preached the sermon, 'A plea for peace.' Mr A E Tuffnell was organist. The parade reformed and marched to the Cenotaph in the Welfare Park. It halted in the Front Street opposite a clock on the Wheatley Hill Modern School, the memorial to those who gave their lives in the Second World War. Organisations' wreaths and private tributes were laid at the Cenotaph.

THORNLEY MAN DIED AT 77

The funeral took place of Mr Sylvester Dinsley (77), 18 Ruskin Crescent, Thornley. The service took place in Sunderland crematorium.

Mr Dinsley, whose wife died six years ago, was born in Richmond, Yorkshire, and is survived by a married son. He went to Thornley as a child and most of his working life was spent as a miner at Thornley Colliery. He was a stoneman but after an accident in 1950 became horsekeeper from which position he retired after 50 years in the coal industry.

In the First World War, Mr Dinsley served with the Royal Horse Artillery and reached the rank of Sergeant Major.

Mr Dinsley was always interested in football and cricket. He was for some years trainer to Wheatley Hill Juniors and under his tuition the team gained some notable success. He has been a member of Thornley and Cassop Workmen's Clubs for more that 50 years.

15 November 1968

SURPRISE PARTY FOR WHEATLEY HILL GOLDEN COUPLE

Though it was Wednesday when a well-known Wheatley Hill couple Mr and Mrs Benjamin Blenkinsopp, of 2a Quetlaw Road, celebrated their golden wedding, their celebration party, a surprise one, was held four days earlier.

Last Saturday when they were whisked off to the home of their only daughter, Mrs Chrissie Tuesday, at Bowburn, they found a cake, decorated in gold icing, waiting for them.

Mr Blenkinsopp told our reporter this week, "It was a complete surprise but a lovely one and I am still spellbound with it."

Both Mr Blenkinsopp (71) and his wife Jennie have spent all their lives in the village, they have known each other since their schooldays.

Church Links
They have had a life-long association with All Saints Church, Wheatley Hill, where they were the first couple to be married at a Holy Communion service on November 20, 1918.

They are also members of the village's Over-60 Club. Mr Blenkinsopp and his daughter are members of the concert party. He is the compere and his daughter producer and accompanist.

Said Mr Blenkinsopp, "I have always been interested in music and singing".

Mr Blenkinsopp formerly sang in the church choir and for many years was a member of the former Wheatley Hill and Thornley Welfare Male Voice Choir. He retired from work at Thornley Colliery when he was 65 after been employed there, mostly as an engineman, the whole of his working life.

Mr and Mrs Blenkinsopp have one daughter and one grandson who is serving in the Royal Air Force.

22 November 1968

WHEATLEY HILL TEETOTALLER SPEAKS UP
"GOOD CLEAN ENTERTAINMENT" PLEA
AT OPENING OF NEW CLUB HQ

The need for the club to provide "good clean entertainment" at all times was stressed by the president, Mr Fred Simpson, a retired colliery undermanager, when he spoke at the official opening of the new headquarters of the Wheatley Hill Discharged and Demobilised Soldiers and Sailors' Club.

"And by this," he added, "I mean entertainment where every member who is married can be proud to bring his wife, and the younger members can be proud to bring their friend."

Mr Simpson, who was introduced by the chairman of the club, Mr E Stanford said "Everyone must be very much impressed with the fine premises and the committee are to be congratulated on their farseeing efforts in getting this building. It behoves us all now to take a real interest in the club, give it our best support and see that it continues its successful way."

Not Just A Building

Mr Simpson reminded the members that the club was "not just a building", it was, he said, "an association of people with a common interest" and the common interest in this case was " the well-being of the club."

The club was opened by Mr Edward Cain, a life-long teetotaller and non-smoker, who has spent most of his life in Wheatley Hill, where he has been actively associated with many local organisations and was formerly an official of the miners' lodge for many years.

Seventy-seven-year-old Mr Cain, who is a retired magistrate, recalled that originally the club was "an old Army hut."

571

When they returned from the 1914-18 war members of the Forces living in the village banded together to form the club with the aim of continuing the comradeship they had enjoyed during the war years.

Mr Cain went on, "This club can really be looked upon as a memorial to the lads who fell in the war. Let it not be forgotten that they died so that you can be free and enjoy yourselves in places like this."

The club secretary, Mr Ernest Curry, welcomed the large crowd of members and visitors who packed the beautifully-decorated concert room and thanked Mr Cain and Mr Simpson for the part they played in the ceremony.

As a memento of the occasion Mr Simpson on behalf of the management committee presented Mr Cain with a barometer.

The new club, which has about 300 members, was converted from a former drapery store in the village's Front Street at a cost of some £25,000, this sum includes the cost of a new house for the club steward, Mr William Hackworth.

29 November 1968

£180 FOR NEW BUILDING FUND

A highly successful Christmas Fayre was organised by the New Building Fund of Thornley Methodist Church, with Mr J H Pattison as chairman, Mr J Mather as secretary and Mr Kenneth Hetherington as treasurer.

The effort was held in the Thornley Bow Street Youth Centre, which was tastefully decorated. It realised approximately £180.

Mr J H Pattison (society steward) presided and introduced Mrs James Plant, of Easington Colliery, who opened the Fayre and appealed for generous support so that the new building opened in September could be free from debt. The project is going well and she expressed the hope that the new church would enjoy a successful future.

Mrs Louisa Hedley presented Mrs Plant with a bouquet of carnations. Mrs Plant was for many years a member of the Bow Street Church and then the amalgamated Methodist's Church in Thornley, St Stephen's. There was a fine display of needlework, Christmas gifts, groceries and cakes.

Stallholders

Sisterhood (draperies), Mesdames J Thornton, J Mather, G Hutchinson and G Hetherington. Sunday School (toilet requisites), Mesdames B Wood and C Bullock. Fellowship (cakes), Mesdames E Greener, H Ashford, R Gilding, E Musgrave and D Pugh and Miss Banks. Choir (confectionery), Mesdames W Davies, E Maitland and Miss M Dent. Girls' Guildry and Boys' Brigade (goods and gifts), Mrs R Speckman and the Misses A Robson and L Cooper.

Youth Club (refreshments), Mesdames F Williams, J Robinson, S Laverick and Miss Ann Williams. Society (groceries). Mesdames Spence, Walls, J Wigham, Misses J Watson and H Woodward. Sisterhood (teas), Mesdames T Lincoln, A Gulliver, B Hedley, J Wilkinson, Miss B Smart and Mr T Lincoln.

Door stewards were Messrs G Hetherington and H Robson.

CHRISTMAS GIFTS FOR RETIRED MINERS

A final Christmas gift of 12s each is to be given on Saturday from the Wheatley Hill Aged Miners' Treat Fund to retired miners at Wheatley Hill Colliery and their wives and widows 55.

"Though the colliery closed earlier this year," Mr Jack Hedley, who has been treasurer of the Fund for the past 20 years, told our reporter, "We are able to make this final pay-out through contributions coming from other funds which have closed down."

They had, he said, been given the surplus which remained in the colliery's and hospital fund when they were wound up after the pit closed.

No Christmas gifts were made last year, said Mr Hedley, but in the summer a trip was organised to Redcar for the retired miners and their wives and widows and they received £2 each.

About 350

The Christmas gifts will be distributed from Wheatley Hill aged miners' hostel on Saturday between 1 and 3 pm. About 350 will benefit and the officials in charge will be Messrs W Young (chairman of the fund), Mr R Cook (secretary) and Mr Hedley.

WHEATLEY HILL

A verdict of accidental death was recorded at the inquest on the death of Sheila Cowan (21), 12 Dalton Terrace, Wheatley Hill, in Durham Town Hall, last week.

RETIREMENT - After almost 45 years in Local Government, Mr Dixon Walton of the Gables, Thornley, retired on reaching the age limit. Mr Walton, who has spent all his life in Thornley, commenced as a clerk in the Easington Rural District Council's Architect's office at Wingate in 1924. In 1937 the office was moved from Wingate to the Council Offices at Easington and later taken over by the Engineer and Surveyor. Some years ago Mr Walton was appointed assistant quantity surveyor the position he held at the time of his retirement.

At a gathering of his colleagues to mark his retirement, the Engineer and Surveyor, Mr R R Lumsden, introduced Coun M Patterson, of Blackhall, chairman of the Rural District Council. In handing over to Mr Walton an electric clock and scroll, Mr Patterson paid tribute to his very long and loyal service. He also expressed the hope that he would enjoy a long and happy retirement. Mr Lumsden with whom Mr Walton had a very long association also paid tribute to the great and loyal service given to him over such a long period. Accepting the gifts, Mr Walton suitably responded.

20 December 1968

LUDWORTH HEAD SPEAKS OF PUPILS' DEBT TO PARENTS

A large attendance of parents, scholars and friends attended the 9th annual school concert and prizegiving, of Ludworth School. The chairman was Coun J T Hedley, supported by County Coun D Thornton and Mr G Prichard, school managers, in the absence of Coun G W Smith, who was represented by Mrs Smith. The rector of Shadforth, the Rev C E Woolstenholmes, was also present.

Coun Thornton presented the prizes after the headmaster, Mr R Simpson, had read an encouraging report of the past year. He spoke of a variety of topics, and referred to forthcoming improvements in the school building, for example further modifications to the heating system this autumn have satisfactorily raised the operating temperature.

Arrangements have been made so that it will be possible for the mobile dental unit to operate at the school, and plans were well advanced for the building of indoor toilets. In addition, designs are now being worked out to develop the school building in terms of the up-to-date specifications of the Ministry.

This later project will cause a major change in the internal design of the school, but promises to be an exciting development, using totally new ideas and materials to enable more valuable use to be made of the space available as well as to enable a less rigid organisation of groups and classes to be adopted.

Staff Changes

Staff changes were referred to, Mr W H Lowrie had been appointed headmaster to a school in Spennymoor. In his place, Mr Welsh had joined the staff.

Mrs Walton, who had been at Ludworth School for 19 years, would retire at the end of term. Mr Simpson spoke of outside normal activities there had been a number of visits which included pantomime, zoo, parish church and sea port, the immediate neighbourhood as well as inter-school visits.

In conclusion the headmaster reminded the children that to date their parents had done a great deal for them, so he said to them "appreciate your parents and remember that you can never do too much for them." Mr Thornton in his remarks dwelt upon another aspect in a similar strain when he said that children would not give of their best if the parents were not interested and for a child to reach the Grammar School the parents must be persistent and patient.

Award Winners

For Progress, 4th year Junior, Shirley Morgan, S Hodge, A Morgan. 3rd year Junior, W Young, Denise Stephenson. 2nd year Junior, Denise White, Mary Widdowfield. 1st year Junior, G Bennett, K Hammond, S Jackson.

Infants, J Bell, Julie Stannard, Joy Vasey, N Savage, D Morgan, Denise Stones, Carole White.

Unbroken attendance for 2 years, Janice Widdowfield. For 1 year, Shirley Graden, Julie Stannard, J Bell, W Geddes, M Widdowfield, Sandra Graden, G Bennett, P Whittle, A Phenny, Denise Stephenson, Alison Carr, Elizabeth Hutchinson.

Special prizes, Reading, G Stephenson. Drama, Paul Whittle. Art, K Raine. Football, S Wilson, Headmasters' prize, Marion Marley.

The vocal items by the choirs included Sea Shanty, folk songs and carols by the 28 strong junior choir, carols by the infant choir of 28 voices and Ten little song birds was sung by the infants.

The play The Turnip, was performed by George Stephenson, Denise Stones, Joy Vasey, Heather Peachy, Kay Osbaldstin, Alison Vasey, Julie Grainger, Ian Worthington and Neil Savage with chorus of Beverley Carr, Sharon Huntington, Josephine Peachy, Gillian Smith, Carol White, Anthony Devenport, David Morgan and John White.

Play, The Hippocrump performed by children of Class 1 Junior was put over by Kenneth Hammond, Stephen Jackson, Walter Geddess, Mary Todd, Stephen Wilson, John Lee, Raymond Peachey, Susan Hutchinson, Pearl Whittle, Gary Bennett, John Bell, John Hutchinson, Julie Stannard, Julie Vasey.

Song Birds

The Ten Little Song Birds were Josephine Smith, Ann Bell, Shirley Graden, Gillian Smith, Lynn Hutchinson, Heather Peachey, Joy Vasey Josephine Peachey, Kathleen Gibb and Raymond Youll.

The final play Royal Choice was acted by the children of the Junior II class as follows, Valerie Brown, Denise Stephenson, Paul Whittle, Keith Cartwright, Sandra Graden, Anne Smith, Julie Bennett, Keith Savage, Gary Nicholson, William Young, Marion Marley, Keith Raine, Alison Carr, Anne Dunbar, Blanche Peachey, Denise White, Janice Widdowfield, Jane Armstrong, Brian Agar, Thomas Harrison, Graham Hall, Arthur Phenny, Joseph Turnbull, John Vasey.

The arrangements were carried out by the school staff, Mr R Simpson ,headmaster with Mrs Walton, Mrs Kirkup, Mrs Fox and Mr Welsh and the parents assisted in many ways with dresses and properties, etc.

20 December 1968

1969

HISTORY WAS MADE at Wheatley Hill last weekend when Anglican, Methodists and Roman Catholics joined together in a united carol service. The large congregation met in Our Lady of the Queen RC Church, and more than 300 heard Father Meagher open the service and say the bidding prayer. Mr A T Tuffnell was organist. The Rev G G Graham, Vicar of All Saints Church, conducted the combined choir of 50. Lessons were read by Mr W Marshall (churchwarden), Mr M B Holmes (a student), the Rev M Henderson and Mr A Howarth (Methodists), The Rev Father Meagher, Mr M Pinna and Mr J Hoban (Roman Catholics). Collection was for Christian Aid.

SCOUTS RAISE £62 – A record sum of £62 was raised by Wheatley Hill Old Scouts with their annual carol singing round of the village during the festive season. They spent four nights singing carols in various parts of the area. The amount raised was £2 higher than last year's record figure of £60. "As usual," the secretary of the Old Scouts' Association, Mr Ralph Watson, told our reporter this week, "the money will be spent on the children's ward of Durham County hospital". The Scouts 'adopted' this ward 17 years ago and since then they have entertained the young patients every Christmas, taken them presents and bought something useful for the whole ward. The Scouts annual reunion supper and social evening is to be held on 11 January.
3 January 1969

A FORMER HEADMISTRESS DIES AGED 96
The death has occurred at the age of 96 of Miss Margaret Helen Ainscow, of 14 North Crescent, Durham, who for 25 years was headmistress of Wheatley Hill Senior Girls' School.

Miss Ainscow took up her appointment at Wheatley Hill in 1908, after leaving training college in North Wales and teaching for a time at Blyth. After her retirement she went to live in Chesire, but returned to Durham City in 1945.

A founder member of the Head Teachers' Association, Miss Ainscow was a guest of honour five years ago at their annual dinner in Durham Town Hall. She visited London, Geneva and Dublin as representative of the World Council of Education, and when in Dublin was presented to Mr de Valera. She also travelled quite widely in Europe.

Miss Ainscow was the first president of Wheatley Hill Women's Institute, and was a member of the Friends of Durham Cathedral. She attended services until the last few years of her life.

Service at Durham crematorium was conducted by the Rev A Herbert, Vicar of St Cuthbert's Parish Church.
10 January 1969

WHEATLEY HILL SCOUTS TRIBUTE TO GOLD AWARD WINNER

When the 2nd Wheatley Hill Group of Boy Scouts held their 36th annual re-union supper and social evening in the Welfare Hall on Saturday night, congratulations were extended to a senior Scout, Mr Ben Aitken, who recently qualified for his Duke of Edinburgh Gold award.

To mark his success, Mr Aitken, now a student at Manchester, was presented with a wallet of notes by Mr Les Barker, the Group Scoutmaster, on behalf of the old Scouts. Mr Barker expressed best wishes to Mr Aitken for his future.

The District Commissioner, Mr J F Ashton, who, with his wife, was among the guests, also presented new flags to the Cub pack and the Scout Troop on behalf of the old Scouts. Other guests included Mr Fred Simpson, retired under-manager of Wheatley Hill Colliery and Miss Simpson, Sister Hutton and Mr Waugh, from Durham County Hospital.

During supper a birthday cake made by one of the Scouts' oldest supporters, 75-year-old Mrs S Watson, and iced by Mrs L Brain, was cut by Mr Ashton, who wished the Group continued success in their activities. Thanks were expressed to Mrs Watson, who had made the birthday cake every year since the first reunion.

Sing Song

The supper was served by members of the Scouts' Committee, namely Mesdames Watson, Hodgson and Rowlands, Miss Shutt and Mr A Watson.

During a campfire sing-song which followed, organised by Mr Barker, a sketch, "Scouting through the ages", was presented by the following cubs: M Carr, M Robson, K Robson, K Mather, F Brownless, G Hall, C Swinburne, T Bell, G Abbs and S Metcalfe.

Secretarial duties were carried out by Mr Ralph Watson, assisted by Mr Barker, and also helping with the arrangements for a most successful evening were Senior Scoutmaster W White, Scoutmaster Colin Thackeray and Cubmaster W Saxby.

17 January 1969

WHEATLEY HILL MAN DIES DOWN THE PIT

A datal worker at Easington Colliery, Mr Philip Brown (54), of 5 Stanhope Street, Wheatley Hill, collapsed while on his way out-by at the end of his shift at the colliery on Tuesday night and died before reaching the surface. The facts have been reported to the Coroner.

Mr Brown, who had appeared in his usual good health when he left home for work, had been employed at Easington since the closure of Wheatley Hill colliery last May. He had spent all his life in Wheatley Hill, working at the colliery there until it closed down.

A lifelong churchman, he was a member of the Parochial Church Council of All Saints Church at Wheatley Hill. He is survived by his widow and two sons, one of whom is married.

24 January 1969

THORNLEY METHODISTS YEAR OF PROGRESS

The annual review of the year's work took place in the annual Society meeting of Thornley Methodist Church,. The superintendent minister, the Rev Robert Thompson, presided and gave a short address on the constitution and work of the society meeting.

Representatives to Leaders' and Quarterly meetings were Mrs J Bott, Mrs G Wigham, Mrs B Wilson, Mr R Hedley and Mr T Lincoln. The membership stands at 139.

Mr J H Pattison (senior society steward) reported on the financial position. He stressed the fact that the Sodiety Fund had the duty of fulfilling the Church's financial obligations to the circuit. This meant that £760 per annum had to be raised for this purpose alone.

The Trust Fund needed for lighting and cleaning over £5 per week. Some £18 a week was needed to keep the church open and meeting her commitments.

In the absence of Captain Mrs R Speckman, Lieut Miss A Griffiths reported a good year for the church's Girls' Brigade. There were four officers, Capt Speckman, Lieut A Griffiths, Mrs T Lincoln and Mrs J Appleby. The Brigade has 38 members.

The Thornley Company was responsible for a used book stall at the North East Division Spring Fair.

Sunday School

Mr Peter Wood (General Superintendent) reported on Sunday School affairs, and said, "Parents are sending their children to Sunday School in larger numbers. The increase has been largely in the junior age group, 2-6. In the Primary Department alone, Miss Griffiths and Mrs Wood have had to cater for over 100 youngsters.

Mr Kenneth Hetherington, treasurer of the New Building Fund, gave an encouraging report. Membership had met the challenge of the New Building scheme generously. Even after allowing for generous grants in the £18,000 scheme, the members aimed to raise £7000, by their own efforts.

"Our own people have raised over £6300", said Mr Hetherington. "We only have about £700 to raise and then our goal will have been reached".

WHEATLEY HILL MAN FOUND DROWNED

Two days after he had been reported to the police as missing from home, the body of Mr James Lowther (64), of 1 Fifth Street, Wheatley Hill, was recovered from a pond near the village on Sunday morning. Nothing had been seen of him since 10.30pm last Friday.

Police officers went to the pond known as Burns Pond, after a report that a body had been seen floating there. After recovering the body they tried artificial respiration without success.

Mr Lowther, who was a bachelor, lived with a younger brother. He had recently been in hospital. The facts have been reported to the Coroner.
31 January 1969

OPEN VERDICT ON DROWNED MINER

Although evidence was heard that a redundant miner found drowned in a pond at Wheatley Hill had been depressed and worried about his health, it would be wrong to assume that he deliberately took his life, the Coroner, Mr Peter Ord, said at a Peterlee inquest this week.

He recorded an open verdict on James Lowther, 64, a bachelor, of 1 Fifth Street, Wheatley Hill.

Mr Raymond Lowther, 44, also a bachelor, said that on the morning of 24 January his brother said he was going out. It was 'unusual' for him to go out like this and when he had not returned by night he told the police.

"He had been in hospital and seemed to be worried about his health, but he had never threatened to do anything to himself", said Mr Lowther.

PC Ron Maxwell said he recovered Mr Lowther's body about 10ft from the edge of a pond at Wheatley Hill. The pond was very deep but shallow at the side. It was surrounded by a wire netting fence but there was an opening for fishermen to get through.

Dr K A Irvine said death was due to asphyxia by drowning. A post-mortem showed that Mr Lowther had a congenital heart disease.
14 February 1969

WHEATLEY HILL CHURCH DEDICATION SERVICE

The dedication of a new entrance and re-opening service following interior decorations was held in Wheatley Hill Methodist Church on Saturday.

The structural alterations cost £610.11s.11d and the decorations cost £124.7s.10d. The membership had to find £734.19s.9d. This cost would have been considerably higher but for voluntary work by the men craftsmen of the church.

For many years the church in Patton Street has had no pretentions to architectural beauty. Like many churches in County Durham, it had a close association with the colliery company and so long as a church was there to worship in little notice was taken of design.

The new entrance is imposing, built into the centre of the south wall of the church, leading on to a central aisle. There is an inner vestibule, with an inside glass door. The new alterations and decorations are a great improvement and will be an aid to worship.

The service was attended by a congregation of 240 members and friends of other denominations. Opening ceremony was performed by the present minister of the church, the Rev Maurice Henderson, and the Rev George L Nelson (Horden), who was minister at Wheatley Hill for ten years.

The service was conducted and dedicatory prayers were offered by the superintendent minister, the Rev Robert S Thompson (Thornley).

Lessons were read by the Rev G G Graham, Vicar of All Saints, and the circuit steward, Mr J Craig (Trimdon Grange). The sermon was preached by the Chairman of the Darlington Methodist District, the Rev E Lincoln Minshull. Organist was Mrs A Shutt.

Mr Arthur Leverton (circuit steward and Trust Treasurer) gave a financial statement. He intimated that £350 from the sale of the Church Street church had been allocated to the cost of the scheme. Special efforts by individual members had realised £120.1s.3d. Saturday's financial gains were £30, making a total of £500.1s.3d towards the total cost. The balance has been met from church funds.

Presentations of watches or clocks were made to the bricklayers for their work – Messrs A Lambert, W Poulson, J Swift and R Walker. Joiners who helped in the project were Mr J Bennett and Mr J Baron. Mr L Barker did the electrical work. Men of the church laboured for the craftsmen.

Tea was served by ladies of the church.

21 February 1969

GOLDEN EVENT FOR WHEATLEY HILL PAIR

Though he has been an invalid for the past six years and is only able to get about outside, in a wheelchair, Mr William Clish, 2 Aged Miners' Homes, Wheatley Hill, who celebrated his golden wedding on Tuesday, was one of the area's most active sportsmen in his younger days.

He played cricket, football, tennis, croquet and bowls, and proudly recalls he won no fewer than six gold medals in local soccer cup competitions. "But", he told our reporter this week, "I gave them all away and so have nothing to show for the success my team enjoyed". Mr Clish always played in the defence – at half back or full back.

To the Welfare

Nowadays he retains a cheery outlook on life despite his ill-health and in the summer months enjoys being wheeled to the local Welfare Park to watch others taking part in the various recreational activities.

Mr Clish and his wife Ethel, whose maiden name was Goyns, have spent all their married life in the village. They were married at the former Wesleyan Methodist Church at Wingate on 4 March 1919, and on Tuesday held a family party at their home to celebrate their 'golden' anniversary.

Mr Clish, who was 77 last month, was born at Haswell Plough and began work at Shotton Colliery when he was 15. A year later he transferred to Wheatley Hill Colliery, where he remained, doing most jobs underground, until his retirement 12 years ago after a 50-year mining career.

Since a Girl

Mrs Clish (72), was born at Wingate but has lived in Wheatley Hill since she was a girl of 5. She enjoys good health and gives her husband undivided care and attention. For the past four years she has been a member of Wheatley Hill Mothers' Club.

The saddest day of Mrs Clish's life was when an explosion ripped through Easington Colliery in 1951 – two of her brothers, Messrs Ernest and Herbert Goyns, were among those who were killed.

Mrs Clish still has four brothers and a sister living, and her husband has two brothers and three sisters.

The couple have an only daughter, Mrs Ethel Jones, of Peterlee, whose husband Clifford is headmaster of Trimdon Village Parochial School. They also have two grandchildren.

7 March 1969

VANDALS 'TEST STRENGTH' ON WAR MEMORIAL

A public war memorial clock at Wheatley Hill, which for years has given the council a headache, and a war memorial at Wingate which has been damaged by vandals, both sparked off a long discussion at Wingate Parish Council this week.

Experts had examined the clock, said the Clerk, Mr J G Alderton, and had concluded that the present movement should be scrapped and replaced with an up-to-date one which should ensure the correct time even allowing for interruptions in the electricity supply. The cost would be £112.

Coun Mrs D Dodds commented: "The people of Wheatley Hill have given up this clock as a bad job. They just don't expect it to go or, when it is going, to give the correct time".

Year after year the council spend money trying to keep the clock right but they were still getting no satisfaction, said the chairman, Coun J H Charlton.

It was agreed to defer until the next meeting a decision on whether to accept the latest repair estimate. In the meantime the Clerk is to enquire if anyone living in the vicinity would be prepared "to keep an eye on it".

14 March 1969

WHEATLEY HILL IS PROUD OF THESE PEOPLE

Tribute to their sterling work for the club was paid to the former chairman, Mrs E Amies, and treasurer, Mrs I Hodgson, when presentations were made to them in appreciation for their services at the annual meeting of Wheatley Hill Over-60 Club.

Both resigned during the past year after filling their respective positions for eight years. Each was presented with a clock, Mr W Henderson, the present chairman, made the presentation to Mrs Amies, and the treasurer, Mr J W Burrell, made the other presentation.

Reports of excellent progress were presented by the secretary, Mrs M E Richardson and treasurer. The finances, reported Mr Burrell, were in a very healthy state and he thanked the members for their loyal support.

Team Work

Mrs Richardson said that the success of the club, with its 300-odd members, was due not only to the members themselves but also to other people in the village, including the tradespeople, who gave such generous support to their efforts.

It was announced that the annual outing will be held at Redcar on 19 June.

Officers elected were: President, Mrs E Amies; chairman, Mr W Henderson; vice-chairman, Mrs I Robinson; treasurer, Mr J W Burrell; assistant treasurer, Mr J Hammond; secretary and entertainments secretary, Mrs M E Richardson, Assistant Secretary, Mrs J Harper; auditors, Mr J Harper and Mr T Taylorson; committee, Mesdames E Adams, H Saxby, H Worthington, M Charlton, E Charlton, L Turner and D Nicholson and Messrs G Adams, A Martin, S Mitcheson, J Hedley and G Farrar.

LEGION – When Mr R Smith presided over the fortnightly meeting of Thornley British Legion, in the Thornley Officials Club, he welcomed 37 members. Mr W Johnson (secretary) read minutes and correspondence. Mr W Brereton announced that arrangements have been made for pilgrimages to Anzio in May; and to Holland in May, June and August for the purpose of visiting War Cemeteries. Legion personnel are asked to give their names to Mr W Johnson, 40 Thornlaw North, Thornley, if they are desirous of making a reservation for either of these pilgrimages.

LEGION EASTER BONNET PARADE – Mrs Clark presided and welcomed over 70 members to the meeting of Thornley Women's Section of the British Legion. Mrs Bromilow (secretary) read business details. Mrs Harvey and Mrs Willey were MCs for competitions and games. There were 22 entries for the Easter bonnet parade judged by Mrs M Barrass and Mrs D Wright. Prizes were awarded to Mesdames Brazier, Ross and Clark, and the dyed egg competition was won by Mrs Davies. All eggs were taken to St Margaret's Hospital, Durham. Judges were Mrs Bowes and Mrs Hird. Other competition winners were Mesdames L Osbaldestin, E Middleton and P Luke.

11 April 1969

WHEATLEY HILL COMMUNITY ASSOCIATION

Mr Jack Dormand, Education Officer to the Easington Excepted District Education Committee, had one discordant note to strike when he attended the official opening of Wheatley Hill and District Community Association last week.

Referring to vandalism as "the one black spot" in the area, he said it was costing the ratepayers thousands of pounds a year to put right, and he appealed to parents and others to do all in their power to help to combat it.

The Community Association was formed last July soon after Wheatley Hill Colliery was closed and eventually the former Miners' Welfare Hall was acquired for its headquarters.

"The Education Committee", said Mr Dormand, "have taken a very close interest in the development of this Association – and for a very good reason. It is the first Miners' Welfare Association to be taken over by the Education Committee in the Easington Rural District. It has happened in other parts of the county and the country with varying degrees of success, but it is the first time here and it represents a challenge to the people of this village".

Mr Dormand added: "We are pleased with the progress made in such a short time".

582

The official opening was performed by Mr Roderick Griffiths, of Tyne-Tees Television news staff, who was introduced by the chairman of the Association, Coun A D Wharrier.

WHEATLEY HILL WON CIRCUIT BANNER

Thornley Methodist Circuit Youth Eisteddfod closed with a display of needlework and handicrafts in Wheatley Hill Church, and a final concert, given by prize-winners. Over 1000 people visited the event during its ten-day run and 400 attended the final concert, presided over by Mrs Olive Stoves, who presented trophies and certificates.

Leading churches were: Wheatley Hill (118½ points), Trimdon Station (73½), Thornley (57), Fishburn (34½), Trimdon Grange (33½), Kelloe St Pauls (22).

Trophies were awarded to the following: Circuit banner, Wheatley Hill; Lewis Alan cup (runners-up), Trimdon Station; J W Collingwood trophy (highest individual points in handicrafts section), Mrs R Harriman (16 points); Thomas Strong Memorial trophy (highest individual points in other sections), Stephen Pugh (7 points).

James Howie Shield for senior choirs, Thornley Fellowship; William Kirk Cup (photography), David Stoves; Scotex Trophy (junior choirs under 11 years), Wheatley Hill and Thornley; John Wilson Hays Bowl (painting and penmanship), Vera Golightly; J T Galley Cup (public speaking), Wheatley Hill; Doreen Pattison Memorial Cup (vocal solo – girls), Ann Barker; Thornley Circuit Subscription Cup (elecution), Maureen Fulton; Wheatley Hill Church Street Memorial Trophy (pianoforte), Jean Gething and Carolyn Stubbs; Friendship Bowl (modelling), Phillip Harriman and Maurice Nixon.

Memorial Trophy (Bible reading – girls), Judith Wade; J Reg Barker Trophy (Bible reading – boys), David Dunn; Joseph Pattison Cup (needlework), Mrs R Harriman; Dorcas Trophy (cookery), Mrs I Wheatley; Mr and Mrs M F Stephenson Memorial Trophy (recorder), Carolyn Stubbs; Unity Cup (decorated eggs), Mrs R Harriman.

9 May 1969

WHEATLEY HILL GOLDEN WEDDING

The days when it was firmly believed that fairies had been seen dancing on a plot of land at Hetton-le-Hole are recalled by Mrs Ellen Adams, of 3 Eighth Street, Wheatley Hill, who celebrated her golden wedding with her husband George at the weekend.

So strong was the belief that 'fairies cradle' had been found said Mrs Adams, that when houses were built on the site the street was named Fairy Street and a plaque was erected on the wall of No 12 recording the fact that a 'fairies cradle' had been found there.

"I suppose," smiled Mrs Adams, "you could call this a fairy story – but I am firmly convinced it is a true one. I lived with my parents in Fairy Street – No 41 – and well remember people talking about fairies dancing at the bottom of the garden, but I myself never saw them. They used to say they came out at night when everyone was asleep".

"One day", says Mrs Adams, "a 'fairies cradle' was found there. Nobody knew where it had come from – but they said the fairies had brought it", and as far as she can recall, Mrs Adams says it eventually found its way into a museum.

Mrs Adams, who will be 70 in November, and her husband were married at Houghton-le-Spring on 10 May, 1919. They have lived for the past 36 years at Wheatley Hill, where they are well-known and respected.

Both are members of the village's Over-60 Club concert party and serve on the committee. Said Mrs Adams, "It is good fun being in the concert party – we visit other clubs all over the county and really enjoy ourselves".

She and her husband can always find something to do, said Mrs Adams, "We both do the garden – I have one side and he has the other – and I am often busy, either knitting, crocheting or matting", she added.

They also do all their own house decoration and Mr Adams, who will be 74 next month, is often pottering about his workshed. He said, "I love jobbing about and making bits of furniture".

Mr Adams was born at Shotton Colliery but all his mining career of 51 years was spent at Thornley Colliery, where he retired in 1960. For most of the time he was a wagonwaymen.

Mr and Mrs Adams, who are in good health, lived at Hutton Henry for four years and then at Thornley before going to Wheatley Hill. Mrs Adams was formerly actively associated with the Good Templars' movement at Wheatley Hill and was superintendent of the lodge for some time.

The couple, have an only son George, who lives at Cassop, two grandchildren and two great grandchildren. Their only daughter, Mrs Hannah Christopher, who lived at Wynyard, near Wolviston, died five years ago.

16 May 1969

WHEATLEY HILL MAN OFF TO TEACH IN
NEW ZEALAND

Newly out of college, a young Wheatley Hill man, Mr Colin Bramfitt, elder son of Mr and Mrs C Bramfitt, of 13 Wharrier Square, flew thousands of miles away this week to New Zealand, to take up his first teaching post – and join a new soccer club.

At first 22-year-old Colin toyed with the idea of taking up a teaching job he was offered in Canada. "But", he told our reporter this week before leaving home, "I spent last summer in the States working at an educational camp, and thought it would be quite a change exploring another part of the world".

Colin first thought of going to New Zealand when, earlier this year, a friend told him about a football club there which was looking for players from this country.

Accepted

"I have always been keen on soccer", said Colin, "and so I wrote to the club and was accepted by them and they put me in touch with a school where I could teach".

Colin's application to the school – the Southwell School in Hamilton, the biggest preparatory school in the country – was successful and they have fixed him with a flat ready for his arrival.

"They wanted a physical education teacher and so it just suited my ambition", said Colin, who has just finished his final examinations at the Loughborough College of Education for the degree of Bachelor of Education.

Played for Wellfield

Colin played both soccer and rugby for Wellfield A J Dawson Grammar School, Wingate, where he was a student before entering college. For a time he captained the Durham County Youth soccer team and also played for the county Grammar Schools XI. He was 'capped' also for the county under-15 rugby 15.

While at college Colin has been playing for an amateur soccer club in the Midlands and also had two games for Burton Albion in the Premier Division of the Southern League.

Unfortunately he was injured while playing ten weeks ago. He said, "This was a bit of a worry when I was all signed up to go to New Zealand, but I am now back in training and more or less fit again".

In New Zealand Colin will play for Claudeland Rovers FC. He has signed a two-year contract at the school where he is to begin his teaching career. "And at the end of that I will probably come back home for a holiday", he said.

Colin, whose father is a miner at Blackhall Colliery, was born at Wheatley Hill and went to a Secondary Modern School there before qualifying for the Grammar School.

He was 'looking forward tremendously' to his new life in New Zealand, he said, adding, "It'll be quite an experience".

30 May 1969

MANY COUPLES LOOK BACK TO THEIR WEDDING DAY AT WHITSUN, 1919
Wheatley Hill Couple 50 years Wed

A Wheatley Hill couple, Mr and Mrs Ernest Donkin, of 8 Ryan Terrace, celebrated their golden wedding with a quiet family gathering.

Mr Donkin who is 73, was born at Easington Lane but spent nearly all his life at Wheatley Hill. He started work as a boy at the colliery, and completed almost 40 years before leaving the pits to work for a hardware firm in Wheatley Hill until he retired.

Serving in the 1914-18 War with the DLI in France, he was awarded the Military Medal for conspicuous gallantry in the field and on his return after the end of hostilities was presented with a gold watch by village organisations.

He was an active Methodist in his younger days. His hobbies are gardening and bowls, but he is unable through illness to pursue either at present.

Eliza, his wife, was born 72 years ago at Thornley, and the couple were married at Thornley Methodist Church. Both are former members of the Over-60 Club. Mrs Donkin is the eldest of eight girls (all living).

Mr and Mrs Donkin have two daughters, one son and six grand-children.

Mr and Mrs Poulson, Wheatley Hill

Mr Thomas Poulson, of 6 Thirteenth Street, Wheatley Hill, who spent the whole of his mining career of nearly half a century at Wheatley Hill Colliery, mostly as an official, celebrated his golden wedding on Monday.

He and his wife Elizabeth have spent all their married life in the village, where they are held in the highest esteem among a wide circle of friends.

Mr Poulson, who was 72 on Tuesday, was born at Whitburn but was only 4 years old when he moved with his family to Wheatley Hill.

He started work at Wheatley Hill colliery as a lamp carrier when he left school at 14. "The working shift had just been reduced from ten hours to eight when I started", Mr Poulson told our reporter this week, "and my early pay was at the rate of 9s.6d for five shifts".

Mr Poulson did all kinds of work underground and was on deputy work when he was 26. Later he was an official for nearly 30 years, most of the time as back shift overman. When he was 63 he broke his left leg in a pit accident. "And it was then that I decided to pack up work altogether, with being so close to retirement", said Mr Poulson.

For 20 years Mr Poulson was a member of the colliery underground rescue team of the Houghton Rescue and Fire Brigade.

Mrs Poulson, whose maiden name was Cook, was born at Kelloe 70 years ago. She and her husband are both members of Wheatley Hill over-60 Club and Mrs Poulson was formerly a member of the local branch of the Women's Institute.

Mr and Mrs Poulson, both in pretty good health, have an only son Tom, who is a police sergeant at Blackhall, and a daughter, Mrs Margaret Conron, who lives at Peterlee. They also have three grandchildren and one great-granddaughter.
13 June 1969

A THORNLEY COUPLE –
THE COUNTY'S OLDEST-WEDS?

Shortly after the turn of the century a Thornley couple, Mr and Mrs Robert William Forster, walked up the wedding aisle at a parish church on Tyneside ... and this week, still in fairly good health, they were reminiscing on that happy day when they celebrated their 69th wedding anniversary quietly at home. They are believed to be the oldest married couple in East Durham, if not in the county.

Only a fortnight ago the couple, after spending most of their married life in the same house – at 7 Percy Street, Thornley – moved into a new council bungalow at 3 Cooper's Close in the village.

"It was quite an upheaval leaving the house where we had spent so many years together, but now we are beginning to get nicely settled down in our new bungalow and we like it very much", said Mr Forster, who celebrated his 89th birthday last month, told our reporter.

Mr Forster's wife Jane is a year older than him – she was 90 on 17 May, four days before his birthday.

Invalid

For the past five years she has been an invalid, the result of breaking her leg twice.

The first time she broke it when she slipped at home she also broke her wrist and spent 16 weeks in hospital. And then she had not long been out of hospital when she broke the same leg again and was back in hospital again for another nine weeks.

Like her husband, she is in full possession of her faculties and takes a keen interest in what is going on around her. "But", she said, "I cannot get about outside these days".

Her husband is quite active – he was, in fact, cooking their lunch when our reporter called. He said, "I have always had pretty good health until about six months ago – since then I have had more doctor's medicine and pills that I have ever had in the whole of my life!"

The couple, who were married in Heworth Parish Church, on 16 June 1900, have had a family of ten, of whom four daughters and three sons are still living, and there are over 30 grandchildren.

Mr Forster was only 12 when he began work down the pit at Wardley colliery, earning "about 1s.2d" *(approx 7p)* for a ten-hour shift. After a mining career of nearly 54 years Mr Forster retired from work at Wheatley Hill colliery. He worked there for more than 30 years, travelling from Thornley, often in severe wintry weather.

Gardener

Gardening, with leek-growing his speciality, has been Mr Forster's life-long hobby. As well as winning dozens of prizes as an exhibitor at local and county shows, he was well-known as a leek show judge.

The couple are still using articles of furniture Mr Forster won for his expert leek-growing. "In fact", he said, "I won the bed we are still sleeping on!" He cultivated an allotment "from the first sod I cut until it was taken over by the council for building", until he was turned 80.

20 June 1969

WHEATLEY HILL CARNIVAL JUSTIFIED CA WORK

Over 2000 villagers took advantage of the sunny weather on Saturday to attend the Wheatley Hill Community Association first garden party sports day in Wheatley Hill Modern School playing fields.

This association, formed just about a year ago, has taken over the Welfare Hall and grounds when the Wheatley Hill pit closed. The closure of mines is bringing a new element into the life of the County, active Community Associations.

Organising secretary was the Rev Maurice Henderson, sports secretary, Father Meagher; chairman, Coun Anthony Wharrier and treasurer, Mr J Oswald.

The smart uniforms of jazz bands and the picturesqueness of the fancy and comic dress added a touch of colour to the parade through the village.

Results

Sgt Pickering and PC J Carr were judges in the jazz band section. There were many interesting entries in the fancy dress parade. Judges were Miss Harbottle and Miss Elsie Harbottle, Dr and Mrs Penrose and Mrs M Henderson.

Fancy Dress

Results: **Fancy Dress:** 1 Jeanette and Shirley Parkin (off to the fair); 2 Dorothy Parnham (Spanish Lady); 3 Deborah Carr (Bounty). **Original:** 1 Albert Dowson (Welcome to the Moon); 2 William Thompson (Field Marshall Rommel); 3 Margaret Preece and Karen Dinsdale (John and Yoko).

Comic: 1 Lynne Soppitt and Brenda Hammond (litter bug); 2 Kathleen Thubron and Susan Carr (8 draws in a line); 3 Dawn Stephenson and Ellen Peacock (Andy Capp and Flo). **Adult:** 1 Ralph Craggs (tramp); 2 Nat Cook (blind man).

A four mile race provided a close competition. Placings: 1 M Waistell; 2 J Burke; 3 M Hepple; 4 G Ayre; 5 N Cook.

Children's Races

Boys: 5 years: 1 D Dixon; 2 D Barron; 3 C Barron. **6 years:** 1 N Worthington; 2 P Darby; 3 G Atkinson. **7 years:** 1 K Lonsdale; 2 J Hall; 3 M Young. **7 plus years:** 1 J Walker; 2 A Wood; 3 A Walker. **8 years:** 1 A Turnbull; 2 P Niles; 3 G Coxon. **9 years:** 1 G Pugh; 2 S Robinson; 3 J Appleby. **10 years:** 1 I Burnham; 2 J Gutcher; 3 G Pattison. **11 years:** 1 T Hagan; S Hagan; 3 J Bartley. **12 years:** 1 J Carr; 2 G Rowbotham; 3 M Million. **13 years:** 1 D Million; 2 D Welsh; 3 P Appleby. **14 years:** 1 R Martin; 2 G Lambert.

Girls: 5 years: 1 T Wood; 2 S Routledge. **6 years:** 1 A Graney; 2 R Scott. **7 years:** 1 E Parnham; 2 E Bulmer; 3 A Swallow. **7 plus years:** 1 L M Chapman; 2 J Law; J Aspinall. **8 years:** 1 A Amies; 2 C MacDonald; 3 L Warnes. **9 years:** 1 L Robson; 2 P McDonald; 3 S Dobbin. **10 years:** 1 S Dixon; 2 P Attwood; 3 L Patterson. **11 years:** 1 P Hepple; 2 J Hepple; 3 K Rutherford. **12 years:** 1 J Carr; 2 M Bartley. **13 years:** 1 O Telford; 2 P Hitch. **14 years:** 1 M Bulmer; 2 K Waistell; 3 A Battye.

Teas and refreshments did a roaring trade and personnel were provided by Wheatley Hill WI, Mothers' Club, Ladies Bowls Club and British Legion.

The effort realised over £300.

Coun A Wharrier (chairman) said that he and his officials and committee thanked the tradespeople of the village for their fine support.

He appealed for the village's continued support in all Community efforts so that we might keep alive the community spirit which was such a vital characteristic in a mining area. We must not lose that spirit with the closing of our mines.

27 June 1969

THORNLEY GOLDEN

On 6 July 1919, Mr and Mrs George Atkin, both 72, of 8 Coopers Terrace, Thornley, were married in the Rainton Gate Methodist church. They celebrated their Golden

Wedding with a family party on Saturday. 30 of their relatives and friends met in their new bungalow, in which they have lived for a month.

The couple have two daughters, Mrs Smith (Billingham) and Mrs Dinning (Ryton). Another expected guest was Mrs Atkin's sister, Mrs Prudence Attenbury, who flew from Winnipeg in Canada.

Although Mrs Atkin suffered a serious accident some years ago, and is only able to get outside her home with the aid of a wheelchair, she remains a cheerful person with a genius for happiness. Mr Atkin was born at Thornley and has spent all his life in the village. He worked at Thornley Colliery for 51 years. As coal hewer and stone man he worked underground and a serious accident in 1948 caused him to transfer to lighter work. For many years he was a store keeper.

Mr Atkin is a noted gardener and a very successful exhibitor of prize leeks.

He is a regular worshipper at Thornley St Bartholomew's Anglican Church.
11 July 1969

SCOUTS FIELD DAY SUCCESS

Under blazing sunshine and blue skies members of Wheatley Hill Old Scoutsd Association held a successful field day in Wheatley Hill Peterlee Modern School playing fields.

The event was supported by over 1000 villagers, Assistant Scout leader Sidney Saxby was organising secretary. Over £130 was raised for association funds, which are largely used to assist the village's present Scouts and Cubs.

Local Scout groups took part in a camping display. Groups represented were 2nd Wheatley Hill, Colonel Burdon's No 1 Wingate and the 1st and 2nd Peterlee Troops. Each group received a set of cooking pans for their efforts.

A tug-of-war between a team from the Wheatley Hill Fire Station and the Old Scouts Association was won by the Old Scouts.
Stalls
Stalls and sideshows were manned by present and past Scouts. Those assisting were: Messrs W Corner, D Hedley, R Gratton, T Walker, N Waugh, C Thackeray, J Horrocks, R Woodward, D Metcalfe, E Hutchinson, J Cowan, J Metcalfe, R Hunter, A Jamieson, A Watson, W Saxby, W Walker, R Watson, T Meechin, R Elliott, G Anderson, C Gregory, G Hinds, L Barker. Members of the Ladies' Scout Committee were in charge of teas and refreshments.
18 July 1969

THORNLEY SA CORPS STILL A "GOING CONCERN"

Thornley Salvation Army Corps, its headquarters a sturdy red brick building sandwiched between the Miners' Welfare Hall and a disused cinema hall, is still thriving despite reports to the contrary.

The Corps, not as strong in members, as it used to be, holds a Sunday morning service for young soldiers and the Home League meets on Mondays.

Mrs Violet Dowson, Home League secretary for the past 45 years, said she was upset to read that the citadel had closed.

Mrs Dowson, who has sold the Army magazine in the village every week for the past 25 years, added: "I felt as though I was cheating going round selling the War Cry in the name of a Corps which apparently did not exist. The 'Army' was established in Thornley more than 80 years ago and there is no sign of it shutting down. We have 20 Home League members.

Affection

Thornley people of all denominations have an affection for the 'army' and give generously", said Mrs Dowson. "I always get a good reception on visiting the public houses and clubs to sell the War Cry. It is very encouraging. Granted, we are depleted in numbers, but not in spirit", said Mrs Dowson, who is a member of the Senior Census Board and the Church Council for Women's World Day of Prayer.

"So far as I am concerned I will be selling the War Cry in the name of Thornley Corps for many more years".

Captain Freda Armstrong, Commanding Officer of Wingate Corps, who is also responsible for Thornley Corps, said, "Since I took over the command of both Corps a few weeks ago there has been no official move to close Thornley Hall. If there was a move I would be the first to know".

1 August 1969

WHEATLEY HILL GOLDEN PAIR ARE 'DARBY AND JOAN'

A Wheatley Hill couple, known as 'Darby and Joan' at the Over-60 Club they attend in the village because they go everywhere together, celebrated their golden wedding on Monday.

They are Mr and Mrs Fred Alderton, of 100 Johnson Estate, who were married at the Primitive Methodist Church, Thornley, on 4 August 1919, nine months after Mr Alderton was 'demobbed' from the Army.

"We have always gone about everywhere together", Mrs Alderton, whose maiden name was Mary Hannah Jones, told our reporter this week. She added, "We have never been parted all the 50 years – where he goes, I go – and I can honestly say we have always got on very well together".

Mr Alderton enjoys good health but his wife has not been so well recently. "But he is always doing odd jobs in the house for me – he cannot sit still – and he does nearly all the messages", said Mrs Alderton.

Only a Month's Difference

The couple are both 73 – only a month separates their ages – and practically all their married life has been spent in Wheatley Hill, where they have been members of the Over-60 Club for the past 12 years. Mr Alderton was formerly a member of the concert party.

"We thoroughly enjoy the Over-60's and we often go away with them when they are entertaining other clubs – in fact, I have heard the concert party so often that I know the whole programme off by heart!" said Mrs Alderton. Mrs Alderton is also a member of the local women's section of the British Legion.

Mr Alderton started work at Wheatley Hill colliery the day after leaving school at 14. He worked there for 45 years until his neck was broken by a flying wire rope. "That finished my mining career", he said, "I have never been able to work since".

With DLI

During the 1914-18 War Mr Alderton served for three years with the 20th DLI and most of the time was in France and Italy. Only a month before the war ended, his left hand was badly wounded by shrapnel in the battle of the Somme. "I was home on leave in the September and had not long been back in France when I was wounded", he said.

Mr Alderton is one of a family of 14, the first break in which came only six weeks ago when he lost one of his brothers, Mr Albert Alderton, who was best man at his wedding. He still has living seven brothers and five sisters. "I think this must be something a family record", he said. Mrs Alderton's only sister, Mrs Elizabeth Adams, who was her bridesmaid 50 years ago, lives at Essyn House, Easington Village. She is 77.

Mr and Mrs Alderton have had a family of seven, of whom two sons and two daughters are living. They also have 14 grand-children and one great-grandchild. Last Saturday their family provided a celebration party for them at the home of the elder daughter, Mrs Mary Hanley of York Street, Wheatley Hill, where they were the recipients of many good wishes for their future good health and happiness.

BLACK CAT WAS LUCKY FOR GOLDEN PAIR
50 YEARS AGO

Married in All Saints Church, New Shildon, 50 years ago on 4 August, Mr and Mrs William Lloyd, of Morris Crescent, Thornley, celebrated the anniversary with a family party at their home.

"We walked to church for our wedding, and when I stepped out of the house that day a black cat walked in front of me and I was told that was a sign of good luck. Well, we have had good luck since", said Mrs Lloyd.

Mr Lloyd, born at Shildon 72 years ago, was 13 when he started work on the surface at New Shildon Colliery, but after a few weeks he was ordered back to school.

A year later he returned to the colliery, and after a year as a surface worker he started in the pit.

The colliery closed in 1928, so Mr Lloyd moved to Thornley pit and remained there until retiring at 65. At Thornley he was a member of the first team of coal-cutters on machines operated by compressed air. For 52 years Mr Lloyd was a member of Durham Area of the National Union of Mineworkers.

In his younger days he played left-half for Shildon Rovers FC. Mr Lloyd is a member of the local Over-60 Club, at one time serving on the committee.

In 1916, he joined the King's Own Hussars, a cavalry regiment, and served in Northern Ireland. He won many prizes for rifle-shooting.

Mrs Lloyd, born at Spennymoor 72 years ago, was four years old when the family moved to Shildon. "I was 16 when I started courting Bill, and it was the best thing that happened in my life".

WI Member

Mrs Lloyd, a life-long member of the Church of England, is an active member of Thornley St Bartholomew's Church Mothers' Union, and for 38 years has been a member of the local Women's Institute.

She served on the committee of the local Over-60 Club and is a member of the club's concert party.

From the Over-60 Club, Mr and Mrs Lloyd received a silver cake stand, and from the club concert party a gold flower vase. Mr H Pattison, the concert party compere, presented them with a fruit dish. The golden wedding cake was made by Mr and Mrs Cutter, relations.

Mr and Mrs Lloyd have two sons and a daughter all married, and two grandchildren. One of the sons, Mr Stanley Lloyd, of Cleethorpes, near Grimsby, played for Sunderland FC and then for Grimsby FC, and Scunthorpe United FC.

8 August 1969

FOOTBALLER DIES AFTER WHEATLEY HILL GAME

While captaining Wheatley Hill Workmen's Club SC soccer team in their Durham Club Union League match against Murton British Legion Club at Wheatley Hill last Saturday, Mr James Robert Cowan (25), of 48 Wheatley Terrace, Wheatley Hill, collapsed and was rushed to Dryburn Hospital, Durham, where he died three hours later.

Jim Cowan with his Workmen's Club SC Soccer Team
Back L-R: Dave Young, David Robson, Morris Nichols, Colin Smith, George Cook, Sid Jobes
Front L-R: Ralph Winter, Jim Cowan, Alf Purvis, Alan Hawkes, Eddy Newby

It was during the first half that Mr Cowan – well known in the village as Jimmy – collapsed while playing in the left back position. He was in his second year as captain of the team.

Mr Cowan, who had lived in Wheatley Hill all his life, worked as a joiner for a firm near Darlington. He served on the committee of Wheatley Hill Workmen's Club, and was also a meber of the village's Old Scouts' Association.

The son of a widow, Mrs Elizabeth Cowan, Mr Cowan was one of a family of 11 – he had four brothers and six sisters. One of his sisters, Miss Sheila Cowan, who was 21, was killed last October when involved in a collision with a workmen's bus she had gone to catch near her home to go to work at a Spennymoor factory.

Mr Cowan had been married three years. He is survived by his wife and a baby daughter of 17 months.

Following a service in All Saints' Church, Wheatley Hill, on Wednesday, conducted by the Vicar, the Rev G Gordon Graham, Mr Cowan was cremated at Durham.

22 August 1969

CIU LEAGUE PAYS TRIBUTE TO JIM COWAN

At all eight matches in the Club Institute Union League programme on Saturday, teams observed a silence before the kick off, and all players wore black arm bands, to the memory of James R Cowan, the Wheatley Hill Club captain, who died in hospital after collapsing during the game against Murton British Legion a week earlier.

"Jimmy was one of our most enthusiastic players, a sportsman in every sense of the word, and popular with all players in the league; he will be a great loss to sport", said Mr Joe Hayes, secretary of the league.

The league committee have agreed to the postponed Easington Central-Houghton Social game being played on Bank Holiday Monday, at Easington (10.30am) when the proceeds will be donated to his widow.

29 August 1969

BENEFIT MATCH AT WHEATLEY HILL

As a benefit match for the dependants of the late Mr Jimmy Cowan, the team captain, who died suddenly last month, Wheatley Hill Workmen's Club SC are to play Murton British Legion Club at Wheatley Hill on Sunday morning (kick-off 10.15am).

Mr Cowan, who was 25, collapsed on the field while playing for Wheatley Hill against Murton British Legion on 16 August and died three hours later in hospital. He was in his second year as captain of the team, which competes in the Durham Club Union League. Mr Cowan was married and had a baby daughter.

12 September 1969

THORNLEY WOMAN LOOKS BACK OVER 90 YEARS

Mrs Elizabeth Lowther, 34 Greenwood Cottages, Thornley, has reached 90 years of age this week and celebrated the event with a family party at her son's home in Durham. With the exception of three years in Wingate as a child, the rest of her long life has been spent in Thornley.

Mrs Lowther, was a member of a family of 15. She married the late Mr Robert Jordison, a miner, who died as a result of illness, whilst doing service in the First

World War. The couple had three sons, Arnold, residing at Darlington; George at Durham; and Norman at Wheatley Hill.

Later in life, she married Mr Thomas Henry Lowther, and was widowed again after 28 years.

Mrs Lowther recalled the early struggles the Durham miners had. She commented, "I remember one serious incident when I was a child. There had been trouble at Thornley pit. The previous day the men had found there was no wages for them at the end of the fortnight. On the Sunday afternoon the men thronged the market place and in angry mood created near riot conditions. The police were called to control an ugly situation. We were in Sunday School at the time and some of our parents and church officials led us home in safety".

Mr Arnold Jordison (Darlington), was a church organist at Thornley for some years and was a noted pianist. Mrs Lowther is proud of the fact that his father gave him his original tuition and fostered the love of music in his son.

Methodist

A Methodist for over 60 years, she was an ex-Wesleyan and her service was largely given to the Waterloo Street Methodist Church in Thornley. She remembers the landmarks in the history of that church; the putting in of a gallery to accommodate the increasing membership; the introduction of a pipe organ in worthip; the advance from gas lighting to electric light.

When Waterloo Street was closed and joined with the Bow Street society to form the new Methodist Church in Thornley, Mrs Lowther transferred her allegiance. She said, "It was a heart-break to us to see the church in which we had been christened, married and many of our families buried, close down. But we realise that the move was necessary.

Era of Change

Mrs Lowther has lived through an era of change. She remarked "People today, particularly young people, have no idea of conditions which prevailed at the beginning of the century. Today we don't see miners taking barrows and horses and flatcarts going round the villages begging food and clothing while their colliery is on strike. That was a regular sight at one time. Today the ugly back-to-back rows of grey colliery houses have given way to the modern home".

Mrs Lowther was a former member of the Thornley Over-60 Club. Today she is the oldest member of Thornley Methodist Church Sisterhood and attends its meetings.
12 September 1969

RECORD STANDS AT WHEATLEY HILL SHOWS

The annual leek show at the New Tavern, Wheatley Hill, on Saturday, drew 24 leek entries and over 100 in other sections. Organising secretary was Mr J Richardson and Mr Walter Myers (Sedgefield) was judge.

The outstanding exhibitor was Mr William Curry, who took seven firsts and three seconds.

Mr T Foster took the Nimmo Cup for the leek championship and Mr E H Ward had the best leek.

Results: Leeks: 1 T Forster (110.2 cu in); 2 E H Ward; 3 T Mole; 4 R Patterson; 5 J Scott; 6 S Scott.

Flowers: Bunch: 1 S Scott; 2 W Curry; 3 J Scott. Button Hole: 1 W Curry; 2 J Williamson; 3 J Frampton. Decorative Dahlias: 1 T Kellett; 2 J Frampton; 3 C Bramfitt. Pompom Dahlias: 1 I Richardson; 2 E H Ward; 3 W Hall. Cactus Dahlias: 1 W Curry; 2 S Parnham; 3 W Hall.

Vegetables – Onion: 1 W Hall; 2 and 3 T Mole. Celery: 1 and 2 W Curry; 3 D Knowles. Parsnips (long): 1 W Curry; 2 S Swallow; 3 T Mole. Carrots (long): 1 W Curry; 2 J Richardson; 3 J Frampton. Cauliflowers – 1 W Curry; 2 T Kellet; 3 J Frampton. Kidney potatoes: 1 T Kellett; 2 W Curry; 3 S Parnham. Round potatoes: 1 S Parnham; 2 W Curry; 3 N Franklin.

CONSTITUTIONAL CLUB

From a record number of stands – 43 – at the annual leek show in Wheatley Hill Constitutional Club, Mr S Raffell won first prize with leeks measuring 77.18 cubic inches. The runner-up was Mr R Forster (77.25 cubic inches).

The quality of the exhibits – leeks, vegetables and flowers – was outstanding and the judge, Mr S Poulson, had anything but an easy tak in naming the winners. Prizes valued at more than £500 were awarded and officials were Messrs R Forster (chairman), C Rose (treasurer) and C Frampton (Secretary).

Winners

Pot Leeks (in order of merit): R S Raffell; R Forster; W T Bell; J Orchard (also best single leek in show); I Wilson; G Worthington; S Scott; J Gair; L Young and G Hewitson. Intermediate leeks: 1 C W Rose; 2 and 3 R Forster.

Other vegetables – Intermediate leeks: 1 C W Rose; 2 and 3 R Forster. Celery: 1 C Frampton; 2 A Sutherland; 3 J Gair. Parsnips: 1 E Lowther; 2 and 3 R Cook. Long carrots: 1 R Forster; 2 A Sutherland; 3 E Lowther. Short carrots: 1 C Worthington; 2 E Lowther; 3 R Forster. Onions (with tops): 1 W Elcoat; 2 M Curry; 3 W Curry. Cauliflowers: 1 R Cook; 2 S Hewitson; 3 A Holden. Tomatoes: 1S Scott; 2 W Curry; 3 A Lambert. Round Potatoes: 1 S Raffell; 2 C Bell; 3 A Sutherland. Kidney Potatoes: 1 and 2 R Cook; 3 S Worthington.

Flowers – Bunch of Flowers: 1 G Hewitson; 2 J Scott; 3 C Frampton. Bowl of Dahlias: 1 S Scott; 2 W Curry. Vase of 12 blooms: 1 A Holden; 2 G Hewitson; 3 K Bell. Three incurved chrysanthemums: 1 R Cook; 2 R Forster; 3 S Metcalfe. Six chrysanthemums (any variety): 1 and 3 R Cook; 2 J Gair. Gladioli: 1 and 2 C W Rose. Three poms (medium or semi-cactus): 1 R Cook; 2 J Gair; 3 A Holden. Three pom-pom dahlias: 1 M Curry; 2 W Curry; 3 S Scott. Gent's Buttonhole: 1 A Holden; 2 J Frampton; 3 G Hewitson. House plant: 1 J Gair; 2 abd 3 G Lambert.

26 September 1969

BLACKHALL ATH 3, THORNLEY YC 6

Blackhall Athletic quickly recovered from an early goal scored against them when they entertained Thornley Youth Club in the Seaham and District League on Saturday and by half-time had established a 3-2 lead.

Later, however, ThorNley came much more into the picture, pressing home some strong attacks, and rattled in four goals to register a convincing win.

It was Dave Smithson, their centre-forward, who put Thornley ahead after ten minutes and after Blackhall had gone into a 3-1 lead with goals from Billy Bell, Ron Wilkinson and Billy Dawson, Walker reduced the arrears shortly before half time.

Saiger, a live wire in the visitor's attack, scored twice in the second half, Smithson got a second goal and two minutes from time Peachey, who had come on as substitute, completed the scoring.

WHEATLEY HILL JUN 3, FERRYHILL JUN 1

The home team gave a good performance to enter into the second round of the County Junior Cup competition. It was a keenly contested first half, there being very few scoring chances due to the firmness of the defence.

"Hill" took the lead in the 55th minute, Cook making a fine solo effort to shOot in. Shortly afterwards, Million increased the lead, and Cook headed on to the bar.

"Hill" were setting the pace at this phase, but in a breakaway the visitors scored. It was a tough struggle for supremacy in the closing stages. Then Starkie settled the issue by converting a penalty in the last minute.

"Mick" Hoban (centre-half) and Brian Foster (right-back) were resolute defenders for the winners, and George Burke (outside-left) was the most effective forward.

31 October 1969

CHRYSANTHEMUMS – With one first, two seconds and a third, Mr W Swindle of Shotton, was the principal prize-winner at the first open chrysanthemum show held this week in Wheatley Hill Discharged and Demobilised Soldiers' and Sailors' Club. The show, which is to become an annual event, was judged by Mr Tom Poulson, of Wheatley Hill. Winners were: Incurves – 1 H Brain (also wins Vaux Silver Tankard); 2 J Nattrass; 3 W Swindle. Reflex – 1 and 2 W Swindle; 3 J Nattrass. Decoratives – 1 J Nattrass; 2 W Swindle; 3 F Hodgkinson.

LEGION BRANCH REVIVED – Wheatley Hill branch of the British Legion, which disbanded some years ago, was re-formed at a meeting of ex-servicemen from the village in the Soldiers' Club. Mr Sydney Craggs, of 60 Johnson Estate, Wheatley Hill, was elected secretary of the new branch, Mr Ernest Curry chairman, Mr William Hackworth vice-chairman and Mr Thomas Hodgson treasurer. Arrangements were made to hold the next meeting at 8pm next Wednesday in the club and an invitation was extended to all ex-servicemen in the village interested in Legion affairs to attend.

GOOD YEAR FOR WHEATLEY HILL BL WOMEN

A year of excellent progress, with an average of about 100 members regularly attending weekly meetings, was reported at the annual meeting of Wheatley Hill women's section of the British Legion, presided over by Mrs D Cowan.

Mrs Cowan welcomed 104 members, including a new one, and the secretary, Mrs F M Carr, reviewed the year's work. A satisfactory financial statement was presented by the treasurer, Mrs E Stainsby.

Officers re-elected unopposed were: President, Mrs L Saxby; vice presidents, Mrs Robinson and Mrs Walls; chairman, Mrs D Cowan; vice-chairman, Mrs G Jones; secretary, press correspondent and standard bearer, Mrs F M Carr; assistant secretary, Mrs E Johnson; treasurer, Mrs E Stainsby; assistant treasurer, Mrs Irene Hodgson; delegate, Mrs P E Morgan; assistant standard-bearer, Mrs V Worthington; sick visitors, Mrs M Saxby and Mrs H Worthington; committee, Mesdames M Saxby, H Worthington, A Mercer, A Booth, E Telford, L Collingwood, M Farrar, V Worthington, M Charlton, E Carter and M Wilson.

As a result of a bring-and-buy sale and the sale of home-made toffee, £14.13s.7d was raised for the Poppy Day Fund. Refreshments were served by the committee and the meeting ended with a programme of games arranged by Mrs Cowan and Mrs Carr.

7 November 1969

THORNLEY COLLIERY LOSES ITS FIGHT FOR LIFE

A nine-month battle waged by 900 miners has failed and Thornley Colliery will close on 31 January.

The pit was placed in 'jeopardy' in February after losing £500,000 in the previous ten months, and though, as a National Coal Board official said this week the men had worked very hard; it was now impossible to keep it going.

It means that 900 men will lose their jobs at the pit, but though about 150 men over 55 will probably be declared redundant, jobs are available at other long life pits in the area for younger men who are able to travel.

Seam Fault

The pit produces coking coal which is in strong demand – but it cannot produce it cheaply enough. Because of the geological conditions, the men have to send 1700 tons to the surface to provide 900 saleable tons. Because of the difficult underground conditions with faulting and stone intrusion into the coal seams, operating costs have become too high.

The decision to close the pit was announced after a meeting yesterday of the Colliery Consultative Committee which was attended by top Coal Board and union officials.

14 November 1969

FAREWELL GIFTS TO WHEATLEY HILL VICAR

A large congregation assembled in All Saints Church, Wheatley Hill, for evensong to say farewell to Rev Gordon G Graham, Mrs Graham and their two daughters, Sidonie and Phillipa. Mr Graham has been vicar of All Saints for 13 years. The occasion was his last service in the parish as vicar. He takes up a similar appointment at Hunwick St Paul's Church.

During his 13 years at Wheatley Hill, Mr Graham has seen a lot accomplished in his own church and in the community. He put in hand schemes for surfacing the drive to the church; had new gates built and added a new vestry. In his time a new altar has been installed in the Lady Chapel and back dorsal curtains subscribed. Mr Graham's ministry has always shown an interest in young people. He founded the church's successful youth club and the Over Twenty Club and was instrumental in having the beautiful memorial stained glass windows put into the East of the church.

He has always enjoyed a good relationship with the village Over-60 Club. Besides attending their Christmas party he has conducted an annual service for the old people. He has also shared services with the Roman Catholics and Methodists.

Mr Graham was chairman of the Community Association, formed when Wheatley Hill Colliery closed down. He was a staunch supporter of the village taking over the Miners' Welfare Hall.

The villagers showed their appreciation of Mr Graham's ministry during Evensong. The Vicar preached and Mr A Tuffnell was organist. On behalf of the church membership, Mr S Woodward (vicar's warden) presented the Rev G G Graham with a cheque and paid tribute to his service. Mrs E Thompson (Mothers' Union enrolling member) presented Mrs Graham with a bouquet.

Boxes of chocolates to the Vicar's children, were the personal gifts of Mr S Woodward. Sunday School teachers, Senior Sunday School scholars and members of the junior choir gave Mr Graham a black calf skin wallet of notes. The presentation was made by Margaret Ann Amies.

CUPS FOR WHEATLEY HILL BL WOMEN

When she attended the recent annual county conference of the British Legion (women's section) Mrs P E Morgan, delegate for the Wheatley Hill women's section, was presented with three cups by Lady Havelock Allen – one of them, the Park Cup, was won by the section for the second year running for the biggest increase in membership.

The Lady Havelock Allen Cup for Durham Quilting was awarded to Mrs Gallon, a member of the Wheatley Hill section, and another member, Mrs I Robinson, won the cup for the member proposing most new members.

Mrs Morgan reported on the conference at the section's weekly meeting and was thanked by the president, Mrs L Saxby.

Mrs D Cowan presided and members stood in silence in memory of Mrs Annie Hughes, who had died since the last meeting. The business items were dealt with by secretary, Mrs F M Carr, and Mrs M Saxby reported on sick visiting. An auction of goods realised £3.2s.9d for Poppy Funds.

Mrs Carr was pianist for a musical parcel competition, which was won by Mrs Symons and Mrs Clark. Mrs F Routledge, won the weekly Legion prize. The committee served refreshments and the meeting ended with a programme of games organised by Mrs Cowan and Mrs Carr.

28 November 1969

THORNLEY BAZAAR RAISED £240

A former member of Thornley Waterloo Street Methodist Church and Sunday School teacher, Mrs Joyce Howie (Wingate) returned to the village to open a successful Christmas bazaar held in the local Welfare Hall, in aid of the Thornley Methodist Church. She was introduced by Mr Joseph H Pattison (society steward and Trust secretary) who presided. Pauline Barker presented a bouquet and Allison Bullock gave a buttonhole spray to Mrs Howie.

The effort raised over £240. Mrs J Mather acted as organising secretary, with Mr J H Pattison as treasurer. Stallholders were: Sisterhood: Mesdames J Mather, N Fort, G Watson, G Hetherington, J Bullock, W Henderson, J Thornton and Miss I Smart. Society: Mesdames G Walls, G Wigham, E Walls. Sunday School: Mesdames T Wood, C Bullock and Miss N Armstrong. Choir: Mesdames W Davies and E Maitland. Girls' Brigade: Mesdames R Speckman, J Crisp. Friends of the Church: Coun Miss A Griffiths, Misses Margaret Jackson, Lindy Fisher. Cakes: Mesdames F Pugh, E Greener, E Musgrave. Photography: Mr T Robinson. Pottery: Messrs J Mather, R Hedley, A L Miller. Christmas cards: Mrs J Bennett. Games and sideshows: Officers and members of the Boys' Brigade under Capt R Speckman.

Tea and refreshments: Mesdames M Hedley, J Bott, F Middlemas, J Hedley, A Appleby, M Barrass, E Middleton, R E Gratton, A Gulliver, S Lee, J Oswald, O Lincoln, P Wood.

Also assisting were Mr Tom Lincoln, Mr George Hetherington and Mr Harry Robinson.

5 December 1969

TURKEY FOR THORNLEY BL WOMEN

Christmas has come early for Thornley Women's Section of the British Legion. They gathered for the Christmas party in the Argus Butterfly Hotel, Peterlee, and Mrs E Robson (chairman) welcomed 70 members to a meal of turkey with all the traditional trimmings. The dinner was organised by Mrs Joan Forster.

Mrs Robson made presentations to two officers who had served the Legion for many years before their retirement this year. Handbags went to Mrs E Clark, who had served as chairman for 25 years, and to Mrs G M Bromilow, secretary. Games and dancing followed; music was by George (pianist) and Syd (drums). MC's Mrs B Musgrave and Mrs E Smailes. Musical items were contributed by Miss Julie Day, Mr E Peachey, sen, Mr W Parker (comedian), all of Thornley. Prize-winners were

Mesdames E Woodhead, M Hood, E Baldasera, E Middleton, M Hodgson, E Hird, E Gordon, B Osbaldestin, S Richardson and M Myers.

12 December 1969

LUDWORTH SCHOOL SPEECH DAY

There was a good assembly of parents and scholars at the annual prize giving and speech day in the Ludworth County Junior Mixed and Infants School. An encouraging report was given by the headmaster, Mr R B Simpson, who was supported by his staff, Mr G Kirkup, Mrs B Morris and Miss D Turnbull. The chairman was Mr G Pritchard, of Shadforth, school manager, and others present were Coun J T Hedley, school manager and chairman of Shadforth Parish Council and County Coun D Thornton.

It his address Mr Simpson said among the occasions that we tend to look both back and forward to, were the Christmas festivities, concerts and parties.

This year, again they had a successful sports day, but with a difference – it was held on the newly completed School Sports Field. In the past the school had to rely on the generosity of Mr Davison, and during the past decade, of the Welfare and Recreation Committee for the use of a field.

One pleasant surprise was the spurt made by the school football team rather late in the season and it led to their appearing in two cup semi-finals, one of which was lost and the other won in a replayed match away from home. The team had to face the Champion team of a larger schools league. Although the Ludworth team was beaten, every credit was due to the boys for their determination and never-say-die spirit.

During the Summer Term, the schools in the area were able to share a totally new (for this area) experience. It was agreed that the schools supplying pupils to the Sherburn Secondary School should arrange a festival of movement, mine and music.

Nearly 45 per cent of the children of Ludworth School took part and had representatives in each part of the programmes which proved to be one of great success.

The greater value was that they were learning to live and work with children of other villages and to become acquainted with the children and teachers with whom they would see later at the Secondary School.

Speaking upon the school buildings, Mr Simpson told his hearers that at the moment planning was going ahead rapidly for the modifications to the existing school buildings.

Prizewinners

Mr Hedley presented prizes to the following: **For progress**: April Stones, Stephen Jackson, Keith Briggs, Mary Widdowfield, Kay Osbaldestin, Sandra Gradon, Heather Peachey, Denise White, Carole White, Keith Cartwright, Joy Vasey, Keith Raine, Neil Savage, William Young, Julie Stannard, Anne Dunbar, John Bell, Kanice Widdowfield, Gary Bennet, Denise Stephenson.

Special Prizes: For effort: Arthur Phenny; **for initiative**: Paul Whittle; **for helpfulness:** Sharon Huntingdon; **Headmasters prize**: Denise White; **Unbroken**

attendance: Two years – Sandra Gradon, Julie Stannard, Arthur Phenny, Mary Widdowfield; **One year** – Allison Vasey, Beverley Carr, Gillian Smith, Kathleen Gibb, Keith Briggs, Stephen Huntington, Brian Ingleby, Valeria Brown, Anne Dunbar.

For entertainment this year the school had sought to develop a programme out of the work done by the children during the present term, and the children attempted to portray the story of Aladdin by means of movement, mime, choral speech and vocal and instrumental music.

19 December 1969

1970

THORNLEY 'DIAMOND'

On 4 January 1910, Mr and Mrs Rowland Johnson, 1 Aged Miners' Homes, Thornley, were married in Thornley St Bartholomew's Church by the Rev J Hodgson. A small family party will celebrate the event, on Sunday quietly in their home. The couple have one married daughter, Mrs Ethel Goodwin, and three grandchildren and three great-grandchildren. Their other daughter, Mrs Ella Proudlock, is deceased.

Mr Johnson was born in the village 79 years ago and started work at Thornley Pit when he was 13. He served 52 years in the one colliery and finished as a stone-man at 65.

Mr Johnson served in 1914-1918 War with the 10th Northumberland Fusiliers and fought in France. He was in the Battle of the Somme and was severely wounded in the Nieuport sector of the line.

Football and gardening were Mr Johnson's main hobbies. He was a noted leek grower and won many prizes. His daughter, Mrs Ethel Goodwin, has in her possession, and still in use, a dinner service which her father won in a leek show in 1925. She has had it since her marriage in 1930. Mr Johnson was for many years a member of Thornley Workmen's Club.

Mrs Sarah Ellen Johnson is 78 and does her own work. She was born in Tanfield and moved to Thornley as a baby. Her only outside interest is her church, St Bartholomew's. For many years she has been a regular worshipper there and is a member of the Mothers' Union. In her younger days she helped in church social activities.

2 January 1970

WHEATLEY HILL MINER RETIRES

After nearly 50 years service in the mining industry, most of which was spent at Wheatley Hill Colliery, Mr Mark Alderton, of 63 Wordsworth Avenue, Wheatley Hill, has retired through ill-health. He celebrated his 64th birthday yesterday.

"I only had a year left to go to pension age", Mr Alderton told a 'Chronicle' reporter, "but decided to retire because I have not enjoyed the best of health for the last year or two".

Mr Alderton, who has served on Wingate Parish Council for the past nine years – he is the present Chairman – has also decided to retire from this authority.

For most of his life Mr Alderson has taken an active interest in the trade union, political and social life in Wheatley Hill.

He was compensation secretary for Wheatley Hill miners' lodge for 16 years and he has served on the local Aged Miners' Homes Committee for the past 15. For two years he was secretary of the Aged Miners' Treat Fund and was formerly secretary of the local Welfare Committee for two years.

For more than 30 years Mr Alderton has been a member of the Civil Defence Corps and he holds a long-service medal.

He began work at Wheatley Hill colliery when he was 14. Four years ago, when the Harvey seam was closed, he transferred to Easington Colliery.

Mr Alderton is married, with an only daughter, Irene, a policewoman in Bradford.

9 January 1970

LEGION PROGRESS – Good progress was reported when the recently-formed Wheatley Hill branch of the British Legion resumed its weekly meetings. Six new members were welcomed by the chairman, Mr E Curry. Mr Curry said that the draw to raise funds for the branch had been very successful and plans were now in hand for a social evening, to which neighbouring branches would be invited.

CAROL SINGING - Though the money they have raised by carol singing in the village over many years has been spent on the children's ward of Durham County Hospital, which they "adopted", Wheatley Hill Old Scouts' Association are to give the record sum of £65 they raised during the recent festive season to another charitable organisation and not to the children's ward. "We have been delighted over a long period to provide extras for the children's ward", an official said this week, "but this year we decided to make a change, although we have not yet settled on which organisation will benefit".

PIT CLOSURE

With the closure of Thornley Colliery at the end of this month, the meals-on-wheels service run at Wingate and Wheatley Hill for elderly people of these villages has come to an abrupt end. "We are extremely disappointed that we have had to suspend this service, but, with the dinners collected from the canteen at Thornley Colliery no longer available, there was, of course, no other choice", Mrs Hilda Kilgour, the Easington Area WRVS Organiser, told a Chronicle reporter this week.

At Wingate, where there was a twice-weekly delivery of meals to 15 elderly folk, and at Wheatley Hill, where 12 meals went out for the last time last week. Because of the gradual run-down of the colliery canteen the Luncheon Club at Thornley, which provided 30 meals twice a week, ceased about a month before Christmas after being in existence for about five years.

New Source

It was impossible to say when there would be a resumption of the meals service, said Mrs Kilgour, but certainly every avenue was being explored to find a new source of supply.

Mrs Kilgour said she had already been in touch with the Medical Officer of Health for the Easington Rural Area to try and "sort out the problem" of meals supply. She added: "The ideal solution, of course, would be a central meals kitchen which could supply the whole area, especially since we can no longer really depend on NCB canteens because of pit closures".

The voluntary workers at Wingate and Wheatley Hill, who were responsible for taking out the meals were themselves disappointed at the end of the service, said Mrs Kilgour, for they felt that it was during the winter months that the elderly people were most in need of the meals

Mrs Kilgour added: "Both schemes were running very well and at Wingate we had been hoping to start a Luncheon Club". Mrs Myra Bell was in charge of the scheme at Wingate, which was launched 14 months ago, and responsible for the rota at Wheatley Hill, where the service was introduced about four years ago, was Mrs Thackeray. Mrs Grieves was the Luncheon Club organiser at Thornley.

16 January 1970

EX-MINERS JOIN JOBLESS QUEUE

At intervals, in alphabetical order, 170 ex-Thornley miners signed the unemployed register at the Wingate office of the Department of Employment and Productivity on Monday.

The majority were 55 years and over made redundant by the NCB. "They are all eligible for employment, but in most cases their chances of getting work are very limited", said a spokesman at the office this week.

Most of them will have worked 40 or more years in the pits and are set in their ways. Factories needing men for re-training will not be keen to take them because of the risk of not getting back money spent on training.

There was no time on Monday to interview the men, said the spokesman, but they would get round to this in due course and some would be offered suitable work.

One of the men in the queue to sign was Mr Michael Darby, aged 61, who had worked 47 years in the pits. "I am sure I am expressing the feelings of most miners in their 60's when I say that we have had enough,

"Considering the contribution we have made to the wellbeing of the country over a long period in uncongenial conditions, I think, like the pit ponies, we should be put out to grass and left to live out the remainder of our lives in comfort", he said.

There are now 650 people on the Wingate register of unemployed.

6 February 1970

LEGION SALE - Wheatley Hill Women's Section of the British Legion raised £8.2s, with a bring-and-buy-sale at their weekly meeting to help towards the cost of a new standard for the recently-formed men's branch. Mrs D Cowan presided and secretary Mrs F M Carr, read the minutes and correspondence. The weekly Legion prize was won by Mrs G Jones, and Mrs E Kendal won the special competition prize. Games were organised by Mrs Cowan and Mrs Carr.

LEGION MEETING - Three months after the formation of the branch, membership now totalled 50, the secretary, Mr S Craggs, reported at the weekly meeting of the Wheatley Hill branch of the British Legion. Good progress had been made, he said, but there was still plenty of room for more members and he hoped that all ex-Servicemen in the village would join the branch. Mr E Curry presided and the

treasurer, Mr T Hodgson, presented a satisfactory financial statement. A report of the No 10 Group conference was given by the delegate, Mr W Poole. The meeting ended with a dominoes drive arranged by the social secretary, Mr G Hewitson.
20 February 1970

COMMUNITY ASSOCIATION AT THORNLEY

"This will keep the heart of the village throbbing", declared Dr John Gray, at a public meeting in Thornley Welfare Hall on Monday night when his proposal that a village Community Association be formed was carried unanimously. The proposal was seconded by the village's representative on Durham County Council, Coun Edward Carter.

The meeting was convened by Easington Rural District Education Committee to discuss the future of the Miners' Welfare Scheme following the closure of Thornley Colliery at the end of January.

All the villagers over 18 had been invited by circular letter to attend and the District Education Officer, Mr Jack Dormand, who explained the aims and objects of the association, said he was pleased to see such a wide range of citizens present – from the younger element to the senior citizens. "This augurs well for the future success of the association", he said.

Mr Dormand, who was introduced by the chairman of the district youth and social services' committee, Coun A D Wharrier, said that the Welfare Hall had been generously put at their disposal by the Coal Board Social Welfare Organisation as the headquarters for a Community Association.

Said Mr Dormand: "Had we been able to sit down and design a purpose-built Community Centre it is doubtful whether we could have got a building better than this one. It has all the ingredients and facilities of a successful centre".

A Community Association, said Mr Dormand, would provide a "focal point" for all the village's activities – it could form a very important and, indeed, a crucial link between all the various organisations.

New Group

It was not just a question of taking over the Welfare Hall, said Mr Dormand. He added: "We would hope that all kinds of social and recreational groups would be formed and new suggestions made to improve the village life, all under the umbrella of the association".

They wanted to encourage every organisation in the village to become affiliated to the association, said Mr Dormand, and he hoped that every villager would join to make it a really successful venture.

Turning to the cost of running the association, Mr Dormand said that up to 75 per cent would be met by the youth and social services' committee. The members themselves would be responsible for raising the rest of this money – this could come from affiliation and membership fees and special efforts.

Mr Dormand added: "We are challenging the people of Thornley not only to come together as a Community Association but to make it the envy of the whole of the Easington Rural District. I am confident they can do it!"

Mr J Coates, social welfare officer for the South Durham Area of the Coal Board, said his organisation was quite ready to hand over as a gift the Welfare Hall for the benefit of the Thornley community.

There would be "no strings attached", said Mr Coates, and, in fact, they would be ready to help in any way and even carry out the legal formalities with the Ministry to transfer the building to the local authority on behalf of the Community Association.

Mr Coates added: "We know the people of Thornley are capable of making a really "good go" of this Community Association".

When questions were invited of the large representative audience one of them asked if any estimate could be given of the cost of running the Welfare Hall. The Welfare secretary, Mr R Patterson, said that the cost this past year was in the region of £3700. Up to three-quarters of the cost, however, as already explained, would be met by the youth and social services' committee.

Thanks to Mr Dormand for so clearly outlining the position and to the villagers for turning up in such large numbers and giving such enthusiastic support were expressed by Coun W H Tate, vice-chairman of the Education Committee.

Coun Tate said, "When a pit dies it is very regrettable, but when the community spirit dies in a village, that is pathetic. But by coming here tonight the people of Thornley have proved that their community spirit will never die but, in fact, will flourish stronger than ever".

A "caretaker" committee of 15 was elected as follows: Dr John Gray, Rev P G Mold (Vicar of Thornley), Dr H McNeil (St Godric's RC Church), Rev R Thompson (Methodist minister), Mr W Brereton (over-60 Club), Mr J Wright (Labour Party), Mrs E Gratton (Women's Institute), Mr R Speckman (Methodist Church), Mr J Ellis (Old Time Dancing Club), Mr K Bradley, County Coun E Carter, Mrs Swinburne, Mr Brian Bell, Mr J Bosomworth and Mrs O Lincoln.

Officials will be chosen at the first meeting of the committee when the future policy of the association and membership fees will be discussed.
6 March 1970

DEATH OF WHEATLEY HILL AMBULANCE WORKER

A well-known figure in ambulance circles in Wheatley Hill, where he had spent all his life, Mr Richard Wheatley Storey, of 3 Durham Street, died on Sunday, aged 51. He had been in poor health for the past eight months.

Mr Storey had taken a lifelong interest in first-aid and was secretary of the Wheatley Hill ambulance class for about 30 years. He began work at Wheatley Hill Colliery when he left school at the age of 14 and worked his way up through the various grades until becoming a deputy and then a master shifter. Later he was fore-shift overman until the pit was closed nearly two years ago, when he was transferred – again as an official – to Blackhall colliery, where he had since been employed.

Mr Storey was formerly secretary of Wheatley Hill lodge of the Durham County Colliery Deputies Association for a number of years. He leaves a widow.

After a service in All Saints Church, Wheatley Hill, on Wednesday, Mr Storey was cremated at Durham.

13 March 1970

CONCERN OVER THORNLEY PATH

Coun J Wright took the chair and welcomed members to a meeting of Thornley Parish Council, held in the Welfare Hall. Concern was expressed by Coun A Griffiths about the realignment of the footpath between Thornley Junior School and Ludworth owing to the establishment of a new playing field for the school. Coun Griffiths stated that the footpath was a right of way and any realignment of the path could interfere with the right of way. It was decided to obtain a plan of the proposed playing field to see exactly how it affected the footpath.

Mr R Speckman gave the cemetery caretaker's report.

A report was given on the meeting that was held to form a Community Association at Thornley to take over the Miners' Welfare Scheme now that Thornley Colliery had closed. Members were told that the Community Association would only be responsible for the upkeep of the Welfare Hall and it was agreed that the clerk approach Easington RDC and the Miners' Welfare Committee with a view to the parish council taking over the Welfare Park and the pavilion.

A complaint was received about the state of the footpath and road between Thornley and Wheatley Hill owing to vehicles loading soil on to a site bordering the road. The chairman, Coun J Wright, said that the footpath and road were covered with several inches of mud and that it was impossible to walk between Thornley and Wheatley Hill. It was agreed to contact Easington RDC about the matter and request a speedy solution.

LONG SERVICE TRIBUTES AT
WHEATLEY HILL BRITIGH LEGION WOMEN

Five long-service members of the section, with a total of 203 years' service among them, were among the guests welcomed by the chairman, Mrs D Cowan, at the 40th birthday party of the British Legion.

They were founder-members, Mrs Jane Barker, with 43 years' Legion work to her credit, and Mesdames Maria Brain, Winnie Bowes, Nora Cain and Mary J Kime, all with 40 years' service. Tribute was paid to their loyal service and a toast to the continued success of the section was proposed by Mrs E Telford.

About 130 members and friends were present and other guests included the county secretary, Mrs A Hamilton of Darlington, the county treasurer, Mrs A Johnson of South Hetton and the group representative, Mrs E Clark, of Thornley.

The county chairman, Mrs Lily Park of Blackhall, who was also a guest, presented the county certificate to the president of the section, Mrs L Saxby. During supper, a birthday cake, made and iced by Mrs Saxby was cut. Entertainment was provided by Mr Eddie Kitto (organist), Thornley, Miss Shirley Winter (vocalist) and Mr Jack Calvert (comedian), of Easington. Members of the recently-formed men's section at Wheatley Hill were invited for the entertainment and a competition organised for them was won by Mr G Hewitson and Mr J Richardson.

Six of the original members of Wheatley Hill Women's Section of the British Legion, started in 1930, were at the Legion's 40th birthday party held in the Workingmen's Club, Wheatley Hill. Back row, left to right: Mrs. M. Brain and Mrs. W. Bowes. Front, Mrs. N. Cain, Mrs. Kime, Mrs. Bradley and Mrs. Barker.—[Photo: Harriman].

An iced Easter cake made by Mrs Saxby was won by Miss C Lewins and the door prize went to the secretary, Mrs F M Carr. Spot dance winners were Mesdames Humes, V Worthington, I Jones, M Foster snr and Moses.

20 March 1970

NEW LEGION CHAIRMAN - Mr W Poole has been elected the new chairman of Wheatley Hill branch of the British Legion in succession to Mr E Curry, who had filled the position since the branch was re-formed last year. Mr Curry has resigned because of pressure of other work and at the weekly meeting appreciation was recorded of his service. The treasurer, Mr T Hodgson, presented a satisfactory financial statement. Mr J Harper was chosen to attend the National Leadership Forum in London in September. Mr Poole reported on county and group meetings and Mr J Million won the weekly competition prize.

DEATH OF WHEATLEY HILL'S 95-YEAR OLD

Wheatley Hill's oldest inhabitant, Mrs Mary Barker, of 3 Nimmo's Cottages, was buried at Wheatley Hill Cemetery on Friday – her 95th birthday.

Mrs Barker was born in the neighbouring village of Wingate and had spent the whole of her life in the area – she had lived in Wheatley Hill since 1907 moving there from Thornley. In her younger days she was associated with the Methodist Church at Thornley.

Mrs Barker had an excellent memory and could often clearly recall events of her girlhood days. She lived at 3 Second Street, Wheatley Hill, before moving about 18 years ago to the house where she died.

Her husband John died 17 years ago and of a family of 17 she leaves seven sons and three daughters. She was the head of five generations, a number of great-great-grandchildren being among her descendants.

The funeral service, attended by many relatives and friends, was conducted in Wheatley Hill Methodist Church by the Rev R S Thompson of Thornley.

THORNLEY MAN IN RDC ELECTIONS

Councillor James Nicholson (50), a member of the labour Party for 20 years and one of Thornley's most prominent personalities, is to contest the Thornley ward of Easington Rural Council next month. He describes himself as an Independent Labour candidate.

"This does not imply that I am turning my back on the Labour Party principles", said Coun Nicholson. "I am an inveterate Socialist and I will be doing everything in my power to bring about the election of Mr Jack Dormand as Easington Division Member of Parliament for Labour".

Mr Nicholson, who has represented Thornley Ward on Easington Rural Council for the past 14 years and is chairman of the District Education Committee, a position he has held for seven years, was not selected by the Thornley Ward Labour Party as a candidate for the forthcoming district council election.

"During my first eight years as a district councillor I lost well over £1000 in earnings but I did not mind that because I got a lot of satisfaction in helping the community", said Coun Nicholson.

"I never had any ambition to be on the county council because I realised I would be remote from the Thornley people. I knew I could serve them better on the district council".

A Miner

Coun Nicholson, a miner at Thornley Colliery from the age of 14 until he was made redundant when the colliery closed in February, is still financial secretary of Thornley Miners' Lodge. He served on the Lodge committee for many years, was on the consultative board and safety committee, and is vice-chairman of the Colliery Federation Board. He was Durham area delegate to the National Union of Mineworkers centenary conference at Blackpool last year.

Coun Nicholson served as sub-agent for Mr Emmanuel Shinwell in Parliamentary elections many times. He is Thornley Ward delegate to the Easington Divisional Labour Party and has served on the Parish Council for 20 years.

In his younger days he was well-known as a goalkeeper for teams in the Northern League and Wearside League.

10 April 1970

MUD ON THE ROAD AGAIN
CRITICISED AT THORNLEY

Mr J Wright took the chair at the monthly meeting of Thornley Parish Council, in Thornley Community Centre, and welcomed 11 members

The state of the road between Thornley and Wheatley Hill again came under fire from members. Mud was being deposited inches deep on this road and this was causing great inconvenience to pedestrians and drivers alike.

The mud was falling from lorries carrying soil from roadworks at Castle Eden to a land reclamation scheme at Thornley and it was claimed the responsibility for clearing away the mud lay with Easington RDC.

The Clerk of the Parish Council, Mr J Taylor, had been in touch with Easington RDC on this matter and they stated that everything possible was being done to keep the road and footpath clear of mud. The members accepted this explanation but commented that the efforts of the Rural District council did not appear to be meeting with much success.

Aid Request

A request for financial aid was received from the newly formed Thornley Community Association and it was agreed to give the association a grant of £500, if an emergency precept for this amount was allowed. It was also agreed that the Parish Council take over the running of the Thornley Colliery Welfare Sports Ground.

24 April 1970

WI BIRTHDAY PARTY – Thornley WI celebrated its 45th birthday with a party when Mrs R E Gratton, president, welcomed 100 members and friends to the function. Mrs S Fort was organising secretary. Supper was enjoyed and a birthday cake, made and decorated by Mrs M Hodgson, was cut by a founder member, Mrs G Hodgson. Proposing the toast of the Institute, Mrs Hodgson reminded members that in the early days the Institute was shared with their neighbours at Wheatley Hill. A programme of games and dancing followed, with Mr Jack Jordan as MC.

22 May 1970

BROTHERS REMANDED ON MURDER CHARGE

Two Peterlee brothers were jointly charged at Peterlee this week with the murder of John Robert Kears, 42, an ex-miner, of Stanhope Street, Wheatley Hill. Leslie Burrell, 19, of Dickens Walk and Alex Burrell, 18, of Eden Lane, were remanded in custody to Durham Prison until Thursday.

Applying for the remand, Chief Supt H F Marsden, Peterlee sub-division commander, said the body of Mr Kears was found lying on a patch of grass in front of some bungalows in Church Street, Wheatley Hill, at 10.50pm on Sunday. He had severe facial injuries and died from these injuries. The chairman of the bench, Mr H O'Neill, granted legal aid.

29 May 1970

THORNLEY FAMILY BOUND FOR CANADA

Emigrating to Canada are Mr and Mrs Rowley Brooks, of St Bede's Crescent, Thornley, and at a social in the officials club they received gifts from the Thornley branch of the Legion.

Mr Brooks, branch treasurer for three years, received an engraved wrist watch, and Mrs Brooks, at one time treasurer and then secretary of the women's section, a compact.

The gifts were handed over by the branch chairman, Mr Ronald Smith, and tributes to the couple were also expressed by Mr William Johnson (secretary).

Mr and Mrs Brooks were formerly employed at Smart and Browns, Spennymoor.

Mr Brooks served in the 4th Battalion, Duke of Wellington Regiment in the Korean War. The couple, with their only child, ten-year-old Yvonne, fly to Toronto, on 19 June. "I believe the prospects are much better out there", said Mr Brooks. "There is far too much taxation here".

THORNLEY CENTRE READY FOR THE OPENING

A new phase in the social life of Thornley will begin tomorrow when Thornley and District Community Centre, will be officially opened by Mr Jack Dormand. The centre was formerly the Miners Welfare Hall.

The Rev Dr McNeil, chairman of the centre, will preside. After the opening, entertainment will be provided and refreshments served.

"We are expecting that the centre will be the venue of all indoor social life in the village", said Mr Jonathan Bosomworth (honorary secretary).

"This is the best hall in the village, including a large billiards room with four billiards tables, a spacious ballroom, a reading room and other rooms for miscellaneous activities".

Those interested in promoting social life were now under an obligation to do their utmost to make the centre a going concern, said Mr Bosomworth.

Guests at tomorrow's function will include members of the former Colliery Welfare Committee and Mr Hubert Tunney, who performed the official opening of the buildings about 20 years ago. Thornley Colliery Prize Brass Band will give items.
19 June 1970

OLD SCOUTS' FIELD DAY AT WHEATLEY HILL

Over 1000 villagers attended the annual field day of Wheatley Hill Old Scouts' Association. About £200 was raised for charity. Organisers, backed by a strong committee were Mr L Barker (chairman), Mr S Saxby (secretary), Mr J Fishwick (treasurer), Mr R B Elliott (field events), Mr R Watson (social evening).

Six jazz bands paraded: Ferryhill Bugle Band, South Hetton Royal Scots, South Hetton Supremes, Elemore Sunbeams, Newton Aycliffe Monarchs and Penshaw Hillsiders. Also in the parade was Wheatley Hill Modern School Boys' Silver Band. The Music Cup was awarded to South Hetton Royal Scots and the marching and formation trophies were presented to Newton Aycliffe Monarchs.

A wheelbarrow race was won by 1, John Taylorson and George Reed; 2, Enid Simons and Joan Long; 3, J W Woodward and J Hall. Boys from Wheatley Hill

Modern School gave a display of gymnastics, and Mr L Barker was in charge of the fire engine and equipment.
26 June 1970

WHEATLEY HILL FIELD DAY A BIG SUCCESS

At the annual field day of the Wheatley Hill and District Community Association, the event and parade through the village attracted well over 2000. Heading the organising committee, were Coun A Wharrier (chairman), Rev M Henderson (secretary), Mr C Oswald.

A four mile race which attracted nine entrants: 1, Michael Waistell; 2, John Million; 3, William Carter; 4 Brian Foster.

Fancy Dress results: Children – Fancy: 1, J Lawson; 2, G and N Peart; 3, C Abbs. Original: 1, J Kenny; 2, W Thompson; 3, V Ryder. Comic: 1, P Ryder; 2, M Carr and J Ogden; 3, R Craggs. Adult: Miss S Parkin, Miss M Durkin.

Children's races winners included: R Race, P Connor, D Peacock, C Watson, P Carr, N Metcalfe, D Atkinson, C Young, P Darby, J Walker, D Carr, F Bradley, D Durkin, A Harker, E Blakemore, M Walker, G Pugh, M Carr, G Coxon, S Million, J Bradley, S Stephenson, L Cairns, D Jackson, S O'Connor, A Carr, M Million, R Lambert, I Collin, D Million, F Wood, J Harvey, J Armstrong, K Wilkinson, G Hepple, M Rutherford, A Hepple, D Dixon, C Barren, E Bulmer, E Parnham, J Hodgson, C Dyson, S Wilkinson, M Chapman, T Ord, M Aimes, L Warnes, C Million, L Robson, L Hunter, P McDonald, T Hagan, J Gutcher, D Parsley, P Attwood, C Welsh, Gratton, S Kendal, D Stephenson, P Hitch, L Soppitt, S Lee.

Sideshows were organised and manned by personnel of the Wheatley Hill Old Scouts' Association.
10 July 1970

MINERS' OFFICIAL'S WARNING

At a two-hour meeting at Durham's NUM headquarters to discuss the Coal Board's pay offer, Mr Kit Robinson (general secretary) warned that unofficial action could harm the negotiations.

The winners are claiming a £20 minimum for surface workers, £22 for underground men and £30 for those at the face. The Board's offer could give surface workers £17.10s and underground men £18.10s.

Mr Robinson told representatives from 34 Durham pits at the meeting to wait until the national ballot on the Board's offer was known.
25 September 1970

A TALK ON the new decimal currency was given by Mr Jones, of Sunderland, at Wheatley Hill Women's Institute. He was thanked by Mrs Thackeray.

Mrs J Moorin presided and members stood in silence in memory of a member, Mrs B Robson, who had died since the last meeting. In the Golden Thread series of household hints, Mrs D Carr spoke on how to keep brasses clean.

612

The secretary, Mrs J Milne, read the minutes and correspondence, and names were taken for the group conference to be held on 20 October, with Wheatley Hill the hostess institute.

The competition for the best fruit cake made from a set recipe, judged by Mrs Collingwood, was won by Mrs J Hughes. Miss E Simpson won the door prize.

Mrs W Poulson introduced a newly-formed folk group from All Saints' Church, Wheatley Hill, who provided the entertainment.
16 October 1970

All Saints Folk Group
Back L-R: Jean Oliver, Tommy Hodgson, Margaret Carr,
Pauline Nicholson
Front L-R: Robert Waite, Derek Ayre (manager)

REMEMBRANCE - An impressive service of dedication and remembrance took place around the War Memorial in Front Street, Ludworth. It was attended by British Legion men and women, and *Al Saints Church Folk* the parade was headed by Thornley Colliery Band. Mr T T Johnson conducted the service which was well attended.

13 November 1970

SHADFORTH PARISH AFFAIRS

Mr A St Julien presided at a meeting of Shadforth Parish Council.   On   Learning that the Ludworth branch store of Sherburn Hill Co-operative Society (now the North East Co-operative Society) was to close, the clerk reported writing to the society protesting in the strongest possible terms to the closing of this shop which was the largest one trading in the village and stressing the hardship which would be caused to members to journey to Sherburn Village, the nearest premises to Ludworth.   This protest, however, was without avail.

The need for public conveniences at Sherburn Hill and Ludworth was raised and the clerk was asked to take up this matter with the rural council.

27 November 1970

CAROL SERVICE PLANNED AT THORNLEY

Thornley and District Community Association is to hold a carol service in the Community Centre on 21 December.

Organisations taking part will be the three churches – Catholic, Methodist and the Anglican, the Salvation Army, the Women's Institute, the Mothers' Club, British Legion, Youth Club, Boys' Brigade and the Over-60 Club.

Music will be provided by Thornley Prize Brass Band. "This will be something novel in the village", Mr Jonathan Bosomworth, association secretary, said.

"It is the first festival of its kind to be held in the village. We are expecting a very large gathering for the celebration of this Christian event".

The hall will be decorated and the Youth Club has provided a Christmas tree. There will be community singing of carols of the traditional kind and of the modern version.

18 December 1970

JUNIOR COPORAL Sid Race, 17, receives the Director of Music's prize for the Junior Bandsman who has made the best progress during the term. The presentation was made by his Commanding Officer, Lt Colonel Mark Chirnside, during a ceremony at the Junior Leaders' Regiment of the Royal Armoured Corps at Bovington Camp, Dorset. He also received a prize for being the best trumpeter of the term and for his appointment as Commanding Officer's trumpeter for next term. Sid, whose parents, Mr and Mrs S Race, live at 7 St Chad's Square, Thornley, has been with the Regiment since May 1969. He is learning to play the trombone. In his leisure time he has represented the Regiment at football and also shown a keen interest in cycling. Before joining the Junior Leaders he attended Wheatley Hill Secondary Modern School.

Junior Corporal Sid Race

614

ENTERTAINED – Ludworth Old People's Christmas party took place in the Youth Club Centre when 157 veterans were entertained to supper, and during the meal were each handed a gift of ten shillings. The treat was organised by the Ludworth Sports and Recreation Fund Women's Committee (Mesdames Maddison, Winter, M Hutchinson, S Smith, P Smith and A Hutchinson). After supper the old folk went across to the British Legion Club Hall where a concert was provided. Organisers of the Old People's Treat Fund were Mr M Hammond, supported by Mr W Hyland, Mr D Crisp, Mr G Hyland and Mr T V Kelly.
25 December 1970

1971

OLD SCOUTS GIFT TO EARLS HOUSE IS A GRAND "PETS' CORNER"

For some months now members of the Wheatley Hill Old Scouts Association have devoted their Sunday mornings to building a "Pets' Corner" at the Earls House Hospital for handicapped children at Durham ... and on Saturday afternoon at the official "handing-over" ceremony the Old Scouts were warmly congratulated for yet another good deed.

Throughout the post-war years the Association members have always had the welfare of children at heart, especially those in hospitals and institutions. They "adopted" a children's ward at Durham County Hospital and regularly, Christmas after Christmas, visited the patients there, distributing gifts and often providing some extra special amenity for the ward.

Popular

But this last year they decided to do something for the Earls House Hospital and there is little doubt that the "Pets' Corner" with its variety of birds and pet animals, will be a popular attraction among the young patients.

Under the leadership of Mr Les Barker, chairman of the Association, the Old Scouts laid a large paving-stone floor and en-

Bill Cook, Derek Metcalf, Norman Waugh, Ralph Watson Les Barker and Jack Fishwick

closed the area with a chain link and interwoven fencing.

"We made wooden huts and hutches at our headquarters at Wheatley Hill", one of the helpers told our reporter, "and then one by one transported them to the hospital grounds and fitted them snugly into the pets' corner in a really professional pattern".

Even a Goat

The huts, he said, "will house pigeons, guinea fowl, birds, rabbits, hamsters ... and even a goat. There will be a separate hut for the storage of feeding stuffs and cleaning equipment.

The spokesman added, "We feel sure the children will enjoy themselves there – there will be something to interest them all. We are glad we have been able to bring some new pastime into their lives".

Money raised by the Old Scouts from carol-singing was used to buy all the equipment and stock needed.

15 January 1971

PLANE SEAT IN POND

A three-man fox hunting expedition led to the discovery of one more piece of the Vulcan bomber which crashed at Wingate two weeks ago.

At the weekend Richard Carr, 29, Jack Mason, 32 and Jack Mitchison, 36 , of Gore Hill Estate, Thornley, were passing Kirk's Pond, when they noticed a half submerged object.

At first the men thought it was a one-armed-bandit but, after pulling it out of the water, they found it to be one of the ejector seats from the bomber which crashed five miles away.

"The police contacted the RAF who immediately came to rescue the seat. A police spokesman at Peterlee: "We would still welcome information which could lead to further recoveries".

29 January 1971

WOMAN FC SECRETARY AT THORNLEY

The fair sex are not usually associated with local soccer administration, but at Thornley the village's Youth Club team, which competes in the Seaham and District League, has one of its staunchest supporters – a woman – as secretary.

Miss Joyce Taylor, a part-time leader at Thornley Community Centre's Youth Club, has been secretary of the soccer team for the past two years. "And I love the work – there are few games I miss, home or away", she told us.

Miss Taylor, who lived at Wheatley Hill until moving to Hartlepool three years ago, is on the unattached list of teachers employed by the Durham County Education Committee. Her work takes her to schools all over the area – at the moment she is teaching at Chilton.

Both at school – she was a pupil of Wellfield A J Dawson Grammar School – and at college, she took a keen interest in all types of sport, playing hockey, tennis and netball.

When she took over as secretary of the Thornley team, Miss Taylor confessed she "knew little about football. But since then", she smiled, "I have learned a lot about the game and enjoy going around with the lads for their Saturday fixtures".

Fared Quite Well

Though not in the running for championship honours, the team has fared reasonably well this season. Recently they reached the quarter-final of the League Challenge Cup only to lose 3-0 away to Blackhall Athletic.

Miss Taylor said she had not come across any other woman secretaries in her two years of soccer travel. She is certainly the only one in the Seaham and District League. "And she keeps the club ticking over nicely – we'd be lost without her", eulogised one of the club's supporters.

Wembley Footnote

Miss Taylor has seen few big soccer matches, but next month she is hoping to take a party of school-boys to a schoolboy international at Wembley – it will be her first trip to England's most famous football pitch.

28 March 1971

EX-WHEATLEY HILL MAN GETS QUEEN'S MEDAL

A former Wheatley Hill man, who joined the Police Force shortly before the outbreak of the last war and now works from New Scotland Yard as a Detective Chief Superintendent, has been awarded the Queen's Police medal.

He is Detective Chief Superintendent George Clarkson, of Stirling Road, Wood Green, who in his younger days was a pupil at Wellfield A J Dawson Grammar School, Wingate. He and his wife, Irene, a native of Horden, were married at Horden 30 years ago and they have a married daughter and a son.

All The Chief Superintendent's police career has been spent in the London area. At first he was attached to the City Road Police Station and then in 1943 he was granted leave of absence to become a pilot with RAF Coastal Command.

Rejoined

After the war he rejoined the Police Force and in 1952 was promoted Detective Sergeant. Eight years later he was promoted Detective Inspector and in another three years was made Detective Chief Inspector.

He was promoted to his present rank in 1967 and since June, 1968, has been second-in-command for the No 1 Area of the Metropolitan Police.

Chief Superintendent Clarkson has led successful investigations into five separate murders and has been commended on no fewer than 15 occasions.

Before joining the police force he was employed as an assistant in the architect's department of Easington Rural Council.

Chief Superintendent Clarkson, who is to be presented with his medal at Buckingham Palace in a week's time, pays frequent visits to his relations back in Durham County. His two sisters, Mrs Ellen Urwin and Mrs Doreen Aspinall, and one of his brothers, Robert, live at Wheatley Hill, and one of his wife's sisters, Mrs Connie Smith, lives in Durham City.

2 April 1971

LUDWORTH GOLDEN COUPLE

Mr and Mrs G Appleby, of 70 Barnard Avenue, Ludworth, celebrate their golden wedding on Good Friday. They were married at St Cuthbert's Church, Shadforth, on 9 April, 1921. Mr Jack Raine was best man and Mr Appleby's sister Catherine was bridesmaid.

Mr Appleby moved to Ludworth from Thornley as a boy and has lived in Ludworth ever since. During the 1914-18 War he served with the Royal Garrison Artillery and was wounded at the Battle of Ypres. Apart from that period he worked at Thornley Colliery commencing at the age of 14 years.

Mr and Mrs Appleby have three sons and two daughters, all married, 21 grandchildren and six great-grandchildren.

9 April 1971

"PAT ON THE BACK" FOR COUNTY

Durham County Council received a "pat on the back" last week from visiting Secretary of State for the Environment, Mr Peter Walker.

Mr Walker, who was making a tour of the six counties worst affected by a legacy of industrial derelict land, said that he was delighted by what had been achieved in County Durham. "I have received nothing but good co-operation from Durham County Council. They needed no urging to tackle this problem", he said.

Mr Walker continued that one of the best ways of improving the quality of the environment was to clear up the scars of industry. "But it is not good enough just to pass legislation and hope", he said.

He visited derelict land reclamation schemes at Willington, Spennymoor and Wheatley Hill. The Government pays for 91% of the cost of the reclamation work, and already twice as much is being spent this year as before. The estimated cost of work to be undertaken during the coming year is £1,270,000.

Since work started, some 1500 acres have been cleared within the county. But there are still 7000 acres to go. Mr Walker said that one of the reasons for his tour was to urge local authorities to set themselves more ambitious targets in land reclamation. His own target is to clear all major areas of derelict land within a decade. One of the aims of his Ministry is not merely to conserve areas where the environment is good, but to clear up the bad spots.

This present scheme is, he said, very exciting. Once the pit heaps have gone there will be encouragement to start small landscaping schemes which will generate completely new environments in the areas at present derelict.

30 April 1971

CORONER WARNS OF FIRE DANGER

The North West Durham Coroner, Mr Lance Heron, warned last week at the inquest on a 33-year-old Thornley man, of the dangers of using a paraffin heater to heat a garage where petrol and oil fumes could ignite.

The jury at the inquest on Patrick Carr of Thornlaw North, Thornley, heard how he and another man, John Burgin of Hartlepool Street, in Thornley, were repairing the leaking joint of a petrol tank in the pit of a garage.

Mr Burgin who had his back to the heater spoke of seeing a 'ball of fire' come over his shoulder from the heater. The pit became an inferno trapping the two men beneath the car, away from the steps. Mr Carr had tried to run through the flames and as a result his clothing had caught fire.

Mr Burgin eventually was able to get from beneath the car, rescue his friend and call for help. "He had the presence of mind to close the garage doors, thus containing the fire", said Fire Officer Bough.

"In the circumstances", said Mr Heron, "Mr Burgin was lucky to escape with his own life".

A verdict of accidental death was recorded.

THORNLEY FAIR RAISED £180

A Spring fair was held by Thornley Methodist Church. Organising secretary was Mrs J Mather with the society steward, Mr J H Pattison as treasurer. The effort raised £180 for church funds. Mr J H Pattison presided and devotions were led by the superintendent minister, Rev Robert S Thompson. The fair was opened by Mrs D Swinburne, a teacher on the staff of Wheatley Hill County Infants' School. She was presented with a bouquet by Anne Lowther.

Stalls were provided by the church organisations, Mrs W Davies, Mrs E Maitland, Mesdames Spencer, G Wigham, Fisher, Walls, Coun Miss A Griffiths, Mrs R Speckman, Mrs W Crisp, Mrs Brandling, Mr Fisher, Mrs Bullock, Messrs R Hedley and J Mather, Captain R Speckman, Lieuts K Hetherington, J Bennett, C Davies, Mesdames G Hetherington, J Mather, J Watson, A Appleby, G Watson, A Calam, Miss B Smart and helpers. Mesdames Pugh, B High and helpers. Catering was by the Sisterhood secretary and treasurer, Mrs R Hedley and Mrs J Thornton.

21 May 1971

DAY OUT AT LUDWORTH

LUDWORTH Sports and Recreation Fund's annual sports day began with a parade, headed by Thornley Community Band and Jazz Bands, to the Recreation Ground, where the judging took place. Results: Jazz Bands parade, Band Major – Sacriston Juvenaires; drum-major bass drummer, Elemore; display, Elemore and Sacriston (tie); drum major, Elemore and Sacriston (tie); band-master, Elemore; bass drummer, Sacriston; mascot, South Hylton; music, Sacriston.

Fancy dress, juniors section 1 G Parsons; 2 T Devenport; 3 P Leather. Senior section 1 Mrs E Stannard; 2 Mr T Bowes.

Races

Sprints for all ages were run, plus a cross country race. Boys' winners: P Race, D Briggs, N Robson, D Harrison, K Barrasford, K Briggs, C Bennett, G Thompson, S White, S Wilson, W Young, J Vasey and G Stannard.

Girls' winners: J Jones, A Youll, D Ingleby, B Carr, S Gradon, P Whittle, S Hutchinson, V Brown, E Hutchinson.

Women's: Mrs Hall, Mrs Parsons, Mrs Winter and Mrs Leather.

Cross-country: I Dunbar, N DeLuce, J Graham.

Wheatley Hill Scouts and Old Scouts were in attendance and gave valuable help in the manning of the various stalls, and also judged the fancy dress. The Women's Section Mesdames Maddison, T Winter, R Smith, M Hutchinson, R Peachey, M Hayes, E Hutchinson, T Hutchinson and P Smith provided tea and the food stall. A Karate display was given by the Tyne Tees Club.

The chairman (Mr F Hutchinson) secretary (Mr W Hyland) and treasurer (Mr T V Kelly) thank the police, Scouts and Mr George Copeland, of Shotton, for his entertainment. Coun D Thornton presented the prizes.

13 August 1971

WHEATLEY HLL YOUTH TO VISIT GERMANY

Two apprentice fitters from the North-East coking plants have been selected by the Coal Products Division of the National Coal Board to take part in a 10-day study tour in Germany starting next week. They are Malcolm Bell, aged 19, who works at Norwood coking plant and 19-year-old John Hodgson of Fishburn coking plant. Malcolm lives at Swalwell and John at Wheatley Hill.

The party, which will also include two other Coal Products apprentices from the Midlands and Wales, will be led by Mr J Cornish, of Durham City, electrical engineer with the East Durham Coking Management Unit.

The study tour lasts from 8 to 18 September and will include visits to coking and allied industries mainly in the Essen and Hamburg areas. There also will be visits to a mining exhibition, power station and steel works. The apprentices will see the Mohne dam and will make an underground visit at a coal mine.

3 September 1971

LUDWORTH MEETING

There was a good attendance at a public meeting at Ludworth Youth Club Centre, the purpose of which was to discuss playing fields and the centre. Owing to increased costs of maintaining equipment, it was decided to ask Durham Rural Council to take over the playing fields and also if possible to turn the Youth Centre into a Community Hall. Coun D Thornton presided.

5 November 1971

MACKAYS DOWN AT THORNLEY

Mackays Sports Club forfeited two Durham and District League points to Thornley CA on Saturday by two goals to nil.

Thornley CA, kicking up the slope with the wind in their favour, dominated the early exchanges and took the lead after ten minutes through Strong, who brilliantly headed the ball just inside the post.

Mackays tried hard but could not break Thornley's midfield domination, where Weatherall and Warne held sway. Just before half-time Burnett hit the post in a breakaway for Mackay's.

After Smithson had had a shot kicked off the line early in the second half Thornley took command and Strong, Todd and Million all had shots well saved.

Despite having advantage of the strong wind the visitors could not beat the strong Thornley defence well marshalled by centre-half Jordan.

Thornley's controlled football paid off when Todd collected Weatherall's through ball to draw the goalkeeper and register a second goal.

Weatherall and Warne (Thornley) and Dawson (Mackay's) were players to catch the eye.

12 November 1971

(We believe that the 'Mackay's' team is that of the Hugh Makay carpet company in Durham City, at this time operating in Freemans Place, opposite the Ice Rink)

THORNLEY'S SIX AGAINST WHITE TUN UNITED

Thornley CA entertained White Tun United under Durham League auspices on Saturday and scored six goals without reply. Thornley were denied an early goal by fine goalkeeping. After 15 minutes, however, he was beaten when Million crossed the ball and Smithson outjumped all opposition to head a fine goal. This was followed by constant Thornley pressure during which Howe, Cook and Smithson all scored to make it 4-0 at half-time.

On resuming, the siege of the White Tun goal continued and on three occasions only the woodwork saved more goals. Thornley were in full command, with Strong and Wetherell particularly tormenting gallant defenders, and it came as no surprise when Strong scored, from fully 25 yards. Cook added No 6, and the rout was completed. White Tun made many friends by the sporting way they accepted defeat, always playing clean and fair.

Thornley have now gone six successive games without defeat, and the side are to be congratulated on this success which is bringing back the crowds.

10 December 1971

1972

THE STRIKE. SPECIAL CENTRES FOR FAMILY BENEFITS SET UP

With the national coal strike in its fifth day, Durham's 34,200 miners are solidly behind their local and national leaders in the fight for an increased wage offer.

Spearheading their efforts are the Durham miners' leaders Mr John C (Kit) Robinson, general secretary, and Mr Walter Malt, president, together with the various lodge officials all over the county who have called upon their members to do all they can to ease the burden of lack of coal supplies to hospitals, clinics and other similar institutions, together with schools and old age pensioners.

The miners had agreed nationally to let normal coal supplies through to hospitals and other institutions and this week pit liaison committees have been busy identifying the various places in the county where stocks have been getting low.

Very Pleased

Earlier this week Mr Robinson, speaking on behalf of the Durham Miners' Association, said, "We have been very pleased that our drivers have been ensuring in many cases that supplies of coal have gone to pensioners and local hospitals. Now we have said that we will include schools in the same category. We want to see that the children's education carries on despite the strike. We cannot understand how any school can run out of coal so quickly, but if they have, then we appeal to them to contact us.

On Wednesday it was reported that some County Durham schools may have to close by this weekend because of the strike. Some, it was stated, are left with fuel which will only last for two days.

Statement

In a statement issued from the Miners headquarters at Red Hill, Durham, with regard to safety measures at the pits, it stated that "no major difficulties are being experienced except in regard to reported total or partial non-manning of safety jobs by our members, The Area Union has circularised lodges advising them to allow members normally employed on safety jobs to go to work.

A number of social security special centres has been set up where the miners will be able to obtain limited benefits for their wives and families.

14 January 1972

THE COUNTY CUP

Brandon Juniors entertained Wheatley Hill Juniors in the third round of the Durham County Junior Cup on Brandon Welfare ground and won by two goals to nil.

Wheatley Hill were straight into the attack, but this was broken up by Tobin and Morgan. Five minutes from half-time Wheatley Hill should have taken the lead when they were awarded a penalty for hands against Thompson, Starkey shot over the bar.

From the kick-off in the second half Brandon swept into the attack, and after a few minutes, Adamson put them ahead scoring with a fine header from a centre by Redden.

Brandon were now more in control and if Yates, the Wheatley Hill goalkeeper, had not brought off so many fine saves the score could have been a lot higher. Brandon went further into the lead when Thompson sent the ball down the centre to Humble, who put it to Adamson. He centres into the Wheatley Hill goalmouth for Hesp to slam into the net. For the last five minutes of the game Wheatley Hill tried desperately to get on level terms. Penrose, however, missed two excellent chances. Outstanding players for Brandon were Franklin, Tobin, Morgan, Pears, Redden and Gibson. For Wheatley Hill Yates, Hutchinson, Pattinson, Brown, Penrose and Foster did well.

HAMSTEELS BEATEN AT THORNLEY

Thornley Community Association entertained Hamsteels CW in a Durham and District League game and took the initiative from the start, attacking through Strong, Todd and Smithson, who all went very close to scoring. They were denied by good goalkeeping and bad luck, but urged on by midfield men Wetherall and Warne, Thornley pressed even harder. After 40 minutes Smithson scored after being put clear by Todd.

After the interval Hamsteels found new energy and attempted to wipe out their deficit. Mains in goal showed excellent form and Routledge, Snowdon, Jordan and Pattison held all attacks with skill and courage.

A hotly disputed penalty awarded to Hamsteels was missed and almost at once Thornley substituted Cook for Million, suffering an injury. Goal No 2 came after a scramble in the Hamsteels penalty area, Smithson forcing the ball across the line.

Hamsteels reduced the arrears and this roused Thornley, who went straight on the attack. Strong beat two men and crashed a shot at goal. An opponent made a flying save but used his hands. The penalty was converted by Strong. So a fast exciting match ended 3-1 in favour of Thornley.

21 January 1972

WIDENING SUPPORT
AS FOLK LEARN TO LIVE WITH THE STRIKE

As the coal strike ends its third week, there is still no signs of a settlement and both sides seem firmly entrenched in their attitudes. In the meantime as stocks of coal run low more and more people are beginning to feel the effects of the prolonged stoppage.

This week the Coal Board deputy chairman, Mr William Sheppard, warned that some of the nation's strike bound pits are threatened with permanent closure because of the lack of safety cover. Closure of these would mean the equivalent in redundancies of shutting down between 40 and 50 pits.

In South Durham the Board is worried about four "wet pits", Horden, Fishburn, East Hetton and Blackhall. They say that even with limited safety work, these are causing problems.

No Incidents

This week at the Durham Miners' Association headquarters at Redhill, Durham, organisation of further picketing in the coalfield has proceeded without incident, a spokesman told us.

They were also receiving considerable support from other unions, mainly from the Transport and General Workers' whose members were refusing to cross picket lines and dockers at Teesside have refused to unload 20,000 tons of American coal brought in by the ship World Explorer.

A considerable amount of money has been received at Redhill from unions and others in support of the miners, ranging from small postal orders to cheques for thousands of pounds. These are all being sent to Headquarters Strike Committee in London in support of the national fund.

Old Folk's Need

As the miners' strike begins to take effect, social workers have been swamped with requests from old people for coal. All the requests have to be checked to make sure that they are genuine, and if requests continue to come in such numbers, the WRVS may be called in to help.

White Collar Support

Over 24,000 white collar workers in the North East pledged their support at the weekend to the miners out on strike.

Delegates of the North Eastern District National and Local Government Officers Association (Nalgo) unanimously passed a motion condemning the Government's attitude over the strike.

28 January 1972

THORNLEY'S SUCCESS AGAINST DURHAM CIVIL SERVICE

Thornley C A, playing away to Durham Civil Service in a Durham and District League game won 1-0 and extended their unbeaten record to 12 games.

From the onset Thornley laid siege in their opponents half, but found Civil Service in a defensive mood. This negative approach frustrated the more skilful Thornley side, whose nearest approach to a goal was to hit the woodwork at least seven times. Mains in goal for Thornley did not have one shot to save up to half-time.

On resuming Strong, Cook and Warne worked hard to penetrate their opponents' defence and on the wings Smithson, Million and later substitute J Routledge won corner after corner, but to no avail.

With only eight minutes left justice was done when Snowdon took a long throw on the right, Warne won possession, flicked the ball to Strong who smashed it into the net for victory to Thornley.

625

COAL IS ON THE MOVE TO YOU

The big drive to get coal moving for householders in the North-East got under way on Wednesday when fleets of lorries and rail wagons carried loads from pits and stocking sites in the region.

The Coal Board said that about 6,000 tons of house coal and about 3,000 tons of hard coke would be made available for coal merchants this week.

Members of the Coal Merchants' Federation were called to a meeting at the Coal Board's regional headquarters at Team valley on Tuesday, when the Board's marketing team led by Mr Eddie Milburn, explained the plans to reopen the domestic market.

After the meeting Mr Milburn said, "Real progress in this direction can only be made if the miners vote to accept the Wilberforce recommendations and get back to work."

Domestic coal stocks are being lifted from Ashington pit in Northumberland and from Westerton stocking site in County Durham. At Westerton the depot is being manned round the clock so merchants can get coal at any time.

An NCB spokesman said this week that there would be a progressive build up and at the end of next week it was expected that local merchants would be receiving 90 per cent of their normal allocation.

Since Monday the Board has moved an average of 30,000 tons a day by road, rail and sea to power stations in the North East, the North West and North Yorkshire.

In addition supplies of coking coal have been rushed to Consett Iron works and to the British Steel Corporation complex on Teesside.

25 February 1972

THANKS FOR SYMPATHY AND SOLIDARITY

Sir- The Durham Miners seek the facilities of your newspaper to express their warm affection and appreciation to fellow trade unionists, organisations and individual well-wishers throughout the region for the messages of support, donations, food parcels and vouchers, and acts of solidarity in the recent industrial action undertaken to achieve a fair wages settlement. There will always be a place under our banner for you and yours.

We welcome the goodwill, sympathy and understanding of the community in general, and even though we acted from the outset to minimise hardship by delivery of fuel to Social Security priority cases, hospitals, schools etc and by other local activities, we regret any inconvenience which may have had to be borne in our struggle.

Yours etc

W MALT

NETTLESWORTH TEAM FAILED AT LUDWORTH

The Hut (Nettlesworth) travelled to Ludworth without a recognised goalkeeper and a heavy defeat was expected. Their fears were confirmed when Ludworth gained two goals within the first five minutes. However, The Hut refused to submit and they began to play some attractive football, although the home team provided the danger.

626

The visitors' defence stood firm until just before half-time when they conceded a third goal.

The second half was evenly balanced with both teams playing open attacking football. However, further goals had to come and it came as no surprise when Ludworth added two further goals. The visitors scored a merited consolation goal when a Ludworth defender headed an own goal while under intense pressure.

Ludworth Legion eventually won by five goals to one.

17 March 1972

THORNLEY 10, DURHAM RANGERS 1

Thornley entertained Durham Rangers in a Durham and District League game and gained two points even more easily than the score suggests. Thornley went straight onto the attack and were rewarded after ten minutes when Naylor scored. Three more, by Todd (2) and Million, and a goal by Rangers found Thornley 4-1 ahead.

On resumption, Thornley lay siege on Durham's goal and further goals were scored by Todd (2), Strong (3) and Million. This entertaining game had several moments of very good football, all from Thornley. Mains in Thornley's goal, was almost a spectator, as Routledge, Snowdon, Jordan and Peachey snuffed out Rangers forward line, until they were unable to even get within 30 yards of goal.

The midfield supremacy won by Wetherell and Warne ensured plenty of good service to home forwards Million, Todd, Strong and Naylor who responded with a degree of skill and speed which reduced Rangers defence to tatters. Thornley substitute Edelson replaced Wetherell who received a knock.

Two records were made by Thornley with this score, the most goals for, and highest individual score for a season by Todd.

This week Thornley are hosts to University SC in the J W Morgan Memorial Cup, kick off 3 pm

14 April 1972

LUDWORTH

At Ludworth annual sports, Dr Mark Hughes, MP, judged the fancy dress. County Coun D Thornton presented trophies to the jazz bands and to other prizewinners. Wheatley Hill Old Scouts manned the stalls. Proceeds go to the sports fund. The women's section provided the food stall and also supplied refreshments. The sports were organised by the Ludworth Sports and Recreation Fund officials and committee.

Race results, Mixed 2 to 3 years: 1 Colleen Dougherty, 2 S E Forster, 3 J Phenny. 3 to 4 years: 1 Rose A Miller, 2 W Stones, 3 Linda Holmes. 4 to 5 years: 1 Alan Huntington, 2 Karen Briggs, 3 F Lavell.

BOYS

Boys, 5 to 6: 1 D Devonport, 2 I Miller, 3 P Jones. 6 to 7: 1 H F Hall, 2 D Harrison, 3 C Race. 7 to 8: 1 K Barrasford, 2 S P Donnelly, 3 P Hutchinson. 8 to 9: 1 K A Briggs, 2 N Shepherd, 3 G A Slater. 9 to 10: 1 B Ingleby, 2 D Wright, 3 I Jackson. 10 to 11: 1 G Thompson, 2 D Morgan, 3 N Savage. 11 to 12, 1 S White, 2 K Osbaldestin, 3 S Huntington. 12 to 13: 1 S Wilson, 2 S Jackson, 3 K Hammond. 13 to 14: 1 B Ager, 2 A Phenny, 3 P Whittle. 14 to 15: 1 J Vasey, 2 J Armstrong, 3 J Deluce.

GIRLS

Girls 5 to 6: Nicola Robson, 2 Susan Leathers. 6 to 7: 1 Alison J Youll, 2 Judith Jones, 3 Heather Burrell. 7 to 8: 1 Donna Armstrong, 2 Lesley Gibson, 3 Margaret Bennett. 8 to 9: 1 Kay Osbaldestin, 2 Dianne Ingleby, 3 Karen Turnbull. 9 to 10: 1 Beverley Carr, 2 Marilyn Ager, 3 Carole White, 10-11: 1 Josephine Smith, 2 Shirley Gradon, 3 Lynne Hutchinson. 11-12: 1 Julie Stannard, 2 Karen Ager, 3 Pearl Whittle.

12-13: 1 Katherine Lavelle, 2 Susan Hutchinson, 3 Margaret Bennett. 13 to 14: 1 Sandra Gradon, 2 Denise White. 14 to15: 1 Dorothy Winter, 2 Alison Carr, 3 Valerie Brown.

Women over 40: 1 Mrs B Parsons, 2 Mrs N Hunter, 3 Mrs J Hutchinson. Women under 40: 1 Mrs W Stones, 2 Mrs H Hall, 3 Miss M Slater.

Adult fancy dress: Mrs Stannard, mobile shop. Children's fancy dress: Keith Parsons Zulu. Cross-country run: 1 Alan Hutchinson, 2 Kevin Brown.

14 July 1972

FORMER DURHAM PAIR BACK ON VISIT FROM CANADA

Back here on a six-week holiday from Canada, to where they emigrated 24 years ago, a former Wheatley Hill couple, Mr and Mrs Mark Waters Brain, said that emigrating was the finest thing they ever did.

"You cannot help feeling homesick at first when you tear up your roots and start a new life in a new country", said Mr Brain's wife Edna. "But once you get over that, you are all right. Mind you I could have come back to England many a time in those first two years out there".

Mr and Mrs Brain, who are staying with Mrs Brain's parents, Mr and Mrs Sidney Hird, at 3 Moore Street, Wheatley Hill, are flying back to their home on Vancouver Island on 21 September. Last weekend they left for a fortnight's holiday in Switzerland and on their return Mr Brain is fitting in a short fishing trip in Wales before bidding farewell to their relations, his widowed mother, Mrs Maria Brain, also lives in Wheatley Hill.

Employed as a shipwright in the naval dockyards, Mr Brain said they were able to enjoy an extended holiday in this country through working overtime. He explained, "When you work overtime there you can either be paid for it or have it added to your annual holidays, I chose to take holiday in lieu so that we could have a long trip back home.

Visits

Mr Brain, who will be 50 this month, worked as a miner at Wheatley Hill colliery in his younger days and then was an apprentice pork butcher with Sherburn Hill Co-operative Society. He served for five-an-a-half years in the RAF and it was about two years after being demobilised that he and his wife decided to emigrate with their baby son.

Their son Keith, now 25, had a university education, and works for a business machine company in Vancouver, and their 21-years-old daughter Patty is employed by a telephone company.

Although thousands of miles separate the Brains from their "folk back home" there have been frequent visits between them over the past 13 years.

Mr and Mrs Hird spent a nine-week holiday with them in 1959 and since then they have been back twice together, the last time in 1970 when the visit coincided with their golden wedding.

Mrs Brain made her first return trip to England with her daughter five years ago and two years later spent another holiday here with her husband, last year their daughter was here with a girl friend for six months and five years ago their son flew here alone for a similar holiday.

"We like to keep in close touch with each other," said Mrs Brain. "Although we love the life in Canada it is nice to come back to England again to meet all our family and friends." Her parents are already planning to have another holiday in Canada next year.

8 September 1972

WHEATLEY HILL BOWLS CLUB PRESENTATION

Cups and prizes won by members of the men's and women's sections of Wheatley Hill Bowls Club last season were presented when they held their annual joint supper and social evening in the Community Centre.

Mrs Chapell, president of the North-Eastern Women's League, who congratulated the bowlers on the fine progress they had made, presented the awards. All three trophies in the women's section, the Championship Cup, the William Jones Cup and the Festival Bowl, were won by the secretary, Mrs Edna Hall. Mrs Joyce Berry was runner-up in all three competitions. Winners of the men's section trophies were Messrs H Poole, H Peacock, J Hennessey and Watson.

15 December 1972

HORNES 'A' BEAT LEAGUE LEADERS LUDWORTH

On Sunday Hornes A visited league leaders Ludworth, and were convincing 6-3 winners. The match opened briskly with both sides going close before Hornes took the lead with a goal by T Bell from a K Mayne cross. Hornes maintained their pressure and came close to scoring on several occasions before R Potts got the equaliser before half-time.

Hornes attacked straight from the kick-off and scored two goals through C Reed and M Gill from 30 yards. Ludworth hit back and T Davies beat P Walker with a penalty. Hornes immediately took up the offensive and Mayne increased the lead after being put through by D Lonsdale. This was followed up with another goal by C Reed before Ludworth were awarded another penalty and T Hoban scored. Mayne recorded Hornes' sixth and final goal

22 December 1972

LUDWORTH – One hundred and forty eight people attended the annual party of Ludworth Sports and Recreation fund held in the youth centre. Members of the women's section, Mesdames P Smith, T Winter provided high tea with the aid of helpers. Each person was presented with a gift of money. After tea, entertainment was in the ex-servicemen's Club by Mr W Maddison and party. The cake was cut by Miss Lister.

29 December 1972

1973

LUDWORTH'S CUP-TIE WIN OVER NALGO

In a hard and exciting game Ludworth Legion beat NALGO in a second round tie of the Guards Cup of Durham and District Sunday League.

Ludworth opened the scoring through Potts after ten minutes. Two minutes later Brown made it 2-0. NALGO pulled a goal back in the 30th minute when Burlison finished a long run with a hard left foot drive, giving the goalkeeper no chance.

In the second half Ludworth did most of the attacking and only good defensive work and fine goalkeeping by Gardiner kept the score down. Five minutes from the end Kipling made sure of a third round game for Ludworth by scoring from a well-taken corner.

2 February 1973

LUDWORTH LEGION'S GOOD AWAY WIN

In Division II of Durham Sunday League, Blue Star (Willington) went down 3-2 at home to promotion candidates Ludworth Legion. Ludworth were one down after ten minutes with a goal from R Dixon. Davies, Ludworth's centre-half, equalised from a corner before the interval.

Early in the second half T Strong, after eluding his "shadow" R Pardew, drove an unstoppable shot past Gibson from 25 yards. M Heslop made it 3-1 soon afterwards, when Gibson failed to hold a hard low drive. R Dixon brought Blue Star back into the game but Ludworth's hard-worked defence, with Joe Armstrong outstanding, held firm to collect the two points.

23 March 1973

RETIRED MINER DIES SUDDENLY

Mr John Youll of 28 Barnard Avenue, Ludworth, has died at his home suddenly at the age of 76 years. The Rev C W Woolstenholme conducted the funeral service at St Cuthbert's Church, Shadforth. Interment followed at Shadforth cemetery.

Mr Youll began work in the mines as a boy and continued as a miner until his retirement at 65. He was union representative to the checkweighman for a number of years for the Ludworth and Thornley Collieries.

He played football for Thornley in his youth. During the 1914-1918 War he served with the East Yorkshire Regiment and as a sergeant in the 22nd Battalion Home Guard, during the 1939-45 War. He was a regular member of the British Legion.

13 April 1973

SOLDIER DIES IN ULSTER

One of two soldiers who died after being lured to a Belfast factory and then had a mine blown up in their face, came from Thornley.

The terrorists have robbed the Gaskell family of East Lea, Thornley, of their second twin. Pte John Gaskell, 21, was one of seven. His twin died of a serious illness when he was young.

Mr and Mrs Gaskell said yesterday that next month John was due to return to his 18-year-old wife, Martha, and their six-month-old baby, who are living in Colchester.

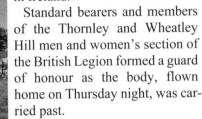

He was on his second tour of duty in Ireland.

Standard bearers and members of the Thornley and Wheatley Hill men and women's section of the British Legion formed a guard of honour as the body, flown home on Thursday night, was carried past.

The service was conducted by the Rev Phillip Mold of St Bartholomew's. The Rev Alan Homer, padre with the 2ⁿᵈ Battalion in Northern Ireland read the lesson. Also present was Lt Col McGregor-Oakford, Capt Christopher Deeds, second-in-command of B Company and 2ⁿᵈ Lt David Thomas, platoon commander.

Afterwards, as the funeral procession wound its way towards the churchyard, the streets were filled with Thornley people paying their last respects. A triple salute was fired over the grave by a firing party from the 5ᵗʰ Battalion Light Infantry.

19 May 1973
The Northern Echo
(*we have cited this newspaper as our research is usually from the Durham Advertiser series*)

FARM VISIT

At Durham City Young Farmers, members visited Thornley Hall Farm, Thornley, the home of Mr and Mrs Robinson. Tony gave a sheep shearing demonstration and members were shown round the farm.

The tug-of-war team practised for the rally, before going indoors for refreshments provided by Mrs Robinson. Brian Rutherford proposed the vote of thanks.

1 June 1973

LUDWORTH CHILDREN'S SPORTS DAY

Headed by Wheatley Hill Modern School Band, members of the general public, competing adults, children in fancy dress paraded the village of Ludworth, escorted by the police with three jazz bands in attendance at Ludworth Children's annual sports day.

Judges of the fancy dress were two Wheatley Hill old Scouts. Children's results: Graham Parsons (Zulu); Garry Bennett and Thomas Harrison (mummies); Angela Mills (Little Bo Peep). Adults: Mr T Bowes (High Chapparel), Mrs Stannard (day and night).

Children's race results: Andrew Gibbons, Daren K Miller, Colin Ager, Ian Raine, Tracey Craggs, Colleen Doughty, Ray Whittle, Linda Holmes, Rose Anne Miller, Karen Maitland, Karen Gibbons, Nicola J Robson, Alison J Youll, Judith Jones, Anne M Turnbull, Donna Armstrong, Maxine Lavelle, Leslie Gibson, Margaret Bennett, Anthony Metcalfe, Ian Barrasford, Paul Smith, Ivor Miller, Peter Jones, David Davenport, Henry F Hall, Keith Barrasford, Daren Ingleby, Carole White, Lynn Hutchinson, Karen Ager, Neil Shepherd, David Wright, Gary Thompson, Shawn White, Susan Hutchinson, Sandra Gradon, Valerie Brown, Stephen Wilson, Brian Ager, John Vasey.

Prizes were presented by County Coun D Thornton. Dr Mark Hughes, MP paid a brief visit.

Sports were organised by the men's committee. The women's section provided tea. Wheatley Hill Old Scouts organised the side shows and were responsible for the marquee.

13 July 1973

JUVENILE BANDS IN GALA PROCESSION

The number of brass bands and banners in the annual procession on Durham Miners Gala Day has steadily declined with the closing of collieries during the past 20 years.

But in the gala tomorrow, four juvenile jazz bands are to take part in the procession. "This is more or less a tentative move", said Mr Tony Graham, secretary of the Northern Area of the National Jazz Bands Association.

"We discussed the matter with Mr W Malt, Durham Area of the NUM official, "and he agreed it was something worthy of a try", said Mr Graham.

"The jazz bands will not be intermixed with the brass bands. We are scheduled to start marching at 11.00am when the colliery bands and banners will have completed their procession", said Mr Graham.

"There would probably be more jazz bands next year", said Mr Graham. "They will at least add a touch of colour and please the children and the teenagers", added Mr Graham.

20 July 1973

TOUGH START FOR THORNLEY

In preparing for the start of the season, Thornley played three friendlies all away from home in which they won one, drew one and lost one, scoring six goals and conceding three. John Todd scored four, Glyn Hutchinson and Keith Carter one year. Tomorrow Thornley entertain Durham and District League champions, Langley Park CW in their first league fixture, kick off 3.00pm.

Team from: Yates, Maines, Featherstone, A Pattison, Griffiths, Warne, Carter, Kipling, Evans, Franks, Banks, Brown, Hutchinson, Todd, Million, J Pattison.
24 August 1973

THORNLEY 1, LANGLEY PARK 4

In a great first half, in which Thornley and Langley Park played some excellent football, the teams went to the dressing rooms all level at one each.

Langley Park took the lead through a defensive mistake in which Willis got the ball and pushed it past Maines giving him no chance. Thornley fought for the equaliser they deservedly got when Brown pushed the ball forward for Hutchinson to stab it into the net from about six yards. Langley Park's experienced side soon showed what they could do, coming out to the second half and scored three more times.
31 August 1973

DEATH OF MR R NIXON

Wheatley Hill lost one of its best known residents when Mr Ralph Nixon, of 20 Alexandra Terrace, died at his son's home at Solihull Warwickshire, where he was on holiday. He was a member of a family with long business connections in the Wheatley Hill area.

After attending various schools he continued his education at the Henry Smith School, Hartlepool, and then he entered the business as a grocer with his father, Mr John Nixon and his brother, Maurice.

He married Miss Elizabeth Thompson of Wingate and it survived bys his wife, a son John (a civil servant in Birmingham), daughter-in-law Elizabeth, a grand-daughter Sarah, a sister Mrs T Valks, brothers William (retired headmaster), Walter (headmaster Henry Smith School, Hartlepool) and several nephews and nieces.

He was well known in Methodist and choral circles, having been a lifetime church member and also a member of male voice choirs and church choirs. At the time of his death he was still a member of the Trimdon and District Male Voice Choir.

He had a long record of public-service. At the start of the 1939-45 War he was a member of the Durham Division Special Constabulary and after the War served in charge of the Thornley section of the Castle Eden Division. His War service was in The Royal Army Service Corps.

He was in rather poor health but continued his activities, including Community Centre work, choirs and bowling club.

He was cremated after a service at the Robin Hood Crematorium, Solihull. The service was conducted by the Rev E (Ted) Harrison, himself a Wheatley Hill man and a member of a family closely associated with Mr Nixon's family.
14 September 1973

THORNLEY FC 2, DURHAM NALGO 0

Under bad conditions in which no team could have played well, NALGO were beaten by Thornley who were the more superior side. NALGO held the Thornley forwards for the first forty-five minutes. After half-time Thornley piled on the pressure and

634

then came the onslaught. Hutchinson put Thornley ahead with a well struck shot. Million finally sealed this win for Thornley with a shot from 20 yards.

30 November 1973

1974

MINERS BEGIN STRIKE TOMORROW MIDNIGHT

Nearly a year ago the Durham miners voted decisively against striking for more pay. This time, even more overwhelmingly, they support the call for a national coal strike, which will begin at midnight tomorrow.

Nearly 15,000 of the county's 17,000 miners are in favour of strike action, giving an 85.7 per cent majority.

Only South Wales (93.15 per cent), Yorkshire (90.5), Kent (89.7), Cumberland (88.07), Scotland (87.40) and Derbyshire (86.54) had higher majorities.

Durham Mechanics voted for a strike by more than 77 per cent and the Durham Enginemen, the smallest NUM section in the region, were 60 per cent in favour.

Neither of Durham's two members on the national executive, Mr Tom Callan (president) and Mr Walter Malt (secretary), were in favour of last month's decision by the executive, which was carried by 16 votes to ten, to call for a strike ballot among the miners.

Mr Malt explained at that time, "We went to the meeting to reflect the views of our members and the last time we met them they voted for a continuation of the overtime ban".

The result of the ballot, showing the extent of the support for a strike by the Durham miners, was "better than I had thought", he said this week.

Mr Callan's comment was that no-one could now doubt the mood of the miners.

The starting date for the strike was decided on Tuesday after a four-hour meeting of the executive in London.

8 February 1974

THORNLEY FC 3 – UNIVERSITY SC 0

Thornley kicked off with the wind in their favour and soon had the visitors in trouble with Pratt, Hutchinson and Saiger all going close to scoring.

John Saiger gave Thornley a two-goal interval lead with fine goals. After the interval it was much the same story, with Thornley doing most of the attacking, although Mains brought off two excellent saves from long-range shots.

Thornley created enough chances to win by double figures, but only fine goal-keeping kept the score down. Ronnie Robson scored his first goal for Thornley, to put the issue beyond doubt.

Tomorrow, Thornley entertain Bishop Middleham in the National Orphanage Cup quarter-final replay. Team from: Mains, Warne, Weatherall, Patterson, Pattison, Griffiths, Kitson, Nattrass, Strong, Pratt, Hutchinson, Robson, Saiger, Todd.

8 February 1974

COAL FOR ELDERLY IS ASSURED

Coal supplies to the old and infirm are being closely watched during the present emergency and every effort is being made to let those in need know of the arrangements.

This news was given to members of the County Social Services Committee by Miss Dorothy Meek, Assistant Director of the Social Services at a meeting at County Hall on Thursday.

She said that in conjunction with the NUM, the NCB and the Social Services Department they had embarked on a widespread programme of letting people know where to get the necessary certificates for coal and if need be would pay for the allowance agreed, to be repaid over the period to which the supply would relate.

Emergency rest centres would also be opened in Durham County if power cuts are introduced. Places in homes for the elderly were being provided in case the situation worsened.

Miss Meek said they were doing all they could to get friends and neighbours to help old people and the handicapped. She paid tribute to the National Union of Mineworkers and the Coal Board for doing all they could in the present crisis to help the old people.

22 February 1974

SURPRISE FROM USA FOR EX-WHEATLEY HILL MINER

When his picture was taken as he was casting his vote at the pithead during the miners' strike ballot earlier this year, a former Wheatley Hill miner never dreamed it would be published in America ... but not only did this happen, but later an American who saw his cheerful coal-begrimed face, wrote to him enclosing a cutting from the paper and a taped message, "It was the surprise of my life", said 56-year-old Mr Jim Morton, who worked at Wheatley Hill colliery until its closure six years ago, and then moved to the Midlands to continue his mining career at Coalville, near Leicester.

At first the letter addressed to "Coalville pit-head England", caused a letter-bomb scare because the package was more bulky than ordinary mail. Carefully it was opened in the post – but it contained nothing more lethal than the tape-recorded voice of Mr Charles (Chuck) Woodward, of Denver, Colorado, along with the newspaper cutting, a letter and a poem.

After being sent to the local Coal Board headquarters the package was delivered to Mr Morton at his home, 4 Melrose Road, Thringstone. Mr Morton's picture in his pit clothes at the end of his shift at Snibston colliery had been taken by an American agency and published in the Rocky Mountain News at Denver. When Mr Woodward, himself a miner's son, saw it he was so impressed by Mr Morton's cheerful face that he promptly sent off a letter, enclosing a tape recording of a song he had written himself entitled "A coalminer's son".

Mr Morton, who is married with a son and daughter, was well-known in the Wingate and Wheatley Hill area before moving to the Midlands. He has written to his widowed sister at Peterlee, Mrs Mary Foggin, of 28 Helford Road, telling of his surprise communication from America.

REQUIEM FOR MR H TUNNEY

The death took place in hospital of Mr Hubert Tunney (84), of 4 St Chad's Square, Thornley. At Thornley RC Church of the English Martyrs', Requiem Mass was celebrated by Rev Dr H McNeill. Interment followed at Thornley.

Mr Tunney leaves a wife, three sons and two daughters and 11 grandchildren. Born at Davey Lamp, Kelloe, he played a prominent part in mining, political and public bodies. He started work at 12 in Kelloe pit and then transferred to Thornley Colliery. In the Second World War he was appointed to the Ministry of Fuel and Power in Newcastle. In 1948 on the introduction of nationalisation, Mr Tunney took up the position of Deputy Labour Director of the Durham Division of the National Coal Board.

For many years he served as secretary of the Thornley Colliery Miners' Lodge and then served as Lodge chairman for a number of years. He was secretary of the Welfare Committee.

As a young man he worked for Ramsey McDonald when he stood for Seaham. For many years he was a member of Easington Rural District Council and served his year as chairman. In the same year he became vice-chairman of the newly-constituted Easington Guardians Committee. He served for many years on Thornley Parish Council and was chairman there. During these years he launched and fought for the Crimdon Park project. On the death of Peter Lee, Mr Tunney fought a County Council election as an unofficial Labour candidate and lost to Mr Francis Quinn, the official nominee.

Hospital

Mr Tunney did valuable work as chairman of the Durham County Hospital Finance Committee and was active in furthering the hospital's appeal for increased contributions for mineworkers. For 11 years he was secretary of Thornley Aged Miners' Homes Committee.

He visited Germany on a fact-finding mission on German mining conditions and also wrote a reference book on mining conditions in Durham.

Family mourners included Mrs E Tunney (wife); Mr and Mrs L Tunney (son and daughter-in-law); Mr and Mrs T Tunney (son and daughter-in-law); Mr and Mrs A Atkinson (son-in-law and daughter); Mrs C Rowley (daughter); Mr and Mrs E Tunney (son and daughter-in-law), Mrs Z Tunney (daughter-in-law),

26 April 1974

GOLDEN DAY
AT WHEATLEY HILL

Mr and Mrs William Carr, of Sandwick Terrace, Wheatley Hill, who have spent the last 40 years of their married life in the village, celebrated their golden wedding on Saturday with a party for 100 of their family and friends in Wheatley Hill Community Hall.

The couple were married in Thornley Parish Church and they lived in Thornley before moving to the neighbouring village.

Mr Carr, who is 71, was born at Eaglescliffe and moved to Wheatley Hill as a boy. He was only 12½ when he began work on Greenhills Farm for a half-a-crown *(25p)* a day. "In those days", he said "this was quite a lot of money for a lad starting his first job but, believe me I worked hard for it!" His day's work started at 5.30am and it was often eight at night before he was finished.

He said, "I did all kinds of work on the farm, including milking and ploughing – and I also had a milk round". The only time he had free was a few hours on a Sunday afternoon.

Mr & Mrs W Carr (Centre & Right)
With Steve Poulson, Best Man (Left)

When he was 15 Mr Carr left the farm to start work as a miner at Wheatley Hill colliery, where he remained until his early retirement at 62 for health reasons. He was a deputy for seven years and then an overman for the last 28 of his career.

His wife Isabella, who is 72, was born in Ludworth. After a short spell in 'place' at a private school in Redcar, she moved back to Ludworth and worked as housekeeper for the schoolmaster there, Mr White. Mrs Carr enjoys good health and is very active in the house. "I do all my own wallpapering and decorating", she said proudly. In fact Mrs Carr was painting a bedroom when our reporter called. Her husband has been a keen gardener all his life and his beautifully-kept back garden is clear proof of the care he lavishes on it. The couple have two married sons and two grand-daughters.

LUDWORTH CHILDREN'S SPORTS

Ludworth Sports and Recreation Fund Committee held their annual children's sports day on Saturday in sunny conditions. Their special guest was Mr Mark Hughes, MP for Durham, and Mr Peter Snow, the Cleveland Constabulary Solicitor was there to act as judge of the parade.

The highest markings in the bands presentations went to Newton Aycliffe Jazz Band who received first prize with Hall Lane second and Witton Gilbert third.

In the fancy dress section, Mrs Stannett was given first prize for her presentation of a Mexican Lady, while Mr Bowes who had obviously come direct from the High Chapparal won second prize.

In the Junior Section Graham Parsons dressed as a Zulu won first prize, with Gillian Smith second, as an old hag, and Arthur Phenny third as a washerwoman.

The winners in the field events were: Age 2-3 years: A Donnelly; 3-4 years: Gail Robson; 4-5 years: Tony Kennedy and Stephen Elcoat; 5-6 years: Karen Hutchinson and Ray Whittle; 6-7 years: Karen Maitland and Alan Huntington; 7-8 years: Nicola J Roeson and Michael D Hall; 8-9 years: Alison J Youll and Henry F Hall; 9-10 years: Donna Armstrong and Keth Barresford; 10-11 years: Dianne Ingleby and Neil Shepherd; 11-12 years: Jay Vasey and Ian Jackson; 12-13 years: Josephine Smith and Gary Thompson; 13-14 years: Karen Agar and Shaun White; 14-15 years: Susan Hutchinson and Stephen Wilson; 15-16 years: Denise White and Arthur W Phenny.

There were sideshows under the care of Wheatley Hill Old Scouts. A tea-tent was run by the ladies; the sporting events, parade etc were the responsibility of the men of the committee.

Sweets and ice-cream were supplied to all the children.

19 July 1974

LABOUR AND LOVE – AGED MINERS HOMES

Joseph Hopper, founder of the Aged Miners' Homes in County Durham, was born at Windy Nook in 1856 and died in 1909. His experience as local preacher, county councillor, of school boards and as a member of the Gateshead board of guardians, made of him a reformer of overwhelming zeal, from which grew his scheme for the relief of hardship in poverty. He was a miner who completed his own education in the scant leisure hours after work in pit or quarry.

To relieve poverty in general, but especially among the aged, was his ambition, and in 1894 he made his first public move at the annual meeting of the Miners' Permanent Relief Fund when he proposed "That it be an instruction to the Executive Committee to devise some scheme for aged miners' homes".

For the next two years he campaigned for the scheme in the face of discouragement from colleagues and against much ridicule. He contended with very stiff prejudice, but as he persisted he also gained support, and in 1896 he met a tiny gathering of followers in a Newcastle cafe.

Levy

There they held what later became accepted as the foundation meeting of Gateshead District Aged Mineworkers Homes. Until then Joseph Hopper had tried to establish the scheme through the Relief Fund (established by public subscription after the Hartley pit disaster in 1862, and which was eventually used to help dependents of miners killed or injured at work). Funds were kept up by a levy on miners' wages, but there was a reluctance to use this money for homes. In 1896 tactics were changed, and an independent organisation was set up with the specific aim of providing "ordinary separate dwellings". From then on the movement went from strength to strength.

The first homes were opened in 1899 by John Wilson MP at Haswell Moor. They were disused colliery houses bought cheaply because of pit closure, and they provided homes and gardens for 114 couples. In 1900, 65 dismantled colliery houses at Shincliffe were given to the Association, followed shortly after by the purchase of houses at Shotton Colliery and the leasing of cottages at Houghall. By the end of 1905 £16,500 had been spent, 200 homes were owned, and a community home for single men at Haswell Moor was established. Here the men provided their own food, but washing and cooking was done for them. By 1924 over 1000 properties were owned, and in that year the "Joseph Hopper Memorial Homes" were opened at Windy Nook.

Attractive

The present secretary is Tom Madrell, third consecutive local preacher to hold the office, and president is Edward Cain, MBE, JP, 84 years old and for 50 years closely involved with the Association and its affairs. He lives at Wheatley Hill just round the corner from 24 Aged Miners' bungalows. Twelve were built in 1923 followed two years later by another twelve. The first group included a hostel for eight men (in the centre with six bungalows either side). In November last year the hostel was taken over by the local authority and converted to Community Centre and warden's bungalow. Here lives Mrs Cook who's responsible for the comfort and security of residents of the Aged Miners' Homes as well as tenants of local authority bungalows nearby.

The community centre is bright and attractive, with golden coloured lino on the floor and gay curtains at each window. Smart modern chairs and tables, piano and television furnish the room, which adjoins a fully-equipped kitchen where Thursday's coffee morning is prepared and in which suppers of pies and peas can be kept hot. Friday night is Bingo night. Wednesday afternoon dominoes and Thursday is for whist.

During conversion of the hostel three inscribed tablets were lost. Every bungalow has one under the front window and they commemorate people and associations responsible for foundation laying. Mr Cain (his stone is one that disappeared) remembers that "it cost a £5 donation to have your name on a stone".

He's probably the only survivor of the names that make fascinating reading. Donors formed a wonderful cross section of the community and prove the alert social conscience that preceded today's Welfare State. The doctor, the schoolteacher, the butcher, the newsagent. Mine owners, mine agents, mine workers, Co-operative Societies, secretaries of Mechanics, Educational Staff and just one "In Memory" – that was for the Member of Parliament, John Wilson.

The bungalows were well built, of good red brick (stairfoots I think) and wind and weather has dealt kindly with all but the foundation tablets on the newest bungalows. Mr and Mrs Poulson at No 18 were kind enough to show me the neat sitting room, bedroom, kitchen and bathroom of their home. A back porch covers toilet and coal store, and leads to a tiny back garden where Mr Poulson grows leeks, onions, cabbages and lettuce. They live in the group built in 1925, and across the road, backing to the grounds of the Welfare Hall, is the group that was built two years earlier.

Aged Miners' Homes of this decade are all improved to modern standards. Twenty years ago, during modernisation, the aim was said to be "bathrooms, hot water systems, sink units and electric boilers to replace set-pot boilers".

The Association's theme at inception was "Labour and Love". Earl Attlee said of it many years after: " ... it is one of the greatest philanthropic schemes run by workers anywhere in the world".

Fifty years after erection, the Wheatley Hill group is a perfect example of the farsightedness of the Association's founders. Its integration with local authority bungalows is a tribute to the work done for the scheme since its foundation. The motto may be "Labour and Love", but with the benefit of hindsight, do you not think that a better and truer motto might have been "Labour of Love?

9 August 1974

LUDWORTH GOLDEN

Mr John W Williams and his wife Christina have just been celebrating their golden wedding in their Ludworth home. They were married on 30 August, 1924, at the Register Office at Easington Colliery.

Living originally at Wheatley Hill, they moved to Ludworth 47 years ago into a colliery house for what was intended to be a temporary period, but their stay at this village still continues. Mr Williams working life has been shared between Wheatley Hill and Sherburn Hill collieries with the exception of a brief period spent with Durham County Council on their road works. A Sunderland Football Club supporter for many years, he has latterly been denied this pleasure because of rowdyism and fighting on the terraces. They have two sons and three daughters and nine grandchildren, one of their sons is a serving soldier stationed in Germany.

6 September 1974

PARISH VIEWS ON LUDWORTH RECLAMATION TO BE HEARD

Shadforth Parish Council proposed the style in which key areas of Ludworth should be reclaimed. The County Council has agreed to consider parish views at the earliest possible stage and a site meeting is scheduled for 25 October.

The future of the village's abandoned pit heap seems in doubt, it was partially landscaped and planted with trees and heather some years ago, but some trees have been damaged by vandals. However, saplings and over 20 species of wild flower flourish on its grassy slopes and the general feeling is that an attractive feature of the village should not be flattened but re-contoured at the edges and the vandalised trees replaced.

"It is also vital that the reclamation of the old golf links should take cognisance of the excellent landscaping done by the District Council on the opposite side of the road", said Coun Bill Hyland, chairman.

The outpost of Lynn Terrace, in Shadforth Parish, but geographically several miles away, near Wheatley Hill, was the source of several complaints to the council. Dustbins had not been emptied regularly for several weeks and the beck, parallel to the street, was brimming with sewage. The Clerk was asked to write to the appropriate authority before the situation reached crisis level.

LUDWORTH MAN GOT HIGH LABOUR SWING

David Taylor-Gooby, the Ludworth man who has twice fought Scarborough for the Labour Party, netted almost the highest swing to Labour in the country in the general election. Increasing his vote by 43% over the February total, Mr Taylor-Gooby ran the Liberal to within 200 votes for second place, in this traditional Conservative stronghold.

A teacher in Peterlee, David twice fought council seats before being adopted for Scarborough in 1973 and intends to continue in the Parliamentary stakes. In Ludworth, he hopes to restart the Youth Club now the election is over. He is standing in as Clerk to Shadforth Parish Council while his wife, Vera, is in London reading for the Bar.

18 October 1974

643

1975

MIDDLESTONE MOOR 2, WHEATLEY HILL 2

A draw was a fair result of the quarter-final of the Staffieri Cup competition, in which extra time was played.

"Hill" went into the lead after ten minutes. Barry Grant, after beating four men, succeeded from 12 yards, and 15 minutes later George Trewhitt increased the lead by lobbing over the keeper's head from 15 yards. In the 40th minute Holden replied for Middlestone, and 15 minutes later Shoulder equalised with a header. Bill O'Neil for Hill, failed to convert a penalty kick.

Play was end to end for the 120 minutes with both defences putting up stubborn resistance. For Wheatley Hill, Harry O'Neil and Trevor Strong were most successful in midfield and Grant and John Parkinson were very effective in the front line.
3 January 1975

WHEATLEY HILL 6, THE HUT 1

Soon after the start it was obvious Wheatley Hill would pass into the semi-final of the President's Cup competition. They were quicker and more constructive, and had chances to widen the goal gap. Ronnie Robson (sub) brought on for the last 20 minutes completed a hat-trick. The other scorers were Tony Mooney (2) and George Trewhitt. Hill intermediate men, Trevor Strong, Jim Jackson and John Parkinson were responsible for most of the attacking.
24 January 1975

NEWTON ALL STARS 2, WHEATLEY HILL 1

Newton All Stars moved into the semi-final of the Staffieri Cup with a deserved victory over Wheatley Hill on Sunday.

The visitors attacked strongly in the first half but All Stars defence was always sound and Harris in goal was outstanding. All Stars always looked dangerous when breaking out and from one such move Parsons supplied the pass for Blacklock to make the interval score 1-0. The home side gradually got on top and despite a penalty miss by Chivers scored their second when Parsons was on hand to get the vital touch in a goalmouth melee.

Wheatley Hill never looked like getting on level terms after this but managed a consolation goal five minutes from the end. All Starts are away to Ouston Red Lion in the semi final.

SHERBURN 4, THORNLEY 2

Sherburn Hill reached the final of the Brandon Aged Miners Cup, with a 4-2 win over Thornley. It was a hard cup tie with both teams playing some fine football. Sherburn Hill took the lead on the half hour, when Derrick Aylesbury scored direct from a corner.

The Hill never looked back after this fine start, although Thornley put them under tremendous pressure, they defended well. The lead was increased by Keith Harrison, who tucked a fine shot past Hodgson. Chas Armstrong made it three shortly afterwards, when he went round Hodgson to score a fine goal.

Thornley then pulled one back through Todd, but the game was put beyond doubt, when the Hill were awarded a penalty for pushing against Fox. Derrick Aylesbury made no mistake and scored his second of the match. Thornley scored another late goal in the final minutes to make the scoreline a little more respectable.

7 March 1975

THORNLEY FUNERAL

After the sudden death of Mr Robert Wigham (76), 23 Greenwood Cottages, Thornley, a funeral service was conducted in St Bartholomew's Church by Rev P G Mold. Interment was at Quarrington Hill churchyard. Married for more than 50 years, Mr Wigham leaves his wife, Mrs Mary J Wigham, two sons and a daughter all married. He was born at Wheatley Hill and spent most of his married life in Thornley. He was a one-colliery man and started work at Thornley pit at 14. He studied for certificates and became a deputy and progressed to overman. He retired after 51 years.

In his younger days Mr Wigham was a keen sportsman, playing football for local teams. He won a few cup and league medals. He served as a machine gunner in the first world war. He was a founder member of the Thornley Officials Club.

Family mourners included Mrs M J Wigham (widow), Mr and Mrs R Wigham (son and daughter-in-law), Mr and Mrs A Carr (son-in-law and daughter), Mr and Mrs P Wigham (son and daughter-in-law), grandchildren, Miss L Wigham, Miss H Carr, Mr D Wigham. Mr and Mrs F Wigham) brother and sister-in-law), Mr and Mrs G Wigham (brother and sister-in-law), Mr and Mrs R McKay (brother-in-law and sister), Mr and Mrs E Wilson (brother-in-law and sister), Mr and Mrs W Wigham (brother and sister-in-law), Miss H Wigham (sister), Mr and Mrs T L Robson (brother-in-law and sister).

16 May 1975

CITY ANGLERS DEFEAT WHEATLEY HILL

The weekly Durham City Angling Club sweepstake series match was fished at Tursdale Pond on Tuesday, 8 July. The winner was R Fox, 2lb.8oz; 2 G Skirrey, 2lb.2oz, 8dr; 3 T Wood, llb.8oz. Once again catches consisted of mainly perch.

At the same venue on 9 July, the first round of the Fred Evans knockout competition was fished. The teams were ten men each, Durham City Angling Club versus Wheatley Hill. It was an overwhelming victory for DCAC team with 13lb.6oz total weight. Wheatley Hill AC total weight was 7lb.5oz. Individual weights were: 1 D Fox, DCAC, 2lb.8oz; 2 S Atkinson, DCAC, 1lb.13oz; joint 3 K Simpson, Wheatley Hill and R Wood, DCAC llb.9oz. This match was an efficient start to the competition series for DCAC with a good average catch per team member.

18 July 1975

CATHEDRAL SACRIST FOR WHEATLEY HILL LIVING

The Rev Dr Timothy John Fawcett, who has been sacrist at Durham Cathedral since 1972, has been appointed Vicar of All Saints Church, Wheatley Hill, and will be instituted and inducted to the living by the Bishop of Durham, Dr John Habgood, and the Archdeacon of Durham, the Ven M Perry on Monday, 8 September, at 7.00pm.

Dr Fawcett sang in the choir of Durham Cathedral as a boy, when a pupil of the Chorister School, and later continued his education in Rossall School, near Fleetwood. He then studied at King's College, London, where he graduated with an honours Bachelor of Divinity degree, and in 1967 was ordained and became curate at the Church of St Stephen-on-the Cliffs at Blackpool.

During his two years service there, he was seconded to London University for further research and was an honorary curate at All Saints' Church in Margaret Street.

In 1970, in the same year that he was awarded the degree of Doctor of Philosophy, Dr Fawcett was married and was appointed curate at another church in London, St Michael-at-Bowes. He remained there until his appointment as sacrist at Durham Cathedral.

Dr Fawcett, who has already taken up residence in the Vicarage at Wheatley Hill with his wife and three young children – three-year-old twin girls and a four-month-old baby boy – has succeeded the Rev A R G Pugh who, for health reasons, retired in April after nearly five years at Wheatley Hill.

Dr Fawcett has done a lot of research into liturgy and recently had a book published entitled "The Liturgy of Comprehension". While working as a curate in London he was deputy chaplain at the Middlesex Hospital.

5 September 1975

FUNERAL OF FORMER LICENSEE

The funeral service took place last week, in the Methodist Church, of Mr William (known as Ginger) Dawson, 17 Gorehill Estate, Thornley, conducted by Rev Robert S Thompson. Interment followed in Thornley cemetery. He was the husband of Mrs Margaret Ann Dawson, who died ten years ago.

One of the village's best-known octogenarians, he was 87. Born at Sacriston, he spent most of his life in Thornley. He started work at Thornley pit and worked in the mine till his early 30's. Mr Dawson then turned to business. He built up a thriving fish and chips business and served the community in that capacity for ten years. He then took the Railway Tavern in Thornley and for over 35 years became a popular licensee.

He served in the First World War for four years in the Royal Artillery.

Mr Dawson is survived by three sons and two daughters, 11 grandchildren and 15 great grandchildren. He was 78 when he retired from the Tavern.

Family mourners were Mr and Mrs J R Johnson (son-in-law and daughter), Mr John Dawson (son), Mr and Mrs Robert Dawson (son and daughter-in-law), Mr William Dawson (son), Mr and Mrs L Stogdale (son-in-law and daughter).

WHEATLEY HILL STANDARD DEDICATED

A new standard for the Wheatley Hill branch of the Royal British Legion Women's Section was dedicated at Wheatley Hill All Saints' Parish Church.

Standard bearers from Easington Colliery, Langley Park, Murton, Houghton, Shotton, Thornley, Norton, Sacriston, Blackhall, Fishburn, Trimdon Village, Great Lumley and Lowerth all took part. With them was the standard bearer for Durham County.

Mr Fishwick, of Langley Park, was parade marshall, and the parade was led by the Wheatley Hill Boy's School Brass Band, under the leadership of Messrs Jones and Kitto, two schoolmasters.

Boy Scouts, Girl Guides, Cubs and Brownies took part, with members of Wheatley Hill Workingmen's Club, community centre members, the domino and whist clubs and the ladies' bowls club. Mr Edward Cain, Dr Todd and members of the Old Scouts Association were also present.

Standard Bearers

The new standard was carried by Mrs M Holdcroft, and the old one by the section's standard bearer, Mrs S Humes. The new standard was handed over to Mrs F M Carr, who then gave it to Mrs Humes and the Rev T Fawcett to be dedicated.

Rev Fawcett was assisted in the dedication by Rev R Thompson and Rev R Richmond.

Among the speakers were Mrs M Holdcroft, chairman of Wheatley Hill Women's Section; Mrs Parkes, County Chairman; Mr R A Douglas, County Poppy Day Appeal representative; the county secretary, Mr Simmons and Mr William Hall, chairman of Wheatley Hill Men's Section of the Royal British Legion.

10 October 1975

WHEATLEY HILL WMC 2, CARLISLE UTD SC 1

This All-England Sunday Cup game drew a large crowd on Ludworth ground. From a free-kick from Harry O'Neil, Charlie Gott headed Hill into the lead in the sixth minute. In the 60th minute Robinson equalised. In the fifth minute of the 30 minutes extra time Fred Crowe, receiving from George Trewhitt, ran through to gain the decisive goal by lobbing over the keeper's head.

31 October 1975

LONG SERVICE GIFT AT LUDWORTH

The president, Mrs Morgan, opened the meeting of Ludworth Royal British Legion Women's Section. Officials re-elected were: Chairman, Mrs A Hutchinson; secretary, Mrs E Stannard; treasurer, Mrs I Cowan; poppy organiser, Mrs M Hughes; standard bearer, Mrs E Stannard. A copper vase was presented to Mrs Winter on her retirement due to ill-health, after 15 years as chairman. The treasurer gave a favourable report on the previous year's achievements.

5 December 1975

WHEATLEY HILL COLLIERY SOLD

G H Edkins and Son, estate agents, of Bishop Auckland, Durham City and branches, report one of their more unusual sales. They have agreed to sell the former Wheatley Hill Colliery together with the spoil heap adjoining to the Easington District Council for reclamation.

It is not often that a privately-owned colliery site comes on the market. The price has not been disclosed, but Mr Denis Edkins, principal of the firm, indicated that the figure was not a very high one due to the cost of the removal of the buildings and spoil heap on the site. In fact, he said, "It would hardly buy a decent terraced house these days".

LUDWORTH – The amount raised this year by the Ludworth Branch Royal British Legion was £122.50. Mr Smith the secretary thanks everyone who helped, especially Sherburn Village Jolly Boys who did a charity show.

12 December 1975

THORNLEY BL WOMEN MEET

Members of Thornley Women's Section of the Royal British Legion heard that their chairman, Mrs E Clark, had been re-elected as a member of the County Standing Orders Committee and the County Executive Committee. Mrs Clark, presiding announced that the Thornley total for the Earl Haig Fund on Poppy Day was £249.06. She thanked all who had helped in the effort, particularly Mrs S Bell, the Poppy Day organiser. Mrs Bell said that the service of the women's section was largely responsible for this excellent achievement.

Minutes and correspondence were read by Mrs B Musgrave. Mrs Clark reported on the official opening of Thornley Men's Section Club, which was formerly The Spearman's Arms. A bring and buy stall was well supported. Mrs M Purvis was MC for games and competitions. Prizewinners were Mesdames M Stewart, L Woodhead, M Barrass, D Laverick and F Nicholson. Tea hostesses were Mesdames M Hewitson, M M Bean and M Matthews.

19 December 1975

1976

WHEATLEY HILL WMC 10, NEWTON ALL STARS 0

As the score indicates, "Hill" found it easy maintaining their 100 per cent record in the Durham and District League. Right from the start they converged on the visitors goal, soon it was obvious they would win by a large margin. The scorers were Brian Greenwood (3), John Jordan and Charley Gott (2 each), Ron Robson, Brian Magee and Jim Jackson. "Hill" now have 55 goals for and only three against.

10 January 1976

WHEATLEY HILL WMC 4, LUMLEY WARRIORS 2

Goals by George Trewhitt (2) and Brian Magee and Brian Greenwood gave Hill a 4-1 interval lead, in this Durham and District Sunday League Challenge Cup game. The visitors, with the aid of the wind for the second half, came more into the picture as attackers, but were easily contained by a strong defence in which Jim Jackson, Frank Ayre and Brian Magee played a major part. Hill now have 101 goals and only five against.

23 January 1976

POLICE TO LOOK INTO HOSPITAL DEATH

A report is to be sent to the Director of Public Prosecutions following the death of a mentally handicapped patient at Durham's Earls House Hospital.

An inquest in Durham on Wednesday heard 44-year-old Mr Leslie Greenwell died as a result of "heavy bleeding resulting from perforations of the rectum in three places with penetration into the abdominal cavity".

Dr Harvey McTaggart, pathologist at Hartlepool General, said he believed the injuries were caused by a metal arrow shaft. The inquest was adjourned to a later date.

Mr Greenwell, formerly of Johnson's Estate, Wheatley Hill, died in the early hours of last Thursday.

It is understood he was taken to Dryburn Hospital after staff had found him bleeding in his dormitory bed, but the full extent of his injuries was not realised at first. He died later at Dryburn.

The arrow was discovered in the dormitory at Earls House Hospital. It is believed another mentally sub-normal patient was involved in the matter.

Police investigations into the death were led by the deputy head of Durham County CID, Detective Superintendent Clayton Whittaker.

He said his enquiries were now concluded and a report would be submitted to the DPP. He also said he found nothing wrong with the hospital.

A seven-man inquiry board has been set up at the hospital consisting of hospital officials, doctors and a member of the Area Health Authority to look into the death.

Mr John Baines, the Durham district health administrator and a member of the inquiry team, said they would be interviewing both staff and patients at the hospital.

He added: "We are collecting facts, but we will not sift through the evidence or reach any conclusions until after the coroner's inquest".

At the opening of the inquest, Mr George Scrafton, of Lingholme, Chester-le-Street, said Mr Greenwell had been at Earls House Hospital for three years following the deaths of his mother and father.

Mr Greenwell's uncle, Mr William Ward, of Dalton Terrace, Wheatley Hill, said his nephew was as quiet as a mouse.

"He was child-like really, and used to watch television a lot. He didn't recognise most people when they went to see him".

27 February 1976

LUDWORTH LEGION WOMEN'S BIRTHDAY PARTY

Ludworth Royal British Legion Women's Section celebrated their 28th birthday party on Tuesday. A hot meal was enjoyed. Mrs Morgan president called upon Mrs Maitland to cut the birthday cake, because at 89 years of age she is the oldest Legion member.

5 March 1976

JUVENILE CHARGED AFTER
MENTAL PATIENT DIES OF ARROW WOUNDS

A 15-year-old juvenile has been charged with manslaughter following the death from arrow wounds of a mentally handicapped patient at a Durham Hospital in February.

A police spokesman confirmed this week a summons had been issued and served on the juvenile.

Mr Leslie Greenwell, 44, a patient at Earls House Hospital for three years died at Dryburn Hospital where he had been taken after he was discovered bleeding in the early hours of 19 February.

At the opening of an inquest into his death it was stated he died as a result of "heavy bleeding resulting from perforations of the rectum in three places with penetration into the abdominal cavity".

A pathologist said he believed the wounds were caused by a metal arrow shaft.

A police investigation into Mr Greenwell's death was led by the deputy head of Durham County CID, Detective Superintendent Clayton Whittaker.

His report was sent to the Director of Public Prosecutions who has now decided to go ahead with proceedings.

It is not known when the juvenile, who has not been named, will appear in court.

9 April 1976

RESCUERS FIGHT FOR BOY IN PIT SHAFT

A desperate attempt to rescue a teenager trapped in a 1000 ft deep mine shaft could continue for the next two days.

The boy, Frank Lye, slipped and fell into a mass of water and slurry while exploring a disused pit at Thornley yesterday lunch-time.

And as darkness fell last night the NCB said, "It looks like a recovery rather than a rescue operation now".

Frank and his friend, Dale Beeston, climbed a 30ft wall, scrambled along a ten-feet tall girder just six inches wide, and climbed into the shaft head building through a high window.

Inside, says the National Coal Board, safety fencing ringing the treacherous shaft had been removed.

The alarm was raised by 16-year-old Dale Beeston. The Mine Rescue Service was first on the scene. Rescue teams used search-lights, infra-red binoculars, grappling irons and ropes.

Black Slurry

Just after six last night firemen broke a three-foot hole into the shaft head – working in near darkness and in cramped conditions.

At ten, National Coal Board took over from the fire brigade. Shifts of men worked through the night to set up pumping equipment that should be working by mid-day today.

The mine has been closed since 1970 and since then the shaft filled with black slurry from a washery that operated until the start of this year.

Tons of water and stone have poured into the shaft which has a 200ft drop and 50ft of water.

Quiet Boy

Frank's mother has already given up hope that her eldest son could be rescued alive.

As relatives comforted Mrs Jane Lye, she said the shaft was filled with water and broken girders.

"I don't know what he would have been doing there. He's a quiet boy who loved collecting antiques". Boy Scout Frank – he has helped with a milk-round in Thornley for years – has just left school and hoped to start work soon at a factory.

As news of the accident spread, shocked villagers said they thought the shaft had been sealed off.

But the NCB said, "We have done everything we possibly can to keep the kids out. Security men visit the place regularly and checks were made twice on Saturday".

7 June 1976
The Northern Echo
(*we have cited this newspaper as our research is usually from the Durham Advertiser series*)

RESCUE MEN REACH PIT SHAFT BODY

A boys body was brought from the 1000ft disused pit shaft at Thornley Colliery yesterday.

The final winching of the special cage began slowly just after 1.30pm, 48 hours after recovery operations started, and police and NCB experts stood by waiting for the final ascent.

A police van was backed up to the scene, to obscure the view of onlookers who were still gathering on an overlooking hill, and at 1.45pm workers carried a casket from the pit shaft building and placed it in a small blue police van.

The van drove slowly away en route for Dryburn Hospital where the body of 16-year-old Frank Lye will be formally identified this afternoon.

The recovery marked the end of an enormous operation mounted by firemen, police and the NCB since the alarm was raised on Sunday lunchtime by Dale Beeston, Frank's friend.

The two boys who had entered the pit shaft building through a window 18ft above ground, had been exploring when Frank, the eldest of three brothers, slipped and fell.

Parents Relieved

Rescue workers faced the hazards of old shaft gear and a 16ft diameter shaft which had been filled with slurry since the pit ceased working six years ago. Three-man teams made two 200ft descents on Monday to drag the 50ft depth of water, but pumping out began late on Monday evening.

Yesterday morning with 9ft of water left, one shoe was discovered and workers decided to continue pumping risking the loss of submersible pumping gear. But a girder blocked the way – believed to have been thrown down by the boys – and another descent to free it was made before the final recovery could begin.

Mr Peter Heron, NCB Press Officer, said the parents of the dead boy were relieved the body had been found. "Work would have gone on to dredge the tailings which had settled under the water. It would have meant men going down and scooping out the stuff, bringing it back to the surface and going back to continue the work".

Frank, of Handel Terrace, Wheatley Hill, was a quiet boy who liked collecting antiques. He had just left school and was hoping to start work in a plastic sack factory.

Repeat Warnings

The colliery, disused since 1970, but used as a washery until earlier this year, is due for demolition, and Durham County Council is waiting to start phase two of reclamation operations.

The old buildings, when reduced to rubble, will be thrown into the two pit shafts which will then be sealed.

Yesterday, Mr Heron said reclamation would be going ahead. "It will take some time to remove all the gear brought in for the recovery and then the place will be manned 24 hours a day until demolition begins. This has been extremely tragic and we can only repeat our warnings to parents to keep children away from NCB property".

9 June 1976
The Northern Echo
(we have cited this newspaper as our research is usually from the Durham Advertiser series)

THORNLEY BRING AND BUY SALE

A bring and buy sale was well supported in aid of funds at the weekly meeting of Thornley Women's Section of the Royal British Legion in the Catholic Club. Special prizes were donated by Mrs B Musgrave and Mrs P Woodhead, which were won by Mrs F Peacock and Mrs F Simpson. Draw tickets were sold in support of the County Arts and Crafts exhibition. MC for games was Mrs B Atkin. Prize-winners were Mrs M Cooper and Mrs M Oswald. Mrs E Clark presided and Mrs B Musgrave read the minutes and correspondence. Tea hostesses were Mesdames T Walker, M Bean and M Mather.

SCOUTS' FIELD DAY AT WHEATLEY HILL

Wheatley Hill Old Scouts' Association held its annual field day in the Wheatley Hill Secondary School playing field on Saturday. The event attracted a record attendance of approximately 3000 and is expected to yield a record financial return. The money each year is raised for Scouting activities and other charitable objects. Mr Ralph Watson was organising secretary.

A colourful parade marched through the village headed by Thornley Community Association Silver Band. They were followed by six jazz bands from Tyneside, and a Pipe Band. A wheelbarrow race in the streets was won by Messrs Carr and Purvis.

The placings for the Jazz Bands overall competition were as follows: 1 Byker Imperials; 2 Long Benton Fairways Vikings; 3 West Walker Warriors. An appreciative audience acclaimed a concert given by the Thornley Community Association Band under its leader, Mr J Baldasera. Marching and pipe playing was well received from the Houghton and District Pipe Band. Another popular event was the karate exhibition by the Houghton Burn and Eaglescliffe Karate team. A rolling pin throwing competition caused a lot of fun and was won by Mrs J Pratt.

Ladies of the Scouts Parents Committee played their part in serving teas and refreshments; Miss B Johnson, Mesdames Coun R Watson, G Walker, G Richardson, B Andrews and R Armstrong, Scouts and Cubs under Scoutmaster C Thackeray, Guides and Brownies turnout out in uniform for the parade and assisted with sideshows.
11 June 1976

PIT TRAGEDY BOY BURIED

Frank Lye, the 16-year-old boy who fell to his death last weekend in a disused Thornley pit shaft, was buried at Wheatley Hill on Saturday.

Frank, of Handel Terrace, the eldest of three brothers and a Ranger Scout, was carried by members of Wheatley Hill Scout Association to the packed church for the burial service.

14 June 1976

Frank Lye
Died after falling down the pit shaft at
Thornley in 1976

FATALITIES AT
THORNLEY, LUDWORTH & WHEATLEY HILL COLLIERIES

Between 1930 and 1976

Over the course of carrying out research for the series of books dealing with the development and then demise of the three collieries above, our researchers have collated all mentioned fatalities which have occurred in the three pits since the 1830's until the unfortunate accident of a young boy in 1976, and now present them in alphabetical order, giving as much information as space allows here.

This will be by no means a definitive list and for that we apologise, for whilst every effort has been made to investigate and record all known fatalities, it is inevitable that some will have gone unreported/unrecorded and may be known only to family members.

If there is a fatality which does not appear on our list, and of which you are aware, the History Club would be grateful for your contribution in order to keep our lists up to date.

NAME	AGE	JOB	CAUSE OF DEATH	DATE OF DEATH	COLLIERY
ABRAHAM, William E J	16	Putter Boy	Explosion of gas	26.9.1876	Wheatley Hill
ADAMSON, Frederick	21	Wagonwayman	Crushed by two trucks	27.5.1914	Thornley
ADDISON, Matthew	10			3.3.1859	Ludworth
ANDERSON, Herbert	22	Putter	Pony bolted	1.1.1931	Thornley
ANDERSON, Irvine	29	Sinker	Thrown out of corf	Dec 1844	Ludworth
ARMSTRONG, John	13	Putter	Explosion	5.8.1841	Thornley
ARMSTRONG, R	12			7.2.1867	Thornley
ARNOLD, J	16	Landing Lad	Knocked down by set of tubs	17.12.1812	Thornley
ATCHINSON, Thomas H	16	Landing Lad	Dragged under tub of coal	20.12.1943	Thornley
ATKIN, Richard C	32	Engineman	Fell down pit shaft - 120 yards	14.8.1924	Ludworth
ATKINSON, George	64	Overman	Struck by fall of stone	14.10.1941	Thornley
ATTACK, James Kelly	21	Hewer	Explosion of gas	26.9.1876	Wheatley Hill
AVERY, William	14	Lamp Keeper	Crushed by cage at shaft bottom	1.10.1855	Thornley
BAILES, T H	28	Stoneman	Injured by fall of stone 27.1.25	19.2.1925	Wheatley Hill
BAKER, James	59	Shifter	Struck by prop	24.4.1931	Wheatley Hill
BAKER, Robert	50			31.5.1905	Thornley
BARKER, Thomas	64	Stoneman	Crushed by fall of stone	24.10.1910	Wheatley Hill
BARKER, William	60	Timber Leader	Injury to thumb	19.11.1904	Wheatley Hill
BARNARD, Howard	16	Driver	Injuries received 22.12.1905	19.7.1913	Wheatley Hill
BARRASS, John	11	Driver	Run over by coal wagon	10.7.1843	Thornley

NAME	AGE	JOB	CAUSE OF DEATH	DATE OF DEATH	COLLIERY
BATES, Joseph	31	Hewer	Crushed by fall of stone	26.2.1936	Thornley
BELL, Brian	16	Datal Worker	Caught by set of tubs	3.1.1957	Thornley
BELL, George A	37	Shaftman	Fell from cage in No 1 pit - 24 fathoms	10.8.1915	Wheatley Hill
BELL, John	70	Labourer	Fell over pit heap wall - 14ft	27.2.1849	Thornley
BELL, John	30	Stoneman	Drowned in inundation	19.1.1871	Wheatley Hill
BELL, William	13	Switch Keeper	Run over by set of 12 coal wagons	12.8.1846	Thornley
BERRY, James	41	Pitman	Thrown out of cage	10.12.1855	Ludworth
BETTS, George	50	Stoneman	Accident caused by lifting heavy stone	15.5.1916	Wheatley Hill
BICKERTON, Herbert	57	Stoneman	Injury to head caused by baulk in roof	1.5.1909	Wheatley Hill
BLAKEMORE, John	38	Stoneman	Run over by runaway tubs	15.9.1930	Wheatley Hill
BOLTON, John	35	Hewer	Jammed between coal tub and roof	4.5.1880	Thornley
BONES, George	32	Shaftman	Broken cage rope - fell to bottom of shaft	10.8.1844	Thornley
BOOTH, Lancelot F H	28	Under Manager	Crushed against steel support by fall	28.12.1931	Thornley
BOWES, James W	14	Driver Boy	Caught between tub and roadway	10.12.1918	Wheatley Hill
BRADLEY, Edmond	47	Miner	Accidentally killed	2.7.1908	Thornley
BRADLEY, Richard	56	Pitman	Crushed between water tub and wall	7.2.1852	Thornley
BRADSHAW, Kenneth	28	Miner	Accidentally killed	9.3.1954	Thornley
BRADY, Edward	56	Pitman	Crushed by a roof fall	4.5.1855	Thornley
BRIGGS, William	52	Stoneman	Crushed by fall of stone in Hutton Seam	11.11.1937	Thornley
BRODRICK, William T	24	Spareman	Crushed by fall of stone from roof	30.5.1910	Thornley

NAME	AGE	JOB	CAUSE OF DEATH	DATE OF DEATH	COLLIERY
BROUGHTON, Herbert	64	Miner	Struck on the head by handle of winch	25.11.1930	Wheatley Hill
BROWN, John	16	Pitman	Crushed by large stone	14.3.1853	Thornley
BROWN, William M	56	Master Shifter	Caught by the cage in Five Quarter Seam	21.2.1902	Ludworth
BUNTING, Rober M	19			29.7.1898	Thornley
BURNHAM, John	47	Deputy Overman	Crushed by a roof fall	15.2.1854	Thornley
BURNS, John	48			15.6.1908	Wheatley Hill
CARR, Alfred	43	Miner	Died from pneumonia following accident	1.2.1921	Wheatley Hill
CHAMPLEY, John	22	Miner	Falling down shaft of new pit	10.6.1907	Thornley
CHAPMAN, John	42		Knocked down by moving trucks	8.12.1908	Thornley
CHARLTON, Robert	59	Miner	Died through injuries received	10.1.1906	Wheatley Hill
CHATT, John	57	Sinker	Thrown out of kibble and fell down shaft	15.1.1870	Wheatley Hill
CHISHOLM, George	46	Pitman	Thrown out of cage	10.4.1845	Thornley
CHISHOLM, William	46	Miner	Accidentally killed	19.9.1916	Wheatley Hill
CHRISTOPHER, John	13	Pit Boy	Head crushed between tub and wall	16.3.1847	Thornley
CHRISTOPHER, William	14	Pit Boy	Crushed between cage and shaft bottom	24.6.1854	Thornley
CLARKE, Edward	15			25.5.1870	Thornley
CLARKSON, Robert	41	Filler	Crushed by fall of stone in Low Main	15.6.1909	Wheatley Hill
CLEGHORN, William	34	Miner	From injuries received	11.5.1932	Thornley
COLLINS, Arkless	41	Pitman	Injury to back on 1.11.1878	21.11.1878	Wheatley Hill
COLLINS, Henry	26	Sinker	Fell down the shaft	9.12.1870	Wheatley Hill
CONWAY, Thomas H	21	Horse Keeper	Fell down shaft from Hutton Seam - 100ft	13.7.1930	Thornley

NAME	AGE	JOB	CAUSE OF DEATH	DATE OF DEATH	COLLIERY
COOPER, George	13	Helper up	Drowned in inundation	19.1.1871	Wheatley Hill
CRAGGS, Benjamin C	66	Shifter	Injury to back and hip on 15.1.1916	1.1.1923	Thornley
CRAGGS. Ralph	19	Putter	Crushed by fall of stone	23.2.1926	Thornley
CRAIG, Thomas	18	Miner		7.10.1904	Wheatley Hill
CRAIG, William	39	Deputy Overman	Crushed by fall of stone	7.5.1880	Ludworth
CRAWFORD, Thomas W	45	Timber Drawer	Buried by fall of stone	17.7.1942	Thornley
CROSSGROVE, Robert	30	Shaftman	Cage rope snapped	10.8.1844	Thornley
CRUDDAS, James	4		Attempting to cross railway line	29.1.1850	Ludworth
CRUDDAS, Matthew	60	Miner	Severely crushed by roof fall	6.9.1844	Thornley
DALEY, William	22			19.3.1868	Thornley
DAVIS, Richard	58			16.1.1900	Thornley
DAVIS, Samuel	58	Stoneman	Slipped and fell onto rails	24.1.1936	Thornley
DAW, James	16	Pit Boy	Injured on 25.11.1878	1.12.1878	Wheatley Hill
DAY, Thomas R	15	Pit Boy	Crushed by timber	11.12.1925	Thornley
DENT, William	34	Miner	Died through injuries received	18.7.1903	Thornley
DIALL, Thomas	63			2.12.1858	Thornley
DIVINE, John	17	Pit Boy	Crushed between a laden tub & side of	16.12.1854	Thornley
DOBINSON, George D	34	Overman	Explosion of gas	26.9.1876	Wheatley Hill
DOUGLAS, Thomas	30	Stoneman	Buried in a fall of stone	11.2.1914	Wheatley Hill
DOVE, George	18	Stone teemer		17.12.1900	Wheatley Hill
DOWNISON, Peter	15			27.10.1868	Thornley

659

NAME	AGE	JOB	CAUSE OF DEATH	DATE OF DEATH	COLLIERY
DOWSON, Thomas	15		Seriously injured 21.11.1908	29.9.1909	Thornley
DOYLE, Catherine	6		Run down by an engine in Goods Station	13.6.1924	Thornley
DOYLE, Nancy	3		Run down by an engine in Goods Station	13.6.1924	Thornley
DRENNAN, James H	52	Miner	Crushed by fall of stone on 18.10.1936	1.11.1939	Thornley
DUFFEY, William	35	Fireman	Boiler explosion in Low Main	18.1.1878	Thornley
DUNLEAVY, Thomas	64	Miner	Injury to leg on 29.10.1917	21.9.1923	Thornley
EBDALE, Joseph	33	Hewer	Crushed by fall of stone in No 2 Pit	3.5.1916	Thornley
ELLIOTT, George	8		Run over by laden wagons on pit heap	12.7.1858	Thornley
ELLIOTT, Norman S	16	Pony Driver	Crushed by laden coal tubs	11.11.1937	Thornley
ELSDON, Joseph	26	Sinker	Thrown out of corf in shaft	Dec 1844	Ludworth
ELWICK, John	42	Pitman	Crushed by a roof fall	4.8.1853	Thornley
ENGLISH, George T	65	Miner	Died through an accident	14.4.1940	Wheatley Hill
EVANS, Arthur	64	Shifter	Caught between set and a sheave	25.10.1918	Wheatley Hill
EVANS, John	14	Trapper	Head jammed between plank and roof	17.4.1874	Thornley
EVANS, William E	30	Coal Filler	Crushed by a fall of stone	11.2.1958	Wheatley Hill
FARNWORTH, George	36	Stoneman	Crushed by a fall of stone	9.3.1932	Wheatley Hill
FARRELL, Patrick	58	Miner	Crushed by a fall of stone	11.12.1919	Wheatley Hill
FARROW, Joseph	33	Deputy Overman	Crushed by roof fall	1.3.1848	Ludworth
FARROW, Joseph	42	Sinker	Precipitated down the shaft 17.4.1871	20.4.1871	Wheatley Hill
FAWKES, Robert	45	Shaftman	Fell down shaft - 20 fathoms	3.2.1911	Wheatley Hill

NAME	AGE	JOB	CAUSE OF DEATH	DATE OF DEATH	COLLIERY
FERRY, William R	25		Crushed by coil of wire	17.5.1910	Thornley
FLEMING, Martin	16	Pit Boy		15.9.1883	Thornley
FLETCHER, John	31	Pitman		20.3.1883	Ludworth
FORSTER, William	57	Pitman	Crushed by a roof fall	2.3.1848	Thornley
FOSTER, Albert	43	Rolleywayman	Crushed between tub and roof	12.3.1940	Wheatley Hill
FOSTER, Robert	60	Pitman	Killed by machinery - pumping engine	30.12.1872	Thornley
FRANCIS, Charles	25	Hewer	Overcome by poisonous gas in old working	20.12.1909	Wheatley Hill
FULCHER, Russell E	42	Miner	Struck by girder during fall of stone	27.3.1968	Thornley
FULLER, Robert	39	Miner	Died from an injury received in pit	21.4.1913	Wheatley Hill
GARDNER, Jonathan	16	Putter	Killed by explosion	5.8.1841	Thornley
GARDNER, Robert	9	Trapper	Killed by explosion	5.8.1841	Thornley
GIBSON, George	38	Pitman	Falling of cage in the shaft	23.3.1852	Ludworth
GLEGHORN, William	16	Pit Boy	Killed in shaft of new pit	18.1.1912	Thornley
GLENN, Allen	22	Hewer	Crushed by fall of stone	20.9.1868	Thornley
GORDON, James	53	Miner	Crushed by fall of stone in Low Main	21.12.1927	Wheatley Hill
GORMAN, Patrick	47	Miner	Accidentally killed	18.12.1907	Wheatley Hill
GRAYDON, Peter	11	Driver	Killed by explosion	5.8.1841	Thornley
GRAHAM, John	16	Putter	Killed by explosion	5.8.1841	Thornley
GREENER, Norman	17	Datal Worker	Caught between two coal tubs	20.2..1867	Thornley
GREENWELL, Thomas	21	Loco Fireman	Crushed by empty wagons	15.12.1837	Thornley

NAME	AGE	JOB	CAUSE OF DEATH	DATE OF DEATH	COLLIERY
GREENWELL, William	23	Pitman	Run over by a set of coal tubs	2.9.1881	Wheatley Hill
GRIMWOOD, Alfred	28	Coal Hewer	Gas explosion in Main Coal Seam	25.3.1878	Wheatley Hill
HADDICK, Craik	26	Sinker	Thrown out of corf in shaft	Dec 1844	Ludworth
HAGAN,			Buried on duff heap by quantity of coal	28.3.1886	Thornley
HALL, Edward	48	Coal Cutter Op	Crushed between machine and prop	30.8.1957	Thornley
HALL, George	39	Masons Labourer	Fell down shaft - 21 fathoms	22.7.1849	Thornley
HALL, James	42	Hewer	Drowned in inundation	19.1.1871	Wheatley Hill
HALL, Thomas	18	Putter	Killed by explosion	5.8.1841	Thornley
HANBY, George	37	Shaftman	Crushed by cage on 13.12.1877	21.12.1877	Wheatley Hill
HARBRON, John	18	Pitman	Crushed by stone fall	10.8.1846	Thornley
HARGREAVES, Robert	17m		Run over by locomotive engine	19.3.1927	Wheatley Hill
HARGREAVES, Frederick,	52	Stoneman	Crushed by fall of stone in Harvey Seam	1.10.1917	Thornley
HARPER, Joseph	32	Miner	Accidentally Killed	22.4.1927	Wheatley Hill
HACKWORTH, Thomas	39	Stoneman	Crushed by fall of stone	21.3.1938	Wheatley Hill
HASTINGS, Matthew	50	Hewer	Crushed by fall of stone in Harvey Seam	10.6.1929	Wheatley Hill
HASTINGS, Thomas	22	Pitman		29.11.1880	Thornley
HASWELL, Thomas	42	Hewer	Killed by explosion	5.8.1841	Thornley
HAYS, Alexander	34	Stoneman	Crushed by fall of stone	8.12.1922	Wheatley Hill
HEALE, William H	25	Miner	Died from injuries received	22.4.1950	Thornley
HEDLEY, Thomas	20	Pitman	Falling of the cage in shaft	23.3.1852	Ludworth
HEDLEY, William	24	Pitman	Falling of the cage in shaft	23.3.1852	Ludworth

NAME	AGE	JOB	CAUSE OF DEATH	DATE OF DEATH	COLLIERY
HEPPLE, Richard	44			May 1865	Thornley
HERRON, Joseph E R	43	Filler	Crushed by fall of stone in Harvey Seam	4.10.1937	Thornley
HETHERINGTON, T	40	Miner	Crushed by fall of stone	8.2.1906	Wheatley Hill
HEWITSON, Matthew	49	Shaftman	Explosion in shaft	23.8.1865	Thornley
HICKS, John	25	Hewer	Crushed by fall of stone	8.3.1875	Wheatley Hill
HODGSON, John	15	Miner		22.9.1904	Thornley
HOOD, Alfred	34	Shaftman	Fell from cradle in No 1 Pit	25.7.1914	Thornley
HOPE, James	39			12.12.1866	Thornley
HORN, William	62	Deputy Overman	Fractured spine in accident Aug 1936	Jan 1954	Wheatley Hill
HOWE, Robert	70	Miner	Accidentally killed	14.3.1946	Thornley
HUGHES, John Joseph	2		Run over by laden coal truck	1.11.1909	Thornley
HUMES, Ward	42	Filler	Crushed by fall of stone	8.6.1939	Wheatley Hill
HUNTER, John	28	Sinker	Thrown out of corf in shaft	Dec 1844	Ludworth
HUTCHINSON, Edward T	23	Miner	Accidentally killed	15.5.1933	Thornley
HUTCHINSON, John	20	Screenman	Fell from machinery - 30ft	27.11.1858	Thornley
HUTCHINSON, Robert	53	Wagonwayman	Run over by wagon	Nov 1870	Thornley
ILEY, William	28	Clicker	Crushed between set of tubs	20.1.1878	Ludworth
IVESON, George	21	Miner	Accidentally killed	2.6.1944	Thornley
JACKSON, William	58	Pitman	Fell down a staple - 14ft	12.7.1877	Wheatley Hill
JOBLING, Albert	41	Stoneman	Crushed by fall of stone in Hutton Seam	21.5.1928	Thornley
JOHNSON, James	37	Miner	Accidentally killed	6.4.1927	Wheatley Hill

663

NAME	AGE	JOB	CAUSE OF DEATH	DATE OF DEATH	COLLIERY
JOHNSON, Ralph	12	Driver	Crushed by fall of stone	10.6.1859	Ludworth
JOHNSON, Thomas	11	Driver	Head jammed between tub and tram	1.9.1852	Ludworth
JOLLY, James	12	Horse Driver	Crushed by two laden rolleys	17.7.1854	Thornley
JONES, Edward	39	Miner	Run over by set of tubs	12.4.1925	Wheatley Hill
JONES, John E	64	Miner	Injury to the knees on 9.4.1922	5.1.1926	Thornley
JONES, John W	64	Miner	Accident at pit	31.1.1917	Wheatley Hill
JONES, Norris	37	Hewer	Crushed by fall of stone in Harvey seam	11.6.1921	Thornley
JUSTICE, James	66	Furnace Man	Crushed by roof fall	5.6.1850	Ludworth
KEEGAN, Charles	21	Pitman	Broken cage rope	26.7.1840	Thornley
KELLY, William	37	Coal Cutting Team	Drowned in Hutton seam	6.5.1949	Thornley
KERR, Robert	35	Enginewright	Struck by engine beam and crushed	10.4.1848	Thornley
KIDD, James W	22	Miner	Accidentally killed	19.1.1953	Thornley
KNIGHT, John	49	Miner	Crushed by fall of stone in Harvey seam	3.9.1894	Wheatley Hill
KYLE, Edward S	53	Compressor minder	Had a fall in engine house	31.1.1916	Ludworth
LAMB, Curry	12	Rolley Driver	Crushed between coal tubs	21.9.1844	Thornley
LAMB, Jacob	46	Pitman		21.12.1877	Wheatley Hill
LAMB, John	59	Stoneman	Crushed by fall of stone	6.5.1953	Wheatley Hill
LARK, Joseph	36	Hewer	Crushed by fall of stone in Harvey Seam	17.4.1923	Thornley
LAW, Ida Elizabeth	3		Injured by railway locomotive	10.7.1905	Thornley
LAWRENCE, Jesse	44	Stoneman	Crushed by fall of stone 14.11.1923	6.6.1924	Thornley

NAME	AGE	JOB	CAUSE OF DEATH	DATE OF DEATH	COLLIERY
LAWS, John W	18	Landing Lad	Caught between tub and roadside	13.1.1913	Wheatley Hill
LEE, James	60	Hewer	Crushed by fall of stone 4.10.1923	30.1.1924	Wheatley Hill
LEE, John W J	21	Pony Putter	Crushed by fall of stone October 1933	22.8.1934	Wheatley Hill
LEONARD, William H	45	Sinker	Precipitated down the shaft	17.4.1871	Wheatley Hill
LEWINS, Martin	50	Deputy	Crushed by fall of stone	15.7.1871	Wheatley Hill
LINDSAY, John W	35	Master Shifter	Crushed by a fall of stone	1.7.1933	Wheatley Hill
LISTER, Joseph	12	Rolley Driver	Crushed by a laden rolley	11.6.1852	Thornley
LOWES, Arthur B	20	Miner	Accidentally killed	28.6.1915	Thornley
LOWES, Norman	51	Electrician	Knocked down by set of tubs	7.12.1951	Wheatley Hill
LOWTHER, Joseph D	43	Miner	Crushed by fall of stone	21.11.1966	Thornley
LYE, Frank	16		Accidentally killed in mineshaft	6.6.1976	Thornley
MACHAN, Henry	14	Putter	Head crushed between tub and roof	7.1.1860	Thornley
MADDISON, William	52	Engineman	Boiler explosion in the Low Main	27.1.1878	Thornley
MARGETSON, Robert H	33	Miner	Crushed by fall of stone in Harvey Seam	17.2.1906	Wheatley Hill
MATHER, John	34	Stoneman	Crushed by fall of stone in Harvey Seam	1.6.1922	Thornley
MAUDLING, James	62	Overman	Run over by set of tubs	28.7.1864	Thornley
McCARROLL, John	44	Miner	Fall of stone in 1911	20.4.1912	Wheatley Hill
McCOY, Malcolm	17	Miner	Crushed by a fall of stone	24.3.1938	Wheatley Hill
McCURK, Joseph	17	Pit Boy		12.6.1883	Thornley
MERCER, Thomas	24	Power Loader	Fatally injured in shot firing accident	21.9.1966	Wheatley Hill

NAME	AGE	JOB	CAUSE OF DEATH	DATE OF DEATH	COLLIERY
MILLER, Edward	45	Onsetter	Boiler explosion in Low Main	18.1.1878	Thornley
MILLER, T	59	Deputy	Crushed by fall of stone 14.1.1924	30.1.1924	Wheatley Hill
MITCHELL, A C	33	Stoneman	Injuries to spine on 11.11.1919	20.11.1919	Thornley
MOLE, Thomas	32	Hewer	Crushed by fall of stone in the Low Main	21.12.1927	Thornley
MONAGHAN, Edward	58	Stoneman	Fall of stone - May 1920	1.7.1922	Thornley
MOOR, Thomas	26	Banksman	Struck by portion of broken pulley wheel	13.1.1847	Ludworth
MOORE, Catherine	20		Sunk in coal dust on pit heap	1.4.1880	Thornley
MORALEE, Thomas	16	Labourer	Fell down pit shaft	16.10.1889	Wheatley Hill
MORTON, George	11	Trapdoor Keeper	Jammed between a prop and coal tub	18.9.1846	Ludworth
MULLEN, Arthur P	25	Hewer	Crushed by fall of stone in Busty Seam	17.8.1950	Wheatley Hill
NATRESS, Robert	34	Deputy overman	Crushed by fall of stone in Harvey Seam	12.5.1919	Thornley
NEASHAM, Arthur	71	Pitman	Slipped on metal plates at shaft bottom	23.7.1843	Thornley
NELSON, Robert	18	Conveyor Minder	Run over by tubs in Harvey Seam	22.9.1936	Thornley
NICHOL, Thomas	14	Putter	Run over by a coal tub	15.5.1906	Wheatley Hill
NICHOLSON, Ralph	66	Pitman	Run over by set of tubs	23.12.1856	Thornley
NORMAN, Robert	73	Miner	Crushed whilst at work in 1906	15.8.1916	Wheatley Hill
NURSER, George	11	Rolley Driver	Jammed between a tub and side of pit	24.7.1855	Thornley
O'BRIEN, Stephen	9	Rolleywayman	Caught by a truck on colliery railway line	30.11.1965	Thornley
OLLIMAN, John	50	Hewer	Boiler explosion in the Low Main Seam	23.1.1878	Thornley
ORD, Frederick	37	Hewer	Crushed by fall of stone in Hutton Seam	20.1.1931	Thornley
ORD, George	17	Flatman	Killed by an explosion	5.8.1841	Thornley
PARKINSON, Thomas	68	Shifter	Injured on 19.5.1915 by fall of stone	21.2.1919	Wheatley Hill

NAME	AGE	JOB	CAUSE OF DEATH	DATE OF DEATH	COLLIERY
PEACHEY, Ernest	35	Coal Cutting Team	Crushed by fall of stone in Harvey Seam	10.9.1937	Thornley
PEACOCK, J W	27	Onsetter	Died through injuries received 15.6.1929	29.10.1929	Wheatley Hill
PEEL, James	38			22.8.1872	Thornley
PERKINS, John	64	Miner	Accidentally killed	30.1.1931	Thornley
PIERCY, Thomas W	43	Conveyorman	Killed by fall of stone	12.8.1952	Wheatley Hill
PORTER, John	64	Pitman	Right leg caught between cage & scaf-	12.11.1874	Ludworth
POTTES, Edward	15	Rolley Driver	Crushed between a rolley & side of pit	22.8.1853	Thornley
POUNDER, Henry	29	Banksman	Crushed between cage and flat sheets	6.8.1896	Wheatley Hill
PRENTICE, James	37	Loco Fireman	Leg and back injuries 22.4.1903	28.6.1915	Thornley
PRINGLE, James T	55	Miner	Died through an accident	3.3.1941	Thornley
PURVIS, Frank	27	Hand Putter	Crushed by fall of stone in Harvey Seam	20.1.1932	Wheatley Hill
PURVIS, Matthew	43	Coal Cutting Team	Drowned in Hutton Seam	6.5.1949	Thornley
QUINN, Thomas	22	Hewer	Explosion of gas	26.9.1876	Wheatley Hill
RACE, W	22	Engineman	Crushed by drawing engine	11.10.1854	Thornley
RAFFELL, Thomas	59	Miner	Accidentally killed	11.3.1924	Wheatley Hill
RAINE, J W	16	Datal Worker	Died from injuries received 11.11.1942	18.3.1943	Wheatley Hill
REDSHAW, John H	33	Hewer	Crushed by fall of stone on 26.12.1911	1.6.1919	Thornley
RENWICK, Peter	61	Wagonway timber-er	Crushed by a fall of stone	8.9.1914	Wheatley Hill
RICE, John	16	Stable boy	Riding improperly on top of the cage	17.3.1901	Thornley
RICHARDSON, Gardner	14	Rolley Driver	Crushed by rolley	30.7.1850	Thornley

667

NAME	AGE	JOB	CAUSE OF DEATH	DATE OF DEATH	COLLIERY
RICHARDSON, George W	39	Miner	Accidentally killed	9.9.1945	Thornley
RICHARDSON, Margaret	16		Entombed beneath material on heap	29.4.1873	Thornley
RICHIE, Isabella	18		Entombed beneath material on heap	29.4.18783	Thornley
RICHMOND, John	37	Hewer	Crushed by fall of coal	22.10.1900	Wheatley Hill
RILEY, George	18	Pitman	Crushed by fall of stone	10.3.1845	Thornley
ROBERTS, William	50	Onsetter	Fell down the shaft - 20 fathoms	5.11.1873	Thornley
ROBINSON, James	54	Miner	Crushed by a fall of stone	15.11.1916	Thornley
ROBINSON, John	44	Pitman	Crushed by two rolleys laden with coal	3.10.1857	Thornley
ROBINSON, Robert	4		Run over by trucks	16.5.1945	Thornley
ROBINSON, Thomas	20	Hewer	Crushed by fall of stone in Harvey Seam	10.10.1917	Thornley
ROBSON, Benjamin	70	Wasteman	Crushed by a coal tub in March 1881	August 1884	Ludworth
ROBSON, James	21	Miner	Crushed by a fall of stone	3.3.1920	Wheatley Hill
ROBSON, Joseph	28	Sinker	Thrown out of corf in the shaft	Dec 1844	Ludworth
ROBSON, Matthew	29	Hewer	Crushed by fall of stone	5.9.1899	Thornley
ROBSON, William	12			26.7.1870	Thornley
ROSE, Richard	37	Wagon Driver	Run over by wagon loaded with shale	2.10.1878	Ludworth
ROUTLEDGE, Alexan-	44	Miner	Crushed by fall of stone in Hutton Seam	15.7.1932	Wheatley Hill
ROWLEY, Thomas	59	Shifter	Injuries received on 8.6.1910	16.11.1910	Wheatley Hill
RUDD, James	23	Miner	Crushed by fall of stone in Harvey Seam	28.12.1932	Thornley
RUDKIN, Walter	33	Coal Cutting Team	Drowned in Hutton Seam	6.5.1949	Thornley

NAME	AGE	JOB	CAUSE OF DEATH	DATE OF DEATH	COLLIERY
RUTHERFORD, John	50	Miner	Crushed by fall of stone	2.10.1934	Thornley
SCOTT, Joseph	17	Pit Boy	Crushed by fall of stone	9.4.1860	Thornley
SIMPSON, Thomas	25	Pitman	Thrown out of cage	10.4.1845	Thornley
SMITH, Robert	28	Hewer	Drowned in inundation	19.1.1871	Wheatley Hill
SMITH, Thomas	58	Pitman	Crushed by cage	16.12.1943	Wheatley Hill
SMYTH, Patrick	58	Timber Drawer	Injured by fall of stone Sept 1939	1.12.1843	Wheatley Hill
SNOWDON, Eric W	43	Fitter	Died from injuries received	24.11.1966	Wheatley Hill
SOULSBY, Joseph	17	Landing Boy	Run over by two tubs in Hutton Seam	30.1.1928	Thornley
SPENCE, Robert	38	Surface Worker	Knocked down by lorry in colliery yard	1.10.1933	Thornley
STEPHENSON, James	32	Hewer	Crushed by fall of stone	22.10.1860	Ludworth
STOKER, Robert	68	Coal shifter	Lifting a full tub on the wagonway	18.5.1916	Wheatley Hill
STOREY, George	22	Pony Putter	Crushed by a fall of stone	14.11.1924	Thornley
STOREY, Wilfred	24	Miner	From injuries received on 18.3.1933	16.4.1933	Wheatley Hill
STOUT, John	59	Stoneman	Crushed by fall of stone	14.5.1881	Wheatley Hill
SUMMERS, Mark	18	Pony Driver	Run over by a tub	21.11.1925	Thornley
SURTEES, Thomas Y	40	Stoneman	Crushed by fall of stone in No 1 Pit	21.10.1913	Thornley
SWAN, John	20	Putter	Lifting a tub of stone - muscular strain	16.3.1925	Thornley
SWEENEY, Anthony	12	Pit Boy	Crushed between the cage and bunting	18.11.1876	Ludworth
TATE, John	39	Hewer	Crushed by roof fall	16.6.1854	Thornley
TATE, Jon	60	Coll Bricklayer	Injured by fall of steel girder	28.1.1929	Wheatley Hill

NAME	AGE	JOB	CAUSE OF DEATH	DATE OF DEATH	COLLIERY
TATE, John	28			14.8.1894	Thornley
TAYLOR, John	57	Labourer	Foot crushed whilst emptying tubs	30.7.1893	Ludworth
TELFAIR, James	15	Pit Boy		12.9.1870	Wheatley Hill
THOMPSON, George	13	Wagon Driver	Run over by a laden coal wagon	15.3.1848	Ludworth
THOMPSON, Oliver	35	Shaftman	Fell from platform in the shaft	8.12.1879	Wheatley Hill
THOMPSON, William	13			7.12.1866	Thornley
THORNTON, James M	14	Pony Driver	Run over by coal tubs in the Hutton Seam	28.8.1928	Wheatley Hill ''
THORNTON, John	13	Putter	Burns received by gas explosion 5.1.1874	20.1.1874	Thornley
TODD, William R	54	Blacksmith	Fall of iron sleeper on his foot	1.6.1916	Wheatley Hill
TOWNLAND, John	24	Miner	Died through injuries received	5.7.1928	Thornley
TUNSTALL, James W	15	Pony Driver	Run over by tub on 17.12.1915	19.12.1915	Thornley
TURNER, David	14	Putter	Crushed between cage and bunton	5.6.1875	Wheatley Hill
TYSON, Thomas M	20	App Electrician	Crushed by trucks	11.2.1926	Wheatley Hill
ULATT, Henry Dixon	23	Putter	Crushed by fall of stone in Hutton Seam	11.1.1912	Thornley
UNSWORTH, Owen	38	Coal Cutting Team	Crushed by fall of stone	28.3.1942	Thornley
VENABLES, Joseph	50	Deputy Overman	Stuck on the head by fall of stone	1.12.1937	Wheatley Hill
WALKER, John	21	Hewer	Drowned in inundation	19.1.1871	Wheatley Hill
WALKER, John	68	Miner	Cage injury incurred 23.10.1902	1.8.1921	Wheatley Hill
WALKER, John	60	Datal Worker	Died from injuries received	4.7.1960	Thornley
WALKER, Joseph	36	Deputy Overman	Gas explosion in Main Coal Seam	25.3.1878	Wheatley Hill

NAME	AGE	JOB	CAUSE OF DEATH	DATE OF DEATH	COLLIERY
WALKER, Thomas	24	Hewer	Crushed by fall of coal	11.7.1857	Thornley
WALKER, Thomas	18	Pony Putter	Slipped whilst pushing a tub 28.1.1920	13.2.1920	Thornley
WALLACE George	41	Shaftman	Explosion in the shaft	23.8.1865	Thornley
WALLACE, Liddell	31	Shaftman	Explosion in the shaft	23.8.1865	Thornley
WALLACE, William	48	Stoneman	Crushed by fall of stone in No 1 Pit	3.4.1913	Thornley
WALLER, Robert	35	Stoneman	Drilling a hole for shot-firing operations	24.11.1936	Thornley
WALTON, Utrick	21			17.2.1898	Thornley
WALTON, William	58	Colliery Mason	Severe injury to foot on 15.4.1921	1.7.1921	Thornley
WARD, James W	19	Putter	Died through injuries received	9.5.1899	Wheatley Hill
WARDLE, John	15	Putter	Crushed by fall of stone	16.9.1881	Thornley
WARNES, Edward R	49	Miner	Died through injuries received	29.8.1941	Wheatley Hill
WATSON, George	57			18.1.1898	Thornley
WATSON, Thomas	31	Shaftman	Fell from platform in shaft	8.12.1879	Wheatley Hill
WATSON, William	11	Pit Boy	Falling of cage in shaft	23.3.1852	Ludworth
WESTERMAN, Charles	56	Miner	Died through injuries received	12.10.1912	Thornley
WETHERELLL, John	61	Pitman	Run over by a coal tub on 17.11.1881	18.11.1881	Wheatley Hill
WHITE, Robert	62	Pitman		25.10.1877	Ludworth
WHYSALL, Isaac	76	Miner	Accidentally killed	10.11.1904	Thornley
WIGNALL, William	54	Electrician	Injuries received when he fell from ladder	31.8.1954	Thornley
WILKINSON, John	12	Pit Boy	Accidentally knocked down portion of shaft	12.11.1846	Ludworth

NAME	AGE	JOB	CAUSE OF DEATH	DATE OF DEATH	COLLIERY
WILLETTS, Edward R	15			8.2.1901	Thornley
WILLIAMS, Andrew	47			17.3.1903	Thornley
WILLIAMS, John	23	Pitman	Crushed by fall of stone	18.1.1875	Wheatley Hill
WILLIAMS, Joseph	41	Labourer	Struck by a baulk on 2.6.1918	8.10.1921	Thornley
WILLIAMS, Thomas F	20	Endless Haulage	Run over by a set of tubs in shaft sidings	30.12.1935	Thornley
WILSON, Dorothy	10		Jammed between laden coal wagons	22.5.1854	Thornley
WILSON, John	14	Rolley Driver	Run over by a coal wagon	2.6.1846	Thornley
WILSON, John	28	Sinker	Thrown out of kibble	6.7.1870	Wheatley Hill
WILSON, Robert	17	Asst Onsetter	Boiler explosion in Low Main Seam	20.1.1878	Thornley
WILSON, William	33			26.10.1899	Thornley
WINTER, Harry	55		Knocked down by moving trucks	8.12.1908	Thornley
YATES, Thomas	36			1.5.1859	Thornley
YOUNG, George	28	Miner	Accidentally killed	25.1.1907	Wheatley Hill
YOUNG, Joseph	18	Putter	Died through injuries received	8.9.1908	Wheatley Hill